Hellenistic Commentary to the New Testament

Hellenistic
Commentary
to the
New Testament

Edited by

M. Eugene Boring

Klaus Berger

Carsten Colpe

ABINGDON PRESS / Nashville

HELLENISTIC COMMENTARY TO THE NEW TESTAMENT

Translation from the German language with the approval of the Publishing House Vandenhoeck and Ruprecht, Göttingen. © Vandenhoeck & Ruprecht, Göttingen.

This book is printed on acid-free, recycled paper.

Library of Congress Cataloging-in-Publication Data

Hellenistic commentary to the New Testament / edited by M. Eugene Boring, Klaus Berger, Carsten Colpe.
   p. cm.
   Includes bibliographical references and indexes.
   ISBN 0-687-00916-2 (alk. paper)
   1. Bible. N.T.—Extra-canonical parallels. 2. Bible. N.T.—Commentaries. 3. Greek literature—Relation to the New Testament. 4. Rome—Religion. I. Boring, M. Eugene. II. Berger, Klaus, 1940– . III. Colpe, Carsten, 1929– .
BS2341.2.H44 1995
225.9'5—dc20   95-17982
                                                                  CIP

95 96 97 98 99 00 01 02 03 04—10 9 8 7 6 5 4 3 2 1

MANUFACTURED IN THE UNITED STATES OF AMERICA

To the Memory

of

Gerhard Friedrich

8/20/1908 — 1/18/1986

and

Georg Strecker

3/15/1929 — 6/11/1994

Contents

Preface to the English Edition 9

Introduction to the English Edition 11

Foreword to the German Edition 18

Original Introduction to the German Edition 19

The Gospel of Matthew (and Parallels) 33

The Gospel of Mark (and Parallels) 169

The Gospel of Luke (and Parallels) 182

The Gospel of John (and Parallels) 238

The Acts of the Apostles 309

The Letters of Paul 335

The Letter to the Hebrews 509

The Letter of James 523

The First Letter of Peter 528

The Second Letter of Peter 537

The Letters of John 540

The Letter of Jude 546

The Revelation to John 548

Acknowledgments 587

Comparison Chart of Text Numbers 590

Bibliography. 594

Ancient Author Index 602

Subject Index (Selective) 614

Scripture Index 620

Preface to the English Edition

The commonplace that "every book is the product of many hands" is particularly true in the present case. Wilhelm Richmann's (Göttingen) comprehensive collection and translation of Hellenistic texts was adopted, adapted, expanded, and annotated by Professor Klaus Berger (Heidelberg) and Professor Carsten Colpe (Berlin) to form the *Religionsgeschichtliches Textbuch zum Neuen Testament*, which led to and became the core of the present volume. Professor Georg Strecker and Professor Gerd Lüdemann (both Göttingen) were gracious hosts while I was working on this project in Göttingen, providing office and library support. In particular, Georg Strecker was most cooperative in making available for my perusal and use the work already done on the Neuer Wettstein.[1] His name has been added to the dedication as a small token of personal friendship and respect for the contribution he has made to the field of New Testament studies. Professor Udo Schnelle (Halle), who assumed direction of the Neuer Wettstein project after Strecker's untimely death, continued his gracious cooperative spirit. Dipl. Theol. G. Seeling, Wiss. Mitarbeiter in the Göttingen Theologicum, who manages the day-by-day research on the project, was also most helpful, in sharing not only prepublication copies of Neuer Wettstein materials, but also his own depth of knowledge in the field of Hellenistic texts.

The editors at Abingdon Press have been most cooperative and supportive in a project that has grown to much larger proportions than any of us envisioned when it was begun: Davis Perkins, Ulrike Guthrie, and Steve Cox have contributed much to the book. Arndt Ruprecht of Vandenhoeck & Ruprecht has been most cooperative in permitting the expansion of the German edition.

David L. Balch and David E. Aune both found time during their sabbaticals (Rome and Tübingen respectively) to read carefully the penultimate draft of this book. Each is more knowledgeable in this field than I, and each made many valuable suggestions I have incorporated. While they are in no way responsible for remaining errors and idiosyncratic perspectives, I felt much more confident going to press with this product after they had examined it.

Whoever finds this a useful book owes a depth of gratitude to each of the above, as do I. Our collective debt extends especially to two people. I would never have begun such a detailed and arduous project without being able to count on the help of Edward J. McMahon and Lana N. Byrd. Ed McMahon has located most of the English translations used in this book, and has meticulously edited and proofread the entire volume at more than one stage of its development. Lana Byrd has typed all the translations, organized and managed the enormous task of seeking permissions, and carried on a vast correspondence related to the volume. They have both invested themselves in the project beyond all that anyone could reasonably anticipate, and have persevered to the end despite changing professional niches in the years since the project was begun. Both have contributed to making a laborious task interesting and enjoyable. In addition, the timely help in the final stages of the project from Wendy D. McClung, student in the Department of Religion, and Joseph A. Weaks, student in Brite Divinity School, is much appreciated.

---

1. See "How this book came to be" in the Introduction to the English Edition.

Introduction to the English Edition

M. Eugene Boring

"Even a smell of a primary source is better than a shelf of secondary sources."[1] With these words, in his opening lecture to my first New Testament class at Vanderbilt Divinity School in the fall semester of 1963, Leander Keck encouraged us to interpret the New Testament in its historical context, and to engage this context as directly as we did the Bible itself. The Bible is indeed a foreign book, whose message is expressed in the language, thought world, and cultural presuppositions of another time and place.[2] This is a fact, but it is a fact to be celebrated, not lamented. The historical-conditionedness of the New Testament can be celebrated not only by Christians who believe in the incarnation, that in Jesus of Nazareth the Absolute has entered the relativities of history, but by anyone who wishes to understand the New Testament in its own context rather than misunderstand it by reading into it one's own modern cultural presuppositions. Whatever illuminates the world of the New Testament facilitates a hearing of its message in its own terms. Such illumination is provided by collections of texts from the Hellenistic world. In 1963, Keck recommended C. K. Barrett's *New Testament Background: Selected Documents* (New York: Harper & Row, 1956), which immediately became for me an indispensable source of insight into the world of the New Testament, and thence into the canonical texts themselves. I have since benefited from several such books (see Bibliography); the present volume stands in their tradition and owes much to them.

How this book came to be

Shortly after its publication by Vandenhoeck and Ruprecht in 1987, I discovered Berger and Colpe's *Religionsgeschichtliches Textbuch zum Neuen Testament* on the shelves of Deuerlich's bookstore in Göttingen. I was immediately impressed by its usefulness and helpfulness as an exegetical tool:

1) Berger and Colpe had selected several hundred texts from the Hellenistic world, if "Hellenistic world" is defined somewhat loosely.[3] By "Hellenistic world" I mean roughly those large portions of the extended Mediterranean basin characterized by the interaction of Greek language and culture with the variety of local languages and cultures, in the period from Alexander to Constantine, 330 BCE to 300 CE, the "Greco-Roman world."[4]

---

1. Leander Keck, in an unpublished lecture in the course "New Testament History and Literature," September 1963. Less pungently but in a more biblical idiom, cf. the similar sentiment from the Preface of Everett Ferguson's helpful textbook, *Backgrounds of Early Christianity* (Grand Rapids: Eerdmans, 2nd ed., 1993), xv: "To paraphrase the apostle Paul, 'Five words in an original source are worth a thousand words in a secondary source.'"

2. See Bruce Malina, *The New Testament World: Insights from Cultural Anthropology* (Louisville: Westminster/John Knox, rev. ed., 1993), pp. 1-5, under the heading "Bible Study and Cultural Anthropology: Interpreting Texts Fairly."

3. There are 626 sections with lead text, as well as scores of other texts cited and discussed in the Annotations.

4. Cf. the discussion on classification and dating in §2.4 of Berger and Colpe's Introduction, pp. 22-23.

This was the world into which Christianity was born and became a world religion, the context for the formation of the New Testament and the development of Christian theology. Though for the most part Berger and Colpe's volume contained texts that originated in this period and context, numerous texts were included from the pre-Hellenistic classical period, and a few from the post-Hellenistic Byzantine and even Medieval period. The classical texts are easy to justify as included in a "Hellenistic" collection: the texts that influenced and characterized the Hellenistic world were by no means all created then. Classical texts circulated in the Hellenistic world and were widely influential. This means that the Hellenistic reading of classical texts such as Plato and Aristotle was an influential factor in the thought world from which early Christianity was born. The few post-Hellenistic texts contained in the collection are also properly included, if they document and illustrate ideas that were current earlier.

2) Berger and Colpe had selected these texts on the basis of their illumination of the text from a history-of-religions perspective,[5] as indicated by their title, *Religionsgeschichtliches Textbuch zum Neuen Testament,* literally "Religion-historical Textbook to the New Testament."[6] Discussion of the history-of-religions connections of New Testament texts and ideas with their religious and cultural contexts is facilitated by bringing New Testament texts into conjunction with relevant primary sources from the Hellenistic world.

3) Thus a distinct advantage was provided by arranging the texts not by date, topic, or author, but in relation to the canonical texts they were thought most directly to illuminate, somewhat in the manner of H. L. Strack and P. Billerbeck, *Kommentar zum Neuen Testament aus Talmud und Midrasch.* The present work might be thought of as a "Hellenistic Strack-Billerbeck," and uses the term "Commentary" in the same sense.

4) Berger and Colpe provided their texts with brief annotations, to set them in their own historical and cultural context or to provide suggestions as to how they were thought to illuminate the New Testament text to which they were juxtaposed. A variety of kinds of relationships between ideas in Hellenistic texts and those of the New Testament was posited, not merely "parallels."[7]

My positive impressions of the volume were confirmed by discussion with several German New Testament scholars who also welcomed its publication. This evaluation was subsequently confirmed by scholarly reviews, almost uniformly positive.[8] I decided that

---

5. A core of such texts had already been provided Berger and Colpe by the collection of Wilhelm Richmann of Göttingen, as acknowledged in their Foreword.

6. This title could not be preserved in English, not only due to the lack of a good translation for the adjective *religionsgeschichtlich* ("history-of-religions"), but because "textbook" in English does not mean "collection of primary texts." Thus "Hellenistic Commentary to the New Testament" was chosen to denote that not only the annotations, but primarily the texts themselves provide the kind of illumination on the text of the New Testament that is the goal of a commentary.

7. See the discussion and classification in Berger and Colpe's original Introduction, §3, which develops and illustrates twenty-three categories of relationship between Hellenistic texts and the New Testament in addition to "parallels." While the classification may be too refined and the illustrations sometimes forced, the basic idea that illumination of New Testament texts by their Hellenistic contexts occurs in a variety of ways (not only as "parallels") is a helpful insight and a curb against misuse of the Hellenistic texts.

8. E.g., Willem S. Vorster, *Neotestamentica* 23 (1989), 359: "Because of the importance of reading the New Testament in its own world, this book is an excellent tool for any serious interpreter of the New Testament. It is highly recommended."

translating the book into English would make it more accessible not only to American students, but to the worldwide readership for whom English is more accessible than German. Every publisher I approached was interested. Davis Perkins, then of Abingdon Press, was enthusiastic, and the project was launched.

I have made the following changes and expansions of the German collection:

1) I have occasionally included a longer section of the text cited by Berger and Colpe in order to include the immediate context. Likewise, I have occasionally augmented their annotations, especially to include more recent bibliography or English-language works (without attempting anything like bibliographic completeness).

2) The number of texts and annotations has been considerably expanded. The 626 primary texts have become 976, with many more additional texts added in the annotations. The collection now contains well over a thousand primary texts that illuminate the New Testament in one way or another.

3) Berger and Colpe had restricted their perspective to history-of-religions concerns, and had purposely omitted texts judged to be familiar from standard collections, as well as concentrating on texts from the pagan context rather than from Jewish, early Christian, and Gnostic "parallels."[9] In selecting additional texts for inclusion, I cast my net wider. Texts are included that illuminate exegetical and hermeneutical issues implicit in the texts, along with their theological ideas, not only history-of-religion points of contact. The only category of texts I explicitly excluded were those relevant primarily to the social and political history of the times.[10] I wanted to include the "standard" texts that had served to illustrate key points in other collections and in various commentaries, so that the student could have in one volume a comprehensive collection of texts that a variety of scholars had found helpful, and that had often played a key role in exegetical discussions of particular texts and issues. Many of these were included because they had become significant to me over the years, and several others were gleaned from various collections. In particular, I became aware that Georg Strecker was directing a project in Göttingen to completely revise, expand, correct, and republish the collection of texts in J. Wettstein (ed.), *Novum Testamentum Graecum* I-II, Graz, 1962 (= Amsterdam, 1751/52).[11] Professor Strecker and his successor as Director of the project, Professor Udo Schnelle of Halle, graciously made their collection of texts for the *Neuer Wettstein* project available to me.[12] Although Wettstein, old and new, is more oriented to linguistic and stylistic parallels than is the present volume,

---

9. See Berger and Colpe's Introduction, §2.1.c.

10. For such texts, see H. G. Kippenberg and G. A. Wewers, *Textbuch zur neutestamentlichen Zeitgeschichte* (GNT; NTD-Ergänzungsreihe 8. Göttingen, 1979); C. K. Barrett, *The New Testament Background: Selected Documents* (San Francisco: Harper & Row, Publishers, rev. and expanded ed., 1989); J. Leipoldt and W. Grundmann (eds.), *Umwelt des Urchristentums I. Darstellung des neutestamentlichen Zeitalters, II. Texte zum neutestamentlichen Zeitalter, III. Bilder zum neutestamentlichen Zeitalter* (Berlin) (4th ed.) 1975. (3rd) 1972. (3rd) 1973.

11. For Strecker's own description of the project, see "Das Göttinger Projekt 'Neuer Wettstein,'" *ZNW* 83 (1992), 245-52; cf. also Pieter Willem van der Horst, "Johann Jakob Wettstein nach 300 Jahren: Erbe und Anfang," *Theologische Zeitschrift* 49 (1993), 267-80.

12. Georg Strecker and Udo Schnelle, eds., *Neuer Wettstein: Texte zum Neuen Testament aus Griechentum und Hellenismus* (Berlin: DeGruyter). Volume 2, presenting texts related to Romans-Revelation, will appear in 1995, with Volume 1 (Matthew-Acts) to follow in 1997. The Matthew-Acts material was not yet available, but the collection of texts for Romans-Revelation was made accessible to me. This was particularly helpful, since the Berger-Colpe collection had concentrated more on the Gospels than the Epistolary literature.

I found many helpful pointers in their collection and incorporated and annotated several texts their research first disclosed to me (see Preface).

4) Berger and Colpe had ordered their texts according to the commonly accepted theories of sources, authorship, and date of the New Testament documents, so that in the Synoptic Gospels the material is organized according to Marcan, Q, peculiarly Matthean, and peculiarly Lucan texts, and in the Pauline materials Colossians precedes Ephesians. The scheme, though having its strong points, became increasingly difficult to carry out as the material grew more massive, and was abandoned. The present volume arranges all texts in canonical order. Thus if a text occurs in all three Synoptics, it is found at its Matthean location, with cross-references to Mark and Luke. Material generally assigned to Q is found in its Lucan location, as has become customary. Otherwise, only material peculiar to or distinctive of Mark or Luke is found in its Marcan or Lucan location. Practically all the Johannine material is unique to the Fourth Gospel, but in a few places where Johannine and Synoptic texts overlap, the material may be found in its appropriate Synoptic location. Since all texts in the headings are also indexed in the Scripture Index, judgment calls can easily be located.

5) I have retained all the cross-references in the original volume and added numerous new ones. Occasionally, I have duplicated a text, in whole or in part, in order to locate it with the appropriate New Testament text and to give it a new set of connotations.

6) The usefulness of the Berger-Colpe volume was hampered by its lack of indexes. When a Hellenistic text could reasonably be associated with more than one New Testament text, the reader had to guess at its location. The finding of any text in the present volume is facilitated by the addition of extensive indexes and cross-references. The complete index of Scripture texts now included in this volume facilitates the finding of every Hellenistic text in the collection associated with any scriptural text, regardless of its location.

7) Two other indexes have been compiled for this edition. The Ancient Author Index and the selective Subject Index enable the reader to locate relevant Hellenistic texts for New Testament interpretation independently of their association with a particular New Testament text. Since some extracanonical texts can apply to and illuminate a great many New Testament texts (e.g. texts related to "Son of Man"), it seemed useless to attempt to cross-reference them at every relevant location. I have thus printed and discussed them at some relevant location, and indexed relevant topics in the Subject Index. Thematic studies and studies of the influence of a particular Hellenistic author on the New Testament are thus facilitated.

8) To facilitate the study of the Hellenistic texts in their own literary contexts, the German translations of ancient texts included in and made by Berger and Colpe are replaced in this volume where possible with standard and easily accessible English translations.[13]

Dangers and disclaimers

1) The texts themselves are the heart of the book. Each is provided with its date and authorship where these are known, the source of the English translation, and a brief

---

13. See Bibliography. Many of these were of course made before contemporary sensibilities to inclusive language had developed. In accord with standard practice, I have adopted current American spellings. Where standard English translations were not available, I have translated the German text found in Berger/Colpe. These translations are indicated by "MEB/Berger." My own translations of original texts are indicated by "MEB."

annotation, which often contains citations of other texts. The annotations are provided to give some suggestions as to how the Hellenistic text might illuminate the canonical text. They are in no way to be regarded as an alternative to the traditional commentary. The Berger-Colpe annotations were oriented primarily to history-of-religions concerns. While acknowledging that this perspective is an indispensable component of responsible interpretation, my own annotations are oriented more in the direction of theological exegesis. The annotations are not intended to be definitive; often they provide only a springboard for reflection on the illumination the extracanonical text might provide for the meaning of the New Testament. The contribution that this volume might make is focused on the Hellenistic texts themselves, not the annotations.

2) The texts are excerpts from larger wholes. Readers of the New Testament are aware of how easily the canonical texts can be misunderstood by citing small segments out of context. The same is true of each of the Hellenistic texts here presented. Both the New Testament and the Hellenistic corpus can become the object of random raids in search of portable valuables.[14] If context is the first rule of all interpretation, then it must not be forgotten that all the texts quoted, even the longer ones, are excerpts (sometimes even snippets). Unwary or uncritical readers can easily place too much confidence in their understanding of the Hellenistic texts on the basis of having read a few such excerpts. Each text is an extract from a world, a systemic whole. Just as readers familiar with the New Testament are aware of the danger of supposing one has understood Paul's thought on the basis of a paragraph excerpted from Galatians or 1 Corinthians, so students should not suppose that the brief selections contained here are adequate for understanding the thought of the authors they represent. There are secondary resources helpful in doing this, but the most helpful resource is again the larger context of the primary sources themselves (see the Bibliography). The selections assembled in this volume may be thought of as the entrée into this larger world.

Each text quoted thus forms only a doorway into a larger world. This volume will help the reader to discover a number of such doorways that might otherwise be neglected. But once discovered, such doorways must be entered. The list of primary sources in the Bibliography presents the opportunity to pursue each of the excerpts in its own context. Such thorough study should be done before basing too much on the excerpts offered in this volume. This was one of the dangers pointed out by Samuel Sandmel in his 1961 presidential address to the Society of Biblical Literature, entitled "Parallelomania." The essay has become something of a classic, and several of its warnings are still relevant:

"We might for our purposes define parallelomania as the extravagance among scholars which first overdoes the supposed similarity in passages and then proceeds to describe source and derivation as if implying literary connection flowing in an inevitable or predetermined direction. . . . I am not seeking to discourage the study of these parallels . . . I am speaking words of caution about exaggerations . . ."

"It would seem to me . . . that . . . in dealing with similarities we can sometimes discover exact parallels, some with and some devoid of significance; seeming parallels which are so only imperfectly; and statements which can be called parallels only by taking them out of context. . . . I encounter from time to time scholarly writings which go astray in this last regard. . . . the danger of studying parallels only in excerpts."

---

14. Cf. David Aune's introduction to *Greco-Roman Literature and the New Testament: Selected Forms and Genres* (Atlanta, Ga.: Scholars Press, 1988).

"NT scholars devoid of rabbinic learning have been misled by Strack-Billerbeck into arrogating to themselves a competency they do not possess. Strack-Billerbeck confers upon a student untrained and inexperienced in rabbinic literature not competency but confusion."[15]

The warnings of Sandmel, Charlesworth, and Sanders are directed primarily to modern Christian scholars' use of rabbinic materials on the basis of such collections as Strack-Billerbeck and the Dead Sea Scrolls, but they apply just as well to pagan Hellenistic texts.[16] These texts also are foreign documents, which must be understood in their own terms. In our effort to utilize them to avoid reading our modern preconceptions into the New Testament, we must also take care not to understand the Hellenistic texts themselves in terms of these same modern preconceptions. Superficial but erroneous "parallels" can be found by reading our culture into the texts from the Bible's own world.

My colleagues in the field of New Testament studies are aware that I claim no particular expertise in the vast reservoir of primary sources and that this collection of texts owes much to its predecessors. On the other hand, I do think that I have an eye for what is illuminating and helpful to the exegete, biblical theologian, and historian of the religion of early Christianity. From the ocean of material, I have selected items that seemed to me to be particularly illuminating and helpful. We cannot all, of course, become steeped in the rabbinic and pseudepigraphical literature of Judaism, or the classics of ancient Greece and Rome. Hence the value of collections such as this one. If we use it critically, aware both of the book's and the reader's limitations, such a collection can be very useful.

Suggestions on how to use this book

1) As a commentary and reference book, it is assumed that the most common use of the volume will be to turn to the texts corresponding to the canonical text being studied to see what the *Hellenistic Commentary* offers. Thus one studying the story of Jesus' encounter with Nicodemus (John 3:1-21) will turn directly to §§380-95. This approach makes available some of the resources of this book in the most direct and immediate way. The student may then wish to consult the Scripture Index to see if other relevant texts are located elsewhere

---

15. Samuel Sandmel, "Parallelomania," *JBL* 81 (1962), 1, 7, 9. One also thinks of James H. Charlesworth's scathing denunciation of those who suppose they "know" 4 Ezra, for example, because they have studied it for a week or so (*The Old Testament Pseudepigrapha and the New Testament: Prolegomena for the Study of Christian Origins* [Cambridge: Cambridge University Press, 1985], p. 48), and of E. P. Sanders on the misuse of Strack-Billerbeck (*Paul and Palestinian Judaism* [Philadelphia: Fortress Press, 1977], pp. 42-44 and passim).

16. Cf. David Aune's caustic comment about Bible scholars who are neophytes in classical and Greco-Roman studies but who "use" them to "illuminate" the New Testament: "If I have conveyed the notion that a naive intrusion into the world of classical philology is analogous to a blindfolded man staggering through a minefield, then my caveat has been successful" (in "The Problem of the Genre of the Gospels: A Critique of C. H. Talbert's *What Is a Gospel*," in R. T. France and David Wenham, eds., *Gospel Perspectives* II [Sheffield: JSOT Press, 1981], 9). Similarly F. W. Danker warns that "only those who have explored the labyrinth of Greco-Roman studies can appreciate the hazards that await the unwary, not to speak of the avalanche of specialized publications that threatens to destroy anyone's hope of definitively mapping even some part of the route," in *Benefactor: Epigraphic Study of a Graeco-Roman and New Testament Semantic Field* (St. Louis: Clayton Publishing House, 1982), p. 7.

in the *Commentary*, and will be led to nos. 56, 218, 364, 375, 410, 451, 480, 481, 558, and 910. In addition, relevant topics such as "rebirth" may be identified in the Subject Index, which will lead to other texts such as nos. 20, 129, 130, 477, 555, 572, 590, 707, 839, and 843.

2) Alternatively, one may begin with a topic and use the Subject Index to find texts, both canonical and extracanonical, to which this theme is related. Thus the texts related to the theme "homosexuality" are associated with different New Testament texts and accordingly located at different points in the *Commentary*, but may all be found by using the Subject Index.

3) If one is interested in studying the points of contact between particular Hellenistic authors and the New Testament, this is facilitated by the Ancient Author Index. One can quickly find, for example, all the places where Epictetus, *1 Enoch,* or the Dead Sea Scrolls (or any one of them) is cited, and form an impression of the extent to which their idea worlds are related to the New Testament by the number of texts quoted and their location.

4) All such judgments can be only impressionistic, of course, since this volume contains nothing like a complete citation of Hellenistic texts relevant to New Testament study. Especially for the novice, however, even this impressionistic use of the volume is not to be disdained, if its dangers are kept in mind (see above). There is in fact considerable value in simply leafing through the volume as a whole—not to speak of reading it in its entirety—in order to gain a firsthand impression of the points of contact between the New Testament and its world. An even more powerful impression can be gained by even a cursory perusal of the *Neuer Wettstein*, which cannot but leave the reader with an overwhelming impression of how much of the texture of the language of the New Testament is shared with the Hellenistic world. Without this, students are entirely too inclined to read the New Testament in terms of their own language and idioms, or in terms of the Old Testament, often the only body of primary sources from the ancient world with which students of the New Testament are more or less familiar. The student who is accustomed to thinking only of the Hebrew Bible as the "background" for New Testament ideas may receive a revelatory shock from the impression of the hundreds of relevant Hellenistic texts, quite apart from their careful study for the explication of particular New Testament texts.

Foreword
to the
German Edition

The selection of texts contained in this book has been made from the point of view of the history of religions understood rather narrowly, with the emphasis on the *religious* dimension of this phrase. The texts are thus presented in the order of the New Testament writings.

This book is the history-of-religions counterpart to H. G. Kippenberg and G. A. Wewers, *Textbuch zur neutestamentlichen Zeitgeschichte* (Grundrisse zum Neuen Testament; NTD-Ergänzungsreihe Bd. 8, Göttingen, 1979).

In the course of the preliminary work for this project, Herr Dr. Wilhelm Richmann (Göttingen) contributed a comprehensive collection and translation of an extensive section of texts. In the cases where his preliminary work could be utilized, this is explicitly noted. I would like here to express my sincere gratitude for this work. For assistance in reading the proofs, we would like to thank Frau Susanne Imhof, Herr Dr. Christoph Elsas, and Herr Rainer Bätzing.

The book is dedicated to the memory of Gerhard Friedrich. A preliminary version of the manuscript of this book was the last work he, as editor of this series, was able to discuss before his death, and for which he gave a number of valuable suggestions.

Klaus Berger
Carsten Colpe
Heidelberg and Berlin, September 1986

Original Introduction to the German Edition

§1. The Theological Significance of History-of-Religions Studies

History-of-religions comparison is not the whole of exegesis, but it is a necessary, indispensable part, for such comparison lifts the biblical text out of its isolation and relates it to noncanonical texts from its environment. The exegete is thereby enabled to reconstruct the dialogue (in the broadest sense of the word) of which the biblical text was once a partner. In this manner the question to which the biblical text was once a response is freshly posed, the expectations with which it was once associated are brought again into view, along with the presuppositions which once formed the basis on which it was accepted, and the alternatives which were present, given the same or similar presuppositions.

By doing such comparative study, the exegete places a text in relation to other materials and learns to see the biblical text itself in different, new perspectives.[1] The exegete thus establishes or discovers relationships which give the biblical text a certain profile. Such comparative study can also be one of the means of impeding a purely monological and eisegetical dealing with the text by the modern interpreter. Since the exegete can then see the text as itself involved in a dialogue in its own time, he or she will experience a certain essential and advantageous estrangement from the biblical text, an estrangement which can become the occasion of a more patient and respectful listening. The text then attains its proper standing as an independent conversation partner and not a mere quarry of information for the interpreter's own purpose. By reconstructing the relationship between the biblical text and texts from its environment, the exegete attempts to bring integrity to the role of mediator between past and present.

It will frequently be the case that the interpreter will reconstruct a comparison with which the biblical authors were themselves already concerned and had already expressed. Such a comparison occurred in an exemplary manner in the translation of the Septuagint. To take just one example: by seizing the terms used for deity in their environment (Gk. θεός or ὕψιστος), the translators "took them away from" the Greek gods and applied them exclusively to Yahweh, thus accomplishing an (implicit) history-of-religions comparison between the religion of Israel and the religions of the Greek world. This comparison was of the greatest significance for theological understanding. By taking over the same terminology for God, the religious experience of their neighbors was brought into

---

1. These other materials may either be texts from the same document (e.g., a comparison of Matthew 13:24-30 and Matthew 5:39), texts from the same collection (e.g., a comparison of Paul/Matthew or Paul/Deutero-Isaiah), or texts from the same historical situation (e.g., a comparison of Paul/contemporary Judaism) or texts from a distant setting in the history of religions (e.g., a history-of-religions comparison between Mark 14:22-25 and the Assyrian cuneiform text from about 700 BCE in K. Berger, *Exegese des Neuen Testaments, UTB 658,* 2nd ed. (Heidelberg: Quelle & Meyer, 1984), p. 183]).

comparison with their own and respected as religious experience, while at the same time its content was taken over in a one-sided manner, being recoined in a new form and brought to a new realization. Such a view of the matter makes it advisable to avoid studying ancient religious documents as though they were based on fixed religious concepts. They should rather be seen as representing a process of competition and dialogue, discussion and self-definition, antithesis and transformation. Even when foreign gods are described as demons (e.g., 1 Cor 10:20-21), the alien experience is still considered to be religious, since in the Jewish religion experiences with these powers also have something to do with God.

Another significant dimension of the relation of history-of-religions study and Christian theology is the issue of how revelation is understood. Must "revelation" always be understood as the incomparably new, and correspondingly must "world" always be regarded merely as something which revelation overcomes? Does not the concept of revelation always imply that the purported revelation has proved its worth by being tested, a dialogical element capable of joining in a consensus? In the comparative study of religions, the issue of revelation is raised within the horizon of the possibilities presented by the ancient world. Revelation stands in relation to these possibilities; it is not isolated and homeless, but lives by its interrelationship with the other options, in both comparison and contrast. The religious practices of the early Christians can only be discussed within the possibilities of the world of that time; this is the only way they can be perceived in their concrete reality.[2]

One can thus readily understand that history-of-religions comparison has no compulsion to prove the "absoluteness" and "uniqueness" of Christianity.[3] Many attempts have been made to give scientific evidence for the uniqueness and truth of Christianity by pointing to the originality of its ideas and content. That project, however, is extremely questionable in terms of both method and substance. Methodologically, it means that one must tremble at the rediscovery of every ancient document. The subject matter also makes such an approach completely superfluous, since the uniqueness of Christianity is sufficiently established by the fact of its own history and historical individuality—just as other movements also are historically unique and individual. If one wants to go beyond this kind of uniqueness, then two aspects are to be mentioned. First to be named is the fact that religious content and experience cannot be verified by historical proof, but only by religious evidence itself (and it then always becomes one of the tasks of theology to describe this). In the second place, one can point to elements that mediate between historical uniqueness and religious evidence: universal perspectives which extend beyond the interests of a particular group and stand the test of a more general claim (solidarity with sinners, equality and fraternity of all in the community, care for the disadvantaged).

In the discussion of the absoluteness of Christianity—especially if the discussion is being carried on in the apologetic mode—one often meets the conceptual model according to which Christian texts are only similar to (Jewish and) pagan texts in ways that are merely formal and external, but when their content is examined they are supposedly seen to be very different. Such a separation of form and content has repeatedly

---

2. Cf. K. Müller, "Die religionsgeschichtliche Methode. Erwägungen zu ihrem Verständnis und zur Praxis ihrer Vollzüge an neutestamentlichen Texten," BZ NF 29 (1985), p. 167.

3. Cf. ibid., pp. 168-69.

been called into question, however.[4] Even the description of the form and genre of a text is not possible without consideration of its content, as this is usually understood.[5] The positive significance of this is that a purely external connection between comparable texts cannot be accepted. Even if it is only a matter of "adaptation" of a foreign form, that certainly has consequences for the whole of what is adopted and communicated. Language is not finally a changeable garment for an intended meaning quite independent of it, as though "meaning" could be stripped of its external clothing. Nor is language a mere instrument. A "kernel of content" that transcends the language is neither theoretically nor practically available, and the discovery of presumed anthropological constants may be an illusion.[6] The process of translation and comparison does not deal with kernels of content that transcend language, but with analogies that are constantly new and which must be explained otherwise.

Finally, we need to point out that history-of-religions comparison is not guided by the intention of destroying the "historicity" of reported events;[7] that is not at all possible, since exegesis can prove nothing either positive or negative about whether an event reported in the Bible happened as it is described. In reality, the task and purpose of this comparison is not destructive, but historical, since it seeks to apprehend the location of a statement within the stream of history. The issue is therefore: what is the significance of this kind of contingent history for Christian faith? Is this not the true field of operations for faith, in which faith is constantly engaged with all the risks involved in its concrete historical form?

To be sure, critical academic theology means that religious convictions are temporarily held at a distance. In the exegetical process, this attaining of distance from oneself is the truly fascinating human act. It is not only the case that reflection on one's own religious faith gives rise to Christian theology, this theology in turn has its effect on the religiosity of the exegete, which may be experienced either as liberating or as a loss of immediacy. Positively regarded, history-of-religions comparison could lead precisely to a more critical perception of what belongs to that self from which one actually lives. So research could have a critical effect on one's ultimate concern, and by clarifying and purifying it, make it all the more intensive.

§2.   The Structure and Objectives of This Book

1. On the Conception of the Book

a) The selection of texts is not based on isolated concepts, but whole sections of text as linguistic units are placed in relation to each other. Section 3 below provides in advance a systematic presentation of the different types of connections which exist between the biblical texts and the texts with which they are compared.

---

4. Cf. ibid., p. 177. Especially in the light of semantic fields, the elements usually distinguished as form and content are seen to belong closely together. Cf. Berger, *Exegese*, §20, "The Purpose and Goal of the Study of Semantic Fields," and *Einführung in die Formgeschichte*, UTB 1444 (Heidelberg: Quelle & Meyer, 1987), §7.

5. Contra W. Richter, *Exegese als Literaturwissenschaft* (Göttingen, 1971), pp. 174ff.

6. Cf. the critique of K. Müller, "Die religionsgeschichtliche Methode," pp. 177-79.

7. On the nineteenth-century conflict concerning historicity and the burdensome consequences of this debate, see K. Berger, *Exegese und Philosophie* (Stuttgart, 1986), p. 65.

b) In accord with this, each passage is accompanied by a brief explanation as an aid to reading, as well as references to related biblical texts and important secondary sources particularly relevant to this comparison.

c) Since commentaries and secondary literature generally introduce Jewish, early Christian, and Gnostic "parallels," texts from the *pagan* environment of the New Testament are here preferred. We do this not only to avoid repeating that which is already familiar, but also because the use of texts from the pagan world is burdened with far bigger problems from a methodological and systematic-theological point of view. We would like to offer models for resolving these more difficult problems.

2. On the Choice of Materials

Due to the prescribed limited range of this book, and because it is directed toward the focal points of contemporary theology, the selection of materials can only be illustrative. A truly adequate picture of the connections between the New Testament and its environment could only be offered by a *Corpus Hellenisticum Novi Testamenti* and *Corpus Iudaicum Novi Testamenti*. It is not possible or desirable that this book attempt to be either. Still, the widest possible range of ancient sources should be included, to serve as a reminder of the diversity of contacts between the New Testament and its religious world. In addition, we considered as important parallels not only those that "leap out at" the reader because they manifest an almost verbatim agreement. Rather, the decisive factors in selection were whether the connections between the biblical and extrabiblical text were interesting, illuminating, methodologically important, and needed in order to complete the full spectrum of methodological possibilities. The selection is thus determined by the methodological approaches formulated in §3. Other principles would necessarily have resulted in a different kind of selection.

The texts offered here are therefore not statistically representative of the religious inventory of "the" environment of the New Testament, but rather those that stand out when one looks for those texts that present the variety of possible connections. The book is thus intended to provoke reflection and study. While very many of the texts presented here are evaluated as "parallels," one may also be inclined to emphasize their *dis*similarity to the New Testament. And as is almost always the case in the history-of-religions approach, it is not a matter of one's ability to prove this or that, but of a deeper comprehension brought about by juxtaposition and comparison.

3. On the Translations

The translations are often intended to provide a substitute for the original texts, preserving even the word order of the original, in order to keep the range of interpretations as open as possible. Older translations have been used if they are historically significant or appear to be "unsurpassable"; these translations are indicated in each case. (Translator's note: For translation policy in the English edition, see the New Introduction to the English Edition.)

4. On Classification and Dating

With regard to classification, we need to say something here about the categories "Jewish" and "Hellenistic." Not only those items are to be considered Jewish that can be derived from and explained in terms of the Old Testament stream of tradition with a certain degree of "authenticity." There is also that category of texts and materials that became Jewish, represented by the phenomenon of the Judaizing of pagan texts. The same, of course, applies to the Christianity, whether "Hellenistic" or "Jewish," of the period in which we are interested. For the classification as "Hellenistic," we use the definition of A. Momigliano, that Hellenizing was "the Hellenization of an unknown entity." The factor of Hellenization should be considered with regard to the origin or at least the historical mediation of every text presented in this book. This means participation in the Greek-Oriental melting pot which had been developing since the time of Alexander the Great, inclusive of its popular-philosophical and folkloristic elements. Within this framework the "philosophical type of reflection characteristic of the imperial age," with its series of fixed characteristics, attained a special prominence (see below under no. 427). On the question of dating, certain difficulties were presented by the desire of the deceased editor of the German series for which this book was prepared, G. Friedrich, that thorough attention be given to the dating of rabbinic texts, since it is often the case that the parallel texts to be discussed originated in Talmudic or later times, or at least were first written down then. The following possibilities exist: older common traditions were preserved; or, the later rabbinic texts originated on the basis of the catalyzing presence of the New Testament texts (on this, cf. §3); or, they are a later form (or metamorphosis) of independent parallel tradition; there are other possibilities as well.

§3. Categories for Designating the Relation Between Early Christian Texts and Texts from the Environment

There is no such thing as "the history-of-religions method" in and of itself;[8] one can only speak of the general class of methods by which texts are compared (the texts of the New Testament being only one example to which these methods are applied). Form-critical questions, for example, play an important role in history-of-religions work.[9] We are thus here concerned to reflect on the categories used for the comparison of texts.[10] It is frequently the case that in the older literature the relationship of texts to each other was understood only within the general category of literary dependence. There is nothing surprising in this characteristic of the nineteenth century, which concentrated on the investigation of "sources." The model on which this understanding is based is of course all too clearly that of the scholar at his desk, compiling a work from sources. The form-critical method has broadened the perspective to include other kinds of relationships, and has increasingly shifted the focus from the product to the process of transmission. An example: Paul probably became aware of the pagan formulae reflected in 1 Corinthians 8:6 not via a literary source, but more likely from seeing inscriptions (graffiti) or hearing the missionary slogans of the devotees of Serapis.

Still, the comparative categories are too often used in an unreflective manner without sensitivity to the content involved. That applies to the talk of "influence" (an astrological

8. Contra Müller, "Die religionsgeschichtliche Methode," passim.

9. Cf. K. Berger, *Formgeschichte.*

10. Cf. especially C. Colpe, *Theologie, Ideologie, Religionswissenschaft. Demonstrationen ihrer Unterscheidung,* Theol. Bücherei 68 (Munich, 1980), pp. 270-88.

mentality that blocks off the possibility of endogenous development), of "native soil" (a romantic-biological category, oriented to monocausality), of "dependence" (leaves the nuanced forms of reciprocity out of consideration), of the "pattern" of an older linguistic usage (mediation by the historical process plays no role), of common "structures" (danger of an unhistorical mentality).

The categories named below are of a formal sort. They are, however, not meant in a universal sense, but here always refer to the interrelated cultural complex of the Near East and the Mediterranean. This restriction has the intention of keeping the concrete historical relationships and points of contact constantly in mind, for the comparative study undertaken here is not a matter of the pure history of ideas. The categories are organized in terms of contrasts (Group A) and similarities (Group B). In each subgroup the examples listed are composed of all the texts in this book which the authors judge to fit the respective categories. (Translator's note: This applies only to the texts of the original German edition. For chart identifying these, see pp. 590-93.) There are of course overlapping categories, so that the same text may be listed in more than one place.

Group A: Categories That Comprise
Contrast and Differentiation

I. Metamorphosis

A concept with several powerful elements passes through a number of different phases within which it is so strongly affected by the different milieus and purposes for which it is used that the function of the whole is changed and only certain structural configurations are preserved that can henceforth only be perceived as abstractions. The phases are discontinuous and independent.

Example: The atoning death of a person: Phase 1: In the framework of the Hellenistic prodigies, the wrath of the gods is placated by the blood of a human being. Phase 2: Application of this idea to the Jewish martyrs who die for the Law and so cause God's wrath to cease. Phase 3: Application to the once-for-all death of Jesus Christ made effective by "faith." The elements of continuity are comprised by the cultic interpretation of the violent death of a person and averting of the wrath of the deity.

Text nos. 8, 193, 382, 447, 502, 562, 585, 593, 958.

II. Adoption with the Contrary Tendency

Concepts or semantic fields are taken over, but are so deployed that the foreign religious claim is disputed and the idea is reclaimed for one's own religious frame of reference. Here we have continuity among opposed or competing religious frames of reference.

Example: The use of the Greek word θεός (god) or κύριος (Lord) for Yahweh with the claim that he alone, no longer the others, is the bearer of this concept. Or: εὐαγγέλιον (good news, gospel) is no longer used with reference to the joyous birth of a ruler, but is "depoliticized" and brought into relation with God's kingship. The same thing happens to the concept σωτήρ (savior).

Text nos. 178, 230, 477, 510, 549, 639.

III. Intentional Contrast

Within the framework of a specific genre and tradition, the expectation of the hearer/reader is overturned and corrected at a decisive point. The recipients experience a contrast to what they expected. This presupposes that a firm expectation can be demonstrated.

Example: In 1 Corinthians 8:6 the schema of comparable pagan formulae (the name of a deity combined by prepositions with "all"-expressions) is deformed by placing alongside the "one God" an affirmation about the "one Lord."

Text nos. 13, 85, 87, 773, 867.

IV. Implicit Antithesis

This category works in both directions. The biblical text may present an implicitly formulated antithesis to a position formulated more explicitly in a pagan text; in this case the position advocated by the biblical text can be inferred only by its allusions or by its counterpart. Or the reverse situation may exist in which the biblical text openly expresses something at which the pagan text only hints.

Example: The opponents in 2 Peter manifest a clear affinity to the Cynic position as popularly understood, the kind of skepticism expressed in Plutarch's "On the Delays of the Divine Vengeance" (cf. Philo's "On Providence" and SyrBar 21:15). The opponents obviously deny that God is concerned with the world, and especially that he will act with regard to the world in the future. On the one hand 2 Peter makes statements which are documented much more clearly in the pagan writings (compare 2 Pet. 3:4 with the denial of judgment, immortality, and retribution cited in Plutarch's document). On the other hand, 2 Peter openly formulates what the opponents did not say so openly, that which their position only implied (according to 2 Pet. 2:10, the blasphemous denial of the working of divine power in the world). On the whole matter, cf. K. Berger, "Streit um Gottes Vorsehung. Zur Position der Gegner in 2. Petr," in *FS J. Lebram* (Leiden: E. J. Brill, 1985), pp. 121-35.

Text nos. 256, 357(?), 407(?), 541, 671.

V. Reversal of Relations

Here it is a matter of structural changes. In the biblical text the relation of element A to element B is the contrary of the relations of these two elements in pagan examples.

Example: The appropriate attitude of a person to his or her parents is universally described in pagan wisdom and gnomic tradition as "honor" or the like, but in the opposite manner for Jesus' disciples in Luke 14:26 as "hate." Or: According to pagan texts the deity's rulership is thought of as the support and legitimation of earthly royal power, while in biblical texts God's rule is potentially the end of the power of earthly kings.

Text nos. 120, 234, 577.

VI. Abolition

Constitutive elements of the pagan concept are either adopted only marginally or completely rejected.

Examples: In the development of the apocalyptic doctrine of the two eons, the pagan conception of an infinite number of eons was dropped and the number was limited to two.

And: In distinction from the understanding of the annually repeated event of the deity's death and new life based on nature mythology, the element of annual repetition is missing in the death and resurrection of Jesus and is replaced by its having happened once-for-all.

Text no. 768.

VII. Divergence

(See its counterpart *Convergence* under B.V.): The basis of a common older foundation or earlier structural relationship is perceptibly abandoned, so that the phenomena have developed in disparate directions. The similarity still recognizable in the texts being compared is a late stage, in contrast to the closer relationship of the earlier traditions on which the texts are dependent. Here we have a similarity in which the dimension of historical development is manifest.

Example: In Matthew 2 the star only announces the Messiah, while in Ignatius of Antioch, *Ephesians* 19:2, the Messiah is himself named the "star." The divergence is to be explained on the basis of a widespread oriental and Roman tradition in which "star," in the framework of political astrology, was a sign for the new, longed-for, better ruler. Cf. also Numbers 23:7, 24:17.

Text nos. 54, 55, 57, 58, 97, 100, 102, 107, 171, 173, 174, 192, 194, 196, 204, 290(?), 332, 348(?), 380, 397, 438, 459, 463, 580, 600, 611, 694, 713(?), 726, 759, 790, 811, 865(?), 869, 876, 889, 899, 958.

VIII. Borrowing That Generates an Alien Sense

A tradition is borrowed in a relatively intact form, but receives a surprising new function by being referred to new persons, or placed in a new setting or combination.

Example: The self-predication "I am + metaphor" was probably first used by Egyptian deities, then by Jewish representatives of God (angels, Wisdom), and finally by Jesus as the messenger of God (the "I am" sayings of the Fourth Gospel). We do not have a "metamorphosis," since the form remains entirely intact, but the generated alien sense consists in the fact that the human being Jesus now uses a form of speech with reference to himself which previously had been devoted to the gods or heavenly messengers. The function of self-presentation remains.

Text nos. 230, 405, 615, 732, 754, 792, 903, 955, 956, 957.

IX. Transposition

Borrowed linguistic material is transplanted into an essentially different thematic context. Especially prominent in this category are archaizing and eschatologizing.

Example: The pagan concept that everything is permeated by the deity (e.g. of Aratus, cf. the commentaries on Acts 17:28) is reformulated in Colossians and Ephesians to express an eschatological process that is not yet complete. The filling of all things by God is transposed into an eschatological key. An example of archaizing is the taking of statements about God's rule of the world through the Logos and using them in such a way that they no longer describe the present state of affairs, but are interpreted protologically as the mediating function of the Logos at the beginning of creation.

Text nos. 53, 123, 220, 482, 952.

X. Elaboration or Reduction

Concepts, semantic fields, and linguistic elements that played only a minor role with only marginal relevance in the surrounding culture from which they are borrowed are extensively elaborated and become quantitatively dominant in the religion that borrows them—and vice versa. It is a matter of the quantitative dissemination and dominance in linguistic usage.

Example: The term ἀγάπη (love) that had only marginal usage previously was adopted by Judaism and Christianity as a key term to express the relationship and conduct that God requires between human beings. The concept πίστις (faith) became a catchword used to describe Christian existence as a whole.

Text no. 896.

Group B: Categories That Emphasize Similarity

I. Presupposition

The key to explaining the similar phenomena found in a religious movement and its surrounding culture is the fact that this religion shares the same history and participates in the same culture in which these characteristic features are widespread.

Example: In relation to the Judaism of the first and second centuries CE there is a disproportionately strong preponderance of miracle tradition in the New Testament. The explanation for this, in the sense of its historical presupposition, is the "new irrationalism" widespread in the paganism of the first and second centuries CE, a cultural attitude which encouraged belief in magic and faith in miracles.

Text nos. 12, 18, 21, 22, 25(?), 48, 62, 89(?), 110, 112, 131, 160, 163, 175, 202, 228, 229, 231, 243, 257, 290, 312, 344, 364, 393, 403, 410, 422, 446, 450, 452, 474, 492, 494, 499, 500, 531, 543, 546, 556, 564, 566, 582, 584, 589, 618, 655, 659, 663, 673, 679, 696, 698, 701, 713, 737, 749, 755, 763, 787, 789, 802, 805, 815, 827, 837, 840, 856(?), 865(?), 870, 880, 887, 897, 912-15, 969.

II. Reference

In order to make theological content operational, ideas that have already been developed in the surrounding culture are commandeered. Such requisitioned concepts provide a helpful clarification for the recipients.

Example: For the readers of Hellenistic biography, it was expected that the "hero" of a biography was a "son of a god." For the Jews, however, it was a completely unacceptable idea that God himself would have actual contact with a human female. If one wanted nevertheless to make the idea of divine sonship understandable to Hellenistically oriented readers in narrative form (and not merely to use the title), there was available—as a compromise, so to say—the idea already found by Plutarch in Egypt, namely that the hero was conceived by the divine spirit (Plutarch, "Life of Numa" 4). In this way the pagan expectation could be satisfied, without damage to Jewish ideas. One could therefore venture the thesis that the corresponding statements of the New Testament originated with reference to Egyptian religiosity. That is, one can readily imagine an Egyptian Hellenistic Judaism, in which the theological work of figures such as Philo could be thought of as playing a mediating role (cf. Philo, "On the Cherubim" 46; "Allegorical Interpretation of Genesis" 3.180).

Text nos. 36, 141, 180, 273, 311, 322, 399, 535, 626, 654, 709, 714, 724, 725, 756, 813, 878, 973.

III. Parallels

As in the case of the "Reference" category above, in this category too there is a close correspondence in form and function, without there being evidence of direct borrowing. The resemblance is rather a matter of elements that exist side by side in the same culture, responding in similar ways to the broader horizon of common historical conditions.

Example: What the healed blind man in Mark 8:24 sees ("people like trees") is reminiscent of the inscription from Epidaurus (no. 238; Dittenberger, Syll 3.4 1168/9, according to R. Herzog A 18: ". . . there he at first saw the trees in the holy place," namely after the god had opened his eyes). The common presupposition (in the sense of B.I.) is the faith that the healing of blindness is possible by God's help. The "parallel" is that the healed person at first sees trees. It is hardly possible that Mark was personally acquainted with the inscription mentioned above; it is rather more likely that experiences interpreted in a similar manner lie at the basis of both traditions.

Text nos. 10, 14, 22, 45, 46, 51, 53, 57, 66, 83, 88, 101, 104, 105, 111, 122, 126, 127, 132, 147, 148, 152, 153, 155, 170, 172, 176(?), 205, 213, 215-19, 221, 222, 227, 228, 229, 235, 236, 238, 242, 264, 290(?), 299, 314, 315, 319, 341, 342, 354, 358, 369, 372, 374, 389, 392, 398, 401, 404, 406, 407, 409, 411, 424, 425, 437, 441, 442, 454-55, 471, 472, 532, 534, 542, 552, 570, 612, 614, 644, 648, 657, 661, 662, 674, 676, 681, 699, 719, 735, 736, 748, 769, 770, 775, 776, 784, 791, 798, 800, 817, 835, 843, 853, 854, 861, 868, 871, 872, 875, 885, 907, 916.

IV. Faint Similarity

This kind of analogy does not consist in thorough, detailed, or verbatim agreement, but agreement in only one or a few areas (morphology; structure; function). A common or parallel historical origin is not demonstrable (that is the difference from the category "Parallels" under B.III). After all, within the framework of a common culture similarities of this sort are to be expected.

Examples: (1) Jesus' last supper and pagan cultic meals. (2) The imagery of the body and its members in 1 Corinthians 12 and in Livy, *History of Rome,* 2.32.8ff. (3) Jesus' death and resurrection in comparison to the death and new life of pagan deities (Adonis; Dionysus).

Text nos. 42, 44, 49, 54(?), 58, 59, 96, 104(?), 119(?), 121, 157, 179, 245, 246, 267, 326, 339, 355, 371, 381, 394, 419, 420, 423, 432, 439, 487, 547, 572, 619-22, 627, 722, 740, 742, 743, 794, 858, 917, 940, 953.

V. Convergence

Despite the difference in character of their religious and historical origins, concepts become nearer and more similar to each other on the basis of common conditions in a later historical framework.

Examples: Within the framework of the nationalism provoked among the different peoples of the eastern Mediterranean by the Diadochoi and the Roman rulers, Jewish and Iranian apocalypticism became more and more similar, especially in regard to the significance of human messianic redeemer figures. Parallel to this development—on the basis of the same historical conditions—martyr stories were told (Jewish and Christian, and in Alexandria of pagan martyrs as well) of heroic members of one's own people who withstood the Roman tyrants to their face, and who suffered death.

Text nos. 38, 41, 71, 90, 106, 144, 148, 176(?), 197, 224, 272, 275, 276, 296, 298, 301, 317, 346, 453, 461, 486, 587, 592, 602, 629, 637, 638, 647, 652, 653, 658, 664-68, 689, 690, 692, 697, 706, 710, 729, 731, 733, 734, 744, 752, 758, 763, 764, 771, 780, 821, 836, 884, 962.

VI. Witnesses for a Common Basis

An original historically conditioned common element is perceived on the basis of later texts that have undergone development along different paths. It is possible both to infer the common basis and to explain the differing developments.

Example: The wisdom tradition shared by the whole Near East ("international wisdom") is still perceivable centuries later in collections of Greek sentences, in New Testament parenesis, and in Egyptian sentences. Distinct layers of development can be recognized, to which belong the weaving together of thematic collections of material ("nests") as in the "Haustafeln" and later the tractates. A further example is provided when the New Testament "sacraments" share a common basis with the symbolic actions of the mystery cults. An everyday act is abstracted from its ordinary context, of the nature of a fundamental activity of life such as eating or washing, which by a metaphorically interpreted procedure attains for the candidate participation in the life of the deity and/or fullness of life. This is a "sacramental" procedure which represents the wholeness of things, and is thus built hermeneutically into a comprehensive context ("myth").

Text nos. 5, 7, 11, 15, 18, 21, 25(?), 29, 33, 34, 67, 68, 69, 75, 84, 89(?), 97, 128, 135, 137, 145, 154, 158, 200, 201, 209, 216, 240, 251, 280, 290, 305, 338, 348(?), 356, 362, 363, 368, 373, 391, 395, 400, 405, 412, 424, 427, 431, 433, 443, 444, 448, 451, 459(?), 463, 485, 488, 497, 501, 502, 548, 553, 555, 557, 559, 573, 575, 576, 578, 586, 588, 590, 591, 594, 596, 600, 603, 611(?), 630, 645, 660, 680, 681, 707, 711, 718, 723, 727, 728, 730, 739, 741, 747, 757, 767, 778, 786, 795, 812(?), 819, 824, 839, 851, 855, 866, 869, 874, 877, 881, 889, 891, 901, 905, 906, 909, 912-15, 951.

VII. Borrowing

In distinction from the category "Reference" above, here it is not a matter of helpful clarification of content for particular recipients, but the foreign item remains "borrowed," alien and relatively unmediated. The points of contact are minimal, and such borrowings are not at all to be explained from the religious movement's own stream of tradition (e.g., for Christianity, the Jewish–Old Testament stream).

Example: The myth of the woman, the birth of the child, and the flight into the wilderness of Revelation 12 is a borrowing from pagan mythology (Roman: Rhea-myth; Greek: Leto-Apollo myth; Egypt: Isis-Horus myth). Points of contact are available here only by means of allegorical interpretation.

Text nos. 136, 449.

VIII. Imitation

Reception of material under a strong external orientation, in which agreement in linguistic form and the structure of particular external markers is more important than the relevance of substantial theological matter.

Example: The sudden turning around characteristic of those who report visionary experiences (John 20:14; Rev 1:12) has become in the New Testament merely a signal marking a transition in the scene, but in Greek literature and art it is related to the fear inherent in the ambivalence of the appearance, an ambivalence which must first be clarified. The reception of this feature in the New Testament (it is not found in the Old Testament or Jewish literature) is therefore purely external.

Text nos. 201, 633.

IX. Adaptation

The result of the interaction of two traditions both of which are considered relatively binding; the "genuine" indigenous tradition is adjusted to the tradition dominant in the environment, so that the "genuine" tradition appears in a kind of disguise or superficial transformation.

Example: New Testament encomia to Christ are adapted to the style of the pagan hymns to the gods (e.g., in the "all"-formulations). Or: in 1 Corinthians 15 Paul adapts the traditional understanding of resurrection of the body to the pagan conception that the dead are "transformed" (cf. the topos of the *consolatio,* the topics of comfort and consolation often found in Greek literature). Note the difference from the category "Metamorphosis" under A.I.

Text nos. 571, 804, 807.

X. Common Conventions

Elements simply possessed in common, documented as contemporary and supra-regional ("Hellenistic customs"), and as such resulting from political, social, or economic causes.

Examples: The bylaws of ancient cultic associations and the regulations of the early Christian congregations resemble each other due to the conditions of their common social framework. Or: *Proskynese* as an expression for the honor given by a devotee. Or: Introductory formulae in letters.

Text nos. 27, 28, 32, 50, 63, 64, 65, 73, 74, 78, 79, 81, 87, 92, 98, 108, 118, 119(?), 129, 130, 138, 139, 156, 166, 188, 190, 191, 195, 196, 199, 208, 237-39, 249, 250, 256, 330, 398, 413, 418, 434, 474, 484, 512, 616, 635, 636, 656, 669, 687, 703, 716, 720, 721, 760, 765, 766, 774, 810, 820, 831, 859, 908, 942, 949.

XI. Allusion or Quotation

In distinction from simple "reference" (see above under B.II.), in these cases it is clear that the author refers to a fixed text.

Example: First Corinthians 15:12*b* ("There is no resurrection of the dead") exactly corresponds to the formulations of the popular-Epicurean skepticism ("There is no judgment," "no retribution," "no punishment," etc.).

Text nos. 310, 493, 520, 777, 814, 829.

XII. Common Wisdom Traditions

This category reflects reworking of experiences from common life in a region with extensive common cultural elements, e.g. gnomic formulations and the common stock of imagery used in similitudes and parables.

Example: The distinction between reality and appearance, as "wisdom" provides a reflective means for the righteous on earth to cope with the evil they experience (e.g., Plato as cited in no. 205 below, and the statements about suffering in 1 Peter).

Text nos. 31, 47, 70, 99, 124, 134, 140, 143, 150, 151, 159, 181, 182, 234, 241, 244, 274, 277, 279, 281, 282, 284(?), 285, 286, 287, 291, 292, 294, 295, 308, 313, 316, 318, 320, 321, 324, 328, 329, 331, 332, 333, 334, 335, 337, 338, 340, 343, 347, 429, 440, 445, 544, 565, 601, 609, 678, 746, 803, 812, 828, 829, 834, 838, 873, 882, 883.

XIII. Topoi

A *linguistic* kind of convention (different from that in B.X. above), referring to elements appearing repeatedly in the framework of specific oral and written genres.

Example: Within the framework of biographies, the end of the hero's life is foreshadowed or accompanied by premonitions of disaster.

Text nos. 263, 421, 456, 464-67, 468, 475, 476, 478, 479, 483, 495, 504, 579, 604, 672, 793, 830.

XIV. Catalytic Presence

The mere existence of a certain material or literary product—even if one does not know the course of affairs more precisely—provides the stimulus and occasion for the production of competitive or alternative texts. In this process the material already present is not changed, but works "catalytically" merely by its presence.

Examples: The existence of the New Testament canon was a factor in the Corpus Hermeticum's attaining a canonical form (similarly in the case of Plotinus' *Enneads*). Or: By the mere fact of their existence, the Gospels could have contributed to the formation of Philostratus' *Life of Apollonius of Tyana*—even if there is no further literary dependence or points of contact in the history of their traditions. Direct documentation of the particulars of this category is difficult.

Text nos. 98, 119, 132, 240, 290.

For the practical application of the above categories, the following points of view are important to keep in mind:

a) These categories can also function in combination, e.g. B.I. and B.VII when common presuppositions are the basis for borrowing. B.VI. and B.VII. provide an especially interesting case when a common basis in the past, no longer completely remembered, functions as the framework within which a later borrowing takes place. An additional example would be the combination of B.I. and B.III.

b) In those cases for which one does not have adequate material or historical points of contact available, one will lay hold of categories which, regarded historically, remain more superficial and have in view only the two texts being currently compared (e.g., an orientation toward B.II. and B.III, and away from B.V. and B.VI.).

c) There are certain pragmatic values in this approach. The significance of pagan traditions provides greater illumination on the transmission and adaptation of the earlier foundational theological affirmations of the New Testament than on the original formation of these statements. The reception of "institutions" (formulae, prayers, rites, festivals) happened easier than in the case of elements bound up with unique historical events. Instead of thinking in terms of direct reference or the like, one should more often consider endogenous developments, with the result that one can only speak of "parallels" (i.e., lines of development that never actually touch).

d) In comparing texts, particular attention should be paid to similarities in "structure" (plot, course of action, line of argument), function in the literary or historical context and in semantic fields (cf. K. Berger, *Exegese des Neuen Testaments,* UTB 658 [Heidelberg, 1984], §20f.).

e) The categories B.I. and B.VII. focus attention on the remarkable fact that parallel phenomena are developed almost simultaneously (e.g., apocalyptic eschatology and the way in which being taken to the divine world is represented as "ascension").

f) It is recommended that with each comparison of texts, categories from series A be related to their appropriate counterparts in series B.

The Gospel of Matthew (and Parallels)

1. Matthew 1:1-25/ Luke 1:26-38; 2:1-7

Diogenes Laertius, *Lives of Eminent Philosophers*, "Plato" 3.1-2, 45 (3 cent. CE)

Plato was the son of Ariston and a citizen of Athens. His mother was Perictione (or Potone), who traced back her descent to Solon. For Solon had a brother, Dropides; he was the father of Critias, who was the father of Callaeschrus, who was the father of Critias, one of the Thirty, as well as of Glaucon, who was the father of Charmides and Perictione. Thus Plato, the son of this Perictione and Ariston, was in the sixth generation from Solon. And Solon traced his descent to Neleus and Poseidon. His father too is said to be in the direct line from Codrus, the son of Melanthus, and according to Thrasylus, Codrus and Melanthus also trace their descent from Poseidon.

Speusippus in the work entitled *Plato's Funeral Feast,* Clearchus in his *Encomium on Plato,* and Anaxilaîdes in his second book *On Philosophers,* tell us that there was a story at Athens that Ariston made violent love to Perictione, then in her bloom, and failed to win her; and that, when he ceased to offer violence, Apollo appeared to him in a dream, whereupon he left her unmolested until her child was born.

Apollodorus in his *Chronology* fixes the date of Plato's birth in the 88th Olympiad, on the seventh day of the month Thargelion, the same day on which the Delians say that Apollo himself was born. (LCL)

Clearly, Diogenes Laertius intends to portray Plato as the supernaturally conceived son of the god Apollo.

With regard to the New Testament birth stories, cf.:

1) For Diogenes Laertius, this divine birth was the basis for Plato's amazing intellectual ability, the gift of the god for human salvation. This is expressed in one of the "epitaphs" he composed for Plato:

"If Phoebus did not cause Plato to be born in Greece, how came it that he healed the minds of men by letters? As the god's son Asclepius is a healer of the body, so is Plato of the immortal soul." (LCL)

This is in contrast to Matthew and Luke, neither of whom ever refer to the virginal conception after the birth story, and neither base Jesus' divine power on his supernatural birth.

2) Plato is born of a divine father and a human mother (but not of a virgin). This still gives Diogenes Laertius no hesitation in referring to Ariston as his father. Cf. Plutarch, who wrote of Alexander's divine conception, yet spoke of Philip as his father (Cf. *Moralia* III—"Sayings of Kings and Commanders: Philip the Father of Alexander" [*Alexander* 2.1–3.2]). Similarly, Philo can speak of Moses and the patriarchs as both born of God and of human parents (see no. 8 below).

3) Likewise, the combination of a genealogy of his earthly father with the story of a supernatural birth poses no problems for Diogenes. As in the Lucan genealogy, his earthly father's genealogy is also traced back to its divine origin (Luke 3:23-38), and the date of his birth is related to "secular" Greek history (cf. Luke 3:1-2).

Origen, *Against Celsus* 1.37, refers to this as a well-known story so similar to the Gospel stories of Jesus' birth that he must offer a response.

2. Matthew 1:1-25/ Luke 1:26-38; 2:1-7

Iamblichus, *The Life of Pythagoras* 2.3-5 (4 cent. CE)

The story goes, then, that Ancaeus who dwelt in Same in Cephallenia was sired by Zeus. But whether he gained this reputation by moral excellence or by greatness of soul, he surpassed the other Cephallenians in judgment and renown. He received an oracle from the Pythia to assemble a colony from Cephallenia, Arcadia, and Thessaly, . . .

The tradition is that Mnemarchus and Pythais, Pythagoras' parents, were from the household and family started by Ancaeus who founded the colony.

Although this noble origin is told by the citizens, a Samian poet says that Pythagoras was son of Apollo. He spoke thus:

Pythagoras, whom Pythais bore for Apollo, dear to Zeus,
she who was loveliest of the Samians. (Dillon and Hershbell)

Iamblichus does not accept this poetic statement as literal truth himself, i.e. he argues that the view that a god physically impregnated Pythagoras' mother was simply a rumor. He does regard the poet's declaration as having a certain truth, however, stating that ". . . no one would dispute, judging from his very birth and the all around wisdom of his life, that Pythagoras' soul was sent down to humans under Apollo's leadership, either as a follower in his train, or united with this god in a still more intimate way" (Dillon and Hershbell).

As in Matthew and Luke, statements about the hero's ancestry are combined with affirmations of a supernatural birth. For Iamblichus, however, the genealogy is given to account for the hero's amazing ability, since the progenitor of the family line was himself "begotten by Zeus." For Matthew and Luke, the genealogy is to fit Jesus into the line of saving history. In the Gospels, neither the genealogy nor the miraculous birth are the basis for Jesus' abilities and deeds. The "dualism" of Iamblichus (a human body born in the natural manner but a divine soul that came from heaven) is also in contrast to the Gospels' lack of interest in the "nature" of Jesus, as is Iamblichus' attempt to combine a kind of "preexistence" with a human birth.

3. Matthew 1:1-25/ Luke 1:26-38; 2:1-7

Diodorus Siculus, *Library of History* 4.9.1-10 (1 cent. BCE)

This, then is the story as it has been given us: Perseus was the son of Danaê, the daughter of Acrisius, and Zeus. Now Andromeda, the daughter of Cepheus, lay with him and bore Electryon, and then Eurydicê, the daughter of Pelops, married him and gave birth to Alcmenê, who in turn was wooed by Zeus, who deceived her, and bore Heracles. Consequently the sources of his descent, in their entirety, lead back, as is claimed, through both his parents to the greatest of the gods, in the manner we have shown. The prowess which was found in him was not only to be seen in his deeds, but was also recognized even before his birth. For when Zeus lay with Alcmenê he made the night three times its normal length and by the magnitude of the time expended on the procreation he presaged the exceptional might of the child which would be begotten. And, in general, he did not effect this union from the desire of love, as he did in the case of other women, but rather only for the sake of procreation. Consequently, desiring to give legality to his embraces, he did not choose to offer violence to Alcmenê, and yet he could not hope to persuade her because of her chastity; and so, deciding to use deception, he deceived Alcmenê by assuming in every respect the shape of Amphitryon.

When the natural time of pregnancy had passed, Zeus, whose mind was fixed upon the birth of Heracles, announced in advance in the presence of all the gods that it was his intention to make the child who should be born that day king over the descendants of Perseus; whereupon Hera, who was filled with jealousy, using as her helper Eileithyia her daughter, checked the birth-pains of Alcmenê and brought Eurystheus forth to the light before his full time. Zeus, however, though he had been outgeneraled, wished both to fulfill his promise and to take thought for the future fame of Heracles; consequently, they say, he persuaded Hera to agree that Eurystheus should be king as he had promised, but that Heracles should serve Eurystheus and perform twelve Labors, these to be whatever Eurystheus should prescribe, and that after he had done so he should receive the gift of immortality. After Alcmenê had brought forth the babe, fearful of Hera's jealousy she exposed it at a place which to this time is called after him the Field of Heracles. Now at this very time Athena, approaching the spot in the company of Hera and being amazed at the natural vigor of the child, persuaded Hera to offer it the breast. But when the boy tugged upon her breast with greater violence than would be expected at his age, Hera was unable to endure the pain and cast the babe from her, whereupon Athena took it to its mother and urged her to rear it. And anyone may well be surprised at the unexpected turn of the affair; for the mother whose duty it was to love her own offspring was trying to destroy it, while she who cherished towards it a stepmother's hatred, in ignorance saved the life of one who was her natural enemy.

After this Hera sent two serpents to destroy the babe, but the boy, instead of being terrified, gripped the neck of a serpent in each hand and strangled them both. (LCL)

This story combines the elements of one who is born as a son of god, and is thus divine by nature, and one who is human and becomes immortal as the reward for outstanding achievements. The interest in the details of the divine conception, which is understood as the result of physical union between a deity and a human being, and the incorporation of the birth story into a larger mythological story of the activities of the gods all stand in contrast to the New Testament accounts.

4. Matthew 1:2-17 / Luke 3:23-38

Pesiqta Rabbati 40.3-4 (6–7 cent. CE)

He will judge the world [of Israel] and declare it acquitted; but He will minister judgment to the heathen peoples according to the upright (Ps. 9:9). What is meant by according to the upright? R. Alexandri said: He will minister judgment to the heathen peoples by citing as examples the upright ones among them, the example of Rahab, of Jethro, of Ruth. How will He do so? He will say to each man of the peoples of the earth,

"Why didst thou not bring thyself close to Me?" and each man of them will answer: "I was wicked, so steeped in wickedness I was ashamed." And God will ask: Wast thou more so than Rahab whose house was in the side of the wall so that on the outside she would receive robbers and then whore with them inside? Nevertheless, when she wished to draw near Me, did I not receive her and raise up Prophets and righteous men out of her? Or behold Jethro who was a priest unto idols. When he came to Me, did I not receive him and raise up Prophets and righteous men out of him? Or behold Ruth the Moabitess—when she came to Me, did I not receive her and raise up kings out of her? (Braude)

Although this text is late, it is without Christian influence, and shows that the affirmation of Gentiles who have converted to Judaism, and are even included in the lineage of the Messiah, is not a Matthean innovation, but is developed from the stream of Jewish tradition that emphasized the importance of proselytes. (See on no. 168 at Matt 23:15). This text would seem to indicate that the importance of the women in Matthew's genealogy is not simply that they were women, nor that they were all associated with some sexual irregularity, but that they were Gentiles. The insertion of Gentile women was Matthew's only way of introducing Gentiles into his genealogy. Luke's genealogy (3:23-38) seems to have the same concern but utilizes a different method: despite Luke's concern to emphasize women, including in the birth narratives, his genealogy is strictly male, but includes a Gentile element by tracing Jesus' genealogy beyond Abraham to Adam (and God).

5. Matthew 1:18-25

From the document on the priesthood of Methusalam, Nir, and Melchizedek, Appendix to *2 Enoch* 71:1-11 (1 cent. BCE)

Behold, the wife of Nir, [whose] name was Sopanim, being sterile and never having at any time given birth to a child by Nir—

And Sopanim was in the time of her old age, and in the day of her death. She conceived in her womb, but Nir the priest had not slept with her, nor had he touched her, from the day that the Lord had appointed him to conduct the liturgy in front of the face of the people.

And when Sopanim saw her pregnancy, she was ashamed and embarrassed, and she hid herself during all the days until she gave birth. And not one of the people knew about it. And when 282 days had been completed, and the day of birth had begun to approach, and Nir remembered his wife, and he called her to himself in his house, so that he might converse with her. [And] Sopanim came to Nir, her husband; and, behold, she was pregnant, and the day appointed for giving birth was drawing near.

And Nir saw her, and he became very ashamed. And he said to her, "What is this that you have done, O wife? And [why] have you disgraced me in front of the face of these people? And now, depart from me, and go where you began the disgrace of your womb, so that I might not defile my hand on account of you, and sin in front of the face of the Lord."

And Sopanim spoke to Nir, her husband, saying, "O my lord! Behold, it is the time of my old age, and the day of my death has arrived. I do not understand how my menopause and the barrenness of my womb have been reversed."

And Nir did not believe his wife, and for the second time he said to her, "Depart from me, or else I might assault you, and commit a sin in front of the face of the Lord."

And it came to pass, when Nir had spoken to his wife, Sopanim, that Sopanim fell down at Nir's feet and died.

Nir was extremely distressed; and he said in his heart, "Could this have happened because of my word, since by word and thought a person can sin in front of the face of the Lord? Now may God have mercy upon me! I know in truth in my heart that my hand was not upon her. And so I say, 'Glory to you, O LORD, because no one among mankind knows about this deed which the LORD has done.'" (*OTP* 1:204, 206)

This is an etiological legend for the understanding documented in Hebrews 7:3 and elsewhere, that Melchizedek was born without father, mother, and genealogy. A motif like that reported about Joseph in Matthew 1:19*b* is here extensively developed. In contrast to Matthew 1, it is not the Spirit, but God himself who is the source of the pregnancy (cf. the concluding line in the story above).

On the appearance to Joseph in Matthew 1:20, cf. also Josephus, *Antiquities* 2.212-13.

6. Matthew 1:18-25 / Luke 1:26-38

Plutarch, *Parallel Lives*, "Life of Alexander" 2.1–3.2 (45–125 CE)

As for the lineage of Alexander, on his father's side he was a descendant of Heracles through Caranus, and on his mother's side a descendant of Aeacus through Neoptolemus; this is accepted without any question. And we are told that Philip, after being initiated into the mysteries of Samothrace at the same time with Olympias, he himself being still a youth and she an orphan child, fell in love with her and betrothed himself to her at once with the consent of her brother, Arymbas. When, then, the night before that on which the marriage was consummated, the bride dreamed that there was a peal of thunder and that a thunder-bolt fell on her womb, and that thereby much fire was kindled, which broke into flames and traveled all about, and then was extinguished. At a later time, too, after the marriage, Philip dreamed that he was putting a seal upon his wife's womb; and the device of the seal, as he thought, was the figure of a lion. The other seers, now, were led by the vision to suspect that Philip needed to put a closer watch upon his marriage relations; but Aristander of Telmessus said that the woman was pregnant, since no seal was put upon what was empty, and pregnant of a son whose nature would be bold and lion-like.

Moreover, a serpent was once seen lying stretched out by the side of Olympias as she slept, and we are told that this, more than anything else, dulled the ardor of Philip's attentions to his wife, so that he no longer came often to sleep by her side, either because he feared that some spells and enchantments might be practiced upon him by her, or because he shrank from her embraces in the conviction that she was the partner of a superior being.

But concerning these matters there is another story to this effect: all the women of these parts were addicted to the Orphic rites and the orgies of Dionysus from very ancient times (being called Klodones and Mimallones [Macedonian names for Bacchantes]), and imitated in many ways the practices of the Edonian women and the Thracian women about Mount Haemus, from whom, as it would seem, the word "threskeuein" (θρησκεύειν) came to be applied to the celebration of extravagant and superstitious ceremonies. Now Olympias, who affected these divine possessions more zealously than other women, and carried out these divine inspirations in wilder fashion used to provide the reveling companies with great tame serpents, which would often lift their heads from out of the ivy and the mystic winnowing baskets, or coil themselves about the wands and garlands of the women, thus terrifying the men.

However, after his vision, as we are told, Philip sent Chaeron of Megalopolis to Delphi, by whom an oracle was brought him from Apollo, who bade him sacrifice to Ammon and hold that god in greatest reverence, but told him he was to lose that one of his eyes which he had applied to the chink in the door when he espied the god, in the form of a serpent, sharing the couch with his wife. Moreover, Olympias, as Eratosthenes says, when she sent Alexander forth upon his great expedition, told him, and him alone, the secret of his begetting, and bade him have purposes worthy of his birth. Others, on the contrary, say that she repudiated the idea, and said: "Alexander must cease slandering me to Hera" (the lawful spouse of Zeus Ammon). (LCL)

Alexander had thought of himself as the adopted son of Zeus, which he later came to interpret in a special way. He was apparently influenced by the pronouncement of an Egyptian prophet at the oracle of Zeus-Ammon at the Oasis of Siwah in north Africa (see David Aune, "Christian Prophecy and the Messianic Status of Jesus," in James H. Charlesworth, ed., *The Messiah: Developments in Earliest Judaism and Christianity* [Minneapolis: Fortress Press, 1992], p. 412, and the literature he gives). It was only after Alexander's death that legends began to circulate that he had been born son of Zeus. This is analogous to the development of Christology in the New Testament, which proceeded "backward" by conceiving of Jesus to be the son of God who would descend from heaven in the future, then as already son of God at his resurrection or ascension, then to having been son of God already during his ministry, then to stories in which he was born as son of God (cf. Raymond Brown, *The Birth of the Messiah* [New York: Doubleday, 1993], pp. 29-32).

One may further note the large role dreams play in both the Alexander and Matthean stories (but not the Lucan birth stories).

The manner of conception is very different in the biblical stories, which have no suggestion of copulation between the divine father and the human mother.

7. Matthew 1:18-25 / Luke 1:26-38

Plutarch, *Parallel Lives*, "Life of Numa" 4.2-4 (45–125 CE)

However, that this story resembles many of the very ancient tales which the Phrygians have received and cherished concerning Attis, the Bithynians concerning Herodotus, the Arcadians concerning Endymion, and other peoples concerning other mortals who we thought to have achieved a life of blessedness in the love of the gods, is quite evident. And there is some reason in supposing that Deity, who is not a lover of horses or birds, but a lover of men, should be willing to consort with men of superlative goodness, and should not dislike or disdain the company of a wise and holy man. But that an immortal god should take carnal pleasure in a mortal body and its beauty, this, surely, is hard to believe.

And yet the Egyptians make a distinction here which is thought plausible, namely, that while a woman can be approached by a divine spirit [πνεῦμα] and made pregnant, there is no such thing as carnal intercourse and communion between a man [ἀνδρί] and a divinity. But they lose sight of the fact that intercourse is a reciprocal matter, and that both parties to it enter into a like communion. However, that a god should have affection for a man [ἄνθρωπον] . . . is fit and proper. (LCL)

In his "Table Talk" 8.1-3, Plutarch takes up the idea again. Among birds also, conception can take place by means of a wind (πνεῦμα can mean "wind" as well as "spirit"). And since the essence of gods consists of wind and spirit, one could in this way be impregnated with the divine semen.

The middle way suggested here must have been particularly attractive for Hellenistic Jewish Christians: since physical intercourse of God with a human female was out of the question, the idea was formed that it was a matter of the divine "spirit" (= wind), an ideal hermeneutical bridge between the conceptuality of Jewish Christianity and Hellenistic descriptions of the lives of great men. On this cf.:

1) Plutarch, "Fabius Maximus," §1 (the ancestor originated from a relationship between Hercules and a nymph).

2) Plutarch, "Alexander," §2 (in the night before their first sexual contact, a lightning bolt entered the body of the bride; a snake was seen beside the woman's body).

3) Plutarch, "Fortune Alexander," §5 (the ruler Dionysius the Younger claims to be the son of Apollo and a Doric mother).

4) Plutarch, "Fortune Romans" 10. See no. 126 (Servius born of the union of Vulcan and the slave Ocrisia).

5) Philostratus, *Life of Apollonius* 1.4: "To his [Apollonius'] mother, just before he was born, there came an apparition of Proteus, who changes his form so much in Homer, in the guise of an Egyptian demon. She was in no way frightened, but asked him what sort of child she would bear. And he answered: 'Myself.' 'And who are you?' she asked. 'Proteus,' answered he, 'the god of Egypt'" (LCL). The story continues with a portrayal of the miraculous birth by means of a lightning bolt that strikes the ground.

6) Suetonius, *Lives*, "Deified Augustus" 94. See no. 14.

8. Matthew 1:18-25/ Luke 1:26-38

Philo, *On the Cherubim* 44-48 (15 BCE–50 CE)

He [the Father of All] then sows, but the fruit of His sowing, the fruit which is His own, He bestows as a gift. For God begets nothing for Himself, for He is in want of nothing, but all for him who needs to receive. I will give as a warrant for my words one that none can dispute, Moses the holiest of men. For he shows us Sarah conceiving at the time when God visited her in her solitude [Gen. xxi. 1], but when she brings forth it is not to the Author of her visitation, but to him who seeks to win wisdom, whose name is Abraham.

And even clearer is Moses' teaching of Leah, that God opened her womb [Gen. xxix. 31]. Now to open the womb belongs to the husband. Yet when she conceived she brought forth not to God (for He is in Himself all-sufficing for Himself), but to him who endures toil to gain the good, even Jacob. Thus virtue receives the divine seed from the Creator, but brings forth to one of her own lovers, who is preferred above all others who seek her favor. Again Isaac the all-wise besought God, and through the power of Him who was thus besought Steadfastness or Rebecca became pregnant [Gen. xxv. 21]. And without supplication or entreaty did Moses, when he took Zipporah the winged and soaring virtue, find her pregnant through no mortal agency [Exod. ii. 22].

These thoughts, ye initiated, whose ears are purified, receive into your souls as holy mysteries . . . [i.e., who have] the knowledge of the Cause and of virtue, and besides these two, of the fruit which is engendered by them both. (LCL)

While the Old Testament narratives leave no doubt about the fact that in each case the human husband was the father of the child, Philo's interpretation of these stories in terms of an allegorizing catechesis for "initiates" brings in the idea that the births were the result of divine fathering. The view postulated by Philo, that Scripture has the quality of mystery as understood in the mystery cults, becomes the vehicle of introducing mythical ideas. It thus remains an open question whether Philo reckoned divine begetting on the plane of real history. He speaks plainly about the matter only when he is speaking allegorically of the birth of virtues.

On Luke 1:32, 35 (title), cf. no. 531.

9. Matthew 1:18–2:23

Plutarch, *Moralia*, "Dinner of the Seven Wise Men" 159A; "On Inoffensive Self-Praise" 589D (45–125 CE)

[Dreams are] . . . our most ancient and respected form of divination. . . . In popular belief it is only in sleep that men receive inspiration from on high. (LCL)

Plato had developed a sophisticated philosophical argument for divine communication through mania and dreams, by which the soul, untrammeled by the material body, could receive communication with the divine world of forms. In the Hellenistic age, it was sometimes thought that the soul disengaged from the body during sleep and wandered about gaining information not otherwise available (cf. Everett Ferguson, *Backgrounds of Early Christianity* [Grand Rapids: Wm. B. Eerdmans, 1993], p. 206). Although God communicated by dreams in some OT narratives (Gen, Dan, 1 Kgs), claims to revelation through dreams were suspect by the prophets (Jer 23:27-28; Deut 13:1-5). Matthew here reflects the popular Hellenistic view, not the prophetic Jewish view.

10. Matthew 1:19

Pseudo-Herodotus, *Life of Homer* (date unknown, between 3 cent. BCE and 2 cent. CE)

[Melanopos had pledged his daughter Cretheis to the Argive Cleanax in marriage.] But as the time for the wedding drew near, it happened that the young woman was secretly with another man and became pregnant. At first this remained hidden. But when Cleanax became aware of it, he was angry and called Cretheis to him and privately leveled harsh accusations against her, holding before her the shame this had brought to them both in the eyes of the citizenry. . . . [Cleanax dismissed Cretheis quietly, and she gave birth to Homer, had to work with her own hands to raise him, etc.] (MEB/Berger)

As in other biographies of important people (cf. no. 7), so also in the case of Homer, already his birth is irregular. Here however, in distinction to the usual, the father is not a divine being, but the circumstances as a whole are deplorable, bordering on the asocial.

11. Matthew 2:1-12

From the Syrian *Chronicle of Zuqnin* (final redaction ca. 775 CE)

But when the time came for the fulfillment of what had been written in the scriptures concerning the revelation of the light of that hidden star, would that we were worthy that it/he should come in our day and we receive it/him with joy. . . . And every single one of us saw wonderful and different visions, which had never been seen by any of us before. . . . And we came, each of us from our place of residence, in accord with our earlier custom, in order to climb the mountain of victory and to immerse ourselves in the spring of purification, to wash ourselves according to our usual custom. And we saw a light in the form of a pillar of inexpressible light, that descended and stopped over the mysteries. We were afraid and perplexed, as we saw it, and above it the shining star, the light of which we are not able to speak . . . and we climbed up and found the pillar of light in front of the cave. . . . And before our very eyes there came forth from the pillar of light and from the star something like the hand of a small man, which we could not observe more closely, and it strengthened us. . . . And we took our crowns and placed them under his feet. (MEB/Berger)

On the discussion of this text: see G. Widengren, *Iranisch-semitische Kulturbegegnung in parthischer Zeit* (Cologne: Opladen, 1960), 71-86. A similar text (expectation of a star by Magi, and a cave in the cliff of the mount of victory) is handed on (only lightly Christianized) in the "Opus imperfectum" in Matthaeum (*PG* 56. 637-38, the Book of Seth). The conjunction between light and a cave is first found in Christian tradition in the Protevangelium of James 18-21 in connection with the birth of Jesus. Already Justin, *Dial* 78.5, has Jesus born in a cave (cf. no. 13). The primary constituent is the expectation of a star that portends salvation (cf. Num 24:17), then Persian and Christian traditions experienced a cross-fertilization. Cf. further no. 450!

Important from the point of view of church history was the annual celebration of the birth of the Aeon from the Virgin (Kore) in the night of the fifth to the sixth of January, for this date was adopted in the East for the birth of Jesus. (See the report by Epiphanius, *Heresies* 51.22.)

"The leaders of the idolaters . . . in many places hold a great feast on the very night of Epiphany, so that those who have placed their hopes in what is error may not seek the truth. First of all, in Alexandria they hold festival in what is called the Coreum, which is a great temple, namely the sacred precinct of Core. They stay awake the whole night singing hymns to the idol to the accompaniment of flutes. Asked what the rite means, they say: Today at this hour Core [meaning the virgin] engendered [gave birth to] Aeon" (Amidon). On the date, cf. also no. 372.

Suetonius (born ca. 70 CE), *Life of the Caesars* 88, reports that a comet lit up the heavens for seven days, and was taken to be the soul of the dead Caesar.

12. Matthew 2:1-12

Cicero, *On Divination* 1.46 (106–43 BCE)

Why need I bring forth from Dino's Persian annals the dreams of that famous prince, Cyrus, and their interpretations by the magi? But take this instance: Once upon a time Cyrus dreamed that the sun was at his feet. Three times, so Dinon writes, he vainly tried to grasp it and each time it turned away, escaped him, and finally disappeared. He was told by the magi, who are classed as wise and learned men among the Persians, that his grasping for the sun three times portended that he would reign for thirty years. And thus it happened; for he lived to his seventieth year, having begun to reign at forty.

It certainly must be true that even barbarians have some power of foreknowledge and of prophecy . . .

Everybody knows that on the same night in which Olympias was delivered of Alexander the temple of Diana at Ephesus was burned, and that the magi began to cry out as the day was breaking: "Asia's deadly curse was born last night." (LCL)

As in Matthew 2 the Magi are regarded as interpreters of astrological signs referring to rulership. Pliny the Elder reports in his *Natural History* 30.6 of the Magus Tiradates who came to Nero to predict both Nero's and Armenia's subjection. Then Nero had himself initiated into the rites and arts of the magi.

In connection with the birth of Alexander the Great, Pliny 1.47 reports: "The Magi had announced that plague and destruction for Asia would be born in the coming night" (LCL). Cf. F. Pfister, *Kleine Schriften zum Alexanderroman* (1976) 307-8, "Alexander the Great in the revelations."

For Cicero's elaboration of the prevalence of divination among Hellenistic peoples, and the positive view of it from this sophisticated author, see also *Divination* 1.43.

13. Matthew 2:1-16/ Luke 2:4, 15

Jerome, *Letter 58 to Paulinus* §3 (345–419 CE)

The original persecutors, indeed, supposed that by polluting our holy places they would deprive us of our faith in the passion and in the resurrection. Even my own Bethlehem, as it now is, that most venerable spot in the whole world of which the psalmist sings: "The truth hath sprung out of the earth," was overshadowed by a grove of Tammuz, that is of Adonis; and in the very cave where the infant Christ had uttered His earliest cry lamentation was made for the paramour of Venus. (NF)

Tammuz is a Babylonian (originally, Sumerian) fertility god, whose disappearance into the underworld was annually announced by the dying of vegetation. Also Adonis is a "dying" semidivine vegetation deity. It is less likely that it is a case of secondary paganization of an originally Christian cultic site than that the continued existence of pagan folk religion in Bethlehem presented the Christians with a point of contact for the development of their own cultic site. On the "cave," cf. also C. Colpe, "Die Mithrasmysterien und die Kirchenväter" in *Romanitas et Christianitas* (Festschrift for

Waszink) (Amsterdam: North-Holland, 1973), 39-40 (there also a discussion of Isa 33:16-17 LXX and further literature).

14. Matthew 2:1-23

Suetonius, *Lives of the Caesars*, "The Deified Augustus" 2.94 (early 2 cent. CE)

Having reached this point, it will not be out of place to add an account of the omens which occurred before he was born, on the very day of his birth, and afterward, from which it was possible to anticipate and perceive his future greatness and uninterrupted good fortune.

In ancient days, when a part of the wall of Velitrae had been struck by lightning, the prediction was made that a citizen of that town would one day rule the world. Through their confidence in this the people of Velitrae had at once made war on the Roman people and fought with them many times after that almost to their utter destruction; but at last long afterward the event proved that the omen had foretold the rule of Augustus.

According to Julius Marathus, a few months before Augustus was born a portent was generally observed at Rome, which gave warning that nature was pregnant with a king for the Roman people; thereupon the senate in consternation decreed that no male child born that year should be reared; but those whose wives were with child saw to it that the decree was not filed in the treasury, since each one appropriated the prediction to his own family.

I have read the following story in the books of Asclepias of Mendes entitled *Theologumena*. When Atia had come in the middle of the night to the solemn service of Apollo, she had her litter set down in the temple and fell asleep, while the rest of the matrons also slept. On a sudden a serpent glided up to her and shortly went away. When she awoke, she purified herself, as if after the embraces of her husband, and at once there appeared on her body a mark in colors like a serpent, and she could never get rid of it; so that presently she ceased ever to go to the public baths. In the tenth month after that Augustus was born and was therefore regarded as the son of Apollo. Atia too, before she gave him birth, dreamed that her vitals were borne up to the stars and spread over the whole extent of land and sea, while Octavius dreamed that the sun rose from Atia's womb.

The day he was born the conspiracy of Catiline was before the House, and Octavius came late because of his wife's confinement; then Publius Nigidius, as everyone knows, learning the reason for his tardiness and being informed also of the hour of the birth, declared that the ruler of the world had been born. Later, when Octavius was leading an army through remote parts of Thrace, and in the grove of Father Liber consulted the priests about his son with barbarian rites, they made the same prediction; since such a pillar of flame sprang forth from the wine that was poured over the altar, that it rose above the temple roof and mounted to the very sky, and such an omen had befallen no one save Alexander the Great, when he offered sacrifice at the same altar. Moreover, the very next night, he dreamt that his son appeared to him in a guise more majestic than that of mortal man, with the thunderbolt, scepter, and insignia of Jupiter Optimus Maximus, wearing a crown begirt with rays and mounted upon a laurel-wreathed chariot drawn by twelve horses of surpassing whiteness. When Augustus was still an infant, as is recorded by the hand of Gaius Drusus, he was placed by his nurse at evening in his cradle on the ground floor and the next morning had disappeared; but after long search he was at last found lying on a lofty tower with his face toward the rising sun.

As soon as he began to walk, it chanced that the frogs were making a great noise at his grandfather's country place; he bade them be silent, and they say that since then no frog has ever croaked there. As he was lunching in a grove at the fourth milestone on the Campanian road, an eagle surprised him by snatching his bread from his hand, and after flying to a great height, equally to his surprise dropped gently down again and gave it back to him.

After Quintus Catulus had dedicated the Capitol, he had dreams on two nights in succession: first, that Jupiter Optimus Maximus called aside one of a number of boys of good family, who were playing around his altar, and put in the fold of his toga an image of Roma, which he was carrying in his hand; the next night he dreamt that he saw this same boy in the lap of Jupiter of the Capitol, and that when he had ordered that he be removed, the god warned him to desist, declaring that the boy was being reared to be the savior of his country. When Catulus next day met Augustus, whom he had never seen before, he looked at him in great surprise and said that he was very like the boy of whom he had dreamed.

Some gave a different account of Catulus's first dream: when a large group of well-born children asked Jupiter for a guardian, he pointed out one of their number, to whom they were to refer all their wishes, and then, after lightly touching the boy's mouth with his fingers, laid them on his own lips.

As Marcus Cicero was attending Gaius Caesar to the Capitol, he happened to tell his friends a dream of the night before; that a boy of noble countenance was let down from heaven on a golden chain and, standing at the door of the temple, was given a whip by Jupiter. Just then suddenly catching sight of Augustus, who was still unknown to the greater number of those present and had been brought to the ceremony by his uncle Caesar, he declared that he was the very one whose form had appeared to him in his dream. (LCL)

A surprising number of contacts with the Matthean story of Jesus' birth are found concentrated in Suetonius' account of Augustus, who was emperor when Jesus was born: dreams and oracles; the threat to the child's life; a supernatural birth; the "father" receives a dream; the story concerns a king to be born. There are also points of contact with other New Testament passages, e.g. that the world is in labor pains to bring forth the new king (cf. the ὠδίνες of Mark 13:8/ Matt 24:8, and Rom 8:22 συνωδίνω).

By being deposited in the state treasury a decision became legally in force. As in Matthew, here the story concerns the reaction to a prodigy announcing a change in rulership. But in contrast to Matthew, here the senate fears monarchy as such, and the decision never became official law.

On related legends in Judaism about the murder of children in connection with the birth of Abraham, cf. A. Wünsche, *Aus Israels Lehrhallen* (Leipzig, 1907) (= Hildesheim, 1967), 1.1, 3, "Abraham und Nimrod," pp. 14-34; 4, "The Story of Abraham's Birth and Youth," pp. 35-41; 5, "Abraham's Birth," pp. 42-45. On the connections with Moses-traditions, cf. Josephus, *Antiquities* 2.205-12. For bib., cf. G. Binder, *Die Aussetzung der Königskinder Kyros und Romulus* (1964).

15. Matthew 2:5-6/ Luke 2:4-20

Lamentations Rabbah (1–2 cent. CE)

There was a man who was ploughing, and one of his oxen lowed.
An Arab came by and said to him, "What are you?"
He said to him, "I am a Jew."
He said to him, "Untie your ox and your plough."

He said to him, "Why?"

He said to him, "Because the house of the sanctuary of the Jews has been destroyed."

He said to him, "How do you know?"

He said to him, "I know from the lowing of your ox."

While he was engaged with him, the ox lowed again.

He said to him, "Harness your ox and tie on your plough, for the redeemer of the Jews has been born."

He said to him, "What is his name?"

He said to him, "His name is Menahem [Redeemer]."

"And as to his father, what is his name?"

He said to him, "Hezekiah."

He said to him, "And where do they live?"

He said to him, "In Birat Arba in Bethlehem in Judah."

That man went and sold his oxen and sold his plough and bought felt clothing for children. He went into one city and left another, went into one country and left another, until he got there. All the villagers came to buy from him. But the woman who was the mother of that infant did not buy from him. He said to her, "Why didn't you buy children's felt clothing from me?"

She said to him, "Because a hard fate is in store for my child."

He said to her, "Why?"

She said to him, "Because at his coming the house of the sanctuary was destroyed."

He said to her, "We trust in the Master of the world that just as at his coming it was destroyed, so at his coming it will be rebuilt."

He said to her, "Now you take for yourself some of these children's felt garments."

She said to him, "I haven't got any money."

He said to her, "What difference does it make to you! Take them now, and after a few days I'll come and collect."

She took the clothes and went away. After a few days that man said, "I'm going to go and see how that infant is doing."

He came to her and said to her, "As to that child, how is he doing?"

She said to him, "Didn't I tell you that a hard fate is in store for him? Misfortune has dogged him.

"From the moment [you left], strong winds have come and a whirlwind and swept him off and have gone on."

He said to her, "Did I not say to you that just as at his coming it was destroyed, so at his coming it will be rebuilt?" (Neusner, *Lamentations Rabbah*)

On the day when the temple was destroyed, the Messiah was born. This is the sign that allows the farmer, who is wholly dedicated to finding the Messiah, to discern the true identity of the child. His being spirited away by the wind and storm indicates that he is being kept in heaven until the appointed time for his appearance in power (cf. no. 957).

The Messiah is here named "Menachem" ("comforter"), as also frequently elsewhere (so also in the text preserved in a Christian context as an oracle *PG* 107, 1137). Here, this Menachem is son of Hezekiah, a figure who played a role in the resistance against Rome, who is related genealogically to Judas the Galilean (cf. H. Gressmann, *Der Messias* [Göttingen: Vandenhoeck & Ruprecht, 1929], 458ff.).

On the story as a whole, cf. similarly j. Ber. 5a. The important points of contact are (1) Bethlehem as the city of the Messiah's birth, as also in the targum on Micah 5:1: "And you, O Bethlehem Ephrathah, you who were too small to be numbered among the thousands of the house of Judah, from you shall come forth before me the anointed One, to exercise dominion over Israel, he whose name was mentioned from of old, from ancient times" (Cathcart and Gordon). Should we consider the tradition quite old, since it presupposes that the name "Bethlehem" had not yet been monopolized in the standard Christian interpretation? (2) In this text, the Messiah has already been born in Bethlehem. Does this mean it is a pre-Christian, or does it enter into competition with the Christian Gospels? (3) The text offers impressive documentation for the view also presupposed in Mark 14:58 (John 2:19-21), that the Messiah has some connection with the destruction of the temple in 70 CE, and its eschatological restoration. This text makes the view of the Gospels more plausible. (4) In this text the Messiah is pictured as being whisked away after his birth, as is also presupposed in Revelation 12:5 as a Jewish tradition. Cf. also R. Meyer, *Der Prophet aus Galiläa* (Leipzig, 1940; repr. Darmstadt: Wissenschaftliche Buchgesellschaft, 1970), 76-77. On the incognito Messiah, cf. no. 422.

16. Matthew 3:1-2/ Mark 1:4-8/ Luke 3:1-18

Josephus, *Antiquities* 18.116-19 (37–100 CE)

But to some of the Jews the destruction of Herod's army seemed to be divine vengeance, and certainly a just vengeance, for his treatment of John, surnamed the Baptist. For Herod had put him to death, though he was a good man and had exhorted the Jews to lead righteous lives, to practice justice toward their fellows and piety toward God, and so doing to join in baptism. In his view this was a necessary preliminary if baptism was to be acceptable to God. They must not employ it to gain pardon for whatever sins they committed, but as a consecration of the body implying that the soul was already thoroughly cleansed by right behavior. When others too joined the crowds about him, because they were aroused to the highest degree by his sermons, Herod became alarmed. Eloquence that had so great an effect on mankind might lead to some form of sedition, for it looked as if they would be guided by John in everything that they did. Herod decided therefore that it would be much better to strike first and be rid of him before his work led to an uprising, than to wait for an upheaval, get involved in a difficult situation and see his mistake. Though John, because of Herod's suspicions, was brought in chains to Machaerus, the stronghold that we have previously mentioned, and there put to death, yet the verdict of the Jews was that the destruction visited upon Herod's army was a vindication of John, since God saw fit to inflict such a blow on Herod. (LCL)

The description of John and his message is adjusted to fit Josephus' religiopolitical sensitivities, omitting the eschatological and messianic element of his preaching, which forms its central focus in the New Testament. Josephus' report of Herod's fear of John's influence shows that the eschatological and messianic dimension was present in the tradition used by Josephus. Likewise, the explanation of John's baptism is purged of its eschatological dimension and is domesticated into a harmless bodily purification and general moralism, losing its radical eschatological challenge.

Without the political motivation, the *Ep. Arist.* 306 also minimizes the sacral and ritual dimension of Jewish lustrations in order to make them more understandable to Hellenistic readers: "Following the custom of all the Jews, they [the LXX translators] washed their hands in the sea in the course of their prayers to God, and then proceeded to the reading and explications of each point. I asked this question, 'What is their purpose in washing their hands while saying their prayers?' They explained that it is evidence that they have done no evil, for all activity takes place by means of the hands. Thus they nobly and piously refer everything to righteousness and truth." (*OTP* 2:33)

17. Matthew 3:4/ Mark 1:6

Josephus, *Life of Josephus* 9-12 (37–100 CE)

At about the age of sixteen I determined to gain personal experience of the several sects into which our nation is divided. These, as I have frequently mentioned, are three in number—the first that of the Pharisees, the second that of the Sadducees, and the third that of the Essenes. I thought that, after a thorough investigation, I should be in a position to select the best. So I submitted myself to hard training and laborious exercises and passed through the three courses. Not content, however, with the experiences thus gained, on hearing of one named Bannus, who dwelt in the wilderness, wearing only such clothing as trees provided, feeding on such things as grew of themselves, and using frequent ablutions of cold water, by day and night, for purity's sake, I became his devoted disciple. With him I lived for three years and, having accomplished my purpose, returned to the city. Being now in my nineteenth year I began to govern my life by the rules of the Pharisees, a sect having points of resemblance to that which the Greeks call the Stoic school. (LCL)

Josephus pictures the Jews as having philosophical schools like the Greeks (for his detailed descriptions, see *War* 2.119-66 [no. 19]; *Antiquities* 13.171; 18.11). After "passing through all their courses" he also studied with an ascetic teacher who stood outside the structured religious groups of Judaism. Other points of contact with John the Baptist: (1) he dwelt in the "wilderness" (ἐρημία); (2) wore natural, not manufactured, clothing; (3) ate natural, not processed, food; (4) used water for ritual purification; (5) had disciples. There are important differences as well: Bannus has no eschatological message, does not preach to crowds, and his "baptism" is only for himself, not an eschatological sign of repentance urged upon his hearers. However, like the Pharisees, Sadducees, and Essenes, the description of Bannus may have been adapted to suit Josephus' own purposes.

18. Matthew 3:4/ Mark 1:6

Ascension of Isaiah 2:7-11 (1 cent. BCE–1 cent. CE)

And when Isaiah the son of Amoz saw the great iniquity which was being committed in Jerusalem, and the service of Satan, and his wantonness, he withdrew from Jerusalem and dwelt in Bethlehem of Judah. (8) And also there he found great iniquity; and he withdrew from Bethlehem and dwelt on a mountain in a desert place. (9) And Micah the prophet, and the aged Ananias, and Joel and Habakkuk, and Josab his son, and many of the faithful who believed in the ascension into heaven, withdrew and dwelt on the mountain. (10) All of them were clothed in sackcloth, and all of them were prophets; they had nothing with them, but were destitute, and they all lamented bitterly over the going astray of Israel. (11) And they had nothing to eat except wild herbs [which] they gathered from the mountains. . . . (*OTP* 2:158)

In this text from the politically explosive time of the first century BCE Isaiah becomes a prototype of charismatic resistance to oppressive rulers in Israel. He is pictured as being surrounded by a group which may portray the kind of religious milieu from which John the Baptist and Jesus derive, or in any case related charismatic groups. The "ascension into heaven" refers to visions or visionary tours of heaven.

19. Matthew 3:7

Josephus, *Jewish War* 2.119-66 (37–100 CE)

Jewish philosophy, in fact, takes three forms. The followers of the first school are called Pharisees, of the second Sadducees, of the third Essenes.

The Essenes have a reputation for cultivating peculiar sanctity. Of Jewish birth, they show a greater attachment to each other than do the other sects. They shun pleasures as a vice and regard temperance and the control of the passions as a special virtue. Marriage they disdain, but they adopt other men's children, while yet pliable and docile, and regard them as their kin and mold them in accordance with their own principles. . . .

Riches they despise, and their community of goods is truly admirable; you will not find one among them distinguished by greater opulence than another. They have a law that new members on admission to the sect shall confiscate [sic] their property to the order, with the result that you will nowhere see either abject poverty or inordinate wealth; the individual's possessions join the common stock and all, like brothers, enjoy a single patrimony. . . .

A candidate anxious to join their sect is not immediately admitted. For one year, during which he remains outside the fraternity, they prescribe for him their own rule of life, presenting him with a small hatchet, the loin-cloth already mentioned, and white raiment. Having proof of his temperance during this probationary period, he is brought into closer touch with the rule and is allowed to share the purer kind of holy water, but is not yet received into the meetings of the community. For after this exhibition of endurance, his character is tested for two years more, and only then, if found worthy, is he enrolled in the society. But, before he may touch the common food, he is made to swear tremendous oaths: first that he will practice piety toward the Deity, next that he will observe justice toward men: that he will wrong none whether of his own mind or under another's orders; that he will forever hate the unjust and fight the battle of the just; that he will forever keep faith with all men, especially with the powers that be, since no ruler attains his office save by the will of God; that, should he himself bear rule, he will never abuse his authority nor, either in dress or by other outward marks of superiority, outshine his subjects; to be forever a lover of truth and to expose liars; to keep his hands from stealing and his soul pure from unholy gain; to conceal nothing from the members of his sect and to report none of their secrets to others, even though tortured to death. He swears, moreover, to transmit their rules exactly as he received them; to abstain from robbery; and in like manner carefully to preserve the books of the sect and the names of the angels. Such are the oaths by which they secure proselytes. . . .

The war with the Romans tried their souls through and through by every variety of test. Racked and twisted, burnt and broken, and made to pass through every instrument of torture, in order to induce them to blaspheme their lawgiver or to eat some forbidden thing, they refused to yield to either demand, nor ever once did they cringe to their persecutors or shed a tear. Smiling in their agonies and mildly deriding their tormentors, they cheerfully resigned their souls, confident that they would receive them back again. . . .

Of the two first-named schools, the Pharisees, who are considered the most accurate interpreters of the laws, and hold the position of the leading sect, attribute everything to Fate and God; they hold that to act rightly or otherwise rests, indeed, for the most part with men, but that in each action Fate cooperates. Every soul, they maintain, is imperishable, but the soul of the good alone passes into another body, while the souls of the wicked suffer eternal punishment.

The Sadducees, the second of the orders, do away with Fate altogether, and remove God beyond, not merely the commission, but the very sight, of evil. They maintain that man has the free choice of good or evil, and that it rests with each man's will whether he follows the one or the other. As for the persistence of the soul after death, penalties in the underworld, and rewards, they will have none of them.

The Pharisees are affectionate to each other and cultivate harmonious relations with the community. The Sadducees, on the contrary, are, even among themselves, rather boorish in their behavior, and in their intercourse with their peers are as rude as to aliens. Such is what I have to say on the Jewish philosophical schools. (LCL)

There are many points of contact with several aspects of New Testament religion and thought, which are noted in the appropriate places in this volume. The lengthy passage is reproduced here as a whole to give the reader a more extended firsthand impression of how an educated Palestinian Jew who spent his later life in the Roman court portrayed the main currents of Jewish religion to his Hellenistic contemporaries.

20. Matthew 3:13-17 / Mark 1:9-11 / Luke 3:21-22

Magical Papyrus *PGM* 475-829 (uncertain date)

This is the invocation of the spell: first origin of my origin, AEEIOYO, first beginning of my beginning, PPP SSS PHR[E], spirit of spirit, the first of the spirit / in me, MMM, fire given by god to my mixture of the mixtures in me, the first of the fire in me, EY EIA EE, water of water, the first of the water in me, OOO AAA EEE, earthy material, the first of the earthy material in me, / YE YOE, my complete body, I, NN whose mother is NN, which was formed by a noble arm and an incorruptible right hand in a world without light and yet radiant, without soul and yet alive with soul, YEI AYI EYOIE: now if it be your will, . . .

I may gaze upon the immortal / beginning with the immortal spirit, . . .

that I may be born again in thought, . . .

and the sacred spirit may breathe in me, . . .

so that I may wonder at the sacred fire, . . .

that I may gaze upon the unfathomable, awesome water of the dawn, . . .

and the vivifying / and encircling ether may hear me, . . .

for today I am about to behold, with immortal eyes—I, born mortal from mortal womb, but transformed by tremendous power and an incorruptible right hand / and with immortal spirit, the immortal Aion and master of the fiery diadems—I, sanctified through holy consecrations—while there subsists within me, holy, for a short time, my human soul-might, which I will again / receive after the present bitter and relentless necessity which is pressing down upon me . . .

Since it is impossible for me, born / mortal, to rise with the golden brightness of the immortal brilliance, . . .

stand, O perishable nature of mortals, and at once [receive] me safe and sound after the inexorable and pressing / need. For I am the son . . .(Betz)

After reciting this incantation, the initiate/magician inhales the rays of the sun, separates from the body, and leaves it behind as he rises into the sky. Common elements are the water, the holy spirit, the reference to fire (cf. Matt 3:10-12/ Luke 3:9-17), and the identification as "Son." There is no reference to a bird, the messenger of the gods, in this text, but in a similar text, *PGM* 4.154-221, a great sea hawk swoops down to signal the initiate to rise into his deified state. The uncertain date of the papyri make it impossible to exclude Christian influence, but both texts appear to be independent. This is not to suggest that such ideas were in the mind of Jesus or John the Baptist when Jesus was baptized, but the possibility does exist that the early Christians who formulated the stories were influenced by such ideas.

21. Matthew 3:13-17/ Mark 1:9-11/ Luke 3:21-22

Testaments of the Twelve Patriarchs, "Testament of Levi" 18:4-12 (2 cent. BCE–2 cent. CE)

[Describing the eschatological priest from the tribe of Levi:]
(4) This one will shine forth like the sun in the earth;
he shall take away all darkness from under heaven,
and there shall be peace in all the earth.
(5) The heavens shall greatly rejoice in his days
and the earth shall be glad;
the clouds will be filled with joy
and the knowledge of the Lord will be poured out on the earth like the water of the seas.
And the angels of glory of the Lord's presence will be made glad by him.
(6) The heavens will be opened,
and from the temple of glory sanctification will come upon him,
with a fatherly voice, as from Abraham to Isaac.
(7) And the glory of the Most High shall burst forth upon him.
And the spirit of understanding and sanctification
shall rest upon him [in the water].*
(8) For he shall give the majesty of the Lord to those who are his sons in truth forever.
And there shall be no successor for him from generation to generation forever.
(9) And in his priesthood the nations shall be multiplied in knowledge on the earth,
and they shall be illumined by the grace of the Lord,
but Israel shall be diminished by her ignorance
and darkened by her grief.
In his priesthood sin shall cease
and lawless men shall rest from their evil deeds,

and righteous men shall find rest in him.

(10) And he shall open the gates of paradise;

he shall remove the sword that has threatened since Adam,

(11) and he will grant to the saints to eat of the tree of life.

The spirit of holiness shall be upon them.

(12) And Beliar shall be bound by him.

And he shall grant his children the authority to trample on wicked spirits. (*OTP* 1:794-95)

*"In the water" is apparently an interpolation based on Jesus' having received the spirit at baptism (Mark 1:9-11), which is also linked with a heavenly voice. (H. C. Kee's footnote in *OTP*)

Even if it should be the case that this text has itself been influenced by Mark 1, it still represents a development from traditional Jewish materials. It has been understood as a Christian adaptation of an earlier text on the basis of the reference "in the water" in v. 7; but cf. the connection between "knowledge" and "water" that is already made in v. 5. Still, in contrast to Mark 1 there is no reference to being baptized nor to a proclamation of divine sonship, while on the other hand the gift of exorcism plays a role here, though it is developed only later in the Marcan text. It is thus a matter of comparable charismatic installation into an office without literary dependence (cf. Berger, *Formgeschichte*, §75). Is the imagery associated with Romans 1:4*a* to be thought of in a similar manner?

22. Matthew 3:17/ Mark 1:11/ Luke 3:22

Targum Pseudo-Jonathan on Genesis 22:10 (1 cent. BCE–3 cent. CE)

The eyes of Abraham were looking at the eyes of Isaac, and the eyes of Isaac were looking at the angels on high. Isaac saw them, but Abraham did not see them. The angels on high exclaimed: "Come, see two unique ones who are in the world; one is slaughtering, and the other is being slaughtered; the one who slaughters does not hesitate, and the one who is being slaughtered stretches forth his neck." (Maher)

Isaac has a vision of angels, who describe the event in terms of the election and uniqueness of the persons concerned. Those who have compared this text with Mark 1:10 have sometimes regarded the two texts as sharing a common genre, the interpretative vision. In this genre, the earthly event (here, the baptism of Jesus) receives an interpretation and commentary by means of a vision. (See also Matt 3:17; Luke 3:22.)

23. Matthew 3:17/ Mark 1:11/ Luke 3:22

b. Baba Mezia 59b (1 cent. CE tradition; written much later)

On that day R. Eliezer produced all of the arguments in the world, but they did not accept them from him. So he said to them, "If the law accords with my position, this carob tree will prove it."

The carob was uprooted from its place by a hundred cubits—and some say, four hundred cubits.

They said to him, "There is no proof from a carob tree."

So he went and said to them, "If the law accords with my position, let the stream of water prove it."

The stream of water reversed flow.

They said to him, "There is no proof from a stream of water."

So he went and said to them, "If the law accords with my position, let the walls of the school house prove it."

The walls of the school house tilted toward falling.

R. Joshua rebuked them, saying to them, "If disciples of sages are contending with one another in matters of law, what business do you have?"

They did not fall on account of the honor owing to R. Joshua, but they also did not straighten up on account of the honor owing to R. Eliezer, and to this day they are still tilted.

So he went and said to them, "If the law accords with my position, let the Heaven prove it!"

An echo came forth, saying, "What business have you with R. Eliezer, for the law accords with his position under all circumstances!"

R. Joshua stood up on his feet and said, "It is not in Heaven" [Dt. 30:12].

What is the sense of, "It is not in heaven" [Dt. 30:12]?

Said R. Jeremiah, "[The sense of Joshua's statement is this:] For the Torah has already been given from Mount Sinai, so we do not pay attention to echoes, since you have already written in the Torah at Mount Sinai, 'After the majority you are to incline' [Ex. 23:2]." (Neusner, *Talmud*)

"Echo" here is *Bat Qol,* "daughter of a voice," a heavenly voice not judged to be of the same order as the word of God that came to the prophets.

In first-century CE rabbinic tradition, the dominant view was that direct revelation had long since ceased, that prophetic revelation would return during the eschatological times, but did not happen in the present. God's word spoken at Sinai, preserved in both the written Scripture and the oral tradition, when interpreted by authorized rabbis was the definitive revelation of God's will. Thus not only John's prophetic speech, but the heavenly voice that came at Jesus' baptism would not necessarily be doubted as having "actually happened," but they would not prove anything. (Cf. nos. 113-17 on Matt 15:1-9/ Mark 7:1-8.)

24. Matthew 4:12-17/ Mark 1:14 -15/ Luke 4:14-15

Testament of Moses 10 (1 cent. CE)

Then his kingdom will appear throughout his whole creation.
Then the devil will have an end.
Yea, sorrow will be led away with him.
Then will be filled the hands of the messenger,
    who is in the highest place appointed.
Yea, he will at once avenge them of their enemies.
For the Heavenly One will arise from his kingly throne.

Yea, he will go forth from his holy habitation
    with indignation and wrath on behalf of his sons.
And the earth will tremble, even to its ends shall it be shaken.
And the high mountains will be made low.
Yea, they will be shaken, as enclosed valleys will they fall.
The sun will not give light.
And in darkness the horns of the moon will flee.
Yea, they will be broken in pieces.
It will be turned wholly into blood.
Yea, even the circle of the stars will be thrown into disarray.
And the sea all the way to the abyss will retire,
    to the sources of waters which fail.
Yea, the rivers will vanish away.
For God Most High will surge forth,
    the Eternal One alone.
In full view will he come to work vengeance on the nations.
Yea, all their idols will he destroy.
Then will you be happy, O Israel!
And you will mount up above the necks and the wings of an eagle.
Yea, all things will be fulfilled.
And God will raise you to the heights.
Yea, he will fix you firmly in the heaven of the stars,
    in the place of their habitations.
And you will behold from on high.
Yea, you will see your enemies on the earth.
And recognizing them, you will rejoice.
And you will give thanks.
Yea, you will confess your creator.
(*OTP* 1:931-32)

This text, probably written during the lifetime of Jesus, illustrates the apocalyptic form of the hope for the coming of the kingdom of God that was held by some Jews. There is no Messiah; "the Eternal One alone" brings the kingdom. Cf. the apocalyptic imagery of Acts 2:17-21; Rev. 6:12-17.

25. Matthew 4:12-17/ Mark 1:14-15/ Luke 4:14-15

Targum of Ezekiel 7:7, 10 (1 cent. BCE–3 cent. CE)

The kingdom will be revealed over you, O Earth dweller. The time of ruin has arrived, the day of distress has come near. . . . Behold, the day of recompense has arrived, behold it comes, the kingdom will be revealed, the reign will blossom forth. (MEB/Berger)

The Judaism of Jesus' time spoke only rarely of the kingdom of God. Among the rabbis, it was primarily a matter of the kingdom understood as a present reality ("to take the kingdom on oneself" = to place oneself under the yoke of the Torah). The Targums manifest a developed eschatological understanding, and speak primarily of the future revelation of the kingdom of God.

An alternate translation, with more of the context, is provided by Samson H. Levey, *The Aramaic Bible*, vol. 13, *The Targum of Ezekiel* (Wilmington: Michael Glazier, 1987), p. 32, which also gives critical notes on translation problems: "The kingdom has been revealed to you O inhabitant of the land! The time of misfortune has arrived, the day of tumultuous confusion is near, and there is no escaping to the mountain strongholds. Now, soon, I will pour out my wrath upon you, and My anger shall be spent in you, and I will exact payment from you in accordance with your ways, and I will visit upon you all your abominations. My Memra will not spare you, and I will have no pity. I will requite you according to the sins of your ways, and the punishment for your abominations shall be in the midst of you; and you shall know that I the Lord have brought this blow upon you. Behold the day of retribution! Behold it is coming! The Kingdom has been revealed! The ruler's rod has blossomed!"

26. Matthew 4:17/ Mark 1:15/ Luke 4:14-15

Papyrus of unknown date, a platitude from a child's exercise book (3 cent. BCE–3 cent. CE)

What is a god? That which is strong. What is a king? He who is equal to the divine. (Nock, *Conversion*)

Everett Ferguson's comments on this text are insightful: "This is very revealing about the Hellenistic conception of deity, kingship, and the presuppositions behind the cult of rulers. The deities provided the only point of comparison for the power wielded by Hellenistic kings, and divine honors the only adequate expression of homage to such power. . . . What did it mean to be a king *(basileus)*? It was not monarchy in the modern sense of a ruler over a clearly defined territory. A kingdom was rather a sphere of power. Where we say 'state' or 'Seleucid kingdom,' the ancients said 'subjects of king so and so'" (*Background*, p. 191).

27. Matthew 4:18-22/ Mark 1:16-20/ Luke 5:1-11

Aristotle, "On Philosophy" 1.53 (384–322 BCE)

This man [namely, the partner of Themistius], after some slight association with my studies or amusements—whichever you call them—had almost the same experience as the philosopher Axiothea, Zeno of Citium, and the Corinthian farmer. Axiothea, after reading a book of Plato's *Republic,* migrated from Arcadia to Athens and attended Plato's lectures for a long time without being discovered to be a woman—like Lycomedes' Achilles. The Corinthian farmer after coming into contact with Gorgias—not Gorgias himself but the dialogue Plato wrote in criticism of the sophist—forthwith gave up his farm and his vines, put his soul under Plato's guidance, and made it a seed-bed and a planting ground for Plato's philosophy. This is the man whom Aristotle honors in his Corinthian dialogue. The facts about Zeno are well known and are recounted by many writers—that the *Apology* of Socrates brought him from Phoenicia to the painted Stoa. (Ross)

For comments cf. on no. 28.

28. Matthew 4:18-22/ Mark 1:16-20/ Luke 5:1-11

Diogenes Laertius, *Lives of Eminent Philosophers* **2.48, "Xenophon" (3 cent. CE), on Socrates (469–399 BCE) and Xenophon (430–354 BCE)**

Xenophon, the son of Gryllus, was a citizen of Athens and belonged to the deme Erchia; he was a man of rare modesty and extremely handsome. The story goes that Socrates met him in a narrow passage, and that he stretched out his stick to bar the way, while he inquired where every kind of food was sold. Upon receiving a reply, he put another question, "And where do men become good and honorable?" Xenophon was fairly puzzled. "Then follow me," said Socrates, "and learn." From that time onward he was a pupil of Socrates. (LCL)

This and the preceding text are call stories from the world of philosophy. The call occurs in the process of reading or as the personal challenge of Socrates. The challenge to leave home and country and the authoritative call to follow may also be compared with 1 Kings 19:19-21. The stories from each realm had a mutual influence on each other, and both had an impact on the developing Gospel stories.

29. Matthew 4:19/ Mark 1:17/ Luke 5:10

Joseph and Aseneth **21:21—Aseneth's Psalm (1 cent. BCE)**

[Aseneth on Joseph:] [He] made me humble after my arrogance,
and by his beauty he caught me,
and by his wisdom he grasped me like a fish on a hook,
and by his spirit, as by bait of life, he ensnared me. (*OTP* 2:237)

The picture of hunting, fishing, and ensnaring human beings is frequently a topos of the anti-Sophist polemic which was then used negatively (A. Städele, ed. *Die Briefe des Pythagoras und die Pythagoreer* [Meisenheim am Glan: Anton Hain, 1980], 2.3; Diogenes Laertius, *Lives*, "Polemo" 8:36). This, however, is not always the case. In Diogenes, *Lives* 4.16 [10b], it is said of the lad (Polemo), "as he listened, by degrees was taken in the toils. He became so industrious as to surpass all the other scholars, and rose to be himself head of the school in the 116th Olympiad" (LCL). In *Joseph and Aseneth* 21, as in the Gospels, a metaphor is present that obviously already had a tradition in the philosophical schools (winning of disciples and adherents over to their cause), and which then had already been used in the Jewish mission (as in *Jos. Asen.*) before being adopted by early Christianity. Cf. Wilhelm H. Wuellner, *The Meaning of "Fishers of Men"* (Philadelphia: Westminster Press, 1962).

30. Matthew 5–7/ Luke 6:20-49

Philo, *Every Good Man Is Free* **75-80 (15 BCE–50 CE)**

Palestinian Syria, too, has not failed to produce high moral excellence. In this country live a considerable part of the very populous nation of the Jews, including as it is said, certain persons, more than four thousand in number, called Essenes. Their name which is, I think, a variation, though the form of the Greek is inexact, of ὁσιότης (holiness), is given them, because they have shown themselves especially devout in the service of God, not by offering sacrifices of animals, but by resolving to sanctify their minds. The first thing about these people is that they live in villages and avoid the cities because of the iniquities which have become inveterate among city dwellers, for they know that their company would have a deadly effect upon their own souls, like a disease brought by a pestilential atmosphere. Some of them labor on the land and others pursue such crafts as cooperate with peace and so benefit themselves and their neighbors. They do not hoard gold and silver or acquire great slices of land because they desire the revenues therefrom, but provide what is needed for the necessary requirements of life. For while they stand almost alone in the whole of mankind in that they have become moneyless and landless by deliberate action rather than by lack of good fortune, they are esteemed exceedingly rich, because they judge frugality with contentment to be, as indeed it is, an abundance of wealth. As for darts, javelins, daggers, or the helmet, breastplate or shield, you could not find a single manufacturer of them, nor, in general, any person making weapons or plying any industry concerned with war, nor, indeed, any of the peaceful kind, which easily lapse into vice, for they have not the vaguest idea of commerce either wholesale or retail or marine, but pack the inducements to covetousness off in disgrace. Not a single slave is to be found among them, but all are free, exchanging services with each other, and they denounce the owners of slaves, not merely for their injustice in outraging the law of equality, but also for their impiety in annulling the statute of Nature, who mother-like has born and reared all men alike, and created them genuine brothers, not in mere name, but in very reality, though this kinship has been put to confusion by the triumph of malignant covetousness, which has wrought estrangement instead of affinity and enmity instead of friendship. As for philosophy they abandon the logical part of quibbling verbalists as unnecessary for the acquisition of virtue, and the physical to visionary praters as beyond the grasp of human nature, only retaining that part which treats philosophically the existence of God and the creation of the universe. But the ethical part they study very industriously, taking for their trainers the laws of their fathers, which could not possibly have been conceived by the human soul without divine inspiration. (LCL)

As described by Philo (which may be a somewhat idealized picture), the Essenes are a community advocating and living by an ethic that bears comparison with the ethic of the Christian community represented by the Sermon on the Mount. They put a low priority on material wealth. They are opposed to militarism. Strikingly, they not only do not practice slavery themselves, but denounce slave owners and oppose the institution of slavery as such, on the basis that all human beings are created equal members of the one human family. This is in contrast with Jesus, the New Testament, and the whole of early Christianity, which not only never opposed the institution of slavery in principle, but assumed it as a given element in society (cf. Luke 7:1-10; Phlm; 1 Cor 7:20-24; Col 3:22-25; Eph 6:5-8; 1 Pet 2:18-19). On the contrast between animal sacrifice and "spiritual sacrifices" of the "mind," cf. Romans 12:1; 1 Peter 2:2, 5.

31. Matthew 5:17-19

Plutarch, *Moralia*, "Sayings of Spartans: Agesilaus the Great" 73 (45–125 CE)

[Agesilaus the Great, the Lawgiver:] I would not become a lawgiver to enact another set of laws, for in the present laws I would make no addition, subtraction, or revision. It is good that our present laws be in full force, beginning with the morrow. (LCL)

Plutarch's respect for the law is also manifest in his consoling writing to Apollonius, §18: "We are not in the world in order to give laws, but . . . in order to obey the commands of the gods." For contrast, cf. no. 158. Cf. Revelation 22:18.

32. Matthew 5:19

Dio Chrysostom, *The Thirty-First Discourse: The Rhodian Oration* 86 (40–120 CE)

Again, if any one chisels out only one word from any official tablet, you will put him to death without stopping to investigate what the word was or to what it referred; and if anyone should go to the building where your public records are kept and erase one jot of any law, or one single syllable of a decree of the people, you will treat this man just as you would any person who should remove a part of the Chariot. ["Chariot" probably refers to the chariot of the sun god drawn by a team of four.] (LCL)

The speech criticizes the practice that had become usual in Rhodes of the reuse of honorary statues by changing the inscriptions, and compares it to the [considered obvious] criminal outrage of changing the law. On the same subject, cf. the so-called canon formulae such as Revelation 22:18-19. On respect for laws, see also Plutarch, "Sayings of Spartans" 73.

33. Matthew 5:21-28

Plutarch, *Moralia*, "To an Uneducated Ruler" 6 (45–125 CE)

For in weak and lowly private persons folly is combined with lack of power and, therefore, results in no wrongdoing, just as in bad dreams a feeling of distress disturbs the spirit, and it cannot rouse itself in accordance with its desires; but power when wickedness is added to it brings increased vigor to the passions. . . . Wickedness, when by reason of power it possesses rapid speed, forces every passion to emerge, making of anger murder, of love adultery, of covetousness confiscation. (LCL)

Points of contact with Matthew: (1) In the first and second antitheses of the Sermon on the Mount the relation of anger/murder and lust/adultery is similar to that in Plutarch, but not identical.

Matthew identifies the two, while in Plutarch the relation is such that the acquisition of power allows the internal desire to become the external deed. We consider the widespread understanding of such an association to be the theoretical background (in terms of individualistic psychology) of the first two Matthean antitheses. (2) The social psychological reflections of Plutarch concerning the "suppressed class" (ταπεινοί) and the relationship he describes between power and sin fit in with common observations made about Matthew: the community is addressed as the lowly and "little people," which corresponds to his ethic of renunciation of power.

34. Matthew 5:28

Aelian, *Variae historiae* 14.42 (2 cent. CE)

Xenocrates, the companion of Plato, said that it made no difference whether one set one's eyes in a strange house, or placed one's feet there. For the one who looks on forbidden places is guilty of the same sin as the one who goes there. (LCL)

As in several further texts of Greek ethics, transgression is already regarded as present in the thought (Epictetus, *Fragments* 100; Diogenes Laertius, *Lives* 1.36), or in the intention (Aelian, *Variae historiae* 14.28), or merely in showing interest in something. The application is already made with reference to women by Plutarch, "On Being a Busybody" 13: "So too Alexander would not go to see Darius's wife who was said to be very beautiful, but although he visited her mother, an elderly woman, he could not bring himself to see the young and beautiful daughter. Yet we peep into women's litters and hang about their windows, and think we are doing nothing wrong in thus making our curiosity prone to slip and slide into all kinds of vice" (LCL).

Aristotle: "What is a crime for a person to do, is a crime for a person to think" (Magna Moralia).

Cicero: "As it is a sin to betray one's country, to use violence to one's parents, to rob a temple, where the offense lies in the result of the act, so the passions of fear, grief, and lust are sins, even when no extraneous result ensues" (*Goods and Evils* 3.9.32) (LCL).

"Pittacus of Mitylene, on being asked if anyone escapes the notice of the gods in committing some sinful act, said: 'No, not even in contemplating it'" (Hock and O'Neil).

The Habakkuk-Midrash 1QpHab 5.7 recognizes that "whoring originates behind the eyes."

Cf. also nos. 75, 544; on Matthew 5:29-30, cf. no. 136.

35. Matthew 5:31-32; 19:3-7/ Mark 10:2-4

Divorce Certificate from Masada (ca. 111 CE)

On the first day [of the month] Marcheshvan, the sixth year, in Masada.

By my own decision I, Jehoseph bar Niqsan of [ ]h, resident of Masada, today release and dismiss you, Miriam, daughter of Jehonathan of Hanablata, resident of Masada, you who were formerly my wife, so that you have permission to go of your own free will and to be married to any other Jewish man whom you wish to marry. For my part, I hereby present to you the certificate of dismissal. In addition, I give you the morning gift, and you are to be reimbursed for all your [goods] that have been damaged or destroyed, as is lawful, and

I pay fourfold for them. And if you so request, I will replace the written document, as long as I am still alive.

    [On the back side:] Joseph bar Niqsan for himself
              Eli'azar bar Malka, witness
              Jehoseph bar Malka, witness
              El'azar bar Hanana, witness
              (MEB/from *Discoveries in the Judean Desert*)

Although all law was religious law in Judaism, the official but "secular" nature of the divorce contract is noted, as well as its unilateral character (in contrast to the Gentile in no. 142). The divorced woman does however receive reimbursement and is treated with respect.

36. Matthew 5:33-37

2 Enoch 49:1 (1 cent. CE)

For I am swearing to you, my children—But look! I am not swearing by any oath at all, neither by heaven nor by earth nor by any other creature which the Lord created. For the Lord said, "There is no oath in me, nor any unrighteousness, but only truth." So, if there is no truth in human beings, then let them make an oath by means of the words "Yes, Yes!" or, if it should be the other way around, "No, No!" (*OTP* 1:176)

In distinction from Matthew 5:33-37, here it is a matter of a substitute oath-formula. The following sentence in 2 Enoch begins with "And I make an oath to you—'Yes! Yes!,'" similar to the conclusion of Matthew 5:37. It is hardly likely that the saying in 2 Enoch is a Christian addition, even if the passage is lacking in the shorter recension; the longer recension lacks any Christian elements. James 5:12 shows the saying is rooted in Judaism. Cf. nos. 394, 884.

37. Matthew 5:38-42

Diogenes Laertius, *Lives of Eminent Philosophers*, "Socrates" 2.21 (3 cent. CE)

[Socrates] discussed moral questions in the workshops and the marketplace . . . frequently, owing to his vehemence in argument, men set upon him with their fists or tore his hair out; and . . . for the most part he was despised and laughed at, yet bore all this ill-usage patiently. So much so that, when he had been kicked, and someone expressed surprise at his taking it so quietly, Socrates rejoined, "Should I have taken legal action against a donkey, supposing that he had kicked me?" (LCL)

The conduct is similar to that of Jesus, but the motivation is different. Jesus operates on the basis of love for the other (Matt 5:43), while Socrates has a superior disdain for the other. Yet Socrates' reply may reflect only the surface reason; his engaging people on moral issues, and tolerating the abuse he received for his efforts, was itself an expression of love for humanity—though of a different sort than that commended and lived out by Jesus.

So also Paul commends that one suffer evil rather than resort to secular human courts (1 Cor 6:1-8), again with a different motivation than either Jesus or Socrates: the imminent eschatological judgment makes all human forensic efforts futile, and in the meantime the saints, that are to judge angels, are competent to try their own cases.

38. Matthew 5:38-42

Epictetus, *Discourses* 4.1.79 (55–135 CE)

You ought to treat your whole body like a poor loaded-down donkey, as long as it is possible, as long as it is allowed; and if it be commandeered and a soldier lay hold of it, let it go, do not resist nor grumble. If you do, you will get a beating and lose your little donkey just the same. (LCL)

In contrast to Matthew, there is no voluntary second mile. In Epictetus, this is part of a discussion affirming that the body and all its desires is something foreign to the real self, so one is able to renounce it. In Matthew, the context has to do with making an end of human relationships that depend on legal compulsion.

On Matthew 5:40-48, see nos. 272-77, 280.

39. Matthew 5:39

Seneca, *On Anger* 2.34.1 (4–65 CE)

A contest with one's equal is hazardous, with a superior mad, with an inferior degrading. (LCL)

Seneca too commends nonviolence, but on the basis of common-sense rules for the ordinary person who wants to get along in society. In Matthew, Jesus' command is based on his radical eschatological ethic and God's own impartial love even for the oppressor.

40. Matthew 5:43

1QS 1:9-10 (2–1 cent. BCE)

[Book of the Community Rule:] Seek God . . . do what is good and right before him . . .; love all the sons of light, each according to his lot in God's design, and hate all the sons of darkness, each according to his guilt in God's vengeance. (Vermes)

There is no command to hate the enemy in the Old Testament, yet there are statements that God "hates all evildoers" (Ps 5:5; cf. 31:6) and statements that imply that others do, and should do, the same (Deut 23:3-7; 30:7; Ps 26:5; 139:21-22). This is made explicit in the Qumran text, that understands "children of light" to be members of the Qumran community, and "children of darkness" to include all others.

41. Matthew 5:45-48

Marcus Aurelius, *Meditations* 7.70 (121–180 CE)

The gods who have no part in death, are not grieved because in so long an eternity they will be obliged always and entirely to suffer so many and such worthless men; and besides they take care of them in all kinds of ways. Yet do you, who are all but at the point of vanishing, give up the struggle, and that though you are one of the worthless? (*The Meditations of Marcus Aurelius;* in the trans. of A. S. L. Farquharson. [Oxford: Oxford University Press, 1944])

As in Matthew, the behavior of the gods is taken as a model for considering human behavior, precisely at the point of their universal care for humanity. Differently from Matthew, here it is only a matter of patient toleration, based on an inference from the greater to the lesser. Thus the argument has to do with how far patience with others should extend.

42. Matthew 6:1-4

Cicero, *The Republic* 6.23 (25) (106–43 BCE)

[Africanus said to Scipio in a dream:] Consequently, if you despair of ever returning to this place, where eminent and excellent men find their true reward, of how little value, indeed, is your fame among men, which can hardly endure for the small part of a single year? Therefore, if you will only look on high and contemplate this eternal home and resting place, you will no longer attend to the gossip of the vulgar herd or put your trust in human rewards for your exploits. Virtue herself, by her own charms, should lead you on to true glory. Let what others say of you be their own concern; whatever it is, they will say it in any case. (LCL)

As in Matthew, an orientation toward heaven and heavenly praise for one's deeds is placed over against merely human praise. In contrast to Matthew, it is not "your Father" who rewards you, but "virtue itself" is its own reward. This distinction is also met in the confrontation of biblical thought with idealistic philosophy.

43. Matthew 6:7

Plato, reporting the prayer of Socrates, *Phaedo* 279B-C (ca. 390 BCE)

O beloved Pan and all ye other gods of this place, grant to me that I be made beautiful in my soul within, and that all external possessions be in harmony with my inner man. May I consider the wise man rich; and may I have such wealth as only the self-restrained man can bear or endure. (LCL)

Jews tended to demean pagan prayers to make their own piety shine the brighter. Matthew stands in this tradition. Later Christians demeaned Jewish prayers for the same reason. There were selfish and petty pagan and Jewish prayers, just as there have been such Christian prayers. But there were prayers with a depth of religious feeling and conviction, such as that of Socrates. One may also note that Pan ("All") is addressed as the representative god, and in a deeply spiritual manner. The kind of syncretism that developed and deepened in the Hellenistic period is already visible. (For a representative example, see Cleanthes, "Hymn to Zeus" below on Acts 17:22-31, no. 518.)

44. Matthew 6:10*b*

Epictetus, *Discourses* 2.17.22-26 (55–135 CE)

Give up wanting to remain in Corinth, and, in a word, give up wanting anything but what God wants. And who will prevent you, who will compel you? No one, any more than anyone prevents or compels Zeus.

When you have such a leader as Zeus and identify your wishes and your desires with His, why are you still afraid that you will fail? Give to poverty and to wealth your aversion and your desire: you will fail to get what you wish, and you will fall into what you would avoid. Give them to health; you will come to grief; so also if you give them to offices, honors, country, friends, children, in short to anything that lies outside the domain of moral purpose. But give them to Zeus and the other gods; entrust them to their keeping, let them exercise the control; let your desire and your aversion be ranged on their side—and how can you be troubled any longer? (LCL)

It is questionable whether already Matthew 6:10*b*, like Mark 14:36, must be understood in the sense of resigning oneself to suffering. Perhaps Matthew 6:10*b* is concerned with the implementation of God's will as the governing power of the universe (as *b. Ber.* 29b), and the text in Epictetus makes clear how this sentence could be understood by Hellenistic readers. In Epictetus, in any case, it has to do with the giving up of all desire and all binding oneself to material goods. Mark 14:36 presents the martyrological variation thereto. In contrast to Jesus (e.g. Matt 5:44), Epictetus represents an externalization and neutral distance from other people ("friends, children").

45. Matthew 6:13*b*

b. Berakoth 60A-60B

He who is going to sleep in his bed says . . . May it please you, Lord my God, to make me lie down in peace, give me my lot in your Torah, make it my custom to do religious duties, do not make it my custom to do transgressions nor bring me into the power of sin, violation, temptation, or humiliation. May the impulse to do good control me, and may the impulse to do evil not control me. And save me from unfortunate accidents and ailments. (Neusner, *Talmud*)

The Jewish evening prayer is a good commentary on the concluding petition of the Lord's Prayer, since it designates its content more concretely. According to Hierocles the Stoic (2 cent. CE), it is not the gods that are the cause of evil, but baseness and matter (in Stobaeus, *Anthologium*, vol. 2, 181:8ff.).

46. Matthew 6:34

b. *Sanhedrin* 100b

"Do not worry about tomorrow's sorrow, For you do not know what a day may bring forth" (Prov. 27:1). Perhaps tomorrow you will no longer exist and it will turn out that you will worry about a world that is not yours. (Neusner, *Talmud*)

This section from a parenetic series has the same goal, but another basis than the saying of Jesus: what does not belong to one with certainty is not really a matter of one's own concern.

47. Matthew 6:34*b*

b. *Berakoth* 9b

Said the Holy One, blessed be he, to Moses, "Go, say to the Israelites: 'I was with you in this subjugation, and I shall be with you when you are subjugated to the [pagan] kingdoms.'" He said to him, "Lord of the world, sufficient for the hour is the trouble [in its own time. Why mention other troubles that are coming?]" (Neusner, *Talmud*)

The meaning is probably that future troubles need not be announced in advance. The basis is the same as in Matthew 6:34*b*. The common affirmation is that to be too occupied with the future, or to have knowledge of it, would make the burden of the present unbearable, which is already heavy enough. Cf. also no. 883.

Cf. also Plutarch, *Pelopidas* 10 (conclusion). On "judging others" in Matthew 7:1-5, cf. no. 545.

48. Matthew 8:1-4/ Mark 1:40-45/ Luke 5:12-16

The Prayer of Nabonidus, *4QPrNab* (2 cent. BCE)

The words of the prayer uttered by Nabunai King of Babylon, [the great] king, [when he was afflicted] with an evil ulcer in Teiman by decree of the [Most High God].

"I was afflicted [with an evil ulcer] for seven years . . . and an exorcist pardoned my sins. He was a Jew from among the [children of the exile of Judah, and he said], 'Recount this in writing to [glorify and exalt] the name of the [Most High God.' And I wrote this]: in Teiman [by decree of the Most High God]. For seven years [I] prayed to the gods of silver and gold, [bronze and iron], wood and stone and clay, because [I believed] that they were gods . . . "[. . .] he strengthened it, I was healed." (2) [And he said to me, 'See], you are [again strong as] a cedar and [for] ever healthy.' [And as] (3) his friends . . . me . . . I could not [. . . .] (4) 'How are you like to the . . . [!] '(5) . . . ." (Vermes/MEB/Berger)

This text, which is related to Daniel 3:31–4:34, but to an earlier stage of tradition (Nabonidus instead of Nebuchadnezzar II), speaks of punitive suffering and healing. At the end there probably stood a "Praise God." As in Mark 1 and parallels, it is a matter of a miracle that sets aside the most severe uncleanness, in the context of mission. While the Gentile Nabonidus must first convert to the true God in order to be healed, the taking away of impurity in the Gospel story is attributed to Jesus himself. He represents in himself the bridge to God and thus concentrates in himself more "authority" than the "Jewish soothsayer" of Qumran.

49. Matthew 8:1-4/ Mark 1:40-45/ Luke 5:12-16

Herodotus, *The Histories* 1.138 (484 BCE)

The citizen who has leprosy or the white sickness may not come into a town or consort with other Persians. They say that he is so afflicted because he has sinned in some wise against the sun. (LCL)

This text is one documentation for the fact that leprosy was considered unclean "internationally." As in the previous text, a religious basis is given for the uncleanness. This is lacking in the Synoptic text.

On "sun," cf. nos. 869, 962.

50. Matthew 8:4/ Mark 1:44/ Luke 5:14

Magical Papyrus *PGM* 1.130-32 (From a papyrus collection copied 4–5 cents. CE)

[After the communication of a magical formula:] Share this great mystery with no one [else], but conceal it, by Helios, since you have been deemed worthy by the lord [god]. (Betz).

The magical formula itself is a sacred text which may be shared with only select individuals, to keep it from being profaned and thereby becoming ineffective. The commands to silence in the miracle stories have sometimes been associated with commands related to such prohibitions regarding magical formulae in an effort to explain them in history-of-religions terms. But a story is not a formula, nor is it a magical, sacral text.

51. Matthew 8:14-15/ Mark 1:29-31/ Luke 4:38-39

b. Nedarim 41a (ca. 270 CE)

R. Alexandri also said in the name of R. Hiyya b. Abba: "Greater is the miracle wrought for the sick than for Hananiah, Mishael, and Azariah. [For] that of Hananiah, Mishael, and Azariah [concerned] a fire kindled by man, which all can extinguish; whilst that of a sick person is [in connection with] a heavenly fire [i.e., his temperature rises], and who can extinguish that?" (Soncino)

The proper answer to this school question is, of course, that only God can extinguish the fever. Whoever heals a person with fever operates with the power of God. At the same time, the charismatics of the past were typologically upgraded through this text.

52. Matthew 8:14-17/ Mark 1:29-34/ Luke 4:38-41

Inscriptions from Epidaurus (late 4 cent. CE)

Cure affected by Apollo and Asclepius. Ambrosia of Athens, blind in one eye. She came with supplications to the god, and as she walked round the temple she smiled at the accounts of some of the cures which she found incredible and impossible, accounts which related how the lame and blind had been cured by a vision which came to them in a dream. She fell asleep and had a vision. The god appeared before her, telling her that she would be cured and that she had to dedicate in the sanctuary a pig made of silver as a token of her ignorance. Having said this he cut out the bad eye and immersed it in a medicine. She awoke at dawn, cured.

A man with an ulcer in his stomach. While he slept he had a dream. The god appeared to him and ordered his assistants to hold him so that the god could cut out the affected part. The man tried to escape but he was seized and fastened to a door. Asclepius then opened up his stomach, cut out the ulcer, sewed him up again, and finally released him. The man awoke cured, but the floor of the *abaton* was covered with blood. (trans. from Giannelli, *The World of Classical Athens* [New York: Putnam, 1970]; cf. Ferguson, *Background*, p. 211)

I. Kleo was pregnant for five years. After she had been pregnant for five years, she came to the god as one seeking help and slept in the Healing Room; as soon as she came forth from it and left the sanctuary, she bore a young boy, who immediately after his birth washed himself in the waters of the spring, and walked around with his mother. After receiving this great favor [from the god], she had the following written on the dedicatory gift: "It is not the size of the tablet that is wonderful, but the grace of the god, that Kleo who had borne a burden in her body for five years until she slept in the healing room and he restored her to health." (MEB/Leipold and Grundmann, 68)

Near the end of the fourth century CE, the priests of Epidaurus had the earlier reports of healings attributed to Asclepius collected and inscribed on large stone tablets, of which three and fragments of a fourth have survived. The stories themselves are thus in many cases much earlier than the inscription. The last example may reflect the difference between original report by the beneficiary as found on the dedicatory inscription, and its later interpretations, illustrating the growth of legendary miraculous material around a central core. Although we have no firsthand reports from those healed by Jesus and the apostles, an analogous type of development of miraculous traditions can be observed in the New Testament.

While there is no direct connection between the Epidaurus catalogs and the New Testament healing stories, there is a developmental formal connection: the role played by the god in a dream is filled by the earthly Jesus. See K. Berger, "Hellenistische Gattungen im Neuen Testament," *ANRW* II 25. 2 (Berlin: de Gruyter, 1984), 1216; and Michael Wolter, "Inschriftliche Heilungsberichte und neutestamentliche Wundererzählungen: Überlieferungs und formgeschichtliche Betrachtungen" in K. Berger, et al., eds., *Studien und Texte zur Formgeschichte* (Tübingen: Franke Verlag, 1992), 135-76. Wolter disputes Berger's view that there is a formal connection between the Epidaurus reports and New Testament healing stories.

53. Matthew 8:23-27 / Mark 4:35-41 / Luke 8:22-25

j. Berakoth 9.1 (4 cent. CE based on earlier tradition)

Said R. Tanhuma: "Once a boat-load of gentiles was sailing the Mediterranean. There was one Jewish child on the boat. A great storm came upon them in the sea. Each person took his idol in his hand and cried out. But it did not help them.

"Once they saw that their cries were of no avail, they turned to the Jewish child and said, 'Child, rise up and call out to your God. For we have heard that he answers you when you cry out to him, and that he is heroic.'

"The child immediately rose up and cried out with all his heart. The Holy One, blessed be He, accepted his prayer and quieted the seas.

"When the ship reached dry land [at the port], everyone disembarked to purchase his needed staples. They said to the child, 'Don't you wish to buy anything?'

"He said to them, 'What do you want of me? I am just a poor traveler.'

"They said to him, 'You are just a poor traveler? They are the poor travelers. Some of them are here, and their idols are in Babylonia. Some of them are here, and their idols are in Rome. Some of them are here and their idols are with them, but they do them no good. But wherever you go, your God is with you.' " (Neusner, *Talmud of the Land of Israel*)

In the New Testament, the miracle story is christological. In the talmudic story the miracle is no less spectacular, but has a different point. The little Jewish boy does not have any religious status confirmed by the miracle, but the role of Israel in the world among the idolatrous nations is illustrated. Though the miracle itself is similar to that of the Gospels, its function is closer to that of Jonah 1:1-16 than to the Gospel story.

54. Matthew 8:23-27 / Mark 4:35-41 / Luke 8:22-25

Plutarch, *Moralia*, "Obsolescence of Oracles" 30 (45–125 CE)

That other concept is, I think, more dignified and sublime, that the gods are not subject to outside control, but are their own masters, even as the twin sons of Tyndareüs [Castor and Pollux, the protectors of sailors] come to the aid of men who are laboring in the storm,

> Soothing the oncoming raging sea,
> Taming the swift-driving blasts of the winds,

not, however, sailing on the ships and sharing in the danger, but appearing above and rescuing . . . (LCL)

The twin sons of Tyndareüs are the Dioscuri (sons of Zeus). They also appear in Lucian (cf. no. 55). In the first text they calm the storm, in the second they guide the ship out of danger. In the Jesus tradition, in contrast, Jesus is together with the disciples in the boat, as in the Jonah tradition. But different from the Jonah story, Jesus himself accomplishes the mighty deed which is otherwise ascribed only to divine beings. The Dioscuri tradition is also discussed by Plutarch, *Moralia*, (45–125 CE) 2.18: "Concerning the so-called Dioscuri: Xenophanes considers those stars which appear over ships to be small clouds that shine and sparkle by the nature of their movement. Metrodor explains them as a shimmering before the eyes of the observers, caused by fear and consternation" (MEB/Berger). The latter text documents the striving for a natural explanation.

55. Matthew 8:23-27 / Mark 4:35-41 / Luke 8:22-25

Lucian, "The Ship" or "The Wishes" 9 (120–185 CE)

[A.] This is what the captain said they found when it was still night and pitch dark. But the gods were moved by their lamentations, and showed fire from Lycia, so that they knew the place. One of the Dioscuri [Castor and Pollux, guides to mariners] put a bright star [St. Elmo's Fire] on the masthead, and guided the ship in a turn to port into the open sea, just as it was driving onto the cliff. (LCL)

In the background stands the Dioscuri tradition, which also is expressed in the 33rd Homeric hymn, "To the Dioscuri":

[B.] When Leda had lain with the dark-clouded Son of Cronos, she bore them beneath the peak of the great hill Taÿgetus—children who are deliverers of men on earth and of swift-going ships when stormy gales rage over the ruthless sea. Then the shipmen call upon the sons of great Zeus with vows of white lambs, going to the forepart of the prow; but the strong wind and the waves of the sea lay the ship under water, until suddenly these two are seen darting through the air on tawny wings. Forthwith they allay the blasts of the cruel winds and still the waves upon the surface of the white sea: fair signs are they and deliverance from toil. And when the shipmen see them they are glad and have rest from their pain and labor. (LCL)

In a similar vein, Philostratus' *Life of Apollonius* 4.13, written at the beginning of the third century CE (though its hero lived in the first century CE) reports that in the autumn when Apollonius was ready to put to sea, numbers of people wanted to travel with him in the boat even though it was much too small for such a large group, because they thought of him as master of storm, fire, and perils of all sorts. Porphyry has an almost verbally identical passage about Pythagoras (*Life of Pythagoras* §29; 234–305 CE), and Iamblichus (fourth cent. CE) reports the calming of the waves of flood and sea so that those in danger could pass without difficulty (Iamblichus, *Pythagoras* §135). Additional examples can be found in R. Pesch, *Das Markusevangelium* (HTKNT II:1. Freiburg: Herder, 1984), p. 274. The texts manifest basically two types of "solution," both of which are already present in the New Testament: either the deity appears to those in danger on the sea (epiphany, as in Mark 6:42-52 par. and John 6:15-21), or the human miracle worker is already present in the boat with those who are threatened, and helps them in this way (Mark 4:35-41 par., and cf. also Acts 27). Jonah occupies a middle position in that his prayer to God brings help (Jonah 1 and the Armenian version of Philo, "On Jonah," in the translation of F. Siegert, *Drei hellenistisch-jüdische Predigten* [Tübingen: J. C. B. Mohr (Paul Siebeck), 1980]).

56. Matthew 8:23-27/ Mark 4:35-41/ Luke 8:22-25

Armenian Philo, "On Jonah" §8 (15 BCE–50 CE)

. . . And they stretched out their hands in prayer, but in response to their prayer the storm did not abate in the least. (MEB/Berger)

The motif of the fruitless prayers of all others in the story except the one who then finally brings deliverance derives from the story of Jonah (1:5: "Then the mariners were afraid, and each cried to his god"). In Jonah the motif is already related to foreign gods (". . . to his god"). In the story above the motif is separated from the person of Jonah and developed toward the idea that not the pagan gods, but only the Jewish God is able to deliver (apologetic). In Mark 4 and parallels, on the other hand, completely different features of the Jonah story are developed (though others are preserved, such as the motifs of sleeping/waking and reproach). Prayer is replaced by the sovereign command of Jesus. The attribution of the miracle in the rabbinic story to God's "being with" the child corresponds to the case of Jesus, whose power to do miracles can be derived from God's "being with" him (John 3:2).

57. Matthew 8:23-27/ Mark 4:35-41/ Luke 8:22-25

b. Baba Mezia 59b (end of 1 cent. CE [?])

R. Gamaliel too was traveling in a ship, when a huge wave arose to drown him. "It appears to me," he reflected, "that this is on account of none other but R. Eliezer b. Hyrcanus." Thereupon he arose and exclaimed, "Sovereign of the Universe! Thou knowest full well that I have not acted for my honor, nor for the honor of my paternal house, but for Thine, so that strife may not multiply in Israel!" At that the raging sea subsided. (Soncino)

As in the Jonah story, but different from that in Mark 4 and parallels, the experience of trouble on the high seas is linked to the personal lapse of the man of God. But since he humbles himself before God, contact with God is restored and his prayer is heard. In the case of Jesus, it is neither a matter of a personal lapse nor of the power of his prayer, for he commands the sea on his own authority.

58. Matthew 8:23-27; 14:22-33/ Mark 4:35-41; 6:45-52/ Luke 8:22-25

Plutarch, Moralia, "Precepts of Statecraft" 19 (45–125 CE)

[The statesman] . . . must not create storms himself, and yet he must not desert the State when storms fall upon it; he must not stir up the State and make it reel perilously, but when it is reeling and in danger, he must come to its assistance and employ his frankness of speech as a sacred anchor [i.e. the emergency anchor] heaved over in the greatest perils. Such were the troubles which overtook the Pergamenes under Nero and the Rhodians recently, under Domitian and the Thessalians earlier under Augustus, when they burned Petraeus alive.

"Then slumb'ring thou never wouldst see him,"

nor cowering in fear, the man who is really a statesman, nor would you see him throwing blame upon others and putting himself out of danger, but you will see him serving on embassies, sailing the seas, and saying first not only

"Here we have come, the slayers; avert thou the plague, O Apollo,"

but, even though he had no part in the wrongdoing of the people, taking danger upon himself in their behalf. (LCL)

The passage about not slumbering comes from the *Iliad* 4.223 (about Agamemnon, but on the battlefield, not on a ship). There is a series of features in common with the Gospel story (ship, storm, help from the hero, as in Matt 8:25, the call for salvation to a divine being). Differences are that the Plutarch text uses the language only metaphorically, while in the Gospels a story is narrated as a report—which in Matthew may already, of course, be understood entirely as a metaphor referred to the church in distress on stormy seas (cf. Günther Bornkamm, "The Stilling of the Storm in Matthew," in Günther Bornkamm, Gerhard Barth, and Heinz Joachim Held, *Tradition and Interpretation in Matthew* [Philadelphia: Westminster, 1963], 52-57).

59. Matthew 8:25

Achilles Tatius, *Clitophon and Leucippe* 3.4 (2 cent. CE)

"Have pity," I [Clitophon] wailed and cried, "Lord Poseidon, and make a truce with us, the remnants of your shipwreck, we have already undergone many deaths through fear." (LCL)

One in peril on the sea calls out to the Lord of the sea for mercy. Similarly, Jesus is addressed as κύριος in the Matthean version of the story.

60. Matthew 8:28-34 / Mark 5:1-20 / Luke 8:26-39

Magical Papyrus *PGM* 4.3007-3085 (ca. 300 CE)

A tested charm of Pibechis for those possessed by daimons:
Take oil of unripe olives, together with the herb
mastigia and the fruit pulp of the lotus, and boil them with colorless marjoram,
saying: "IOEL OS SARTHIOMI,
EMORI, THEOCHIPSOITH, SITHEMEOCH, SOTHE,
IOE, MIMIPSOTHIOOPH, PHERSOTHI, AEEIOYO,
IOE, EO CHARIPHTHA: come out of NN (add the usual)"

The phylactery: On a tin lamella write
IAEO ABRAOTH IOCH PHTHA MESENPSIN IAO PHEOCH IAEO CHARSOK, and hang
it on the patient. It is terrifying to every daimon, a thing he fears. After placing the patient
opposite [to you], conjure. **This is the conjuration:** "I conjure you by the god of the
Hebrews,
Jesus. IABA IAE ABRAOTH AIA THOTH ELE ELO AEO EOY IIIBAECH ABARMAS
IABARAOU ABELBEL LONA ABRA MAROIA BRAKION, who appears in fire, who is in
the midst of the land, snow, and fog, Tannetis; let your
angel, the implacable, descend and let him assign the daimon flying around this form,
which god formed in his holy paradise, because I pray to the holy god, [calling] upon
AMMON IPSENTANCHO (formula). I conjure you, LABRIA IAKOUTH ABLANATHA-
NALBA AKRAMM (formula) AOTH IATHABRATHA CHACHTHABRATHA CHAMYN
CHEL ABROOTH OUABRASILOTH HALLELOU IELOSAI IAEL. I conjure you by the
one who appeared to Osrael in a shining pillar and a cloud by day,
who saved his people from the Pharaoh and brought upon Pharaoh the ten plagues
because of his disobedience. I conjure you, every daimonic spirit, to tell whatever sort you
may be, because I conjure you by the seal which Solomon placed on the tongue of Jeremiah,
and he told. You also tell whatever sort you may be, heavenly or aerial, whether terrestrial
or subterranean, or nether worldly or Ebousaeus or Cherseus or Pharisaeus, tell
whatever sort you may be, because I conjure you by god, light bearing, unconquerable,
who knows what is in the heart of every living being, the one who formed of dust the race
of humans, the one who, after bringing them out from obscurity, packs together the clouds,
waters the earth with rain
and blesses its fruit, [the one] whom every heavenly power of angels and of archangels
praises. I conjure you by the great god SABAOTH, through whom the Jordan River drew
back and the Red Sea,
which Israel crossed, became impassable, because I conjure you by the one who introduced
the one hundred forty languages and distributed them by his own command. I conjure
you by the one who burned up the stubborn giants with lightning,
whom the heaven of heavens praises, whom the wings of the cherubim praise. I conjure
you by the one who put the mountains around the sea [or] a wall of sand and commanded
the sea not to overflow. The abyss obeyed; and you obey,
every demoniac spirit, because I conjure you by the one who causes the four winds to move,
together from the holy aions, [the] skylike, sealike, cloudlike, light-bringing unconquerable [one]. I conjure [you] by the one in holy Jerusalem, before whom the
unquenchable fire burns for all time, with his holy name IAEOBAPHREMENOUN (formula), the one before whom the fiery Gehenna trembles, flames surround, iron bursts
asunder, and every mountain is afraid from its foundation.
I conjure you, every daimonic spirit, by the one who oversees the earth and makes its
foundations tremble, [the one] who made all things which are not into that which is."

And I adjure you, the one who receives this conjuration,
not to eat pork, and every spirit and daimon, whatever sort it may be, will be subject to you.
And while conjuring, blow once, blowing air from the tips of the feet up to the face, and
it will be assigned. Keep yourself pure, for this charm is Hebraic
and is preserved among pure men. (Betz)

This text shares with the Synoptic Gospels the worldview in which demons are real and exorcistic measures can be taken against them. But there is a great contrast between the picture of Jesus (and the apostles) in the Synoptic Gospels and Acts and this spell. Jesus and the apostles cast out demons because the power of God or the Holy Spirit is personally present in them; here, the power is in the spell itself, which works of itself independently of the exorcist, if the words are correctly pronounced. Though not Christian or Jewish, the spell has obviously incorporated elements of garbled Jewish and Christian lore. (NN in the translation is the translator's indication that the appropriate name or act was to be inserted into the formula at this point.)

On Mark 5:1-20 par. and exorcisms, cf. nos. 230-31.

61. Matthew 8:28-34/ Mark 5:1-20/ Luke 8:26-39

Philostratus, *Life of Apollonius of Tyana* 4.20 (Apollonius, 1 cent. CE; Philostratus, early 3 cent. CE)

Now while he was discussing the question of libations, there chanced to be present in his audience a young dandy who bore so evil a reputation for licentiousness, that his conduct had long been the subject of coarse street-corner songs. His home was Corcyra, and he traced his pedigree to Alcinous the Phaeacian who entertained Odysseus. Apollonius then was talking about libations, and was urging them not to drink out of a particular cup, but to reserve it for the gods, without ever touching it or drinking out of it. But when he also urged them to have handles on the cup, and to pour the libation over the handle, because that is the part of the cup at which men are least likely to drink, the youth burst out into loud and coarse laughter, and quite drowned his voice. Then Apollonius looked up at him and said: "It is not yourself that perpetrates this insult, but the demon, who drives you on without your knowing it." And in fact the youth was, without knowing it, possessed by a devil; for he would laugh at things that no one else laughed at, and then he would fall to weeping for no reason at all, and he would talk and sing to himself. Now most people thought that it was the boisterous humor of youth which led him into such excesses; but he was really the mouthpiece of a devil, though it only seemed a drunken frolic in which on that occasion he was indulging. Now when Apollonius gazed on him, the ghost in him began to utter cries of fear and rage, such as one hears from people who are being branded or racked; and the ghost swore that he would leave the young man alone and never take possession of any man again. But Apollonius addressed him with anger, as a master might a shifty, rascally, and shameless slave and so on, and he ordered him to quit the young man and show by a visible sign that he had done so. "I will throw down yonder statue," said the devil, and pointed to one of the images which was in the king's portico, for there it was that the scene took place. But when the statue began by moving gently, and then fell down, it would defy anyone to describe the hubbub which arose thereat and the way they clapped their hands with wonder. But the young man rubbed his eyes as though he had just woke up, and he looked toward the rays of the sun, and assumed a modest aspect, as all had their attention concentrated on him; for he no longer showed himself licentious, nor did he stare madly about, but he had returned to his own self, as thoroughly as if he had been treated with drugs; and he gave up his dainty dress and summery garments and the rest of his sybaritic way of life, and he fell in love with the austerity of philosophers, and donned their cloak, and stripping of his old self modeled his life in the future upon that of Apollonius. (LCL)

This is a model and often-cited text illustrating several points of contact with New Testament exorcisms in general and Mark 5:1-20 par. in particular:

1) Dialogue between the exorcist and the demon (cf. on Mark 1:21-28 par.)

2) The stern, authoritarian manner of address of the exorcist (cf. Mark 1:25; 5:8; 9:17-26)

3) After the exorcism, the grateful delivered victim wants to become a follower of the exorcist (in Mark 5 par.; mostly, those delivered simply return to their normal life and go their way).

Differences:

1) In Philostratus, the demon is unnoticed by others including the demonized, who give other explanations of the demonic behavior, and the exorcist is the first to correctly diagnose the problem. In the New Testament, the plight of the possessed is already recognized.

2) In Philostratus, the observers are provided with empirical proof that the demon has come out. In the New Testament, this is immediately obvious without other evidence.

3) Strangely enough, the connection between conversion from moral perversity to a good ethical life and being delivered from the demonic power is made explicitly in Philostratus, who even uses the New Testament language of conversion ("returned to his own self," "stripping off his old self"), while the New Testament does not use deliverance from demons as a symbol for individual conversion, but as a sign of the advent of the kingdom of God.

62. Matthew 8:28/ Mark 5:2-3/ Luke 8:27

Jubilees 22:16-17 (145–140 BCE)

[The testament of Isaac directed to Jacob:] And you also, my son, Jacob, remember my words, and keep the commandments of Abraham, your father. Separate yourself from the gentiles, and do not eat with them and do not perform deeds like theirs. And do not become associates of theirs. Because their deeds are defiled, and all of their ways are contaminated, and despicable, and abominable. They slaughter their sacrifices to the dead, and to the demons they bow down. And they eat in tombs. And all their deeds are worthless and vain. (*OTP* 1:98)

The text gives a summary list of pagan impurity, for which, as in Mark 5 par., the association of the dead and the demonic is characteristic. Cf. also the features denoting a possessed person in j. Ter. I:I [40b] [V.A]: "(1) One who goes out [alone] at night, (2) who sleeps in a graveyard, (3) who rips his clothing and (4) who loses what is given him" (Neusner, *Talmud of the Land of Israel*).

63. Matthew 8:31-32/ Mark 5:12-13/ Luke 8:32-33

Callimachus, *Aitia*, Book 3.75 (born before 300 BCE)

. . . in the afternoon an evil pallor came upon her; the disease seized her, which we banish on the wild goats and which we falsely call the holy disease. (LCL)

Epilepsy is what is here pictured. The Greek verb corresponds to the technical term for "sending forth" (ἀποπομπή). The sickness was supposed to be healed by transferring it to wild goats. In Mark 5 par. the transfer is to swine—who are already unclean in any case.

To Mark 5:8-12 par., see no. 636.

64. Matthew 8:31-32/ Mark 5:12-13/ Luke 8:32-33

A Greek Prayer

[Address to a demon:] Now look, don't go into my servant, but flee and depart into the wild mountains and enter into the head of a bull. There eat flesh and suck blood, there destroy the eyes, there darken the brain, confuse, pervert . . . (MEB/from F. Pradel, *Griechische und süditalienische Gebete, Beschwörungen und Rezepte des Mittelalters* [RVV 3:13] [Giessen, 1907], pp. 267-68, 358)

In ancient popular literature ideas of folk religion are expressed more clearly and graphically than in the New Testament, as illustrated by comparing the above magical text which has already been Christianized with the Gospel story. Such ideas, even if they are temporally later than New Testament texts, are thus still worthy of note.

65. Matthew 9:1-8/ Mark 2:1-12/ Luke 5:17-26

Plutarch, *Moralia*, "Questions on Roman Customs" 5 (45–125 CE)

Why is it that those who are falsely reported to have died in a foreign country, even if they return, men do not admit by the door, but mount upon the roof-tiles and let them down inside?

Varro gives an explanation of the cause that is quite fabulous. For he says that in the Silician war there was a great naval battle, and in the case of many men a false report spread that they were dead. But, when they had returned home, in a short time they all came to their end except one who, when he tried to enter, found the doors shutting against him of their own accord, nor did they yield when he strove to open them. The man fell asleep before his threshold and in his sleep saw a vision, which instructed him to climb upon the roof and let himself down into the house. When he had done so, he prospered and lived to an advanced age; . . . for the Greeks did not consider pure, nor admit to familiar intercourse, nor suffer to approach the temples any person for whom a funeral had been held and a tomb constructed on the assumption that they were dead.

Hence it is nothing surprising if the Romans also did not think it right to admit by the door, through which they go out to sacrifice and come in from sacrificing, those who are thought to have been buried once and for all and to belong to the company of the departed, but bade them descend from the open air above into that portion of the house which is exposed to the sky. And with good reason, for, naturally, they perform all their rites of purification under the open sky. (LCL)

It has often been supposed that the making of an opening in the roof corresponded to an exorcistic practice (cf. Hedwig Jahnow, "Das Abdecken des Daches Mc 24, Lc 519," *ZNW* 24 [1925], 155-58; and Otto Böcher, *Christus Exorcista* [Stuttgart: Kohlhammer, 1972], pp. 72-73 and n. 488), but documentation for this view was lacking from the historical environment. From the Plutarch text it becomes clear that ritually unclean persons could not pass over the threshold without suffering harm themselves or causing it to others. Should this idea be in the background of the New Testament story, then it would have a Greco-Roman milieu. On the introduction of the motif of the man being carried on a litter, cf. Lucian, "Lover of Lies" 11 (120–185 CE).

66. Matthew 9:1-8 / Mark 2:1-12 / Luke 5:17-26

Lucian, *Demonax* 7 (120–185 CE)

He [Demonax] never was known to make an uproar or excite himself or get angry, even if he had to rebuke someone; though he assailed sins, he forgave sinners, thinking that one should pattern after doctors, who heal sicknesses but feel no anger at the sick. He considered that it is human to err, divine or all but divine to set right what has gone amiss. (LCL)

As in the Gospel story, the healing of sickness is associated with conduct with regard to sins, both in the relation between the people concerned (the sick, sinners) and the helper (physician, teacher). In Lucian, however, both are located on another plane than in the New Testament. In Lucian it is a matter of the technique of the physician and the pedagogical conduct of the teacher, while in the Gospel story it is a matter of the divinely given "effortless" exercise of authority. But also in Lucian the dealing with sins is related to God and the godlike man (cf. Mark 2:7 par.).

67. Matthew 9:2 / Mark 2:5 / Luke 5:20

Jubilees 41:23-24 (2 cent. BCE)

And he [namely, Judah] began to mourn and make supplication before the LORD on account of his sin. And we [namely, the angels] told him in a dream that it was forgiven him because he made great supplication and because he mourned and did not do it again. (*OTP* 2:131)

Also elsewhere angels give an authoritative communication that prayers have been heard, including prayers of repentance. In *Jubilees* the angel announces to Judah the forgiveness of sins. Thus the objection of Mark 2:7 par. becomes understandable: only God can forgive sins, and whoever on earth speaks of the forgiveness of sins would have to at least be God's messenger and announce God's word.

68. Matthew 9:2 / Mark 2:5 / Luke 5:20

Targum of Isaiah 53 (possibly as late as 1 cent. CE, or as early as 2 cent. BCE)

53.4 Then he will beseech concerning our sins and our iniquities for his sake will be forgiven; yet we were esteemed wounded, smitten before the LORD and afflicted. 53.5 And he will build the sanctuary which was profaned for our sins, handed over for our iniquities;

and by his teaching his peace will increase upon us, and in that we attach ourselves to his words our sins will be forgiven us. 53.6 All we like sheep have been scattered; we have gone into exile, every one his own way; and before the LORD it was a pleasure to forgive the sins of us all for his sake. 53.11 . . . by his wisdom shall he make innocents to be accounted innocent, to subject many to the law; and he shall beseech concerning their sins.

53.12 . . . yet he will beseech concerning the sins of many, and to the rebels it shall be forgiven for him. (Chilton)

The figure of the Servant of Yahweh is here interpreted messianically, as also elsewhere in the Targum of the prophets. The Messiah is here related to the forgiveness of sins. Specifically, forgiveness occurs (1) through his intercession and (2) by the obeying of his word. (3) God forgives entirely "for his sake." (4) According to v. 11 there may even be intercession for those already counted righteous, so it is assumed that even their sins are charged even after they have been justified. In distinction to this Jewish text, in Mark Jesus himself pronounces the word of forgiveness, of course as God's spokesperson, and so functions as Messiah in a different role than the figure in the *Targum of Isaiah*.

69. Matthew 9:5-6/ Mark 2:9-10/ Luke 5:23-24

Josephus, *Antiquities* 10.28 (37–100 CE)

[Concerning King Hezekiah and Isaiah:] . . . and so Hezekiah asked Isaiah to perform some sign or miracle in order that he might believe in him when he said these things, as in one who came from God. For, he said, things that are beyond belief and surpass our hopes are made credible by acts of a like nature. (That is, incredible statements can be accepted only when supported by equally incredible acts.) (LCL)

Forgiveness of sins and healing stand in a similar relation to each other as the two phases of the miracle: at first only announced, but now already accomplished and visible. Cf. also b. Nedarim 41a:

"R. Alexandri said in the name of R. Hiyya b. Abba: A sick man does not recover from his sickness until all his sins are forgiven him, as it is written, Who forgiveth all thine iniquities; who healeth all thy diseases (Ps. CIII, 3)." (Soncino)

70. Matthew 9:12/ Mark 2:17/ Luke 5:31

Diogenes Laertius, *Lives of the Philosophers*, "Antisthenes" 6.6 (3 cent. CE)

One day when he (namely, Antisthenes) was censured for keeping company with evil men, the reply he made was, "Well, physicians are in attendance on their patients without getting the fever themselves." (LCL)

The story is of a similar genre to that in Mark: those who criticize the conduct of a teacher are met with a striking retort. But the thrust is different, even though both responses have to do with physicians. Antisthenes, however, emphasizes the distance and nonparticipation in sin, while Jesus points to the neediness of the sick. (Cf. also Diogenes Laertius, *Lives*, "Aristippos" 2.70, no. 66 above; and Berger, *Formgeschichte*, §§25-29.)

71. Matthew 9:18-26 / Mark 5:21-43 / Luke 8:40-56

Targum to Habakkuk 3:1

The prayer which Habakkuk the prophet prayed when it was revealed to him concerning the extension of time which he gives to the wicked. This is the prophet Habakkuk who drew a circle and stepped into the middle of it. Then he lifted up his voice and spoke as follows. "Living and steadfast is your name. I will not leave this circle unless visions come of the judgment that is already prepared for the deeds of people." Then came the Spirit of Holiness and said the following to him . . . (*Targum of the Minor Prophets;* MEB/Berger from codex Reuchlinianus)

In dealing with God the prophet applies the necessary magical means (circle drawing) and prayer, in order to receive a revelation. His prayer is answered. There is a similar story about Moses in *Abot. R. Nat.* A §9.

72. Matthew 9:18-26 / Mark 5:21-43 / Luke 8:40-56

b. Ta'anith 23a (1 cent. CE tradition, written much later)

Once it happened that the greater part of the month of Adar had gone and yet no rain had fallen. The people sent a message to Honi the Circle Drawer, Pray that rain may fall. He prayed and no rain fell. He thereupon drew a circle and stood within it in the same way as the prophet Habakkuk had done, as it is said, *I will stand upon my watch, and set me upon the tower,* etc. (Hab. II, 1) He exclaimed [before God], Master of the Universe, Thy children have turned to me because [they believe] me to be a member of Thy house. I swear by Thy great name that I will not move from here until Thou hast mercy upon Thy children! Rain began to drip and his disciples said to him, We look to you to save us from death; [The meaning of the Hebrew phrase is doubtful] we believe that this rain came down merely to release you from your oath. Thereupon he exclaimed: It is not for this that I have prayed, but for rain [to fill] cisterns, ditches and caves. The rain then began to come down with great force, every drop being as big as the opening of a barrel and the Sages estimated that no one drop was less than a log. His disciples then said to him: Master, we look to you to save us from death; we believe that the rain came down to destroy the world. Thereupon he exclaimed before [God], It is not for this that I have prayed, but for rain of benevolence, blessing and bounty. Then rain fell normally until the Israelites [in Jerusalem] were compelled to go up [for shelter] to the Temple Mount because of the rain. [His disciples] then said to him, Master, in the same way as you have prayed for the rain to fall pray for the rain to cease. He replied: I have it as a tradition that we may not pray on account of an excess of good. Despite this bring unto me a bullock for a thanksgiving offering. They brought unto him a bullock for a thanksgiving offering and he laid his two hands upon it and said, Master of the Universe, Thy people Israel whom Thou hast brought out from Egypt cannot endure an excess of good nor an excess of punishment; when Thou wast angry with them, they could not endure it; when Thou didst shower upon them an excess of good they could not endure it; may it be Thy will that the rain may cease and that there be relief for the world. Immediately the wind began to blow and the clouds were dispersed and the sun shone and the people went out into the fields and gathered for themselves mushrooms and truffles. Thereupon Simeon b. Shetah sent this message to him, Were it not that you are Honi I would have placed you under the ban; for were the years like the years [of famine in the time] of Elijah [Cf. 1 Kings XVII, 1ff.] (in whose hands were the keys of Rain) would not the name of Heaven be profaned through you? [Honi would not have hesitated to force, so to speak, the hand of Heaven even in the face of an oath such as Elijah had made in the name of God that there would be no rain for years (1 Kings XVII, 1ff.).] But what shall I do unto you who actest petulantly before the Omnipresent and He grants your desire, as a son who acts petulantly before his father and he grants his desires; thus he says to him, Father, take me to bathe in warm water, wash me in cold water, give me nuts, almonds, peaches, and pomegranates and he gives them unto him. Of you Scripture says, *Let thy father and thy mother be glad, and let her that bore thee rejoice* [Prov. XXIII, 25].

Our Rabbis have taught: What was the message that the Sanhedrin [lit., "the Men of the Hall of Hewn Stone." The Sanhedrin met in the Hall of Hewn Stone.] sent to Honi the Circle Drawer? [It was an interpretation of the verse,] *Thou shalt also decree a thing, and it shall be established unto thee, and light shall shine upon thy ways,* etc. [Job XXII, 28ff.] *"Thou shalt also decree a thing:"* You have decreed [on earth] below and the Holy One, Blessed be He, fulfills your word [in heaven] above. *"And light shall shine upon thy ways:"* You have illumined with your prayer a generation in darkness. (Soncino)

While quite frequent in Latin and especially Greek literature, the picture of the miracle-working sage or rabbi, while present, is rare in rabbinic literature (see Morton Smith, *Tannaitic Parallels to the Gospels,* SBLMS 6 [Philadelphia: Society of Biblical Literature, 1968, corrected repr. of 1951 ed.], pp. 81-83).

The following is significant in this narrative:

1) The miracle worker is before God a "son of the house[hold]" (Heb. בֶּן בַּיִת, *ben bayit*), and thus stands in a relation of intimacy to God like Jesus in Hebrews 3:6 (alternatively: a member of a rabbinic "house," i.e. school, such as the "House of Hillel"). God unconditionally fulfills even the most bizarre and, as to their results, contradictory wishes of his child. The miracle worker thus has a relation to God like that expressed in the New Testament "abba" address to God, and like that of the lost son of Luke 15.

2) The magical misuse of the name of God must be punished by placing the violator under the ban. Josephus reports (*Antiquities* 14.22-25) of Onias (obviously identical with this Honi) that he was stoned for the practice of his charismatic office (in his prayer he had practiced love for the enemy). Only the fulfilling of the wish justifies this kind of urgent, direct pressure on God, since it shows that the miracle worker really could relate to God like a little child to its papa. Magic is then only objectionable when it is practiced by someone who does not stand in this intimate relation to God. Early Christianity too knows of a case of such direct intimate pressure on God, namely by James, who is otherwise only described as a model of Jewish piety; according to Jerome, *Illustrious Men 2* (Frag. 7), the Gospel of the Hebrews reported that James had sworn to eat no bread until he had seen the Risen One.

3) According to Mark, several miracles were performed by Jesus specifically as Son of God (e.g. 3:11; 5:7), and the separation of the three disciples in Mark 5:37 to witness the miracle alone is a signal for the revelation of the special office of Jesus. In Mark 5:41 Jesus heals without prayer, in a somewhat magical manner—differently from the Old Testament model for the story.

73. Matthew 9:18-26/ Mark 5:21-43/ Luke 8:40-56

Genesis Apocryphon 20:28-29 (1 QapGen) (1 cent. BCE)

[Pharaoh prays, after he had given Sarah back to Abraham, for deliverance from the plague, i.e. from spirit that caused the evil sores of Genesis 20:26:] And now pray for me and my house that this evil spirit may be expelled from it. So I prayed [for him] . . . and I laid my hands on his [head]; and the scourge departed from him and the evil [spirit] was expelled [from him], and he lived. (Vermes)

Hands, and correspondingly the finger of God (Luke 11:20), are critical means of thaumaturgical practice. To be noted, in contrast to New Testament texts, is the connection between laying on of hands and exorcism (in the New Testament exorcisms are predominantly by command), and the combination of both elements with prayer. The traditional understanding of Abraham as intercessor was here the point of contact for the development of this idea.

74. Matthew 9:20-21/ Mark 5:27-28/ Luke 8:44

Arrian, *Anabasis of Alexander* 6.13.3 (ca. 90–170 CE)

. . . when Alexander drew near his pavilion he dismounted from his horse, so that the army beheld him walking. Then they all ran toward him from this side and that, some touching his hands, some his knees, some his garment; others just looked on him from near at hand, and with a blessing upon him went his way; some cast wreaths upon him, some such flowers as the country of India bare at that time. (LCL)

Especially in the case of rulers, their power is frequently transmitted by the mere touch, as for example in Plutarch, *Life of Sulla* 35 (474 C): Valeria approaches Sulla from behind, extends her hand after him, and pulls a fluff of wool from his garment. When challenged to explain, she responds that she wanted to obtain some of his good fortune. So also in Tacitus, *Histories* 4, 81.1 (contact with the sole of his foot brings healing; cf. no. 88). It is important to see that the contact was made not alone for the purpose of healing, but also in order to participate in the ruler's "power," "blessing," and "good fortune."

75. Matthew 9:20-21/ Mark 5:27/ Luke 8:44

Plutarch, *Moralia,* "Table Talk" Book 5.7.1-2 (45–125 CE)

And yet the so-called Thibaeans, who anciently lived near the Pontus, were, according to Phylarchus, deadly not only to children but to adults. He says that those who were subjected to the glance, breath, or speech of these people, fell ill and wasted away. . . . Just so, there is no reason to doubt that contact between human beings may prove in some cases beneficial and in others rough and harmful. . . . "Indeed," I answered, "in a way you yourself have found the track and trail of the reason at the point where you came to effluences from bodies. For odor, voice, and breathing are all emanations of some kind, streams of particles from living bodies, that produce sensation whenever our organs of sense are stimulated by their impact. Living bodies are, because of their warmth and motion, far more likely in reason to give off these particles than are inanimate bodies, inasmuch as breathing produces a certain pulsation and turmoil whereby the body is struck and emits a continuous stream of emanations." (LCL)

Plutarch here attempts a natural, "scientific" explanation for magical phenomena (especially such that happen by means of looking at a person or object), and thus presents a contribution to the reconstruction of the worldview that also stands behind Mark 5 par., reflected with more or less clarity. In his own way, Plutarch makes it clear that for him looking at something is more than the mere subjective act of seeing. This means that we should also ask in regard to texts such as Matthew 5:28-29 whether in historical interpretation the one-sided personalistic and idealistic aspect of a "more subtle ethic" should not be corrected by attending more carefully to the circumstances surrounding their formation in the framework of the ancient ways of thinking (historical psychology, so-called magical ideas, and such). The same question could be raised in regard to "sins of the tongue."

76. Matthew 9:24/ Mark 5:39/ Luke 8:52

Celsus, *On Medicine* 2:6 (early 1 cent. CE)

[In a discussion about possible misinterpretation of the signs of death in a patient:] . . . some signs, stated as approximately certain, often deceive inexperienced practitioners, but not good ones; for instance, Asclepiades, when he met the funeral procession, recognized that a man who was being carried out to burial was alive; and it is not primarily a fault of the art if there is a fault on the part of its professor. (LCL)

Celsus refers to a scene that became traditional and was sometimes reported in great detail (Pliny, *Natural History* 7.37; 26.8; Apuleius, *Florida* 19). Celsus' point that expert physicians can detect signs of life that escape their less experienced colleagues is a defense of the medical profession, and different from the Marcan story, in which the girl was really dead. Jesus' comment in Mark 5:39 par. is not to be taken literally, as it was in the nineteenth-century rationalizing explanations of Gospel miracles (e.g., H. E. G. Paulus, *Das Leben Jesu als Grundlage einer reinen Geschichte des Urchristentums* [Heidelberg: C. F. Winter, 1828], labeled this category of gospel stories not "raisings from the dead" but "deliverances from premature burial"). Cf. further no. 290 on Luke 7:11-17, where the scene of Asclepiades' stopping the funeral procession was recounted in a strikingly similar manner.

77. Matthew 10:1, 7-8/ Mark 6:7/ Luke 9:1-2

Empedocles, *On Nature*, fragment (483/1–423 BCE)

You will learn about medicines, as many as there are, and helps against evils and old age, because for you alone I will accomplish all this.
You will halt the power of untiring winds which move over the earth, and by their blowing destroy the seedland; and again, if you have the will, you will summon the winds to return.

You will make from dark rain, dryness for men in its season; you will make summer drought into streams that nourish trees, pouring down from the sky.

You will lead out from Hades the power of a dead man. (Franklin)

Empedocles speaks of having power over sickness, nature, and even death. The Synoptic Jesus gives his disciples authority over the demonic powers that afflict human beings. Matthew explicitly includes raising the dead. In contrast to Empedocles, the Synoptic sayings confer this power on the disciples as an aspect of the irruption of the kingdom of God into this world in the ministry of Jesus.

78. Matthew 10:5-12 / Mark 6:8-11 / Luke 9:2-5

Iamblichus, *On the Pythagorean Way of Life* 23 (105) (4 cent. CE)

[Some examples of Pythagorean teaching through symbols:] "As secondary purpose of a journey neither enter a temple nor worship at all, not even if you be passing before the very doors." "Sacrifice and worship unshod." "Walk on paths, avoiding roads traveled by the public." "Do not talk about Pythagorean matters without light." (Dillon and Hershbell)

Cf. Epictetus, *Discourses* 3.2.2. As in Matthew 10 par., the instructions have to do primarily with the life of wandering. Cultic concerns are not to be attended to even in passing. The other instructions are purity regulations and liturgical stipulations. In Jesus' missionary discourse too, the purity rule plays a role (Matt 10:5, 8).

For an allegorical interpretation cf. no. 98. On Matthew 10:21, cf. no. 83.

79. Matthew 10:7-14 / Mark 6:8-10 / Luke 9:3-5; 10:1-16

Josephus, *Jewish War*, 2.124-27 (37–100 CE)

On the arrival of any of the sect from elsewhere, all the resources of the community are put at their disposal, just as if they were their own; and they enter the houses of men whom they have never seen before as though they were their most intimate friends. Consequently, they carry nothing whatever with them on their journeys, except arms as a protection against brigands. . . . They do not change their garments or shoes until they are torn to shreds or worn threadbare with age. There is no buying or selling among themselves, but each gives what he has to any in need and receives from him in exchange something useful to himself. (LCL)

Josephus here pictures the traveling arrangements between Essene groups. Typical are (1) the ascetic tendency of the whole and (2) the great importance that settled members of the group have for taking care of traveling, itinerant members. For the rest, Josephus follows the topos of the ideal picture of eastern philosophical associations, as presented for example in Plutarch's *Moralia*, "Fortune of Alexander," 10: "Even there it is said that there are certain holy men, a law unto themselves, who follow a rigid gymnosophy [cf. *Life of Alexander*, chaps. 64, 65 (700 F-701) for Alexander's dealings with the Gymnosophists] and give all their time to God; they are more frugal than Diogenes since they have no need of a wallet. For they do not store up food, since they have it ever fresh and green from the earth; the flowing rivers give them drink and they have fallen leaves and grassy earth to lie upon" (LCL).

80. Matthew 10:9-10/ Mark 6:8-9/ Luke 9:3-4

Epistles of Diogenes, No. 7, "To Hicetas" (2 cent. CE)

Diogenes to Hicetas. Do not be upset, Father, that I am called a dog and put on a double, coarse cloak, carry a wallet over my shoulders, and have a staff in my hand. It is not worthwhile getting distressed over such matters, but you should rather be glad that your son is satisfied with little, free from popular opinion, to which all, Greeks and barbarians alike, are subservient. Now the name, besides not being in accord with my deeds, is a sign that is notable as it is. For I am called heaven's dog, not earth's, since I liken myself to it, living as I do, not in conformity with popular opinion but according to nature, free under Zeus, and crediting the good to him and not to my neighbor. As for my clothing, even Homer writes that Odysseus, the wisest of the Greeks, so dressed while he was returning home from Ilium under Athena's direction. And the vesture is so fine that it is commonly acknowledged to be a discovery not of men but of the gods.

"First she gave him a cloak, tunic and mantle, seedy, dirty, stained by filthy smoke. She put around him a large, hairless hide of swift deer and gave him a staff and a poor leather pouch, riddled with holes, with a knapsack strap on it" (Homer, *Odyssey* 13.434-38).

Take heart, Father, at the name which they call me, and at my clothing, since the dog is under the protection of the gods and his clothing is god's invention. (Malherbe)

"Cynics" derived their name from the Greek word for "dog," κύων (cf. "Dominican," "the Lord's dog"). The description of the wandering philosopher's clothing and equipment may be compared and contrasted with that of the Christian missionaries in Mark 6:8-9 and parallels. Most notable is the sense of freedom from all human authority, ambitions, and conventions, reminiscent of the famous story told of the Cynic founder Diogenes: "When he was sunning himself in the Craneum, Alexander came and stood over him and said, 'Ask of me any boon you like.' To which he replied, 'Stand out of my light'" (Diogenes Laertius, *Lives of the Philosophers*, 6.38) (LCL).

Since this letter is pseudonymous but nonetheless has the personal touch, it may be compared to pseudonymous New Testament letters such as Colossians and the Pastorals. In addition, one may note how Homer is cited in a quasi- "scriptural" manner for justification of current practice.

81. Matthew 10:9-10/ Mark 6:8-9/ Luke 9:3; 10:4

Musonius Rufus, *On Clothing and Shelter* 19 (30–100 CE)

It does not improve the appearance of the body to cover it completely with many garments, to smother it with tight wrappings, and to soften the hands and feet by close fitting gloves or shoes unless perhaps in the case of illness. It is not good to be entirely without experience of cold and heat. . . . Wearing one chiton is preferable to needing two, and wearing none but only a cloak is preferable to wearing one. Also going barefoot is better than wearing sandals, if one can do it, for wearing sandals is next to being bound, but going barefoot gives the feet great freedom and grace when they are used to it. (Lutz)

Musonius then proceeds to speak against unnecessary luxury in the construction of housing. To spend one's money on doing good and winning friends is more important (cf. Luke 16:9, and no. 335). The freedom from the products of civilization is for Musonius the sign of an inner liberation; in the missionary discourse in the Synoptics this freedom from cultural accoutrements is oriented to practical action. Still, Matthew 6:25-33 par. shows that the other aspect is also present, of course in the sense of freedom to practice righteousness.

82. Matthew 10:19/ Mark 13:11/ Luke 21:14-15; 12:11-12

Plato, *Apology of Socrates* 28D-29 (428/427 BCE–349/348 BCE)

Strange indeed, would be my conduct, O men of Athens, if I who, when I was ordered by the generals whom you chose to command me at Potidaea and Amphipolis and Delium, remained where they placed me, like any other man, facing death—if now, when, as I conceive and imagine, God orders me to fulfill the philosopher's mission of searching into myself and other men, I were to desert my post through fear of death, or any other fear; that would indeed be strange, and I might justly be arraigned in court for denying the existence of the gods, if I disobeyed the oracle because I was afraid of death. . . . And I shall repeat the same words to every one I meet, young and old, citizen and alien, but especially to the citizens, inasmuch as they are my brethren. For I know that this is the command of God; and I believe that no greater good has ever happened in the state than my service to the God. For I do nothing but go about persuading you all, old and young alike, not to take thought for your persons or your properties, but first and chiefly to care about the greatest improvement of your soul. (LCL)

It was not only cranks and fanatics who sometimes believed they were inspired by the divine spirit or had a mission to humanity as the result of a divine call. At his defense Socrates (expressed in Plato's words) claims a divine revelation as the basis of his mission and message. He is referring to the oracle from Apollo he received at Delphi, and also to the inner spirit, his "daemon," he believed accompanied him and provided divine guidance. Other points of contact: (1) The divine spirit gives him courage to testify before the court even in the threat of death. (2) He considers his commission of ultimate importance taking precedence over all else, and that not just for himself. The chief difference: the early Christian prophets and missionaries' message centered on the redemptive act of God, i.e. it was kerygmatic, a gospel, rather than on the philosophical message of self-examination and self-improvement by turning toward noble ideals. This means that the person of the Christian missionary himself or herself did not stand at the center but was rather incidental; it was the message of something that had happened quite apart from their own apprehension of it that was to be proclaimed even at the cost of suffering and death.

83. Matthew 10:21/ Mark 13:12

b. Sotah 9.15 (49b)

Rabbi Eliezer the Great says, "Since the day when the Temple was destroyed, the Sages began to act like [children's] school teachers, and school teachers like synagogue janitors, and synagogue janitors like the [ignorant] people of the land. . . . On whom should we lean? On our Father in Heaven. With the advent of the Messiah, presumptuousness shall be great and produce shall soar in price; the vine will yield its fruit but the wine will be costly; and the heathen [idol worshipers] will be converted to heresy and there will be no one to rebuke. . . . The wisdom of the Scribes shall be decadent and those who fear sin shall be hateful to others; and truth shall be absent. The young shall put the elders to shame . . . (as it is written) the son dishonoreth the father, the daughter riseth up against her own mother . . . a man's enemies are the men of his own house (Micah 7:6) . . . and on whom are we to lean? On our Father in Heaven. R. Phineas ben Jair says, Zeal leads to cleanliness, and cleanliness to purity, and purity to self-restraint, and self-restraint leads to humility, and humility leads to the fear of sin, and the fear of sin leads to piety, and piety leads to divine intuition [literally, "the Holy Spirit"], and divine intuition leads to the resurrection of the dead, and the resurrection of the dead shall come through Elijah of blessed memory." Amen. (Soncino)

The second-century rabbis, influenced by the tradition of the terrors of the destruction of Jerusalem to which they looked back, pictured the future advent of the Messiah as preceded by similar signs. The OT topos (cf. Micah 7:6) is elaborated into a portrayal of social chaos. The Gospels are influenced by the same tradition, as they look forward to the (second) advent of the Messiah. They focus the coming terrors particularly on the persecution of the disciples of Jesus. Cf. also 2 Tim 4:1-3; 2 Tim 3:1-9. Further:

84. Matthew 10:40

Josephus, *Jewish Antiquities* 8.220-21 (37–100 CE)

So bitter did they feel toward him and so great was the anger they nourished that, when he sent Adōramos, who was in charge of the levies, to appease them and soften their mood by persuading them to forgive what he had said if there had been in it anything rash or ill-tempered owing to his youth, they did not let him speak but threw stones at him [Adōramos] and killed him. Roboamos, seeing this and imagining himself the target of the stones with which the crowd had killed his minister, was afraid that he might actually suffer this dreadful fate and immediately mounted his chariot and fled to Jerusalem. (LCL)

The incident illustrates the statement widespread in rabbinical writings, "The one sent is like the person himself." Similarly in Josephus, *Antiquities* 3.85-87, "In His name, then, and in the name of all that through Him has already been wrought for us, scorn not the words now to be spoken, through looking only on me, the speaker, or by reason that it is a human tongue that addresses you. Nay, mark but their excellence and ye will discern the majesty of Him who conceived them and, for your profit, disdained not to speak them to me. For it is not Moses, son of Amaram and Jochabad, but He who constrained the Nile to flow for your sake a blood-red stream. . . . He it is who favors you with these commandments, using me for interpreter" (LCL). Similarly, Josephus paraphrases the text of Deuteronomy 34:7-8 (*Antiquities* 4.329): "As a general he [Moses] had few to equal him, and as a prophet none, insomuch that in all his utterances one seemed to hear the speech of God Himself" (LCL). Here a particular understanding of inspiration is related to the application of the law of the messenger to God's messenger (cf. on this especially J. Bühner, *Der Gesandte und sein Weg im 4. Evangelium* [Tübingen: J. C. B. Mohr, 1977], pp. 270ff.; here, p. 300). The meaning is that in his messengers God himself is met, so that the response to them is response to God. Cf. no. 135 and John 12:44-45; 13:20.

85. Matthew 11:28-29

Plutarch, *Moralia*, "On Praising Oneself Inoffensively" 15 (45–125 CE)

Consider first, then, whether a man might praise himself to exhort his hearers and inspire them with emulation and ambition, as Nestor by recounting his own exploits and battles incited Patroclus and roused the nine champions to offer themselves for the single combat. For exhortation that includes action as well as argument and presents the speaker's own example and challenge is endued with life: it arouses and spurs the hearer, and not only awakens his ardor and fixes his purpose, but also affords him hope that the end can be attained and is not impossible. (LCL)

Matthew 11:28-29, 72, is also an example of the genre of self-commendation; cf. Berger, *Formgeschichte* 265-66. Plutarch's reflection on this genre is oriented to the connection between the word of the teacher and his own conduct offered as a model. In Matthew, it is the passion story that provides the key illustration of the teaching.

86. Matthew 11:30

Diogenes Laertius, *Lives of Eminent Philosophers*, "Cleanthes" 7.170 (3 cent. CE)

And he [Cleanthes] used to put up with gibes from his fellow pupils and did not mind being called the ass, telling them that he alone was strong enough to carry the load [φορτίον] of Zeno. (LCL)

The common element in the two pictures: the disciple carries the burden of the teacher (= he takes over his teaching and commandments and mediates it to others). Jesus challenges people to become his followers, because his burden is not heavy (not oppressive, since it gives "rest"). Differently from the rabbinic tradition, which also speaks of taking the "yoke" of the commandments (adopted from the Hellenistic philosophical tradition?), the philosophical tradition speaks of the yoke/burden of a particular teacher, as in Matthew 11.
Cf. also no. 790 (near the conclusion). On Matthew 12:44-45, cf. no. 155.

87. Matthew 12:1-8/ Mark 2:23-28/ Luke 6:1-5

Philo, *On the Life of Moses* 2.22 (15 BCE–50 CE)

For the holiday [Sabbath] extends also to every herd, and to all creatures made to minister to man, who serve like slaves their natural master. It extends also to every kind of trees and plants; for it is not permitted to cut any shoot or branch, or even a leaf, or to pluck any fruit whatsoever. All such are set at liberty on that day, and live as it were in freedom, under the general edict that proclaims that none should touch them. (LCL)

It is noteworthy that Philo, who otherwise appears not to know Halachah, in the case of Sabbath rules seems to have accurate information even to details. This stands in a certain tradition, however (cf. Josephus, *Apion* 2.282, prohibition of fasting and lighting a lamp on the Sabbath; *Jubilees* 50:7-13; CD 10-11), which is to be explained in terms of the Diaspora situation in which strict observance of the Sabbath was an important mark of Jewish identity that distinguished them from their surroundings.

88. Matthew 12:9-14 / Mark 3:1-6 / Luke 6:6-11

Tacitus, *Histories* 4.81 (55–120 CE)

During the months while Vespasian was waiting at Alexandria for the regular season of the summer winds and a settled sea (such as he would have in June and July), many marvels occurred to mark the favor of heaven and a certain partiality of the gods toward him. One of the common people of Alexandria, well known for his loss of sight, threw himself before Vespasian's knees, praying him with groans to cure his blindness, being so directed by the god Serapis, whom this most superstitious of nations worships before all others; and he besought the emperor to deign to moisten his cheeks and eyes with his spittle. Another, whose hand was useless, prompted by the same god, begged Caesar to step and trample on it. Vespasian at first ridiculed these appeals and treated them with scorn; then, when the men persisted, he began at one moment to fear the discredit of failure, at another to be inspired with hopes of success by the appeals of the suppliants and the flattery of his courtiers: finally, he directed the physicians to give their opinion as to whether such blindness and infirmity could be overcome by human aid. Their reply treated the two cases differently: they said that in the first the power of sight had not been completely eaten away and it would return if the obstacles were removed; in the other, the joints had slipped and become displaced, but they could be restored if a healing pressure were applied to them. Such perhaps was the wish of the gods, and it might be that the emperor had been chosen for this divine service; in any case, if a cure were obtained, the glory would be Caesar's, but in the event of failure, ridicule would fall only on the poor suppliants. So Vespasian, believing that his good fortune was capable of anything and that nothing was any longer incredible, with a smiling countenance, and amid intense excitement on the part of the bystanders, did as he was asked to do. The hand was instantly restored to use, and the day again shone for the blind man. Both facts are told by eyewitnesses even now when falsehood brings no reward. (LCL)

Agreements between this story and Mark 3:1-6 par., as well as Mark 8:22-26, consist in the following elements: (a) similarity in the structure of the narrative: portrayal of the affliction, approach to the miracle worker, mention of the healing technique, description of the public nature of the event (a mass of witnesses), the success of the healer. (b) The temporal adverb "instantly" at the conclusion of the narrative corresponds to the frequent use of εὐθύς ("immediately") in Mark, including miracle stories such as 2:12. (c) The note about eyewitness reports continuing to be repeated even now corresponds to 1 Corinthians 15:6 (cf. the Quadratus Fragment), where it refers to an appearance of the risen Lord. (d) For connotations important to the discussion of Christology it is important that here it is the *ruler* who is the miracle worker (cf. the story of the sweating bust of Serapis before the emperor Trajan according to the "Acta Hermaisci," part of the *Acts of the Pagan Martyrs*, ed. H.

Musurillo [Oxford: Clarendon, 1954]). A difference especially to be noted is the whole middle section of the story telling of the emperor's conversation with his physicians and their examinations, which of course functions to slow the story down and build up dramatic tension. From the perspective of form criticism the combination of the two healing stories is important, since such serial arrangement (obviously for the purpose of strengthening the testimony) can also characterize miracle stories in the Gospels (e.g. Mark 5:21-43). Cf. also Philostratus, *Life of Apollonius* 3.39 (beginning of 3 cent. CE), which gives a list of miracles, including the healing of a blind person and an afflicted hand. For the restoration of a withered hand by prayer of the afflicted person to God, see *T. Sim.* 2:11-14.

89. Matthew 12:9-14 / Mark 3:1-6 / Luke 6:6-11

Musonius Rufus, *That Kings Also Should Study Philosophy* (30–100 CE)

Do not imagine, he [namely, Musonius] said, that it is more appropriate for anyone to study philosophy than for you [namely, a Syrian king], nor for any other reason than that you are a king. For the first duty of a king is to be able to protect ["save"] and benefit ["do good for"] his people. (Lutz)

The Greek verbs "save" (σώζω) and "do good" (εὐεργετέω) are combined in a way analogous to Mark 3:4. According to Musonius the king must practice philosophy because he is called to save people and be their benefactor, and therefore must understand what is good for them and what is bad for them. Jesus' action in the Gospel story therefore corresponds completely to the contemporary picture of the public benefactor. Like a philosopher king, he lays claim to the right to determine the criteria for right and wrong conduct himself.

On Mark 3:11, see nos. 71, 72.

90. Matthew 12:12 / Mark 3:4 / Luke 6:9

b. Yoma, 85 a/b (2 cent. CE [?])

R. Ishmael, R. Akiba, and R. Eleazar b. Azariah were once on a journey, with Levi ha-Saddar and R. Ishmael son of R. Eleazar b. Azariah following them. Then this question was asked of them: Whence do we know that in the case of danger to human life the laws of the Sabbath are suspended? R. Ishmael answered and said: *If a thief be found breaking in* [Ex. XXII, 1, in which case, in spite of all the other considerations, it is lawful to kill him]. Now if in the case of this one it is doubtful whether he has come to take money or life; and although the shedding of blood pollutes the land, so that the Shechinah departs from Israel, yet it is lawful to save oneself at the cost of his life—how much more may one suspend the laws of the Sabbath to save human life! R. Akiba answered and said: *If a man come presumptuously upon his neighbor, etc. thou shalt take him from My altar, that he may die* [Ex. XXI, 14] i.e., only off the altar, but not down from the altar. [If he came as priest to do his service, one may take him off the altar, but if he had commenced on it, one may not take him down.] And in connection therewith Rabbah b. Bar Hana said in the name of R. Johanan: That was taught only when one's life is to be forfeited, [85b] but to save life one may take one down even from the altar. Now if in the case of this one, where it is doubtful whether there is any substance in his words or not, yet [he interrupts] the service in the Temple [which is important enough to] suspend the Sabbath, how much more should the saving of human life suspend the Sabbath laws! [If one had been sentenced to death, there is ample provision for a revision, if even at the last moment someone claims to have found evidence of the accused's innocence. If a priest has such evidence, or is only believed to have it, he would be taken down from the altar even after he had commenced, and before having completed, his service.] Now if in the case of this one, where it is doubtful whether there is any substance in his words or not, yet [he interrupts] the service in the Temple [which is important enough to] suspend the Sabbath, how much more should the saving of human life suspend the Sabbath laws! R. Eleazar answered and said: If circumcision, which attaches to one only of the two hundred and forty-eight members of the human body, suspends the Sabbath, how much more shall [the saving of] the whole body suspend the Sabbath! [The circumcision must take place on the eighth day, even if that day falls on the Sabbath, suspending the law of the Sabbath, which prohibits operation, as well as preparations leading to it.] (Soncino)

In all three cases the inference proceeds from small to great *(a minore ad maius)*. (1) A thief caught in the act may be killed, according to Exodus 22:1, since it could of course mean that he thereby saves his own life. That is legal, even though shedding blood defiles the land. So how much more is it permitted to save a life on the Sabbath, since it involves no shedding of blood, defiling of the land, and the resultant expulsion of God's presence from Israel. (2) In the case of anticipated or possible situations in which human life is in danger, a priest may interrupt the temple service. Now the temple service takes precedence over the Sabbath (the Sabbath must be broken in order to carry out temple ritual procedures). So if the possibility of saving life can interrupt the temple service, which is even more important than the Sabbath, how much more can the opportunity to save a life take precedence over the Sabbath. (3) Circumcision breaks the Sabbath—so how much more must the Sabbath be broken when not just one part of the body, but the whole body is at stake. The line of argument shows how, over against the rigorous sharpening of the laws of Sabbath observance in the second and first centuries BCE (*Jub.* 50 and CD) people were concerned to justify a more humane practice of the Sabbath with the justification of the Scripture. The weight of the supporting authorities speaks for itself.

91. Matthew 12:22-37 / Mark 3:22-30 / Luke 11:14-23; 12:10

Testament of Solomon 6:1-11 (date uncertain; possibly 1–2 cent. CE)

Then I summoned Beelzeboul to appear before me again. When he was seated, I thought it appropriate to ask him, "Why are you alone Prince of the Demons?" He replied, "Because I am the only one left of the heavenly angels [who fell]. I was the highest-ranking angel in heaven, the one called Beelzeboul. There also accompanied me another ungodly [angel] whom God cut off and now, imprisoned here, he holds in his power the race of those bound by me in Tartarus. He is being nurtured in the Red Sea; when he is ready, he will come in triumph."

I said to him, "What are your activities?" He replied, "I bring destruction by means of tyrants; I cause the demons to be worshiped alongside men; and I arouse desire in holy men and select priests. I bring about jealousies and murders in a country, and I instigate wars."

Then I said to him, "Bring to me the one you said is being nurtured in the Red Sea." He retorted, "I will bring no one back to you. But there will come a certain demon whose name is Ephippas who will bind him and bring him up out of the abyss." I responded, "Tell me why he is in the abyss of the Red Sea and what his name is." He, however, said, "Do not ask me; you are not able to learn that from me. He will come to you because I, too, am with you." So I said to him, "Tell me in which star you reside." "The one called by men the Evening Star," he said.

Then I said, "Tell me which angel thwarts you." "The Almighty God," he replied. "He is called by the Hebrews Patike, the one who descends from the heights; he is [called] by the Greeks Emmanouel. I am always afraid of him, and trembling. If anyone adjures me with the oath [called] 'the Elo-i,' a great name for his power, I disappear."

Now when I, Solomon, heard these things, I commanded him to cut blocks of Theban marble. As he was beginning to cut, all the demons cried out with a loud voice because [he was their] king, Beelzeboul.

Nevertheless, I, Solomon, persisted in interrogating him, saying, "If you wish to obtain a release, inform me about heavenly things." Beelzeboul replied, "Listen, King, if you burn oil of myrrh, frankincense, and bulbs of the sea along with spikenard and saffron, and light seven lamps during an earthquake, you will strengthen [your] house. And if, being ritually clean, you light [them] at the crack of dawn, just before the sun comes up, you will see the heavenly dragons and the way they wriggle along and pull the chariot of the sun." When I, Solomon, heard these things, I rebuked him and said, "Be silent and continue cutting marble just as I ordered you." (*OTP* 1:967-68)

With its late confused jumble of religious ideas illustrating folk magical ideas, the text can hardly provide much illumination on the background of Mark 3:22-30, except for the way that some early readers may have understood the figure of Beelzeboul. Other points of contact with the New Testament: Solomon as "healing Son of David," i.e. an exorcist, and gematria, the number symbolism of names such as is presupposed in Revelation 13:18.

92. Matthew 12:31-32/ Mark 3:28-29/ Luke 12:10

Gospel of Nicodemus/ Acts of Pilate 4:3 (4 cent. ?)

The Jews answered Pilate: "It is contained in our law, that if a man sins against a man, he must receive forty strokes save one, but he who blasphemes against God must be stoned." (Hennecke-Schneemelcher)

We have here a remarkable analogy to the distinction between two kinds of blasphemy especially as it is made in Matthew 12:32, of which the one sort is forgivable or may be atoned for by punishment, while the other is not forgivable because it is directed against God himself. For Mark 3:28-29 par. this parallel affirms that in the reality "Spirit," God himself is touched and infringed upon, so that the one who speaks against the Spirit active in Jesus cannot be forgiven. This does not apply to speaking against the Son of Man (Matt 12:32*a*), since this figure is understood in terms of the sequence "lowliness" and "exaltation," and the words are spoken against him during the time of his incognito lowliness. But it is a different matter to speak against the Spirit in him and who represents God immediately.

On blasphemy, cf. no. 763.

On Mark 3:31-35 par., cf. nos. 148, 235, 264.

93. Matthew 13:1-52/ Mark 4:1-34/ Luke 8:1-18

Aesop, *Fables* 172 (collection since 5 cent. BCE)

A farmer who was dying wanted his sons to become good agriculturalists. He summoned them and said: "I, my boys, am about to leave this world. You must search for what I have hidden in the vineyard. You will find there all I have to give you." They thought there was a treasure buried somewhere in the vineyard, and after their father was dead they dug every inch of the soil. There was no hidden treasure to be found, but the vines were so well dug that they yielded a bumper crop.

This story teaches us that the fruits of toil are man's best treasure. (Handford)

In the wake of Joachim Jeremias, *The Parables of Jesus* (rev. ed., trans. S. H. Hooke [New York: Charles Scribner's Sons, 1963]), it has been widely assumed that "Jesus' parables . . . were something completely new" (p. 8 of German 7th ed.). Jeremias based his statement on extensive research in rabbinic literature. But were there Hellenistic analogies to Jesus' parables? This depends in part on how "parable" is defined. It has also been widely assumed that the New Testament parables are fundamentally different from fables such as Aesop's, which often lack the "realism" of Jesus' parables, dealing with talking animals, plants, and the like. But, as Adolf Jülicher already pointed out (*Die Gleichnisreden Jesu*, 2 vols. [Tübingen: J. C. B. Mohr, 1910; repr. Darmstadt: Wissenschaftliche Buchgesellschaft, 1972], 1:98), not all Aesop's fables are "unrealistic," and Jesus' parables resemble some of them quite closely.

The above example shows in any case that there were Hellenistic stories somewhat analogous to Jesus' parables. The one cited above has a moralizing conclusion similar to those added to Jesus' parables in the course of transmission, and is itself an engaging illustration of a commonplace point. The story contrasts with Jesus' parables in that a connection with anything like "kingdom of God" is lacking, as is the surprising twist in the narrative that calls everyday wisdom into question and shakes up the mental world of the hearer. For the latter feature, however, see the following text no. 94. On the whole subject of Hellenistic analogies to Jesus' parables, see Michael Ernst, "Hellenistische Analogien zu ntl. Gleichnissen: Eine Sammlung von Vergleichstexten sowie Thesen über die sich aus der parabolischen Redeweise ergebenden gesellschaftspolitischen Konsequenzen," in Friedrich V. Reiterer, ed., *Ein Gott, Eine Offenbarung: Beiträge zur biblischen Exegese, Theologie und Spiritualität* (Festschrift für Notker Füglister, OSB zum 60. Geburtstag [Würzburg: Echter Verlag, 1991], 461-80).

94. Matthew 13:1-52/ Mark 4:1-34/ Luke 8:1-18

Aesop, *Fables* 299 (collection since 5 cent. BCE)

A man had two Daughters, one of whom he gave in marriage to a gardener, and the other to a potter. After a time he thought he would go and see how they were getting on; and first he went to the gardener's wife. He asked her how she was, and how things were going with herself and her husband. She replied that on the whole they were doing very well: "But," she continued, "I do wish we could have some good heavy rain: the garden wants it badly." Then he went on to the potter's wife and made the same inquiries of her. She replied that she and her husband had nothing to complain of: "But," she went on, "I do wish we could have some nice dry weather, to dry the pottery." Her father looked at her with a humorous expression on his face. "You want dry weather," he said, "and your sister wants rain. I was going to ask in my prayers that your wishes should be granted; but now it strikes me I had better not refer to the subject." (Jones)

Though still lacking the eschatological dimension and relation to something analogous to the "kingdom of God," this story is closer to Jesus' parables in the way it functions. Despite the concluding "moral," the parable in fact has a surprising, provocative turn that resists summary in a discursively stated "point." The reader might anticipate that the story would be used to argue for the futility of prayer in general, or the dilemma in which the gods are placed when prayers are only selfish shopping lists addressed to the deity. Rather, the story ends with the dilemma of the father, and provokes to further thought in more than one direction.

95. Matthew 13:1-23/ Mark 4:1-20/ Luke 8:4-15

Plutarch, *Moralia*, "On Listening to Lectures" 48 (45–125 CE)

But as for those lazy persons whom we have mentioned, let us urge them that, when their intelligence has comprehended the main points, they put the rest together by their own efforts, and use their memory as a guide in thinking for themselves, and, taking the discourse of another as a germ and seed, develop and expand it. For the mind does not require filling like a bottle, but rather, like wood it only requires a kindling to create in it an impulse to think independently . . . (LCL)

Mark, like Plutarch, uses the metaphor of the ground's reception of seed to emphasize the importance of hearing in the reception of the message; the decisive factor is the receiver of the word. The metaphorical material is thus not unusual. On the other hand, Plutarch's analogy does not reckon with varying qualities of ground, but leaves the metaphor simple in order to emphasize, more strongly than would be conceivable for Mark, the individual accomplishment of the hearers.

96. Matthew 13:1-23/ Mark 4:1-20/ Luke 8:1-15

4 Ezra 8:41-45 (late 1 cent. CE)

[The angel (God) speaks to "Ezra":] For just as the farmer sows many seeds in the ground and plants a multitude of seedlings, and yet not all that have been sown will come up in due season, and not all that were planted will take root; so also those who have been sown in the world will not all be saved. 42 I answered and said, "If I have found favor in your sight, let me speak. 43 If the farmer's seed does not come up, because it has not received your rain in due season, or if it has been ruined by too much rain, it perishes. 44 But people, who have been formed by your hands and are called your own image because they are made like you, and for whose sake you have formed all things—have you also made them like the farmer's seed? 45 Surely not, O Lord above! But spare your people and have mercy on your inheritance, for you have mercy on your own creation." (NRSV)

Though comparable to the Synoptic text in both form ("parable" + interpretation) and content (seed and field; most seed is unproductive), the function is different. In 4 Ezra, the text is part of the angel's "explanation" for the great number that shall be damned and the few that shall be saved, drawing support from an agricultural commonplace. "Ezra" argues with the "explanation," which he accepts as a commonplace illustration, but finds the theological application incompatible with his understanding of a merciful creator. In the Synoptics (i.e. in the pre-Marcan tradition), Jesus' original startling polysemic parable, which begins in the everyday world but climaxes in an extravagant, unexpected harvest, has been interpreted by an allegorical didactic piece on the fate of the gospel as it is preached in a pluralistic world. Fourth Ezra and the Marcan text have in common, however, the image of sowing in which most of what is sown is lost. For the imagery of the divine sowing of good seed in ground that does not produce, cf. also 4 Ezra 3:20; 9:17, 31-37.

97. Matthew 13:1-23/ Mark 4:1-20/ Luke 8:4-15

4 Ezra 9:30-37 (late 1 cent. CE)

"Hear me, O Israel, and give heed to my words, O descendants of Jacob. For I sow my law in you, and it shall bring forth fruit in you, and you shall be glorified through it forever." But though our ancestors received the law, they did not keep it and did not observe the statutes; yet the fruit of the law did not perish—for it could not, because it was yours. Yet those who received it perished, because they did not keep what had been sown in them. Now this is the general rule that, when the ground has received seed, or the sea a ship, or any dish food or drink, and when it comes about that what was sown or what was launched or what was put in is destroyed, they are destroyed, but the things that held them remain; yet with us it has not been so. For we who have received the law and sinned will perish, as well as our hearts that received it; the law, however, does not perish but survives in its glory. (NRSV)

Already in 8:41-45 and 9:17 the author had reflected on the relation of ground and seed: "As the ground, so the seed," a perspective that is fundamental for the parable in Mark 4 par. In the quotation above, however, the matter is seen from another aspect. As in Mark 4 par. it deals with (a) a call to hear, (b) the relation of seed, ground, and fruit, the role of "ground" being assumed by the hearers. Differently from Mark, however, here—explicitly (!) contrary to the logic of the metaphorical plane—the destruction of the receiving "ground" (= Israelite hearers) stands in the foreground. While in Mark 4 par. what is sown is mostly lost, in 4 Ezra 9 this is precisely what is preserved. The Law remains; it is only its tradents that perish, because they were not worthy of it. Thus in 4 Ezra it is a matter of the contrast between the holy Law and the guilty culprits, while in Mark 4 par. it is a matter of the different qualities of the recipients of the message, with the implied warning not to belong to the unfruitful category. In 4 Ezra, on the other hand, the Sitz im Leben is that of an apologia for the Law.

98. Matthew 13:10-17/ Mark 4:11-12/ Luke 8:9-10

Iamblichus, *Life of Pythagoras* 23.104-5 (4 cent. CE)

But in accord with the "silence" legislated for them by Pythagoras, they engaged in divine mysteries and methods of instruction forbidden to the uninitiated, and through symbols, they protected their talks with one another and their treatises. And if someone, after singling out the actual symbols [σύμβολα], does not explicate and comprehend them with an interpretation free from mockery, the things said will appear laughable and trivial to ordinary persons, full of nonsense and rambling. When, however, these utterances are explicated in accord with the manner of these symbols, they become splendid and sacred instead of obscure to the many, rather analogous to the prophecies and oracles of the Pythian god. And they reveal marvelous thought, and produce divine inspiration in those scholars who have grasped their meaning. It is well to mention a few in order that the general character of their teaching may become clearer: "as secondary purpose of a journey neither enter a temple nor worship at all, not even if you are passing before the very doors." "Sacrifice and worship unshod." "Walk on paths, avoiding roads traveled by the public." "Do not talk about Pythagorean matters without light." Such, in outline, was the manner of his teaching through symbols [διὰ συμβόλων διδασκαλία]. (Dillon and Hershbell)

Analogies to Mark: (1) Instruction of the disciples is a riddle to outsiders unless it is explained. (2) The analogy to Apollonian oracles is explicitly drawn by Iamblichus, and—within the framework of Jewish tradition—it stands, from the point of view of form criticism, behind the series of picture, blame/question, and exposition by allegorical interpretation in Mark 4 (cf. Berger, *Formgeschichte*, §18). Differences: (1) The symbolic sayings of Pythagoras are not parables, and therefore do not rest on the use of more or less usual metaphors, and at first glance it is completely unclear as to why they should receive an allegorical interpretation at all. That is to say, their symbolic character itself is concealed. (2) There is no real "hardening" theory associated with the Pythagorean symbolic speech, as in Mark. (3) The parable theory of the evangelist has the function of challenging to discipleship—the hardening theory in Mark has the character of an appeal. In Iamblichus it is a matter of a report about an elite who wants to remain elite.

99. Matthew 13:12/ Mark 4:25/ Luke 8:18

4 Ezra 7:25 (late 1 cent. CE)

[After the disobedience to God's commands has been pictured:] That is the reason, Ezra, that empty things are for the empty, and full things are for the full. [There follows a picture of the advent of the future invisible city.] (NRSV)

The Arabic translation published by H. Ewald interprets the passage in 4 Ezra, "Therefore I have delivered the weak to vanities and the full to perfections." The principle is that each one should expect an eschatological destiny on the basis of similarity. One receives eschatologically the radical, perfected state of what one already is now. In 4 Ezra the statement is a bridge between the portrayal of the destiny of the wicked and the reward of the righteous.

100. Matthew 13:24-30

Philo, *On Providence* 2.35-36 (15 BCE–50 CE)

[Discussing the nature and delays of divine judgment:] And if some of the men of violence still left unmentioned, insurgents who seized power over the populace and enslaved not only other peoples but their own countries, continued unpunished, why should we wonder? For in the first place the judgments of men and God are not alike. For we inquire into what is manifest but He penetrates noiselessly into the recesses of the soul, sees our thoughts as though in bright sunlight, and stripping off the wrappings in which they are enveloped, inspects our motives in their naked reality and at once distinguishes the counterfeit from the genuine. Let us never then prefer our own tribunal to that of God and assert that it is more infallible and wiser in counsel, for that religion forbids. Ours has many pitfalls, the delusions of the senses, the malignancy of the passions and most formidable of all the hostility of the vices; while in His there is nothing that can deceive, only justice and truth, and everything that is judged according to these standards brings praise to the judge and cannot but be settled aright. (LCL)

This is to be supplemented with Philo's statement that God does not punish sinners immediately, but gives them time for repentance and healing (*Allegorical Interpretation* 3.106).

In common with Matthew 13: (a) Renunciation of judgment of good and bad in the present. (b) The basis for this is a teleological conception of history that transcends the human perspective, a conception of history grounded in God: everything will come to its appointed and appropriate end.

The differences: (a) Jesus judges eschatologically, Philo in terms of providence. These two views could exist alongside each other within the framework of first-century Judaism. (b) The statements rest on different foundations. For Jesus, the good are not to be "rooted out with" the evil; for Philo, no human being knows all the hidden elements. (c) Missing from Jesus' parable is the view that the interim period in which people still have the opportunity to repent exists by virtue of God's patience (cf. also Philo, *Providence* 1.54). In Matthew, it is not the possible repentance of the wicked, but the possible harm to the good, that is in view. Philo is concerned to avoid placing blame on Providence, while in Matthew the interest is in avoiding premature judging and condemning.

Cf. also no. 903.

101. Matthew 13:31-32/ Mark 4:30-32/ Luke 13:18-19

Seneca, *Epistles*, "Letter to Lucilius" 4.38.2 (4–65 CE)

[Concerning philosophical discourse . . .] Words should be scattered like seed; no matter how small the seed may be, if it has once found favorable ground, it unfolds its strength and from an insignificant thing spreads to its greatest growth. Reason grows in the same way; it is not large to the outward view, but increases as it does its work. Few words are spoken; but if the mind has truly caught them, they come into their strength and spring up. Yes, precepts and seeds have the same quality; they produce much, and yet they are slight things. (LCL)

Cf. also the comparison of Athens and Rome in Polybius, *Histories*, 6.

In common with the New Testament: The picture of small beginning and great end, also in Seneca expressed as the contrast between "very small" and "very great," the connection between teaching/preaching, perhaps also the function of the parable as encouragement.

Differences from the New Testament: The aspect of the "good ground," which is the point in Mark 4:3-9 par., is only an afterthought in Seneca. The parable of Jesus goes beyond Seneca in that it points to a universal kingdom by evoking the overtones of various Old Testament passages (Ezek 17:22-24; 31:5-6; Dan 4:7-10, 17-19). Seneca, on the other hand, uses the imagery in an individual-psychological way.

The same imagery is used in a very different way by Philo, "Eternity" 100. What is generated from seed is greater than that from which it is produced. "Thus trees which soar to heaven often spring from a very small grain, and animals of great corpulence and stature come from the emission of a little moisture." But the opposite is the case with regard to the universe.

Here a brief comment on the relation of exegesis and the selection of "parallels": In this passage, the parallel was selected from the perspective of the contrast great/small in the growth process. That this is the "point" of the parable is the result of preceding exegesis (based on the structure of the context). But this is of course not the only possible exegesis. Whoever thinks, for example, that the "point" of the parable has to do with continuing growth will seek and find other parallels.

102. Matthew 13:44-46

Testament of Job 18:6-8 (1 cent. BCE–1 cent. CE)

[First-person report of Job:] And I became as one wishing to enter a certain city to discover its wealth and gain a portion of its splendor, and as one embarked with cargo in a seagoing ship. Seeing at mid-ocean the third wave and the opposition of the wind, he threw the cargo into the sea, saying, "I am willing to lose everything in order to enter this city so that I might gain both the ship and things better than the payload." Thus, I also considered my goods as nothing compared to the city about which the angel spoke to me. (*OTP* 1:846-47)

(Cf. Berger, "Materialen zu Form und Überlieferungsgeschichte neutestamentlichen Gleichnisse" *NovT* 15 [1973], 1-9.) Common elements: The attainment of the kingdom or the glory of the city is considered to be so valuable that one is ready to sacrifice everything else for it. Earthly possessions are considered of lesser worth. It is a matter of the relationship that exists between obtaining the kingdom of heaven and possessing earthly treasures. It is important that also in *Testament of Job* it is a question of being converted (here, to Judaism).

103. Matthew 13:44-46

Mekilta of R. Simon b. Jochai 14.5 (2 cent. CE, from older tradition)

[It is like] one to whom there fell in inheritance a residence in a seaport city and he sold it for a small sum and the purchaser went and dug through it and found in it treasures of silver and treasures of gold and precious stones and pearls. The seller almost strangled [for rage and grief]. So did Egypt because they sent away [Israel] and did not know what they sent away. (Smith, *Tannaitic Parallels*)

The separate motifs of the two Matthean parables are here combined. The "parallel" is different at the crucial point, in that the rabbinic story is an objectifying illustration, a conventional point that can be stated in discursive, nonparabolic language: the "treasure" is Israel, and Egypt was frustrated and angry when they later realized what a treasure they had let slip through their fingers. In Matthew, the story is a genuine parable communicating something about the kingdom of God that cannot be otherwise stated.

104. Matthew 13:53-58/ Mark 6:1-6/ Luke 4:16-30

Plutarch, *Parallel Lives*, "Life of Romulus" 7.3-4 (45–125 CE)

When Numitor came home, after getting Remus into his hands, he was amazed at the young man's complete superiority in stature and strength of body, and perceiving by his countenance that the boldness and vigor of his soul were unsubdued and unharmed by his present circumstances, and hearing that his acts and deeds corresponded with his looks, but chiefly, as it would seem, because a divinity was aiding and assisting in the inauguration of great events, he grasped the truth by a happy conjecture, and asked him who he was and what were the circumstances of his birth . . . (LCL)

Common element: amazement at his arrival leads to the question of his hidden identity. In addition, wisdom and work complement each other in Mark 6:2 par. like appearance and deed in Plutarch's report. Both point in the direction of the divine realm. On the question of the identity of one who appears in such wondrous fashion, cf. Berger, "Hellenistische Gattungen" 1262 (listing the alternatives). A difference here is the absence of the aesthetic element in the Jesus story (but cf. Moses, Heb 11:23), and the absence in the Remus story of the motif of rejection in the home territory.

105. Matthew 13:53-58/ Mark 6:1-6/ Luke 4:16-30

Plutarch, *Moralia*, "On the Fortune of the Romans" 8.320-21 (45–125 CE)

And this, methinks, is what Fortune says to the Virtue of Romulus: "Brilliant and mighty are your deeds, and in very truth you have proved yourself to be divine in blood and birth. But do you observe how far you fall behind me?" (LCL)

The artificial dialogue between Virtue and Fortune presupposes that divine origin is demonstrated by great deeds. This conception is significant for the composition of the Gospels as a whole, especially for the idea of Jesus' divine sonship. It is obviously related to the biographical genre. Cf. Berger, *Formgeschichte*, §§99-100.

106. Matthew 13:57/ Mark 6:4/ Luke 4:23-24/ John 4:44

Apollonius of Tyana, Letter 44 (d. ca. 97 CE)

Other men regard me as the equal of the gods, and some of them even as a god, but until now my own country alone ignores me, my country for which in particular I have striven to be distinguished. What wonder is there in this? (LCL)

Cf. also Plutarch, *Moralia*, "Exile" 7:13: "On this account you will find that few men of the greatest good sense and wisdom have been buried in their own country, and that most of them, under compulsion from no one, weighted anchor of their own accord and found a new haven for their lives" (LCL).

Cf. also Dio Chrysostom, *Discourses* 47:6: "'What of it,' some one in this audience has been saying long since, 'are you comparing yourself with Homer and Pythagoras and Zeno?' Nay, by Heaven, not I, except that it was the opinion of all the philosophers that life in their own native land was hard" (LCL).

It is interesting that the closest parallels to the saying of Luke 4:24 are found in the pagan philosophical tradition.

107. Matthew 14:1-12/ Mark 6:14-29

Josephus, *Antiquities* 18.116-19 (37–100 CE)

But to some of the Jews the destruction of Herod's army seemed to be divine vengeance, and certainly a just vengeance, for his treatment of John, surnamed the Baptist. For Herod had put him to death, though he was a good man and had exhorted the Jews to lead righteous lives, to practice justice toward their fellows and piety toward God, and so doing to join in baptism. In his view this was a necessary preliminary if baptism was to be acceptable to God. They must not employ it to gain pardon for whatever sins they committed, but as a consecration of the body implying that the soul was already thoroughly cleansed by right behavior. When others too joined the crowds about him, because they were aroused to the highest degree by his sermons, Herod became alarmed. Eloquence that had so great an effect on mankind might lead to some form of sedition, for it looked as if they would be guided by John in everything that they did. Herod decided therefore that it would be much better to strike first and be rid of him before his work led to an uprising, than to wait for an upheaval, get involved in a difficult situation, and see his mistake. Though John, because of Herod's suspicions, was brought in chains to Machaerus, the stronghold that we have previously mentioned, and there put to death, yet the verdict of the Jews was that the destruction visited upon Herod's army was a vindication of John, since God saw fit to inflict such a blow on Herod. (LCL)

As in Mark 6:16 par., so also here the inference is that the murder of the Baptist would necessarily lead to bad consequences for Herod (the appearance of Jesus or the annihilation of an army). Different from Mark, the reason for Herod's wanting to put John to death is seen not in the ethical preaching of the Baptist, but in Herod's anxiety about a possible uprising among the people, since the Baptist was regarded as having much influence among the people (this aspect is entirely missing in Mark 6 par.; in addition, Josephus knows of no disciples of John the Baptist). The antisacramental interpretation of John's baptism by Josephus contrasts with that of the Gospels. In Mark 1:4 and Luke 3:3b, baptism is the means of forgiveness of sins, after which good works are required. (Cf. Luke 3:8; has Luke already arranged the material according to the schema of the postbaptismal exhortation?)

In a manner reminiscent of Mark 6 par., there is a connection between a story from the royal court and the story of a martyrdom made in Plutarch (45–125 CE), "Cleomenes" 33-39: the king has been mentally incapacitated by wine and women, his paramour is taking care of the government, the king decides to kill Cleomenes, whose corpse is placed in animal skins and crucified, but then on the basis of events that happen after his death he is believed to be a son of the gods.

108. Matthew 14:6 / Mark 6:22

Tomb inscription in Antibes (2 cent. or earlier CE)

To the divine manes [spirits of the dead]. [Tombstone] of the boy Septentrio, twelve years old, who danced for two days in the theater of Antipolis and aroused pleasure. [Latin *saltavit et placuit,* the same phrase as the Vulgate of Matt 14:6!] (MEB/Berger's trans. of F. Cumont, *La stèle du danseur d'Antibes et son décor végétal. Étude sur le symbolisme funéraire des plantes* [Paris, 1942], p. 3.)

Michelet, *Histoire de France I,* 1833, 1871, on this inscription: "I know of nothing that is more tragic in its brevity, nothing that could let one perceive the hardness of the Roman world. He appeared two days in the theater of Antibes, danced and pleased the spectators. No regrets, no sorrow. Is this not in fact a well fulfilled destiny? There is no mention of parents; the slave had no family" (MEB/Berger). The text is here cited, since one can perceive with F. Cumont that in both cases we have "the language of the theater" (p. 2).

On Mark 6:34-44 par., see no. 419.

109. Matthew 14:13-21 / Mark 6:32-44 / Luke 9:10-17 / John 6:1-13

b. *Tannith* 24b-25a (Hanina ben Dosa 1 cent. CE; written 4 cent. CE)

Rab Judah said in the name of Rab: Every day a heavenly voice is heard declaring, The whole world draws its sustenance because [of the merit] of Hanina my son, and Hanina my son suffices himself with a *kab* of carobs from one Sabbath eve to another. Every Friday his wife would light the oven and throw twigs into it so as not to be put to shame. She had a bad neighbor who said, I know that these people have nothing, what then is the meaning of all this [smoke]? She went and knocked at the door. [The wife of R. Hanina] feeling humiliated [at this] retired into a room. A miracle happened and [her neighbor] saw the oven filled with loaves of bread and the kneading trough full of dough; she called out to her: You, you, bring your shovel; for your bread is getting charred; and she replied, I just went to fetch it. (Soncino)

Bread is miraculously provided, but to save the rabbi from disgrace and to embarrass a neighborhood busybody. The Gospel story's connotations of eschatological plenty (cf. no. 375 below, 2 Baruch 29:1-8 on John 2:1-11), Messianic Banquet, and compassion for hungry multitudes are missing.

110. Matthew 14:22-33 / Mark 6:45-52 / John 6:15-21

Job 9:8 in the LXX

[Referring to Yahweh:] . . . the one who alone has stretched out the heavens, and who walks on the sea as on firm ground. (MEB)

The MT has only "who alone stretched out the heavens and trampled the waves of the sea." Cf. W. Berg, *Die Rezeption alttestamentlicher Motive im Neuen Testament—dargestellt an den Seewandelerzähl-ungen* (Hochschulsammlung Theologie, Exegese Band 1. Freiburg, 1979), 79-81. While the MT presents the image that Yahweh walks on the back of the sea god monster and thus prevails over it (cf. NRSV alternate translation, "trampled the back of the sea dragon"), in the LXX *this* mythical element is no longer visible. Rather, the power of God is revealed in the ability to walk on the sea as on firm ground. Cf. also nos. 55, 111.

111. Matthew 14:22-33/ Mark 6:45-52/ John 6:15-21

Fragment 182 of Eratosthenes, from Hesiod's
The Astronomy 4 (700 BCE)

Hesiod says that he [Orion] was the son of Euryale, the daughter of Minos, and of Poseidon, and that there was given him as a gift the power of walking upon the waves as though upon land. (LCL)

It could well be that the variation from the MT of the LXX of Job 9:8 stands under the influence of this pagan tradition. It is important to note that Orion's power is portrayed as conveyed directly by his divine father. Apollodorus (1 cent. CE) reports the same about Orion, *Library* 1.4 ("to walk through the sea"). Also in Job 9:8 it is a matter of specifically divine capability.

112. Matthew 14:22-33/ Mark 6:45-52/ John 6:15-21

Dio Chrysostom, *The Third Discourse on Kingship* 30 (40–120 CE)

[During a debate on the true greatness of humanity, Socrates' conversation partner argues that visible, impressive power is a sign of divine greatness:] Socrates' interrogator put the following question to him: "Socrates," said he, "you know perfectly well that of all men under the sun that man is most powerful and in might no whit inferior to the gods themselves who is able to accomplish the seemingly impossible—if it should be his will, to have men walk dryshod over the sea, to sail over the mountains, to drain rivers dry by drinking—or have you not heard that Xerxes, the king of the Persians, made of the dry land a sea by cutting through the loftiest of the mountains and separating Athos from the mainland, and that he led his infantry through the sea, riding upon a chariot just like Poseidon in Homer's description? And perhaps in the same way the dolphins and the monsters of the deep swam under his raft as the king drove along." (LCL)

In the context, Xerxes has this power to walk on the water (so also in Isocrates [4 cent. BCE], *Panegyricus* 88-89), which is explicitly considered a divine power. Not only Xerxes is like the gods, but so is everyone who can walk on the sea. According to Lucian (120–185 CE), "Lover of Lies" 13, the Hyperboreans have the ability to fly through the air, "to walk on water," and to walk through fire (which Lucian, of course, considers nonsense).

Iamblichus, *Life of Pythagoras* 91, attributes this wonderful power to Pythagoras by virtue of a magical arrow given him by the god Apollo: "For Abaris came from the Hyperboreans, a priest of Apollo there, an old man and most wise in sacred matters. He was returning from Hellas to his own people, in order to deposit the gold that had been gathered for the god in the temple of the Hyperboreans. Passing through Italy and seeing Pythagoras, he recognized in him a particular likeness to the god whose priest he was. Indeed he believed him to be truly none other than Apollo himself, and not just a mortal resembling a god. In consequence of the greatness which he saw in Pythagoras and the tokens of recognition which in his priestly capacity he recognized beforehand, he gave to Pythagoras an arrow which he had when he left his temple, and which would be useful to him in the many difficulties encountered on a very long journey. For riding on it he crossed impassable places; for example, rivers, lakes, swamps, mountains, and the like. And talking to the arrow, so goes the story, he performed purifications and drove off plagues and winds from the cities which asked for his assistance" (Dillon and Hershbell).

113. Matthew 15:1-20 / Mark 7:1-23

m. Yadaim 4.6 (2–3 cents. CE)

The Sadducees say, we cry out against you, o ye Pharisees, for ye say, "The Holy Scriptures render the hands unclean," [and] "the writings of Hamiram do not render the hands unclean." Rabban Johanan ben Zakkai said, Have we naught against the Pharisees save this!—for lo, they say, "The bones of an ass are clean, and the bones of Johanan the High Priest are unclean." They said to him, As is our love for them so is their uncleanness—that no man make spooks of the bones of his father or mother. He said to them, Even so the Holy Scriptures: as is our love for them so is their uncleanness; [whereas] the writings of Hamiram which are held in no account do not render the hands unclean.

The Sadducees say, We cry out against you, O ye Pharisees, for ye declare clean an unbroken stream of liquid. The Pharisees say, we cry out against you, O ye Sadducees, for ye declare clean a channel of water that flows from a burial ground. (Danby)

That the technical term for sacred, canonical Scriptures was "writings that defile the hands" is sufficient evidence that "cleanness" and "uncleanness" were ritual terms that had nothing to do with hygiene. Holiness and unholiness, cleanness and uncleanness, were thought of in quasi-physical terms, as powers that could be transferred from one object to another, somewhat as we think of electricity or radiation. As radiation can be a positive, beneficial power or a negative, threatening one, so with ritual uncleanness. We speak of objects being "contaminated" (in laboratory slang, also of being "dirty" and needing to be "cleaned up," with no thought of hygiene). Like electricity and radiation, the power of ritual cleanness/uncleanness was dangerous, and needed to be controlled, so careful rules were needed to define what was clean and what was not, what "defiled" and what did not.

114. Matthew 15:1-20 / Mark 7:1-8

The Fathers according to Rabbi Nathan 15 (3–4 cent.; compilation 7–9 cent.)

What was this impatience of Shammai the Elder? The story is told:

A certain man once stood before Shammai and said to him: "Master, how many Torahs have you?"

"Two," Shammai replied, "one written and one oral."

Said the man: "The written one I am prepared to accept, the oral one I am not prepared to accept."

Shammai rebuked him and dismissed him in a huff.

He came before Hillel and said to him: "Master, how many Torahs were given?"

"Two," replied Hillel, "one written and one oral."

Said the man: "The written one I am prepared to accept, the oral one I am not prepared to accept."

"My son," said Hillel, "sit down."

He wrote out the alphabet for him [and pointing to one of the letters] asked him: "What is this?"

"It is *'Aleph*," the man replied.

Said Hillel: "This is not *'aleph* but *bet*. What is that?" he continued.

The man answered: "It is *bet*."

"This is not *bet*," said Hillel, "but *gimmel*."

[In the end] Hillel said to him: "How dost thou know that this is *'aleph* and this *bet* and this *gimmel*? Only because so our ancestors of old handed it down to us that this is *'aleph* and this *bet* and this *gimmel*. Even as thou hast taken this in good faith, so take the other in good faith." (Goldin)

Like no. 116 below, this anecdote illustrates the Pharisaic conviction that the written text alone is utterly ambiguous, requiring the oral tradition and faith in the community that transmitted it before it can function at all.

115. Matthew 15:1-20/ Mark 7:1-8

m. Aboth 1:1-3, 12, 15 (2–3 cent. CE)

Moses received the law from Sinai and committed it to Joshua, and Joshua to the elders, and the elders to the Prophets; and the Prophets committed it to the men of the Great Synagogue. They said three things: Be deliberate in judgment, raise up many disciples, and make a fence around the Law.

Simeon the Just was of the remnants of the Great Synagogue. He used to say: By three things is the world sustained; by the Law, by the [Temple]-service, and by deeds of loving-kindness.

Antigonus of Soko received the Law from Simeon the Just. He used to say: Be not like slaves that minister to the master for the sake of receiving a bounty, but be like slaves that minister to the master not for the sake of receiving a bounty; and let the fear of heaven rest upon you. . . .

Hillel and Shammai received [the Law] from them. Hillel said: Be of the disciples of Aaron, loving peace and pursuing peace, loving mankind and bringing them nigh to the Law. . . . Shammai said, "Make thy [study of the Law] a fixed habit; say little and do much, and receive all men with a cheerful countenance." (Danby)

The Law is here the oral tradition, believed by the Pharisees to have been given to Moses at Sinai and handed on in an unbroken chain from one authorized set of teachers in each generation to the next. It was considered to be the elaboration and explanation of the written Law, with which it was not in conflict. "Making a fence around the Law" was the making of additional commandments as an explanation of and safeguard against transgressing the original commandment, the whole tradition including its later accretions being considered part of the Sinai revelation. Cf. Num. R., Naso 14.10, "God gave the Israelites two Laws, the Written Law and the Oral Law."

116. Matthew 15:1-20/ Mark 7:1-8

Seder Eliahu Zuta 2

A Rabbi narrated: "while traveling, a man met me and continued on the way with me. He said: 'Rabbi it is my belief that only the Torah was given on Mount Sinai, but not the Mishnah.'

"I replied: 'Nay, my son, both were given to Moses on Mount Sinai. Are you open to reason?'

"'Yes,' he replied.

"I said: 'When you recite a definite number of benedictions in the Amidah, is the number inscribed in the Torah? When you hold Services, is the procedure definitely inscribed in the Torah? In every Mitzvah you must refer to the Traditional Law concerning the manner of its performance. Therefore, the Traditional or Oral Law must have originated at Sinai.'" *(Talmudic Anthology)*

The citation, expressing the Pharisaic point of view, seems defensive, but it is difficult to determine whether the detractors are fellow Jews who dispute the validity of the Oral Torah championed by the Pharisees (e.g. Sadducees), or whether they were Christians. The latter seems to be the case in the following quotation from Pesiq. R. 5: "Moses asked that the Mishnah also be in written form, like the Torah. But the Holy One, blessed be He, foresaw that the nations would get to translate the Torah, and reading it, say, in Greek, would declare: 'We are Israel; we are the children of the Lord.' And Israel would declare: 'We are the children of the Lord.' The scales would appear to be balanced between both claims, but then the Holy One, blessed be He, will say to the nations: 'What are you claiming, that you are My children? I have no way of knowing other than that My child is he who possesses My secret lore.' The nations will ask: 'And what is Thy secret lore?' God will reply: 'It is the Mishnah'" (Braude). Both quotations give the inner-Jewish view of tradition, while Mark gives the polemical outsider's view. For Pharisaic Judaism, as soon as one attempts to put the Torah into practice, it becomes clear that the written Torah alone is inadequate to instruct the believer as to what must be done (i.e. just what things may be done on the Sabbath without profaning it, and what things must not be done). From this point of view, "sola Scriptura" is not only perverse, it is impossible, and there can be no conflict between Scripture and Tradition because it is precisely Tradition that allows Scripture to be effective. Further:

117. Matthew 15:1-9/ Mark 7:1-8

b. *Baba Mezia* 59b (1 cent. CE tradition; written much later)

On that day R. Eliezer produced all of the arguments in the world, but they did not accept them from him. So he said to them, "If the law accords with my position, this carob tree will prove it."

The carob was uprooted from its place by a hundred cubits—and some say, four hundred cubits.

They said to him, "There is no proof from a carob tree."

So he went and said to them, "If the law accords with my position, let the stream of water prove it."

The stream of water reversed flow.

They said to him, "There is no proof from a stream of water."

So he went and said to them, "If the law accords with my position, let the walls of the schoolhouse prove it."

The walls of the schoolhouse tilted toward falling.

R. Joshua rebuked them, saying to them, "If disciples of sages are contending with one another in matters of law, what business do you have?"

They did not fall on account of the honor owing to R. Joshua, but they also did not straighten up on account of the honor owing to R. Eliezer, and to this day they are still tilted.

So he went and said to them, "If the law accords with my position, let the Heaven prove it!"

An echo came forth, saying, "What business have you with R. Eliezer, for the law accords with his position under all circumstances!"

R. Joshua stood up on his feet and said, "It is not in Heaven" [Dt. 30:12].

What is the sense of, "It is not in heaven" [Dt. 30:12]?

Said R. Jeremiah, [the sense of Joshua's statement is this:] "For the Torah has already been given from Mount Sinai, so we do not pay attention to echoes, since you have already written in the Torah at Mount Sinai, 'After the majority you are to incline [Ex. 23:2].'" (Neusner, *Talmud*)

The rather playful-sounding story is entirely serious, portraying the profound respect in which the oral and written Torah were held. Both were believed to come from God's revelation at Sinai (see nos. 23, 57, 114-16 above). This divine revelation was not to be superseded by miracles, nor were disputed points of interpretation to be settled by miraculous demonstrations. The story does not doubt that such miracles happened, but presents them as not settling anything. Rabbinic discussion that interpreted and transmitted the oral tradition was the final authority, which even heavenly voices could not challenge.

118. Matthew 15:2/ Mark 7:3

Sibylline Oracles 3.591-94a (140 BCE)

[Describing the Jews:] for on the contrary, at dawn they lift up holy arms toward heaven, from their beds, always sanctifying their flesh [Clement, *Protrepticus* 6.70; MSS read "hands"] with water, and they honor only the Immortal who always rules, and then their parents. (*OTP* 1:375)

The washing of hands appears here as precisely the decisive characteristic of the ethnic distinctiveness of the Jews and their national identity, so it is mentioned in the same breath with their monotheism. As in Mark 7 par., this is here related to the command to honor one's parents. According to *Ep. Arist.* (2 cent. BCE) 305, the washing of hands is the presupposition of prayer to God, a good commentary on 1 Timothy 2:8.

On the evaluation of ritualism, cf. no. 500. On Mark 7:24-30 par. (healing at a distance), cf. John 4:46-54 (no. 404). On Mark 7:33 (healing with saliva), cf. on Mark 8:22-26 (nos. 237-38).

119. Matthew 15:21-28/ Mark 7:24-30

Philostratos, *Life of Apollonius of Tyana* 1.19 (3 cent. CE)

It was a lazy fellow and malignant who tried to pick holes in him, and remarked that he had recorded well enough a lot of things, for example, the opinions and ideas of his hero, but that in collecting such trifles as these he reminded him of dogs who pick up and eat the fragments which fall from a feast. Damis replied thus: "If banquets there be of gods, and gods take food, surely they must have attendants whose business it is that not even the parcels of ambrosia that fall to the ground should be lost." (LCL)

This chreia (on the genre, cf. Berger, *Formgeschichte*, §§25-29) refers to the title of the journal kept by Damis, "Ἐκφατνίσματα, " i.e. "Scraps" (from eating, especially from the manger). As in Mark, the initially negative image is given a positive application. In Mark the metaphor of v. 27 is used in a positive argument in v. 28. With Damis, it is a matter of two images of the work of an author: dogs, or servants of the gods. Here the argument is: it is not dogs that are to be named as the point of comparison, but servants of the gods. In Mark, the punch line sticks with the canine imagery, while Damis replaces it with a different picture.

On Mark 8:11, see no. 213.

120. Matthew 16:13-20/ Mark 8:27-30/ Luke 9:18-21

Plutarch, *Moralia*, "On Inoffensive Self-Praise" 12 (543 D-E) (45–125 CE)

. . . When the praise runs on the contrary to extravagance, as with the invidious flattery used by many, it permits one to say: "No god am I; why likenest thou me to the immortals? [Homer, *Odyssey* 16.187] If you know me truly, commend my probity, temperance, reasonableness, or humanity." For to him who declines the greater honors envy is not displeased to grant the more moderate, and does not cheat of true praise those who reject what is false and vain. Hence those kings who were unwilling to be proclaimed a god (among the Seleucids Antiochus II, IV, and VI and Demetrius II and III bore the title "god"; and of course all deified rulers were "gods") or son of a god were ungrudgingly honored by those who gave them these noble yet human titles. . . . Whereas the rhetorical sophists who at their displays of eloquence accept from the audience the cries of "how divine" and "spoken like a god" lose even such commendation as "fairly said" and "spoken as becomes a man." (LCL)

(LCL note: "Thus Alexander was called 'son of Zeus' [cf. *Life of Alexander* 27.9, 680 F], Demetrius Poliorcetes 'son of Poseidon' [cf. Athenaeus, 6.62, 253 c, e], but rather Philadelphus [that is 'lover of his (her) brother (sister)'], a title of the Seleucids Demetrius II, Antiochus XI, and Philippus or

Philometor [that is, 'lover of his (her) mother'], a title of Ptolemy VI, VII, X, and XI, Cleopatra II and III, or Euergetes [that is, 'benefactor'], a title of Alexander Balas, Antiochus VII, and Ptolemy III, VI, and VII, or Theophiles, [that is 'dear to God (a god)'].)"

Among enlightened Greeks the tradition of rejecting divine predications about human beings was widespread, especially in connection with Alexander the Great, sometimes with reference to their all-too-human needs. Thus Plutarch's *Moralia*, "Sayings of Kings and Commanders": Antigonus 7, "When Hermodotus in his poems wrote of him as 'The Offspring of the Sun,' he said, 'The slave who attends to my chamber-pot is not conscious of that!'"

121. Matthew 16:21-23/ Mark 8:31-33/ Luke 9:22

Pseudo-Callisthenes, *The Life and Deeds of Alexander of Macedonia* (The "Alexander Romance") 3.17.7-11 (3 cent. CE)

But it happened as the sun set: an Indian voice came from the tree, but the Indians with him were afraid and did not want to translate. After some thought, Alexander took them aside individually. And they whispered in his ear, "King Alexander, soon you must die at the hands of your own people." All present were thunderstruck, but Alexander wanted to receive another oracle. Having heard the future, he went in and asked that he might embrace his mother, Olympias. And when the moon rose, the tree said in Greek, "King Alexander, you must die in Babylon and you will be killed by your own people and you will not be able to return to your mother, Olympias."

Alexander was amazed and wanted to put magnificent garlands on the trees, but the priests told him: "This is not permitted. But if you are going to use force, do what you will: for a king every law is canceled." Alexander was very upset, and, rising at first light, he went back into the shrine with the priests, his friends, and the Indians. After a prayer, he went up with the priest and, placing his hand on the tree, asked if the years of his life were complete—as this was what he wanted to know. And as soon as the sun began to rise and cast its rays on the top of the tree, a voice came out, explicitly declaring: "The years of your life are complete, and you will not be able to return to your mother, Olympias; instead, you must die in Babylon. And shortly afterward your mother and your wife will die miserably at the hands of your own people. Ask no further questions about these matters: you shall not hear anything more." (Reardon)

The whole framework of the story of the life and death of Alexander is comparable to the concept of the Gospels (cf. M. Reiser, "Der Alexanderroman und das Markusevangelium," in H. Cancik, *Markus-Philogie* WUNT 33 [Tübingen: J. C. B. Mohr, 1984], 131-63). Different from Mark, where Jesus himself makes the prophecy of his death, another voice announces it to Alexander. But as in Mark, this happens three times, and, it is important to notice, with increasing elaboration and precision with regard to details.

Cf. also Matthew 17:22-23/ Mark 9:30-32/ Luke 9:43-45; Matthew 20:17-19/ Mark 10:32-34/ Luke 18:31-34.

122. Matthew 16:21-23/ Mark 8:31-33/ Luke 9:22

Plutarch, *Moralia*, "On the Fortune or the Virtue of Alexander" 11 (45–125 CE)

I shall be thought to be making a strange statement, yet what I shall say is true: it was because of Fortune that Alexander all but lost the repute of being the son of Ammon! For what offspring of the gods could have toiled through such hazardous, toilsome, and painful Labors save only Heracles, the son of Zeus? . . . But upon Alexander it was Virtue who laid the kingly and god-like Labor . . . to order all men by one law and to render them submissive to one rule and accustomed to one manner of life. (LCL)

As for Peter in Mark 8:32 par., so also for the followers of Alexander, the announcement of the necessity of suffering and death conflicted with their perception of what a "son of God" should experience. Only Hercules can be named as a "model" for Alexander, but then he is considered to be the ideal of the ruler and benefactor of humanity. So one must reflect on the possibility that precisely the combination of the ideas of the royal son of God and the necessity and capacity of suffering and death was not a completely unfamiliar tradition. The Christian message did not necessarily fall on completely "deaf ears" on this point.

Cf. also Matthew 17:22-23/ Mark 9:30-32/ Luke 9:43-45; Matthew 20:17-19/ Mark 10:32-34/ Luke 18:31-34.

123. Matthew 16:25/ Mark 8:35/ Luke 9:24; 17:33

Tyrtaeus, Fragment 8.11-13 (7 cent. CE)

For those who dare something, stick together, and venture into fights and wars, these die more seldom, and they save the people who are behind them. (MEB/Berger)

This is almost a topos of the general's speech to his troops: whoever risks his life in the end actually preserves it more often—and the life of the people as well. The topos is clearly adopted by Ps.-Menander, "Never lose heart. Do not fall back in battle; for whosoever does not fall back in battle and gives himself unto death, shall immediately find life and a good name and he shall be praised" (*OTP* 2:601). The battle context is never given in the New Testament. In Luke 17:33 the literal meaning of "life" is preserved, while in Mark 8:35 and parallels the meaning fades into "eternal life." The paradoxical affirmation about seeking to preserve one's life which in fact causes one to lose it has here received a completely different sense.

124. Matthew 16:26/ Mark 8:36-37/ Luke 9:25

***2 Baruch* 51:15-16 (end of 1 cent. CE)**

Because of what have men lost their life and for what have those who were on the earth exchanged their soul? For once they chose for themselves that time which cannot pass away without afflictions. And they chose for themselves that time of which the end is full of lamentations and evils. (*OTP* 1:638, adapted)

Common denominator: both texts are directed against a senseless exchange, in which people trade "life" or "soul" (the Syrian text uses both words) for an extremely doubtful profit. While in the Gospel text both rhetorical questions are to be answered with "Nothing!" (i.e. the value of the soul/life is irreplaceable), in the Jewish apocalypse the evil end of the bad trade is painted in lurid colors. The context, however, makes a decisive difference: in Mark it is a matter of missionary conduct, in order to ward off an opportunistic approach, while in *2 Baruch* it is a more general point of people's rejection of truth.

125. Matthew 17:1-9 / Mark 9:2-10 / Luke 9:28-36

Homeric Hymns, 2, 275-80 (prior to 7 cent. BCE)

[Demeter has disguised herself as an old woman and hired herself out as a nurse for the royal family of Eleusis. But she finally] changed her stature and her looks, . . . beauty spread round about her and a lovely fragrance was wafted from her sweet-smelling robes, and from the divine body of the goddess a light shone afar . . . , so that the strong house was filled with brightness as of lightning. (LCL)

Cf. F. W. Beare, *The Gospel According to Matthew* (Peabody, Mass.: Hendrickson, 1987 [repr. Harper & Row, 1981]), 363: "Through Moses' communion with God on Mount Sinai, 'the sight of the skin of his face was glorified' (δεδόξασται, LXX, Exod 34:29-35). The verb of the LXX is not taken up here; it is perhaps echoed in the Lucan version, where we are told that the disciples 'saw his glory' (Luke 9:32). In the Hebrew of Exodus, the text reads: 'The skin of his face shown.' The Marcan story does not mention the face of Jesus, but only the whiteness of his clothes."

126. Matthew 17:1-9 / Mark 9:2-10 / Luke 9:28-36

Plutarch, *Moralia*, "The Fortune of the Romans" 10 (45–125 CE)

[The slave Ocrisia has become pregnant through a divine appearance by the protector-god of the house, or from the god Vulcan:] At any rate, it resulted in the birth of Servius, and, while he was still a child, his head shone with a radiance very like the gleam of lightning. But Antias and his school say not so, but relate that when Servius's wife Gegania lay dying, in the presence of his mother he fell into a sleep from dejection and grief; and as he slept, his face was seen by the women to be surrounded by the gleam of fire. This was a token of his birth from fire and an excellent sign pointing to his unexpected accession to the kingship. (LCL)

In various, but always significant circumstances, to have a brilliant light shine upon one is an important omen of future greatness. Cf. *1 Enoch* 106:2-6, of the birth of Noah, "His body was white as snow and red as a rose; the hair of his head as white as wool [Gp adds 'and curly and glorious'] and his *demdema* [This Eth. word has no equivalent in English. It refers to long and curly hair combed up straight, what one calls *gofare* in several modern Ethiopian languages, or 'afro' in colloquial English] beautiful; and as for his eyes, when he opened them the whole house glowed like the sun—[rather] the whole house glowed even more exceedingly. And when he arose from the hands of the midwife, he opened his mouth and spoke to the Lord with righteousness. And his father, Lamech, was afraid of him and fled and went to Methuselah his father; and he said to him, 'I have begotten a strange son: He is not like an [ordinary] human being, but he looks like the children of the angels of heaven to me; his form is different, and he is not like us. His eyes are like the rays of the sun, and his face glorious. It does not seem to me that he is of me, but of angels; and I fear that a wondrous phenomenon [Lit. "a wonder, miracle, wonderment"] may take place upon the earth in his days'" (*OTP* 1:86). Here too the phenomenon of light on the little child is an omen, and as in Plutarch it is regarded as a sign (for Lamech in any case) of a supernatural paternity. Similarly Aramaic Enoch, according to K. Beyer *Die arämatischen Texte vom Toten Meer* (Göttingen: Vandenhoeck & Ruprecht, 1984): "And as Lamech saw that his body was whiter than snow and redder than roses and the hair of his head whiter than wool, and that his eyes illuminated the dark chambers of the house like the rays of the sun . . ." (v. 13 refers to the fall of the angels).

All texts mentioned above suggest that the phenomenon of light on the face or the whole body points as such to one's nature as son of God, and in these texts suggests that human fatherhood is excluded. Thus the problem of light emerges especially in connection with small children. A different line of thought comes to expression in Jewish texts (cf. under no. 128). Thus a mediating position is occupied by the following example.

127. Matthew 17:1-9 / Mark 9:2-10 / Luke 9:28-36

Lives of the Prophets 21 "Elijah" (earliest form written before 70 CE)

When he was to be born, his father Sobacha saw that men of shining white appearance were greeting him and wrapping him in fire, and they gave him flames of fire to eat. And he went and reported [this] in Jerusalem, and the oracle told him, "Do not be afraid, for his dwelling will be light and his word judgment, and he will judge Israel." [Most MSS, including E and D, add "with sword and fire." Elijah was frequently assigned a role in the judgment of the deceased (Ginzberg, *Legends*, vol. 6, p. 324).] (*OTP* 2:396)

Here, too, we have a story of light and fire prodigies with reference to a small child. But here, this phenomenon is not generated by birth without a human father, but by two men of the same character, who speak to Elijah. The light phenomenon affects specifically Elijah's clothing. There is a noticeable agreement with Mark 9 par. in the motifs of the shining garment and the conversation with glowing, transcendent figures. In Mark 9 par. Jesus is the subject, here Elijah. In Elijah's case, the other figures are thought of as the mediators of the fiery quality. In Mark 9 par., however, it seems the transformation had already occurred (?). Mark emphasizes the independence of the radiance of the chief figure, Jesus. To converse with exalted authorities of the past is a means of legitimation of the first order, as in the anonymous Akhmimic *Apocalypse of Zeph.*, 9:1-5. The angel proclaims to the visionary that his name stands written in the book of the living. The visionary wants to kiss him, but his glory was too great. In the same sense his (the angel's) glory was confirmed by the following: "Then he ran to all the righteous ones, namely Abraham and Isaac and Jacob and

Enoch and Elijah and David. He spoke to them as friend to friend speaking to one another" (*OTP* 1:514). (Cf. no. 835.)

128. Matthew 17:1-9/ Mark 9:2-10/ Luke 9:28-36

Philo, *On the Virtues* 217 (15 BCE–50 CE)

[Concerning Abraham:] For the society also which he sought was not the same as they sought, but oftener under inspiration another more august. Thus whenever he was possessed, everything in him changed to something better, eyes, complexion, stature, carriage, movements, voice. For the divine spirit which was breathed upon him from on high made its lodging in his soul, and invested his body with singular beauty, his voice with persuasiveness, and his hearers with understanding. (LCL)

Here the presence of God's spirit in Abraham as a missionary effected a kind of "transfiguration," as similarly is reported in the case of Stephen during his "missionary" function (Acts 6:15), of Daniel (Hippolytus, *Commentary on Daniel* 3:7: Daniel takes on the form of an angel and receives a glowing countenance. He appears sometimes as a human being, sometimes as an angel. Moses is specifically mentioned), of Jeremiah ("A Coptic Jeremiah Apocryphon," K. G. Kuhn *Museón* 83 (1970) 95-135, 291-350: "Then Abimelech saw the prophet Jeremiah . . . glowing like the sun"), of the Jewish high priest Hananiah (W. Wright, *Apocryphal Acts of the Apostles* [Amsterdam: Philo Press, 1968], p. 84): "And they saw that his countenance was like the angel of the Lord"), and of early Christian apostles. Similarly in *Lev. Rab.* 1:1 (on Judges 2:1), "The truth is, said R. Simon, that the face of Phinehas, when the Holy Spirit rested upon him, flamed like a torch (which gave him the awe-inspiring look of an angel)" (Soncino).

It is consistently a matter of God's messenger and representative in the situation of speaking a decisive word. Probably the tradition of Moses' glowing face stands in the background, though it has become an independent motif in the above examples. Cf. also nos. 728, 795.

The Gospel story could thus be understood both from the Jewish background of the messenger of God and from the Greek background of the son of God (no. 126).

129. Matthew 17:9-13/ Mark 9:9-13

Corpus Hermeticum 13.1 (2–4 cent. CE)

My father, you spoke indistinctly and in riddles when talking about divinity in the *General Discourses;* claiming that no one can be saved before being born again, you offered no revelation. But after you talked with me coming down from the mountain, I became your suppliant and asked to learn the discourse on being born again since, of all the discourses, this one alone I do not know. And you said you would deliver it to me when "you were about to become a stranger to the cosmos." I have prepared myself, and I have steeled my purpose against the deceit of the cosmos. Grant me what I need and give me—whether aloud or in secret—the [discourse on] being born again that you said you would deliver. I do not know what sort of womb mankind is born from, O Trismegistus, nor from what kind of seed. (Copenhaver)

The mountain is here—as in the New Testament transfiguration story—the place of special revelation resulting in election. The descent from the mountain is here as there the occasion for a dialogue in which the disciples ask the teacher to explain a puzzling discourse. It is a matter of a common arsenal of motifs in the general framework of revelation literature in which Mark also shares. On the Corpus Hermeticum see W. C. Grese, *Corpus Hermeticum XIII and Early Christian Literature* (Leiden: Brill, 1979). On rebirth, see nos. 380-88.

130. Matthew 17:9 / Mark 9:9

Corpus Hermeticum 13:22 (2–4 cent. CE)

[Hermes speaks by revelation to his son Tat.:] I rejoice that the truth has borne good fruit for you, my child, an undying crop. Now that you have learned it from me, promise to be silent about this miracle, child, and reveal the tradition of rebirth to no one lest we be accounted its betrayers. For each of us has done enough study—I the speaker, you the hearer. You know yourself and our father intellectually. (Copenhaver)

The command to silence is here intended to prevent the teaching that is here communicated from becoming a topic of common conversation and thereby being "talked to death" and disdained. Analogous commands to silence are regularly communicated to the readers in written form (and so are already exclusive). Cf. the material in Klaus Berger, *Die Auferstehung des Propheten und die Erhöhung des Menschensohnes* (SUNT 13) (Göttingen: Vandenhoeck & Ruprecht, 1976), p. 492 n. 211, and no. 131 below.

131. Matthew 17:12 / Mark 9:13

Coptic Apocalypse of Elijah 4:7-15 (3 cent. CE)

Then when Elijah and Enoch hear that the shameless one has revealed himself in the holy place, they will come down and fight with him, saying,
Are you indeed not ashamed?
When you attach yourself to the saints,
because you are always estranged.
You have been hostile to those who belong to heaven.
You have acted against those belonging to the earth.
You have been hostile to the thrones.
You have acted against the angels.
You are always a stranger.
You have fallen from heaven like the morning stars.
You were changed, and your tribe became dark for you.
But you are not ashamed,
when you stand firmly against God.
You are a devil.

The shameless one will hear and he will be angry, and he will fight with them in the marketplace of the great city. And he will spend seven days fighting with them. And they will spend three and one half days in the marketplace dead, while all the people see them. But on the fourth day they will rise up . . . (*OTP* 1:747-48)

A series of parallel texts are treated in Berger, *Auferstehung des Propheten*, 38-109, 650. Cf. as an ancient witness on the death of Elijah in the endtime also Pseudo-Philo *LAB* (1 cent. BCE ?) 48:1 (God said to Phinehas that he would return as Elijah:) "And afterward you will be lifted up into the place where those who were before you were lifted up, and you will be there until I remember the world. Then I will make you all come, and you will taste what is death" (*OTP* 2:362). In both parallel texts, Elijah does not die alone, but others who had been taken to heaven without dying will die with him, but still he is singled out as an individual in both texts, either specifically or cryptically. In Mark 9:13 par. the rejection of either John the Baptist (as unambiguously Matt. 17:12-13) or Jesus is spoken of (cf. Berger, *Auferstehung des Propheten*, 302 n. 197). In Mark, Jesus could also be portrayed as Messiah by using the imagery of Elijah, since in the Judaism of this time Elijah had received the role of the eschatological representative of God before the new eon (the kingdom of God).

132. Matthew 17:14-21 / Mark 9:14-29 / Luke 9:37-43

Philostratos, *Life of Apollonius of Tyana* 3:38 (beginning of 3 cent. CE)

And he brought forward a poor woman who interceded in behalf of her child, who was, she said, a boy of sixteen years of age, but had been for two years possessed by a devil. Now the character of the devil was that of a mocker and a liar. Here one of the sages asked, why she said this, and she replied: "This child of mine is extremely good-looking, and therefore the devil is amorous of him and will not allow him to retain his reason, nor will he permit him to go to school, or to learn archery, nor even to remain at home, but drives him out into desert places. And the boy does not even retain his own voice, but speaks in a deep hollow tone, as men do; and he looks at you with other eyes rather than with his own. As for myself I weep over all this, and I tear my cheeks, and I rebuke my son so far as I well may; but he does not know me. And I made up my mind to repair hither, indeed I planned to do so a year ago; only the demon discovered himself, using my child as a mask, and what he told me was this, that he was the ghost of a man, who fell long ago in battle, but that at death he was passionately attached to his wife. Now he had been dead for only three days when his wife insulted their union by marrying another man, and the consequence was that he had come to detest the love of women, and had transferred himself wholly into this boy. But he promised, if I would only not denounce him to yourselves, to endow the child with many noble blessings. As for myself, I was influenced by these promises; but he has put me off and off for such a long time, that he has got sole control of my household, yet has no honest or true intentions." Here the sage asked afresh, if the boy was at hand; and she said not, for, although she had done all she could to get him to come with her, the demon had threatened her with steep places and precipices and declared that he would kill her son, "in case," she added, "I haled him hither for trial." "Take courage," said the sage, "for he will not slay him when he has read this." And so saying he drew a letter out of his bosom and gave it to the woman; and the letter, it appears, was addressed to the ghost and contained threats of an alarming kind. (LCL)

Agreements: The possessed son is not brought; he has had the sickness a long time; the goal of the demon is the death of the child.

Differences: In the Gospel story the spirit is mute (as in Plutarch, "Obsolescence of Oracles," 438 B [ch. 51]: an evil and mute spirit throws the Pythia to the ground and jerks her this way and that; *PGM* 13.242ff.: the demon-possessed person will speak when sulfur and bitumen are placed up to his nose. Jesus' command of Mark 9:25 stands in the place of the authoritative heavenly letter of Apollonius. Jesus needs no heavenly letter. On foaming at the mouth in Mark 9:18, cf. Lucian (120–185 CE) "Lover of Lies," §16 (about a Syrian in Palestine who healed a possessed epileptic who foamed at the mouth). On the command of Mark 9:25 par. and the forbidding of the spirit to return, cf. the exorcism of *PGM* 7.331: "Come on, come on; immediately, immediately; quickly, quickly; and speak concerning those things about which I questioned you" (Betz), and Philostratos, *Life of Apollonius* 4.20 at no. 61 above (the demon gives assurance that he will leave the young man and never again fall upon another human being).

That the disciples are unable to do as much as the master (Mark 9:28-29 par.), an important theme of this narrative, is pictured by Lucian in his "Lover of Lies" 36-37, the immediate source for Goethe's poem of the magician's apprentice.

133. Matthew 17:24-27

b. Sabbath 119a

Joseph who-honors-the-Sabbath had in his vicinity a certain gentile who owned much property. Some Chaldeans said to him: Joseph who-honors-the-Sabbath will consume all your property. He [the gentile] went and sold all his property and bought a precious stone with the proceeds, which he set in his turban. As he was crossing a bridge, the wind blew it off and cast it into the water; a fish swallowed it. The fish was hauled up and brought [to the marketplace] on the Sabbath eve toward sunset. They said: Who will buy at this hour?

They said to them: Go and take it to Joseph who-honors-the-Sabbath, as he is in the habit of buying [to stop commerce before the Sabbath]. So they took it to him. He bought it, opened it, and found the jewel therein, and sold it for thirteen roomfuls of gold denarii. A certain old man met him and said: He who lends to the Sabbath, the Sabbath repays him. (Soncino)

As in Matthew, those who honor the Torah (or the Tradition), doing even more than is required, are rewarded. The treasure is found in a fish in each case. The primary differences: (1) The Talmudic story concerns Sabbath keeping, a clear obligation of every Jew, while the Matthean story is about the temple tax, a disputed point among Torah-observant Jews. (2) The Talmudic story celebrates a Jew who obtains a gentile's property despite his efforts to preserve it. In the Matthean story on the other hand, the treasure had not previously belonged to anyone (but cf. Matt 13:44!).

134. Matthew 18:1-5 / Mark 9:33-37 / Luke 9:46-48

Plutarch, *Moralia*, "Whether an Old Man Should Engage in Public Affairs" 8 (45–125 CE)

. . . in public life one must escape, not from one tyrant, the love of boys or women, but from many loves which are more insane than that: love of contention, love of fame, the desire to be first and greatest, which is a disease most prolific of envy, jealousy, and discord. (LCL)

Such quotations point us to the fundamental significance which ancient conceptions of the guidance of the state have for the regulation of early Christian congregational and church problems. Not only those cited here, but also the other political-ethical writings of Plutarch present rich resources for this.

135. Matthew 18:5/ Mark 9:37/ Luke 9:48

Te'ezaza Sanbat (an Ethiopic-Jewish Falasha writing, probably still 1 cent. CE)

[God speaking to the personified Sabbath:] Those who honor you honor me, and those who reject you reject me. And those who serve you serve me. And those that I accept are those who accept me, and they do me the honor of observing the Sabbath, and they are as those who loan to me. (MEB/Berger)

Here God addresses the Sabbath as his messenger whom he is sending to humanity. The Sabbath here assumes the role not only of Wisdom, but of the sole messenger from God to humanity. The text is important for illuminating Jewish concepts of the divine messenger (cf. also Johannine Christology). In connection with Mark 9:36-37 the passage from *b. Ber.* 64 is also often mentioned: "If one partakes of a meal at which a scholar is present, it is as if he feasted on the effulgence of the Divine Presence" (Soncino). Here, too, the principle of interchangeable effects applies, i.e., "Who does something for A has really done something for B, (and who does something for B has really done it for C = God)" (Cf. Berger, *Formgeschichte,* §§184-85).

Cf. also Matthew 10:40; Luke 10:16; no. 84 above.

136. Matthew 18:6-9/ Mark 9:42-50/ Luke 17:1-2, 14, 34-35

Plato, *Symposium* 204c, e (428/27–349/48 BCE)

. . . but if love is such as you describe him, of what use is he to mankind? . . . For men are prepared to have their own feet and hands cut off if they feel these belongings to be harmful. The fact is, I suppose, that each person does not cherish his belongings except where a man calls the good his own property and the bad another's; since what men love is simply and solely the good. (LCL)

Similarly Xenophon (d. 429 BCE), *Memorabilia* 1.54: Despite all our love for our bodies, one removes that which is useless such as nails and hair and "lets the surgeon cut and cauterize him, and aches and pains notwithstanding, feels bound to thank and fee him for it," (LCL) for otherwise there is no usefulness but only damage. The application is made to relationships with relatives and friends (the goal: be useful to those by whom one wants to be noticed and appreciated).

This same tradition is found in Aristotle, *Eudemian Ethics* 7:1 (concerning people who base friendship on usefulness): One removes hair, saliva, nails, and "extracts useless parts of the body."

Porphyry (234–305 CE) also has words in this tradition, "Letter to Marcella" 34: "Often people amputate some limb to save their lives; you should be prepared to amputate the whole body to save your soul" (Wicker). On the whole subject, cf. H. Hommel, "Herrenworte im Lichte sokratischer Überlieferung," *ZNW* 57 (1966), 1-23.

General characteristics of all texts: (1) The background of the imagery is formed by medical practice. (2) Metaphorical application deals with the relation of cost to use in the sense of clever choices (to avoid a total loss, even that which is valuable must be sacrificed). (3) Particular emphasis is placed on the fact that in critical situations this simple principle means that even extremely valuable and intimate members of the body may have to be sacrificed. If the Greek tradition deals metaphorically with the regulation of social relationships, in Matthew 5:29 as in Porphyry it probably deals with the actual physical body (though not in the sense of literally tearing out members), thus coming back to the original source of the imagery (similarly Philo, "Worse Attacks Better," §§174-75, referring to "martyrs"). In Mark 9 par., in view of v. 42, it could deal with social relationships (separation of seducers from the community), for it is unlikely that a new theme emerges in v. 43 (but if so, then it is to be understood in the sense of Matt 5:29).

137. Matthew 18:10

Plutarch, *Moralia*, "Isis and Osiris" 26 (45–125 CE)

. . . he [Xenocrates] believes that there exists in the space about us certain great and powerful natures, obdurate, however, and morose, which take pleasure in such things as these, and, if they succeed in obtaining them, resort to nothing worse.

Then, again, Hesiod calls the worthy and good demigods "holy deities" and "guardians of mortals" and "givers of wealth, and having therein a reward that is kingly."

Plato calls this class of beings an interpretative and ministering class, midway between gods and men, in that they convey thither the prayers and petitions of men, and thence they bring hither the oracles and the gifts of good things.

Empedocles says also that the demigods must pay the penalty for the sins that they commit and the duties that they neglect . . . (LCL)

The text shows that demonology and angelology were not the exclusive property of Judaism and early Christianity. (1) For the "air" as the place of demons, cf. Ephesians 2:2. (2) On good angels as watchers and protectors of human beings, Matthew 18:10. (3) On angels as servants and mediators between deity and humanity, especially for prayers from humans to God and gifts from God to humans, Revelation 8:3-5; Galatians 3:19; Revelation 22:8-9. (4) Condemned to serve a sentence, Jude 6 and the tradition of the fallen angels in *1 Enoch*. (5) In general, the dividing up of the transcendent world between earth and heaven into the realms of angels and demons (= Christian interpretation for good spirits and evil spirits).

On the whole subject see C. Zintzen, article "Geister" (Dämonen) B.III.c, "Hellenistische und kaiserzeitliche Philosophie," in *RAC* 9:640-68, esp. 641-42: "The demonology of the old Stoa followed in part Xenocrates. Diogenes Laertius 7.151 gives the core of this doctrine: the demons are bound to human beings by sympathy and are their overseers" (MEB from *RAC*). On Plutarch, see cols. 644-47.

138. Matthew 18:15-18

Plutarch, *Moralia*, "How to Tell a Flatterer from a Friend" 32 (45–125 CE)

. . . we must be very careful about the use of frank speech toward a friend before a large company . . .

For error should be treated as a foul disease, and all admonition and disclosure should be in secret, with nothing of show or display in it to attract a crowd of witnesses and spectators.

I imagine also that it was not so much the wine that caused Cleitus to be so exasperating to Alexander, as that he gave the impression of trying to curb him before a large company. (LCL)

Plutarch deals with the candid reprimanding of a brother in his writing "On Brotherly Love," §10. Further:

139. Matthew 18:15-18

1QS 5:24–6:1 (1 cent. BCE)

They shall rebuke one another in truth, humility, and charity. Let no man address his companion with anger, or ill-temper, or obduracy, or with envy prompted by the spirit of wickedness. Let him not hate him [because of his uncircumcised] heart, but let him rebuke him on the very same day lest [6] he incur guilt because of him. And furthermore, let no man accuse his companion before the Congregation without having first admonished him in the presence of witnesses. (Vermes)

Similar instruction is found in CD 9:3-4. As in Matthew 18, 1QS presents a three-stage process: private conversation between two, then reprimand before witnesses, then bringing the matter before the whole congregation. Cf. further *Epistula Apostolorum* 47 (58). Like Plutarch (cf. no. 138 above), 1QS emphasizes the duty of reprimanding as such. While in Plutarch going before other witnesses is considered impossible, it is provided for both by 1QS and Matthew, to be sure only as a next step. In this much more strictly developed process of group discipline, the distinction to the ethic of popular philosophy is clear.

140. Matthew 18:23-35

b. *Rosh Hashanah* 1, 2 17b (1 cent. CE)

Bluria the proselyte put this question to Rabban Gamaliel: It is written in your Law, [she said], *who lifteth not up the countenance,* and it is also written, *The Lord shall lift up his countenance upon thee.* R. Jose the priest joined the conversation and said to her: I will give you a parable which will illustrate the matter. A man lent his neighbor a *maneh* and fixed a time for payment in the presence of the king, while the other swore to pay him by the life of the king. When the time arrived he did not pay him, and he went to excuse himself to the king. The king, however, said to him: The wrong done to me I excuse you, but go and obtain forgiveness from your neighbor. So here: one text speaks of offenses committed by a man against God, the other of offenses committed by a man against his fellow man. (Soncino)

The "antithesis" between the two passages is thus explained: For sins against God (here: an unfulfilled condition that had been sworn before God), God turns toward the sinner and forgives him or her. Reference is made to Numbers 6:26. As in Matthew 18, God's forgiveness is granted in advance. But then, after this time of the mercy of God, Deuteronomy 10:17 becomes effective. This text speaks of God as the impartial judge who distributes justice without respect of persons. This judgment takes into consideration whether people have come to terms with one another, and forgiven one another. Then the judgment proceeds without respect of persons. After the time of mercy comes the time of judgment—as in Matthew 18. Differently from Matthew 18, it is not a matter of two debts, but of one, so it is not the case here that the one who has been forgiven by God must also forgive the one indebted to him or her (as in Matt 18). In relation to one's fellow human beings, it is a matter of being on good terms with them as such, which is each person's own responsibility, and into which God's forgiveness does not extend.

On Matthew 19:12, cf. nos. 652, 657.

141. Matthew 19:3-9/ Mark 10:2-12

Damascus Rule 4:20–5:2 (CD) (original document 2–1 cent. BCE)

The "builders of the wall" [Ezek. 13:10] who have followed after "precept"—"Precept" was a spouter of whom it is written, *they shall surely spout* [Mic. 2:6]—shall be caught in fornication twice by taking a second wife while the first is alive, whereas the principle of creation is, *Male and female created He them* [Gen. i, 27]. Also, those who entered the Ark went in two by two. And concerning the prince it is written, *He shall not multiply wives to himself* [Deut. xvii, 17]. (Vermes)

As in Mark 10:6 par., Genesis 1:27 is used as a basis of the argument, and an additional argument is introduced from the ark (like Gen 1:27, from P, and representing the same conceptual pattern) and from Deuteronomy 17:17. In contrast to Mark 10 par., there is no appeal here to Genesis 2:24 and God's having made the two into a unity. Also in CD the emphasis is entirely on the fact of two wives, with no reference to divorce. It is, however, similar to the ideal formulated in Titus 1:6 (on which see K. Berger, *Die Gesetzesauslegung Jesu* I [Neukirchen-Vluyn: Neukirchener, 1972], 524-26, 547-48).

On reservations about and prohibitions of divorce in the pagan realm, cf. Plutarch, "Life of Romulus," §22 (Romulus' social ordinance: the wife may not leave her husband at all, and the husband may divorce the wife only in case of capital crimes; otherwise the wife receives a part of his property and he must offer sacrifice to the gods of the underworld). Plutarch obviously regards this as an ideal regulation.

142. Matthew 19:3-9/ Mark 10:2-9

A Deed of Divorce (13 BCE)

To Protarchus from Zois daughter of Heraclides, with her guardian her brother Irenaeus son of Heraclides, and from Antipater son of Zenon. Zois and Antipater agree that they have separated from each other, severing the union which they had formed on the basis of an agreement made through the same tribunal in Hathur of the current 17th year of Caesar, and Zois acknowledges that she has received from Antipater by hand from his house the material which he received for dowry, clothes to the value of 120 drachmae and a pair of gold earrings. The agreement of marriage shall henceforth be null, and neither Zois nor other person acting for her shall take proceedings against Antipater for restitution of the dowry, nor shall either party take proceedings against the other about cohabitation or any other matter whatsoever up to the present day, and hereafter it shall be lawful both for Zois to marry another man and for Antipater to marry another woman without either of them being answerable. In addition to this agreement being valid, the one who transgresses it shall moreover be liable both to damages and to the prescribed fine. The 17th year of Caesar, Pharmouthi 2. (LCL)

This is one instance of the variety of marriage laws and customs that prevailed during the time the New Testament was written. The differences between Mark 10:10-12 and Matthew 19:9 reflect this variety. That the strictness of some New Testament codes of marriage and divorce is not unique to early Christianity is seen, for example, in the rule of Qumran (cf. no. 141 above). Here too, we have an eschatological sect that appeals to the order of creation rather than the current interpretation of the Law of Moses.

143. Matthew 19:6/ Mark 10:9

Musonius Rufus, *Is Marriage a Handicap for the Pursuit of Philosophy?* (30–100 CE)

How great and worthy an estate is marriage is plain from this also, that gods watch over it, great gods, too, in the estimation of men; first Hera (and for this reason we address her as the patroness of wedlock), then Eros, then Aphrodite, for we assume that all of these perform the function of bringing together man and woman for the procreation of children. (Lutz)

Similarly, in the Isis aretalogies, Isis says of herself, "I have brought woman and man together" (*SIG* 3.1267). We may then suppose that the rabbinic tradition of God as the bridal escort at the wedding of Adam and Eve rests on pagan models. Mark 10:9 would then be the first example from the Jewish tradition. This does not make the concept of God as attendant to the bride a biblical idea in origin, however. Rather, it is rabbinic. Like Mark 10, early Judaism (e.g. *Jub.* 3:7) knows God as the founder of marriage (among other images, of course). (Cf. also no. 443.)

144. Matthew 19:16-22/ Mark 10:17-22/ Luke 18:18-23

Letter of Diogenes 24, to Alexander (1 cent. BCE–3 cent. CE)

If you wish to become good and upright, throw aside the rag you have on your head and come to me. But you certainly cannot, for you are held fast by the thighs of Hephaestion. (Malherbe)

The formulation corresponds especially to Matthew 19:21 ("If you will be perfect, go, sell . . ."). The challenge to Alexander the Great, as Diogenes sees in advance, will not avail due to Alexander's attachment to his friend Hephaestion. The challenge to the rich young man fails due to his possessions, which he is not willing to sell. The text belongs in the series of numerous analogies between Cynic wandering philosophers and early Christian wandering missionaries. Cf. also nos. 148, 296, 298, 453.

145. Matthew 19:21/ Mark 10:21/ Luke 18:22

2 Enoch 50:5–51:2 (1 cent. CE)

Let each one of you put up with the loss of [his] gold and silver on account of a brother, so that he may receive a full treasury in that age.
Widows and orphans and foreigners, do not distress, so that God's anger does not come upon you; . . . stretch out your hands [to the needy] in accordance with your strength. (*OTP* 1:178)

On the more comprehensive idea of the treasury of deeds or good works in heaven, cf. R. Heiligenthal, *Werke als Zeichen* (Tübingen: J. C. B. Mohr, 1983), pp. 239-41, and Klaus Koch, "Der Schatz im Himmel," *Festschrift für H. Thielicke* (1968), pp. 47-60. The close connection with almsgiving is also present in Tobit 4:9 (cf. 4:8). The relationship between one's deeds and how one gets along in the world is here modified in an eschatological and transcendent direction.

146. Matthew 19:26/ Mark 10:27/ Luke 18:27

Philo, *Life of Moses* 1.31.174 (15 BCE–50 CE)

[Moses' speech to Israel trapped at the Red Sea:] "Do not lose heart." He said, "God's way of defense is not as that of men. Why are you quick to trust in the specious and plausible and that only? When God gives help He needs no armament. It is His special property to find a way where no way is. What is impossible to all created beings is possible to Him only, ready to his hand." (LCL)

The premise is the same in both Philo and the Gospel story: salvation comes from God alone. The difference is that in the situation described by Philo from Exodus 14, the human impossibility of salvation is obvious. In the Gospel story, the "rich young ruler" seemed the most likely candidate for salvation.

147. Matthew 19:29/ Mark 10:29/ Luke 18:29

Testament of Job 4:6-9 (Hellenistic-Jewish, 1 cent. BCE or 1 cent. CE)

But if you are patient, I will make your name renowned in all generations of the earth till the consummation of the age. And I will return you again to your goods. It will be repaid to you doubly, so you may know that the Lord is impartial—rendering good things to each one who obeys. And you shall be raised up in the resurrection. For you will be like a sparring athlete . . . (*OTP* 1:841)

The angels' promise to Job when he was converted to the God of Israel corresponds to Jesus' promise to those who follow him in the following elements: (1) Both texts know three temporal stages: the present trouble or giving up of material possessions—restoration on earth, all the more abundantly, of the things that had been given up—eschatological reward as resurrection or eternal life. So also in no. 817. (2) It is a matter of a promise made with the condition that the conversion lasts. The difference consists in the fact that for Mark par. the restitution in this world is obviously accomplished in the realm of the "community" (10:30), and so is not free from persecution (since the community is a persecuted community). For Job, on the contrary, it is a matter of being rewarded twice with rewards that are unconditionally good. Obviously texts such as this from the *Testament of Job* are the foil that allows the meaning of Jesus' words to be perceived all the more clearly, and that by means of "redaction" or by an "adjustment in the exchange rate."

148. Matthew 19:29/ Mark 10:30; 3:34

Epictetus, *Discourses* 3.22.81-82 (55–135 CE)

[On the Cynics, who are unwilling to marry and beget children:] Man, the Cynic has made all mankind his children; the men among them he has as sons, the women as daughters; in that spirit he approaches them all and cares for them all. Or do you fancy that it is in the spirit of idle impertinence he reviles those he meets? It is as a father he does it, as a brother, and as a servant of Zeus, who is Father of us all. (LCL)

The common element is the emphasis on the bonds of kinship. But in Mark this happens with a view to a particular group (perhaps not yet a "church"), which is characterized by doing the will of God (Mark 3:35). In Epictetus, on the other hand, in the foreground stands (a) the cosmopolitan aspect and (b) the unsparing "Socratic" critique. The role of the authoritative father is just as carefully avoided by the Christians (cf. also Matt 23:9) as is a new relationship to the spouse, however metaphorically this is conceived. Cf. also no. 264.

149. Matthew 20:1-16

p. Berakhoth 2.7c.   (ca. 2–3 cent. CE?)

To what [story] may [the life of] R. Bun bar R. Hiyya be compared? [To this story.] A king hired many workers. One worker excelled in his work. What did the king do? He took him and walked with him back and forth [through the rows of crops and did not let him finish his day's work]. Toward evening, when all the workers came to be paid, he gave him a full day's wages along with [the rest of] them.

The workers complained and said, "We toiled all day, and this one toiled only two hours, and he gave him a full day's wages!"

The king said to them, "This one worked [and accomplished] more in two hours than you did in a whole day."

So R. Bun toiled in the study of the Torah for twenty-eight years, [and he learned] more than an aged student could learn in a hundred years. (Neusner, *Talmud of the Land of Israel*)

This is part of the eulogy of Rabbi Zeeira at the funeral of a gifted scribe, Rabbi Bun ben Hiyya, who had died at the age of twenty-eight. In contrast to Matthew, it is not a parable of unmerited grace, but of amazing concentrated achievement.

150. Matthew 20:1-16

Tanchuma Ki teze 110a (300 CE)

"The sleep of the worker is sweet, whether he eats plenty or little . . ." Rabbi Levi told a parable. With what may this be illustrated? It is like a king, who hired workers for his work. While they were working, the king took one of them for a walk. At evening the workers came to receive their wages. The worker who had taken a walk with the king appeared with them to receive his pay. Can the king say to him, "You only worked two hours with them, so you get paid only for two hours work?" Then he could say to the king, "If you hadn't let me rest by taking me on a walk, my pay would be greater!" So it is with God, blessed be His name. The king is God. The workers are those who study the Torah. Those who have studied the Torah for fifty years, and those who have studied only twenty or thirty years can say, "If you had not taken me away, I could have studied the Torah even longer." That is why Solomon too can say, whether one may eat much or little, their reward is the same. (MEB/Strack-Billerbeck)

As is the case with Matthew, so also here the relationship between work and pay is emphasized. While Matthew is thinking, however, of how much time has elapsed since one's entry into the Christian community, the rabbinic story deals with the end of one's life appointed by God, i.e. with how long God permits one to live for "work." As in Matthew, the length of time one has "worked" plays no role.

151. Matthew 20:1-16

Midrash Tehillim on Ps 37:13

With whom may David be compared? With a laborer who worked all his days for the king. When the king did not give him his hire, the laborer was troubled and said: "Am I to go forth with nothing in my hands?" Then the king hired another laborer who worked for the king but one day, and the king laid meat before him, gave him drink, and paid him his hire in full. The laborer who had worked all his days for the king said: "Such reward for this one who did no more than work but one day for the king? For me who have been working for the king all the days of my life, how much more and more my reward!" The other laborer went away, and now the one who had been working all his days for the king was glad in his heart. (Braude)

In common is the image field: one employer, two workers who labor different periods of time, and reflection on their respective wages. Differences: the rabbinic parable emphatically affirms the difference in pay, while the offense against the principle of justice is precisely what is bothersome in the Matthean story. Different from the rabbinic parable, in Matthew the principle that one's pay should correspond to one's work is broken, and precisely by the way in which mercy and goodness play a role that transcends justice (cf. K. Erlemann, *Das Gottesbild in den synoptischen Gleichnissen* [Stuttgart: Kohlhammer, 1988], pp. 93-114). But rabbinic parables also are acquainted with grumbling about the same pay for different periods of work (e.g., p. Ber. 2, 8 [5c]), but this is justified by the fact that the one who worked the shorter period still accomplished more than the others, so that he (e.g. because he had studied the Torah more intensively) still received the same pay. So in this case God's justice is preserved, with the help of the quantity/quality distinction. In Matthew, however, the employer does in fact deal "unjustly."

152. Matthew 20:22/ Mark 10:38

Martyrdom and Ascension of Isaiah 5:13 (1 cent. BCE–1 cent. CE)

. . . to the prophets who [were] with him he [Isaiah] said before he was sawed in half, "Go to the district of Tyre and Sidon, because for me alone the LORD has mixed the cup." [Then follows the account of his being sawed in half and the charismatic speaking.] (*OTP* 2:164)

As in Mark par., the story is concerned with the relation of the master and his disciples in view of the coming martyrdom. Isaiah sends his disciples away, and the intention of Mark 10:35-45 par. could be to show that in view of the doubtful way of martyrdom, the way of discipleship and service is unambiguously following in the way of the Son of Man. Martyrdom as a way of discipleship is clearly relativized. In *Ascension of Isaiah* too, martyrdom is determined only for the prophets.

153. Matthew 20:28/ Mark 10:45

Demetrios Lacon the Epicurean, *Life of Philonides* (200 BCE)

For the one most loved or his closest friend, he would be ready to offer his neck. (MEB/Berger)

On this characteristic of the ethic of friendship, cf. already Aristotle, *Nic. Eth.* 9.8 (1169a) (doing anything for the friend's sake, including, if necessary, laying down one's life); Epicurus (347–271), according to Diogenes Laertius, *Lives*, 10.121 (the wise man must be able to die for his friend); Seneca (4–65 CE), "Letter to Lucilius" 1, 9:10 ("For what purpose, then, do I make a man my friend? In order to have someone for whom I may die, whom I may follow into exile, against whose death I may stake my own life, and pay the pledge too" [LCL].); Philostratus, *Life of Apollonius* 7.11. Cf. also Martin Hengel, *The Atonement* (Philadelphia: Fortress Press, 1981), 6-15, 19-28. On "service," cf. no. 346. Cf. Romans 5:7.

154. Matthew 20:28/ Mark 10:45

2 Maccabees 7:37-38 (1 cent. BCE)

. . . I, like my brothers, give up body and life for the laws of our ancestors, appealing to God to show mercy soon to our nation and by trials and plagues to make you confess that he alone is God, and through me and my brothers to bring to an end the wrath of the Almighty that has justly fallen on our whole nation. (NRSV)

Similarly 4 Maccabees 6:27-29: 27 "You know, O God, that though I might have saved myself, I am dying in burning torments for the sake of the law. 28 Be merciful to your people, and let our punishment suffice for them. 29 Make my blood their purification, and take my life in exchange for theirs" (NRSV). Cf. also 4 Maccabees 17:21-22: "The tyrant was punished, and the homeland purified—they having become, as it were, a ransom for the sin of our nation. 22 And through the blood of those devout ones and their death as an atoning sacrifice, divine Providence preserved Israel that previously had been mistreated" (NRSV). Ideas of this kind form the contemporary background for some New Testament affirmations of the atonement. A difference: the atonement is here made for Israel, to fill up the lack of those who had not been faithful enough to the Law, rather than for humanity as a whole. God's wrath had fallen on Israel because of the unfaithfulness of the covenant people as a whole, and the faithfulness of the martyrs redresses the balance of the covenant-obedience Israel owed to God. In this light and with the help of these linguistic expressions, Isaiah 53 was read and interpreted from the time of 1 Peter 2:22-24. (There is no proof for this understanding of Isaiah 53 earlier.)

In Jewish tradition such substitutionary death is understood and evaluated from a cultic point of view. (On the connection of Jewish sources with Hellenistic ideas of human sacrifice in order to avert the wrath of the gods, cf. M. Hengel in no. 153 above and K. Berger in "Hellenistisch-heidnische Prodigen," *ANRW* II, 23.2, pp. 1435-36.)

155. Matthew 20:30-31/ Mark 10:47-48

Testament of Solomon 20:1-2 (1–2 cent. CE)

Now it happened that one of the artisans, a dignified man, threw himself down before me, saying, "King Solomon, Son of David, have mercy on me, an elderly man." I said to him, "Tell me, old man, what you want." He replied, "I beg you, King. I have a son, my only son, and every day he does terribly violent things to me, striking me in the face and head and threatening to send me to a terrible death. Because he did this, I came forward [to request] a favor—that you will avenge me." [The demon Ornias then preaches that the old man will kill his own son.] (*OTP* 1:982)

Thanks to his relationship with the demons, Solomon can restore the friendship between father and son. The address here is spoken to the physical son of David. According to Wisdom 7:20, God gave Solomon, among other things, the knowledge of the "powers of the spirits," and the powers of various roots. Josephus, *Antiquities* 8.45-49, says of Solomon, "And God granted him knowledge of the art used against demons for the benefit and healing of men. He also composed incantations by which illnesses are relieved, and left behind forms of exorcisms with which those possessed by demons drive them out, never to return. And this kind of cure is of very great power among us to this day, for I have seen a certain Eleazar, a countryman of mine, in the presence of Vespasian, his sons, tribunes and a number of other soldiers, free men possessed by demons, and this was the manner of the cure: he put to the nose of the possessed man a ring which had under its seal one of the roots prescribed by Solomon, and then, as the man smelled it, drew out the demon through his nostrils, and, when the man at once fell down, adjured the demon never to come back into him, speaking Solomon's name and reciting the incantations which he had composed. Then, wishing to convince the bystanders and prove to them that he had this power, Eleazar placed a cup or foot basin full of water a little way off and commanded the demon, as it went out of the man, to overturn it and make known to the spectators that he had left the man. And when this was done, the understanding and wisdom of Solomon were clearly revealed" (LCL).

Cf. also *Testament of Solomon* 15:14: "At my death I wrote this testament to the sons of Israel and I gave [it] to them so that [they] might know the powers of the demons and their forms, as well as the names of the angels by which they are thwarted" (*OTP* 1:976). In Pseudo-Philo, *LAB* 60, David announces one who will be born from his loins and who will overcome the evil spirits. From this it becomes clear (1) David's son Solomon has power over evil spirits in connection with power over sickness and disease. (2) In contemporary Judaism, exorcisms were accomplished by appeal to the name of Solomon, the son of David. Emphasis is placed on the fact that the spirits do not return (cf. Matt 12:44-45). (3) Especially Matthew emphasizes Jesus' Davidic sonship in connection with healings and thus lets us recognize one of the sources of the process by which the exorcist Jesus could have then been thought of as a messianic figure: "Son of David" is the point of contact between "exorcist" and "Christ." Cf. Dennis C. Duling, "Solomon, Exorcism, and the Son of David," *HTR* 68 (1975) 235-52.

156. Matthew 21:8-9/ Mark 11:8-10/ Luke 19:35-38

Plutarch, *Parallel Lives*, "Life of Cato the Younger" 12 (45–125 CE)

When the time of Cato's military service came to an end, he was sent on his way, not with blessings, as is common, nor yet with praises, but with tears and insatiable embraces, the soldiers casting their mantles down for him to walk upon, and kissing his hands, things which the Romans of that day rarely did, and only to a few of their imperators. (LCL)

What Mark reports concerning Jesus corresponds, including the acclamation, to the contemporary style of ceremonious welcome of a ruler at his entrance into a city. For similar ceremonious entrances see the material in K. Berger, "Die Königlichen Messiastraditionen des Neuen Testaments," *NTS* 20 (1972–73), 30 n. 111.

157. Matthew 21:33-46/ Mark 12:1-12/ Luke 20:9-19

Sifre to Deuteronomy 32:9, §312 (134b) (3 cent. CE)

1. A. For the lord's portion is his people [Jacob his own allotment]:

B. The matter may be compared to a king who had a field, which he handed over to tenant-farmers.

C. The tenant-farmers began to steal [the produce of the field that was owing to the king, so] he took it from them and handed it over to the children.

D. They began to conduct themselves worse than the earlier ones.

E. He took it from their children and handed it over to the children of the children.

F. They began to conduct themselves even worse than the earlier ones.

G. He had a son. He said to them, "Get out of what is mine. I don't want you in it. Give me my portion, which I may get it back."

H. So when our father, Abraham, came into the world, chaff came forth from him, Ishmael and all the children of Keturah.

I. When Isaac came into the world, chaff came forth from him, Esau and all the nobles of Edom.

J. They began to conduct themselves worse than the earlier ones.

K. When Jacob came along, no chaff came forth from him. All the sons that were born to him were proper people, as it is said, "And Jacob was a perfect man, dwelling in tents" [Gen. 25:27].

L. Whence will the Omnipresent regain his share? It will be from Jacob: "For the Lord's portion is his people, Jacob his own allotment."

M. And further: "For the Lord has chosen Jacob to himself" [Ps. 135:4]. (Neusner, *Sifre to Deuteronomy*)

The first tenant farmers are the bad sons of Abraham, the second the bad sons of Isaac, "the son" in contrast is Jacob/Israel. The heavily allegorical tale grounds the election of Jacob as the son of God over against the other offspring of Abraham and Isaac, i.e. against the neighboring peoples. The imagery is the same as in Mark 12 (leasing, misuse, removal, the contrast between tenants and the son). But in this story the goal is the final assignment of the field to Israel itself. In Mark 12, in contrast, it is precisely Israel from whom the vineyard is taken away, representing the removal of Israel's elect position.

158. Matthew 21:33-46/ Mark 12:1-12/ Luke 20:9-19

Mara bar Serapion, Letter to his son (2 cent. CE)

[Punishment for the killing of the defenseless Messiah by taking away the kingship:] When the wise are oppressed by the violence of tyrants, and when their wisdom is rewarded with abuse, and when they are oppressed for their insight without [the possibility of] self-defense, what is there left to say? For what use was the murder of Socrates to the Athenians? Their reward for it was hunger and plague. Or what gain did the inhabitants of Samos receive from the burning of Pythagoras? Their land was suddenly covered with sand, in a single hour. Or the Jews, through the murder of their wise king? For it was precisely from this time on that they lost their kingship. God righteously avenged the rejection of the wisdom of these three. The Athenians died of hunger, the people of Samos were covered by the sea, with no chance to be saved. And the Jews, desolated and driven into exile from their own kingdom, are now dispersed throughout every place. But Socrates is not dead after all—because of Plato, and neither is Pythagoras dead, because of the statue of Juno, and neither is the wise king [of the Jews] dead, because of the new laws which he ordained. (MEB/Berger)

This text, in the framework of a pedagogically oriented wisdom writing (gnomic; cf. Berger, *Formgeschichte*, §19.48), can hardly have been written by a Christian, for otherwise the name of Jesus would occur, he would not be set on a par with Socrates and Pythagoras, and his resurrection would certainly have been mentioned. Thus it is all the more interesting that his effect is described as that of a new lawgiver. He is in fact the "wise king," since by his renunciation of violence he corresponds completely to the contemporary picture of the wise ruler (cf. also Berger, "Königlichen Messiastraditionen," 32-36). A conception analogous to the Deuteronomic picture of history is here applied alike to Athens, Samos, and the Jewish state. The giving over of the vineyard to others in Mark corresponds here to the removal of the kingship (the Syriac word corresponds to the Greek βασιλεία). On the dating, cf. the edition of W. Cureton, pp. xiii-xv.

159. Matthew 22:11-14

Midrash Rabbah on Ecclesiastes 9:8 (8 cent. CE)

LET THY GARMENTS BE ALWAYS WHITE; AND LET THY HEAD LACK NO OIL (IX, 8). R. Johanan b. Zakkai said: If the text speaks of white garments, how many of these have the peoples of the world; and if it speaks of good oil, how much of it do the peoples of the world possess! Behold, it speaks only of precepts, good deeds, and Torah. R. Judah ha-Nasi said: To what may this be likened? To a king who made a banquet to which he invited guests. He said to them, "Go, wash yourselves, brush up your clothes, anoint yourselves with oil, wash your garments, and prepare yourselves for the banquet," but he fixed no time when they were to come to it. The wise among them walked about by the entrance of the king's palace, saying, "Does the king's palace lack anything?" The foolish among them paid no regard or attention to the king's command. They said, "We will in due course notice when the king's banquet is to take place, because can there be a banquet without labor [to prepare it] and company?" So the plasterer went to his plaster, the potter to his clay, the smith to his charcoal, the washer to his laundry. Suddenly the king ordered, "Let them all come to the banquet." They hurried the guests, so that some came in their splendid attire and others came in their dirty garments. The king was pleased with the wise ones who had obeyed his command, and also because they had shown honor to the king's palace. He was angry with the fools who had neglected his command and disgraced his palace. The king said, "Let those who have prepared themselves for the banquet come and eat of the king's meal, but those who have not prepared themselves shall not partake of it." You might suppose that the latter were simply to depart; but the king continued, "No, [they are not to depart]; but the former shall recline and eat and drink, while these shall remain standing, be punished, and look on and be grieved." Similarly in the Hereafter, as Isaiah declares, Behold, My servants shall eat, but ye shall be hungry [Isa. LXV, 13]. (Soncino)

As in Matthew, here it is a matter of the proper dress when invited to a royal meal: violators of the dress code are not only excluded, but punished. The question that often arises in expositions of Matthew 22:11, how people gathered in from the streets could be expected to have the proper wedding attire, is irrelevant to the rabbinic parable, since the king had explicitly commanded those invited to wash their clothes. The remark "Does the king's palace lack anything?" shows that they understood that the meal could begin anytime. In contrast to Matthew 22, the motif of the unexpected hour appears here. Cf. the related story in *b. Sabbath* 153a.

160. Matthew 22:15-22/ Mark 12:13-17/ Luke 20:20-26

Josephus, *Jewish War* 2.117 (37–100 CE)

[Concerning the Roman procurator Coponius in the area of Archelaos:] Under his [Coponius'] administration, a Galilean, named Judas, incited his countrymen to revolt, upbraiding them as cowards for consenting to pay tribute to the Romans and tolerating mortal masters, after having God for their Lord. This man was a sophist [wandering preacher] who founded a sect of his own, having nothing in common with the others. (LCL)

Josephus is the documentation for the view that there were "Zealot" groups (on Judas the Galilean cf. also Acts 5:37) who considered belonging both to God and to human sovereigns to be impossible. In practice, this meant a refusal to pay the Roman taxes.

161. Matthew 22:23-33/ Mark 12:26-27/ Luke 20:27-40

m. Megilla 3:3 (2 cent. CE with older materials)

Moreover R. Judah said: [Even] if a synagogue was in ruins lamentation for the dead may not be made therein, nor may they twist ropes therein or stretch out nets therein, or spread out produce [to dry] on its roof, or make of it a short by-path; for it is written, *And I will bring your sanctuaries into desolation*—their sanctity [endures] although they lie desolate. (Danby)

The text illustrates the kind of rabbinic interpretation of the Bible also used in Mark 12:26-27 par. As in the Gospels, the Mishnah is unconcerned with the original meaning (Exod 3:6 in Mark; Amos 7:9 in the Mishnah), but proves the point in question by the way a word is used in the text. In each case, the point is made on the basis that the text speaks of a historical entity as though it remains in existence after it has disappeared from the earth. In Megilla 3:3, the holy places of the past are still called "sanctuaries" even after their desolation. In Mark 12:26 par., God "is" the God of the patriarchs (not "was"). In neither case does it matter to the interpreter that the original text referred to a reality that once was, not to the reader's present. For modern readers, such arguments do not have probative force, though they may illustrate from the Scripture a conviction held on other grounds. In the rabbinic context, however, it was supposed that such exegesis constituted an argument. Further:

162. Matthew 22:23-33 / Mark 12:26-27 / Luke 20:27-40

Midrash Sifre on Numbers 112 (2 cent. CE with earlier materials)

R. Ishmael says: ". . . his iniquity shall be upon him:" why is this statement made?

Because Scripture says, ". . . visiting the sin of the fathers upon the children" [Ex. 20:5], might one maintain that even the sin of idolatry will be visited on the children to the third and fourth generations?

Scripture says, "his iniquity shall be *upon him*," meaning, "on that soul in particular the sin is suspended, and it is not visited on the children or the third or fourth generations thereafter."

R. Nathan says, "It is a good omen for someone if penalty for his sins is exacted from him after he dies. If, when he dies he is not eulogized or buried, a wild beast eats his corpse, or it rains on his corpse, lo, this is a good sign for someone that penalty for his sins is exacted from him after he has died." [Then he gets his share in the world to come.]

And even though there is no clear proof for the proposition, there is at least an indication of it: "At that time, says the Lord, the bones of the kings of Judah, the bones of its princes, the bones of the priests, the bones of the prophets, and the bones of the inhabitants of Jerusalem shall be brought out of their tombs; and they shall be spread before the sun and the moon and all the host of heaven which they have loved and served [Jer. 8:1]."

Said R. Simeon b. Eleazar, "On the following basis I proved that the versions of Scripture of the Samaritans are forgeries, for they maintained that the dead do not live. I said to them, 'Lo, Scripture says, ". . . that person shall be utterly cut off; his iniquity shall be upon him."'"

For Scripture says, "His iniquity shall be upon him" only so as to indicate that it is destined to give a full accounting of itself on the day of judgment. (Neusner, *Sifre*)

Like the preceding rabbinic quotation and Mark 12:25-26 par., the argument seems strained and unconvincing to us, but illustrates that Mark (and Jesus) interpreted Scripture in a manner appropriate within the customary methods and perspectives of first-century Judaism. Thus the saying of Rabbi Simai, intended not in sarcasm but as a sincere affirmation of rabbinic theology and hermeneutics, "You cannot find any section [of the Hebrew Bible] which does not imply the resurrection of the dead . . . for it is said . . . 'Come, wind, from the four winds'" (*Sifre* on Deut 32:2).

163. Matthew 22:30 / Mark 12:25 / Luke 20:35-36

2 Baruch 51:10 (end 1 cent. CE?)

For they [the righteous] will live in the heights of that world and they will be like the angels and be equal to the stars. And they will be changed into any shape which they wished, from beauty to loveliness, and from light to the splendor of glory. (*OTP* 1:638)

Second Enoch 22:10 also knows the analogous view of the transformation of one who has been taken to heaven into the figure of an angel: "And I looked at myself, and I had become like one of his glorious ones, and there was no observable difference" (*OTP* 1:138). But statements about the lack of sexuality among angels are *not* found in this connection among Jewish texts from this period (but cf. the Persian text no. 710). The interesting feature in Mark 12 par. is that the angels, like the resurrected ones, are *very* similar to God, including their transcendence of sexuality. Is the phenomenon of abstinence from sex and marriage in early Christianity also to be understood from this point of view? Those near God become godlike. Galatians 3:28 realizes that only in a different way. On the resurrection, cf. no. 443.

164. Matthew 22:34-40 / Mark 12:28-34 / Luke 10:25-28

Sifra 19:18 (2 cent. CE, based on older tradition)

This is the great rule of the law. (Smith, *Tannaitic Parallels*)

"This" in *Sifra* refers to the command to love the neighbor, understood as the fellow Israelite. In the Synoptic saying, this is the "second" commandment, inseparable from the "first." This text is often cited as showing that Jewish tradition too distinguished between central and peripheral commands. Yet cf. the warning of Morton Smith: "Sifra speaks of Lev 19:18, Matt of Deut 6:5; 'rule' is not 'commandment'; 'great' in Sifra means 'logically prior'—that rule which includes by implication all the rest, 'great' in Matt means 'morally preeminent'—the most important. In short, the two sentences have nothing in common but their structure and the word 'great,' and I have cited the pair of them only to exclude them specifically from this list [of 'complete parallels']—an exclusion made necessary by the custom of supposing them to be equivalent." (*Tannaitic Parallels*)

165. Matthew 22:34-40 / Mark 12:28-34 / Luke 10:25-28

Philo, *The Special Laws* 2.63 (15 BCE–50 CE)

For the law bids us take the time for studying philosophy and thereby improve the soul and the dominant mind. So each seventh day there stand wide open in every city thousands of schools of good sense, temperance, courage, justice and the other virtues in which the scholars sit in order quietly with ears alert and with full attention, so much do they thirst for the draught which the teacher's words supply, while one of special experience rises and sets forth what is the best and sure to be profitable and will make the whole of life grow to something better. But among the vast number of particular truths and principles there studied, there stand out practically high above the others two main heads: one of duty to God as shown by piety and holiness, one of duty to men as when by humanity and justice, each of them splitting up into multiform branches, all highly laudable. (LCL)

Philo may be thinking of the two tables of the Law, the first setting forth duties to God, the second duties to human beings. He illustrates that Hellenistic Judaism could summarize the law under two great headings, duty to God and duty to other human beings. The explicit reference to love is missing, but love in the New Testament commands is not a matter of emotional feelings, but of active seeking the well-being of the other, so Philo's summary is analogous to that of the New Testament.

166. Matthew 22:34-40/ Mark 12:28-34/ Luke 10:25-28

Iamblichus, *Life of Pythagoras*, §82 (4 cent. CE)

[Concerning the schools that trace themselves back to Pythagoras:] The philosophy of the *acusmatici* consists of oral instructions without demonstration and without argument: e.g. "in this way one must act." . . . All these so-called oral instructions are divided into three kinds: for some indicate what a thing is; others, what is the best in any category; and others, what is necessary to do or not to do. . . . Those on what is best are, for example: what is the most just thing? To sacrifice. What is the wisest? Number. (Dillon and Hershbell)

The issues of what is the maximum or most important (as Mark 12:28, "What is the first, i.e. most important commandment) have become here a firm component of a philosophical school tradition. But questions of this type had belonged for a long time to the genre of chreia (cf. Berger, "Hellenistische Gattungen," 1097: "What is the most beautiful, the most difficult, the happiest?"). This genre does not deal with a compendium of "mosts" in the sense of a book of world records. Rather, the chreia functions as a critique of values and society. On the chreia genre cf. Berger, *Formgeschichte*, §§25-29.

167. Matthew 22:41-46/ Mark 12:35-37*a*/ Luke 20:41-44

Psalms of Solomon 17:21-51 (ca. 50 BCE)

[Immediately preceding: a description of the calamities that have befallen the Jewish people from foreign invaders, and because of their own sins] See, Lord, and raise up for them their king,

the son of David, to rule over your servant Israel
in the time known to you, O God.
Undergird him with the strength to destroy the unrighteous rulers,
to purge Jerusalem from gentiles
who trample her to destruction;
in wisdom and in righteousness to drive out
the sinners from the inheritance;
to smash the arrogance of sinners
like a potter's jar;
To shatter all their substance with an iron rod;
to destroy the unlawful nations with the word of his mouth;
At his warning the nations will flee from his presence;
and he will condemn sinners by the thoughts of their hearts.
He will gather a holy people
whom he will lead in righteousness;
and he will judge the tribes of the people
that have been made holy by the Lord their God.
He will not tolerate unrighteousness [even] to pause among them,

and any person who knows wickedness shall not live with them.
For he shall know them
that they are all children of their God.
He will distribute them upon the land
according to their tribes;
the alien and the foreigner will no longer live near them.
He will judge peoples and nations in the wisdom of his righteousness. Selah.
And he will have gentile nations serving him under his yoke,
and he will glorify the Lord in [a place] prominent [above] the whole earth.
And he will purge Jerusalem
[and make it] holy as it was even from the beginning,
[for] nations to come from the ends of the earth to see his glory,
to bring as gifts her children who had been driven out,
and to see the glory of the Lord
with which God had glorified her.
And he will be a righteous king over them, taught by God.
There will be no unrighteousness among them in his days,
for all shall be holy,
and their king shall be the Lord Messiah.
For he will not rely on horse and rider and bow,
nor will he collect gold and silver for war.
Nor will he build up hope in a multitude for a day of war.
The Lord himself is his king,
the hope of the one who has a strong hope in God.
He shall have compassion to all the nations
[who] reverently [stand] before him.
He will strike the earth with the word of his mouth forever;
he will bless the Lord's people with wisdom and happiness.
And he himself [will be] free from sin [in order] to rule a great people.
He will expose officials and drive out sinners
by the strength of his word.
And he will not weaken in his days, [relying] upon his God,
for God made him
powerful in the holy spirit
and wise in the counsel of understanding,
with strength and righteousness.
And the blessing of the Lord will be with him in strength,
and he will not weaken;
His hope will be in the Lord.
Then who will succeed against him,
mighty in his actions
and strong in the fear of God?
Faithfully and righteously shepherding the Lord's flock,
he will not let any of them stumble in their pasture.
He will lead them all in holiness
and there will be no arrogance among them,
that any should be oppressed.

This is the beauty of the king of Israel
which God knew,
to raise him over the house of Israel
to discipline it.
His words will be purer than the finest gold, the best.
He will judge the peoples in the assemblies,
the tribes of the sanctified.
His words will be as the words of the holy ones,
among sanctified peoples.
Blessed are those born in those days
to see the good fortune of Israel
which God will bring to pass in the assembly of the tribes.
May God dispatch his mercy to Israel;
may he deliver us from the pollution of profane enemies;
The Lord himself is our king forevermore. (*OTP* 2:667-69)

The text represents one stream of messianic expectation shortly before the birth of Jesus. It should not too quickly be taken as an example of the "militaristic" and "national" Messiah of Judaism in contrast with the "spiritual" Messiah of the Christians, since (1) it is an extension of the biblical models represented by Isaiah 11:1-5 and Psalm 2:8-9, texts also basic to Christian Messianism, and (2) some Christian models also use this imagery, such as Revelation 12:5; 19:15. Mark 12:35-37*a*, like Mark as a whole, is cool toward "Son of David" imagery for Christian Christology, while Matthew and Luke reinterpret the imagery and consider it a positive christological title for Jesus.

A similar picture of the expected Messiah is given in the Palestinian *Targum of Pseudo-Jonathan* Genesis 49:10-11 (7 cent. CE, much earlier materials): "Kings and rulers shall not cease from those of the house of Judah, nor scribes teaching the Law from his descendants, until the time the King Messiah comes, the youngest of his sons, because of whom the people will pine away. [11] How beautiful is the King Messiah who is to arise from among those of the house of Judah. He girds his loins and comes down arranging battle lines against his enemies and slaying kings together with their rulers; and there is no king or ruler who can withstand him. He makes the mountains red with the blood of the slain; his garments are rolled in blood; he is like a presser of grapes" (Maher). Cf. Revelation 19:11-21; 21:1–22:5, where this imagery is reinterpreted.

168. Matthew 23:15

Genesis Rabbah 39:14 (5 cent. CE)

. . . whoever brings a gentile close [to the worship of the true God] is as if he had created him anew. (Neusner, *Genesis Rabbah*)

We have documented evidence of a few celebrated cases in which the Pharisees persuaded prominent Gentiles to convert to Judaism, but the existence of a large-scale Pharisaic mission to the Gentiles is unsupported by historical evidence. Yet there are numerous Talmudic sayings praising proselytes and those who convert them to Judaism, e.g.:

"Rabbi Meir said: 'Ye shall therefore keep My statutes and My ordinances, which, if a man do, he shall live by them [Lev. 18:5].' It is not said that priests, Levites, and Israelites shall live by them, but 'a man,' therefore even a Gentile" (b. Sanh. 59A) (Soncino).

Yet the general pattern of these laudatory references to proselytes has the initiative with the would-be convert, rather than with a Jewish "missionary," e.g.: "Our Rabbis taught: A certain heathen once came before Shammai and asked him, 'How many Toroth have you?' 'Two,' he replied: 'the Written Torah and the Oral Torah.' 'I believe you with respect to the Written, but not with respect to the Oral Torah; make me a proselyte on condition that you teach me the Written Torah [only].' [But] he scolded and repulsed him in anger. When he went before Hillel, he accepted him as a proselyte. On the first day he taught him, Alef, beth, gimmel, daleth; the following day he reversed [them] to him. 'But yesterday you did not teach them to me thus,' he protested. 'Must you then not rely upon me? Then rely upon me with respect to the Oral [Torah] too'" (*b. Shab.* 31A) (Soncino). In this case the initiative is with the Gentile to become a proselyte. Once an insider, the rabbi then can issue challenges. So also b. Yeb. 47a, "When a man comes in these times seeking to become a proselyte, he is asked: 'What is your motive in presenting yourself to become a proselyte? Do you not know that in these times the Israelites are afflicted, distressed, downtrodden, torn to pieces, and that suffering is their lot?' If he answer, 'I know; and I am unworthy [to share their sufferings],' they accept him at once, and acquaint him with some of the lighter and some of the heavier commandments" (Soncino).

Although there is much encouragement to Gentiles to become Jewish proselytes, and much encouragement to Jews to accept them as full members of the community (indicating there was reluctance to do so in some circles), there is little trace in Jewish literature of an active "evangelistic" mission to Gentiles.

169. Matthew 23:1-36/ Mark 12:37*b*-40/ Luke 20:45-47

Dio Cocceianus, *Oration 13* (1 cent. CE)

[Against his opponents, whom he calls "sophists":] ". . . ignorant, boastful, self-deceived" [4.33] ". . . unlearned and deceiving by their words" [4.37] ". . . evil-spirited . . ." [4.38] ". . . impious . . ." [11.14] ". . . liars and deceivers . . ." [12:12] ". . . flatterers, charlatans, and sophists . . ." [23.11] ". . . preaching for the sake of gain and glory and only for their own benefit . . ." [32.30] ". . . mindless . . ." [54.1] ". . . boastful and shameless . . ." [55.7] ". . . deceiving others and themselves . . ." [70.10]. (Johnson)

The vitriolic language of Matthew against the Pharisees is characteristic of ancient philosophical and religious polemic. "The way the NT talks about Jews is just about the way all opponents talked about each other back then" (Luke Timothy Johnson, "The New Testament's Anti-Jewish Slander and the Conventions of Ancient Polemic," *JBL* 108 [1989], 430.) Johnson gives many examples from the Hellenistic world, of which Aelius Aristides, *Platonic Discourses* 307.6, is typical: His opponents "despise others while being themselves worthy of scorn. They criticize others without examining themselves. They make a great show of virtue and never practice it."

170. Matthew 24:1-2/ Mark 13:1-2; 14:58/ Luke 21:5-6

b. Yoma 39b

Our Rabbis taught: during the last forty years before the destruction of the Temple the lot ["For the Lord"] did not come up in the right hand; nor did the crimson-colored strap become white; nor did the westernmost light shine; and the doors of the *Hekal* would open by themselves, until R. Johanan b. Zakkai rebuked them, saying *Hekal, Hekal,* why wilt thou be the alarmer thyself? I know about thee that thou wilt be destroyed, for Zechariah ben Ido has already prophesied concerning thee: *Open thy doors, O Lebanon, that the fire may devour thy cedars.* (Soncino)

In the following it is then explained why the temple is compared with Lebanon. A series of signs (prodigies) is pictured, of the type that Josephus knows as well (*Wars* 6.288-300). These are identical in part; cf. Berger, "Hellenistisch-heidnische, Prodigien" 1428ff. The formulation of Johanan b. Zakkai with "I know . . ." indicates an apocalyptic knowledge (cf. K. Berger, "Zur Geschichte der Einleitungsformel «Amen, ich sage euch»," *ZNW* 63 [1972], 45-75, at 68, n. 83). It is to be noted that Rabbi Johanan b. Zakkai does not prophesy against the temple by his own authority (cf. no. 202), but legitimates his words by an allegorical interpretation of the Zechariah passage.

On Mark 13:5-6, 21-23, see nos. 175, 400, 531, 912-15.

171. Matthew 24:1-15/ Mark 13:1-14/ Luke 21:5-20

2 Baruch 7:1–8:5 (end of 1 cent. CE)

[The seer stands on the battlements of the wall of Jerusalem and sees four angels at the four corners of the city. The contents of the Holy of Holies are hidden by an angel. Then follows 7:1–8:5:]

And after these things I heard this angel saying to the angels who held the torches:

Now destroy the walls and overthrow them to their foundations so that the enemies do not boast and say, "We have overthrown the wall of Zion and we have burnt down the place of the mighty God." And they restored me to the place where I once stood.

8 Now the angels did as he had commanded them; and when they had broken up the corners of the wall, a voice was heard from the midst of the temple after the wall had fallen, saying:

Enter, enemies, and come, adversaries, because he who guarded the house has left it.

And I, Baruch, went away. And it happened after these things that the army of the Chaldeans entered and seized the house and all that is around it. And they carried away the people into captivity and killed some of them. (*OTP* 1:623)

The fate of Jerusalem in 70 CE is interpreted in the light of the catastrophe of 586 BCE. The shame of the destruction is averted by explaining that it was not the Romans, but angels who destroyed the city. In *2 Baruch* 13, the author will interpret this as punishment that serves the good purpose of expiation for Israel's sins. Gentiles, on the other hand, did not have this opportunity. In the Synoptics, in contrast, the fate of Jerusalem is considered in relation to the eschatological events, from which it is distinguished (cf. Berger, *Formgeschichte,* §77). *Second Baruch* 48:34-37 below provides supporting documentary evidence.

172. Matthew 24:1-15/ Mark 13:1-14/ Luke 21:5-20

2 Baruch 48:34-37 (end of 1 cent. CE)

And there will be many tidings and not a few rumors, and the works of the phantoms will be visible, and not a few promises will be told, some idle and others affirmed. And honor will change itself into shame, and strength will be humiliated to contempt, and the strong one will be broken down, and beauty will become contemptible. And many will say to many in that time, "Where did the multitude of intelligence hide itself and where did the multitude of wisdom depart?" And when one thinks about these things, jealousy will arise in those who did not think much of themselves; and passion will take hold of those who were peaceful; and many will be agitated by wrath to injure many; and they will raise armies to shed blood; and they will perish with those at the end. (*OTP* 1:637)

V. Ryssel comments on this section: "The proliferation of charlatans and prophets, the withdrawal of responsible leaders and sages and the resultant increase of zeal and passions among the people among whom one would rather not see it, the arrival of the Zealots who excited the people and called them forth to arms, forming large armies, of course only to their own destruction and the destruction of their country—all this points undeniably to the time of the Jewish war" (in E. Kautzsch, *Die Apokryphen und Pseudepigraphen des Alten Testaments,* II [Tübingen: J. C. B. Mohr, 1900], 406-7).

173. Matthew 24:1-15/ Mark 13:1-14/ Luke 21:5-20

4 Ezra 10:21-24 (late 1 cent. CE)

For you see how our sanctuary has been laid waste, our altar thrown down, our temple destroyed; our harp has been laid low, our song has been silenced, and our rejoicing has been ended; the light of our lampstand has been put out, the ark of our covenant has been plundered, our holy things have been polluted, and the name by which we are called has been almost profaned; our children [or: free men] have suffered abuse, our priests have been burned to death, our Levites have gone into [captivity], our virgins have been defiled, and our wives have been ravished; our righteous men [or: our seers] have been carried off, our little ones have been cast out, our young men have been enslaved and our strong men made powerless. And, worst of all, the seal of Zion has been deprived of its glory, and given over into the hands of those that hate us. (NRSV)

The lamentation concerns especially the fate of people of Jerusalem and the temple cultus. In the sequel Ezra sees the new Zion, filled with splendor. Further:

174. Matthew 24:1-15/ Mark 13:1-14/ Luke 21:5-20

Second Apocalypse of James 5:4 (2 cent. CE?)

. . . and he allows me to hear. And play your trumpets, your flutes and your harps [of this house]. The Lord has taken you captive from the Lord, having closed your ears, that they may not hear the sound of my word. Yet you [will be able to pay] heed in your hearts, [and] you will call me "the Just One." Therefore, I tell you: Behold, I gave you your house, which you say that God has made—that [house] in which he promised to give you an inheritance through it. This [house] I shall doom to destruction and derision of those who are in ignorance. (NHL)

This Jewish-gnosticizing text likewise reinterprets the destruction of Jerusalem. The Jews are ignorant of the true God, so the true God, in whose name "James" speaks, will destroy the temple (prophecy of doom as in Mark 13:2 par.). The false god has hardened the heart of the Jews so that they cannot give an obedient response to James either. The Gnostic tractate *Test. Truth* 9.3 speaks of King Solomon's having imprisoned in the temple the very demons who had helped him build it (cf. the *Testament of Solomon*): "He [placed them] into seven [waterpots. They remained] a long [time in] the [waterpots], abandoned [there]. When the Romans [went] up to [Jerusalem] they discovered [the] waterpots, [and immediately] the [demons] ran out of the waterpots as those who escape from prison. And the waterpots [remained] pure [thereafter]. [And] since those days, [they dwell] with men who are [in] ignorance, and [they have remained upon] the earth" (NHL). Here it is demons who inhabit the temple (and now all non-Gnostics).

175. Matthew 24:4-5 / Mark 13:5-6, 21-23 / Luke 21:8; 17:23

Sibylline Oracles 3:63ff. (ca. 140 BCE?)

Then Beliar will come from the Sebastenoi [the line of Augustus] and he will raise up the height of mountains, he will raise up the sea, the great fiery sun and shining moon, and he will raise up the dead, and perform many signs for men. But they will not be effective in him. But he will, indeed, also lead men astray, and he will lead astray many faithful, chosen Hebrews, and also other lawless men who have not yet listened to the word of God. But whenever the threats of the great God draw nigh and a burning power comes through the sea to land . . . (*OTP* 1:363)

Satan's deception is here referred only to Jews and pagans, not to Christians (the section is of Jewish origin). In place of the many deceivers of Mark 13, here there is only one, as in 2 Thessalonians 2. The warning against eschatological deceivers is met especially often in the genre "testaments" (cf. Berger, *Formgeschichte*, §24). Cf. nos. 400, 531, 912-15.

176. Matthew 24:7-9; 10:21:22 / Mark 13:8, 12-13 / Luke 21:10-17

Asclepius 72:16-25; 73:5-12, 18-22
(Egyptian syncretism, beginning of 4 cent. CE)

Darkness will be preferred to light and death will be preferred to life. No one will gaze into heaven. And the pious man will be counted as insane, and the impious man will be honored as wise. The man who is afraid will be considered as strong. And the good man will be punished like a criminal.

. . . [The] wicked angels will remain among men, [and] be with them [and] lead them into wicked things recklessly, as well as into atheism, wars, and plunderings, by teaching them things contrary to nature . . . the air will be diseased. Such is the senility of the world; atheism, dishonor, and the disregard of noble words. (NHL)

This text not only illuminates NT apocalyptic texts such as Mark 13 par.; it is an excellent illustration of how ancient texts, canonical or not, can seem to "predict" the modern interpreter's own time. One can readily imagine the interpretation this text would find in interpreters of "biblical prophecy," if it were in the canon!

177. Matthew 24:15-22/ Mark 13:14-20/ Luke 21:20-24

4 Ezra 5:4-10; 6:17-24 (late 1 cent. CE)

But if the Most High grants that you live, you shall see it ["the land that you now see ruling," i.e. Rome] thrown into confusion after the third period;
   and the sun shall suddenly begin to shine at night,
      and the moon during the day.
Blood shall drip from wood,
   and the stone shall utter its voice;
the peoples shall be troubled,
   and the stars shall fall.
And one shall reign whom those who inhabit the earth do not expect, and the birds shall fly away together; and the Dead Sea shall cast up fish; and one whom the many do not know shall make his voice heard by night, and all shall hear his voice. There shall be chaos also in many places, fire shall often break out, the wild animals shall roam beyond their haunts, and menstruous women shall bring forth monsters. Salt waters shall be found in the sweet, and all friends shall conquer one another; then shall reason hide itself, and wisdom shall withdraw into its chamber. . . .
When I heard this, I got to my feet and listened; a voice was speaking, and its sound was like the sound of mighty waters. It said, "The days are coming when I draw near to visit the inhabitants of the earth, and when I require from the doers of iniquity the penalty of their iniquity, and when the humiliation of Zion is complete. When the seal is placed upon the age that is about to pass away, then I will show these signs: the books shall be opened before the face of the firmament, and all shall see my judgment together. Children a year old shall speak with their voices, and pregnant women shall give birth to premature children at three and four months, and these shall live and leap about. Sown places shall suddenly appear unsown, and full storehouses shall suddenly be found to be empty; the trumpet shall sound aloud, and when all hear it, they shall suddenly be terrified. At that time friends shall make war on friends like enemies, the earth and those who inhabit it shall be terrified, and the springs of the fountains shall stand still, so that for three hours they shall not flow." (NRSV)

As the End approaches, the physical and biological processes of the universe break down, nature convulses with the labor pains of bringing in the Messianic Age. By these signs the approach of the

End can be discerned; insiders to apocalyptic knowledge will recognize it not as mere chaos, but as the prelude to the advent of the Messiah (for Christians, the second advent). The breakdown of normal biological processes makes it an especially bad time for pregnant women and those with young children. It is thus not a good time to marry and start a family (1 Cor 7:25-31!).

178. Matthew 24:22/ Mark 13:20

1 Enoch 80:2 (2 cent. BCE)

[In the days of sinners the winters] are cut short. Their seed[s] shall lag behind in their lands and in their fertile fields, and in all their activities upon the earth. He will turn and appear in their time, and withhold rain; and the sky shall stand still at that time. (*OTP* 1:58)

The shortening of calendrical units at the end time is a motif that occurs often and is used in different ways. While in Mark 13 par. it is God's act for the elect, in *1 Enoch* the same phenomenon is related to sinners and the changes and perversions in the natural order that occur due to their sin. In the Greek Apocalypse of Baruch *(3 Baruch)* 9:7, the shortening of days is an expression of God's wrath as a punishment for the serpent. In the Syrian Apocalypse of Baruch *(2 Baruch)* 20:1, the motif is a part of its near expectation of the end, and thus the closest to Mark 13 in terms of content. Similar, but very abbreviated, is the tradition in 4 Ezra 4:26.

179. Matthew 24:30/ Mark 13:26/ Luke 21:27

Suetonius, *Lives of the Caesars*, "Nero," 6.57 (early 2 cent. CE)

He met his death in the thirty-second year of his age, on the anniversary of the murder of Octavia, and such was the public rejoicing that the people put on liberty-caps and ran about all over the city. Yet there were some who for a long time decorated his tomb with spring and summer flowers, and now produced his statues on the rostra in the fringed toga, and now his edicts, as if he were still alive and would shortly return and deal destruction to his enemies. Nay more, Vologaesus, king of the Parthians, when he sent envoys to the senate to renew his alliance, earnestly begged this too, that honor be paid to the memory of Nero. In fact, twenty years later, when I was a young man, a person of obscure origin appeared, who gave out that he was Nero, and the name was still in such favor with the Parthians that they supported him vigorously and surrendered him with great reluctance. (LCL)

The idea of the (eschatological) return of historical persons was developed in Judaism for Elijah (Mal 3), and in the intertestamental period transferred to Enoch, then later to righteous heroes in general, who together with the prophets will appear for judgment (*Sib. Or.* 2.244ff.). In *2 Baruch* (13:2-3) and 4 Ezra it is applied to those who had been taken to heaven without dying (such as Baruch and Ezra), and according to Revelation 12:5, 19:11-12, to the Messiah. The tradition of Nero redivivus also became significant for the later antichrist idea. On its form in the first century CE, cf. W. Bousset, *Die Offenbarung Johannis* (Göttingen: Vandenhoeck & Ruprecht, 1906), 361, 411-13, who mentions among other details that already by 69 CE there were pseudo-Neros. The constant connection with the Parthians is noticeable. Is the background of the idea of the returning king to be found in the relation of astrology and kingship (the new age of the world as the return of the old)? So also perhaps nos. 912-15. Cf. Revelation 13:1-18; 17:9-11.

180. Matthew 24:30-31 / Mark 13:26-27 / Luke 21:27

1 Enoch 62:13-14 (2 cent. BCE)

The righteous and elect ones shall be saved on that day; and from thenceforth they shall never see the faces of the sinners and the oppressors. The Lord of the Spirits will abide over them; they shall eat and rest and rise with that Son of Man forever and ever. (*OTP* 1:44)

As in Mark 13 par., it concerns the Son of Man and those who belong to him. Here, as in Mark, they are saved (Mark: gathered) from the mass of the rest of humanity and separated from them. In contrast to *1 Enoch,* Mark renounces any description of the heavenly fellowship—a result of the intimate relation to God that is pictured? (Cf. no. 163.)

181. Matthew 24:36 / Mark 13:32

2 Baruch 21:8 (end of 1 cent. CE)

[A hymnic praise to God within a prayer, which ends in the request for God to let his glory appear and to let no more human beings die] You are the one who causes the rain to fall on earth with a specific number of raindrops. You alone know the end of times before it has arrived. Hear my prayer. (*OTP* 1:628)

What in Mark serves as a motivation for watchfulness functions here to describe the glory of God: he causes rain and knows the end of time, i.e. everything is included in God's all-encompassing plan.

182. Matthew 25:1-13

Plutarch, *Moralia,* "Precepts of Statecraft" 1 (45–125 CE)

. . . philosophers who urge people to take lessons from them, but give no real instruction or advice; for they are like those who trim the lamps, but fail to pour in oil. (LCL)

Common image field: for lamps to be useful, oil is essential. If one neglects this, then the lamps that have been brought along and trimmed are still useless. The imagery is used differently: the brief similitude from Plutarch pictures an everyday event, while Matthew's story portrays a scandalous incident.

183. Matthew 25:31-46

1 Enoch 37-71 (selections) (date of this section disputed; probably 1 cent. CE)

[45:1-6] [The narrator is Enoch throughout:] This is the second parable concerning those who deny the name of the Lord of the Spirits and the congregation of the holy ones.

Neither will they ascend into heaven
nor will they reach the ground;
such will be the lot of sinners,
who will deny the name of the Lord of the Spirits,
those who in this manner will be preserved for the day of burden and tribulation.
On that day, my Elect One shall sit on the seat of glory
and make a selection of their deeds,
their resting places will be without number,
their souls shall be firm within them when they see my Elect One,
those who have appealed to my glorious name.
On that day, I shall cause my Elect One to dwell among them,
I shall transform heaven and make it a blessing of light forever.
I shall [also] transform the earth and make it a blessing,
and cause my Elect One to dwell in her.
Then those who have committed sin and crime shall not set foot in her.
For in peace I have looked with favor upon my righteous ones and given them mercy,
and have caused them to dwell before me.
But sinners have come before me so that by judgment
I shall destroy them before the face of the earth.

[46:1-6] At that place, I saw the One to whom belongs the time before time. And his head was white like wool, and there was with him another individual, whose face was like that of a human being. His countenance was full of grace like that of one among the holy angels. And I asked the one—from among the angels—who was going with me, and who had revealed to me all the secrets regarding the One who was born of human beings [or: "that *Son of Man*"], "Who is this, and from whence is he who is going as the prototype of the Before-Time?" And he answered and said to me, "This is the *Son of Man,* to whom belongs righteousness, and with whom righteousness dwells. And he will open all the hidden storerooms; for the Lord of the Spirits has chosen him, and he is destined to be victorious before the Lord of the Spirits in eternal uprightness. This *Son of Man* whom you have seen is the One who will remove the kings and the mighty ones from their comfortable seats and the strong ones from their thrones. He shall loosen the reigns of the strong and crush the teeth of the sinners. He shall depose the kings from their thrones and kingdoms. For they do not extol and glorify him, and neither do they obey him, the source of their kingship. The faces of the strong will be slapped and be filled with shame and gloom. Their dwelling places and their beds will be worms. They shall have no hope to rise from their beds, for they do not extol the name of the Lord of the Spirits."

[48:1-10] Furthermore, in that place I saw the fountain of righteousness, which does not become depleted and is surrounded completely by numerous fountains of wisdom. All the thirsty ones drink [of the water] and become filled with wisdom. [Then] their dwelling places become with the holy, righteous, and elect ones. At that hour, that *Son of Man* was given a name in the presence of the Lord of Spirits, the Before-Time; even before the creation of the sun and the moon, before the creation of the stars, he was given a name in the presence of the Lord of the Spirits. He will become a staff for the righteous ones in order that they may lean on him and not fall. He is the light of the gentiles and he will become the hope of those who are sick in their hearts. All those who dwell upon the earth shall fall and worship before him; they shall glorify, bless, and sing the name of the Lord of Spirits. For this purpose he became the Chosen One; he was concealed in the presence of [the Lord of the Spirits] prior to the creation of the world, and for eternity. And he has revealed the wisdom of the Lord of the Spirits to the righteous and the holy ones, for he has preserved the portion of the righteous because they have hated and despised this world of oppression [together with] all its ways of life and its habits in the name of the Lord of the Spirits; and because they will be saved in his name and it is his good pleasure that they have life. In those days, the kings of the earth and the mighty landowners shall be humiliated on account of the deeds of their hands. Therefore, on the day of their misery and weariness, they will not be able to save themselves. I shall deliver them into the hands of my elect ones like grass in the fire and like lead in water, so shall they burn before the face of the holy ones and sink before their sight, and no place will be found for them. On the day of their weariness, there shall be an obstacle on the earth and they shall fall on their faces; and they shall not rise up [again], nor anyone [be found] who will take them with his hands and raise them up. For they have denied the Lord of the Spirits and his Messiah. Blessed be the name of the Lord of the Spirits!

[69:27-29] [Then] there came to them a great joy. And they blessed, glorified, and extolled [the Lord] on account of the fact that the name of that *[Son of] Man* was revealed to them. He shall never pass away or perish from before the face of the earth. But those who have led the world astray shall be bound with chains, and their ruinous congregation shall be imprisoned; all their deeds shall vanish from before the face of the earth. Thenceforth nothing that is corruptible shall be found; for that *Son of Man* has appeared and has seated himself upon the throne of his glory; and all evil shall disappear from before his face; he shall go and tell to the *Son of Man*, and he shall be strong before the Lord of the Spirits. Here ends the third parable of Enoch.

[71:1-17] [Thus] it happened after this that my spirit passed out of sight and ascended into the heavens. And I saw the sons of the holy angels walking upon the flame of fire; their garments were white—and their overcoats—and the light of their faces was like snow. Also I saw two rivers of fire, the light of which fire was shining like hyacinth. Then I fell upon my face before the Lord of the Spirits. And the angel Michael, one of the archangels, seizing me by my right hand and lifting me up, led me out into all the secrets of mercy; and he showed me all the secrets of righteousness. He also showed me all the secrets of the extreme ends of heaven and all the reservoirs of the stars and the luminaries—from where they come out [to shine] before the faces of the holy ones. He carried off my spirit, and I, Enoch, was in the heaven of heavens. There I saw—in the midst of that light—a structure built of crystals; and between those crystals tongues of living fire. And my spirit saw a ring which encircled the structure of fire. On its four sides were rivers full of living fire which encircled it. Moreover, seraphim, cherubim, and ophanim—the sleepless ones who guard the throne of his glory—also encircled it. And I saw countless angels—a hundred times a hundred thousand, ten million times ten million—encircling that house—Michael, Raphael,

Gabriel, Phanuel, and numerous [other] holy angels that are countless. With them is the Antecedent of Time: His head is white and pure like wool and his garment is indescribable. I fell on my face, my whole body mollified and my spirit transformed. Then I cried with a great voice by the spirit of the power, blessing, glorifying, and extolling. And those are the blessings which went forth out of my mouth, being well-pleasing in the presence of that Antecedent of Time. Then the Antecedent of Time came with Michael, Gabriel, Raphael, Phanuel, and a hundred thousand and ten million times a hundred thousand angels that are countless. Then an angel came to me and greeted me and said to me, "You, *son of man [be'esi]*, who art born in righteousness and upon whom righteousness has dwelt, the righteousness of the Antecedent of Time will not forsake you." He added and said to me, "He shall proclaim peace to you in the name of the world that is to become. For from here proceeds peace since the creation of the world, and so it shall be unto you forever and for ever and ever. Everyone that will come to exist and walk shall [follow] your path, since righteousness never forsakes you. Together with you shall be their dwelling places; and together with you shall be their portion. They shall not be separated from you forever and ever and ever. So there shall be length of days with that *Son of Man [sab'e]*, and peace to the righteous ones; his path is upright for the righteous, in the name of the Lord of Spirits forever, and ever." (*OTP* 1:33-36, 49-50; emphasis added)

The reader familiar with the New Testament will recognize numerous points of contact with this text, which is cited at length here only to provide a contextual sample of Enoch's usage of Son of Man imagery. The origin, history, and meaning of the Son of Man tradition in the Hellenistic world and its incorporation into the New Testament as a christological title is one of the most disputed issues in New Testament scholarship. No effort will be made here even to sketch the nature of the problems. The above selections, the interpretation of which is disputed, provide sample texts in which Son of Man is used of a heavenly being without reference to Jesus (Enoch is identified as "son of man" in the concluding section [71:14], but a different term is used from that in previous references in which the Son of Man is also pictured as a heavenly being having already existed in heaven prior to Enoch's arrival there). "If there were, in the first century A.D., Jews who believed that it was possible for a man to be exalted to heaven so as to be identified with a supernatural being who was called Son of man and was to come in glory as judge and savior, their existence and their belief can hardly fail to be relevant to the study of the Gospels" (Barrett, *New Testament Background*, 344). Further:

184. Matthew 25:31-46

4 Ezra 13:1-56 (end of 1 cent. CE)

After seven days I dreamed a dream in the night. 2 And lo, a wind arose from the sea and stirred up all its waves. 3 As I kept looking the wind made something like the figure of a man come up out of the heart of the sea. And I saw that this man flew with the clouds of heaven; and wherever he turned his face to look, everything under his gaze trembled, 4 and whenever his voice issued from his mouth, all who heard his voice melted as wax melts when it feels the fire.

5 After this I looked and saw that an innumerable multitude of people were gathered together from the four winds of heaven to make war against the man who came up out of the sea. 6 And I looked and saw that he carved out for himself a great mountain, and flew

up on to it. 7 And I tried to see the region or place from which the mountain was carved, but I could not.

8 After this I looked and saw that all who had gathered together against him, to wage war with him, were filled with fear, and yet they dared to fight. 9 When he saw the onrush of the approaching multitude, he neither lifted his hand nor held a spear or any weapon of war; 10 but I saw only how he sent forth from his mouth something like a stream of fire, and from his lips a flaming breath, and from his tongue he shot forth a storm of sparks. 11 All these were mingled together, the stream of fire and the flaming breath and the great storm, and fell on the onrushing multitude that was prepared to fight, and burned up all of them, so that suddenly nothing was seen of the innumerable multitude but only the dust of ashes and the smell of smoke. When I saw it, I was amazed.

12 After this I saw the same man come down from the mountain and call to himself another multitude that was peaceable. 13 Then many people came to him, some of whom were joyful and some sorrowful; some of them were bound, and some were bringing others as offerings.

Then I woke up in great terror, and prayed to the Most High, and said, 14 "From the beginning you have shown your servant these wonders, and have deemed me worthy to have my prayer heard by you; 15 now show me the interpretation of this dream also. 16 For as I consider it in my mind, alas for those who will be left in those days! And still more, alas for those who are not left! 17 For those who are not left will be sad 18 because they understand the things that are reserved for the last days, but cannot attain them. 19 But alas for those also who are left, and for that very reason! For they shall see great dangers and much distress, as these dreams show. 20 Yet it is better to come into these things, though incurring peril, than to pass from the world like a cloud, and not to see what will happen in the last days."

He answered me and said, 21 "I will tell you the interpretation of the vision, and I will also explain to you the things that you have mentioned. 22 As for what you said about those who survive, and concerning those who do not survive, this is the interpretation: 23 The one who brings the peril at that time will protect those who fall into peril, who have works and faith toward the Almighty. 24 Understand therefore that those who are left are more blessed than those who have died.

25 "This is the interpretation of the vision: As for your seeing a man come up from the heart of the sea, 26 this is he whom the Most High has been keeping for many ages, who will himself deliver his creation; and he will direct those who are left. 27 And as for your seeing wind and fire and a storm coming out of his mouth, 28 and as for his not holding a spear or weapon of war, yet destroying the onrushing multitude that came to conquer him, this is the interpretation: 29 The days are coming when the Most High will deliver those who are on the earth. 30 And bewilderment of mind shall come over those who inhabit the earth. 31 They shall plan to make war against one another, city against city, place against place, people against people, and kingdom against kingdom. 32 When these things take place and the signs occur that I showed you before, then my Son will be revealed, whom you saw as a man coming up from the sea.

33 "Then, when all the nations hear his voice, all the nations shall leave their own lands and the warfare that they have against one another; 34 and an innumerable multitude shall be gathered together, as you saw, wishing to come and conquer him. 35 But he shall stand on the top of Mount Zion. 36 And Zion shall come and be made manifest to all people, prepared and built, as you saw the mountain carved out without hands. 37 Then he, my

Son, will reprove the assembled nations for their ungodliness (this was symbolized by the storm), 38 and will reproach them to their face with their evil thoughts and the torments with which they are to be tortured (which were symbolized by the flames), and will destroy them without effort by means of the law (which was symbolized by the fire).

39 "And as for your seeing him gather to himself another multitude that was peaceable, 40 these are the nine tribes that were taken away from their own land into exile in the days of King Hoshea, whom Shalmaneser, king of the Assyrians, made captives; he took them across the river, and they were taken into another land. 41 But they formed this plan for themselves, that they would leave the multitude of the nations and go to a more distant region, where no human beings had ever lived, 42 so that there at least they might keep their statutes that they had not kept in their own land. 43 And they went in by the narrow passages of the Euphrates river. 44 For at that time the Most High performed signs for them, and stopped the channels of the river until they had crossed over. 45 Through that region there was a long way to go, a journey of a year and a half; and that country is called Arzareth.

46 "Then they lived there until the last times; and now, when they are about to come again, 47 the Most High will stop the channels of the river again, so that they may be able to cross over. Therefore you saw the multitude gathered together in peace. 48 But those who are left of your people, who are found within my holy borders, shall be saved. 49 Therefore when he destroys the multitude of the nations that are gathered together, he will defend the people who remain. 50 And then he will show them very many wonders."

51 I said, "O sovereign Lord, explain this to me: Why did I see the man coming up from the heart of the sea?"

52 He said to me, "Just as no one can explore or know what is in the depths of the sea, so no one on earth can see my Son or those who are with him, except in the time of his day. 53 This is the interpretation of the dream that you saw. And you alone have been enlightened about this, 54 because you have forsaken your own ways and have applied yourself to mine, and have searched out my law; 55 for you have devoted your life to wisdom, and called understanding your mother. 56 Therefore I have shown you these things; for there is a reward laid up with the Most High. For it will be that after three more days I will tell you other things, and explain weighty and wondrous matters to you." (NRSV)

The Man is here identical with the Son of Man of Daniel 7 ("Son of Man" is a Hebrew idiom for "man," "human being"; cf. Ps 8:3-4; Ezek 2:1 and passim; "mortal" in NRSV). As in Matthew 25:31-46, the Son of Man is identified with the Son of God. There are extracanonical parallels to "Son of Man" as the heavenly redeemer figure and as (mere) human being, but nothing comparable to the suffering, dying, and rising Son of Man introduced into the Synoptic tradition at Mark 8:31; 9:31; 10:33-34.

185. Matthew 25:31-46

Left Ginza 3.19 (extant texts are late, after 500 CE; some traditions may reach back to 1 cent. CE)

They [the uthras, light-beings similar to angels] spoke to it [the soul]:
"What are your works, soul,

so that we may be your escort on the way?"
It spoke to them:
"My father distributed bread
and my mother dispensed alms.
My brothers recited hymns,
and my sisters administered kûsta" [truth, uprightness, personified as savior]
They spoke to it:
"Your father, who distributed bread,
distributed it for himself.
Your mother who dispensed alms
dispensed them for her own soul.
Your brothers who recited hymns,
will ascend on the path of kûsta.
Your sisters, who admired kûsta,
will Manda dHaiyê [knowledge, Gnosis, the name of the most important savior figure]
support.
But what are your works which you have done for yourself,
So that we may be your escort?"
It spoke to them:
"I have loved the Life,
and allowed Manda dHaiyê to settle in my inner thoughts.
At the close of Saturday in the evening
and at the coming in of Sunday for the good [?]
I put alms in my pocket
and went to the gate of the temple.
I added the alms to the other alms
and the loaf of bread to the community meal.
I found an orphan and sustained it,
I replenished the widow's pocket.
I found a naked person,
and clothed him in a garment for his nakedness.
I found a prisoner,
and released him and sent him back to his village." (Foerster)

Points of contact: (1) The same virtues are valued: care for the poor, vulnerable, hungry, naked. Prisoners are not only visited, but set free (as Luke 4:18). (2) These are what count ultimately, in the eschatological judgment (Matthew) or on the soul's path to its heavenly home (*Ginza*). In the *Ginza,* the point is that one cannot rely on the good works of one's parents and family, but is responsible to perform acts of charity on one's own.

There is however a fundamental difference between this text and Matthew. Although compassion for others is not excluded, the accent is set differently in the *Ginza,* where the issue is whether one has done acts of charity *"for oneself."* There is an element of self-interested calculation absent from Matthew, where those who have been compassionate are surprised to learn that their acts of service to others are the basis of their acceptance at the Last Judgment. Cf. the revelatory proclamation of the "messenger of light" (*Right Ginza* 2.3): "A cry I uttered to the world, from one end of the world to the other. I uttered a cry to the world: let everyone take care of himself. Everyone who takes care of himself will be saved from the consuming fire" (Foerster).

186. Matthew 25:34, 41

Palestinian Targum of Pseudo-Jonathan Genesis 3:24
(7 cent. CE, much earlier materials)

Before he had yet created the world, he created the Law. He established the garden of Eden for the righteous, that they might eat and take delight in the fruit of the tree, for having during their lives cherished the instruction of the Law in this world and fulfilled the precepts. For the wicked he established Gehenna which is like a sharp two-edged sword. (Maher)

There is little mythology in the New Testament in the sense of descriptions of what transpired in the transcendent world before the creation of the world and the beginning of human history. (This is true of what became the main stream of early Christianity, in contrast to Gnosticism.) Early Christianity reflects its rootedness in the Hebrew Bible and Jewish tradition, which likewise rejected speculative mythological explanations of precreation goings-on as the explanation for the harsh realities of history. Yet in both Judaism and earliest Christianity there was a minimal incorporation of the idea that some things were created at or before "the foundation of the world." Here the Targumic tradition elaborates slightly on the Genesis text (which had resolutely resisted mythological explanations, the narrative being limited to what transpires under the hard dome of heaven, after the "beginning," i.e. the creation), by positing the creation of the Law, Paradise, and Gehenna before the creation of the world. (Cf. 4 Ezra 3:6, the garden of Eden was planted before the earth was formed. For the NT, in addition to Matt 25:34, cf. John 17:5, 24; Eph 1:4; 1 Pet 1:20; Rev 13:8; 17:8.) There are few other references in rabbinic Judaism. Cf. *Aboth*, "Seven things were created before the foundation of the world . . ." (none of which are elaborated mythologically).

187. Matthew 25:35-40

Mekilta on Deuteronomy 15.9

And so the Holy One, blessed be He, said to Israel, "My children, whenever you feed the poor I count it up for you as if you fed me." (Smith, *Tannaitic Parallels*)

See on no. 283 on Luke 6:40/ Matthew 10:24-25.

188. Matthew 26:6-13/ Mark 14:3-11/ John 12:1-8

Suetonius, *Lives of the Caesars*, "The Deified Vespasian" 8.4 (b. ca. 70 CE)

Once when he was taking breakfast, a stray dog brought in a human hand from the crossroads and dropped it under the table. Again, when he was dining, an ox that was ploughing shook off its yoke, burst into the dining room, and after scattering the servants, fell at the very feet of Vespasian as he reclined at table, and bowed its neck as if suddenly tired out. (LCL)

As in Mark 14, it is a case of extraordinary events happening during a mealtime. In Suetonius it is animals who do the unusual deeds, while in Mark it is a woman who anoints Jesus. In both cases, however, it is a matter of prodigies. Suetonius represents the great Vespasian as one whom even animals, without any provocation, involuntarily reverence as a master. In Mark, the prodigy points to Jesus' coming death (an anticipation of the anointing of his body for burial), but in 14:9 the lordship of Jesus is also in view. These "personal prodigies" belong to the biographical genre in antiquity. (Cf. Berger, *Formgeschichte*, 350.)

189. Matthew 26:17-29/ Mark 14:12-25/ Luke 22:7-20

m. *Pesahim* 10 (2–3 cents. CE)

On the eve of the Passover, from about the time of the Evening Offering, a man must eat naught until nightfall. Even the poorest in Israel must not eat unless he sits down to table, and they must not give them less than four cups of wine to drink, even if it is from the [Pauper's] Dish. . . .

When [food] is brought before him he eats it seasoned with lettuce, until he is come to the breaking of bread; they bring before him unleavened bread and lettuce and the *haroseth*, although *haroseth* is not a religious obligation. R. Eliezer b. R. Zadok [2 cent. CE] says: It is a religious obligation. And in the Holy City they used to bring before him the body of the Passover offering [no longer possible after the destruction of the temple, 70 CE].

They then mix him the second cup. And here the son asks his father (and if the son has not enough understanding his father instructs him [how to ask]), "Why is this night different from other nights? For on other nights we eat seasoned food once, but this night twice; on other nights we eat leavened or unleavened bread, but this night all is unleavened; on other nights we eat flesh roasted, stewed, or cooked, but this night all is roast." And according to the understanding of the son his father instructs him. He begins with the disgrace and ends with the glory; and he expounds from *A wandering Aramean was my father . . .* until he finishes the whole section [Deut 26:5-9].

Rabban Gamaliel used to say: Whosoever has not said [the verses concerning] these three things at Passover has not fulfilled his obligation. And these are they: Passover, unleavened bread, and bitter herbs: "Passover"—because God passed over the houses of our fathers in Egypt; "unleavened bread"—because our fathers were redeemed in Egypt; "bitter herbs"—because the Egyptians embittered the lives of our fathers in Egypt. In every generation a man must so regard himself as if he came forth himself out of Egypt, for it is written, *And thou shalt tell thy son in that day saying, It is because of that which the Lord did for me when I came forth out of Egypt* [Exod 13:8]. Therefore are we bound to give thanks, to praise, to glorify, to honor, to exalt, to extol, and to bless him who wrought all these wonders for our fathers and for us. He brought us out from bondage to freedom, from sorrow to gladness, and from mourning to a Festival-day, and from darkness to great light, and from servitude to redemption; so let us say before him the *Hallelujah*. (Danby)

All the Gospels locate the last supper of Jesus with his disciples and Jesus' subsequent arrest, trial, and crucifixion in conjunction with the Jewish Passover. The Synoptics follow Mark in making the last supper a Passover meal, though the only elements of the Passover ritual mentioned are bread, wine, and the hymn at the end. In the Fourth Gospel, the last supper is not a Passover meal, but Jesus' death occurs at the same time the Passover lambs are being sacrificed. Thus while historically it is indisputable that Jesus was crucified during the Passover festival, the exact chronology is unclear, since it is conditioned not by strictly historical concerns, but by the theological intentions of the Christian tradition and the evangelists to interpret the meaning of Jesus' suffering and death within the framework of the Passover.

190. Matthew 26:26-29/ Mark 14:22-25/ Luke 22:15-20

Diodorus Siculus, *The Library of History*, 4.3.4 (1 cent. BCE)

And since the discovery of wine and the gift of it to human beings were the source of such great satisfaction to them, both because of the pleasure which derives from the drinking of it and because of the greater vigor which comes to the bodies of those who partake of it, it is the custom, they say, when unmixed wine is served during a meal to greet it with the words, "To the Good Deity!" but when the cup is passed around after the meal diluted with water, to cry out, "To Zeus Savior!" For the drinking of unmixed wine results in a state of madness, but when it is mixed with the rain from Zeus the delight and pleasure continue . . . (LCL)

In the course of ancient dinner parties and banquets, the "cups" were a kind of indication of the points in the progress of the meal, similar to "courses." They were usually numbered, and every new cup could be introduced with religious toasts, or there could also be a libation poured out before each cup in honor of various gods or human beings (as in the bylaws of the club "Andreios" IG 12 3.330; cf. also §670). The Jewish Passover, with its speeches and prayers over individual cups, was only following the common practice of antiquity.

191. Matthew 26:26-29/ Mark 14:22-25/ Luke 22:15-20

P. Oxy. 110 (perhaps end of 1 cent. CE)

[A written invitation:] Chairemon requests your company at dinner at the table of the Lord Serapis, in the Serapaeum, tomorrow the 15th, at 9:00. (Grenfell and Hunt)

A similar invitation is found in P. Köln 57 (in B. Krämer/R. Hübner, *Kölner Papyri* [1976], 175-77). Altogether we now have eleven examples from the papyri of very similar invitations to a banquet involving the Lord Sarapis. Three were added to the collection alone in the year 1976:

"Nikephoros asks you to dine at a banquet of the lord Sarapis in the Birth-House on the 23rd, from the 9th hour."

"Herais asks you to dine in the [dining] room of the Sarapeion at a banquet of the Lord Sarapis tomorrow, namely the 11th, from the 9th hour."

"The god calls you to a banquet being held in the Thoereion tomorrow from the 9th hour" (Horsley, *New Documents* 5). Note here the invitation is from the god himself.

Here we meet a first group of history-of-religions analogies to the Lord's Supper (for the other groups, see below nos. 192-96), in which the deity is host and master of ceremonies for diners who are in this sense guests of the god or goddess. At the head of this series stands the homophagia, the eating of raw flesh, in which the torn meat is the flesh of the deity (Euripides, *Bacchi* 734-47, 100, 618, etc., and Euripides, *Fragments*, 472, 9-15; scholia on Clement of Alexandria, *Protrepikos* 119.1, "For they ate raw flesh, which they dedicated to Dionysus. They celebrated this as a sign of the dismemberment which Dionysus suffered at the hands of the Maenads" [MEB/Berger]). The other view was that the god Dionysus had himself practiced homophagy, and this act was imitated in a sacred ritual at banquets that also included special clothing and names in imitation of the deity. A next stage is reached when animals are no longer torn apart, but small pieces of raw flesh are distributed among the participants (inscription from 276–75 BCE, *LSAM* 48.2-3). The next stage is represented by banquet guests who are themselves ranked with these deities (Livy 39.8.5; in regulation clubhouses, where these cultic practices received a character akin to the mysteries: *CIG* 2052.4, 6). The Essene meals are to be mentioned in this connection (e.g. Philo, "Contemplative Life" 34ff.); cf. also no. 346. The final stage is represented by the already mentioned regular guests at the meals of Isis, Anubis, and Serapis. Josephus (*Antiquities* 18.73) by means of a scandalous affair makes clear that one could anticipate not only a meal, but an embrace from the deity. Especially Serapis was thought of as the master host of elegant meals (partly only for priests) that were held in his name. Tertullian *Apol.* 39.15 compares them with the Christian celebrations of the Lord's Supper.

192. Matthew 26:26-29 / Mark 14:22-25 / Luke 22:15-20

Clement of Alexandria, *Exhortation to the Greeks* 15.3 (late 2 or early 3 cent.)

[Reporting the mysterious speech of the Attis initiates:] I ate from the drum; I drank from the cymbal; I carried the sacred dish; I stole into the bridal chamber. (LCL)

In this second line of tradition which intersects the history-of-religions sphere of the Lord's Supper it is not a matter of the actual meals that are repeated, but an eating and drinking of *symbolic character* in the context of the initiation ceremonies to the mystery cults. The manner of symbolization is important in comparison to the Eucharist. Clement of Alexandria, *Exhortation to the Greeks* 2.18 is to be understood similarly: "And the formula of the Eleusinian mysteries is as follows: 'I fasted; I drank the draught; I took from the chest; having done my task, I placed in the basket, and from the basket into the chest'" (LCL). According to 2.21.4-5, the chest contained a group of fertility symbols: "Are they not sesame cakes, pyramid and spherical cakes, cakes with many navels, also balls of salt and a serpent, the mystic sign of Dionysus Bassareus? Are they not also pomegranates, fig branches, fennel stalks, ivy leaves, round cakes and poppies? These are their holy things! In addition there are the unutterable symbols of Ge Themis, marjoram, a lamp, a sword, and a woman's comb, which is a euphemistic expression used in the mysteries for a woman's secret parts" (LCL). Similar things are reported by Firmicus Maternus and Eusebius. Justin, *Apology* 66:4 reports concerning the Mithras mysteries that in the induction ceremony bread and a cup of water were placed before the new candidates. He recognized the history-of-religions analogy and describes the pagan ceremony as a demonic imitation of the Christian rite. Further:

193. Matthew 26:26-29/ Mark 14:22-25/ Luke 22:15-20

Joseph and Aseneth 16:16 (Hellenistic Jewish missionary document, perhaps 1 cent. BCE)

And the man said to Aseneth, "Behold, you have eaten bread of life, and drunk a cup of immortality, and been anointed with ointment of incorruptibility. Behold, from today your flesh [will] flourish like flowers of life from the ground of the Most High, and your bones will grow strong like the cedars of the paradise of delight of God, . . ." (*OTP* 2:229)

What is described is the character and result of Aseneth's conversion to Judaism, especially the "revelation of the inexpressible mysteries of God" (16:14). It would be easy to suppose that here is portrayed the taking up into Judaism of something analogous to pagan initiation into the mystery cults. A corresponding rite is missing here; the bread for eating and the cup for drinking had become firmly entrenched metaphors for the description of initiation. (Cf. J. Charlesworth, *Old Testament Pseudepigrapha and the New Testament* [Cambridge: Cambridge University Press, 1985], 133-34.)

194. Matthew 26:26-29/ Mark 14:22-25/ Luke 22:15-20

Lucius Apuleius, *The Golden Ass* 11 (ca. 125 CE)

Then they began to solemnize the feast, the nativity of my holy order, with sumptuous banquets and pleasant meats: the third day was likewise celebrated with like ceremonies, with a religious dinner, and with all the consummation of the adept order. (LCL)

In this third type of sacral meal in the environment of the New Testament there stands a regular formal meal at the end of the initiation, for which it might form the crowning climax. Further examples: Livy 39.9.4 (fasting, washing, dedication, eating); Mysteries of Zeus Panamaros (inscription from the 2nd cent. CE, *SEG* 4.247): "The deity invites all people to a meal, and he prepares a common and honorable table for all, whatever their origin" (MEB/Berger).

In summary, the lines of development portrayed in nos. 191-92, 194 are significant for understanding the Christian Lord's Supper in the following ways: (1) Nourishment is a metaphor for life (even of immortality); (2) the religious meal makes clear that the one who partakes participates in the life granted by the deity in a special way; (3) the meal is especially characterized by a sense of fellowship with other participants, either as initiation or as the content of the meetings of the group. Beyond these meals, which were mainly practiced with some relationship to the mystery cults, the following meals of religious character were of significance for the Lord's Supper.

195. Matthew 26:26-29/ Mark 14:22-25/ Luke 22:15-20

Diogenes Laertius (3 cent. CE), *Lives of Eminent Philosophers*, "Epicurus" 10.18 (4 cent. BCE)

[Revenues are to be allocated for sacrifices for the dead and] for the customary celebration of my birthday on the tenth day of Gamelion in each year, and for the meeting of all my School held every month on the twentieth day to commemorate Metrodorus and myself according to the rules now in force. (LCL)

The formulation "to commemorate" (Gk. εἰς μνήμην) corresponds somewhat to 1 Corinthians 11:25; Luke 22:19. It is confirmed by Cicero, *Goods and Evils* 2.101 and Plutarch, *Moralia* 1089C that the monthly memorial to the teacher took place at a mealtime. This too is analogous to the meal celebrated by the disciples of Jesus, since ancient philosophic schools conferred religious honors on their founder in regular observances (cf. R. A. Culpepper, *The Johannine School* [Missoula: Scholars Press, 1975], 101ff.).

196. Matthew 26:26-29/ Mark 14:22-25/ Luke 22:15-20

Jubilees 45:5 (145–40 BCE)

[Jacob's dying blessing on Joseph:] and Joseph and his brothers ate bread before their father, and they drank wine. And Jacob rejoiced very greatly because he saw Joseph eating and drinking with his brothers before him. And he blessed the Creator of all who kept him and kept for him his twelve sons. (*OTP* 2:136)

In *Jubilees* 36:17, after the testamentary speech of Isaac to Jacob and Esau, in which they were both exhorted to brotherly love, it is said, "And he finished commanding them and blessing them. And they ate and drank together before him. And he rejoiced because they were in mutual agreement" (*OTP* 2:124). In view of the fact that their father is dying, the common meal of those who remain behind is especially a realization of the unity to which they are repeatedly challenged in the testamentary literature (cf. Berger, *Formgeschichte*, §24). This was just as important among Joseph and his brothers as between Jacob and Esau. This aspect of the Lord's Supper is especially emphasized by Paul (1 Cor 10:16-17 and 11:17-34). In the Gospel of John as well, this motif plays an important role in the farewell discourses of Jesus, although there is no institution of the Lord's Supper, and the Synoptic Gospels call the reader to reflect on the contrast with the betrayal by Judas that stands in the background of the institution of the Lord's Supper.

On Mark 14:28, cf. no. 152.

197. Matthew 26:39/ Mark 14:36/ Luke 22:41-42

Arrian, *Discourses of Epictetus* Book 3.22.95 (55–135 CE)

[Describing the Cynic's conduct and perspective on life:] . . . and that every thought which he thinks is that of a friend and servant to the gods, of one who shares in the government of Zeus; and has always ready at hand the verse "Lead thou me on, O Zeus, and Destiny," and "If so it pleases the gods, so be it" . . . (LCL)

In Mark 14:32-42 par., Jesus is once again set forth before the chosen witnesses as the Son of God (cf. his address to God in v. 36). As a son, he yields to the will of the Father. In Epictetus, it is not sonship, but friendship with the gods, which leads to the same result. In Mark as in Epictetus the text is formulated as a prayer. The Marcan text is more readily understood from Greek presuppositions of the type illustrated here than from Psalm 40:8 (Torah obedience). Cf. also James 4:15.

198. Matthew 26:47–27:50/ Mark 14:43–15:37/ Luke 22:47–23:46/ John 18:2–19:30

Philostratus, *Life of Apollonius of Tyana* 7.14 (Apollonius, 1 cent. CE; Philostratus, 3 cent. CE)

[After Apollonius had become famous, the Emperor Domitian resolved to destroy him. Of his own accord, Apollonius allowed himself to be arrested and tried in Domitian's court. However, he confided to his disciples:] I myself know more than mere men do, for I know all things . . . and that I have not come to Rome on behalf of the foolish will become perfectly clear; for I myself am in no danger with respect to my own body nor will I be killed by this tyrant. (LCL)

The text from Philostratus illustrates the difficulty in relating the victimization and death of a "divine man." During his trial, Apollonius removes his shackles at will. After hearing Apollonius' defense, Domitian declares that he will not condemn him. But Apollonius considers this a ruse, and responds, "Give me my freedom, if you will, but if not, then send someone to imprison my body, for it is impossible to imprison my soul! Indeed, you will not even take my body, for [quoting Homer, *Iliad* 22:13], 'you cannot kill me since I am not a mortal man,' and, saying this, he vanished from the courtroom, suddenly appearing to his disciple Damis and a friend in another town" (7.5) (LCL). Philostratus proceeds to relate various conflicting accounts of the supposed "death" of Apollonius, attaching the most credence to those stories in which he enters the temple of one of the gods and then vanishes, amid the chorus of heavenly choirs singing "Come up from earth, come to heaven, come" (from M. Eugene Boring, *Truly Human/Truly Divine* [St. Louis: CBP Press, 1984], 20-21).

The Marcan story of the arrest, trial, and death of Jesus is in stark contrast to this, as Jesus suffers and dies a human death. In Matthew and Luke, minimal elements of the divinity of Jesus emerge in the story. In the Fourth Gospel, Jesus is more like a "divine man," and the human elements of victimization and suffering a real death, while still present, are minimized.

199. Matthew 26:57–27:14/ Mark 14:55–15:5/ Luke 22:55–23:5

Acts of the Pagan Martyrs, "Acta Appiani" 33 (2–3 cent. CE)

The emperor [then] recalled Appian. The emperor said: "Now you know whom you are speaking to, don't you?"

Appian: "Yes, I do: Appian speaks to a tyrant."

The emperor: "No, to an emperor."

Appian: "Say not so! Your father, the divine Antoninus, was fit to be emperor. For, look you, first of all he was a philosopher; secondly, he was not avaricious; thirdly, he was good. But you have precisely the opposite qualities: you are tyrannical, dishonest, crude!"

Caesar [then] ordered him to be led away to execution. As Appian was being taken, he said: "Grant me but one thing, my Lord Caesar."

The emperor: "What?"

Appian: "Grant that I may be executed in my noble insignia."

The emperor: "Granted."

Appian [then] took his fillet and put it on his head, and putting his white shoes on his feet, he cried out in the middle of Rome: "Come up, Romans, and see a unique spectacle, an Alexandrian gymnasiarch and ambassador led to execution!" (Musurillo)

In comparison with this text, Jesus is much more quiet (cf. no. 474), but as here he receives the insignia of the status he claims, even if only mockingly. The "Acts of the Alexandrian Martyrs" are papyri which recount the legal trials of Alexandrian aristocrats (gymnasiarchs) who resisted the Roman colonial administration on the basis of their political and ethical ideals and their indigenous patriotism. The speeches are strongly emphasized, especially their courage over against the emperor. Alongside this "dramatic protocol style" the Acts document the heroic disdain of death and present a caricature of the Roman administration. On the tradition of the aggressive words of the martyrs against tyrants, cf. Berger, in "Hellenistische Gattungen," 1251-55.

200. Matthew 26:57–27:14 / Mark 14:55–15:5 / Luke 22:55–23:5

Pseudo-Philo, *Liber Antiquitatum Biblicarum* 6:4-6 (1 cent. CE, probably pre-70)

[A group of twelve righteous men, among them Abraham and Lot, refuse to work on building the Tower of Babel:] And the people of that land laid hold of them and brought them to their chiefs and said, "These are the men who have gone against our plans and would not walk in our ways." And the leaders said to them, "Why were each of you not willing to cast in bricks along with the people of the land?" And those men answered saying, "We are not casting in bricks, nor are we joining in your scheme. We know the one Lord, and him we worship. Even if you throw us into the fire with your bricks, we will not join you." And the leaders were angered and said, "As they have spoken, so do to them. And unless they take part with us in throwing in the bricks, you will have the fire devour them along with your bricks."

And Joktan, who was chief of the leaders, answered,

"No, but let them be given a period of seven days, and if they repent of their evil plans and are willing to cast in bricks with you, they may live. If not, let it be done and let them be burned then in accord with your judgment." He, however, sought how he might save them from the hands of the people . . . (*OTP* 2:310-11)

The text reflects the pattern of anti-Jewish riots among the populace (e.g. as in Philo, *Flaccus* 20-96), which is then repeated in the Christian portrayals of Jewish opposition to Christians (e.g. Acts 17:6-8). The reproduced pattern, which includes the confession of faith and the threat of punishment, corresponds to the scheme of the martyr narratives (cf. 2 Macc, 4 Macc; on the genre cf. Berger, *Formgeschichte*, §97). On the accusation, cf. Wisdom 2:12. The role of Joktan is in part comparable to that of Pilate.

201. Matthew 26:57–27:14/ Mark 14:55–15:5/ Luke 22:55–23:5

"The Acts of SS. Justin and His Companions" (end of 2 cent. CE) (The event narrated took place 163–67 CE)

And so the aforementioned [Justin, Chariton, Charito, Evelpistus, Hierax, Paeon, and Liberian] were arraigned before the urban prefect at Rome, a man named Rusticus.

After they had been brought before his tribunal, the prefect Rusticus said to Justin: "First of all you must obey the gods and submit to the orders of the emperors."

Justin said: "There is no blame or condemnation in obeying the commands of our Savior Jesus Christ."

The prefect Rusticus said: "What are the doctrines that you practice?"

"I have tried to become acquainted," said Justin, "with all doctrines. But I have committed myself to the true doctrines of the Christians, even though they may not please those who hold false beliefs."

The prefect Rusticus said: "What belief do you mean?"

Justin said: "The belief that we piously hold regarding the God of the Christians, whom alone we believe to have been the maker and creator of the entire world from the beginning, both visible and invisible; also regarding the Lord Jesus Christ, the child of God, who was also foretold by the prophets as one who was to come down to mankind as a herald of salvation and a teacher of good doctrines."

The prefect Rusticus said to Evelpistus: "And what are you, Evelpistus?"

Evelpistus, one of the emperor's slaves, answered: "I too am a Christian. I have been freed by Christ and I share in the same hope by the favor of Christ."

The prefect turned to Justin: "You are said to be learned, and you think you know the true doctrine. Now listen: if you are scourged and beheaded, do you suppose that you will ascend to heaven?"

"I have confidence," said Justin, "that if I endure all this I shall possess his mansions. Indeed, I know that for all those who live a just life there awaits the divine gift even to the consummation of the whole world."

The prefect Rusticus said: "You think, then, that you will ascend to heaven to receive certain worthy rewards?"

"I do not think," said Justin, "but I have accurate knowledge and am fully assured of it."

"Well then," said the prefect Rusticus, "let us come to the point at issue, a necessary and pressing business. Agree together to offer sacrifice to the gods."

"No one of sound mind," said Justin, "turns from piety to impiety."

The prefect Rusticus said: "If you do not obey, you will be punished without mercy."

Justin said: "We are confident that if we suffer the penalty for the sake of our Lord Jesus Christ we shall be saved, for this is the confidence and salvation we shall have at the terrible tribunal of our Savior and Master sitting in judgment over the whole world."
(Musurillo)

The distinctive feature of the acts of the Christian martyrs over against the Jewish martyr narratives (cf. nos. 154, 204) from 2 and 4 Maccabees is that the trial proceedings are treated extensively, but the tortures and their endurance by the martyrs is hardly pictured. In this they agree with the pagan acts of the Alexandrian martyrs (no. 199), even if Pseudo-Philo (no. 200) also documents an extensive treatment of the trial in a first-century Jewish martyr narrative. As in Mark 14 par., the scenes prior to the execution represent the *place of confession.*

On the dispute about the true "knowledge," cf. the analogy in the apology of Socrates, no. 618. On Mark 14:56-59 par. (witnesses), cf. no. 763.

202. Matthew 26:61 / Mark 14:58

Josephus, *Antiquities* 10.89-92 (37–100 CE)

And this was what the prophet Jeremiah foretold day after day, how that it was vain for them to cling to their hope of help from the Egyptians and that the city was destined to be overthrown by the king of Babylonia, and King Joakeimos to be subdued by him. These things, however, he spoke to no avail, since there were none who were destined to be saved, for both the people and their rulers disregarded what they heard; and, being angered by his words, they accused Jeremiah of having as prophet used divination against the king, and, bringing him to trial, demanded that he be sentenced to punishment. And so all the others cast votes against him, thereby rejecting the advice of the elders, but these, being of wise understanding, released the prophet from the prison-hall and advised the others to do Jeremiah no harm. For, they said, he was not the only one to foretell what would befall the city, but Michaias before him had announced these things, as had many others . . . (LCL)

The theme is the tradition of "prophesying against the city," as already documented by the prophet Uriah (Jer 26:20-24; cf. the formulation of the death penalty, 26:11). The Hellenistic Jewish "Lives of the Prophets" reports of almost all prophets that they prophesied against Israel (also rejection of the cultus and changing the Law). In the *Ascension of Isaiah,* this prophesying is understood as powerfully effective prophetic speech (3:6, 7, 10; 5:1), because of which the prophet is accused (cf. on no. 952). The distinction made by Josephus between effective prophesying of doom and mere prediction of the future is also found in the Greek recension of the *Ascension of Isaiah* 3:11-12! That a corresponding saying of Jesus, analogous to Mark 14:58 and the parallels (including *Gos. Thom.* 71) could be formulated in the I-style is specifically documented by the text in no. 174 above. Cf. further no. 15, line 21.

On Mark 15:13ff. (the cross), cf. no. 763.

203. Matthew 27:3-10

Suetonius, *Lives of the Caesars,* "The Deified Julius" 1.89 (early 2 cent. CE)

Hardly any of his [Julius Caesar's] assassins survived him for more than three years, or died a natural death. They were all condemned, and they perished in various ways—some by shipwreck, some in battle; some took their own lives with the self-same dagger with which they had impiously slain Caesar. (LCL)

Cf. Plutarch, *Parallel Lives, Caesar* 69.3-5 (45–125 CE): "After he was defeated at Philippi, he [Cassius, one of Caesar's assassins] killed himself with the same dagger which he had used against Caesar" (LCL).

204. Matthew 27:26/ Mark 15:15

Plutarch, *Moralia*, "Whether Vice Is Sufficient to Cause Unhappiness?" §2 (45–125 CE)

. . . And this is the proof: many are silent under mutilation and endure scourging and being tortured by the wedge at the hands of masters or tyrants without uttering a cry, whenever by the application of reason the soul abates the pain and by main force, as it were, checks and represses it . . . (LCL)

This conception of the power of reason in suffering corresponds to the extensive portrayal in 4 Maccabees 6:1-27, representing the Hellenistic Jewish martyr literature. The martyrdom of Eleazar: Antiochus attempts to persuade Eleazar to eat pork. Eleazar's counterargument: "small" and "great" transgressions against the Law are equally serious. The old man is then tortured, bound, and flogged, and finally dies "for the sake of the Law." The conclusion in 6:31 reads: ". . . by his reason held his ground through the very tortures of death for the Law's sake" (*OTP* 2:552). Also the later Christian martyrdoms emphasize the ability to endure corporeal suffering (cf. already 1 Pet 2:23?). It is thus all the more noticeable that the reports of Jesus' passion are entirely free of this trait. Cf. nos. 206, 306.

205. Matthew 27:26/ Mark 15:15

Plato, *The Republic*, Book 2, 5 (428/27 BCE–349/48 BCE)

[On the fate of a just man who lives his life without the outward appearance of righteousness, which brings honor:] . . . that such being his disposition the just man will have to endure the lash, the rack, chains, the branding-iron in his eyes, and finally, after every extremity of suffering, he will be crucified, and so will learn his lesson that not to be but to seem just is what we ought to desire. (LCL)

In the history of interpretation, this section was later understood as a prophecy of Christ, and Plato was numbered among the prophets (e.g. Act Apollonii 40:42; Clement of Alexandria, *Stromata* V.14, 108.1-2; IV.7.52.1-2). Cf. E. Benz, *Der gekreuzigte Gerechte bei Plato, im Neuen Testament und in der Alten Kirche* (Mainz: Akademie der Wissenschaften und der Literatur, 1950). On Matthew 27:28-31/ Mark 15:17-20/ Luke 23:11/ John 19:2-3, see no. 473.

206. Matthew 27:33-54/ Mark 15:21-39/ Luke 23:33-48/ John 19:17-30

4 Maccabees 8:12-15; 9:10-25 (50–150 CE)

When he had said these things, he ordered the instruments of torture to be brought forward so as to persuade them out of fear to eat the defiling food. 13 When the guards had placed before them wheels and joint-dislocators, rack and hooks and catapults and caldrons, braziers and thumbscrews and iron claws and wedges and bellows, the tyrant resumed speaking: 14 "Be afraid, young fellows; whatever justice you revere will be merciful to you when you transgress under compulsion." 15 But when they had heard the inducements and saw the dreadful devices, not only were they not afraid, but they also opposed the tyrant with their own philosophy, and by their right reasoning nullified his tyranny. . . .

9:10 When they had said these things, the tyrant was not only indignant, as at those who are disobedient, but also infuriated, as at those who are ungrateful. 11 Then at his command the guards brought forward the eldest, and having torn off his tunic, they bound his hands and arms with thongs on each side. 12 When they had worn themselves out beating him with scourges, without accomplishing anything, they placed him upon the wheel.. 13 When the noble youth was stretched out around this, his limbs were dislocated, 14 and with every member disjointed he denounced the tyrant, saying, 15 "Most abominable tyrant, enemy of heavenly justice, savage of mind, you are mangling me in this manner, not because I am a murderer, or as one who acts impiously, but because I protect the divine law." 16 And when the guards said, "Agree to eat so that you may be released from the tortures," 17 he replied, "You abominable lackeys, your wheel is not so powerful as to strangle my reason. Cut my limbs, burn my flesh, and twist my joints; 18 through all these tortures I will convince you that children of the Hebrews alone are invincible where virtue is concerned." 19 While he was saying these things, they spread fire under him, and while fanning the flames they tightened the wheel further. 20 The wheel was completely smeared with blood, and the heap of coals was being quenched by the drippings of gore, and pieces of flesh were falling off the axles of the machine. 21 Although the ligaments joining his bones were already severed, the courageous youth, worthy of Abraham, did not groan, 22 but as though transformed by fire into immortality, he nobly endured the rackings. 23 "Imitate me, brothers," he said. "Do not leave your post in my struggle or renounce our courageous family ties. 24 Fight the sacred and noble battle for religion. Thereby the just Providence of our ancestors may become merciful to our nation and take vengeance on the accursed tyrant." 25 When he had said this, the saintly youth broke the thread of life. (NRSV)

The above text represents only a brief excerpt from a long and developed tradition (cf. 2 Macc 6:18–7:42; 4 Macc 6:1–18:24). Although the interpretation of Jesus' death in the New Testament has some points of contact with the tradition of the Maccabean martyrs (see no. 154 on Mark 10:45), the narrative of Jesus' death itself stands in contrast to the way in which the death of the Maccabean martyrs is described.

1) The New Testament does not indulge in sensationalistic detail. The intended effect of the narrative of Jesus' death is not to be produced by graphic description.

2) There are no speeches by Jesus. The Maccabean martyrs are described as "grouped about their mother as though a chorus" (2 Macc 8:4); i.e., it is their speeches that interpret the meaning of the event, as does the chorus in a Greek drama.

3) In the Gospels there is no contrast between "divine reason" and "emotions"; i.e., Jesus' death is interpreted in an entirely different framework from the Stoic understanding adopted by the authors of the Maccabean narratives.

4) There are no vengeful threats against the persecutors, either from Jesus, his disciples, or the narrator.

207. Matthew 27:33-54/ Mark 15:21-39/ Luke 23:33-48/ John 19:17-30

Josephus, *Jewish War* 2.119f. (37–100 CE)

The war with the Romans tried their [the Essenes'] souls through and through by every variety of test. Racked and twisted, burnt and broken, and made to pass through every instrument of torture, in order to induce them to blaspheme their lawgiver or to eat some forbidden thing, they refused to yield to either demand, nor ever once did they cringe to their persecutors or shed a tear. Smiling in their agonies and mildly deriding their tormentors, they cheerfully resigned their souls, confident that they would receive them back again. (LCL)

Josephus' admiring description of the Essenes' noble death as martyrs for the faith is in contrast to the Marcan description of Jesus' death, which presents no picture of Jesus' response to his sufferings except the cry of abandonment and the inarticulate scream as he died. He does not smilingly deride his executioners, does not die in confidence of the immortality of his soul, does not die as a noble martyr. Josephus' description of the Essenes stands directly in the tradition of the Maccabean martyrs (cf. 2 Macc 6:18–7:42 [1 cent. BCE]); Mark's description of Jesus' death does not. (See no. 206 on Mark 15:21-39.)

208. Matthew 27:35/ Mark 15:24/ Luke 23:33/ John 19:18

Cicero, *In Defense of Rabirius* 5.15-16 (106–43 BCE)

How grievous a thing it is to be disgraced by a public court; how grievous to suffer a fine, how grievous to suffer banishment; and yet in the midst of any such disaster some trace of liberty is left to us. Even if we are threatened with death, we may die free men. But the executioner, the veiling of the head, and the very word "cross" should be far removed not only from the person of a Roman citizen but from his thoughts, his eyes and his ear. For it is not only the actual occurrence of these things or the endurance of them, but liability to them, the expectation, nay, the mere mention of them, that is unworthy of a Roman citizen and a free man. Or shall it be said that while a kind master, by a single act of manumission, frees a slave from the fear of all these punishments, we are not to be freed from scourgings, from the executioner's hook, nor even from the dread of the cross . . . (LCL)

The text specifically documents not only the horrifying nature of death by crucifixion, but also the concomitant circumstances, and the dishonor in which slaves were still held.

209. Matthew 27:38-43 / Mark 15:27-32 / Luke 23:25-38

Ascension of Isaiah, Martyrdom of Isaiah 5:2-3 (1 cent. BCE–1 cent. CE)

And while Isaiah was being sawed in half, his accuser, Belkira, stood by, and all the false prophets stood by, laughing and [maliciously] joyful because of Isaiah. And Belkira, through Mekembekus, stood before Isaiah, laughing and deriding. And Belkira said to Isaiah, "Say, 'I have lied in everything I have spoken; the ways of Manasseh are good and right . . .'" (*OTP* 2:163)

Mockery while being killed is the final temptation that must be faced, intended to cause the apostasy of the martyr. This is also clear in 5:8, where Belkira says to Isaiah, "Say what I say to you, and I will turn their heart and make Manasseh, and the princes of Judah, and the people, and all Jerusalem worship you." It is no coincidence that this is reminiscent of Matthew 4:1-11 and Luke 4:1-13. So too, the Synoptic crucifixion stories present analogies to the temptation story, especially challenges such as Matthew 27:40, "If you are the Son of God . . ." are to be compared with Matthew 4:3, 6.

210. Matthew 27:43

Wisdom of Solomon 2:10-20 (150 BCE–50 CE)

[The wicked say:] Let us oppress the righteous poor man;
let us not spare the widow
or regard the gray hairs of the aged.
But let our might be our law of right,
for what is weak proves itself to be useless.
Let us lie in wait for the righteous man,
because he is inconvenient to us and opposes our actions;
he reproaches us for sins against the law,
and accuses us of sins against our training.
He professes to have knowledge of God,
and calls himself a child [παῖς] of the Lord.
He became to us a reproof of our thoughts;
the very sight of him is a burden to us,
because his manner of life is unlike that of others,
and his ways are strange.
We are considered by him as something base,
and he avoids our ways as unclean;
he calls the last end of the righteous happy,
and boasts that God is his father.
Let us see if his words are true,
and let us test what will happen at the end of his life;
for if the righteous man is God's child [υἱός], he will help him
and will deliver him from the hand of his adversaries.

Let us test him with insult and torture,
so that we may find out how gentle [ἐπιείκει] he is,
and make trial of his forbearance.
Let us condemn him to a shameful death,
for, according to what he says, he will be protected. (NRSV)

Wisdom's description of the suffering of the righteous man who called himself God's son had a profound effect on the development of the story of Jesus' passion and on New Testament Christology in general. It is cited here because Matthew seems to allude to it directly. The text shows that "son of God" need not be understood in a metaphysical sense.

211. Matthew 27:45-54/ Mark 15:33-39/ Luke 23:44-46

b. *Berakoth* 61b (2 cent. CE tradition; written much later)

They say that only a few days passed before they arrested and imprisoned R. Aqiba. They arrested and imprisoned Pappos b. Judah nearby. He said to him, "Pappos, who brought you here?"

He said to him, "Happy are you, Aqiba, because you were arrested on account of teachings of Torah. Woe is Pappos, who was arrested on account of nonsense."

The hour at which they brought R. Aqiba out to be put to death was the time for reciting the *Shema*. They were combing his flesh with iron combs while he was accepting upon himself [in the recitation of the *Shema*] the yoke of the Kingdom of Heaven.

His disciples said to him, "Our master, to such an extent?"

He said to them, "For my whole life I have been troubled about this verse, 'With all your soul' [meaning] even though he takes your soul. I wondered when I shall have the privilege of carrying out this commandment. Now that it has come to hand, should I not carry it out?"

He held on to the word, "One," until his soul expired [as he said the word] "one." An echo came forth and said, "Happy are you, Rabbi Aqiba, that your soul expired with the word 'one.'"

The serving angels said before the Holy One, blessed be he, "Is this Torah and that the reward? 'From them that die by your hand, O Lord' [Ps. 17:14] [ought to have been his lot]."

He said to them, "Their portion is in life [Ps. 17:14]."

An echo went forth and proclaimed, "Happy are you, R. Aqiba, for you are selected for the life of the world to come." (Neusner, *Talmud*)

As in the Gospels, a popular Jewish teacher is executed on charges of sedition. The narrator gives the reader a glimpse into the heavenly scene hidden from Akiba, his executioners, and his disciples: angels quote the Psalms (14:13-14) to God on behalf of the executed rabbi, but God defends himself by an interpretation of a later section of the same Psalm, revealing its hidden meaning.

In contrast to Jesus in the Marcan passion story, Akiba is composed and worshipful, is accompanied by his disciples, recites the Shema, and dies an exemplary death, which is confirmed by a heavenly voice. In Mark too, Jesus had affirmed the Shema as the greatest commandment (Mark 12:28-34), and a psalm is quoted. But in Mark, it is the Psalmist's cry of mingled trust and despair that is quoted by Jesus himself. This stark Marcan picture is adjusted in the other Gospels in the direction of the model represented by Akiba's death: his disciples remain by him. In Matthew there are eschatological signs that register God's affirmation of Jesus (Matt 27:51-54); in Luke the cry of dereliction is replaced by a psalm of trust (Luke 23:46 = Ps 31:5); in John his mother and disciples remain by him and are instructed by him from the cross (John 19:25-27).

212. Matthew 27:45-54/ Mark 15:33-39/ Luke 23:44-48

Plutarch, *Parallel Lives*, "Agis and Cleomenes" 39 (45–125 CE)

And a few days afterward those who were keeping watch upon the body of Cleomenes where it hung, saw a serpent of great size coiling itself about the head and hiding away the face so that no ravening bird of prey could light upon it. In consequence of this, the king was seized with superstitious fear, and thus gave the women occasion for various rites of purification, since they felt that a man had been taken off who was of a superior nature and beloved of the gods. And the Alexandrians actually worshiped him, coming frequently to the spot and addressing Cleomenes as a hero and a child of the gods; but at last the wiser men among them put a stop to this by explaining that, as putrefying oxen breed bees, and horses wasps, and as beetles are generated in asses which are in the like condition of decay, so human bodies, when the juices about the marrow collect together and coagulate, produce serpents. (LCL)

Cf. *Lives of the Caesars*, 1.88-89 ("The Deified Julius"), "He died in the fifty-sixth year of his age, and was numbered among the gods, not only by a formal decree, but also in the conviction of the common people. For at the first of the games which his heir Augustus gave in honor of his apotheosis, a comet shone for seven successive days, rising about the eleventh hour, and was believed to be the soul of Caesar, who had been taken to heaven; and this is why a star is set upon the crown of his head in his statue" (LCL).

Cf. Plutarch, *Lives*, "Caesar," 69.3-5, "Among the events of man's ordering, the most amazing was that which befell Cassius; for after his defeat at Philippi he slew himself with that very dagger which he had used against Caesar; and among the events of divine ordering, there was the great comet, which showed itself in great splendor for seven nights after Caesar's murder, and then disappeared; also, the obscuration of the sun's rays. For during all that year its orb rose pale and without radiance, while the heat that came down from it was slight and ineffectual, so that the air in its circulation was dark and heavy owing to the feebleness of the warmth that penetrated it, and the fruits, imperfect and half ripe, withered away and shriveled up on account of the coldness of the atmosphere" (LCL).

As in Mark 15, extraordinary events after the death of the hero are the occasion for his being worshiped as a child of the gods/Son of God. To "child of the gods" corresponds "Son of God": the occurrences are the occasion for witnesses to postulate a theological interpretation of the essential nature of the one who has died. In contrast to Mark, Plutarch adds a "natural, scientific" explanation that frees the author from the suspicion of sharing the superstition himself.

213. Matthew 27:45-54/ Mark 15:33-39/ Luke 23:44-48

Diogenes Laertius, *Lives of Eminent Philosophers*, "Carneades" 4.64 (3 cent. CE)

[Concerning Carneades, a philosopher of the "Middle Academy," and his death] At the time he died the moon is said to have been eclipsed, and one might well say that the brightest luminary in heaven next to the sun thereby gave token of her sympathy. (LCL)

Similarly Virgil, *Georgica* 1.463-68, on the death of Caesar (the sun hid its face in distress, and so terrified the peoples). In Plutarch, *Parallel Lives*, "Pelopidas" 31, the darkness of the sun is a portent that brings bad luck: Pelopidas will die in the battle that begins on this day. The darkness is specifically labeled a "sign from heaven" (Gk. σημεῖον, *semeion*, as in Mark 8:11!). Luke specifically interprets the darkness as an eclipse. Cf. Dionysius of Halicarnassus, *Roman Antiquities* 2.56.6, and no. 349 below.

214. Matthew 27:48/ Mark 15:36/ Luke 23:36

b. Ta'anit 21a

Why was he called Nahum of Gamzu?—Because whatever befell him he would declare, This also is for the best גם זו לטבה [Gam zu letobah]. Once the Jews desired to send to the Emperor a gift and after discussing who should go they decided that Nahum of Gamzu should go because he had experienced many miracles. They sent with him a bag full of precious stones and pearls. He went and spent the night in a certain inn and during the night the people in the inn arose and emptied the bag and filled it up with earth. When he discovered this next morning he exclaimed, This also is for the best. When he arrived at his destination and they undid his bag they found that it was full of earth. The king thereupon desired to put them all to death saying, The Jews are mocking me. Nahum then exclaimed, This also is for the best. Whereupon Elijah appeared in the guise of one of them and remarked, Perhaps this is some of the earth of their father Abraham, for when he threw earth [against the enemy] it turned into swords and when [he threw] stubble it changed into arrows, for it is written, His sword maketh them as dust, his bow as the driven stubble. Now there was one province which [the emperor had hitherto] not been able to conquer but when they tried some of this earth [against it] they were able to conquer it. Then they took him [Nahum] to the royal treasury and filled his bag with precious stones and pearls and sent him back with great honor. When on his return journey he again spent the night in the same inn he was asked, What did you take [to the king] that they showed you such great honor? He replied, I brought thither what I had taken from here. [The innkeepers] thereupon razed the inn to the ground and took of the earth to the king and they said to him, The earth that was brought to you belonged to us. They tested it and it was not found to be [effective] and the innkeepers were thereupon put to death. (Soncino)

A righteous Jew, threatened with execution by the Roman government, is indeed saved by the appearance of Elijah.

215. Matthew 28:1-8/ Mark 16:1-8/ Luke 24:1-12

Diodorus of Sicily, *Library of History* 4.38.3-5 (1 cent. BCE)

The god gave the reply that Heracles should be taken, and with him his armor and weapons of war, unto Oetê and that they should build a huge pyre near him; what remained to be done, he said, would rest with Zeus. Now when Iolaüs had carried out these orders and had withdrawn to a distance to see what would take place, Heracles, having abandoned hope for himself, ascended the pyre and asked each one who came up to him to put torch to the pyre. And when no one had the courage to obey him Philoctetes alone was prevailed upon; and he, having received in return for his compliance the gift of the bow and arrows of Heracles, lighted the pyre. And immediately lightning also fell from the heavens and the pyre was wholly consumed. After this, when the companions of Iolaüs came to gather up the bones of Heracles and found not a single bone anywhere, they assumed that, in accordance with the words of the oracle, he had passed from among men into the company of the gods. (LCL)

The taking up of Hercules into heaven represents a theme of Greek mythology since the sixth century BCE (going to heaven; traveling through the air; transport by means of a cloud; being mixed with the ether; flying to the gods). Cf. also no. 485. But Diodorus is the first to bring the motif of the vain search for the corpse into this context. Since the first century BCE the Hercules tradition had been transferred to Romulus, of whom it was related that he ascended to heaven with horses and carriage (Ovid, *Fasti* 2.475-510), that at his ascension his earthly body was pulverized and received a divine form (Ovid, *Metamorphoses* 14:805-51), or that he "suddenly disappeared" (*De viris illustr* 2.13). Plutarch, *Parallel Lives*, "Life of Numa" 11:2 reports (similarly as Diodorus about Hercules): "Suddenly there was a great commotion in the air, and a cloud descended upon the earth bringing with it blasts of wind and rain. The throng of common folk were terrified and fled in all directions, but Romulus disappeared, and was never found again either alive or dead" (LCL). Speculations then arose about his having been murdered by the patricians, but the view prevailed that "Romulus did not die," and he was accorded divine honors. (On the confirmatory reports of visions, see no. 217.) The text from Diodorus also illustrates the difficulty of picturing the departure of a divine or divinized being as a truly human death. On "death and resurrection" of gods, see no. 447.

216. Matthew 28:1-8/ Mark 16:1-8/ Luke 24:1-12

Testament of Job 39:8–40:4 (Hellenistic Jewish) (1 cent. BCE or CE)

[Satan had demolished the house of Job's children while they were in it; Sitis, Job's wife, cries before him and his friends; Job speaks:] But she began to beg them, saying, "I plead with you, order your soldiers to dig through the ruins of the house that fell on my children so that at least their bones might be preserved as a memorial since we cannot because of the expense. Let us see them, even if it is only their bones. Have I the womb of cattle or of a wild animal that my ten children have died and I have not arranged the burial of a single one of them?"

And they left to dig, but I forbade it, saying, "Do not trouble yourselves in vain. For you will not find my children, since they were taken up into heaven by the Creator their King."

Then again they answered me and said, "Who then will not say you are demented and mad when you say, 'My children have been taken up into heaven!' Tell us the truth now!"

40 And I replied to them and said, "Lift me up so I can stand erect." And they lifted me up, supporting my arms on each side. And then when I had stood up, I sang praises to the Father. And after the prayer I said to them, "Look up with your eyes to the east and see my children crowned with the splendor of the heavenly one."

And when she saw that, Sitis my wife fell to the ground worshiping and said, "Now I know that I have a memorial with the Lord." (*OTP* 1:859-60)

In the Old Testament–Jewish tradition too, the motif is found of the failure to find the corpse despite searching as evidence of having been taken to heaven, as in the case of Elijah. In 2 Kings 2:16-17, Elisha plays the role of Job in the above text: he knows of the whereabouts of Elijah, and advises against the search. In Genesis 5:24 LXX it is said of Enoch "and he was not found" (MT: "and he was not"). In view of the post-Marcan Gospels it is worthy of note that in the *Testament of Job* the failure to find the corpse and the vision of those who had been taken to heaven are integrated within one story (in Mark this is done only by suggestion). The *Testament of Job* testifies to the vitality and dispersion of this tradition in New Testament times.

217. Matthew 28:1-20/ Mark 16:1-20/ Luke 24:1-53/ John 20:1-23

Livy, *History of Rome* 1.16.2-8 (59 BCE–17 CE)

And the shrewd device of one man is also said to have gained new credit for the story. This was Proculus Julius, who, when the people were distracted with the loss of their king and in no friendly mood toward the senate, being, as tradition tells, weighty in council, were the matter never so important, addressed the assembly as follows: "Quirites, the Father of this City, Romulus, descended suddenly from the sky at dawn this morning and appeared to me. Covered with confusion, I stood reverently before him, praying that it might be vouchsafed me to look upon his face without sin. 'Go,' said he, 'and declare to the Romans the will of Heaven that my Rome shall be the capital of the world; so let them cherish the art of war, and let them know and teach their children that no human strength can resist Roman arms.' So saying, he concluded, 'Romulus departed on high.'" (LCL)

Ovid, *Fasti* 2:500-509 reports similarly (with the addition of a description of the appearance: Romulus is clothed with the royal mantle, and commands that he be honored as a god under the name of Quirinus). In Ovid's *Metamorphoses,* in contrast, Hersilie, the wife of Romulus, when she asks to behold the splendor of her husband in heaven, is immediately snatched away by a star and likewise transformed into a goddess.

218. Matthew 28:1-20/ Mark 16:1-20/ Luke 24:1-53/ John 20:1-23

Plutarch, *Parallel Lives,* "Life of Romulus" 28 (45–125 CE)

At this pass, then, it is said that one of the patricians, a man of noblest birth, and of the most reputable character, a trusted and intimate friend also of Romulus himself, and one of the colonists from Alba, Julius Proculus by name, went into the forum and solemnly swore by the most sacred emblems before all the people that, as he was traveling on the road, he had seen Romulus coming to meet him, fair and stately to the eye as never before, and arrayed in bright and shining armor. He himself, then, affrighted at the sight, had said: "O King, what possessed thee, or what purpose hadst thou, that thou hast left us patricians a prey to unjust and wicked accusations, and the whole city sorrowing without end at the loss of its father?" Whereupon Romulus had replied: "It was the pleasure of the gods, O Proculus, from whom I came, that I should be with mankind only a short time, and that after founding a city destined to be the greatest on earth for empire and glory, I should dwell again in heaven. So farewell, and tell the Romans that if they practice self-restraint, and add to it valor, they will reach the utmost heights of human power. And I will be your propitious deity, Quirinus." These things seemed to the Romans worthy of belief, from the character of the man who related them, and from the oath which he had taken; moreover, some influence from heaven also, akin to inspiration, laid hold upon their emotions . . . (LCL)

The following points are important for comparison with the Gospels: (1) The credibility of the witnesses is enhanced by pointing out that they had been friends with the exalted one during his earthly life. (2) The earthly cultic community is filled with enthusiasm and inspiration, and in this way participates in the life of the exalted one (cf. Acts 1–2), which also has similarities with Old Testament stories (2 Kgs 2:9-10). (3) The ascension of Romulus to heaven corresponds to his origin from there (cf. John 3:13); cf. nos. 22, 70, 391. The transcendent one who appears gives assurance of his continuing presence and help (cf. Matt 28:20), and promises future blessing on the condition that the group remain faithful to the essence of its moral values (cf. Mark 16:16-17).

While in the illustrations given so far Romulus appears from heaven, in a different group of reports he is seen during his ascent to heaven, i.e. the witnesses were themselves present at the time of the ascension. This double aspect pertains also to the New Testament reports; witnesses of the ascension itself: Luke 24:51-52; John 20:17; *Gos. Pet.* 10:38-40 (cf. also nos. 224, 485). The following may also be mentioned:

219. Matthew 28:1-20/ Mark 16:1-20/ Luke 24:1-53/ John 20:1-23

Plutarch, *Parallel Lives*, "Life of Numa" 11.3 (45–125 CE)

And Proculus, a man of eminence, took oath that he had seen Romulus ascending to heaven in full armor, and had heard his voice commanding that he be called Quirinus. (LCL)

Similarly in Justin's *First Apology* 21, on the apotheosis of the emperors: "We propound nothing different from what you believe regarding those whom you esteem sons of Jupiter. . . . And what of the emperors who die among yourselves, whom you deem worthy of deification, and in whose behalf you produce some one who swears he has seen the burning Caesar rise to heaven from the funeral pyre?" (ANF). In Dionysius of Halicarnassus (taught 30–38 CE in Rome), *Roman Antiquities* 2.63.2–2.64.1, on the same tradition: "A certain man, named Julius who was a husbandman and of such a blameless life that he would never have told an untruth for his private advantage, arrived in the Forum and said that, as he was coming in from the country, he saw Romulus departing from the city fully armed and that, as he drew near to him, he heard him say these words: 'Julius, announce to the Romans from me, that the genius to whom I was allotted at my birth is conducting me to the gods, now that I have finished my mortal life, and that I am Quirinus'" (LCL). The New Testament itself knows of spectators to the event of ascensions to heaven in Revelation 11:12 (of the two resurrected witnesses) and of Jesus in Luke 24:50-52; Acts 1:9-11, as well as in John 20:14-18 (cf. v. 17).

On the theological significance of the texts in nos. 215-19: (1) Being taken to heaven, including the later vain quest for the corpse, is common Near East tradition concerning human beings of extraordinary importance or semidivine beings. (2) The connection between ascensions and later appearances from heaven is documented for prophets—even though there is considerable time between the events (Elijah, Jeremiah)—in direct line with the Romulus tradition. (3) In view of the contemporary popularity of the Romulus tradition, one can well imagine that the evangelists, especially Luke, portray the Easter events precisely as they do, in order to present the one who during his lifetime had proclaimed the coming kingdom of God as one whose destiny also showed him to be a qualified ruler himself, and that as a clear alternative to the current emperor mythology. This Jesus, not Hercules or Romulus, is the true ruler ($\beta\alpha\sigma\iota\lambda\epsilon\acute{\iota}\alpha$, kingdom, is also translated "empire"; $\beta\alpha\sigma\iota\lambda\epsilon\acute{\upsilon}\varsigma$, king, is also translated ("emperor"). Parallel with this, one can note the political significance of the Antichrist in the confrontation with his killed and raised adversary according to Revelation 11:7-12 and 13:12. (E. Bickermann, "Die römische Kaiserapotheose," *Archiv für Religionswissenschaft* 27 [1929] 1-34).

Cf. also the report from Herodotus (5 cent. BCE), *History* 4.14-15: "It is said that this Aristeas, who was as nobly born as any of his townsmen, went into a fuller's shop at Proconnesus and there died; the fuller shut his workshop and went away to tell the dead man's kinsfolk, and the report of Aristeas' death being now spread about in the city, it was disputed by a man of Cyzicus, who had come from the town of Artace, and said that he had met Aristeas going toward Cyzicus and spoken with him. While he vehemently disputed, the kinsfolk of the dead man had come to the fuller's shop with all that was needful for burial; but when the house was opened there was no Aristeas there, dead or alive. But in the seventh year after that Aristeas appeared at Proconnesus and made that poem which the Greeks now call the Arimaspeia, after which he vanished once again.

"Such is the tale told in these two towns. But this, I know, befell the Metapontines in Italy, two hundred and forty years after the second disappearance of Aristeas, as reckoning made at Proconnesus and Metapontium shows me: Aristeas, so the Metapontines say, appeared in their country and bade them set up an altar to Apollo and a statue for himself" (LCL). As in the Romulus tradition, cultic directives play an important role.

220. Matthew 28:1-20/ Mark 16:1-20/ Luke 24:1-53/ John 20:1-23

Chariton of Aphrodisias, *Chaereas and Callirhoe* 3, 3.1-7 (1–2 cent. CE)

[Chaereas, soon after his marriage with Callirhoe, in a fit of jealousy kicks her so severely that she is taken for dead and is buried. Grave robbers find her alive and take her to Miletus:] At the crack of dawn Chaereas turned up at the tomb, ostensibly to offer wreaths and libations, but in fact with the intention of doing away with himself; he could not bear being separated from Callirhoe and thought that death was the only thing that would cure his grief. When he reached the tomb, he found that the stones had been moved and the entrance was open. He was astonished at the sight and overcome by fearful perplexity at what had happened. Rumor—a swift messenger—told the Syracusans this amazing news. They all quickly crowded round the tomb, but no one dared go inside until Hermocrates gave an order to do so. The man who was sent in reported the whole situation accurately.

It seemed incredible that even the corpse was not lying there. Then Chaereas himself determined to go in, in his desire to see Callirhoe again even dead; but though he hunted through the tomb, he could find nothing. Many people could not believe it and went in after him. They were all seized by helplessness. One of those standing there said, "The funeral offerings have been carried off—it is tomb robbers who have done that; but what about the corpse—where is it?" Many different suggestions circulated in the crowd. Chaereas looked toward the heavens, stretched up his arms, and cried: "Which of the gods is it, then, who has become my rival in love and carried off Callirhoe and is now keeping her with him—against her will, constrained by a more powerful destiny? That is why she died suddenly—so that she would not realize what was happening. That is how Dionysus took Ariadne from Theseus, how Zeus took Semele. It looks as if I had a goddess for a wife without knowing it, someone above my station. But she should not have left the world so quickly, even for such a reason. Thetis was a goddess, but she stayed with Peleus, and he had a son by her; I have been abandoned at the very height of my love." (Reardon)

Chariton is the earliest extant Greek novelist. Important for the comparison with Mark 16 par. are the following points: (1) The scene of the procession to the grave and the discovery of the empty tomb. (2) As in all comparable reports, the corpse was "not found." (3) For the lover, the empty tomb was the occasion to think that the dead person had been taken to heaven by the gods, and to think of the one taken as a divine being. To this it corresponds that, according to Luke 24:52, the disciples fell before Jesus in worship on the occasion of his ascension. (4) The empty tomb itself is a datum that can be interpreted several different ways; neither in the New Testament nor in Chariton is it sufficient of itself. The text of Chariton thus has a critical tendency toward religion: the line between loving adoration and acceptance of the loved one's divine status is perhaps too thin.

221. Matthew 28:1-20/ Mark 16:1-20/ Luke 24:1-53/ John 20:1-23

Onassanius, memorial inscription to his nephew M. Lucceius (Augustine period 63 BCE–14 CE)

It happened, as I lamented my nephew, taken from me by premature death, and bemoaned the fragile threads of fate, that fresh pain tortured me within, as I mourned that I had been robbed, abandoned, and left alone, that I wept tears that could wash away mountains. And then, as night was almost gone and the day [morning star] shone forth its fire and the moist dew arrived on its flying horse, that I saw a figure gliding down from heaven, radiant with light like that of the stars. The youth had not the stiffness of death, but living color and voice, but the figure itself was larger than the familiar appearance of his body. He appeared fiery in the eyes and radiant on the shoulders, and from his rose-red mouth spoke the words: "Honored uncle, why are you weeping that I have been taken to be among the stars of heaven? Stop your crying, for I have indeed now become a god [desine flere deum]. Piety must not, from uncertainty, mourn for the one who has been taken up to his heavenly home, and unhappiness must not offend against the divine beings. I will not come to the river Tartarus full of sadness, will not be as a shade transported on the floods of Acheron, I will not come floating on that dark ship with its oars, nor will I fear you,

Charon, with your face of terror, nor will Minos, that ancient of days, swear an oath to me. I will not haunt dark or watery places. Rather: Stand up! Report to my mother, she must not cry for me night and day, as the mourning mother of Attica [Prokne] cried for Itys. For the holy Venus did not let me learn the places of the silent ones [the dead], but brought me into the bright halls of heaven."

I straightened myself up, for terror had penetrated my being, so that my limbs were as rigid as ice. Meanwhile, the whole place had been bathed in a pleasant, sweet scent. I said, "Divine Nephew, whether you are enjoying the games of Adonis, happily surrounded by a host of lovers, or are joyfully whiling away the time in the company of the Muses, or delighting in the art of Athena—the whole choir of heaven receives you. If you want to decorate the thyrsus [Bacchus staff] with ivy and clusters of blossoms and cover your hair with wreaths, then you will be Liber [the Italian god of fertility and wine, often identified with Bacchus/Dionysus]. If you want to let your hair grow and braid it with laurel, and take a bow and quiver of arrows, then you will be Apollo. Do you want to wear round sleeves and the fur cap of the Phrygians? Then there will no longer be just one Atys who will live through the breast of Cybele. If you want to press your iron spurs into the flanks of a lathery horse, then like Mercury you will have the figure of a well-formed rider. But after whichever heroes or gods you are named—sister and mother and son want to be kept safe and sound. These gifts are more important than anointings and garlands, since greedy time cannot rob them from us . . ." (Latin text in *CIL* VI.3, p. 2244 Nr. 21 521 MEB/Berger)

This remarkable inscription, here for the first time translated into English, has a number of important points of contact with the Easter (and other Jewish and Christian) vision reports. (1) The vision is in the early morning. (2) The appearance resembles an angelophany, and light as Acts 9:3 (cf. Matt 28:3). (3) The first-person I-style of the vision ("I saw . . ."). (4) Describing the lifelike identity ("It is really he"). (5) Motif of "no more crying" (John 20:13). (6) The exalted one communicates that he has ascended to heaven (John 20:7). (7) Charge to tell relatives as Matthew 28:10. (8) Terror as reaction, as Matthew 28:4; Luke 24:36. (9) Especially worthy of note is the affinity of "the whole choir of heaven receives you" with the statement in 4 Maccabees 18:23 ". . . gathered together in the choir of their fathers"; cf. Luke 16:9*b*. On the variability of the form of the Heavenly One, cf. especially Mark 16:12, no. 749.

222. Matthew 28:1-20/ Mark 16:1-20/ Luke 24:1-53/ John 20:1-23

Cicero, *The Republic* 6, 10 (106–43 BCE)

[Vision of Publius Cornelius Scipio Africanus:] I thought that Africanus stood before me, taking that shape which was familiar to me from his bust rather than from his person. Upon recognizing him I shuddered in terror, but he said: "Courage, Scipio, have no fear, but imprint my words upon your memory." (LCL)

This vision of the deceased ancestor is probably stylized in a literary manner and accommodates itself to the usual elements of the visionary tradition: description of the figure; fear as the reaction; encouraging response from the figure; charge to preserve what is transmitted. Cf. from the New Testament Easter stories: Luke 24:37-38; Matthew 28:3, 10 (the figure); Matthew 28:4-5 (terror and command not to fear); Luke 24:48 (witness by preserving and proclaiming). The more extensive post-Easter instructions hinted at in Acts 1:3 are then developed in the apocryphal Gospels. Here there is greater similarity to the Dream of Scipio.

On the theme "resurrection" cf. also no. 447.

223. Matthew 28:13

Claudius' Ordinance, from an inscription near Nazareth (ca. 50 CE)

Ordinance of Caesar. It is my pleasure that graves and tombs remain undisturbed in perpetuity for those who have made them for the cult of their ancestors or children or members of their house. If however any man presents information that another has either demolished them, or has in any other way extracted the buried, or has maliciously transferred them to other places in order to wrong them, or has displaced the sealing or other stones, against such a one I order that a trial be instituted, as in respect of the gods, so in regard to the cult of mortals. For it shall be much more obligatory to honor the buried. Let it be absolutely forbidden for any one to disturb them. In case of contravention I desire that the offender be sentenced to capital punishment on charge of violation of sepulture. (Zulueta)

The text has points of contact with the burial stories of Jesus, especially Matthew's report of the story that the body of Jesus was stolen by the disciples. But there seems to be no direct connection with the Gospels, even though the inscription was discovered near Nazareth.

224. Matthew 28:16-20

Plutarch, *Parallel Lives*, "Life of Theseus" 35.5 (45–125 CE)

In after times, however, the Athenians were moved to honor Theseus as a demigod, especially by the fact that many of those who fought at Marathon against the Medes thought they saw an apparition of Theseus in arms rushing on in front of them against the Barbarians. (LCL)

The scope of this brief notice: The life and work of Theseus continues after his death,* and, be it noted, in situations of distress where his help appears. According to Matthew 28, Jesus' work continues, expressed in terms of his own continuing presence. Similarly in Plutarch, "Greek Customs," §40: The hero/demigod Eunostos is seen after his death as he comes to the sea to take a purifying bath after a woman had trespassed into his sanctuary reserved only for men. Different from the New Testament Easter stories, the apparitions do not speak, nor is there any interest in clarifying the nature and reality of their continued existence beyond death.

*"Die Sache des Theseus geht weiter," literally "the Theseus-thing goes further," a reflection (and something of a parody) of a mottolike way of talking about Jesus' resurrection popularized by Willi Marxsen, "Die Sache Jesu geht weiter," which could be translated "The Jesus-thing continues to happen," i.e. did not cease with his death. See Willi Marxsen, *The Resurrection of Jesus of Nazareth* (Philadelphia: Fortress Press, 1970).

The Gospel of Mark
(and Parallels)

225. Mark 1:1

Inscription from Priene (9 BCE)

Since the Providence which has ordered all things and is deeply interested in our life has set in most perfect order by giving us Augustus, whom she filled with virtue [divine power] that he might benefit mankind, sending him as a savior [σωτήρ], both for us and for our descendants, that he might end war and arrange all things, and since he, Caesar, by his appearance [ἐπιφανεῖν, "epiphany," often used of Hellenistic rulers] [excelled even our anticipations], surpassing all previous benefactors, and not even leaving to posterity any hope of surpassing what he has done, and since the birthday of the god Augustus was the beginning for the world of the good tidings [εὐαγγελίων] that came by reason of him. (Nock, *Early Gentile Christianity*)

In older Greek the original connotation of the prefix "ευ-" "good" had been lost, so that in Hellenistic times εὐαγγέλιον had come to mean "news," "announcement," of whatever sort. Likewise the Hebrew equivalent בשרה *besorah* can be used for all sorts of messages, including bad ones (1 Sam 4:17 for the *defeat* of Israel). Thus the Old Testament alone cannot provide the background for the use of εὐαγγέλιον in the New Testament (though such passages as Isaiah 61:1 are certainly an important factor). Helmut Koester has recently pointed out that inscriptions such as the one above (of which many are extant) "result from the religio-political propaganda of Augustus in which the rule of peace, initiated by Augustus' victories and benefactions, is celebrated and proclaimed as the beginning of a new age. *This* usage of the term εὐαγγέλιον is new in the Greco-Roman world. It elevates this term and equips it with a particular dignity. Since the Christian usage of the term for its saving message begins only a few decades after the time of Augustus, it is most likely that the early Christian missionaries were influenced by the imperial propaganda in their employment of the word. Also the Christian usage is eschatological, as the missionaries proclaim the beginning of a new age and call this proclamation their 'gospel'" (*Ancient Christian Gospels: Their History and Development* [Philadelphia: Trinity Press International, 1990], 4). This background also lends an unmistakable political tone to the term.

226. Mark 1:1

Lucretius, *On the Nature of the Universe* 5.1 (94–55 BCE)

Who has such power within his breast
That he could build up a song
Worthy of this high theme and these discoveries?

No one, I believe, whose body is of mortal growth.
If I am to suit my language to the majesty

Of his revelations—he was a god,
A god indeed who first discovered
That rule of life that now is called *philosophy;*

. . . whose gospel [εὐαγγέλιον],
Broadcast through the length and breadth of empires,
Is even now bringing soothing solace
To the minds of men. (Lathan)

Cf. the Priene inscription, no. 225. This lyrical tribute from Lucretius to his revered teacher shows that divine language could be used not only of emperors, but of teachers who founded communities, as well as illustrating that in the Hellenistic world the boundary between "divine" and "human" was not as sharp as in the Jewish and Christian traditions. As in the Priene inscription, the connection between "God" and "gospel" is a striking point of contact with Mark 1:1.

227. Mark 1:1

Lucian, "Icaromenippus" or "The Sky Man" 34 (120–185 CE)

[Conclusion of the document, after the eyewitness report of the heavenly tour:] You have heard it all, my friend, all the news from Heaven. Now I am going off to carry the glad tidings [εὐαγγελιούμενους] to the philosophers who pace about in the Porch. (LCL)

If one understands Mark 1:1 as "the gospel *about* Jesus Christ," then the term "gospel" can be clarified with the help of the verb used in this passage from Lucian. The verb has clear analogies to the aretalogical function of the "gospel" in Mark (i.e. proclaiming the demonstrations of mighty power) (cf. Berger, *Formgeschichte*, §69).

The proclamation of the series of heavenly events as a whole (primarily the speeches and appearances of gods) is described comprehensively with the word εὐαγγελιούμενος. Similarly, in the sense of an individual message of a particular saving deed: Lucian, "Lover of Lies," §31. Philostratus (beginning of the 3 cent. CE) uses the same verb in a similar context in *Life of Apollonius of Tyana* 1.28 (after the arrival of Apollonius men ran into the palace and told everybody the good news [εὐαγγελιζόμενοι] of the arrival of a wise man sent by one of the gods).

228. Mark 1:13

Testaments of the Twelve Patriarchs, " Testament of Naphtali " 8:4, 6 (2 cent. BCE–2 cent. CE)

If you achieve the good, my children,
men and angels will bless you;
and God will be glorified through you among the gentiles.
The devil will flee from you;
wild animals will be afraid of you,

and the angels will stand by you.
The one who does not do good,
men and angels will curse,
and God will be dishonored among the gentiles because of him;
the devil will inhabit him as his own instrument.
Every wild animal will dominate him,
and the Lord will hate him. (*OTP* 1:813-14)

The same characters appear in both texts (angels, animals, devil, God), and they have the same attitude and conduct toward human beings, including the positive relation in the case of Jesus. There is a difference in literary form: on the one hand, we have a conditional admonitory speech [Cf. Berger, *Formgeschichte*, §51, 2.7], and on the other, a narrative picturing Jesus as God's Chosen One. Righteousness thought of primarily in moral terms may be compared with holiness conferred as a charismatic gift. Additional texts dealing with the relationship between animals and righteous persons: *2 Baruch* 73:6 (in the time of salvation, animals will serve human beings); *b. Sanh.* 59b. reports concerning the ministry of the angels in Paradise: "R. Judah b. Tema would say, 'The first man reclined in the Garden of Eden, and the ministering angels roasted meat for him and strained wine for him. The snake looked in and saw all of this glory [that was coming to Adam] and envied him'" (Neusner, *Talmud*). It cannot be proved, however, that Mark intends to portray Jesus as the "second Adam." The point is a more general one concerning the preferential treatment of the righteous one. An additional example: in Philostratus' *Life of Apollonius* 6.24, none of the wild animals attack Apollonius and his companions. Cf. also no. 188.

229. Mark 1:14-45

Empedocles, "Purifications," fragment 112 (483/82–423 BCE)

But I go about [among] you as an immortal God, no longer as a mortal, honored by all. . . . When I come to them [?] into the busy towns, to men and women, I am honored by them; however they follow after me [ἕπονται], in their thousands, to learn where the path [leads] to gain, some requiring sayings from the oracle [μαντοσυνέων], others seeking to experience a word that brings healing in their manifold sickness, having already long been riddled with severe pain. (Hengel, *Charismatic Leader*)

The connection between discipleship, religious teaching, and healing activity in this I-saying corresponds form-critically to the evangelist's so-called summaries (*Basisberichten*, "foundational reports," cf. Berger, *Formgeschichte*, §96) of Jesus' activities. The analogies to Pythagoras cannot be overlooked. In the first century CE this type of philosopher-healer is represented by Apollonius of Tyana.

230. Mark 1:21-28/ Luke 4:33-37

Lucian, *The Lover of Lies, or the Doubter* 16 (120–185 CE)

"You act ridiculously," said Ion, "to doubt everything. For my part, I should like to ask you what you say to those who free possessed men from their terrors by exorcising the spirits so manifestly. I need not discuss this: everyone knows about the Syrian from Palestine, the adept in it, how many he takes in hand who fall down in the light of the moon and roll their eyes and fill their mouths with foam; nevertheless, he restores them to health and sends them away normal in mind, delivering them from their straits for a large fee. When he stands beside them as they lie there and asks: 'Whence came you into his body?' the patient himself is silent, but the spirit answers in Greek or in the language of whatever foreign country he comes from, telling how and whence he entered into the man; whereupon, by adjuring the spirit and if he does not obey, threatening him, he drives him out. Indeed, I actually saw one coming out, black and smoky in color." "It is nothing much," I remarked, "for you, Ion, to see that kind of sight, when even the 'forms' [i.e. the 'ideas'] that the father of your school, Plato, points out are plain to you, a hazy object of vision to the rest of us, whose eyes are weak." (LCL)

Additional examples for the dialogue between exorcist and demon are not numerous. Philostratus, *Life of Apollonius* 3.38: "The demon had threatened her with steep places and precipices and declared that he would kill her son"; cf. also 4.20 at Mark 5:1-20. In the text above, Lucian ironically portrays the practice, and not without a side jab at Platonism ("ideas" = "demons"), also not without some highlighting of the financial aspect. Lucian knows of Christians, and makes fun of their naivete ("Death of Perigrinus" 10-14). It is not possible to prove, however, that he knew the New Testament or that he could presuppose and allude to this passage.

231. Mark 1:21-28/ Luke 4:33-37

Bentresch Stele, Egypt (525–337 BCE)

[The demon in the sick person speaks to the god incorporated in the statue:] You come in peace, great God, destroyer of the evil ones. Your land is Bechten, its inhabitants are your servants, and I am your servant. I will depart to the land from which I came, in order to satisfy your heart, since that is the reason you have come. But you might command the prince of Bechten to celebrate a festival in my honor. (MEB/Berger)

The demon is the cause of the sickness, he acknowledges the god, who wants to help, and knows how to call him by name. As in Mark 5:12 he insists on a condition. Here as in the previous text, the superiority of the healer over the demon is uncontested. The manner of exorcism in which the demon and exorcist engage in dialogue is possibly altogether of Egyptian origin.

232. Mark 2:27

Philo, *The Special Laws* 2.60-64 (15 BCE–50 CE)

On this day we are commanded to abstain from all work, not because the law inculcates slackness; on the contrary it always inures men to endure hardship and incites them to labor, and spurns those who would idle their time away, and accordingly is plain in its directions to work the full six days. Its object is rather to give men relaxation from continuous and unending toil and by refreshing their bodies with a regularly calculated system of remissions, to send them out renewed to their old activities. For a breathing-space enables not merely ordinary people but athletes also to collect their strength and with a stronger force behind them to undertake promptly and patiently each of the tasks set before them. Further, when He forbids bodily labor on the seventh day, He permits the exercise of the higher activities, namely, those employed in the study of the principles of virtue's lore. For the law bids us take the time for studying philosophy and thereby improve the soul and the dominant mind. So each seventh day there stand wide open in every city thousands of schools of good sense, temperance, courage, justice and the other virtues in which the scholars sit in order quietly with ears alert and with full attention, so much do they thirst for the draught which the teacher's words supply, while one of special experience rises and sets forth what is the best and sure to be profitable and will make the whole of life grow to something better. But among the vast number of particular truths and principles there studied, there stand out practically high above the others two main heads: one of duty to God as shown by piety and holiness, one of duty to men as when by humanity and justice, each of them splitting up into multiform branches, all highly laudable. These things show clearly that Moses does not allow any of those who use his sacred instruction to remain inactive at any season. But since we consist of body and soul, he assigned to the body its proper tasks and similarly to the soul what falls to its share, and his earnest desire was, that the two should be waiting to relieve each other. Thus while the body is working, the soul enjoys a respite, but when the body takes its rest, the soul resumes its work, and thus the best forms of life, the theoretical and the practical, take their turn in replacing each other. The practical life has six as its number allotted for ministering to the body. The theoretical has seven for knowledge and perfection of the mind. (LCL)

Philo illustrates the joy and humanitarian spirit in which Jews observed the Sabbath, which he understands to have been "made for humankind" because it corresponds to his dualistic understanding of human nature. In Philo's situation, the Jewish practice of Sabbath observance was caricatured by Gentiles as an example of "Jewish laziness." Thus one notes a certain defensiveness in Philo's discussion. He defends Sabbath observance on rational grounds he holds in common with his Gentile neighbors, not on the biblical bases of God's command, God's resting on the seventh day after creation, or as a sign of God's deliverance from Egypt (Gen 2:2; Exod 20:11; Deut 5:15).

233. Mark 2:27

Mekilta on Exodus 31:13 (109b) (3 cent. CE)

The Sabbath is given over to you, not you to the Sabbath. (MEB/Berger)

The Sabbath was honored by all Jews, and was one of their distinctive marks noted by Gentiles. It was not considered a burden, but a delight, a special time of rejoicing, a family celebration, a time of worship both in the family circle and in the synagogue. The best food and clothes were reserved for the Sabbath. It was therefore all the more important to observe it correctly (on the different interpretations of the Sabbath law, see on Luke 14:5).

234. Mark 2:27-28

Plutarch, *Moralia*, "Sayings of the Spartans" 230F; Pausanias, the Son of Pleistonax, §1 (45–125 CE)

Pausanias, the son of Pleistonax, in answer to the question why it was not permitted to change any of the ancient laws in their country, said, "Because the laws ought to have authority over the men, and not the men over the laws." (LCL)

The following are comparable elements to Mark 2:27-28: (a) The common genre chreia (cf. Berger, *Formgeschichte*, §§25-29); (b) discussion of the question of the stability of the law; (c) the form of the answer: antithetic parallelism, in which the contrasting terms are "humanity" (lit. "men") and "Law" (in Mark, "Sabbath"); (d) the rare expression "be lord over a law" (Gk. κύριος + gen.). Despite the similarity of materials, the thrust of the two sayings is in opposite directions. In Mark it is a matter of freedom of interpretation of the law (which is still a valid keeping of the law; cf. κυριεύειν and the "command" in Hermas, *Mandates* 5.2.8: "If you master this commandment you will be able to keep the other commandments"). According to Plutarch, on the other hand, Pausanias affirmed the law's unchangeable validity. For similar structures in chreiai, cf. Berger, "Hellenistische Gattungen," 1100 under 2a; and for analogies in Judaism cf. 2 Maccabees 5:19, "But the Lord did not choose the nation for the sake of the holy place, but the place for the sake of the nation," and *2 Baruch* 14:17, "When in the beginning the world did not exist with its inhabitants, you devised and spoke by means of your word and at the same time the works of your creation stood before you. And you said that you would make a man for this world as a guardian over your works that it should be known that he was not created for the world, but the world for him" (*OTP* 2:626).

235. Mark 3:21

Alciphron, *Letters of Courtesans*, "Thais to Euthydemus" 1.34.1-2 (2 cent. CE)

Ever since you took it into your head to study philosophy you have put on airs and have raised your eyebrows above your temples. Then, in a pompous fashion and with a book in your hands, you stalk along to the Academy and walk past my house as if you had never so much as set eyes on it before. You've gone mad, Euthydemus; don't you know what sort of person that sophist is, the man with the solemn countenance who delivers those wonderful lectures to you? (LCL)

Cf. Acts 26:24. Similarly in Alciphron, *Letters of Farmers*, "Euthydicus to Philiscus" 38: "I sent my son to town to sell wood and barley. . . . But a fit of anger—sent by what evil spirit I cannot say—came upon him, utterly transformed him, and drove him out of his mind. The fact is that he gazed on one of those madmen who, because they are affected by the madness of rabies, are ordinarily called Cynics [i.e. 'dogs,' which suffer from rabies], and that, by imitating, he surpassed the founder of that evil sect. And now you may witness a revolting and terrible sight, as he tosses back his filthy locks, a bold, insolent look in his eye, half naked in a ragged old cloak, with a little wallet suspended from his girdle . . . a man of no occupation, not recognizing the farm or us, his parents, but denying us and saying that all things are the work of nature and that birth is occasioned, not by parents, but by the mixture of the elements" (LCL).

In each case the one adept at Cynic philosophy is described as "out of his mind," since he has disdained and abandoned the customary standards of respectability. In relation to Mark 3:31-35, the connection with the severing of relations to one's natural family is important. But the analogy goes no deeper. The Jesus who is "out of his mind" has its cause, in the perspective of the evangelists, in Jesus' "inspiration," while the basis for the Cynic's conduct is his provocative calling into question of everything that is not according to "nature." Cf. no. 442.

236. Mark 3:21

Sibylline Oracles 3.811-18 (ca. 3 cent. BCE)

[I say] these things to you, having left the long Babylonian walls of Assyria, frenzied, a fire sent to Greece, prophesying the disclosures of God to all mortals, so that I prophesy divine riddles to men. Throughout Greece mortals will say that I am of another country, a shameless one, born of Erythrae. Some will say that I am Sibylla born of Circe as mother and Gnostos as father, a crazy liar. But when everything comes to pass, then you will remember me and no longer will anyone say that I am crazy, I who am a prophetess of the great God. (*OTP* 1:380)

As in Mark 3:21-22 Jesus is described as "crazy" and possessed by Beelzebul, and in John 8:48 as a foreigner, a Samaritan and possessed by a demon, so here the Sibyl is described as "raging" and as a "foreigner," or even as the daughter of the inglorious Circe. Only the fulfillment of her prophesying will vindicate her. In the Gospels, it is the Easter events, among others, that have this function. Cf. Job in no. 216.

237. Mark 8:22-26

Tacitus, *Histories* 4.81 (55–120 CE)

[On the Emperor Vespasian in Alexandria:] One of the common people of Alexandria, well known for his loss of sight, threw himself before Vespasian's knees, praying him with groans to cure his blindness, being so directed by the god Serapis, whom this most superstitious of nations worships before all others; and he besought the emperor to deign to moisten his cheeks and eyes with his spittle. (LCL)

Vespasian is at first hesitant, but then performs a successful healing. (Cf. no. 88 on Mark 3:1-6.) Cf. Suetonius, *Vespasian* 7-8; Dio Cassius 66.8. Cf. no. 434.

238. Mark 8:22-26

Inscription from Epidaurus, *Sylloge Inscriptionum Graecarum* 1168/69

[After the god had opened the eyes of a blind man:] . . . there he at first saw the trees in the holy place . . . (MEB/Berger)

See discussion in Introduction to German Edition, above, §3.A.III.

239. Mark 8:23

Plutarch, *Parallel Lives*, "Life of Pyrrhus" 3.4-5 (45–125 CE)

In the aspect of his countenance Pyrrhus had more of the terror than of the majesty of kingly power. He had not many teeth, but his upper jaw was one continuous bone, on which the usual intervals between the teeth were indicated by slight depressions. People of a splenetic habit believed that he cured their ailment; he would sacrifice a white cock, and, while the patient lay flat upon his back, would press gently with his right foot against the spleen. Nor was any one so obscure or poor as not to get this healing service from him if he asked it. The king would also accept the cock after he had sacrificed it, and this honorarium was most pleasing to him. It is said, further, that the great toe of his right foot had a divine virtue, so that after the rest of his body had been consumed, this was found to be untouched and unharmed by the fire. (LCL)

Here the foot of the royal miracle worker is the instrument of healing, even after his death. The religious foundation of the story is clear in both instances (in Mark 8:22-26 by the context), but in neither case does the faith of the healed person play a role. The renunciation of any reward corresponds to this religious element.

240. Mark 8:27-30

Iamblichus, *Life of Pythagoras* 6.30 (4 cent. CE)

. . . they held their possessions in common, as stated before, and reckoned Pythagoras henceforth among the gods, as a beneficent guardian spirit *[daimon]* and most benevolent to humanity. Some spread a report that he was the Pythian Apollo, others that he was Apollo from the Hyperboreans, others that he was Paean, others that he was one of the spirits *[daimones]* dwelling in the moon. Still others reported that he was one of the Olympian gods, claiming that he appeared in human form to those then alive for the benefit and improvement of the mortal way of life, in order that he might give mortal nature a saving spark of well-being and philosophy. (Dillon and Hershbell)

The plethora of speculations concerning the hidden identity of the hero is a reflection of the mélange of numinous responses he evoked. This corresponds to Mark 6:14-16 and 8:28-29. Both Mark and Iamblichus indicate the true solution from their perspective (Iamblichus in 2.8: the soul of Pythagoras stood under the direction of Apollo; he rejects the legends of divine birth). Similarly also in the 44th Letter of Apollonius of Tyana to Hestiaeus, his brother (1 cent. CE, died ca. 97): "Other men regard me as the equal of the gods, and some of them even as a god, but until now my own country alone ignores me, my country for which in particular I have striven to be distinguished" (LCL). Similarly in Philo of Alexandria, *Moses* 2.17: "His associates and everyone else, considered earnestly what the mind which dwelt in his body like an image in its shrine could be, whether it was human or divine or a mixture of both" (LCL). Such discussions, with a listing of the alternatives, belong to the genre of biography (cf. the tabulation in Berger, "Hellenistische Gattungen," 1262). On the role in the chreiai literature (Berger, *Formgeschichte*, §§25-29), cf. Plutarch's *Moralia*, "Sayings of Spartans," Dereylidas 6-7: "If this man is a god, we do not fear him, for we are guilty of no wrong; but if he is a man, he is surely not superior to us" (LCL).

241. Mark 9:50*b*

Plutarch, "Table Talk" 7 (45–125 CE)

Homer calls salt "divine," and a colloquial term for salt is "graces," because when mixed with foods it will render most of them harmonious and agreeable and so "gracious" to our taste. But the most truly godlike seasoning at the dining table is the presence of a friend or companion or intimate acquaintance—not because of his eating and drinking with us, but because he participates in the give-and-take of conversation . . . (LCL)

Cf. also Plutarch's comment in "On Having Many Friends" 3 that the friend is one "who has consumed with us in the course of time the proverbial bushel of salt" (LCL). Already Aristotle, *Nic. Eth.* 8.3 appeals to the proverb that people don't really know each other unless they have eaten the proverbial bushel of salt together, just as he does in *Eudem. Ethic* 7.2.26. Finally, Philo, "Dreams" 2.210 speaks of the "salt of hospitality." The texts leave no doubt that salt was a common allegory for friendship. Thus the context indicates in Mark 9:49-50. Cf. further V. Hehn, *Das Salz*, 2nd. ed. (1901).

242. Mark 10:38*b*-39

Lucian, *Hermotimos, or Concerning the Sects* 7 (120–185 CE)

Riches and glories and pleasures and bodily things are all stripped off the climber and left down below before he makes his ascent. Think of the story of Heracles when he was burned and deified on Mount Oeta: he threw off the mortal part of him that came from his mother and flew up to heaven, taking the pure and unpolluted divine part with him, the part that the fire had separated off. So philosophy like a fire strips our climbers of all these things that the rest of mankind wrongly admires. (LCL)

Similarly Ovid, *Metamorphoses* 9.251 (Hercules: separation of the mortal, maternal part from the immortal, paternal part), and Seneca, *Hercules Oetaeus* 1966-67. In Lucian death is seen as purification ("Orphic"). In Christianity, "the" purification is expected through baptism (a sign of purification from sins; of freedom from the body subject to the powers of sin and death). In the binding of the two ideas together, as happens here in Mark, death can simply be regarded as baptism. In Ovid, Lucian, and in Luke 12:49-53, the additional step is taken of relating this to the concept of separation.

243. Mark 11:16

Josephus, *Against Apion* 2.106 (37–100 CE)

One further point: no vessel whatever might be carried into the temple, the only objects in which were an altar, a table, a censer, and a lampstand. (LCL)

Josephus describes, in the style appropriate to an apology, the temple as altogether pure and holy, similarly as it is formulated in the announcement of salvation in Zechariah 14:20-21 (the holiness of every vessel in Jerusalem, and the absence of all merchants). Jesus acts out, in a symbolic manner, the extension of the accomplished purity of the temple beyond the narrow confines of the cultic area itself, and thereby points to the inbreaking time of the eschatological holiness of Jerusalem and the eschatological incorporation of the Gentiles in the realm of holiness. In contrast, Josephus concerns himself with the apologetic depiction of the ideal state.

244. Mark 12:41-44/ Luke 21:1-4

Euripides, Danae Fragment 329 (485–406 BCE)

Often I see that poor people are more wise than the rich, and with their own hands offer small gifts to the gods and [one sees in them] more piety than those who bring oxen to sacrifice. (MEB/Berger)

Here, the poor are favored against the rich. Differently, Xenophon, *Memoirs* I 3:3, who reports Socrates as considering it to be right to sacrifice only "according to one's means" (and thus not disproportionately, small gifts from poor people).

245. Mark 12:41-44/ Luke 21:1-4

Epigram of the Prefect Julianos of Egypt, *Anthologia Graeca* 6.25 (6 cent. CE)

Old Cinyras, weary of long fishing, dedicates to the Nymphs this worn sweep-net; . . . if the gift is but a small one, it is not his fault, ye Nymphs, for this was all Cinyras had to live on. (LCL)

The experience which lies at the base of this epigram is that in the matter of religious giving, the poor find it easier to give up their possessions than do the rich. Cf. E. Klostermann, *Markus-Kommentar*, 4th ed. (Tübingen: J. C. B. Mohr [Paul Siebeck], 1950), 130.

246. Mark 12:41-44/ Luke 21:1-4

Leviticus Rabbah 3.5 (4–5 cent. CE?)

Once a woman brought a handful of fine flour, and the priest despised her, saying: "See what she offers! What is there in this [for the priests] to eat? What is there in this to offer up?" It was shown to him in a dream: "Do not despise her! It is regarded as if she had sacrificed her own life." (Soncino)

Here too is a woman who brings a very small offering. To the dream of the rabbi there corresponds the amen-saying of Jesus, Mark 12:43b. (Amen-words have a basically revelatory character.) Note especially that here too it is a matter of giving her "life."

247. Mark 13:20

4 Ezra 4:44-52 (late 1 cent. CE)

I answered and said, "If I have found favor in your sight, and if it is possible, and if I am worthy, 45 show me this also: whether more time is to come than has passed, or whether for us the greater part has gone by. 46 For I know what has gone by, but I do not know what is to come."

47 And he said to me, "Stand at my right side, and I will show you the interpretation of a parable."

48 So I stood and looked, and lo, a flaming furnace passed by before me, and when the flame had gone by I looked, and lo, the smoke remained. 49 And after this a cloud full of water passed before me and poured down a heavy and violent rain, and when the violent rainstorm had passed, drops still remained in the cloud.

50 He said to me, "Consider it for yourself; for just as the rain is more than the drops, and the fire is greater than the smoke, so the quantity that passed was far greater; but drops and smoke remained."

51 Then I prayed and said, "Do you think that I shall live until those days? Or who will be alive in those days?"

52 He answered me and said, "Concerning the signs about which you ask me, I can tell you in part; but I was not sent to tell you concerning your life, for I do not know." (NRSV)

As in Mark 13, the time is short, but the knowledge of the revealer is limited as to the precise date. In 4 Ezra, this arrangement is a part of the fictive framework of the narrative inherent in the pseudepigraphical genre. The time is indeed short for the real author, who, like Mark, expected the end to come in his own generation (Mark 13:30). The fictive framework does not allow him to answer the question of whether "Ezra" will still be alive to see the end, since the real author knows that Ezra lived generations in the past. New Testament apocalyptists, believing that the eschatological gift of prophecy had been renewed in their own time, had no need of pseudonymity (Mark 13 should be thought of not as a pseudepigraphical retrojection of a "prophecy" into the mouth of Jesus, but as an example of the renewal of Christian prophecy; see my *Continuing Voice of Jesus* [Louisville: Westminster/John Knox, 1991], pp. 236-42). In Mark, the denial of Jesus' exact knowledge of the end is part of the redactor's discouragement of apocalyptic speculation, while retaining the general apocalyptic worldview. The by-product is to place Jesus in the category of a revelatory angel, less than omniscient deity. Although this text played a role in the later Arian controversy, Christology in this sense is not here Mark's concern.

248. Mark 14:17-25

1Qsa 2:12-22 (1 cent. CE)

He shall come [at] the head of the whole congregation of Israel with all [his brethren, the sons] of Aaron the Priests, [those called] to the assembly, the men of renown; and they shall sit [before him, each man] in the order of his dignity. And then [the Mess]iah of Israel shall [come], and the chiefs of the [clans of Israel] shall sit before him, [each] in the order of his dignity, according to [his place] in their camps and marches. And before them shall sit all the heads of [family of the congreg]ation, and the wise men of [the holy congregation,] each in the order of his dignity.

And [when] they shall gather for the common [tab]le, to eat and [to drink] new wine, when the common table shall be set for eating and the new wine [poured] for drinking, let no man extend his hand over the first-fruits of bread and wine before the Priest; for [it is he] who shall bless the first-fruits of bread and wine, and shall be the first [to extend] his hand over the bread. Thereafter, the Messiah of Israel shall extend his hand over the bread, [and] all the congregation of the Community [shall utter a] blessing, [each man in the order] of his dignity.

It is according to this statute that they shall proceed at every me[al at which] at least ten men are gathered together. (Vermes)

The Qumran text describes regulations for the future Messianic Banquet, when the Prophet and the Two Messiahs (the lay Messiah of Israel and the priestly Messiah of Aaron) shall appear. Points of contact are not only the centrality of bread and wine, the Messiah as presider over the meal, but also (in the Lucan version) the concern over rank.

249. Mark 15:21

Plutarch, *Moralia*, "On the Divine Vengeance" 9.553-54 (45–125 CE)

. . . Whereas every criminal who goes to execution must carry his own cross on his back, vice frames out of itself each instrument of its own punishment . . . (LCL)

Contrary to the Synoptics' picture, the Fourth Gospel emphasizes that Jesus carried the cross entirely by himself (John 19:17). In the Synoptics, the soldiers make use of the right of angary, compelling Simon of Cyrene to help.

250. Mark 16:8*b*

Testaments of the Twelve Patriarchs, "Testament of Levi" 8:18-19 (2–1 cent. BCE)

[Levi had a vision in which seven angels clothed him with priestly garments and made promises concerning his posterity:] When I awoke, I understood that this was like the first dream [2:5–5:7]. And I hid this in my heart as well, and I did not report it to any human being on the earth. (*OTP* 2:791)

Notices concerning the hiding of the mysterious revelations after their reception are a specific literary means of treating the readers with special distinction, for they now have this secret material before them in written form, and only to them is the revelation communicated. Cf. also the texts in Berger, *Auferstehung*, 496 n. 219.

On Mark 16:12, cf. nos. 504, 749.

251. Mark 16:18*a*

t. Berakhoth 3:20 (ca. 2 cent. CE?)

A. One who was standing and reciting the Prayer in a camp or in a wide highway—

B. lo, he may move aside to allow an ass, an ass-driver or a wagon-driver to pass in front of him, but he may not interrupt [his recitation of the Prayer].

C. They related about R. Haninah b. Dosa that once while he was reciting the Prayer, a poisonous lizard bit him, but he did not interrupt [his recitation].

D. His students went and found it [the lizard] dead at the entrance to its hole.

E. They said, "Woe to the man who is bitten by a lizard. Woe to the lizard that bit Ben Dosa." (Neusner, *Tosefta*)

Cf. B. M. Bokser, "Wonder-Working and the Rabbinic Tradition: The case of Hanina ben Dosa," *JSJ* 16 (1985), 41-92. This narrative is found in a comprehensive rabbinic history-of-tradition complex which is at first only concerned (*m. Ber.* 5.1) with not interrupting the stated prayer when a snake appears underfoot. In the Tosefta passage, the point is illustrated by attaching to it a miracle story about Hanina ben Dosa. According to *j. Ber.* 5, 9a, God has a spring of water appear to save him (obviously the story must be protected from the simple idea of imitation). According to *b. Ber.* 5, 1 33a, the story is interpreted moralistically: the story shows that not the snake, but sin, is what kills. The common element with this addition to the original text of Mark is the protection for the elect, to which group early Christianity believed all the messengers of the gospel belonged. Cf. also no. 404. Cf. also Acts 28:3-6.

The Gospel of Luke
(and Parallels)

252. Luke 1:1-4

Josephus, *Jewish War* 1.1.1-3 (37–100 CE)

The war of the Jews against the Romans—the greatest not only of the wars of our own time, but, so far as accounts have reached us, well nigh of all that ever broke out between cities or nations—has not lacked its historians. Of these, however, some, having taken no part in the action, have collected from hearsay casual and contradictory stories which they have then edited in a rhetorical style; while others, who witnessed the events, have, either from flattery of the Romans or from hatred of the Jews, misrepresented the facts, their writings exhibiting alternatively invective and encomium, but nowhere historical accuracy. In these circumstances, I—Josephus, son of Matthias, a Hebrew by race, a native of Jerusalem and a priest, who at the opening of the war myself fought against the Romans and in the sequel was perforce an onlooker—propose to provide the subjects of the Roman Empire with a narrative of the facts, by translating into Greek the account which I had previously composed in my vernacular tongue and sent to the barbarians in the interior. (LCL)

From the point of view of the history of religions, Luke's preface is like that of Josephus' in its lacking any claim to divine inspiration—a lack remedied by the Old Latin MSS b and q, which added *et spiritu sancto* after "I" (so NRSV; "me," RSV; cf. Acts 15:28). Contrast the preface to the Asclepius document, no. 253. Both claim to derive their information from eyewitness accounts: Josephus from his own observation and memory, Luke indirectly through the "ministers of the word" and from earlier documents. Like Luke, Josephus mentions earlier attempts at writing the history, but does not claim them as sources. Both Josephus and Luke disparage earlier accounts as inadequate, and claim to set forth the truth accurately. Josephus clearly identifies himself; "Luke" remains anonymous, and the author's name in the title is from tradition, not the author himself.

253. Luke 1:1-4

Papyrus Oxyrhynchus 1381 (2 cent. CE)

Now I often began the translation of this same book into the Greek tongue [without success] when I finally learned how to make it known [κερῦξαι]. But then in the midst of pouring forth my words, my eagerness was restrained by the greatness of the story [ἱστορία] because I was about to [unlawfully] take it [to give to those] outside [Greek unclear], for the gods alone but not to mortals [is it permitted] rightly to describe [διήγεισθαι] the powers [δύναμαι] of the gods. For if I failed, not only would I be disgraced before men but also [warnings-oracles descending from above] prevented me . . . [text has a break here] . . . through his anger and his immortal virtue [assisting] my weakness to complete the writing. But if I succeeded, my life would be happy and my fame undying. For the god [Asclepius] is always ready to help [as we can see by the fact that] he often saves people after all medical efforts have failed to [liberate them] from the diseases binding them, if only they turn to him in worship, however briefly.

On this account, then, I fled from my rashness and restrained myself until the right moment in old age. For I was delaying in [making good] my promise since youth especially is apt to be indiscreet when its enthusiasm rises quickly and aggressiveness leads the way to seize the thing wanted. When a period of three years had elapsed during which I was still not sick, but during which the god made [his punishment] fall on my mother, afflicting her with quartan fever or chills [malarial fever], at length we came to our senses and appeared before the god entreating him to grant my mother recovery from the disease. He who is kind [χρηστός] toward all in every way appeared to her in dreams and cured her by simple remedies while we returned fitting thanks through sacrifices to our Savior. When I also was suddenly afflicted not long after with a pain in my right side, I quickly hastened to the helper of human nature and again he was more than ever prepared to bestow his mercy [upon me], demonstrating more effectively his unique power for good [εὐεργεσία], which I would give my personal testimony to at this point before I announce [ἀπαγγέλλω] his frightening powers [in the book translated below].

It was night when every living thing except those in pain is asleep but when the supernatural [τὸ θεῖον, lit. "the divine"] manifests itself more effectively. An exceedingly hot fever burned me and I was convulsed with pain in my side because of constant coughing and choking. Groggy and suffering, I was lying there half-asleep and half-awake, being tended by my mother as if I were still a baby for she is by nature affectionate. She was sitting [by my bed] extremely grieved at my agony and not able to get even a little sleep, when suddenly she saw—it was no sleep or dream for her eyes were open immovably, although [admittedly] she was not seeing very distinctly since a supernatural and terrifying vision [φαντασία] came to her which easily prevented her from observing the god [Asclepius] himself or his servant, whichever it was. In any case, it was someone of superhuman size, clothed in shining linen and carrying a book in his left hand. He only examined me from head to foot two or three times and then vanished. When she had recovered, still quaking [with fear] she tried to rouse me. But she discovered that my fever was gone and sweat was pouring off of me, so she gave glory to the god for his appearance and dried me off and woke me up. Now she began to tell me of the virtue [ἀρετη] of the god just revealed, I interrupted her and announced [ἀπαγγέλλω] everything to her first, for what she had seen through her vision I had imagined through dreams. The pain in my side had abated, for the god had given me still one more healing cure, so I proclaimed [κηρύσσω] his benefits [εὐεργεσίαι].

But when we were again seeking his favor by offering all the sacrifices we could afford, he demanded, through the priest who was serving him, the fulfillment of the promise I had long before given him. We knew that we did not lack sacrifices or votive offerings, nevertheless we besought him again with these. But after he repeatedly said that he would not be pleased by these but by that which I had sworn previously, I was quite at a loss, for he was subjecting me to the supernatural duty [τὸ θεῖον χρέος] of [finishing the . . .] book—a task I scarcely took lightly.

However, as soon as thou recognized, O Master, that I was neglecting thy divine book [θεῖα βίβλος], I invoked thy providence, and, being filled by thy divinity [θειότης], I eagerly hastened to the heaven-sent prize of thy narrative [ἱστορία]. For I hope to make thy intention widely known through my prophecy. In fact I have already written a plausible explanation of the story [μῦθος] of the creation of the world [by turning it into] natural concepts [φυσικῷ λόγῳ] closer to the truth.

Throughout the writing I added what was lacking and removed what was superfluous so that I wrote briefly an overly wordy narrative [διήγημα] and told once a repetitive story [ἀλλαττολόγος μῦθος]. Accordingly, O Master, I deem the book to have been finally completed according to thy kindness and not according to my intention. A writing [γραφή] such as this suits thy divinity, O Asclepius, for thou hast disclosed it! Thou, greatest of gods and teacher, shalt be made known by the thanks of all thy people. For every gift of a votive offering or a sacrifice lasts only for the moment, and immediately perishes, while scripture [γραφή] is an undying thanks [ἀθάνατος χάρις] since it rejuvenates the memory [of God's kindness] again and again. And every Greek tongue shall tell of thy story [ἱστορία] and every Greek man shall worship Imouthes of Ptah. (Cartlidge and Dungan)

This is the preface to a Greek translation of the sacred account of the ancient Egyptian healing god Imouthes of Ptah (cf. the last line above), identified in the syncretistic Hellenistic age with the Greek god of healing, Asclepius. Only the preface given here is extant, not the book itself, which apparently recounted the healing stories of Imouthes/Asclepius. Considered as a preface to a document having points of contact with the Gospels, one is immediately struck by its more "religious" orientation in comparison with Luke's, which is more like the "secular" preface of Josephus (cf. no. 252 above), both in its general orientation and its claim to inspiration, lacking from Luke. Luke's preface is also much more brief, even shorter than that of Josephus.

Additional points of contact with the New Testament:

1) The healing miracles of Imouthes/Asclepius resemble those of the Synoptic Jesus, but in contrast Imouthes/Asclepius also causes sickness for punitive or disciplinary purposes.

2) The vision report may be compared to those in the NT, e.g. Acts 22:6-21; Revelation 1:9-20; 10:1-11. There are interesting points of similarity to Revelation, e.g. the gigantic figure, the bright linen, and the book in the hand. In contrast to Revelation, the "subjective" experience is confirmed by experience of an independent observer (cf. however Acts 9:7; 22:9).

3) The author is sincerely convinced that he is translating a sacred text under divine inspiration, and considers the product to be "prophecy" and a "divine book." Nonetheless, his understanding of inspiration means that he does not hesitate to "add what was lacking and remove what was superfluous," and his "translation" is not at all literal but a paraphrase, actually rewriting "an overly wordy narrative" and once eliminating a doublet (contrast Rev 22:18-19). The author is convinced that he is not only telling the deeds of a past hero, but is doing so under the guidance of the heavenly Asclepius whose overruling power has caused the book to be written as Asclepius intends, not as the author intended, so that he can close his preface on the note of adoration and praise.

254. Luke 1:21

m. Yoma 5 (2–3 cents. CE)

[Description of the High Priest's entry into the Holy of Holies on the Day of Atonement:] The outer curtain was looped up on the south side and the inner one on the north side. He went along between them until he reached the north side; when he reached the north he turned round to the south and went on with the curtain on his left hand until he reached the Ark. When he reached the Ark he put the fire pan between the two bars. He heaped up the incense on the coals and the whole place became filled with smoke. He came out by the way he went in, and in the outer space he prayed a short prayer. But he did not prolong his prayer lest he put Israel in terror. (Danby)

Zechariah did not enter into the Holy of Holies, which was done only once every year by the high priest. Yet his burning the incense offering in the Holy Place occurred in the same place as the High Priest's annual prayer, and in dangerous proximity to the sacred ark. The ark was believed to be charged with the threatening power of God's holiness (cf. the Uzzah incident, 2 Sam 6:1-15), so that Zechariah was in mortal danger while inside the curtain. The anxiety of the waiting crowd of worshipers in Luke 1:21 is thus not mere curiosity at his delay, but expresses their view of the awesome holiness of God who may not be approached casually.

255. Luke 1:52

Sirach 10:14 (ca. 180 BCE)

The Lord overthrows the thrones of rulers,
and enthrones the lowly in their place. (NRSV)

The connection of Mary's song with that of Hannah (1 Sam 2:1-10) is well known. But Luke (or his source) draws not only from the more eschatological and revolutionary streams of Israel's tradition in picturing the eschatological turning of the tables, but also on the Wisdom tradition in which God is active behind the scenes to reverse the fortunes of arrogant rulers and God's own humble servants (Gen 39–50; Dan 1–6) in this-worldly events.

256. Luke 1:68-79

Virgil, *Bucolica*, 4 Eclogue (70–19 BCE)

1 Muses of Sicily, essay we now
2 A somewhat loftier task! Not all men love
3 Coppice or lowly tamarisk: sing we woods,
4 Woods worthy of a Consul let them be.
5 Now the last age by Cumae's Sibyl sung
6 Has come and gone, and the majestic roll
7 Of circling centuries begins anew:
8 Justice/the Virgin returns, returns old Saturn's reign,
9 With a new breed of men sent down from heaven.
10 Only do thou, at the boy's birth in whom
11 The iron shall cease, the golden age arise,
12 Befriend him, chaste Lucina; 'tis thine own
13 Apollo reigns. And in thy consulate,
14 This glorious age, O Pollio, shall begin,
15 And the months enter on their mighty march.
16 Under thy guidance, whatso tracks remain
17 Of our old wickedness, once done away,

18 Shall free the earth from never-ceasing fear.
19 He shall receive the life of gods, and see
20 Heroes with gods commingling, and himself
21 Be seen of them, and with his father's worth
22 Reign over a world at peace. For thee, O boy,
23 First shall the earth, untilled, pour freely forth
24 Her childish gifts, the gading ivy-spray
25 With foxglove and Egyptian bean-flower mixed,
26 And laughing-eyed acanthus. Of themselves
27 Untended, will the she-goats then bring home
28 Their udders swollen with milk, while flocks afield
29 Shall of the monstrous lion have no fear . . .
30 . . . Nathless
31 Yet shall there lurk within of ancient wrong
32 Some traces, bidding tempt the deep with ships,
33 Gird towns with walls, with furrows cleave the earth.
34 Therewith a second Tiphys shall there be,
35 Her hero-freight a second Argo bear;
36 New wars too shall arise, and once again
37 Some great Achilles to some Troy be sent.
38 Then, when the mellowing years have made thee man,
39 No more shall mariner sail, nor pine-tree bark
40 Ply traffic on the sea, but every land
41 Shall all things bear alike: the glebe no more
42 Shall feel the harrow's grip, nor vine the hook;
43 The sturdy plowman shall loose yoke from steer,
44 Nor wool with varying colors learn to lie;
45 But in the meadows shall the ram himself
46 Now with soft flush of purpose, now with tint
47 Of yellow saffron, teach his fleece to shine.
48 While clothed in natural scarlet graze the lambs.
49 "Such still, such ages weave ye, as ye run,"
50 Sang to their spindles the consenting Fates
51 By destiny's unalterable decree.
52 Assume thy greatness, for the time draws nigh,
53 Dear child of gods, great progeny of Jove!
54 See how it totters—the world's orbed might,
55 Earth, and wide ocean, and the vault profound,
56 All, see, enraptured of the coming time!
57 Ah, might such length of days to me be given,
58 And breath suffice me to rehearse the deeds,
59 Nor Thracian Orpheus should out-sing me then,
60 Nor Linus, though his mother this, and that
61 His sire should aid—Orpheus Calliope,
62 And Linus fair Apollo. Nay, though Pan,
63 With Arcady for judge, my claim contest,
64 With Arcady for judge great Pan himself

65 Should own him foiled, and from the field retire.
66 Begin to greet thy mother with a smile,
67 O baby-boy! ten months of weariness
68 For thee she bore: Oh baby-boy begin!
69 For him, on whom his parents have not smiled,
70 Gods deem not worthy of their board or bed.
(Rhaodes)

This poem probably represents the oracle of a Sibyl in 40 BCE, which Virgil relates to Hesiod's periodization of history into the four ages (Gold/Silver/Bronze/Iron). The returning Virgin from line 8 is "Justice," who had fled at the beginning of the Age of Iron. Lucina is the divine mother. The child addressed and anticipated in line 22 is possibly the expected son of Octavian. The wedding of Octavian and Cleopatra was part of the celebration of the Peace of Brundisium, which was expected to bring the end to civil war and inaugurate the reign of peace, of which their expected child would be the symbol and means.

As in Luke 1:68-79, the praise of the time of salvation fulfilled by the oracle (Luke 1:70) modulates into direct address to the bearer of salvation (cf. Luke 1:76 with line 22 of Virgil). Both are predictions of a child who is to appear. (Cf. Berger, *Formgeschichte*, §76).

See the treatment of this text in Eduard Norden, *Die Geburt des Kindes: Die Geschichte einer religiösen Idee* (Leipzig: Teubner, 1924; repr. Darmstadt: Wissenschaftliche Buchgesellschaft, 1958). He shows that the vision of the new age inaugurated by the birth of a divine child goes back to ancient Egyptian mythology and mystery language. From this point of origin, the idea affected many traditions of the ancient Near East and the Hellenistic world. Like Virgil's *Eclogue 4*, the biblical pictures of Isaiah 7 and 9 are part of this larger picture and movement. The birth stories of the Gospels cannot thus be understood only in terms of their Old Testament background, for this itself is part of the larger picture. "The titles of the child of Isa 9:6, born to rule the new age, 'Wonderful Counselor, Mighty God, Everlasting Father, Prince of Peace,' are the same as those which were given to Pharaoh at his enthronement" (Koester, *Ancient Christian Gospels*, 305, citing Hans Wildberger, *Jesaja 1-12* [Neukirchen-Vluyn: Neukirchener Verlag, 1972], pp. 376-80).

The *cyclical* understanding of history presupposed in the *Eclogue* is in tension with the fundamentally linear understanding of history of Luke-Acts and the Bible generally, which does not expect the age of salvation to be the return of a past Golden Age, but the new eschatological act of God already inaugurated in the advent of Jesus. For the recent discussion of this text cf. the articles on Virgil by W. W. Briggs, J. van Sickle, W. Kraus, and St. Benko in *ANRW* II 31, 1 (1980), 575-705, and by W. W. Briggs in *ANRW* II, 31, 2 (1981), 1265-1357. (Translator's note: for an elaboration of the contrast between Greco-Roman "cyclical" and Jewish-Christian "linear" understandings of history from a history-of-religions point of view, cf. Mircea Eliade, *Cosmos and History: The Myth of the Eternal Return* [New York: Harper & Brothers, 1954]. For a critique of this view, see Hubert Cancik, "Die Rechtfertigung Gottes durch den 'Fortschritt der Zeiten': Zur Differenz jüdisch-christlicher und hellenisch-römischer Zeit- und Geschichtsvorstellungen," in *Die Zeit*, ed. A. Peisl and A. Mohler [Munich: R. Oldenbourg Verlag, 1983], 257-88.)

257. Luke 2:14

1QH 11, 8-9

In Thy wrath are all chastisements,
but in Thy goodness is much forgiveness
and Thy mercy is toward the sons of Thy goodwill. (Vermes)

Cf. similarly 1QH 4:32-33,

"The way of man is not established
except by the spirit which God created for him
to make perfect a way for the children of men,
that all His creatures may know
the might of His power,
and the abundance of His mercies
towards all the sons of His grace." (Vermes)

Also in Luke 2:14 the text deals with people whom God has chosen according to his good will (cf. also the closing cry of the angel [!] in no. 596!). The old dispute as to whether it deals with God's will or with "people of good will" (so the Vulgate) has now been decided by the Qumran texts.

(This is Berger's judgment. However, since the Qumran text itself may be translated differently, the matter has hardly been decided on this basis. Cf. the translation of T. H. Gaster, *The Dead Sea Scriptures* [Garden City: Doubleday, 1964], p. 151, which concludes: ". . . that all His works may know how mighty is His power, how plenteous His love to all who do His will") (MEB).

258. Luke 2:24

Herondas, *Mime* 4 (3 cent. BCE)

Greetings, Lord Paeeon [epithet of Asklepios], who rulest Trikka and has settled sweet Kos and Epidauros, and also may Koronis who gave thee birth and Apollo be greeted, and she whom thou touchest with thy right hand Hygieia, and those to whom belong these honored altars, Panake and Epio and Ieso be greeted, and the sackers of Laomedon's house and walls, curers of cruel diseases, Podaleirios and Machaon be greeted, and whatsoever gods and goddesses live at thy hearth, father Paeeon: may ye graciously come hither and receive this cock which I am sacrificing, herald of the walls of the house, as your dessert. For our well is far from abundant or ready-flowing, else we should have made an ox or a sow heaped with much crackling, and not a cock, our thank-offering for the diseases which thou hast wiped away, Lord, stretching out thy gentle hands. (LCL)

Mary and Joseph make the offering allowed poor people (Lev 12:2-8) rather than the regular offering. This picture fits Luke's general theme of the gospel as "good news to the poor." The allusion to the biblical poverty-clause would be recognized by many of his readers, while others would recognize a traditional pagan picture. Luke stands astride the biblical and Hellenistic worlds, and pictures Jesus and the early church as belonging to both.

259. Luke 2:41-52

Iamblichus, *Life of Pythagoras* 8-10 (4 cent. CE)

. . . no one would dispute, judging from his very birth and the all-around wisdom of his life, that Pythagoras' soul was sent down to humans under Apollo's leadership, either as a follower in his train, or united with this god in a still more intimate way. . . .

He was thus educated, and having had this good fortune, he became the most handsome and godlike of those ever recorded in history. After his father's death, he grew up to be most dignified and sound-minded, and while still quite young he was already thought worthy of all respect and reverence even by the oldest. Both on sight and at first hearing, he attracted everyone's attention; and on whomever he gazed, he appeared marvelous, so that by the multitude he was naturally confirmed to be a god's child. (Dillon and Hershbell)

Unlike Luke, Iamblichus closely relates the precocious youth of Pythagoras to his supernatural birth and to his status as "son of a god." This single story from Jesus' childhood found in the Gospel of Luke seems to be unrelated to the birth story, both in the tradition and in the Lucan redaction.

260. Luke 2:41-52

Philo, *Life of Moses* 1.18-24 (15 BCE–50 CE)

As he grew and thrived without a break, and was weaned at an earlier date than they had reckoned, his mother and nurse in one brought him to her from whom she had received him, since he had ceased to need an infant's milk. He was noble and goodly to look upon; and the princess, seeing him so advanced beyond his age, conceived for him an even greater fondness than before, and took him for her son, having at an earlier time artificially enlarged the figure of her womb to make him pass as her real and not a supposititious child. God makes all that He wills easy, however difficult be the accomplishment. So now he received as his right the nurture and service due to a prince. Yet he did not bear himself like the mere infant that he was, nor delight in fun and laughter and sport, though those who had the charge of him did not grudge him relaxation or shew him any strictness; but with a modest and serious bearing he applied himself to hearing and seeing what was sure to profit the soul. Teachers at once arrived from different parts, some unbidden from the neighboring countries and provinces of Egypt, others summoned from Greece under the promise of high reward. But in a short time he advanced beyond their capacities; his gifted nature forestalled their instruction, so that his seemed a case of recollection rather than of learning, and indeed he himself devised and propounded problems which they could not easily solve. For great natures carve out much that is new in the way of knowledge; and, just as bodies, robust and agile in every part, free their trainers from care, and receive little or none of their usual attention, and in the same way well-grown and naturally healthy trees, which improve of themselves, give the husbandmen no trouble, so the gifted soul takes the lead in meeting the lessons given by itself rather than the teacher and is profited thereby, and as soon as it has a grasp of some of the first principles of knowledge presses forward like the horse to the meadow, as the proverb goes. Arithmetic, geometry, the lore of meter, rhythm and harmony, and the whole subject of music as shown by the use of instruments or in textbooks and treatises of a more special character, were imparted to him by learned Egyptians. These further instructed him in the philosophy conveyed in symbols, as displayed in the so-called holy inscriptions and in the regard paid to animals, to which they even pay divine honors. He had Greeks to teach him the rest of the regular school course, and the inhabitants of the neighboring countries for Assyrian letters and the Chaldean science of the heavenly bodies. This he also acquired from

Egyptians, who give special attention to astrology. And, when he had mastered the lore of both nations, both where they agree and where they differ, he eschewed all strife and contention and sought only for truth. His mind was incapable of accepting any falsehood, as is the way with the sectarians, who defend the doctrines they have propounded, whatever they may be, without examining whether they can stand scrutiny, and thus put themselves on a par with hired advocates who have no thought nor care for justice. (LCL)

Philo had pictured Moses in somewhat superhuman terms, without making him into a divine being. As he had hinted at a supernatural birth (see no. 8), so here his educational development "seemed a case rather of recollection than of learning." How does one picture the boyhood of such a more-than-human figure? Philo makes Moses into a serious, contemplative youngster who disdains entertainment and sports, while Josephus documents the extraordinary quality of his person by making him excel in the games. Philo ponders how his quasi-divine boy Moses dealt with youthful passions, and while acknowledging that life in the Pharaoh's palace provided opportunity aplenty for their indulgence, assures us that the boy Moses always kept a tight reign on the desires of the flesh. "For it is these impulses which cause both good and bad—good when they obey the guidance of reason, bad when they turn from their regular course into anarchy. Naturally, therefore, his associates and everyone else, struck with amazement at what they felt was a novel spectacle, considered earnestly what the mind which dwelt in his body like an image in its shrine could be, whether it was human or divine or a mixture of both, so utterly unlike was it to the majority, soaring above them and exalted to a grander height. For on his belly he bestowed no more than the necessary tributes which nature had appointed, and as for the pleasures that have their seat below, save for the lawful begetting of children, they passed altogether even out of his memory" (1.26-28) (LCL).

For other pictures of the precocious boy Moses, see no. 260 and Josephus, *Antiquities* 2.224-30, and *Tanhumot, Shemot* 8-9.

The Gospels, oriented to proclamation rather than biography, are not concerned to picture what the boyhood of one who was born Son of God might have been like. Even Luke is not entirely an exception to this statement. On the one hand, Luke's solitary pericope dealing with the "boyhood of Jesus" does have analogies to the pictures of the phenomenally advanced little boy Moses, but even in this respect Luke is more restrained than Philo, Josephus, and the rabbis. On the other hand, when Luke's portrayal of the boy Jesus is compared with the pictures in e.g. the *Infancy Gospel of Thomas,* the lad Jesus, though sincerely religious, appears to have had a childhood in which he grew and developed normally. Such questions as Jesus' sexuality and experiences at school do not come within the purview of the Gospels, including Luke.

261. Luke 2:41-51

Wisdom of Solomon 8:10, 19-21 (150 BCE–50 CE)

> [Solomon speaks:] Because of her [Wisdom] I shall have glory
> among the multitudes
> and honor in the presence of the elders,
> though I am young. . . .
> As a child I was naturally gifted,
> and a good soul fell to my lot;
> or rather, being good, I entered an undefiled body

But I perceived that I would not possess wisdom
unless God gave her to me . . . (NRSV)

"Solomon" confesses that though he was naturally gifted, the wisdom he has is not his own attainment but the gift of God. The way this is expressed, in terms of a preexisting soul entering a human body, is alien to the biblical tradition.

262. Luke 2:41-52

Josephus, *Life of Josephus* 7-9 (37–100 CE)

Distinguished as he was by his noble birth, my father Matthias was even more esteemed for his upright character, being among the most notable men in Jerusalem, our greatest city. Brought up with Matthias, my own brother by both parents, I made great progress in my education, gaining a reputation for an excellent memory and understanding. While still a mere boy, about fourteen years old, I won universal applause for my love of letters; insomuch that the chief priests and leading men of the city used constantly to come to me for precise information on some particular of our ordinances. (LCL)

Though there is doubtless some self-serving exaggeration in Josephus' description of his youth, it also shows that precocity, and not miracle or divinity, is portrayed in such a description (written about the same time as the Gospel of Luke).

263. Luke 2:41-52

Xenophon, *Cyropaedia* 1, 2, 8 (d. 429 BCE)

They teach the boys self-control also; and it greatly conduces to their learning self-control that they see their elders also living temperately day by day. And they teach them likewise to obey the officers; and it greatly conduces to this also that they see their elders implicitly obeying their officers. (LCL)

At the age of twelve Cyrus is superior to all the other boys, is faster than they, and is like an adult, just as is Samuel according to Josephus, *Antiquities* 5.348, and Epicurus according to Diogenes Laertius, *Lives of the Philosophers* 10.14. It is a widespread biographical topos.

On Luke 1–2: Important for understanding the gospel genre as a whole (Berger, *Formgeschichte*, §§99-100, 10a) is the narrative of the birth, divine origin, and miraculous childhood of Heracles, by Diodorus Siculus 4, 9.1-10 and 10.7 (1 cent. BCE). It is also interesting to compare the story of the genealogy, birth, and endangerment of Adonis (the child was hidden in a chest) in the *Bibliotheca of (pseudo-) Apollodorus* 3, 14.3-4 (a handbook of mythology from the 1 cent. CE). An example of combining a genealogy with legends about divine origin, as in Matthew 1, is provided by Diogenes Laertius (3 cent. CE), *Lives* 3.1-2, and in Plutarch (45–125 CE), "Table Talk" 8.1.2.; cf. also Plutarch, "Parallel Histories," §9, §§33-34; "Fortune Romans," §§8, 10; "On the Fortune of Alexander the Great," §5; Dio Chrysostom (ca. 40–120 CE), "Speeches" 15, §12.

264. Luke 2:48-49

Musonius Rufus, *Must One Obey One's Parents Under All Circumstances?* **16 (30–100 CE)**

Your father forbids you to study philosophy, but the common father of all men and gods, Zeus, bids you and exhorts you to do so. His command and law is that man be just . . . (Lutz)

In place of the lack of understanding (and almost "misunderstanding," in the Johannine sense) of the parents in the story in Luke, here is the explicit opposition of two different demands.

265. Luke 2:52

R. Judah b. Tema, cited in *Pirke Aboth* **5:21 (3 cent. CE; cited in later source)**

At five years of age [one is fit] for Scripture; at ten, for the Mishnah; at thirteen for [keeping] the commandments; at fifteen for the Talmud; at eighteen for the bride-chamber; at twenty for pursuing [a calling]. (Danby)

Here is one late picture of what Jewish education was perceived to be. It was centered in the home and on Scripture and tradition, and much more religious than Greco-Roman education in general, for which rhetoric, pointing to political activity, was a leading component. But the particulars of this late picture cannot be taken as the model for Jesus' development or for education in New Testament times.

On 2:41-52, cf. also Josephus, *Antiquities* 5:348, "Samuel had now completed his twelfth year when he began to act as a prophet," (LCL) and Diogenes Laertius, "Life of Epicurus," 10:14: "He [Epicurus] began to study philosophy when he was twelve years old, and started his own school at thirty-two" (LCL).

266. Luke 3:3-17 / Matthew 3:1-12 (Q)

Josephus, *Jewish War* **6.300 (37–100 CE)**

[The signs prior to the destruction of Jerusalem, 66–70 CE:] But a further portent was even more alarming. Four years before the war, when the city was enjoying profound peace and prosperity, there came to the feast at which it is the custom of all Jews to erect tabernacles to God, one Jesus, son of Ananias, a rude peasant, who, standing in the temple, suddenly began to cry out,

"A voice from the east,

A voice from the west,

> A voice from the four winds,
> A voice against Jerusalem and the sanctuary,
> A voice against the bridegroom and the bride,
> A voice against all the people." (LCL)

Prophets, i.e. those who claimed to be messengers from God who spoke by direct inspiration, were not so uncommon in first-century Judaism as is often believed (cf. Boring, *Continuing Voice*, 51-58). The Holy Spirit was identified with the "spirit of prophecy." In some streams of Jewish thought, it was believed that prophecy (and the Spirit) had ceased in the time of Ezra, and would not reappear until the eschatological times. From such a perspective, the advent of John and Jesus as prophets, as well as prophetic phenomena in the Christian community, would be regarded as an eschatological claim, even a blasphemous one (cf. Mark 3:20-30 par.). Yet such prophets as Jesus ben Ananias show that the prophetic phenomenon was not unknown in first-century Judaism. (Cf. Philo on the High Priest's gift of prophecy, no. 446 on John 11:51, and the claims of Philo and Josephus to possess the prophetic gift themselves: Philo, "Cherubim," 9.1: "But there is a higher thought than these. It comes from a voice in my own soul, which oftentimes is God-possessed and divines where it does not know. This thought I will record in words if I can"; [cf. Boring, *Continuing Voice*, 156]. Cf. also the "woe" prophecy described by Josephus during the siege. The oracle of Jesus ben Ananias resembles some streams of NT prophecy in that it is against the temple and religious structures, and that it is a pronouncement of eschatological doom.)

267. Luke 3:7-9, 17/ Matthew 3:7-10, 12

Midrash on Song of Songs (6 cent. CE)

Just as the farmer pays no attention to the baskets of dung or of straw or of stubble or of chaff, because they are not worth anything, so the Holy One, blessed be He, pays no attention to the other nations, because they are not worth anything. . . . The following parable will illustrate this. "The straw, the chaff, and the stubble were arguing with one another, each claiming that for its sake the ground had been sown. Said the wheat to them: 'Wait till the threshing time comes, and we shall see for whose sake the field has been sown.' When the time came and they were all brought into the threshing-floor, the farmer went out to winnow it. The chaff was scattered to the winds; the straw he took and threw on the ground; the stubble he cast into the fire; the wheat he took and piled in a heap, and all the passers-by when they saw it kissed it, as it says, *Kiss ye the corn* (Pss. 11, 12). So of the nations some say, 'We are Israel, and for our sake the world was created,' and others say, 'We are Israel, and for our sake the world was created.' Says Israel to them: 'Wait till the day of the Holy One, blessed be He, comes, and we shall see for whose sake the world was created.'" (Soncino)

The imagery is the same (harvest, separation of wheat from chaff), only it has been fashioned into a fable in the rabbinical text, and referred to the contrast Israel/Gentiles. Q on the other hand certainly thinks of a separation within Israel.

268. Luke 3:10-14

Diogenes Laertius, *Lives of the Philosophers*, "Antisthenes" 6:8 (3 cent. CE)

Phanias in his work on the Socratics tells us how someone asked him what he must do to be good and noble, and he replied, "You must learn from those who know that the faults you have are to be avoided." (LCL)

Cf. responses to similar questions as to what one should do, in the form of chreiai, in Berger, "Hellenistische Gattungen," 1098-99.

269. Luke 3:16-17 / Matthew 3:11-12

b. *Yebamoth* 47a, b (1 cent. CE?)

Our Rabbis taught: If at the present time a man desires to become a proselyte, he is to be addressed as follows: "What reason have you for desiring to become a proselyte; do you not know that Israel at the present time are persecuted and oppressed, despised, harassed and overcome by afflictions?" If he replies, "I know and yet am unworthy," he is accepted forthwith, and is given instruction in some of the minor and some of the major commandments. He is informed of the sin [of the neglect of the commandments of] Gleanings, the Forgotten Sheaf, the Corner, and the Poor Man's Tithe. He is also told the punishment for the transgression of the commandments. Furthermore, he is addressed thus: "Be it known to you that before you came to this condition, if you had eaten suet you would not have been punishable with *kareth*, if you had profaned the Sabbath you would not have been punishable with stoning; but now were you to eat suet you would be punished with *kareth*; were you to profane the sabbath you would be punished with stoning." And as he is informed of the punishment for the transgression of the commandments, so is he informed of the reward granted for their fulfillment. He is told, "Be it known to you that the world to come was made only for the righteous, and that Israel at the present time are unable to bear [47b] either too much prosperity, or too much suffering." He is not, however, to be persuaded or dissuaded too much. If he accepted, he is circumcised forthwith. . . . As soon as he is healed arrangements are made for his immediate ablution, when two learned men must stand by his side and acquaint him with some of the minor commandments and with some of the major ones. When he comes up after his ablution he is deemed to be an Israelite in all respects. (Soncino)

John's call to repentance and baptism may have functioned to treat his Jewish hearers as though they were outsiders to the people of God, requiring the same kind of repentance and baptism of them that they required of proselytes (though the date of this practice is disputed; on Hellenistic evidence for proselyte baptism, see the citation from Epictetus on Gal 2:13, no. 756). The zeal to make proselytes portrayed negatively in Matthew 23:15 is here placed in a different perspective. The place of proselytes was important enough in Jewish life and thought to be the central concern of one of the regular synagogue prayers (the Thirteenth Benediction, cf. no. 304).

270. Luke 4:17-21

Philo, *Embassy to Gaius* 145–49 (15 BCE–50 CE)

This [Augustus] is the Caesar who calmed the torrential storms on every side, who healed the pestilences common to Greeks and barbarians, pestilences which descending from the south and east and coursed to the west and north sowing the seeds of calamity over the places and waters which lay between. This is he who not only loosed but broke the chains which had shackled and pressed so hard on the habitable world. This is he who exterminated wars both of the open kind and the covert which are brought about by the raids of brigands. This is he who cleared the sea of pirate ships and filled it with merchant vessels. This is he who reclaimed every state to liberty, who led disorder into order and brought gentle manners and harmony to all unsociable and brutish nations. . . . He was also the first and the greatest and the common benefactor. . . (LCL)

While the specific background for Luke's picture of the salvation brought by Jesus is Isaiah 61:1-4 and Leviticus 25:10, the list of saving benefits also resonates with the description of Caesar as savior. For Philo, "calming storms" and "healing" were metaphors for political storms and the ills of the body politic. For the New Testament such stories about Jesus often intend to portray actual events, but are also symbolic of the salvation he brought.

271. Luke 5:1-11

Inscription from Epidaurus

Amphimnestos the fish carrier. This man, while carrying fish to Arkadia, vowed to give the tenth of his sale of fish to Asklepios, but he did not fulfill his vow. But while selling fish at Tagea, suddenly gnats appearing from everywhere started stinging him on the body. Since a large crowd stood around the spectacle, Amphimnestos revealed his deceit completely . . . which had occurred previously. And when he entreated the god the latter caused many fish to appear for him, and Amphimnestos dedicated the tenth to Asklepios. (Horsley, *New Documents*)

The text of the inscription is damaged and involves considerable restoration, but the content seems to be clear. The healing god Asclepius of Epidaurus is also able to implement a miraculous catch of many fish. In Luke, Jesus the healer is also master of fishing (cf. also John 21:1-14). Differences: Asclepius does this in response to an appeal; in Luke the initiative is with Jesus. The punitive and bargaining motif is absent from the miracle story in Luke, as in the New Testament generally.

272. Luke 6:27, 32, 35/ Matthew 5:43 (Q)

Seneca, *Moral Essays*, "To Novatus on Anger" 3.24.2 (ca. 4–65 CE)

What right have I to make my slave atone by stripes and manacles for too loud a reply, too rebellious a look, a muttering of something that I do not quite hear? Who am I that it should be a crime to offend my ears? Many have pardoned their enemies; shall I not pardon the lazy, the careless, and the babbler? (LCL)

Stoics do not permit themselves to be overcome by anger, and for this reason do not make retaliation the standard of their conduct. Explicit instruction is given to love one's enemies (cf. also Seneca, "On Leisure," 1.4). It is not a matter here of a theological grounding of the love commandment.

273. Luke 6:27-33/ Matthew 5:38-48 (Q)

2 Enoch 50.2-4 (1 cent. CE)

Now therefore, my children, in patience and meekness abide for the number of your days, so that you may inherit the final endless age that is coming. Every assault and every persecution and every evil word endure for the sake of the Lord. If the injury and persecution happen to you on account of the Lord, then endure them all for the sake of the Lord. And if you are able to take vengeance with a hundredfold revenge, do not take vengeance, neither on one who is close to you nor on one who is distant from you. For the Lord is the one who takes vengeance, and he will be the avenger for you on the day of the great judgment, so that there may be no acts of retribution here from human beings, but only from the Lord. (*OTP* 1:176)

As in Matthew 5, the linguistic data in v. 3 point to Exodus 21:15. Both cases are concerned to overcome the law of retaliation (on the genre, see Berger, *Formgeschichte* §§176-77). Of course, here it is only a matter of patience, not by responding to evil with positive good. Cf. no. 609. Note the eschatological grounding of ethics, as in the Sermon on the Mount/Plain.

274. Luke 6:27-35/ Matthew 5:43-47(Q)

Plutarch, *Moralia*, "Sayings of the Spartans: Ariston" 1 (45–125 CE)

When someone commended the maxim of Cleomenes, who, on being asked what a good king ought to do, said, "To do good to his friends and evil to his enemies," Ariston said, "How much better, my good sir, to do good to our friends, and to make friends of our enemies?" (LCL)

As in Matthew, a maxim that distinguishes between friends and enemies is corrected and dismissed by an appeal to the new authority. In regard to the dictum of Cleomenes, this text corresponds more to Matthew 5:43*b* than to the passage in 1QS 1.9-10: "He [the Master] shall admit into the Covenant of Grace all those who have freely devoted themselves to the observance of God's precepts, that they may be joined to the counsel of God and may live perfectly before Him in accordance with all that has been revealed concerning their appointed times, and that they [the saints] may love all the sons of light, each according to his lot in God's design, and hate all the sons of darkness each according to his guilt in God's vengeance" (Vermes). In Matthew, the "neighbor" is not restricted to the members of the group, as is the case in the Qumran dictum.

275. Luke 6:27-35/ Matthew 5:43-47 (Q)

Epictetus, *Discourses* 3.22.54 (55–135 CE)

For this too is a very pleasant strand woven into the Cynic's pattern of life; he must needs be flogged like an ass, and while he is being flogged he must love the men who flog him, as though he were the father or brother of them all. (LCL)

Context: greatness and suffering belong together. Hercules is the model. Zeus permits suffering in order to prove the validity of the philosopher, thus showing the philosopher's freedom. Similarly *Discourses* 4.1.127 and the Stoic fragment in von Arnim (*SVF* III, 578-80; Seneca in his writing "On the Steadfastness of the Wise"). Cf. Lucian, "Philosophies for Sale," 9: "Leading this life [as a Cynic] you will say that you are happier than the Great King; and if anyone flogs you or twists you on the rack, you will think that there is nothing painful in it" (LCL). Cf. Dio Chrysostom, Discourse 60/61, 41: "They despise him [the philosopher] and say he is crazy. He, however, does not get angry with them nor is he indignant, but, I believe, still wishes him well, like a father to each one, more even than a brother or friend" (MEB/Berger). On charging the philosopher with insanity, cf. Mark 3:21, nos. 235-36.

276. Luke 6:27-35/ Matthew 5:43-47 (Q)

Marcus Aurelius, *The Communings with Himself* 2, 1 (121–180 CE)

Say to thyself at daybreak: I shall come across the busybody, the thankless, the bully, the treacherous, the envious, the unneighborly. All this has befallen them because they know not good from evil. But I, in that I have comprehended the nature of the Good that it is beautiful, and the nature of Evil that it is ugly, and the nature of the wrongdoer himself that it is akin to me, not as partaker of the same blood and seed but of intelligence and a morsel of the Divine, can neither be injured by any of them—for no one can involve me in what is debasing—nor can I be wroth with my kinsman and hate him. For we have come into being for cooperation, as have the feet, the hands, the eyelids, the rows of upper and lower teeth. Therefore to thwart one another is against Nature; and we do thwart one another by showing resentment and aversion. (LCL)

Here it is the sense of a common origin that is the motivation for putting up with the offensive element among one's fellow human beings, and even leads to cooperative work with them. Matthew 5:45-48 argues differently: God is the model, and one becomes God's child when one responds to the evil and the good as does God. In place of the common human nature stands the one God (cf. also no. 148). But on this cf. also Seneca (4–65 CE), "On Benefits," IV.25.2-26.3 (16.1): "If you are imitating the gods," you say, "then bestow benefits also upon the ungrateful; for the sun rises also upon the wicked, and the sea lies open also to pirates" (LCL). Similarly Marcus Aurelius, "Love human-kind. Follow God" (7.31) and "The Gods—and they are immortal—do not take it amiss that for a time so long they must inevitably and always put up with worthless men who are what they are and so many; nay they even befriend them in all manner of ways" (7.70) (LCL). On the body analogy, cf. nos. 694-96, 802-3.

277. Luke 6:29*b* / Matthew 5:40 (Q)

Aramaic *Ahiqar* 57.1 13-14 (5 cent. BCE)

When a blasphemer grabs your garment, let him have it! Shamash is coming near to you in this incident: he will take something from that one and give it to you. (MEB/Berger)

Cf. M. Küchler, *Frühjüdische Weisheitstraditionen* (Göttingen: Vandenhoeck & Ruprecht, 1979), 319ff., 387. The circumstances and the requisite response are analogous. The motivation is different in Matthew (5:48), but similar to a comparable Pauline context (Rom 12:19-20). As the Sun god, Shamash is also responsible for guaranteeing justice.

278. Luke 6:31 / Matthew 7:12 (Q)

Rabbi Hillel, in *b. Shabbath* 30b (early 1 cent. CE)

What is hateful to you, do not to your neighbor. That is the whole Torah, while the rest is commentary; go and learn. (Soncino)

This statement is often rightly cited as a Jewish analogy and predecessor to the "Golden Rule." Its context is also important: A Gentile wanted to become a Jewish proselyte, but on the condition that he be taught the whole Torah while standing on one foot. The text is thus also an example of "summaries of the Law" such as we find in Romans 13:9. There are other rabbinic parallels, e.g. *Abot. R. Nat.* 15: "Rabbi Eliezer says: Let the respect owing to your companion be as precious to you as the respect owing to yourself. And don't be easy to anger. And repent one day before you die.

Let the respect owing to your companion be as precious to you as the respect owing to yourself: how so?

This teaches that just as someone sees to the honor owing to himself, so he should see to the honor owing to his fellow.

And just as a person does not want a bad name to circulate against his honor, so he should not want to circulate a bad name against the honor owing to his fellow" (Neusner, *Rabbi Nathan*). In an honor/shame society such as the ancient Mediterranean, a rule so formulated deals with one's central value system (see Bruce Malina, *The New Testament World: Insights from Cultural Anthropology* [Louisville: Westminster/John Knox, rev. ed. 1993], chap. 2).

On "summaries of the law" cf. Matthew 22:34-40/ Mark 12:28-31/ Luke 10:25-28/ Romans 13:9-10.

279. Luke 6:31 / Matthew 7:12 (Q)

The negative form: Isocrates, "To Demonicus" 1.17 (4 cent. BCE)

But most of all will you have the respect of men, if you are seen to avoid doing things which you would blame others for doing. (LCL)

Similarly: Homer, *Odyssey* 5:188-89; Herodotus, *The Histories* 3.142; *Tg. Yer.* Lev. 19:18: "What you yourself do not like, do not do [to your neighbor]."

The positive form: Isocrates, "To Demonicus" 1.21 (4 cent. BCE)

You will attain such self-control . . . if you manage your temper toward those who offend against you as you would expect others to do if you offended against them. (LCL)

Cf. Demosthenes (384–322 BCE), *Exordia* 22.3: "By rights, of course, all men should feel toward those who are wronged as each would think fit to demand of all others to feel toward himself if something should go amiss, which I pray may not happen" (LCL).

For literature, see A. Dihle, *Die Goldene Regel* (Göttingen: Vandenhoeck & Ruprecht, 1962).

280. Luke 6:36/ Matthew 5:48 (Q)

Philo, *The Special Laws* 1.318 (15–50 CE)

This promise of mine is confirmed by the law, where it says that they who do "what is pleasing" to nature and what is "good" are sons of God. For it says, "Ye are sons to your Lord God," clearly meaning that He will think fit to protect and provide for you as would a father. And how much this watchful care will exceed that of men is measured, believe me, by the surpassing excellence of Him who bestows it. (LCL)

As in Matthew, being a child of God is made dependent on doing the good. In context, this means fulfilling the Law. In contrast to Philo, in Matthew, the providential care of God takes precedence and is directed to all, not primarily to the children of God, although Matthew certainly did not wish to exclude this futuristic aspect. In the *Apocalypse of Paul* (Greek and Syriac), God must command the angels, despite their explicit objections, to grant the good gifts of creation not only to the righteous, but to sinners as well.

281. Luke 6:37-38/ Matthew 7:2 (Q)

Targum Neofiti I on Genesis 38:25-26 (1–3 cent. CE)

It is better for me to burn in this world, with extinguishable fire, that I may not be burned in the world to come whose fire is inextinguishable. It is better for me to blush in this world that is a passing world, that I may not blush before my just fathers in the world to come. And listen to me, my brothers and house of my father: In the measure in which a man measures it shall be measured to him, whether it be a good measure or a bad measure. Blessed is every man who reveals his works. Inasmuch as I took the ornamented garment of my brother Joseph and dipped it in blood of the kid-goat and I said to Jacob: "Examine, examine I pray whether this is the ornamented garment of your son or not." (McNamara)

The fundamental principle behind Jesus' statement is here strengthened by the fact that the nature of one's relations with others in the present age not only is reflected in the age to come, but that the consequences are intensified. In Matthew, the eschatological tone is only derived from the context, while in the story of Judah, the eschatological dimension is made explicit in the "application."

282. Luke 6:39-40/ Matthew 15:14 (Q)

Plutarch, *Moralia,* "To An Uneducated Ruler" 10.2-3 (45–125 CE)

For one who is falling cannot hold others up, nor can one who is ignorant teach, nor the uncultivated impart culture, nor the disorderly make order, nor can he rule who is under no rule. But most people foolishly believe that the first advantage of ruling is freedom from being ruled. Who, then, shall rule the ruler? The "law, the king of all, both mortals and immortals," as Pindar says—not law written outside him in books or in wooden tablets or the like, but reason endowed with life within him, always abiding with him and watching over him and never leaving his soul without his leadership. (LCL)

This observation of wisdom derived from general experience is here applied from the perspective of models used as examples, common in the ancient world. That which is applied by Plutarch to king and the law is generalized by Luke with regard to teachers and students, applied by Matthew to Pharisees and the Law, in Romans 2:19-23 to Jews and the Law. Whoever will teach others must himself follow his own instruction. That was a fundamental principle of Greek *paideia,* especially in the tradition of Socrates. That which was said in the Hellenistic world of rulers is said in the New Testament of religious leaders.

On Luke 14:15-24/ Matthew 22:1-14, cf. nos. 325-26.

283. Luke 6:40/ Matthew 10:24-25/ John 13:16 (Q)

Sifra 25:23 (2 cent. CE from older tradition)

[God is speaking to Israel:] You are my servants. [Sifra comments:] It is enough for the servant that he be as his master. (Smith, *Tannaitic Parallels*)

Morton Smith has pointed out that "so far as I know, parallels of this sort have never hitherto been discussed as a peculiar group, and no student has pointed out the fact that it is common to find a saying which was applied to God in TL [Tannaitic Literature] applied to Jesus in the Gospels. But R. H. Charles had already remarked that the Gospels speak of Jesus as the Old Testament speaks of God" (*Tannaitic Parallels,* 152; the quotation from Charles is from *Religious Development Between the Old and New Testaments* [London: H. Holt and Co., 1914], p. 95).

The phenomenon itself has been noticed, but "what has always been lacking has been the remark, that the Gospels *customarily* put in Jesus' mouth, or say of him, what TL puts in the mouth of, or says of, God" (*Tannaitic Parallels,* 152, emphasis added). As other representative examples, Smith points to Luke 10:16/ Matthew 10:40; Luke 10:24/ Matthew 13:17; Matthew 25:35-40; John 5:46 (see nos. 187, 300, 302, 310, 414).

284. Luke 6:40/ Matthew 10:24-25/ John 13:16 (Q)

Epictetus, *Discourses* 2.23.16 (55–135 CE)

"What then," says an objector, "if the matter stands like *this*, and it *is* possible for that which serves to be superior to what it serves—the horse to the rider, or the dog to the hunter, or his instrument to the harper, or his servants to the king?" (LCL)

A truth from everyday life about the natural order of things, as offered by Epictetus, in Matthew illustrates the equal status of all at the parousia, in Luke and John is a protest against ambition, presenting Jesus as a model in humility.

285. Luke 6:41-42/ Matthew 7:3-5 (Q)

Seneca, *On the Happy Life* 27:6 (4–65 CE)

Why do you not rather look about you at your own sins that rend you on every side, some assailing you from without, others raging in your very vitals. Human affairs—even if you have insufficient knowledge of your own position—have not yet reached the situation in which you may have such superfluity of spare time as to find leisure to wag your tongue in abusing your betters. (LCL)

Cf. similarly Menander 1:1, "If you are inclined to complain about your neighbor, first notice what's wrong with yourself" (MEB/Berger). Such texts document the traditional philosophical position that warns against presumption and arrogance. A close parallel to the saying of Jesus is offered by the *b. Arak.* 16b, "Said R. Tarfon, 'I should be surprised if there is anyone left in this generation who accepts rebuke. If one says to someone, "Remove the chip from your eye," the other party responds, "Take the beam from your eye"'" (Neusner, *Talmud*). Here, however, in distinction from Matthew, the offering of any criticism at all is forbidden. The illustration is only given to show how difficult it is to criticize someone, since every critic immediately gets in response the saying about the chip and the beam.

286. Luke 6:41-42/ Matthew 7:3-5 (Q)

Petronius, *Satyricon* 57.7, "Ascyltos Gets into Hot Water" (d. 66 CE)

But are you so full of business that you have no time to look behind you? You can see the lice on others, but not the bugs on yourself. No one finds us comic but you. (LCL)

Since in Matthew 7:3-5 there is no reference to the kingdom of God or other items specifically Jewish-Christian, our text documents the possibility that Jesus adopted an expression of current wisdom for which the constitutive element was the discrepancy between the way people judge others and the way they see themselves.

287. Luke 6:47-49 / Matthew 7:24-27 (Q)

The Fathers According to Rabbi Nathan 24:1-2
(3–4 cent.; compilation 7–9 cent.)

[Both good deeds and Torah-learning are necessary.]

1. A. Elisha b. Abuyah says, "One who has good deeds to his credit and has studied the Torah a great deal—to what is he to be likened?

B. "To someone who builds first with stones and then with bricks. Even though a great flood of water comes and washes against the foundations the water does not blot them out of their place.

C. "One who has no good deeds to his credit but has studied the Torah—to what is he to be likened?

D. "To someone who builds first with bricks and then with stones. Even if only a little water comes and washes against the foundations, it forthwith overturns them."

2. A. He used to say, "One who has good deeds to his credit and has studied the Torah a great deal—to what is he to be likened?

B. "To lime spread over stones. Even if vast rainstorms come down on them they do not stir the lime from its place.

C. "One who has no good deeds to his credit but has studied the Torah a great deal—to what is he to be likened?

D. "To lime spread over bricks. Even if a sporadic rain falls on the lime, it is forthwith melted and disappears." (Neusner, *Rabbi Nathan*)

The comparative material (building, water, bipartite literary construction) is closely comparable to the saying of Jesus, and the intended application is especially so: hearing and doing vs. hearing without doing.

In common with Q is also the genre and the structure of the parable (cf. Berger, *Formgeschichte*, §51.7, p. 174). The position occupied by the word of Jesus in Q is taken in the rabbinic text by the study of Torah. The claim to confer permanence and stability was especially beloved in the Hellenistic world.

On Matthew 8:5-13, Luke 7:1-10, cf. no. 404.

288. Luke 7:1-10 / Matthew 8:5-13 (Q)

b. Berakoth 34b (1 cent. CE tradition; written later)

Our rabbis have taught on Tannaite authority:

There was the case in which the son of Rabban Gamaliel fell ill. He sent two disciples of sages to R. Hanina b. Dosa to pray for mercy for him.

When he saw them, he went up to his upper room and prayed for mercy for him.

When he came down, he said to them, "Go, for his fever has left him."

They said to him, "Are you a prophet?"

He said to them, "I am not a prophet nor a disciple of a prophet, but this is what I have received as a tradition: *If my prayer is fluent, then I know that he [for whom I pray] is accepted, and if not, then I know that he is rejected.*"

They sat down and wrote down the hour, and when they came back to Rabban Gamaliel, he said to them "By the Temple service! You were neither early nor late, but that is just how it happened. At that very moment, his fever left him and he asked us for water to drink." (Neusner, *Talmud*)

As in the Gospel story, the healing is accomplished at a distance. The dialogue incorporated into the miracle story is the key point in both the Jewish story and the New Testament, but the point is different in each case. Cf. John 4:46-54, esp. 4:52-53.

289. Luke 7:1-10 / Matthew 8:5-13 (Q)

Josephus, *Jewish War* 2.195 (37–100 CE)

When the Jews appealed to their law and the custom of their ancestors, and pleaded that they were forbidden to place an image of God, much more of a man, not only in their sanctuary but even in any unconsecrated spot throughout the country, Petronius replied, "But I too must obey the law of my master; if I transgress it and spare you, I shall be put to death, with justice. War will be made on you by him who sent me, not by me; for I too, like you, am under orders." (LCL)

The nobility of the Roman officer is shown in this scene pictured by Josephus (cf. Luke 7:5!), as well as his sense of being part of a chain of command. Gaius Caligula had given the insane order to install his image in the temple in Jerusalem. Petronius, with three legions under his command, marched reluctantly from Antioch to enforce the decree. When the Jews came out en masse passively to resist this madness, and convincingly indicated they were willing to sacrifice their lives in the protest, Petronius finally backed down and accepted the responsibility himself, indicating it was better for him to die for insubordination than so many innocent civilians. But in the process of negotiating with the Jews, the above statement is made that is not merely the comment of a lackey, but one with a sense of authority and its uses, a sense that he fits into a great chain of command on which the order necessary for human life depends. A difference: Here, the point is that both Petronius and the Jews are *subject* to a higher authority that they must obey. In the Q text, the point is that both the centurion and Jesus *have* authority that commands obedience.

The story presupposes and accepts the validity of the institution of slavery. For the Essenes' repudiation of slavery, see no. 30 on Matthew 5–7.

290. Luke 7:11-17

Philostratos, *Life of Apollonius of Tyana* 4.45 (3 cent. CE)

Here too is a miracle which Apollonius worked: A girl had died just in the hour of her marriage, and the bridegroom was following her bier lamenting as was natural his marriage left unfulfilled, and the whole of Rome was mourning with him, for the maiden belonged to a consular family. Apollonius then witnessing their grief, said: "Put down the bier, for I will stay the tears that you are shedding for this maiden." And withal he asked what was her name. The crowd accordingly thought that he was about to deliver such an oration as is commonly delivered as much to grace the funeral as to stir up lamentation; but he did nothing of the kind, but merely touching her and whispering in secret some spell over her, at once woke up the maiden from her seeming death; and the girl spoke out loud, and returned to her father's house, just as Alcestis did when she was brought back to life by Hercules. And the relations of the maiden wanted to present him with the sum of 150,000 sesterces, but he said that he would freely present the money to the young lady by way of a dowry. Now whether he detected some spark of life in her, which those who were nursing her had not noticed—for it is said that although it was raining at the time, a vapor went up from her face—or whether life was really extinct, and he restored it by the warmth of his touch, is a mysterious problem which neither I myself nor those who were present could decide. (LCL)

Apuleius of Madaura, *Florida* 19:2-6 (125 CE)

It chanced that once, when he [Asclepiades] was returning to town from his country house, he observed an enormous funeral procession in the suburbs of the city. A huge multitude of men who had come out to perform the last honors stood round about the bier, all of them plunged in deep sorrow and wearing worn and ragged apparel. He asked whom they were burying, but no one replied; so he went nearer to satisfy his curiosity and to see who it might be that was dead, or, it may be, in the hope to make some discovery in the interests of his profession. Be this as it may, he certainly snatched the man from the jaws of death as he lay there on the verge of burial. The poor fellow's limbs were already covered with spices, his mouth filled with sweet-smelling unguent. He had been anointed and was all ready for the pyre. But Asclepiades looked upon him, took careful note of certain signs, handled his body again and again, and perceived that the life was still in him, though scarcely to be detected. Straightway he cried out "He lives! Throw down your torches, take away your fire, demolish the pyre, take back the funeral feast and spread it on his board at home." While he spoke, a murmur arose: some said that they must take the doctor's word, others mocked at the physician's skill. At last, in spite of the opposition offered even by relations, perhaps because they had already entered into possession of the dead man's property, perhaps because they did not yet believe his words, Asclepiades persuaded them to put off the burial for a brief space. Having thus rescued him from the hands of the undertaker, he carried the man home, as it were from the very mouth of hell, and straightway revived the spirit within him, and by means of certain drugs called forth the life that still lay hidden in the secret places of the body. (Butler, *Apologia*)

Paraleipomena Jeremiou 7:12-16, 18-20 (1 cent. CE)

. . . When he [the eagle] arrived he rested on a post outside the city in a desert place. And he kept silent until Jeremiah came along, for he and some of the people were coming out to bury a corpse outside the city. (For Jeremiah had petitioned king Nebuchadnezzar, saying: "Give me a place where I may bury those of my people who have died"; and the king gave it to him.)

And as they were coming out with the body, and weeping, they came to where the eagle was. And the eagle cried out in a loud voice, saying: I say to you, Jeremiah the chosen one of God, go and gather together the people and come here so that they may hear a letter which I have brought to you from Baruch and Abimelech.

. . . and the eagle came down on the corpse, and it revived. (Now this took place so that they might believe.) And all the people were astounded at what had happened, and said:

This is the God who appeared to our fathers in the wilderness through Moses, and now he has appeared to us through this eagle. (Kraft and Purintun)

To this category of narrative, stories of resuscitations, one may also compare the miracle worked by Asclepius according to no. 339 below. Common elements (no. 290): The incident takes place just outside the city, as the miracle worker meets the funeral procession. He works the miracle (predominantly) in public view (in contrast to the OT type of resuscitation story, as found in 1 Kgs 17:17-24; 2 Kgs 4:18-37; and Mark 5:21-43 and parallels). In this type of miracle, faith plays no role. Both Luke and Philostratus emphasize that the dead person was of extraordinary importance (the only son of a widow; a bride during the wedding days). The giving back of the revived one to the family is pictured (except in *PJ*). In both Luke and Philostratus, the halting of the procession and the letting down of the bier plays an important dramatic role (so also in the text from Epidaurus in no. 339 below). In Luke, Jesus touches the bier and speaks directly to the corpse; in Philostratus the dead girl is touched.

The miraculous power at work in the event is evaluated in quite different ways. To a certain degree, the one extreme is represented by the reports which regard the resuscitation as the result of medical techniques (besides Apuleius in no. 290, cf. also the brief report about Empedocles in Diogenes Laertius about the "lack of breath," *Lives* 8:60-61, 67; cf. Suidas, *Lexicon* on ἄπνους). At the other extreme God himself works the miracle through his messenger (in Luke, Jesus; in P J, the eagle), the miracle serving as God's legitimation of the messenger. Between these poles stands the report of Philostratus, which possibly has a "naive" miracle story as its basis, for which the present version suggests a rationalistic explanation.

291. Luke 7:24-26/ Matthew 11:7-9 (Q)

A. Aesop, *Fable* (collection since 5 cent. BCE)

A reed and an olive tree were disputing about their strength and their powers of quiet endurance. When the reed was reproached by the olive with being weak and easily bent by every wind, it answered not a word. Soon afterward a strong wind began to blow. The reed, by letting itself be tossed about and bent by the gusts, weathered the storm without difficulty; but the olive, which resisted it, was broken by its violence.

The moral is that people should accept the situation in which they find themselves and yield to superior force. This is better than kicking against the pricks. (Handford)

B. *b. Ta'anith* 20a

Better is the curse which Ahijah the Shilonite pronounced on Israel than the blessings with which Balaam the wicked blessed them. Ahijah the Shilonite cursed them by comparing them with the *"reed"*; he said to Israel, *For the Lord will smite Israel as a reed is shaken in water.* [Israel are as the reed], as the reed grows by the water and its stock grows new shoots and its roots are many, and even though all the winds of the universe come and blow at it they cannot move it from its place for it sways with the winds and as soon as they have dropped the reed resumes its upright position. But Balaam the wicked blessed them by comparing them with the *"cedar,"* as it is said, *As cedars beside the waters;* the cedar does not grow by the waterside and its stock does not grow new shoots and its roots are not many, and even though all the winds of the universe blow at it they cannot move it from its place; if however the south wind blows against it, it can uproot it and turn it over. (Soncino)

The common elements are widespread both in pagan fables (Aesop; cf. Babrios §36 and Avian §16 in H. C. Schnur, *Fabeln der Antike,* 1978) and in rabbinic tradition (Derek Erez 4; *Abot. R. Nat.* 41). The "tree" changes according to geographical location (cedar, oak, olive tree). The text cited here, with its consistent application to the destiny of Israel, shows how a Hellenistic figurative story could be interpreted in a rabbinic manner. In Luke 7:24-26/ Matthew 11:7, only a part of this picture is used, so it is probably superfluous to ask who is to be represented by the oak. Is it a contrast between the prophet (John the Baptist) and the royal palace (Herod Antipas), as G. Theissen supposes (*ZDPV* 101:43-55)? The use of the material in Claudian, *Depracatio ad Hadrianum* 37, would speak for an application from the political perspective.

292. Luke 7:25/ Matthew 11:8 (Q)

Lucian, *Saturnalia* 2.29 (120–185 CE)

[Cronus to His Very Dear Me:] Now if you ignored and despised them and neither turned to look at their silver carriage nor during conversation glanced at the emeralds in their ring and touched their dress in admiration at its softness, but let them be rich for themselves alone, you may be quite sure they would come to you of their own accord and beg you to dine with them so that they might show you their couches and tables and cups, which are no use if people don't see that they're yours. (LCL)

For religiously motivated critique on the evils of wealth, the "Saturnalia letters" of Lucian are of great significance, though long neglected. (They are in the form of letters from Lucian or rich people to the god Saturn, who responds from time to time.) The portrayal of riches and the attitude taken toward them show clear resemblance to Q. The significance of the "kingdom of Saturn" should also be kept in mind with regard to the pagan understanding of the "kingdom of God." Cf. nos. 689-90.

293. Luke 7:31/ Matthew 11:16 (Q)

Josephus, *Jewish War* 6.408 (37–100 CE)

[On the destruction of Jerusalem:] . . . a city undeserving, moreover, of these great misfortunes on any other ground save that she produced a generation such as that which caused her overthrow. (LCL)

As repeatedly in Q (Luke 7:31/ Matt 11:16; Luke 11:29/ Matt 12:39; Luke 11:30-32/ Matt 12:41-42, 45; Luke 11:50-51/ Matt 23:36), it is not Jerusalem as such, but "this generation" that is rebellious and has brought (in Q and the Gospels, "will bring") devastation on the holy city.

294. Luke 7:32/ Matthew 11:17 (Q)

Herodotus, *The Histories* 1.141 (484 BCE)

Once, he [Cyrus of Persia] said, there was a flute-player who saw fishes in the sea and played upon his flute, thinking that so they would come out on to the land. Being disappointed of his hope, he took a net and gathered in and drew out a great multitude of the fishes; and seeing them leaping, "You had best," said he, "cease from your dancing now; you would not come out and dance then, when I played to you." (LCL)

The activities of a flute player and fish are not harmonious. When he plays the flute, they do not want to dance, and when they dance (= wriggle in the net), this is annoying to him. In any case, they do not want to do what he wants.

295. Luke 7:32/ Matthew 11:17 (Q)

b. Sanhedrin 103a (4 cent. CE?)

Said R. Pappa, "This is in line with what people say: 'Weep for the one who does not know, laugh for the one who does not know. Woe to him who does not know the difference between good and bad.'" (Neusner, *Talmud*)

In the context the statement applies to king Amaziah, who worshiped foreign gods whether he was victorious in battle or was defeated by his enemies.

The opposite, positive attitude is called for by Sirach 7:34 and Romans 12:15, though here it is not a matter of dancing. Herodotus could have been aware of the fable from the collection that circulated under the name Aesop (§27 in Halm's collection), and it is possible that Jesus used this tradition in the first part of his saying, and elements such as those in Sirach 7:34 or *b. Sanhedrin* 103a for the second part. But attempting to establish such connections is not important. One only needs to note that such figurative material was current, the broad point being that people are not able to respond to a challenge whether it is offered in this way or in that, so that such language was readily understandable in the situation of Jesus and Q. Cf. A. A. T. Ehrhardt, "Greek Proverbs in the Gospels," *HThR* 46 (1953), 66-68.

296. Luke 9:58/ Matthew 8:20 (Q)

Epictetus, *Discourses* 3.22.45-48 (55–135 CE)

And how is it possible for a man who has nothing, who is naked, without home or hearth, in squalor, without a slave, without a city, to live serenely? Behold, god has sent you the man who will show in practice that it is possible. "Look at me," he says, "I am without a home, without a city, without property, without a slave; I sleep on the ground; I have neither wife nor children, no miserable governor's mansion, but only earth, and sky, and one rough cloak. Yet what do I lack? Am I not free from pain and fear, am I not free?" (LCL)

The one sent from God is here the Cynic. On the various points of contact between Jesus, his disciples, and the Cynic wandering philosophers, see also nos. 144, 148, 298, 317, 325.

297. Luke 9:58/ Matthew 8:20 (Q)

Plutarch, *Parallel Lives*, "Tiberius Gracchus" 9.4 (45–125 CE)

"The wild beasts that roam over Italy," he would say, "have every one of them a cave or a lair to lurk in; but the men who fight and die for Italy enjoy the common air and light, indeed, but nothing else; houseless and homeless they wander about with their wives and children." (LCL)

This is a brief excerpt from a speech by Tiberius (as reported by Plutarch) at the beginning of his reign. The speech was in defense of the law redistributing the land to reward faithful soldiers, a law which generated much anger among the wealthy land-owning class. The similar words have a different function in their Gospel settings.

298. Luke 9:60/ Matthew 8:22 (Q)

Teles, "On Banishment" (ca. 240 BCE)

[Resistance to being buried in foreign soil is being overcome. The way to Hades is in fact quite short, wherever one is buried. The discourse continues:] Or, in the first place, what does it matter to you if you are not buried? "Indeed, the anguish over burial," says Bion, "has composed many tragedies." Just as even Polyneices commands:
But bury me, Mother and you my sister,
In my ancestral land, and calm the angry
City, so that I win at least this much
Of my ancestral soil, though I've lost home.
But if you should not be buried but be tossed out without a grave, what is so annoying about that? Or what is the difference in being burnt up by fire, eaten up by a dog or being devoured by ravens above the ground or by worms below?
And close my eyelids fast with your own hand, Mother.
But should she not "close your eyelids fast," and you should die stark and staring, what will be the difficulty? (O'Neil)

The old Cynic Teles declares his complete indifference with regard to the holiest customs of society: even to remain unburied is no disgrace. Philosophy and doing right are the only values worth striving for. This text is one of a whole series of analogies between the appearance of the messengers sent out by Jesus and the Cynics (cf. nos. 144, 148, 296, 317, 325). Alongside the freedom from worry, here the freedom from any inhibition by conventional piety steps forward. That which in Matthew 8:22 is referred to one's relatives is here applied to the Cynic himself.

299. Luke 10:6 / Matthew 10:13 (Q)

Aristophanes, "The Acharnians" 833 (5–4 cent. BCE)

[After rejecting the customary "farewell":] Then on my head the officious wish return! (LCL) [Comment of the scholiast: "as an accusation against someone, with malicious intent."]

Both the passage from Aristophanes and the NT saying are based on a "materialistic" understanding of language: if the one addressed by a greeting is not worthy, then the greeting returns to the one who spoke it, since it could not find a point of contact with the one addressed.
On Luke 10:16 / Matthew 10:40, cf. no. 135.

300. Luke 10:16 / Matthew 10:40 (Q)

Mekilta of R. Simon b. Jochai 18.12 (2 cent. CE from older traditions)

Whoever receives the Sages [lit. the faces of the Sages] is as if he received the Shekinah [lit. the faces, etc.; most MSS have "whoever receive his companion"]. (MEB/Berger)

See nos. 135, 283 on Luke 6:40 / Matthew 10:24-25.

301. Luke 10:20

Cicero, *The Republic* 6.13 (106–43 BCE)

But, Africanus, be assured of this, so that you may be even more eager to defend the commonwealth: all those who have preserved, aided, or enlarged their fatherland have a special place prepared for them in the heavens, where they may enjoy an eternal life of happiness. For nothing of all that is done on earth is more pleasing to that supreme God who rules the whole universe than the assemblies and gatherings of men associated in justice, which are called States. Their rulers and preservers come from that place, and to that place they return. (LCL)

Old Testament and Jewish parallels to this oriental idea regularly speak of the Book (of Life) and of names being written there, just as in Luke. So too in Cicero the preservation of civil law and the freedom of the state are not conceivable without this certification.
In addition, Jewish texts know the picture of house and dwelling (see Rudolf Schnackenburg, *The Gospel According to St. John* [New York: Seabury Press, 1980], 3:61-62 on John 14:2-3, and cf. no.

460). In *Joseph and Aseneth* 22:9, the "place" is spoken of, as in Cicero. The one sent by God comes from heaven and returns to heaven (cf. nos. 217, 391).

On Luke 11:20, cf. no. 73.

302. Luke 10:24/ Matthew 13:17 (Q)

Mekilta 15:2 (2 cent. CE from older traditions)

"This is my God," R. Eliezer says, "Whence do you [find justification for] saying that a servant girl at the sea saw what Isaiah and Ezekiel did not see? Because it is said . . ." (Smith, *Tannaitic Parallels*)

See no. 283 on Luke 6:40/ Matthew 10:24-25.

303. Luke 10:31

Inscription from the temple of Athena in Pergamum (prior to 4 cent. BCE)

Whoever wishes to visit the temple of the goddess, whether a resident of the city or anyone else, must refrain from intercourse with his wife [or her husband] that day, from intercourse·with another than his wife [or her husband] for the preceding two days, and must complete the required lustrations. The same prohibition applies to contact with the dead and with the delivery of a woman in childbirth. (Grant)

This very old inscription, still valid in the Hellenistic age, illustrates that purity at the temple was a matter of ritual cleanliness, not of morality, and that it was universally understood, not only a matter of priestly lore. The priest of Luke 10:31 may have had the particular injunction against touching dead bodies of Leviticus 21:1-3 and related traditions in mind, but the Hellenistic readership to whom Luke directs the story would get the point without any knowledge of particular Jewish rules.

304. Luke 11:1-4/ Matthew 6:9-15 (prayer) (Q)

The Eighteen Benedictions (elements from 1 cent. CE)

1. Blessed art Thou, O Lord, our God and God of our fathers, God of Abraham, God of Isaac, and God of Jacob, the great, mighty, and revered God, God Most High, who art the Creator of heaven and earth, our Shield and the Shield of our fathers, our confidence from generation to generation. Blessed art Thou, O Lord, the Shield of Abraham!

2. Thou art mighty, who bringest low the proud, strong, and He that judgeth the ruthless, that liveth for ever, that raiseth the dead, that maketh the wind to blow, that sendeth down the dew; that sustaineth the living, that quickeneth the dead; in the twinkling of

an eye Thou makest salvation to spring forth for us. Blessed art Thou, O Lord, who quickenest the dead!

3. Holy art Thou and Thy Name is to be feared, and there is no God beside Thee. Blessed art Thou, O Lord, the holy God.

4. O favor us, our Father, with knowledge from Thyself and understanding and discernment from Thy Torah. Blessed art Thou, O Lord, who vouchsafest knowledge!

5. Cause us to return, O Lord, unto Thee, and let us return anew [in repentance] in our days as in the former time. Blessed art Thou, O Lord, who delightest in repentance.

6. Forgive us, our Father, for we have sinned against Thee; blot out and cause our transgressions to pass from before Thine eyes, for great is Thy mercy. Blessed art Thou, O Lord, who dost abundantly forgive!

7. Look upon our affliction and plead our cause, and redeem us for the sake of Thy Name. Blessed art Thou, O Lord, the Redeemer of Israel!

8. Heal us, O Lord our God, from the pain of our heart; and weariness and sighing do Thou cause to pass away from us; and cause Thou to rise up healing for our wounds. Blessed art Thou, O Lord, who healest the sick of Thy people Israel!

9. Bless for us, O Lord our God, this year for our welfare, with every kind of the produce thereof, and bring near speedily the year of the end of our redemption; and give dew and rain upon the face of the earth and satisfy the world from the treasures of Thy goodness, and do thou give a blessing upon the work of our hands. Blessed art Thou, O Lord, who blessest the years!

10. Blow the great horn for our liberation, and lift a banner to gather our exiles. Blessed art Thou, O Lord, who gatherest the dispersed of Thy people Israel!

11. Restore our judges as at the first, and our counselors as at the beginning; and reign Thou over us, Thou alone. Blessed art Thou, O Lord, who lovest judgment!

12. For apostates let there be no hope, and the dominion of arrogance do Thou speedily root out in our days; and let the Nazoreans and the heretics perish as in a moment, let them be blotted out of the book of the living and let them not be written with the righteous. Blessed art Thou, O Lord, who humblest the arrogant!

13. Toward the righteous proselytes may Thy tender mercies be stirred; and bestow a good reward upon us together with those that do thy will. Blessed art thou, O Lord, the trust of the righteous!

14. Be merciful, O Lord our God, in Thy great mercy toward Israel Thy people, and toward Jerusalem Thy City, and toward Zion the abiding place of Thy glory, and toward Thy glory, and toward Thy temple and Thy habitation, and toward the kingdom of the house of David, Thy righteous and anointed one. Blessed art Thou, O God, God of David, the Builder of Jerusalem!

15. Hear, O Lord our God, the sound of our prayer and have mercy upon us, for a God gracious and merciful art Thou. Blessed art Thou, O Lord, who hearest prayer!

16. Accept us, O Lord our God, and dwell in Zion; and may Thy servants serve Thee in Jerusalem. Blessed art Thou, O Lord, whom in reverent fear we serve!

17. We give thanks to Thee, who art the Lord our God and the God of our fathers, for all the good things, the lovingkindness, and the mercy which Thou has wrought and done with us and with our fathers before us: and if we said, Our feet slip, Thy lovingkindness, O Lord, upheld us. Blessed art Thou, O Lord, unto whom it is good to give thanks!

18. Bestow Thy peace upon Israel Thy people and upon Thy city and upon Thine inheritance and bless us, all of us together. Blessed art Thou, O Lord, who makest peace!

This is still the standard prayer of the synagogue, called the *Amidah* because it is said standing. Its basic elements and structure go back to the first century. There are several translations and editions. The text given here is the presumed early text, based on the reconstruction of Gustav Dalman in *The Words of Jesus* (Edinburgh: T. & T. Clark, 1909). Other translations may be found in C. W. Dugmore, *The Influence of the Synagogue upon the Divine Office* (Oxford: Oxford University Press, 1944), 46-48; and Emil Schürer, *The History of the Jewish People in the Age of Jesus Christ,* revised edition ed. G. Vermes et al. (Edinburgh: T. & T. Clark, 1979), 2:460-61, which also gives the Babylonian recension.

The most disputed section, in both text and interpretation, is the twelfth benediction, which underwent changes during the Middle Ages because of Christian pressure. See translations and discussions in W. D. Davies, *The Setting of the Sermon on the Mount* (Cambridge: Cambridge University Press, 1964), 275ff., G. D. Kilpatrick, *The Origin of the Gospel According to St. Matthew* (Oxford: Clarendon, 1950), 109, and S. Sandmel, *Judaism and Christian Beginnings* (New York: Oxford University Press, 1978), 149, 438. It is generally considered to have been added to the liturgy at the close of the first century CE as a "test benediction." Like the anathemas at the conclusion of Christian creeds, it contains words that no heretic or schismatic could pronounce, and had the effect of banning them from the synagogue. The Johannine community was probably reacting to this pressure (see John 9:34; 16:2), and the Gospel of Matthew's antipathy to "Scribes and Pharisees" may reflect a response to such measures. Cf. further on no. 470.

305. Luke 11:1-4/ Matthew 6:9-15 (Q)

Kaddish prayer (prayer of ancient Judaism, pre-70 CE ?)

Magnified and hallowed be his great name in the world which he created according to his will; and may he make his kingship sovereign in your lifetime and in your days, and in the lifetime of the whole house of Israel speedily, in the near future. Praised be his great name from eternity to eternity. (Singer)

Analogous to the Lord's Prayer are the sanctification of the name and the prayer for the realization of God's kingship, but which is not here thought of eschatologically. Also in Matthew, the "coming of the kingdom" first becomes unambiguously eschatological through the context. As in Matthew, the petitions are not linked to each other. Note too that talk of the "Father in heaven" is not yet met in the Old Testament, but is found in Judaism, in the Targumim, and especially in connection with prayer. E.g. the fragmentary Targum on Genesis 21:33, "And our father Abraham told them of the one who spoke, and the world came into being through his word: 'Pray before your Father who is in heaven, since it is from his bounty you have eaten and drunk'" (McNamara). On the character of the Lord's Prayer as a Hellenistic prayer cf. Berger, "Hellenistische Gattungen," 1169-70.

306. Luke 11:4/ Matthew 6:13 (Q)

4 Maccabees 9:7-8 (50–150 CE)

Therefore, tyrant, put us to the test [πείραζε]; and if you take our lives because of our religion, do not suppose that you can injure us by torturing us. 8 For we, through this severe suffering and endurance, shall have the prize of virtue and shall be with God, on whose account we suffer . . . (NRSV)

The Maccabean martyrs, confident of the power of their "devout reason" to be sovereign over their "emotions" (4 Macc 1:1), invite the persecutor to put them to the test, sure that their faith will not fail. The prayer Jesus taught his disciples is dominated by the eschatological perspective, the "time of trial" (πειρασμός *peirasmos*, from the same root as πείραζε above, traditionally "temptation") being the eschatological terrors. The disciples are not to be confident that their faith will withstand such a test, and are taught to pray that they are not brought into such a situation.

307. Luke 11:27 (cf. 1:28, 42, 48)

Petronius, *Satyricon* 94.1 (d. 66 CE)

Eumolpus cried: "Happy was the mother who bore such a son as you, be good and prosper. Beauty and wisdom make a rare conjunction. And do not think that all your words have been wasted. In me you have found a lover. I will do justice to your worth in verse." (LCL)

The mothers of great men are praised as blessed or happy, as the mother of Baruch in *2 Baruch* 54:10, the mother of the Messiah in *Pesiq.* 149a (H. L. Strack-P. Billerbeck, *Kommentar zum Neuen Testament aus Talmud und Midrash* I [München: C. H. Beck, 1922], 495-96). It may be either an indirect form of praising the great man himself (cf. Berger, *Formgeschichte*, §99), or the praise directed to the great man spills over on his mother.

308. Luke 11:34-36 / Matthew 6:22-23 (Q)

Plutarch, *Moralia*, "The Roman Questions" 72 (45–125 CE)

For the lantern is like the body which encompasses the soul; the soul within is a light. . . . (LCL)

From the allegorical explanation of cultic practices, Plutarch too knows the picture of the light of the body. It is used differently, however: in Matthew the eye stands for "heart," in Luke for "hearing," while in Plutarch it refers to the higher evaluation of the soul in contrast to the body—an example of the multiple functions of metaphorical material. On the basic idea cf. also Epicharmus (pre-Socratic), "If you have a pure mind, you will be pure in all your body" (Freeman). On the figure of light, cf. also Diogenes Laertius, "Aristotle," in *Lives* 5.17, "As sight takes in light from the surrounding air, so does the soul from mathematics" (LCL). The content of this sentence is close to that of Luke 11:34-36.

309. Luke 11:42 / Matthew 23:23 (Q)

Magical Curse (uncertain date)

To the god Jupiter Optimus Maximus there is given that he may hound . . . through his mind, through his memory, his inner parts [?], his intestines, his heart, his marrow, his veins: whoever it was, whether man or woman, who stole away the denarii of Canius [?]

Dignus that in his own person in a short time he may balance the account. There is given to the god above named a tenth part of the money when he has [repaid it?]. (Turner)

If the god executes the curse and causes the stolen money to be returned, he receives a ten percent commission (cf. Gen 28:18-22). While the Hebrew Bible and Jewish tradition is the immediate background of tithing in New Testament texts, there are also points of contact in the pagan Hellenistic world.

310. Luke 11:49-51; 13:34/ Matthew 23:34-37 (Q)

5 Ezra 1:28-30, 32 (1–2 cent. CE)

Thus says the Lord Almighty: Have I not entreated you as a father entreats his sons or a mother her daughters or a nurse her children, so that you should be my people and I should be your God, and that you should be my children and I should be your father? I gathered you as a hen gathers her chicks under her wings. But now, what shall I do to you? I will cast you out from my presence. . . . I sent you my servants the prophets, but you have taken and killed them and torn their bodies in pieces; I will require their blood of you, says the Lord. (NRSV)

Although in 5 Ezra it is God who speaks, the very similar passage in Q is in the mouth of Jesus. In Q, invective and announcement of punishment are more concrete. Important for the difference between the ways God and Jesus are pictured is that the metaphors father/mother/nurse are missing in the saying of Jesus, as is the covenant formula. And while it is the case in Q that two images of the mother almost compete with each other (Jerusalem has children; Jesus wants to gather like a mother hen), the metaphorical usage in 5 Ezra is all on the same line. Finally, Q emphasizes contrary wills of Jesus and those he addresses, while 5 Ezra speaks only of God. When all these aspects are considered, it is quite conceivable that 5 Ezra represents a preexisting Jewish tradition utilized in the Q saying, which transforms the saying of God into a saying of Jesus and dramatically sharpens the conflict. Cf. nos. 187, 283, 300, 302, 414.

311. Luke 11:9-13/ Matthew 7:7-11 (Q)

Testament of Abraham, Recension A 8.7 (1–3 cent. CE)

Truly I say to you that *blessing I will bless you and multiplying I will multiply your seed*, and I will give to you whatever you ask of me . . . (*OTP* 1:886)

Similarly: *Daniel Apocalypse* (Persian), "Then God sent an angel and spoke to me, 'O Daniel, my friend, whatever you ask will be given to you'" (MEB/from Zotenberg ed., p. 393).

Greek Apocalypse of Ezra 7:13, "Ezra, my beloved, I shall grant to each one the things which you asked" (*OTP* 1:579).

Appendix to *3 Enoch* 21:4-5, "Then 'Aktari'el Yah YHWH of hosts answered and said to Metatron, Prince of the Divine Presence, 'Fulfill every request he makes of me. Hear his prayer and do what he wants, whether great or small.' At once Metatron, Prince of the Divine Presence, said to Moses,

'Son of Amram, fear not! for already God favors you. Ask what you will with confidence and boldness, for light shines from the skin of your face from one end of the world to the other'" (*OTP* 1:304).

In all these texts, the promise is made only to a very select few individuals, in most cases to prophets. The New Testament texts, in contrast, give assurance of the unconditional hearing of prayer to all Jesus' disciples.

312. Luke 12:16-21

1 Enoch 97:8-10 (2 cent. BCE)

Woe unto you who gain silver and gold by unjust means;
you will then say, "We have grown rich and accumulated goods,
we have acquired everything that we have desired.
So now let us do whatever we like;
for we have gathered silver,
we have filled our treasuries [with money] like water.
And many are the laborers in our houses.
Your lies flow like water.
For your wealth shall not endure
but it shall take off from you quickly
for you have acquired it all unjustly,
and you shall be given over to a great curse. (*OTP* 1:78)

Cf. also Sirach 11:18-19 and Hosea 12:8-10 (for comparison, see also Berger, *Formgeschichte*, §§207-8). Points of contact with NT text: The theme of riches, the form of quoting what those addressed say to themselves, the dramatic suddenness of their loss, the authoritative, blaming direct address to those charged, the making of independent plans, the excess of goods, the full warehouses. Points of difference: the genre (woe speech; parable), and in Enoch the charge that the riches were gained unjustly (but this is also implicit in Luke).

On Luke 12:19*c*, cf. also no. 709.

313. Luke 12:22-31 / Matthew 6:25-34 (Q)

Dio Chrysostom, *The Tenth Discourse: Diogenes or on Servants* (40–120 CE)

[Concerning a runaway slave:] Sometimes barefooted persons get about more easily than those who are badly shod; and similarly, many live more comfortably and with less annoyance without domestics than those who have many. See what worries the rich have. Some are taking care of their sick slaves and wanting doctors and nurses—

And so it goes; they can neither get away from home easily whenever they like nor have leisure if they stay at home.

Or perhaps you will use the money received for something that will harm you. For by no means in every case does money help those who have gotten it; but men have suffered many more injuries and many more evils from money than from poverty, particularly when they lacked sense. Are you going to try to secure first, not that other thing, which will enable you to derive profit from everything and to order all your affairs well, but in preference to wisdom are you going to seek riches or lands or teams of horses or ships or houses? You will become their slave and will suffer through them and perform a great deal of useless labor, and will spend all your life worrying over them without getting any benefit whatsoever from them. Consider the beasts yonder and the birds, how much freer from trouble they live than men, and how much more happily also, how much healthier and stronger they are, and how each of them lives the longest life possible, although they have neither hands nor human intelligence. And yet, to counterbalance these and their other limitations, they have one very great blessing—they own no property. (LCL)

Dio Chrysostom presents the Cynic Diogenes as speaking. In contrast to Matthew he emphasizes how many worries are involved in having wealth. Jesus speaks only of how useless it is to worry. But as with Jesus, so also here, the freedom from worry enjoyed by (animals and) birds is brought before the mind's eye. Of course, here the argument is not based on the providence of God, but the inherent advantages that derive from the freedom from wealth. Similarly to Matthew 6:33, the exhortation/warning is given (15) to be concerned first with something that is truly useful, but here it is the Cynic lifestyle and not a matter of anything heavenly or eschatological. As is often the case in pagan analogies, so here too any reference to God is lacking. Further:

314. Luke 12:22-31 / Matthew 6:25-34 (Q)

Epictetus, *Discourses* 3.16.12-15 (55–135 CE)

[Invective against a blameworthy philosophy student:] Very well then, lament and groan, and eat [your bread] in fear of not having food tomorrow; tremble about your paltry slaves, for fear they will steal something, or run away, or die! Live in this spirit. . . . But you never desired stability, serenity, peace of mind; . . . you have been devoting your attention to the last of all topics [philosophy], that which deals with immutability, in order that you may have immutable—what? your cowardice, your ignoble character, your admiration of the rich, your ineffectual desire, your aversion that fails of its mark! These are the things about whose security you have been anxious! Ought you not, first, to have acquired something from reason, and then to have made that something secure? (LCL)

As in Q, it is a matter of rejection of false worries about food and property and the naming of that which is of primary importance. In contrast to Q, the assurance is lacking that freedom from worry rests on the all-embracing providence of God. Instead, security and stability are sought in the internal goods of the soul. Further:

315. Luke 12:22-31 / Matthew 6:25-34 (Q)

b. *Qiddushin* 82b (200 CE)

It was taught: R. Simeon b. Eleazar said: In my whole lifetime I have not seen a deer engaged in gathering fruits, a lion carrying burdens, or a fox as a shopkeeper, yet they are sustained without trouble, though they were created only to serve me, whereas I was created to serve my Maker. Now, if these, who were created only to serve me, are sustained without trouble, how much more so should I be sustained without trouble, I who was created to serve my Maker! But it is because I have acted evilly and destroyed my livelihood, as it is said, *your iniquities have turned away these things.* (Soncino)

Even more strongly than in the saying of Jesus, the inference from lesser to greater emphasizes the difference in grade between the world of animals and human existence (hierarchy of service). But in contrast to the saying of Jesus, the paradisical freedom from worry is no longer possible for humans, because of the sin of humanity. In the context of the "realistic" evaluation of the human situation in the Jewish tradition, the sharpness and provocative character of Jesus' saying becomes clear.

316. Luke 12:33-34/ Matthew 6:19-21 (Q)

Sophocles, Fragments 194 (5 cent. BCE)

The acquisition of virtue is the only sure acquisition. (MEB)

As in Q, the uncertainty involved in the bourgeois acquisition of property is compared with the lasting positive benefit of moral conduct. Both cases involve the same kind of symbuleutic logic (cf. Berger, *Formgeschichte,* §30).

317. Luke 12:4-5/ Matthew 10:28 (Q)

Epictetus, *Discourses* 1.9.14-15 (55–135 CE)

Suffer us to go back whence we came; suffer us to be freed at last from these fetters that are fastened to us and weigh us down. Here are despoilers and thieves, and courts of law, and those who are called tyrants; they think that they have some power over us because of the paltry body and its possessions. Suffer us to show them that they have power over no one. (LCL)

The tyrants have no power over the souls, the interior selves, of human beings. Both Epictetus and Q here document a widespread tradition often expressed in resistance to tyrants. (Documentation: Berger, "Hellenistische Gattungen," 1251-56). For Epictetus it is a matter of the strict freedom from all things. For Jesus, on the other hand, it is a matter of what is to be truly feared, for the saying goes on to say who should be really feared.

318. Luke 12:42; cf. 16:1

Plutarch, *Moralia*, "On Listening to Lectures" 6 (45–125 CE)

For as Xenophon asserts that good householders [οἰκονόμικος] derive benefit both from their friends and from their enemies, so in the same way do speakers, not only when they succeed, but also when they fail, render a service to hearers who are alert and attentive. (LCL)

This text is one of many that could be chosen to document and illustrate the very common practice of using household managers as the subjects of analogies and parables in the NT environment.
On Luke 12:49-53, cf. no. 242.

319. Luke 12:45/ Matthew 24:48 (Q)

Plutarch, *Moralia*, "On the Delays of the Divine Vengeance" 2 (45–125 CE)

Patrocleas replied: "The delay and procrastination of the Deity in punishing the wicked appears to me the most telling argument by far. . . . Furthermore, as Thucydides says: 'For no debt as it falls overdue so weakens the cheated victim in his hopes and breaks his spirit, and so strengthens the wrongdoer in confidence and boldness, as the debt of merited punishment . . .'" (LCL)

The problem of the delay of the parousia is basically seen from the same perspective as in this writing from Plutarch, which deals with this phenomenon at least from the negative side (delay of judgment). In the Q parable the arrogance of the wicked is increased by the delay. Cf. no. 903.

320. Luke 13:6-7

Syriac *Ahikar*, a collection of wisdom sayings in the context of the Ahikar legend (1 cent. [?] CE)

My son, you were to me like a palm tree that stood beside the road, but from whom no one ever plucked fruit. Your owner came and wanted to root it up. Then the palm tree spoke to him, "Grant me just one more year, and I will present you with Carthamin [saffron]." Its owner answered, "You miserable tree! You did not bear your own fruit, so how could you bear other fruit?" (MEB/Berger)

Cf. Armenian Philo, *De Jona*, §52, "But I too believe that a farmer . . . who no longer expects any fruit to come from his tree is ready to root up what he has planted. But if he sees buds about ready to burst open, then he will leave it alone in order to gain some fruit. Exactly right! One cuts down a useless tree, but if it produces fruit, one lets it stand" (trans. MEB of F. Siegert, *Drei hellenistisch-jüdische Predigten* [Tübingen: J. C. B. Mohr, 1980], 47-48).
Both texts illustrate the currency of the parable material. In *Ahikar* the perspective is more negative (if in the one case not . . . then in the other case even less . . .), in Pseudo-Philo pedagogically more positive (spare that which shows some positive signs), in Luke it is in the form of an ultimatum.

321. Luke 13:23-24/ Matthew 7:13-14 (Q)

Midrash Schemot Rabbah 30:20 (dating difficult)

With each individual commandment I have given both the punishment for its infraction and the reward for observing it. It is like a king who laid out two roads. The one was full of thorns, thistles, and stinging nettles, while the other was full of aromatic spices. The blind took the bad road, and received from the thorns even more wounds from the thorns, while the clever took the good road, and they along with their children took on a pleasant odor themselves. Thus God too has prepared two roads, one for the godly and one for the ungodly. Those who have no eyes go the way of the ungodly and are punished; they will not last, but are like the infamous Balaam. . . . The righteous, however, who walk in their innocence, will be happy, and so will their children after them. (MEB/Berger)

The rabbinic text illustrates a simple dualism: the blind fools choose the bad road, on which they have troubles. There was never any appearance of good qualities in either the road or its travelers. In Q on the other hand there is not only the dualism wise/foolish, but a double dualism: the way of the foolish appears the more pleasant but in the "transcendent" future turns out to be the opposite—and vice versa. The motif of the two ways was widespread in the ancient world. For literature, see U. Luz, *Matthew 1–7: A Commentary* (Minneapolis: Augsburg, 1989), 433.

322. Luke 13:28/ Matthew 8:11 (Q)

Book of Elijah (Hebrew) (2 cent. CE)

Elijah speaks: "I see Abraham, Isaac, and Jacob and all the righteous sitting, and the earth has been planted before them with every kind of delight, and that tree planted by God stands in the midst of the garden . . ." (MEB/from M. Buttenwieser, *Die hebräische Elia-Apokalypse*, 1897, p. 25).

As in the saying of Jesus, blessedness consists of fellowship with the patriarchs. More strongly than in the New Testament, the paradisical element of the eschatological blessedness is emphasized. The saying of Jesus presents within this tradition a (critical) contribution to the question of who is here to be regarded as "righteous."

323. Luke 14:5/ Matthew 12:11 (Q)

Damascus Rule (CD) 10-11 (2 cent. BCE)

No man shall walk abroad to do business on the Sabbath. He shall not walk more than one thousand cubits beyond his town.

No man shall eat on the Sabbath day except that which is already prepared. He shall eat nothing lying in the fields. He shall not drink except in the camp. If he is on a journey and goes down to bathe, he shall drink where he stands, but he shall not draw water into a vessel. He shall send no stranger on his business on the Sabbath day.

No man shall walk more than two thousand cubits after a beast to pasture it outside his town. He shall not raise his hand to strike it with his fist. If it is stubborn he shall not take it out of his house.

No man shall take anything out of his house or bring anything in. He shall not open a sealed vessel on the Sabbath. . . .

No man shall assist a beast to give birth on the Sabbath day. And if it should fall into a cistern or pit, he shall not lift it out on the Sabbath.

No man shall profane the Sabbath for the sake of riches or gain on the Sabbath day. But should any man fall into water or fire, let him be pulled out with the aid of a ladder or rope or [some such] utensil. (Vermes)

This text reflecting the Qumran interpretation of the Sabbath is different from that presupposed as Jewish practice by Luke 14:5. The Mishnah tractate *Shabbath* gives detailed discussions and instructions for the proper keeping of the Sabbath. "Work" was prohibited, but what constitutes "work"? *B. Shabb.* 7.1-2: "The main classes of work are forty save one: sowing, ploughing, reaping, binding sheaves, threshing, winnowing, cleaning crops, grinding, sifting, kneading, baking, shearing wool, washing or beating or dyeing it, spinning, weaving, making two loops, weaving two threads, separating two threads, tying [a knot], loosening [a knot], sewing two stitches, tearing in order to sew two stitches, hunting a gazelle, slaughtering or flaying or salting it or curing its skin, scraping it or cutting it up, writing two letters, erasing in order to write two letters, building, pulling down, putting out a fire, lighting a fire, striking with a hammer and taking out aught from one domain into another. These are the main classes of work: forty save one" (Soncino).

324. Luke 14:7-11

Plutarch, *Moralia*, "Table-Talk" 1.2, 1-5 (45–125 CE)

My brother Timon, upon an occasion when he was host to a considerable number of guests, bade them each as they entered take whatever place they wished and there recline, for among those who had been invited were foreigners as well as citizens, friends as well as kinsmen, and in a word, all sorts of people.

Now when many guests were already assembled, a foreigner came . . .; and when he had run his eyes round the guests who had settled in their places, he refused to enter, but withdrew and was on his way out when a number of the guests ran to fetch him back, but he said that he saw no place left worthy of him.

[Plutarch's father said] If he had arranged the placing of his guests at the beginning, as I told him to do, we would not be under suspicion of disorderliness and liable to public audit under the rule of a man skillful "in marshaling horses and shield-bearing men" (Plato, *Timaeus* 30A). . . .

Thus it is ridiculous for our cooks and waiters to be greatly concerned about what they shall bring in first, or what second or middle or last—also, by Zeus, for some place to be found and arrangement made for perfume and crowns and a harp-girl, if there is a girl—yet for those invited to this entertainment to be fed at places selected haphazardly and by chance, which give neither to age nor to rank nor to any other distinction the position that suits it, one which does honor to the outstanding man, leaves the next best at ease, and exercises the judgment and sense of propriety of the host. [Plutarch responded:] . . . but if we humble some of them and exalt others, we shall rekindle their hostility and set it aflame again through ambitious rivalry. (LCL)

Plutarch discusses at table, just as happens in Luke 14 (cf. v. 7) questions of arrangement and organization that bear directly on the difference of social class among those present.

325. Luke 14:26/ Matthew 10:37 (Q)

Musonius Rufus, *Must One Obey One's Parents Under All Circumstances?* (30–100 CE)

A certain young man who wished to study philosophy, but was forbidden by his father to do so, put this question to him: "Tell me, Musonius, must one obey one's parents in all things, or are there some circumstances under which one need not heed them?" And Musonius replied, "That everyone should obey his mother and father seems a good thing, and I certainly recommend it. However, let us see what this matter of obedience is, or rather, first, what is the nature of disobedience, and let us consider who the disobedient person is, if in this way we may better understand what the nature of obedience is.

"Now then, take this case. If a father who is not a physician and not experienced in matters of health or sickness should prescribe for his invalid son something which was harmful and injurious, and the son was aware of that fact, surely in not following his father's prescription he is not disobeying and is not disobedient, is he? It would not seem so.

"And so you, my young friend, do not fear that you will disobey your father, if when your father bids you do something which is not right, you refrain from doing it, or when he forbids you to do something which is right you do not refrain from doing it." (Lutz)

Plutarch also reports on the "bourgeois" hindrances that stood in the way of anyone wanting to live the life of a philosopher ("Progress in Virtue," §4: marriage, wealth, friendship, military service; cf. Luke 14:15-24; Matt 22:1-14 par.; *Gos. Thom.* 64). He discusses the philosopher's disdain of biological brothers in the writing "On Brotherly Love," §4. On the other hand, Apollonius of Tyana in his 44th letter (see no. 106) reports the disdain the philosopher receives from family and fatherland.

The command to honor one's parents, to love them and obey them, had the highest rank in Old Testament and Jewish tradition, just as it did in the Stoic school tradition, in both following closely on the command to honor God. If it is neglected or disdained in favor of another obligation or business, then this disruption of the recognized order of things is a provocative alarm signal for the worth and significance of the new, higher priority. In both realms the new priority is expressed in terms of discipleship over against a religious-philosophical authority.

326. Luke 14:26/ Matthew 10:37 (Q)

Philostratus, *Epistles of Apollonius of Tyana* 43 (1 cent. CE)

If anyone professes to be my disciple, let his profession be that he remains within his house, that he abstains from all bathing, that he kills no living creature, nor eats flesh, that he is exempt from feelings of jealousy, of spite, of hatred, of slander, of enmity . . . (LCL)

In Luke 14:26-27/ Matthew 10:37-39 conditions are given, in catalog form, for the style of discipleship formulated in no. 325. The letter of Apollonius gives a similar list, to which is attached a catalog of vices. The genre is the same, though the details of content are different. In early Christianity the revived ideal of the disciples of the prophets (the Elijah-Elisha tradition, cf. Sir 48:8) was combined with contemporary Hellenistic ideas of the ideal disciple in a philosophical school (Cf. M. Hengel, *The Charismatic Leader and His Followers* [New York: Crossroad, 1981]).

327. Luke 14:26-27/ Matthew 10:37 (Q)

Isocrates, Chreia 41 (quoted in Theon)

Isocrates the rhetor used to advise his students to honor their teachers above their parents, because the latter are the cause only of living, while teachers are the cause of living nobly. (Hock-O'Neil)

Not only in the Jewish tradition, but also in the Hellenistic world, to challenge respect for parents was to challenge a fundamental value on which society itself depended. So also, the teaching office was highly respected not only in Judaism, but in the pagan world. The radicality of Jesus' statement can hardly be exaggerated. The chreia illustrates that in the Hellenistic world too, "teacher" was far more than a dispenser of information, but could be a matter of discipleship to one to whom one owed one's life.

328. Luke 14:34-35/ Matthew 5:13 (Q)

Galen, *On the Differences in Impulses* 2 (129–199 CE)

When, he says, water makes one choke, what should we then drink? For when the original function no longer works, to whom should we then go? Who will then correct its defect? (MEB/Berger)

The final result is the same as in Matthew 5:13. The text makes clear that similar considerations existed within the realm of those who devise metaphors.

329. Luke 15:3-10

Midrash Rabbah on the Song of Songs **1.9 (6–8 cent.** CE**)**

The matter may be compared to the case of a king who lost gold in his house or pearls. Is it not through a wick that is worth a penny that he finds it again?

So let a parable not be despised in your view, for it is through the parable that a person can master the words of the Torah.

You may know that that is so, for lo, Solomon through parables mastered the smallest details of the Torah.

R. Phineas b. Yair commenced by citing this verse: "If you seek it like silver [and search for it as for hidden treasures, then you will understand the fear of the Lord and find the knowledge of God]" [Prov. 1:4-5]:

If you seek words of the Torah like hidden treasures, the Holy One, blessed be He, will not withhold your reward.

The matter may be compared to the case of a person, who, if he should lose a penny or a pin in his house, will light any number of candles, any number of wicks, until he finds them.

Now the matter yields an argument *a fortiori:*

If to find these, which are useful only in the here and now of this world, a person will light any number of candles, any number of wicks, until he finds them, as to words of Torah, which concern the life of the world to come as much as this world, do you not have to search for them like treasures? (Neusner, *Song of Songs;* cf. the differing trans. of A. Wünsche [Leipzig, 1882], p. 32)

Both rabbinic parables have to do with the losing, seeking, and finding of some object in the house. In the first parable the contrast consists of the great value of what is sought and the little value of the means by which the search is made. In the second rabbinic parable the contrast consists in the exertion expended in seeking and the relatively small value of the coin that was sought and found. This then is applied, *a minore ad maius* to how intensively one must search for that which is most valuable of all, life in both eons. Luke too uses the same materials to express a contrast: the small value of what is sought: the insignificance of what is sought contrasts with the expenditure of time and energy of the search, and—only in Luke—the joy when it is found (cf. Luke 15:5, 6, 7, 9, 10, 32 as leitmotif). In the rabbinic texts the point has to do with parables and the Torah, in Luke with the repentant sinner. The rabbinic texts illustrate the popularity and wide circulation of common parabolic elements, used by Luke in different ways.

330. Luke 15:11-32

Philo, *On the Virtues* **179 (15** BCE**–50** CE**)**

So therefore all these who did not at the first acknowledge their duty to reverence the Founder and Father of all, yet afterward embraced the creed of one instead of a multiplicity of sovereigns, must be held to be our dearest friends and closest kinsmen. They have shown the godliness of heart which above all leads up to friendship and affinity, and we must rejoice with them, as if, though blind at the first they had recovered their sight and had come from the deepest darkness to behold the most radiant light. (LCL)

The attitude that Philo here commends regarding proselytes is applied by Luke to the lost son who returned home. In Luke, the older brother is invited to join in the celebration (15:32; cf. in context, vv. 6, 9). One may compare Philo's light/darkness with Luke's death/life in 15:24, 32. In both authors the use of this metaphor intensifies the motivation for heeding the admonition. Further:

331. Luke 15:11-32

A. Teles, *On Contentment with One's Self* (3 cent. BCE)

. . . I do not see how circumstances themselves have anything troublesome, not old age or poverty or lack of citizenship. For not ineptly does Xenophon say, "If I show you two brothers who have divided an equal sum, one of whom is in utter distress while the other is quite content, isn't it obvious that the money is not to be blamed but something else?" So if I show you two old men, two poor men, two exiles, one of whom is quite content and tranquil while the other is in total turmoil, isn't it obvious that it is not old age, not poverty, not lack of citizenship that should be blamed but something else? (O'Neil)

The text illustrates the commonness of example stories and parables in which two partners belonging to the same category are juxtaposed.

Quintilian, *Declamatio* 5 (35–100 CE)

Children are obligated to support their impoverished parents, or they deserve to be imprisoned. There was once a man who had two sons. The one was a good manager, the other a spendthrift. Both traveled into a far country and were captured by pirates. While they were captured, the spendthrift became sick. Both wrote home asking to be ransomed. The father immediately converted all his assets into cash and departed to redeem them. The pirates were not satisfied with the sum he had brought with him, saying that it hardly sufficed to ransom one son, and that he would have to make a choice. The father chose the sick son, who died soon after he had been released. Later, the other son managed to escape. Then, the impoverished father called on his son for support. The son refused . . . [from the father's speech:] No concern I have ever had, no memory of my heartbreaking experience, nothing ever led me to suspect that after enduring the danger of the pirates, after the loss of one of my sons, after suffering hunger, my misery would be made the greater by the fact that my other son has now returned. . . . When a father of two sons redeems the sick one from the chains of slavery, this does not mean that he loves him more than the other. And just this, my judges, among all my troubles what grieves me most is that this my son, through his hard-heartedness, through his disdaining of my poverty and dependency, maliciously attacks the good name of his dear departed brother. . . . So grant me support, because I wanted to redeem you, give me my bread, because I did redeem your brother. . . . (MEB/Berger)

Cf. Luise Schottroff, "Das Gleichnis vom verlorenen Sohn," in *ZTK* 68 (1971): 27-52, and, for a different perspective, Wolfgang Poehlmann, *Der Verlorene Sohn und das Haus: Studien zu Lukas 15, 11-32 im Horizont der antiken Lehre von Haus, Erziehung und Akerbau* (WUNT 68. [Tübingen: J. C. B. Mohr (Paul Siebeck)], 1993).

The form in which the case is reported is the same as in our parable. Here as there, the frugal brother protests against the preferential treatment the spendthrift brother receives. But in Quintilian, the spendthrift does not regret, repent, or return home, and in Luke the older brother still has his share of the property. In Quintilian the father justifies his conduct with the help of the distinction between *caritas/pietas* and *miseratio:* his love for both sons was equally great, and this equality was only apparently violated by the fact that the one son was in the greater trouble. This however is no critique against the principle of reward on the basis of accomplishment (against Schottroff): the paradox is precisely this, that the younger was preferred despite the undoubtedly greater virtue of the frugal brother. But when either son is in bad trouble, the question of whether he is the frugal one or the spendthrift is no longer a factor. Now it is a matter of life and death. The principle of reward according to achievement cannot be permitted to challenge the emergency situation. In Luke, the distinction between love and compassion does not come in view.

332. Luke 15:11-32

Apocalypse of Sedrach 6:4-6 (Greek; 1 cent. CE ?)

Tell me, what sort of a father would give an inheritance to his son, and having received the money [the son] goes away leaving his father, and becomes an alien and in the service of aliens. The father then, seeing that the son has forsaken him [and gone away], darkens his heart and going away, he retrieves his wealth and banishes his son from his glory because he forsook his father. How is it that I, the wondrous and jealous God, have given everything to him, but he, having received them, became an adulterer and sinner? (*OTP* 1:610)

The sin of the "lost" son here consists in his leaving his father. The son then serves a foreigner, which is his main sin, not in the squandering of his inheritance or in immoral living. Further:

333. Luke 15:11-32

Mekilta de Rabbi Ishmael, "Beshallah" §4 (3 cent. CE)

R. Absalom the Elder says: "A parable. Unto what is the matter like? It is like one who got angry with his son and drove him out of his house. His friend (i.e., of the father) came to him, requesting that he allow the son to come back to the house. He (the father) said to his friend: 'You are only asking me on behalf of my own son. I am already reconciled to my son.' " (McArthur and Johnston)

Common imagery: father, son, separation of the son from the house, reconciliation, with the initiative from the father. Difference: in Luke, anger and expulsion play no role. Further:

334. Luke 15:11-32

Midrash Debarim Rabba (developed from 450 to 800 CE)

Rabbi Samuel Perergita said in the name of Rabbi Meier: "With what is this matter to be likened? It is like a king's son who had gotten out of hand and was running wild, and the king sent his tutor after him and had him say: 'Search your conscience, feel remorse, my son!' But the son had the tutor say to his father, 'How can I face you, I am too ashamed.' Then his father sent these words to him, 'My son, should a son be ashamed to come back to his father? When you come home, are you not coming home to your father?'" (MEB/from A. Wünsche [Leipzig, 1882], p. 32 = 2:24)

Common imagery: father, son, running wild, return, especially the reflection of the son on his own unworthiness as he returns (Luke 15:19 "unworthy"; rabbinic parable "I am ashamed to face you," which is overcome in both parables from the father's side [running to meet him and embracing him in Luke; emphasis on the lasting father/son relationship in the rabbinic parable]). The rabbinic parable is missing the extravagant picture of the father's "going crazy" at the return of his son, and the motif of joy.

335. Luke 16:1-9

"Teaching of the mayor and vezier of Ptahhotep, under the majesty of King Issi, who lives eternally and forever" (several eds. from 16 to 10 cent. BCE)

Take care to use what has been apportioned to you to keep your close friends happy, as one who has been rewarded by God. There is no one who knows well his plans, who only thinks as far ahead as tomorrow. When another occasion of reward comes, then the people come to him and say "Welcome." (MEB/from Fr. W. Frhr. v. Bissing, *Altägyptische Lebensweisheit* [Zürich, 1955], p. 49)

With this one may compare the translation in James B. Pritchard, ed., *Ancient Near Eastern Texts Relating to the Old Testament* (3rd ed., Princeton, N.J.: Princeton University Press, 1969), 413:
"Satisfy thy clients with what has accrued to thee, (340) what accrues to one whom god favors . . .
"One does not know what may happen, so that he may understand the morrow. If misfortunes occur among those [now] favored, it is the clients who [still] say: 'Welcome!'"
The translation in H. Bolkestein, *Wohltätigkeit und Armenpflege im vorchristlichen Altertum* (Utrecht: A. Oosthoek, 1939), p. 18, is quite different and in part incomprehensible, especially in that he adds a conclusion that can't be verified in the MSS (according to A. Erman, *The Literature of the Ancient Egyptians* [London: Methuen & Co., 1927], p. 94), "Therefore take care to keep the devotion of your friends for the threatening times when you may be out of favor."
In any case, however, the significance of the parallels is in the following: (1) Earthly material possessions are considered to be something given by God, held in trust. (2) A "normal" precaution that only takes care of tomorrow, is not sufficient. Rather, it is a matter of using one's possessions in the present to gain friends, or to keep the friends one already has happy with you. (3) The result will be that at a corresponding later time those who have been taken care of will receive the giver,

according to Luke "into the eternal homes," according to Ptahhotep they will say "welcome." It is quite possible that Luke drew this material (as also that in 16:19ff.) from still living contemporary Egyptian tradition (see no. 338). The Lucan parable could be an illustration of this maxim. A comment by Diodorus Siculus (1 cent. BCE) I.90.2 also points to an Egyptian origin of this idea (hope of being paid back for sharing one's good deeds is considered by the Egyptians a form of life insurance).

Cf. also no. 344 and the context of no. 81.

336. Luke 16:3

Aristophanes, *The Birds* 1430-33 (5 cent. BCE)

[Dialogue between Peisthetairos and a sycophant:]
Pei.: Is this your business? you, a sturdy youngster, Live by informing on the stranger-folk?
Sy.: What can I do? I never learnt to dig.
Pei.: O, but by Zeus, there's many an honest calling Whence men like you can earn a livelihood . . . (LCL)

Cf. also the *Anthologia Palatina* XI.4: In contrast to sailing and farming (Gk. σκάπτω), it is light work to live off other people. The examples are enough to show that Luke here adopts a popular current expression.
On Luke 16:19*b*, cf. nos. 81, 221.

337. Luke 16:13 / Matthew 6:24 (Q)

Pythagorean Sentences 110 (2 cent. CE)

It is impossible for the same person to be a lover of success, the body, and God. For whoever loves success, loves also the body. But whoever loves the body also loves money. But whoever loves money is also necessarily unjust. The unjust person however is an offense against the holiness of God and the laws of humanity. . . . (MEB/Berger)

Cf. no. 746. Cf. also the relationship of the desire for money and virtue according to Plato, *Republic* 550 e. The religious (de-) valuation of riches was obviously common material in the sentence literature (cf. Berger, *Formgeschichte*, §§19-22).

338. Luke 16:19-31

Demotic narrative about Setme Chamois (written on the back side of a papyrus from 46–47 CE)

[Once] it happened that Setme heard [loud funeral] lamentations. [He] looked from [the balcony of] his house [and saw a rich man,] who was being carried to his grave with [loud] cries of lamentation, with much pomp [and richly decorated funeral accessories].

He looked [again, and there he saw] below him a poor man from Memphis being carried to the graveyard, wrapped in a mat . . ., without [anyone at all] following it. [Then said] Setme: "By [Ptah, the great god, how much better off are the rich,] who are buried amidst great lamentation and with great honor, than the poor, who are taken to the graveyard without an escort." [Then said Si-osire: "May it go with you in the realm of the dead, as it will happen to this poor man in the realm of the dead [and not as it will go happen to this rich man] in the place [of judgment.] You will [perceive that, when you] come into the realm of the dead." When he heard these words spoken by his son Si-osire, the heart of Setme was very [grieved. He said, "Is that] the voice [of my son I hear?"] [Lacuna: Si-osire leads Setme through the realm of the dead; the individual halls of the realm of the dead are described.] They enter the seventh hall and there Setme saw the appearance of Osiris, the great god, seated on his throne of pure gold, adorned with the atef-crown, with the great god Anubis on his left and the great god Thoth on his right, while the gods of judgment of those who came to the underworld stood left and right from them, with the balances placed in the midst, their sins being weighed against the good deeds, while the great god Thoth wrote, and Anubis made the announcements to his companions. Those whose sins were more numerous than their good deeds. . . . Then Setme saw an elegant, prominent man, clothed in a garment of fine linen, near the place where Osiris was seated, a man of very high rank. . . . That is the poor man from Memphis you saw being carried to the graveyard, wrapped in a mat, without a funeral procession. He was brought to the underworld, and his good deeds he had done on earth balanced against the sins he had committed. His good deeds were found more numerous than his sins, and since his lifetime that had been granted to him in writing by Thoth had not corresponded to his fortunes on earth, it was commanded before Osiris that the rich funeral vestments of the rich man you saw being carried out with much honor and praise be given to the aforementioned poor man, and that he be given a place among the elevated transfigured ones as a man of god who serves Sokaris-Osiris, near the residence of Osiris.

This rich man whom you saw was brought into the underworld, and his sins were balanced against his good deeds. His sins were found to be more numerous than the good deeds he had done on the earth; it was commanded that recompense be made in the underworld. [He is the man] from whom you have seen how the hinge-pin of the gate to the realm of the dead has been left in his right eye . . . while his mouth is open in loud lamentations. By the great god Osiris, the lord of the underworld, when I said to you on earth, ["may it go with you] as with this poor man and not as with this rich man," I knew how it would go with him. . . . Whoever is good on earth, to that person the underworld is also good, and to whomever is evil on earth, it goes badly [there]. . . . (MEB/from G. Möller, in H. Gressmann, *Vom Reichen Mann und armen Lazarus. Eine literargeschichtliche Studie* [Berlin, 1918], 63-68)

p. Sanhedrin 6:23c, 30-43 (the Jewish version of the story)

There were two holy men in Ashqelon, who would eat together, drink together, and study Torah together. One of them died, and he was not properly mourned.

But when Bar Maayan, the village tax collector died, the whole town took time off to mourn him.

The surviving holy man began to weep saying, "Woe, for [the enemies] of Israel will have nothing."

[The deceased holy man] appeared to him in a dream, and said to him, "Do not despise the sons of your Lord. This one did one sin, and the other one did one good deed, and it went well for [the latter on earth, so while on earth I was punished for my one sin, he was rewarded for his one good deed]."

Now what was the culpable act which the holy man had done?

Heaven forefend! He committed no culpable act in his entire life. But one time he put on the phylactery of the head before that of the hand [which was in error].

Now what was the meritorious deed which Bar Maayan the village tax collector had done?

Heaven forefend! He never did a meritorious deed in his life. But one time he made a banquet for the councilors of his town but they did not come. He said, "Let the poor come and eat the food, so that it not go to waste."

There are, moreover, those who say that he was traveling along the road with a loaf of bread under his arm, and it fell. A poor man went and picked it up, and the tax collector said nothing to him so as not to embarrass him.

After a few days the holy man saw his fellow [in a dream] walking among gardens, orchards, and fountains of water. He saw Bar Maayan the village tax collector with his tongue hanging out by a river. He wanted to reach the river but he could not reach it. (Neusner, *Talmud of the Land of Israel*)

For the Greek version of this story, see the preceding section. The historical question of how Luke could have attained this material may perhaps be answered with a reference to Ephesus. The city was important for Paul and the heirs of the Pauline tradition (Acts 20:17ff.), at the same time a bridgehead in Asia for Egyptian culture and religion (cf. G. Hölbl, *Zeugnisse ägyptischer Religionsvorstellungen für Ephesus* EPRO 73 [Leiden: E. J. Brill, 1978], especially on the Ephesian novels).

H. Gressmann, *Der Messias* (Göttingen: Vandenhoeck & Ruprecht, 1929), 59, names seven Jewish versions of the legend/tradition, and supposes that Jews in Memphis had learned the material during the Hellenistic period. Only the pre-Christian Jewish form on which Luke was dependent has not been preserved. In the Egyptian as in the rabbinic stories, the contrast in the manner of burial played an important role, for it signals and sums up the injustice that prevails on earth. An awareness of the Egyptian origin of the story was also preserved in the Middle Ages, since the rich man was also called "Amonofis," which presupposes an Egyptian version that dealt with a pharaoh. Perhaps Luke presupposed a version in which—as was the case with his own story—both figures already had contact in this world; that would better explain several features of the later tradition.

Only in Luke is the second part, vv. 27-31, found. Although Luke reports on the other world, still the emphasis in what he says lies on his declaration that one already knows what to do on the basis of the Law, without such a report from the other world. To this it corresponds that in his case the source of the report is neither a trip to the underworld nor a dream, but the authority of the narrator himself. The point of the story in Luke remains the equalizing justice of God.

339. Luke 17:11-19

Inscription from Epidaurus (end of 4 cent. BCE)

Sostrata from Pherai was pregnant. Things went in the worst way with her, and she was carried on a litter to the sanctuary and went to sleep. But as she saw no effective dream, she was brought back home. Afterward she was encountered by a certain one near Kornoi, who appeared to those who followed as in the form of a respectable, dignified man. He asked them about her problems, and commanded them to put down the litter on which they were carrying her. He then slit open her stomach and took out a large mass of dough, two footwashing tubs full. He then sewed her stomach back together and made the woman healthy, and he revealed his presence [παρουσία] as Asclepius, and commanded that a thank offering be sent to Epidaurus. (MEB/from Dittenberger, *Sylloge Inscriptionum Graecarum* 3, 4.1168-69, §25)

The scene is as in Luke 7:11-17. The concluding directive reminds one of Mark 1:44 (bringing an offering for purification), which also manifests the tendency to relate extracultic events to the cult center. The text is related to Luke 17 since a successful healing means that the one healed owes thanksgiving to God who is identified with the healer or who stands behind him. (R. Herzog, *Die Wunderheilungen von Epidaurus* [Leipzig, 1931], reads "small animals" instead of "dough.")

340. Luke 17:37

Plutarch, *Moralia*, "The Roman Questions" 93 (45–125 CE)

If Herodotus tells the truth, Hercules delighted in the appearance of vultures beyond that of all other birds at the beginning of any undertaking, since he believed that the vulture was the most righteous of all flesh-eating creatures; for, in the first place, it touches no living thing, nor does it kill any animate creature, as do eagles and hawks and the birds that fly by night; but it lives upon that which has been killed in some other way. Then again, even of these it leaves its own kind untouched. . . . (LCL)

Cf. Plutarch's *Moralia*, "How to Profit by One's Enemies" 3 (45–125 CE):
"Especially does he try to get hold of their [our enemies'] failings and ferret them out. And just as vultures are drawn to the smell of decomposed bodies, but have no power to discover those that are clean and healthy, so the infirmities, meannesses, and untoward experiences of life rouse the energies of the enemy, and it is such things as these that the malevolent pounce upon and seize and tear to pieces" (LCL).
Both texts use the picture of the carcass and the vultures metaphorically, the first text as a picture of righteous conduct, the second of hostile. Both texts are structured dualistically (life/death, faulty/whole). The context from Luke 17:34 is built on the same principle. On the basis of the comparative material, one can say: sin, death, negativity will certainly be condemned—an appeal to decide for the other side.

341. Luke 18:1-8

Plutarch, *Moralia*, "Sayings of Kings and Commanders: Philip the Father of Alexander" 31 (45–125 CE)

When a poor old woman insisted that her case should be heard before him, and often caused him annoyance, he said he had no time to spare, whereupon she burst out, "Then give up being king." Philip, amazed at her words, proceeded at once to hear not only her case but those of the others. (LCL)

The material, which Plutarch has formed into a chreia about Philip's father, Alexander, is used by Luke as a parabolic narrative (cf. Berger, *Formgeschichte,* 1984, §§25-29). In Plutarch, of course both parties become the target group for the saying: judges are told what their job is, while those of little social standing are told that they can appeal to the sense of duty which public officials have. In Luke the story serves as an admonition toward constancy in prayer.

On Luke 18:7, cf. no. 824 (middle part). On Luke 18:7-8, cf. no. 949.

342. Luke 18:10-14

4 Ezra 8:47b-50 (late 1 cent. CE)

[The angel to Ezra:] But you have often compared yourself to the unrighteous. Never do so! But even in this respect you will be praiseworthy before the Most High, because you have humbled yourself, as is becoming for you, and have not considered yourself to be among the righteous. You will receive the greatest glory . . . (NRSV)

Ezra stands for the type of those who are righteous before God. In view of the contrast between God and the world, his self-abnegation is appropriate. As in Luke, the one who counts himself a sinner is counted by God as the righteous one. Since 4 Ezra originates from a Pharisaic milieu, Luke 18 is understandable within the context of an inner-Pharisaic discussion.

343. Luke 19:11-27/ Matthew 25:14-30 (Q)

Yalqut shim'oni 267 a (date unknown)

A king had two servants, one of whom loved him and the other feared him. The king went on a long journey. During his long absence, the servant who loved him worked industriously taking care of the garden and the palace, and preparing delicacies for his return. The servant who feared him but did not love him, did not even think about the king during his absence. Finally the king returned, and gave a friendly smile to the first minister, because of all the care he had taken to have things prepared for his return. And the servant rejoiced because the king was pleased. Then the king turned threateningly toward the second servant, who trembled and turned pale. This is the difference between one who loves God and one who fears him; the share of those who love God is doubled. (MEB/from L. Seligmann, *Das Buch der jüdischen Weisheit* [3rd ed., 1980], p. 66)

Common material: different types of subordinates to a king, who is absent a long time, fearfulness of the one who is condemned (cf. Matt 25:25; Luke 19:21), the situation of giving account upon the king's return. Difference: In Q it is not (directly) a matter of love for the Lord, but of profiteering with the master's money.

Cf. also *b. Shabb.* 152b: "This may be compared to a mortal king who distributed royal apparel to his servants. The wise among them folded it up and laid it away in a chest, whereas the fools among them went and did their work in them. After a time the king demanded his garments: the wise among them returned them to him immaculate, [but] the fools among them returned them soiled. The king was pleased with the wise but angry with the fools. Of the wise he said, 'Let my robes be placed in my treasury and they can go home in peace'; while of the fools he said, 'Let my robes be given to the fuller, and let them be confined in prison.' Thus too, with the Holy One, blessed be He: concerning the bodies of the righteous" (Soncino).

Here too the situation is like that in Q, and here too it is a matter of responsible use of something that has been entrusted to one. But the thrust of the rabbinic story is in the opposite direction from that of the Q story; since the rabbinic story is concerned with maintaining ritual purity, the emphasis is on preserving that which was entrusted just as it was given.

344. Luke 19:12-27 / Matthew 25:14-30 (Q)

2 Enoch 50:6–51:2 (1 cent. CE)

Widows and orphans and foreigners do not distress, . . . stretch out your hands to the needy in accordance with your strength. Do not hide your silver in the earth. Help a believer in affliction, and then affliction will not find you, in your treasuries and in your time of work [= toil, trouble]. (*OTP* 1:178)

In the light of this passage from *2 Enoch*, and in view of the following pericope in Matthew 25:31-46, the disputed question as to what the talents are, which one should not hide in the earth (Matt 25:18, 25-27) is probably to be understood literally, at least for Matthew's meaning. It is a matter of wealth, with which one should do something constructive, as also in the sense of Luke 16:9. (The points of contact between Luke 16:10-12 and the elements of this parable thus also become more clear.) Cf. also no. 336.

345. Luke 22:17-20

Josephus, *Antiquities* 3.89-90 (37–100 CE)

[Paraphrase of the Exodus account of giving the Law.] That said, he [Moses] made the people advance with their wives and children, to hear God speak to them of their duties, to the end that the excellence of the spoken words might not be impaired by human tongue in being feebly transmitted to their knowledge. And all heard a voice which came from on high to the ears of all, in such wise that not one of those ten words escaped them which Moses has left inscribed on the two tables. These words it is not permitted us to state explicitly, to the letter, but we will indicate their purport. (LCL)

There follows a paraphrase of the Decalogue. The idea that the exact wording of the Decalogue is a mystery that must not be revealed to outsiders is unique to this passage in Josephus, where he attempts to make Judaism appear somewhat like the Hellenistic mystery cults. The idea is somewhat reminiscent, however, of the prohibition of pronouncing the sacred name of Yahweh. Josephus also pictures the Essenes, much admired by him, in mystery terms (cf. no. 19 on Matt 3:7).

During New Testament times the church had not developed esoteric secrets to be kept from the unholy eyes and ears of outsiders. The several contacts with mystery cult terminology and conceptuality (cf. index) do not include the command to secrecy (see no. 50 on Mark 1:44). The new faith was public, "not done in a corner" (Acts 26:26). The command *not* to seal up the book of Revelation (Rev 22:10), however, is in contrast not to the secrecy of the mystery cults, but to the typical apocalyptic literary device as illustrated in Daniel 12:4.

By the second century some churches were considering the Eucharist and the Lord's Prayer to be sacred mysteries not to be divulged. It has been argued that this accounts for the short text of Lucan narrative of the Lord's Supper that omits 22:19*b*-20. Joachim Jeremias, *The Eucharistic Words of Jesus* (New York: Scribners, 1966), 125-37, gives an extensive argument that the withdrawal of the sacred formulae from public view was already occurring in the first century, and is reflected in all the Gospels, but many scholars would consider this too early.

346. Luke 22:25-30/ John 13:1-17

Strabo, *Geography* 7, 16.4.26 (64–63 BCE–23 CE)

The Nabataeans are a sensible people, and are so much inclined to acquire possessions that they publicly fine anyone who has diminished his possessions and also confer honors on anyone who has increased them. Since they have but few slaves, they are served by their kinsfolk for the most part, or by one another, or by themselves; so that the custom extends even to their kings. They prepare common meals together in groups of thirteen persons; and they have two girl-singers for each banquet. The king holds many drinking-bouts in magnificent style, but no one drinks more than eleven cupfuls . . .

The king is so democratic (δημοτικός) that, in addition to serving himself, he sometimes even serves the rest himself in his turn. (LCL)

Cultic table fellowship *(marzeah)* with twelve guests was widespread in pagan cults in this time in the environs of Palestine. Cf. J. T. Milik, *Dédicaces faites par des Dieux (Palmyre, Hatra, Tyr) et des thiases sémitiques à l'époque romaine* (Paris, 1972), pp. 119-21. On the renunciation of service from slaves among the Essenes, cf. Philo, "Contemplative Life" 70-72. On abolishing the distinctions between slave and free, and men, women, and children in religious associations and cultic fellowship meals, cf. Milik, p. 123. The kind of cultic fellowship meals that featured pastries and wine as the menu are documented especially in Palmyra and in Nabatean inscriptions. Eusebius (*Hist. Ecc.* 1.3.12; 10.1.8) does not hesitate to use the Greek technical term θίασος for the Christian Lord's Supper fellowship. Cf. also no. 497.

347. Luke 23:28, 31

Plutarch, *Moralia*, "Sayings of Spartans: The Last Agis" 216 (45–125 CE)

[The last of the kings of Sparta had been taken prisoner in an ambush and condemned to death without a trial. He is being led out to be strangled and calls to one of his servants that he sees crying:] Stop your weeping for me, man. For in spite of my being put to death in such defiance of law and justice, I am superior to those who are taking my life. (LCL)

Agreements: the last words of the innocent one unjustly executed, the demand to cry not for the "martyr," but for the guilty (implicit in Plutarch), who are in for a much worse fate. Different from Plutarch, Luke portrays the punishments which the perpetrators of the evil deed have to expect. Luke 23:31 infers from the lesser to the greater, while in Plutarch the comparison is in the "better" form.

348. Luke 23:35

4QMess ar, "The Birth of Noah, God's Elect"

And then he will acquire wisdom and learn und[erstanding] . . . vision to come to him on his knees. And with his father and his ancestors . . . life and old age. Counsel and prudence will be with him, and he will know the secrets of man. His wisdom will reach all the peoples, and he will know the secrets of all the living. And all their designs against him will come to nothing, and [his] rule over all the living will be great. His designs [will succeed] for he is the Elect of God. (Vermes)

Among the many ideal features of Noah, his charismatic-astronomical knowledge is underscored, by virtue of which he has a singular position among all the nations. Elsewhere in the Enoch literature, it is the figure of the Messianic judge who is outfitted with all these characteristics. Of course protection and power are also emphasized, and that points in the direction of "save" in the Lucan text. Noah is protected, and others stand under his protection. That is what one expects from God's elect.

On Luke 24:52 (bowing the knee in worship), cf. no. 485. For the Easter stories, cf. nos. 215-22.

349. Luke 23:45

Philo, *Life of Moses* 1.123 (15 BCE–50 CE)

[Describing the plagues in Egypt:] But, when they were scattered, and the king was sick to death at the thought of releasing the people, a plague arose greater than all that had gone before; for, in bright daylight, darkness was suddenly overspread, possibly because there was an eclipse of the sun more complete than the ordinary, or perhaps because the stream of rays was cut off by continuous clouds, compressed with great force into masses of unbroken density. (LCL)

In both Luke and Philo, the event reported in their tradition as supernatural darkness is given a somewhat "scientific" explanation (cf. NRSV margin). Since both Luke and Philo have no difficulty in accepting miracles, even enlarging those that come to them in Scripture and tradition, this is not a matter of explaining miracles *away,* but illustrates the way educated cosmopolitan types who are writing for the same type of cultivated public tend to set the story in a "secularizing" framework with "naturalistic" *intermediate* causes. Cf. *Life of Moses* 1.185, on Moses' purifying of the bitter waters (cf. Exod 15:22-26): "Hardly had he so prayed, when God sent in advance the power of His grace, and, opening the vigilant eye of the suppliant's soul, bade him lift and throw into the spring a tree which he showed him, possibly formed by nature to exercise a virtue which had hitherto remained unknown, or possibly created on this occasion for the service which it was destined to perform" (LCL). So also on Moses' bringing water out of the rock (*Life of Moses* 1.210-11; cf. Exod 17:1-7 and Num 20:1-13): "Moses, taking that sacred staff with which he accomplished the signs in Egypt, under inspiration smote the steep rock with it. It may be that the rock contained originally a spring and now had its artery clean severed, or perhaps that then for the first time a body of water collected in it through hidden channels was forced out by the impact." Cf. also no. 213 above.

350. Luke 24:44

Sirach, Prologue (125 BCE)

Not only this book, but even the Law itself, the Prophecies, and the rest of the books differ not a little when read in the original. (NRSV)

Sirach himself, ca. 180 BCE, had already referred to "the law of the Most High, the wisdom of all the ancients, and . . . prophecies," but without making clear what had canonical status. In 125 BCE the Law and Prophets seem to be firm bodies of Scripture that may be taken as "canonical," in addition to which there were other "writings" the status of which is unclear. This may be compared with Luke 24:44, written in the church at least two centuries later. There now seem to be three divisions, with "Psalms" constituting or representing the third division, which seems to be included in "canonical" status. Cf. also *Halakhic Letter from Qumran* (4QMMT): "the Book of Moses, the Prophets, and David and the history of the generations"; Philo, "Contemplative Life" 25: "the Law and the Oracles given by inspiration through the Prophets, and the Psalms and the other books"; Josephus, *Apion* 1.7-8, 37-43: "Books of Moses, the Prophets after Moses, Hymns and Precepts for the conduct of life"; some early rabbis, *Baba Bathra* 14b: "Law, Prophets . . ., Sacred Writings."

351. Luke 24:51 / Acts 1:1-11

Ovid, *Metamorphoses* 14.805-51 (43 BCE–17 CE)

Mars put off his gleaming helmet and thus addressed the father of gods and men: "The time is come, O father, since the Roman state stands firm on strong foundations and no longer hangs on one man's strength alone, to grant the reward which was promised to me and to thy worthy grandson, to take him from earth and set him in the heavens. Once to me, in full council of the gods (for I treasured up thy gracious words in retentive mind, and now recall them to thee), thou didst declare: 'One shall there be whom thou shalt bear up to the azure blue of heaven.' Now let the full meaning of thy words be ratified." The omnipotent Father nodded his assent; then, hiding all the sky with his dark clouds, he filled the earth with thunder and lightning. Gradivus knew this for the assured sign of the translation which had been promised him; and, leaning on his spear, dauntless he mounted his chariot drawn by steeds straining beneath the bloody yoke, and swung the loud-resounding lash. Gliding downward through the air, he halted on the summit of the wooded Palatine. There, as Ilia's son was giving kindly judgment to his citizens, he caught him up from earth. His mortal part dissolved into thin air, as a leaden bullet hurled by a broad sling is wont to melt away in the mid-heavens. And now a fair form clothes him, worthier of the high couches of the gods, such form as has Quirinus, clad in the sacred robe.

His wife was mourning him as lost, when regal Juno bade Iris go down to Hersilia on her arching way with these directions for the widowed queen: "O queen, bright glory both of the Latin and of the Sabine race, most worthy once to have been the consort of so great a man, and now of divine Quirinus, cease your laments and, if you would indeed behold your husband, come with me to yonder grove which stands green on Quirinus' hill, shading the temple of the king of Rome." Iris obeyed and, gliding to earth along her rainbow arch, accosted Hersilia in the words which had been given her. She, scarce lifting her eyes and with modest look, replied: "O goddess (for I may not tell who thou art, and yet 'tis plain thou art a goddess), lead, oh, lead me on, and show me my husband's face. If only the fates grant me but once to see him, then shall I say I have gained heaven indeed." Straightway she fared along with Thaumas' daughter to the hill of Romulus. There a star from high heaven came gliding down to earth, and Hersilia, her hair bursting into flame from its light, goes up together with the star into thin air. Her with dear, familiar hands Rome's founder receives, and changes her mortal body and her old-time name. He calls her Hora, and now as goddess is she joined once more to her Quirinus. (LCL)

Ovid gives a slightly different account in *Fasti*, 2.481-509: "With Jupiter's assent, both poles [of the earth] shook, and Atlas moved the burden of the sky. There is a place, called by the old ones the marsh of Caprea. By chance, Romulus, you were there giving laws. The sun disappeared, and rising clouds obscured the sky, and a heavy rain shower fell. Then it thundered, the air was torn by flames. The people fled, and the king [Romulus] flew to the stars on his father's [Mars'?] horses. There was grieving, and certain senators were falsely charged with murder, and that belief might have stuck in the people's mind. But Proculus Julius was coming from the Alba Longa; the moon was shining, he was not using a torch. Suddenly the hedges on the left shook and moved. He shrank back and his hair stood on end. Beautiful and more than human and clothed in a sacred robe, Romulus was seen, standing in the middle of the road. He said, 'Stop the [Romans] from their mourning; do not let them violate my divinity [numina] with their tears; order the pious crowd to bring incense and worship the new Quirinius and to cultivate the arts of their fathers, war.' He gave the order and he vanished to the upper world from Julius' eyes" (Cartlidge and Dungan).

The story has several points of contact with the Lucan account of Jesus' ascension, including (in the *Fasti* version) the understanding that the ascended king left behind a commission to his people. In contrast to the New Testament stories, there is an interest in the "mechanics" of the transition from this-worldly existence to that of the other world. In both versions, the story is seen from the transcendent perspective looking down on this world, rather than from within historical existence, the typically biblical perspective.

352. Luke 24:51/ Acts 1:1-11

Livy, *History of Rome* 1.16 (59 BCE–17 CE)

When these deathless deeds had been done, as the king was holding muster in the Campus Martius, near the swamp of Capra, for the purpose of reviewing the army, suddenly a storm came up, with loud claps of thunder, and enveloped him in a cloud so thick as to hide him from the sight of the assembly; and from that moment Romulus was no more on earth. The Roman soldiers at length recovered from their panic, when this hour of wild confusion had been succeeded by a sunny calm, but when they saw that the royal seat was empty, although they readily believed the assertion of the senators, who had been standing next to Romulus, that he had been caught up on high in the blast, they nevertheless remained for some time sorrowful and silent, as if filled with the fear of orphanhood. Then, when a few men had taken the initiative, they all with one accord hailed Romulus as a god and a god's son, the King and Father of the Roman City, and with prayers besought his favor that he would graciously be pleased forever to protect his children. There were some, I believe, even then who secretly asserted that the king had been rent in pieces by the hands of the senators, for this rumor, too, got abroad, but in very obscure terms; the other version obtained currency, owing to men's admiration for the hero and the intensity of their panic. And the shrewd device of one man is also said to have gained new credit for the story. This was Proculus Julius, who, when the people were distracted with the loss of their king and in no friendly mood toward the senate, being, as tradition tells, weighty in council, were the matter never so important, addressed the assembly as follows: "Quirites, the Father of this City, Romulus, descended suddenly from the sky at dawn this morning and appeared to me. Covered with confusion, I stood reverently before him, praying that it might be vouchsafed me to look upon his face without sin. 'Go,' said he, 'and declare to the Romans the will of Heaven that my Rome shall be the capital of the world; so let them cherish the art of war, and let them know and teach their children that no human strength can resist Roman arms.' So saying," he concluded, "Romulus departed on high." (LCL)

Points of contact with the Lucan story of resurrection and ascension:

1) For both, the ascended one is a son of God. Jesus was killed and raised by God before his ascension. Romulus was exalted to heaven instead of dying.

2) In each case, the ascended one appears and gives a commission to his earthly community. Romulus gives a nationalistic militaristic commission. Jesus gives a commission to preach the gospel and make disciples.

3) Clouds are part of the description of the ascension, though for Luke and Christian tradition, they connote the clouds of the divine presence in biblical and Jewish tradition (cf. e.g. Exod 19:9; Dan 7:13).

The Gospel of John
(and Parallels)

353. John 1:1-18

Wisdom Myth of Early Judaism (Reconstructed)
(2 cent. BCE–1 cent. CE)

Wisdom, a pre-existent being [Job 28:27; Sir 24:9; Wis 7:22; Prov 8:30, 3:19; *2 Enoch* 30:8] was God's partner [or "executive administrator"; depends on pointing of Heb.] at the creation [Prov 8:22-30; Sir 1:1-9, 24:3, 9; Wis 8:3, 9:4, 9. Cf. also Philo].

She sought, and still seeks, a dwelling-place among human beings, but her seeking was in vain [*1 Enoch* 4:1-3; Prov 1:20-32, 9:5-6].

She is universally revealed, in every people and nation [Sir 24:6].

Her preaching was, and is, rejected [Prov 1:23; Sir 6:23; Bar 3:12].

She came to what was her own (for she had created it), but her own did not accept her [Sir 24:6; *1 Enoch* 42:1-3, 84:3].

So she returned to the heavenly world, where she lives in hiding [Job 28:12-17—translators use "it"; Bar 3:15].

Though people seek her now, they can no longer find her. God alone knows the way to her [*1 Enoch* 5:8, 91:10; Wis 7:14, 27; Job 28:20-33; Bar 3:19-31, 37–4:1].

Yet she dwells in the people of Israel [Sir 24:8-12], and is identified with the written Torah, the book of the covenant [Sir 24:23], though remaining mostly unrecognized and unacknowledged.

Nevertheless there are rare exceptions, people to whom Wisdom reveals herself, who accept her, and whom she thereby makes friends of God and prophets [Wis 7:12, 27]. (MEB/from R. Bultmann)

I here depart, for the only time in this volume, from the usual procedure of printing only exact quotations of ancient texts, in order to present the summary of Bultmann's reconstruction of the connected wisdom myth he reconstructs as the basis for the many allusions and oblique references cited above (adapted from R. Bultmann, "Der religionsgeschichtliche Hintergrund des Prologs zum Johannes-Evangelium," H. Schmidt, ed. *EUCHARISTERION, Festschrift für Hermann Gunkel* [Göttingen: Vandenhoeck & Ruprecht, 1923], Part II.1-27.). The complete mythical story as reconstructed above occurs in no single text. The reconstruction is printed here because it is a useful theory that has been extremely influential. See Bultmann's *The Gospel of John* (Philadelphia: Westminster, 1971), 22-23.

Although Bultmann's particular reconstruction of the myth has been severely criticized (cf. e.g. Marshall Johnson, "Reflections on a Wisdom Approach to Matthew's Christology," *CBQ* 36 [Jan. 1974], 44-64), there can be hardly any doubt that something like the above mythical story of Wisdom influenced John's conception of the history of the Logos.

354. John 1:1-14

Oratio Joseph (a Jewish fragment preserved in Origen, *Interpretation of John* 2.189-90) (2–1 cents. BCE)

Jacob, at least, says, "For I who speak to you am Jacob and Israel, an angel of God and a primal spirit, and Abraham and Isaac were created before any work. But I am Jacob, he who was called Jacob by men, but my name is Israel, he who was called Israel by God, a man who sees God because I am the firstborn of every living being which is given life by God."

And he adds, "And when I was coming from Mesopotamia of Syria, Uriel, the angel of God came out and said, 'I descended to the earth and dwelt among men,' and 'I was called Jacob by name.' He was jealous, and fought with me, and wrestled with me [cf. Gen. 32:24, 28], saying that his name preceded my name and that of every angel. And I mentioned his name to him and how great he is among the sons of God: 'Are you not Uriel, my eighth, and I Israel, an archangel of the power of the Lord and chief of the captains of thousands among the sons of God? Am I not Israel, the first minister in the presence of God, and did I not invoke my God by his unquenchable name?'" (Heine)

On this text: J. Z. Smith, "The Prayer of Joseph," in *Religions in Antiquity* (Suppl *Numen* 14), ed. J. Neusner (Leiden: E. J. Brill, 1968), 253-94. The text is a midrash on Genesis 32. Rivalry among the angels is a frequent theme of Jewish mysticism. The goal of this text, however, is to set forth the mysterious nature of Israel; and this is what gives it a point of contact with John 1. (1) A concrete earthly human being, or the people represented by him (cf. also no. 850), is identified with the very first being who stands before God. This is analogous to the relation between Jesus and the Logos. (2) Israel is the one who has seen God; cf. John 1:18. (3) The dwelling of the angelic being among humanity corresponds to the dwelling (lit. "tenting" in each case) of the Logos in John 1:14. Similarly, Wisdom lives among humanity according to Baruch 3:38, even though not as a human being, but as the book of the Law. Likewise in Sirach 24, Wisdom tents among humanity as commanded by God; here too Wisdom has a similar liturgical function to that of Jacob in our text; cf. Sirach 24:8-12.

355. John 1:1

Anaxagoras of Clazomenae fragment 1 (according to Plutarch, *Moralia*, "Placita philosophorum" 1.3) (496–428 BCE)

[He begins his work with the words] in the beginning everything was chaotic; but reason [νοῦς] divided and ordered it. (MEB/Berger)

According to Diels-Kranz, *Fragmente der Vorsokratiker,* the Greek text reads ἀπ ἀρχῆς, but in the translation the editor considers it to be an introductory formula rather than a part of the quotation itself. "Reason" represents the Greek νοῦς, which could also be translated "mind." In any case the subject is that reason that brought order out of the primeval chaos. John 1 presents the contrasting alternative: the Logos stands at the beginning, and his/its opponent is not chaos, but the refusal of humanity to accept him/it. Concretely, this refers to the rejection of Jesus.

356. John 1:1

Hermetica, Fragment 27 (Scott) (according to Cyril) (2–4 cent. CE)

This is what Hermes Trismegistus says about God: "Once having come forth from the Father, all perfect, prolific, and a craftsman in prolific nature, lying low over the prolific water, he made the water conceive." (Copenhaver)

Echoes of Genesis 1:1 are vaguely mixed with general Near Eastern tradition. A characteristic difference from Genesis 1 is seen in that here the creative process is thought of sexually, but on the other hand the mediator of creation is thought of as the Logos, as in John 1.

On the prehistory of Logos speculation in Greek and Hellenistic-Jewish philosophy (cf. C. Colpe, "Gottessohn" in *RAC* 12 [1983], col. 35; C. Colpe, "Von der Logoslehre des Philon zu der des Clemens von Alexandrien," in A. M. Ritter, ed., *Kerygma und Logos* [Fs. C. Andresen] [Göttingen: Vandenhoeck & Ruprecht, 1979], 89-107):

a) Stoicism: God = Logos = cosmos

This idea is found for example in Zenon (according to Diogenes Laertius, *Lives* 7.68, but also in Cleanthes, Hymn to Zeus [Zeus = logos], in Chrysippus, and elsewhere). The equation of providence, destiny, world(-law), nature (natural order), and God (= the all-pervasive world reason).

b) Plato: God and the world are not identical, but are related genealogically (see below, no. 364). The cosmos is only an image of God, or God's son, or the visible manifestation of God in distinction from the invisible, spiritual God. The cosmos is not called "Logos."

c) Philo of Alexandria: a synthesis of Platonic and Stoic formulations. The spiritual God has two sons, the (elder) Logos (the ideal cosmos) and the younger visible cosmos. Philo could say of the visible cosmos that it was created "through the Logos" no. 359 is similar on this point). The thinking human soul is the reflected image of the Logos.

d) Philo can think of the Logos in personal terms, so that he repeats the mythological Greek view according to which the Logos is personified as the all-pervasive world reason (see above under [a], especially Cleanthes' Hymn to Zeus). Philo speaks here of the Firstborn, of the Archangel, but also of Israel, as in *Confusion* 146-48 (Jews as sons of Israel). The whole people is mythologically represented by the Logos = Israel. That is the bridge to no. 354 as well as to the idea represented in Ephesians 1:4-5.

357. John 1:1-2

Iamblichus, *On the Mysteries* 8:2 (4 cent. CE)

Prior to truly existing beings and total principles [or principles that rank as wholes], there is one God, prior to [that deity who is generally believed to be] the first God and king, immovable, and abiding in the solitude of his own unity. For neither is the intelligible connected with him, nor anything else; but he is established as the paradigm of the God who is the father of himself, is self-begotten, is father alone, and truly good. For he is something even greater and prior to this, is the fountain of all things, and the root of the first intelligible forms. (Taylor)

The text is a late witness, in fact a kind of final pagan form of the widespread cosmological reflection on the origin of being—which in any case was not limited to Gnostic texts. The decisive move is always the step from the primeval unity to a second entity which follows from it. As in John 1:1, so also here, the discourse deals with "God," except that in John the one Logos stands in place of the first God/King in Iamblichus, where the system was Primeval Deity → God/King → the other gods. In contrast to John 1, the "second god" is here not the mediator of creation.

358. John 1:1-3

Targum Neofiti Genesis 1:16–2:3 (1–3 cent. CE)

And the Memra of the Lord created the two great lights: . . . And the Glory of the Lord set them in the firmament of the heavens to shine upon the earth. . . . And the Memra of the Lord blessed them saying: "Be strong and multiply and fill the waters in the seas, and let birds multiply upon the earth." And on the seventh day the Memra of the Lord completed his work which he had created. . . . And the Glory of the Lord blessed the seventh day and hallowed it . . . (McNamara)

The Word (Aramaic: *Memra*) of God here clearly functions in the role of creator, as can also be assumed for John 1:3. As its/his counterpart, the Shekinah ("indwelling," i.e. God as the one who is present and active in the world) is entrusted with the task of arranging and developing the creation. In Judaism also, God's Word had a creative function, as for example in Wisdom of Solomon 9:1 ("O God of my ancestors and Lord of mercy, who have made all things by your word [ἐν τῷ λόγῳ], and by your wisdom have formed humankind to have dominion over the creatures you have made" NRSV). But here the word is less an independent being than in John 1. In the often-mentioned wisdom texts Proverbs 8:22ff. and Sirach 24, Wisdom is, while the first created being, still not the mediator of creation. In many interpretations however, in Proverbs 8:30 wisdom participates in the work of creation. That depends on whether one reads '*mwn* as '*amon* = "master workman," as in the MT (cf. LXX "organizer," Vulgate "assembler") or as '*aemun*, "little child" (so Aquila and modern exegetes), because she "plays."

359. John 1:1-3

Philo, *Who Is the Heir of Divine Things?* 205–6 (15 BCE–50 CE)

To his Word, his chief messenger [ἀρχάγγελος], highest in age and honor, the Father of all has given the special prerogative, to stand on the border and separate the creature from the Creator. This same Word both pleads with the immortal as suppliant for afflicted mortality and acts as ambassador of the ruler to the subject. He glories in this prerogative and proudly describes it in these words, "and I stood between the Lord and you," that is neither uncreated as God, nor created as you, but midway between the two extremes, a surety to both sides; to the parent, pledging the creature that it should never altogether rebel against the rein and choose disorder rather than order; to the child, warranting his hopes that the merciful God will never forget his own work. For "I am the harbinger of peace to creation from that God whose will is to bring wars to an end, who is ever the guardian of peace." (LCL)

The Logos is mediator between God and creation. While conceptual consistency should not be required of such discussions, it is perhaps worthy of note that in contrast to (later developed) Christian reflection on Jesus as the incarnate Logos, Philo thinks in the mode "neither/nor" rather than "both/and." For Philo the Logos is neither truly human nor truly divine. While Philo does not share the Platonic disdain of the material world common to the Platonic sources from which he draws, he could never speak of the Logos as having become flesh and dwelling among human beings as a human being (see Philo's comment below, no. 367 at John 1:14).

360. John 1:4

A personalized Aretalogy of Isis, from an inscription in Maroneia (Macedonia) (150–50 BCE)

. . . may words of praise not be lacking in the face of the magnitude of your benefaction. Therefore this encomium entreats you, and praise for my face belongs to a goddess not with a man. So, just as in the case of my eyes, Isis, you listened to my prayers, come for your praises and to hear my second prayer; for the praise of you is entirely more important than my eyes whenever with the same eyes with which I saw the sun I see your world. I am completely confident that you will come again. For since you came when called for my salvation, how would you not come for your own honor? So taking heart I proceed to what remains, knowing that this encomium is written not only by the hand of a man, but also by the mind of a god. And first I shall come to your family, making as the beginning of my praises the earliest beginnings of your family. They say that Ge was the mother of all: you were born a daughter to her first. You took Serapis to live with you, and when you had made your marriage together the world, provided with eyes, was lit up by means of your faces, Helios and Selene. So you are two but have many designations among men. For you are the only ones whom everyday life knows as gods. Therefore, how would the account of your praises not be unmanageable when one must praise many gods at the outset? She with Hermes discovered writing; and of this writing some was sacred for initiates, some was publicly available for all. She instituted justice, that each of us might know how to live on equal terms, just as, because of our nature, death makes us equal. She instituted the non-Greek language for some, Greek language for others, in order that the race might be differentiated not only as between men and women, but also between all peoples. You gave laws, but they were called *thesmoi* originally. Accordingly, cities enjoyed tranquillity, having discovered not violence legalized, but law without violence. You made parents honored by their children, in that you cared for them not only as fathers, but also as gods. Accordingly, the favor is greater when a goddess also drew up as law what is necessary in nature. As a domicile Egypt was loved by you. You particularly honored Athens within Greece. For there first you made the earth produce food: Triptolemos, yoking your sacred snakes, scattered the seed to all Greeks as he traveled in his chariot. Accordingly, in Greece we are keen to see Athens, and in Athens, Eleusis, considering the city to be the ornament of Europe, and the sacred place the ornament of the city. She determined that life should cohere from a man and a woman . . . (Horsley, *New Documents*)

This is the earliest of extant aretalogies of Isis, related to four other texts praising Isis found in inscriptions. The four apparently derive from a common Egyptian source. Although there is in the inscription a certain aspect of propaganda for the Egyptian goddess as her cult spreads throughout the Hellenistic world, the text also expresses genuine piety and devotion. There is no direct contact between this aretalogy and John, but there are points of contact between its thought world and the Johannine idea of the Logos:

1) Isis is herself deity, but is distinguished from and daughter of the mother of all. Here, both the supreme God and this God's representative are all feminine. Cf. the Logos and the Father-language of the Fourth Gospel. A contrast: "beginning" (ἀρχή) occurs twice, but not in connection with the appearance of Isis, who appears "first" (πρώτη). Isis had a definite beginning, was not there "ἐν ἀρχῇ."

2) Like the preexistent Logos of John 1:4, Isis is the light for all humanity. The same note of universalism is struck. It is not only the adherents of Isis who are blessed by her civilizing work for all humanity: the giving of language, establishing of justice, order and obedience in the family. Though called by many names, it is Isis (with her consort Serapis) who in fact presides over all the aspects of human life. They are literally the "light of the world" (cf. John 8:12), the sun and moon representing them in the sky.

3) There is nothing like an incarnation. Isis provides her beneficence always and universally, from the transcendent world. Thus the language of "coming" and "coming again" (lines 10-13) must not of course be mistaken for a Christian pattern, but illustrates how similar phraseology could be used in different religious frameworks to mean entirely different things.

For other texts presenting the all-encompassing deity of Isis, see no. 519 on Acts 17:22-31, and no. 417.

361. John 1:4

Wisdom of Solomon 18:3-4 (150 BCE–50 CE)

Therefore you provided a flaming pillar of fire
as a guide for your people's unknown journey,
and a harmless sun for their glorious wandering.
For their enemies deserved to be deprived of light and imprisoned in darkness,
those who had kept your children imprisoned,
through whom the imperishable light of the law was to be given to the world. (NRSV)

One of many illustrations of a seemingly universal notion, that religious insight and the will of the deity is represented as the gift of light to a darkened world. Here, the symbol functions at two levels: God miraculously provided literal light for the wilderness journey of the Israelites, but they were later to be the vehicles of the giving of God's light to the whole world—the Law. The same author later praises Wisdom:

"For she is a breath of the power of God,
and a pure emanation of the glory of the Almighty;
therefore nothing defiled gains entrance into her.
For she is a reflection of eternal light,

a spotless mirror of the working of God
and an image of his goodness.
Although she is but one, she can do all things
and while remaining in herself, she renews all things;
in every generation she passes into holy souls
and makes them friends of God, and prophets." (7:25-27 NRSV)
See also Hebrews 1:1-4, Colossians 1:15-20.

362. John 1:10

Democritus of Abdera, Fragments (ca. 460–380 BCE)

The world is [only] a tent, life is a transition. You came, you saw, you went forth.
(MEB/Berger, ed. Diels-Kranz II, 165 with no. 115)

Cf. also the other text mentioned above: "The world is change, life is guesswork." In both texts the world is associated with flux, temporality, and uncertainty—a clear indication of a skeptical understanding of the world order. The understanding of the world as a temporary dwelling place (a tent) became very widespread: Epictetus, *Discourses* 2.23.36f.; Seneca, *Letters to Lucilius* 120.14; Cicero, *De senectute* 23.84; in each case however without the use of the concept "world." In contrast to these texts, where the world is evaluated only skeptically because of its temporal nature, the Johannine evaluation is even less favorable, since "world" here is seen in contrast to God, and thus takes on a partly negative tone. This is similar to some apocalyptic writings (*1 Enoch* 48:7; 108:8-9; 4 Ezra). (Cf. also no. 916).

363. John 1:10

Sotades of Maronea, fragment in Stobaeus, *Anthologium* IV 34, 8 (3 cent. BCE)

For he himself, who brings everything forth [namely, the cosmos] and generates everything, does not make just judgments with regard to every human being. For, as regards the world, what has happened has always been evil. The world has always been the cause of evil to its great people. For all who wanted to find something more, whether of technical work or scholarly knowledge, have in fact done something bad—oriented toward death as the goal, in that they suffered evil from the world that gave them being. Socrates was made by the world, and made to be wise; but the world killed Socrates, who died in prison, drinking the hemlock [additional examples follow]. (MEB/Berger)

The point: the personified cosmos is charged with being unjust especially toward those it has made the most richly talented: it judges them worthy of an especially gruesome death. The Begetter kills the best of its children. As in apocalyptic and the Fourth Gospel, "the world" is unjust, not just in contrast to God, but as it were even when measured by its own standards. As in the Johannine community, so also here, the injustice of the world is directed toward an especially qualified group.

364. John 1:14

Plato, *Timaeus* 92 C (428–349 BCE)

For this our Cosmos has received the living creatures both mortal and immortal and been thereby fulfilled; it being itself a visible Living Creature embracing the visible creatures, a perceptible God made in the image of the Intelligible, most great and good and fair and perfect in its generation—even this one Heaven sole of its kind [monogene]. (LCL)

Cf. also Plutarch, *Obsolescence of Oracles*, §23: "Plato, however, is very far from calling the five different divisions of the world five different worlds; and in those passages again in which he contends against those who postulate an infinite number of worlds, he says that his opinion is that this world is the only-begotten [μονογενής] and beloved of God, having been created out of the corporeal whole, entire, complete, and sufficient unto itself" (LCL). As in the texts discussed above, here too it is a matter of a second entity after God. It has attributes, as it does in John 1 and as the Logos does elsewhere: it is an image of something, it is unique (μονογενής, mistranslated as "only begotten" in KJV of John 1:14, 18; 3:16, 18; 1 John 4:9; Heb 11:17, following the vulgate), it is the beloved. But here, this entity is the cosmos, the world as a complete structure without internal tensions, not the Logos. The picture in John 1 (and cf. 3:16) contrasts with this in that Logos and cosmos stand in a tension-filled relationship. Also in Cornutus (1 cent. CE), *Summary of the Traditions concerning Greek Mythology* 27, the cosmos is called the one and only ("μονογενής"). (On cosmos as "son," cf. no. 463.)

365. John 1:14

Diodorus Siculus, *Library of History* 6.1 (1 cent. BCE)

The ancients among men have given to later generations two conceptions concerning gods. They say on the one hand that some are eternal and imperishable such as [gods named after] the sun and the moon and the other stars of heaven . . . but the others they say were earthly men who became gods, attaining immortal honor and glory because of their benefactions toward men, such as Herakles, Dionysos, Aristaios, and others similar to them. (LCL)

Some gods had always been gods, and never became human. Other gods had once lived human lives, even if they were born of divine-human unions, but first became gods themselves by being exalted. That this distinction was not peculiar to the thought of Diodorus is clear from its appearance elsewhere, e.g. in Cicero's 2.8.19: "They shall worship as gods both those who have always been dwellers in heaven, and also those whose merits have admitted them to heaven: Hercules, Liber, Aesclepius, Castor, Pollus, Quirinius . . ." (LCL). On the whole subject, cf. Charles Talbert, *What Is a Gospel? The Genre of the Canonical Gospels* (Philadelphia: Fortress Press, 1977), for an elaboration of these two types and a discussion of their relevance for New Testament Christology. For a sharp critique of Talbert's approach, see David Aune, "The Problem of the Genre of the Gospels," in *Gospel Perspectives,* ed. R. T. France and D. Wenham (Sheffield: JSOT Press, 1981), 2:9-60.

366. John 1:14

Sirach 24:8-10 (ca. 180 BCE)

[Personified Wisdom speaks:] Then the Creator of all things gave me a command, and my Creator chose the place for my tent. He said, "Make your dwelling in Jacob, and in Israel receive your inheritance." 9 Before the ages, in the beginning, he created me, and for all the ages I shall not cease to be. 10 In the holy tent I ministered before him, and so I was established in Zion. (NRSV)

The text illustrates a Jewish view that transcendent preexistent Wisdom with whose aid the world was created came to dwell on earth, and this dwelling is thought of as "tenting," reflecting the view that God dwelt among his people in the tabernacle/tent (Exod 26). The "tenting" vocabulary is reflected in John 1:14 σκηνόω. In contrast to the Johannine Logos, Wisdom is clearly herself a creature.

367. John 1:14

Philo, *Embassy to Gaius* 16:118 (ca. 40 CE)

God would sooner change into a man than man into a god. (LCL)

In arguing against the deification of the emperor, and looking for an illustration of that which is absolutely the most *unlikely* event, Philo comes near to expressing the kind of incarnational doctrine espoused by Johannine Christianity.

368. John 1:16

Philo, *Allegorical Interpretation* 1.44 (15 BCE–50 CE)

For not even the whole world would be a place fit for God to make his abode, since God is his own place, and He is filled by Himself, and sufficient for Himself, filling and containing all other things in their destitution and barrenness and emptiness, but Himself contained by nothing else, seeing that He is Himself One and the Whole. (LCL)

With this may be compared the Hermetic tractate *Asclepius,* §26 (God is the fullness of all, and has what He wants); §32 (He is the fullness of all perceivable things; similarly §29). The concept of God as fullness has its origin in the ancient philosophical speculation concerning the structure of the universe. Cf. Aristotle's discussion concerning "being" as the middle term between "fullness" and "emptiness" *Metaphysics* 1.4. This is the context for understanding such statements as Iamblichus' *Secret Doctrine* 1.8: "But the things on earth have their being through the fullness [lit. "fillings"] that comes from the gods." In Philo this idea was understood primarily in a soteriological sense, as an expression for the unity of creation and redemption, though he also understood it in other ways, cf. *Dreams* 1.62. An additional text important for understanding is Clementine Homilies 17.8.3, which argues that space is simply emptiness, the void, without being in itself; God is the one who fills up space and gives being to that which exists.

369. John 1:29

2 Enoch 64:5 (1 cent. CE)

[The people said to Enoch:] . . . because you are the one whom the Lord chose in preference to all the people upon the earth; and he appointed you to be the one who makes a written record of all his creation, visible and invisible, and the one who carried away the sin of mankind [and to be a Helper for the children of your household]. (*OTP* 1:190; the text is unclear at this point. The final clause is from the translation of G. N. Bonwetsch)

Parallel to "the one who takes away sin" stands "Helper" (if this reading and translation represents the original text). It is clear from 53:1 that there is no (other) Helper who intercedes for sinners before God, so this text deals with the intercession of Enoch himself (the reference is from G. Röhser, *Metaphorik und Personifikation der Sünde* [Tübingen: J. C. B. Mohr (Paul Siebeck), 1985], p. 63). So too in the Gospel of John the taking away of sins must not necessarily be limited to the concept of an atoning death (cf. also "Advocate" in 1 John 2:1). On the other hand, Hebrews 7:25 makes it clear from the context that intercession and atoning death are not mutually exclusive ideas, but may even be complementary: the intercessor bases his intercession on his own death.

370. John 1:38

Sirach, "Prologue" (ca. 125 BCE)

[Grandson of Sirach, in the prologue to the Greek trans. of his grandfather's work:] You are invited therefore to read it with goodwill and attention, and to be indulgent in cases where, despite our diligent labor in translating, we may seem to have rendered some phrases imperfectly. For what was originally expressed in Hebrew does not have exactly the same sense when translated into another language. Not only this book, but even the Law itself, the Prophecies, and the rest of the books differ not a little when read in the original. (NRSV)

John is aware of the need of translating the Hebrew tradition into Greek (1:38, 41, 42; 9:7). Even though the LXX had been used for several generations and became the "standard" Bible of the early church, the New Testament authors were sometimes aware that they stood in the position of the translator attempting to communicate meanings developed in a Hebrew tradition in a language imperfectly adapted to it. At other times, the changes spoken of by Sirach's grandson took place without any consciousness on the part of the author that it was happening.

371. John 2:1-11

Pausanias, *Description of Greece* 6.26.1-2 (2 cent. CE)

The place where they hold the festival they name the Thyia; it is about eight stades from the city. Three pots are brought into the building by the priests and set down empty in the presence of the citizens and of any strangers who may chance to be in the country. The doors of the building are sealed by the priests themselves and by any others who are so inclined. On the morrow they are allowed to examine the seals, and on going into the building they find pots filled with wine. I did not myself arrive at the time of the festival, but the most respected Elean citizens, and with them strangers also, swore that what I have said is the truth. The Andrians too assert that every other year at their feast of Dionysus wine flows of its own accord from the temple. (LCL)

The same tradition is documented by Athenaeus (beginning of 3 cent. CE, in Rome), *The Learned Banquet* 1.34: "Theopompus of Chios relates that the vine was discovered in Olympia, on the banks of the Alpheius; and that there is a district in Elis a mile away, in which, at the festival of Dionysus, the inhabitants shut up and seal three empty cauldrons in the presence of visitors; later, they open the cauldrons and find them full of wine" (LCL). In Diodorus Siculus (1 cent. BCE), *Library of History* 3.66.2 the following account is found: "The Teans advance as proof that the god [Dionysus] was born among them the fact that, even to this day, at fixed times in their city a fountain of wine, of unusually sweet fragrance, flows of its own accord from the earth" (LCL). This story originated in the Dionysus tradition, in which the god sends forth a spring of wine from the earth (Euripides, *Bacchi* 707, "a spring of wine"; Horace, *Odes* 2.19.10). We may consider it firmly established that the context of the idea is everywhere the Dionysus cult, but there is no mention in this tradition of the changing of water into wine. The matter is different in the following texts:

372. John 2:1-11

Pliny the Elder, *Natural History* 2.231 (24–79 CE)

It is accredited by the Mucianus who was three times consul that the water flowing from a spring in the temple of Father Liber on the island of Andros always has the flavor of wine on January 5th: the day is called God's Gift Day. (LCL)

This is in the context of a discussion of whether there is water that makes one drunk like wine (as in Ovid, *Metamorphoses* 15.329ff.). In 31:13, Pliny had mentioned the lake of Clitorius, from which one could drink wine until one is surfeited with it. The only question was whether the drunkenness derived from the lake or from the springs. The passage cited above counts on a temporary transformation (January 5) of the water that normally flows from the spring into a spring of wine. For the date cf. no. 11.

373. John 2:1-11

Philostratus, *Life of Apollonius of Tyana* 6:10 (ca. 210 CE)

[Concerning the Apollo of Delphi:] . . . a person who desires a response, puts his question briefly, and Apollo tells what he knows without any miraculous display. And yet it would be just as easy for him to convulse the whole mountain of Parnassus, and to alter the springs of the Castalian fountain so that it should run with wine, and to check the river Cephisus and stay its stream; but he reveals the bare truth without any of this show or ostentation. (LCL)

Also from Philostratus, *Imagines* 1:14 (Concerning the participants in the festival of Dionysus): ". . . for the Earth will take part with the Fire in the Bacchic revel and will make it possible for the revelers to take wine from springs and to draw milk from clods of earth or from a rock as from living breasts" (LCL).

374. John 2:1-11

Lucian, *A True Story* 1:7 (120–185 CE)

[After a great storm and landing on an unknown island, an inscription is found saying "To this point came Hercules and Dionysus." Nearby, giant footprints are found.] We did obeisance and went on, but had not gone far when we came upon a river of wine, just as like as could be to Chian [the wine of Chios]. The stream was large and full, so that in places it was actually navigable. Thus we could not help having much greater faith in the inscription on the slab, seeing the evidence of Dionysus' visit. I resolved to find out where the river took its rise, and went up along the stream. What I found was not a source, but a number of large grapevines, full of clusters; beside the root of each flowed a spring of clear wine, and the spring gave rise to the river. (LCL)

Lucian too is a witness to the Dionysus tradition. In his evaluation of this passage, I. Broer determines ("Noch einmal: Zur religionsgeschichtlichen 'Ableitung' von Jo 2,1-11," in SNTU 8 [1983], 103-23) that in the majority of the available texts the Dionysus tradition is the determining factor, and that in Pliny and Philostratus (nos. 372, 373) there is explicit reference to changing water to wine. The Old Testament and Jewish tradition does not know this motif, even though in the messianic thought the theme of the eschatological abundance of wine plays a great role (cf. Gen 49:11-12). This could thus have strengthened the motivation for taking over elements of the Dionysus tradition.

375. John 2:1-11

2 Baruch 29:1-8 (ca. 100 CE)

That which will happen at that time bears upon the whole earth. Therefore, all who live will notice it. For at that time I shall only protect those found in this land at that time. And it will happen that when all that which should come to pass in these parts has been accomplished, the Anointed One will begin to be revealed. And Behemoth will reveal itself from its place, and Leviathan will come from the sea, the two great monsters which I created on the fifth day of creation and which I shall have kept until that time. And they will be nourishment for all who are left. The earth will also yield fruits ten thousandfold. And on one vine will be a thousand branches, and one branch will produce a thousand clusters, and one cluster will produce a thousand grapes, and one grape will produce a cor of wine. And those who are hungry will enjoy themselves and they will, moreover, see marvels every day. For winds will go out in front of me every morning to bring the fragrance of aromatic fruits and clouds at the end of the day to distill the dew of health. And it will happen at that time that the treasury of manna will come down again from on high, and they will eat of it in those years because these are they who will have arrived at the consummation of time. (*OTP* 1:629)

Scarcity was the hallmark of normal life, but in the eschatological times there would be abundance of wine. In a vineyard economy such as Hellenistic Palestine and much of the Mediterranean, wine as a symbol of the goodness of life was common and became an eschatological symbol in Judaism (cf. also *1 Enoch* 10:19; Amos 9:13-14; Hos 14:7; Jer 31:12; and as a specific symbol of the "messianic times" already in Gen 49:10-12).

Judaism did not typically adopt the view prevalent in pagan religions (see below) that wine is a symbol of exhilaration and revelatory power which lifted the recipient beyond this world and opened the door to transcendent revelations. Hellenistic Jews such as Philo, however, could intentionally combine traditional Jewish wine symbolism with that of pagan religion: ". . . when the happy soul holds out the sacred goblet of its own reason, who is it that pours into it the holy cupfuls of true gladness, but the Word, the Cup-bearer of God and Master of the feast, who is also none other than the draught which he pours—his own self free from all dilution, the delight, the sweetening, the exhilaration, the merriment, the ambrosian drug (to take for our own use the poet's terms) whose medicine gives joy and gladness?" (*Dreams* 2.249) (LCL). C. K. Barrett, *Gospel According to St. John* 2nd ed. (Philadelphia: Westminster, 1978), 188: "Thus there existed Jewish precedent for speaking of the Logos in pseudo-Dionysiac terminology."

The immediate point of contact with this passage is the extravagant abundance of wine pictured for the eschatological times. For John, the eschatological time is already present in the ministry of Jesus. Additional contacts with Johannine theology are the reappearance of the hidden manna at the eschaton (John 6:49-51), the hungry being fed (John 6:1-13, especially 11-12), and perhaps the wind/spirit (John 3:8). (See also Mark 6:30-44.)

376. John 2:4

Eunapius, *Life of Iamblicus* 549 (4 cent. CE)

This [performance of the requested miracle] is not appropriate for me now, but for the right time [καιρός]. (MEB)

"The hour of Jesus refers to his death on the cross and the exaltation in glory (7:30; 8:20—the 'hour' not yet come; 12:23, 27; 13:1; 17:1—the hour in immediate prospect). It is unthinkable that in this verse ἡ ὥρα should have a different meaning, such as 'the hour for me to supply them with wine,' yet it is legitimate to compare the use of similar expressions in Hellenistic miracle and magical literature [as above]. The essential movement of the life of Jesus is described in Hellenistic as well as Old Testament language" (Barrett, *Gospel According to St. John*, 191). Cf. Bultmann, *Gospel of John*, 117.

377. John 2:11; 20:30

Inscription (107 BCE)

He signified [σημαίνω] beforehand what was about to happen by the signs happening in the holy place. (MEB)

John selects a key word for Jesus' miracles that has theological meaning derived from the Hebrew Bible, and had already developed eschatological overtones in the Christian tradition, but was also known in popular Hellenistic religion. This is another example of his intentional choice of terms that bridge the Hebrew-Jewish religious conceptuality and that of the wider Hellenistic world.

378. John 2:25

3 Enoch 10:3–11:3 (5 cent. CE, with older traditions)

[The ascended Enoch is given a throne; Enoch speaks in the first person:] And the herald went out into every heaven and announced concerning me: "I have appointed Metatron my servant as a prince and a ruler over all the denizens of the heights. . . . Whatever he says to you in my name you must observe and do, because I have committed to him the Prince of Wisdom and the Prince of Understanding, to teach him the wisdom of those above and of those below, the wisdom of this world and of the world to come. . . ." The Holy One, blessed be he, revealed to me from that time onward all the mysteries of wisdom, all the depths of the perfect Torah and all the thoughts of men's hearts. All the mysteries of the world and all the orders of nature stand revealed before me as they stand revealed before the Creator. From that time onward I looked and beheld deep secrets and wonderful mysteries. Before a man thinks in secret, I see his thought; before he acts, I see his act. There is nothing in heaven above or deep within the earth concealed from me. (*OTP* 1:264)

Although this Jewish text is much later than the New Testament, it is not dependent on Christian ideas, and has several points of contact with Johannine ideas:

1) An ascended human figure (Enoch) is invested with divine status and serves as a mediator between the heavenly world and humanity.

2) The divine powers given him include the knowledge of human hearts. This general characteristic of divine beings has a particularly Jewish apocalyptic character in this text, in that the transcendent being who has this knowledge is a "deified" human being who now represents the supreme God. This is at least a two-stage "Christology," human/divine. But it more likely represents a three-stage "Christology," divine/human/divine, since Enoch/Metatron also had a kind of preexistence.

3) Metatron speaks "in my [i.e. God's] name."

379. John 2:24-25

Targum Pseudo-Jonathan on Genesis 3:9 (7 cent. CE; **much earlier materials**)

The Lord God called to Adam and said to him: "Is not the whole world which I created manifest before me, the darkness as well as the light? How then do you imagine in your heart that you can hide yourself from before me? Do I not see the place in which you are hiding?" (Maher)

God's question in Genesis 3:9, "Adam, where are you?" is transformed into an explanation that the God who knows all does not need to ask. Similarly, the Johannine theology in which Jesus represents God results in the transformation of earlier Christian traditions in which Jesus had asked real questions into an explanation of why this is not necessary. The Johannine Jesus never asks questions for information, but is always omniscient.

380. John 3:3-5

Hippolytus of Rome, *Refutation of All Heresies,* Book 5, 8:40-41 (3 cent. CE)

. . . [Now] by night in Eleusis, beneath a huge fire, [the Celebrant,] enacting the great and secret mysteries, vociferates and cries aloud, saying, "August Brimo has brought forth a consecrated son, Brimus"; that is, a potent [mother has been delivered of] a potent child. But revered, he says, is the generation that is spiritual, heavenly, from above, and potent is he that is so born. For the mystery is called "Eleusin," because, he says, we who are spiritual come flowing down from Adam above; for the word "eleusesthai" is, he says, of the same import with the expression "to come." But "Anactorium" is of the same import with the expression "to ascend upward." (ANF)

The text contains an interpretation of the Eleusinian mysteries that is certainly late and perhaps also not one generally known and accepted in the ancient world. That Hippolytus himself is here making use of the language of the Fourth Gospel appears to be excluded, since he usually makes it clear when he is quoting. For the comparison with John 3 it is important that we have translated another as "from above," the only translation supported by Greek usage of that time.

381. John 3:3-5

Marcus Aurelius Antoninus, *Meditations* 10:8 (121–180 CE)

Therefore, if you continue to preserve yourself in these titles [good, self-respecting, true, sane, conforming, high-minded], not aspiring to be called them by others, you will be a changed man and will enter upon a changed life. For still to be such as you have been up to the present, to be torn and polluted in such a way of life, is to be utterly brutalized, to cling to mere life like half-devoured combatants in the arena . . . (Farquharson)

As in John, the new life is bound to entering a new realm. What is understood by Marcus Aurelius in moral and ethical terms (maintaining possession of one's good name), is only secondarily supported by an appeal to the gods. In contrast, for John it is understood in principle as a religious and sacramental matter. (See also nos. 129, 380, 382-88, 410, 843; John 3:13.)

382. John 3:3-5

Philo, *Questions and Answers on Exodus* 2:46 (15 BCE–50 CE)

[On Exodus 24:16b:] Why is the mountain covered with a cloud for six days, and Moses called above on the seventh day?

The even number, six, He apportioned both to the creation of the world and to the election of the contemplative nation, wishing to show first of all that He had created both the world and the nation elected for virtue. And in the second place, because he wishes the nation to be ordered and arrayed in the same manner as the whole world so that, as in the latter, it may have a fitting order in accord with the right law and canon of the unchanging, placeless and unmoving nature of God. But the calling above of the prophet is a second birth better than the first. For the latter is mixed with a body and had corruptible parents, while the former is an unmixed and simple soul [the wording of the original Greek (this sentence and the next are missing from the Greek fragment) was probably "the former is an unmixed and simple sovereign part of the soul,"] which has no mother but only a father, who is [the Father] of all. Wherefore the calling above or, as we have said, the divine birth happened to come about for him in accordance with the ever-virginal nature of the hebdomad. (LCL)

Moses' ascent of the mountain stands for a redemptive event in the psyche, in which the previous entanglement with bodily existence comes to an end. The contrast here is between pure spirit and mixture with matter. Rebirth is understood similarly as the passage discussed under no. 129 from Corpus Hermeticum 13. In Corpus Hermeticum 4:3-4 there is a corresponding account of God's distribution of mind ($\nu o \hat{v} s$) by God:

"He filled a great mixing bowl with it and sent it below, appointing a herald whom he commanded to make the following proclamation to human hearts: 'Immerse yourself in the mixing bowl if your heart has the strength, if it believes you will rise up again to the one who sent the mixing bowl below, if it recognizes the purpose of your coming to be'" (Copenhaver).

In this text, the dipping/baptism is understood only metaphorically. Nor does it speak of rebirth. The significant point of contact with John 3:3-5 is the direction from above to below and from below to above, which is also important for John 3:13.

383. John 3:3-5

Philo, *Life of Moses* 1.50.279 (15 BCE–50 CE)

. . . in virtue of the distinction of their peculiar customs they do not mix with others to depart from the ways of their fathers. Who has made accurate discovery of how the sowing of their generation was first made? Their bodies have been molded from human seeds, but their souls are sprung from divine seeds, and therefore their stock is akin to God. May my soul die to the life of the body that it may be reckoned among the souls of the just, even such as are the souls of these men. (LCL)

This is Balaam's inspired oracle, the blessing on Israel that he had been invited to curse (cf. Num 22–24). All (the first generation of) Israel was divinely begotten, experiencing a spiritual, not a physical rebirth. These are similar ideas as in the Johannine presentation, expressed in Philo's quasi-dualistic terminology. As in John, it is possible for an outsider to be converted and to join this number of the reborn.

384. John 3:3-5

Corpus Hermeticum 13:1-2 (4 cent. CE document incorporating older traditions)

My father, you spoke indistinctly and in riddles when talking about divinity in the *General Discourses;* claiming that no one can be saved before being born again, you offered no revelation. But after you talked with me coming down from the mountain, I became your suppliant and asked to learn the discourse on being born again since, of all the discourses, this one alone I do not know. And you said you would deliver it to me when "you were about to become a stranger to the cosmos." I have prepared myself, and I have steeled my purpose against the deceit of the cosmos. Grant me what I need and give me—whether aloud or in secret—the [discourse on] being born again that you said you would deliver. I do not know what sort of womb mankind is born from, O Trismegistus, nor from what kind of seed.

My child, [the womb] is the wisdom of understanding in silence, and the seed is the true good.

Who sows the seed, father? I am entirely at a loss.

The will of god, my child.

And whence comes the begotten, father? He does not share in my essence [ ].

The begotten will be of a different kind, a god and a child of god, the all in all, composed entirely of the powers.

You tell me a riddle, father; you do not speak as a father to a son.

Such lineage cannot be taught, my child, but god reminds you of it when he wishes. (Copenhaver)

Corresponding to its title "Concerning Regeneration" (*Peri Palingenesias, De Regeneratione,* all of this tractate deals with rebirth. Hermes speaks by revelation to his son Tat. There are similarities to John:

1) The new birth is an absolute necessity for salvation. "No one can be saved before being born again" (13:1).

2) The divine declaration is met by a human response of incredulous questions: "I do not know what sort of womb mankind was born from, O Trismegistus, nor from what kind of seed . . . I am entirely at a loss . . . you tell me a riddle, father" (13:2).

3) The result is that one becomes a child of God. For Hermetic thought, such reborn children of God are themselves divine, "A God and a child of God." This is not an uncommon Gnostic idea.

Cf. *Eugnostos* (from Nag Hammadi Codex 3.71): "Whoever, then, is able to get free . . . is an immortal, who is in the midst of mortal men" (NHL).

4) The new birth is a matter of experience; it cannot be taught in rational terms (13:3).

5) The response of the regenerate person is joy and worship. This CH tractate concludes with a joyful hymn of gratitude for rebirth, including many similarities to Johannine language: "O Life and Light, . . . I thank you . . . through me your word hymns you."

But there are also contrasts:

1) In CH, the metaphor is elaborated and "explained." The role of the father in the generative process is "the will of god," the sperm is "the true good" (the similarity to the Johannine use of "true," ἀληθινός, may be noted), the role of the mother is the Wisdom of the mind. The experience itself is analogous to a dream, when the mind functions independently of the body.

2) In CH, the emphasis is on the deification of the regenerate person. "We have been divinized. . . . Therefore, whoever through mercy has attained this godly birth and has forsaken bodily sensation recognizes himself as constituted of the intelligibles and rejoices" (13:10) (Copenhaver). The reborn one is in fact then All in all, composed of all the powers of the elements.

3) Emphasis is on the fact that the candidate is born *again,* i.e. on the *re*generation of the individual. The key word used repeatedly is παλιγγέννεσις, and the issue is "how many times" one has been born: only once by natural birth, or "again" by wisdom, mind, good, the will of God. In John, the emphasis is on the source of the life by which one lives, and the key word is ἄνωθεν, which means primarily "from above" (as in John 3:31), and is only misunderstood by Nicodemus in terms of a "second" birth. In John, the issue is not "how many times" but "where from?" See C. H. Dodd, *The Interpretation of the Fourth Gospel* (Cambridge: Cambridge University Press, 1953), 10-53, esp. 44-47, and Barrett, *Gospel According to St. John*, 207-9.

(See also Mark 9:9-13 and John 1:12-13.)

385. John 3:3-5

Clement of Alexandria, *Excerpts from Theodotus* 78.2 (2 cent. CE)

Who we were, what we have become;
Where we were, whither we were thrown;
Whither we are hastening, from what we are redeemed;
What birth is, and what rebirth. (Perrin-Duling)

In the Gnostic mood, life is a fate, a "having-been-thrown" into this world, and salvation is redemption from this fate by a knowledge of one's origin, present existence, and destiny. In this schema, "birth" is losing one's true existence in this world, and "rebirth" is the salvation that comes by the saving knowledge of one's true origin and destiny. The manner and degree to which New Testament authors made use of Gnostic conceptuality and vocabulary is much debated, as is the character during the New Testament period of (what later became) Gnosticism. Since the NT authors uniformly view human life as the good gift of the Creator, who is the same God as the Redeemer, the early Christians represented by the NT could not have regarded human life as a negative "thrownness" into a miserable existence, from which the Redeemer God saves, but the vocabulary of rebirth is common to early Christianity and Gnosticism, as well as to other Hellenistic religious movements (cf. nos. 380-84, 386-88, 410, 843).

386. John 3:3-5

"Mithras Liturgy" (Paris Papyrus 574, 2 cent. CE)

Be gracious unto me, O Providence and Psyche, as I write down these mysteries, handed down [not] for gain but for instruction; and for an only child I request immortality, O initiates of this our power (furthermore, it is necessary for you, O daughter, to take [480] the juices of herbs and spices, which will [be made known] to you at the end of my holy treatise), which the great god Helios Mithras ordered to be revealed to me by his archangel, so that I alone may ascend into heaven as an inquirer (485) and behold the universe.

This is the invocation of the ceremony:

"First origin of my origin, AEEIOYO,

first beginning of my beginning, PPP SSS PHR [ ],

spirit of spirit, the first of the spirit (490) / in me, MMM, . . .

now if it be your will, METERTA (500) PHOTH

(METHARTHA PHERIE, in another place) / IEREZATH,

give me over to immortal birth . . .

I, born mortal from mortal womb, but transformed

by tremendous power and an incorruptible / right hand (520)!—

and with immortal spirit, the immortal Aion and / master of the fiery diadems— . . .

Since it is impossible for me, born (530) mortal,

to rise with the golden brightnesses

of the immortal brilliance, OEY AEO EYA EOE / YAE OIAE,

stand, O perishable nature of mortals,

and at once [receive] me safe and sound after / the inexorable and pressing (535) need.

For I am the son PSYCHO [N] DEMOY PROCHO PROA,

I am MACHARPH [.]N MOY PROPSYCHON PROE!")

Draw in breath from the rays, drawing up three times as much as you can, and you will see yourself being lifted up and (540) ascending to the height, so that you seem to be in mid-air. You will hear nothing either of man or of any other living thing, nor in that hour will you see anything of mortal affairs on earth, but rather you will see all immortal things. . . . And you will see the gods staring intently at you and rushing at you.

So at once put your right finger on your mouth and say:

"Silence! Silence! Silence!

Symbol of the living, incorruptible god!

(560) Guard me, Silence, NECHTHEIR THANMELOY!"

Then make a long hissing sound, next make a popping sound, and say:

"PROPROPHEGGE MORIOS PROPHYR PROPHEGGE

NEMETHIRE ARPSENTEN PITETMI MEOY ENARTH

PHYRKECHO PSYRIDARIO (565) TYRE PHILBA."

Then you will see the gods looking graciously upon you and no longer rushing at you, but rather going about in their own order of affairs. . . .

> "Hail, O Lord,
> Great Power, Great Might (640) King, Greatest
>   of gods, Helios, the Lord of heaven and
>   earth, God of gods:
> mighty is your breath;
> mighty is your strength, O Lord.
> If it be your will,
> announce me to the supreme god,
> the one who has begotten and made you: / that a man—
> I, _____ whose mother is _____, (645) who was
>   born from the mortal womb of ____ and from
>   the fluid of semen,
> and who, since he has been born again from you
>   today, has become immortal out of so many
>   myriads in this hour according to the wish
>   of god the exceedingly good—
> resolves to worship (650) you,
> and prays with all his human power
> (that you may take along with you the horoscope
>   of the day and hour today, which has the
>   name THRAPSIARI MORIROK,
> that he may appear and give revelation during
>   the good hours, EORO RORE ORRI ORIOR ROR
>   ROI (655) OR REORORI EOR EOR EOR EORE!)."

After you have said these things, he will come to the celestial pole, and you will see him walking as if on a road . . .

And gaze upon the god while bellowing long; and greet him in this manner:
> "Hail, O Lord, O Master of the water!
> Hail, O Founder of the earth!
> Hail, O Ruler of the wind! . . .

> O Lord, while being born again, I am passing / away;
> while growing and having grown, (720) I am / dying;
> while being born from a life-generating birth,
>   I am passing on, released to death—
> as you have founded,
> as you have decreed,
> and have established the mystery. (Meyer)

Though traditionally designated the "Mithras Liturgy," this text is probably unrelated to Mithraism and may not be liturgical, but represents the popular blend of magic, superstition, and religion in the Hellenistic world. "New birth" language occurred in several religious contexts in the Hellenistic world. Priests who were consecrated by the *taurobolium*, for instance, as they emerged drenched with the life-giving blood of the sacred bull, were said to be *renatus in aeternum*, "born again for eternity" (*CIL*, 6.510). Such language became part of the popular vocabulary of religion and was used rather imprecisely, as a general expression for religious experience, as in contemporary America.

In contrast to the New Testament's understanding of the grace of God, salvation is conceived as the gods being gracious by "going on their own course of business," no longer concerned with the initiate. The freedom brought by salvation is freedom from the gods' threatening attention.

387. John 3:3-5

Apuleius, *Metamorphoses* 11.23-24 (2 cent. CE)

[The goddess appears in a dream, and speaks to Lucius:] I am nature, the Universal Mother, mistress of all the elements, . . . sovereign of all things spiritual, queen of the dead, queen of the immortals, the single manifestation of all gods and goddesses that are. [She recounts the names by which she is known among different peoples.] The Egyptians who excel in ancient learning and worship me with ceremonies proper to my godhead call me by my true name, namely, Queen Isis.

[The priest to Lucius, regarding Isis:] The gates of the underworld and the guardianship of life are in her hands, and the rites of initiation approximate to a voluntary death from which there is only a precarious hope of resurrection. So she usually chooses old men who feel that their end is fast approaching, yet are not too senile to be capable of keeping a secret; by her grace they are, in a sense, born again and restored to a new and healthy life.

[Then follows a purification accomplished by ritual washing and prayers. Lucius was clothed with a new linen robe and led into the inner sanctum. He later reports:] It may be, my studious reader, that you would very much like to know what was said there and what was done. I would tell you if it were lawful for me to tell, and you would know all if it were lawful for you to hear. . . . Hear then and believe, for what I tell you is true. I drew near to the confines of death, treading the very threshold of Proserpine. I was borne through all the elements and returned to earth again. At the dead of night I saw the sun shining brightly. I approached the gods above and the gods below, and worshiped them face to face. See I have told you things which, though you have heard them, you still must know nothing about. (LCL)

Points of contact with the New Testament:

1) Syncretism: Isis represents all the gods. Many therefore worship her without knowing her true name, as do the initiates.

2) The initiation is a kind of death and resurrection (cf. Rom 6:1-11). It is not, however, a being united with the death and resurrection of the goddess, but an anticipation of their own death. It has nothing to do with freedom from the guilt and power of sin, as in Paul's use of the imagery in Romans 6.

3) The initiates are restored to a new life, "in a sense born again," a phrase taken seriously enough that this day was later celebrated as the "birthday" of the initiate. The contacts with John 3:3-5 are mainly terminological, but nonetheless illustrate the proliferation of "new birth" terminology in the Hellenistic world. Thus though the Johannine words "grace," "born again," "life" are used, the meaning is far from Christian gospel and Johannine theology. In each case, one must ask, then and now, what was signified by the phrase. Here, for instance, the meaning is different from the Corpus Hermeticum, where by *gnosis* the believer became a partaker in the divine nature, described as a rebirth (cf. 2 Pet 1:4).

388. John 3:3-5

b. Yebamoth 48B

Rabbi Jose ben Halafta said: "A proselyte who embraces Judaism is like a new-born child. God cannot therefore now chastise him for deeds done or duties neglected before his new birth." *(The Talmudic Anthology)*

Cf. R. Judah, *Gerim* 2.6, declared that a convert is "like a babe one day old." The metaphor of new birth was common enough to be used in Judaism as a premise on which another point could be based: God does not take account of preconversion sins. As is often the case in rabbinic materials, the documentation is later than New Testament times, but may well represent earlier tradition. If the metaphor of becoming a proselyte/new birth was fairly common in first-century Judaism, the Johannine text may represent Jesus as speaking in such manner that readers with a Jewish background would understand him to be saying that "the Jews" must themselves undergo the kind of conversion they required of proselytes (cf. on John the Baptist's preaching, nos. 16, 269). Paul, too, can assume the metaphor, transferred to a Christian context, and use it in a negative way: as newborns, you are not mature enough for solid "food" (instruction) (1 Cor 3:1-4).

389. John 3:3-13

Plutarch, *Moralia*, "On the Fortune (or Virtue) of Alexander" 5 (45–125 CE)

[On Demetrius Poliorketes:] Demetrius, to whom Fortune added the little that she was able to subtract from Alexander's power, allowed himself to be called "The Heaven-descended," and the subject states did not send ambassadors to him, but "Sacred Deputies," and his replies they spoke of as "Oracles" [χρησμοι]. (LCL)

"The one who came down from heaven" was an appellation of Jupiter. There is perhaps an analogy in the statement of Cicero, *On the State* 6:13 (see no. 301 above) that pictures the good ruler as having come from heaven and returning there (cf. no. 218, Plutarch). What is thought of in the Fourth Gospel as the divine messenger (cf. no. 391) can be understood in the Hellenistic milieu also in terms of the religious conception of the ruler, and would therefore partly overlap the meaning of "Messiah"/Son of Man. (See also nos. 391, 407, 445.)

390. John 3:12

Wisdom of Solomon 9:16-17 (150 BCE–50 CE)

We can hardly guess at what is on earth,
and what is at hand we find with labor.
But who has traced out what is in the heavens?

Who has learned your counsel,
unless you have given wisdom and sent your holy spirit from on high. (NRSV)

This contrast was widespread (Jdt 8:14; 4 Ezra 4:11; *t. Job* 38:5; *b. Sanh.* 39a), but John is not merely repeating a commonplace. The Wisdom motif of the Johannine prologue continues here (see on John 1:1-18), as what is declared by the incarnate logos corresponds to the Solomon's declaration about wisdom. The correlation of spirit and wisdom also corresponds to the Johannine view (see also no. 801 on Col 1:15-17).

391. John 3:13

Mekilta on Exodus 19:8 (2 cent. CE)

"And Moses brought the words of the people back to the Eternal." Did Moses have to report the words of the people to the Lord? The Torah alone teaches the way of life. Moses came and brought the response back to the One who had sent him, for Moses spoke as follows: "Although he knows and is the Witness, I will [nevertheless] bring their answer back to the One who sent me." (MEB/Berger)

There are various Hebrew texts. The version given here is a translation of the Hebrew Vorlage of J. Bühner, *Der Gesandte und sein Weg im 4. Evangelium* (Tübingen: J. C. B. Mohr, 1977), p. 307 (= Wünsche, Mechilta, 197).

Here it is a matter of the delegate reporting to the sender, which happens by the one who has been sent returning to the one who sent him. J. Bühner has attempted to understand the Christology of the Fourth Gospel primarily on the basis of the way the authority of the messenger was conceived in the Near East. (See nos. 84, 135, 453.)

392. John 3:14

Pseudo-Callisthenes, *Life and Deeds of Alexander of Macedonia* 2.21:7-11 (3 cent. CE)

Immediately an edict was published in each city, containing the following.

"I, Alexander . . . give these instructions. . . . It was not I who killed Darius; who his killers were, I do not know. I owe it to them to reward them richly and grant them extensive lands, as they killed our enemy . . .

"Accordingly, whether the man who killed him is a Macedonian or a Persian, let him come to me confidently and receive whatever he asks from me; for I swear by Providence above and by the life of my mother, Olympias, that I shall see they are marked out and notable before all mankind."

Bessos and Ariobarzanes came up to Alexander, expecting to receive large gifts from him and said, "Master, we are the men who killed Darius." And straightaway Alexander ordered them to be arrested and to be crucified at Darius's grave. They cried out and said: "Did you not swear that you would see the killers of Darius were marked out and notable?

How is it that you now break your oath and order us to be crucified?" To which Alexander replied: "It is not for your sake, you miserable wretches, that I shall justify myself, but for the mass of troops. Otherwise it would not have been possible to find you so easily or bring you into the open, had I not for a short while applauded the death of Darius. This is what I was praying for: the chance to sentence his killers to the severest punishment. After all, how are men who have slain their own master going to spare me? And as far as you go, you miserable men, I have not broken my oath: I swore I would see you were marked out and notable before everyone, that is, that you would be crucified for everyone to see." At these words everyone cheered him, and the detestable murderers were crucified at Darius's grave. (Reardon)

The point of the Alexander story is the intentional double meaning of "famous" and "to make visible from all sides," including the explanation "that all may see." The murderers understand this announcement to their own advantage, Alexander understands it in the sense of crucifixion. So too in John 3:14 the word "lift up" so that one can better see the one lifted up (ὑψόω) an ambiguous expression, and here too the negative sense means "crucify." This analogy arose in the first place because crucifixion was intended not only to torture and kill, but to have a public effect.

393. John 3:17

Philo, *Concerning God* (Armenian), §7 (15 BCE–50 CE)

Moses says still more clearly: "The Lord your God is a consuming fire"—a fire that consumes not to annihilate, but for salvation, for God's way of working is not to destroy, but to save. (MEB from German of F. Siegert, who translated the Armenian back into Greek and then into German; the path is thus Armenian-Greek-German-English!)

Similarly in the Letter to Diognetus (2 cent. CE) 7:3-4: "Now, did [God] send him [Christ], as a human mind might assume, to rule by tyranny, fear, and terror? Far from it! He sent him out of kindness and gentleness, like a king sending his son who is himself a king. He sent him as God; he sent him as man to men. He willed to save man by persuasion, not by compulsion, for compulsion is not God's way of working" (Richardson).

So also in 10:5: "To be happy does not, indeed, consist in lording it over one's neighbors, or in longing to have some advantage over the weaker ones, or in being rich and ordering one's inferiors about. It is not in this way that any man can imitate God, for such things are alien to his majesty" (Richardson).

The model is that of the Cynic ethic for rulers, according to which the true king is characterized by gentleness, not the use of violence.

394. John 3:18

Josephus, *Jewish War* 2.135 (37–100 CE)

[On the Essenes:] Any word of theirs has more force than an oath; swearing they avoid, regarding it as worse than perjury, for they say that one who is not believed without an appeal to God stands condemned already. (LCL)

The invocation of God in the oath refers the matter to God who will execute judgment if the one who swears does not perform what is promised, or if he has sworn falsely. Among the Essenes such a one is considered to be judged already, since he is already considered unworthy of trust. This severe and immediate judgment is understood by the Essenes as a motivating factor toward an impeccable life. For the Fourth Gospel too it is a motivation, but toward that life that comes through faith in Christ. (See also Matt 5:33-37.)

395. John 3:18

The True Ginza (Treasure), **Mandean writings (7–8 cents. CE, 2–3 cent. traditions)**

The faithful and believing Nazoreans will ascend and view the place of light. The faithful and believing Nazoreans, the excellent ones, will not be held back in this world. Not [in this world] will they be held back, and they will not be held accountable in the great judgment. Over them the judgment will not be spoken, that is to be spoken over all beings. They will not be found guilty before the judgment court, and will not fall into the great Suf-lake . . . (MEB/from Lidzbarski, p. 323, lines 13-22)

"Nazoreans" is an old self-description of the group of the Mandeans (a baptizing sect in Iraq, our oldest texts from 2–4 cents. CE? The oldest kernel of the Haran-Gawaita legend perhaps from the 1 cent. CE). They will avoid the judgment, for they will wander in the place of light beyond this world in advance of the judgment, and with no awareness of it. Here, as in John 3 and Romans 8:1, the possibility of escaping from the final judgment is related to belonging to the right group, and in John and Paul especially to belonging to the savior Jesus Christ.

On John 3:34*b* (God gives the Spirit without measure, i.e. richly): 4Q185 II.10 "with a good measure He measures it; and He will redeem His people," II.15, "with all the strength of his might" (Vermes). In both cases the eschatological quality of the gift of God is indicated by emphasizing (the breaking of) the usual "measure."

396. John 4:2

Josephus, *Antiquities* 20.118; *Life* 269 (37–100 CE)

[Explaining the governor Cumanus' failure to act during a dispute between the Jews and Samaritans:] Hatred also arose between the Samaritans and the Jews for the following reason. It was the custom of the Galileans at the time of a festival to pass through the Samaritan territory on their way to the Holy City. On one occasion, while they were passing through, certain of the inhabitants of a village called Ginaë, which was situated on the border between Samaria and the Great Plain, joined battle with the Galileans . . .

[Describing his decision as a commander during the war:] I further wrote my friends in Samaria to provide for their safe convoy through that district; for Samaria was now under Roman rule and, for rapid travel, it was essential [*edei*, same word translated "he had to"

NRSV] to take that route, by which Jerusalem may be reached in three days from Galilee . . . (LCL)

For a similar note see *Wars* 2:232. Despite the traditional topos of New Testament interpretation that understands the usual pilgrim route from Galilee to Jerusalem to involve a circuitous crossing over into Perea in order to avoid the heretical Samaritan territory and thereby make Jesus' more direct route appear tolerant and open by contrast, the evidence is that the typical pilgrim route was directly through Samaria. The Perean route would involve passing through Gentile territory, which pious Jews would hardly have considered preferable to Samaria. Jesus here takes the normal route. The necessity is simply geographical.

397. John 4:4-15

Macrobius, *Saturnalia* 1:12:28 (ca. 500 CE)

And this is also the reason why in Italy women are not permitted to participate in the rites of Hercules. For as Hercules was leading the cattle of Geryon through the regions of Italy and became thirsty, a woman responded to his request for water by saying that she could provide none, because the special day of the goddess was being celebrated, and that it was not permitted for men to taste of anything prepared for the occasion. Thus Hercules, when about to offer sacrifice, solemnly forbade the presence of women . . . (MEB/Berger)

The point of departure for both narratives is the same: during his wanderings the founder of a religion asks a foreign woman to give him a drink of water. In each case, the woman refuses on religious grounds (John 4:9). But all the other elements in the two narratives are in contrast. While Hercules replied in kind by excluding women from his sacrifice, Jesus programmatically overcame the barriers that separated Jews and Samaritans, and the foreign woman became a bearer of the message (4:39).

398. John 4:14, 19

Memar Marqah 6:3 (Samaritan anthology, final redaction in 4 cent. CE)

Where is there any like Moses, apostle [Sam. *shylch*] of the True One, faithful one of the House of God, and His servant? . . . His mouth was like the Euphrates, rolling with living waters which quench the thirst of all who drink of them. (MacDonald)

The text belongs to the numerous parallels that exist between the Christology of the Fourth Gospel and the views of Memar Marqah concerning Moses (note the idea of the Sent One, also used of Jesus by Justin Martyr [from Samaria!], First Apology 12:9). It does not appear to be established that here we must necessarily reckon this to be a case of dependence of either one upon the other. Rather, it is a case of analogous formation under similar presuppositions and circumstances. See also John 7:37-38 and Hebrews 3:1-6 (house!), as well as no. 423.

399. John 4:19, 25

Addition to the Samaritan Decalogue, Exod. 20:21*b* (from the Samaritan Pentateuch) (Addition made after 200 BCE)

And the LORD spoke to Moses saying [Deut. 5:28], I have heard the words of this people, which they have spoken to you; they have rightly said all that they have spoken [v. 29]. Oh that they had such a mind as this always, to fear Me and to keep My commandments, that it might go well with them and with their children forever! [Deut. 18:18] I will raise up for them a prophet like you from among their brethren; and I will put My words in his mouth, and he shall speak to them all that I command him. [v. 19] And whoever will not give heed to his words while he shall speak in My name, I myself will require it of him. [v. 20] But the prophet who presumes to speak in My name that which I have not commanded him to speak, or who speaks in the name of other gods, that same prophet shall die. (Bowman)

(In the following the criteria for authentic prophecy is named: the word of the authentic prophet comes true.) The expectation of such prophets according to Deuteronomy 18:14-22 is documented for the Samaritans by the Pseudo-Clementine *Recognitions* 1:54:5: "And they [the Samaritans] indeed rightly, from the predictions of Moses, expect the one true prophet."

400. John 4:19, 25

Memar Marqah 3:6 (Samaritan anthology, final redaction in 4 cent. CE)

In the case of a man who declared to you some lying information, keep away from hearing his words. He is the man against whom I warned you, for he typifies seven evils: he likens himself to righteous men who lived in the past, to whom I revealed in night dreams what would bring them honor; he states that he is like Moses in doing a wonder or miracle. (MacDonald)

Cf. ibid. 2:40:28: "The great prophet Moses comes in peace, the one who is faithful to that which he promised, and that which the creatures pray for [or greet]." For other data on the expectation of a prophet like Moses among the Samaritans, cf. H. G. Kippenberg, *Garizim und Synagoge* (Berlin: de Gruyter, 1971), pp. 306-27. Kippenberg also affirms that the figure that could be spoken of in John 4 has nothing to do with the Samaritan Taheb, pp. 276-300.

The prophet like Moses is also a part of the eschatological drama in the Qumran writings (1QS 9:9-11).

401. John 4:22-24

Corpus Hermeticum 5:10 (2–4 cent. CE)

Who may praise you, then, acting on your behalf or according to your purpose? And where shall I look to praise you—above, below, within, without? For there is no direction about you nor place nor any other being. All is within you; all comes from you. You give everything and take nothing. For you have it all, and there is nothing that you do not have. (Copenhaver)

God is so all-embracing, that there is no place that can contain him. (According to chapter 11 of the Hermetica, there is also no particular time in which human beings can praise God.) As in the Gospel of John, the praise of God is here set free from considerations of time and space, but still in John "Spirit and Truth" are certainly bound to a particular Christology. (See Acts 7, nos. 500, 501.)

402. John 4:24

Epictetus, *Discourses*, 2.8.1 (55–135 CE)

God is helpful; but the good also is helpful. It would seem, therefore, that the true nature of the good will be found to be where we find that of God to be. What, then, is the true nature of God? Flesh? Far from it! Land? Far from it! Fame? Far from it! It is intelligence [νοῦς], knowledge [ἐπιστήμη], right reason [λόγος ὀρθός]. Here, therefore, and only here, shall you seek the true nature of the good. (LCL)

Epictetus stands in the broad stream of Stoic tradition that, to be sure, was not theistic in the sense of believing in a personal God, but regarded the immanent intelligence by which the universe was ordered to be the divine principle, in which human beings, as rational beings, also participated. This immanent divine principle was often called "spirit," (πνεῦμα)—Cleanthes, a Stoic of the 3 cent. BCE being the first to do this. Cf. Clement of Alexandria, *Strom.* 5.14: "For the Stoics say that God is spirit by nature." Epictetus uses "mind," "knowledge," and "right reason" as synonyms for "spirit." It is to be noted that not only does Epictetus reject the crass materialism that considered objects to be gods, but also rejects common "this-worldly" values (property, fame) as playing a divine role. Though John makes contact with this Hellenistic idea, he stands primarily in the LXX tradition in which "spirit" does not denote "an order of being over against matter, but life-giving, creative activity" (so Barrett, *Gospel According to St. John*, 238).

403. John 4:25, 42

Memar Marqah 4:12 (4 cent. CE final redaction)

[The context: on the day of wrath, Israel will be redeemed.] The Taheb will come in peace to repossess the place which God chose for those good people. . . .
    The Taheb will come in peace to possess the places of the perfect ones and to manifest the truth. . . .
    The Taheb will arise and the Lord will have compassion. (MacDonald)

The figure of the Taheb originated independently of Deuteronomy 18:18, and was only later identified with the prophet like Moses (cf. no. 399). The parallel with Joseph in our text reveals a messianic view of Joseph, which is also clearly present in Jubilees. John 4 can therefore properly be related to a Samaritan messianic expectation. On the Taheb see also no. 400.

404. John 4:46-54

b. *Berakoth* 34B (1 cent. CE for tradition [?])

There was the case in which the son of Rabban Gamaliel fell ill. He sent two disciples of sages to R. Hanina b. Dosa to pray for mercy for him. When he saw them, he went up to his upper room and prayed for mercy for him.

When he came down, he said to them, "Go, for his fever has left him."

They said to him, "Are you a prophet?"

He said to them, "I am not a prophet nor a disciple of a prophet, but this is what I have received as a tradition: If my prayer is fluent, then I know that he [for whom I pray] is accepted, and if not, then I know that he is rejected."

They sat down and wrote down the hour, and when they came back to Rabban Gamaliel, he said to them "By the Temple service! You were neither early nor late, but that is just how it happened. At that very moment, his fever left him and he asked us for water to drink." (Neusner, *Talmud*)

Many traditions of charismatic activity are associated with Rabbi Hanina ben Dosa. (See nos. 71-72, 251, 288, 404, 529.)

Agreements with John 4:

1) Healing at a distance.

2) The healing happens at the same hour it is pronounced.

3) The expression "the fever left him" is found in the Talmudic story as the assurance given by the healer, in John 4 in the confirming report.

405. John 5:1-15

Aelius Aristides, "Regarding the Well in the Temple of Asclepius," *Speech* 39:14-15 (117–187 CE)

[On the healing power of the well in the Asclepius temple:] But the god also uses it in other ways like any other coworker, and the Well has often assisted many people in obtaining from the god what they desired. For just as the sons of doctors and magicians have been trained to serve them and while they aid them astound spectators and customers, so this Well is the discovery and possession of the great magician who does everything for the safety of mankind. It aids him in everything and for many men is like a drug. [15] For many by bathing in it have recovered their sight, and many by drinking it have been cured of chest trouble and have regained the breath of life. It has cured one man's feet and another part of the body for someone else. Once someone drank it and spoke after being mute, just as those who have drunk the forbidden waters and have become prophetic. For some merely drawing up the water has been like a means of safety. And thus to the sick it is an antidote and a cure, and for those in health who reside nearby it makes the employment of all other waters subject to blame. (Behr)

Cf. similarly §11: "Since it is a servant and coworker of the most generous of gods, it is most ready to serve and is always full. And the god has no leisure to do other than to save mankind, and the Well in imitation of its master always fills the wants of those who need it, and is like some creature or gift of Asclepius, just as Homer depicted the instruments and machines of Hephaestus which move according to his wishes" (Behr).

Cf. also 47:18: "Next it seemed to me that Phoebus was present and encouraged me, so that I entered the water without hesitation" (Behr).

Cf. also K. H. Rengstorf, *Die Anfänge der Auseinandersetzung zwischen Christusglaube und Asklepios-frömmigkeit* (Münster, 1953). Alongside Hercules, Isis, and Mithras, Asclepius was the Hellenistic deity with which Christianity was most in the situation of entering into competition. Cf. also nos. 504, 532. It could well be that just as the evangelist is concerned in John 2 to make contact with the Dionysius tradition, so here he has the Asclepius cult in view (in the 1 cent. the figures of Dionysius and Asclepius were often merged). In each case, Jesus is the one who can fulfill the expectations already there in the culture. That was important, since for people of that time health problems were not only much more obvious than is the case today, but were also bound more closely to religion. The Asclepius temple area should be thought of as an enormous encampment of sick people (Pausanias, *Description of Greece* 2.27.2; 10.32.8; 7.27.5; Aristophanes, *Plutus* 410:653ff.; *Wasps* 122; Strabo, *Geography* 14.1.44; Plautus, *Curc.* 1.1.61; 2.1).

406. John 5:17

Maximus of Tyre, *Dissertations* 15:16:2 (125–185 CE)

But if Hercules had wanted . . . to have leisure . . . no one would have dared to name him "Son of God." For even Zeus does not take time off. (MEB/Berger)

Hercules is here "Son of God" (Gk. παῖς Διός) because his work corresponds to that of deity, namely without needing to pause for rest. Jewish authors too attempted to combine the idea of the Sabbath celebration with the concept of the unceasing activity of God, as did the Hellenistic-Jewish expositor of the Torah Aristobulus in the midst of the second century BCE:

"And it is plainly said by our legislation that God rested on the seventh day. This does not mean, as some interpret, that God no longer does anything. It means that, after he had finished ordering all things, he so orders them for all time" (Fragment 5 in Eusebius, *Praeparatio Evangelica* 13.12.11) (*OTP* 2:841-42).

Also, according to the Letter of Aristeas 210 it can be said of God that he "is continually at work in everything and is omniscient" (*OTP* 2:26).

407. John 5:18

Josephus, *Antiquities* 19:4 (37–100 CE)

He [Caligula] would also have deified himself and demanded from his subjects honors that were no longer such as may be rendered to a man. When he visited the Temple of Jupiter which they call the Capitol and which is first in honor among their temples, he had the audacity to address Jupiter as brother.* (LCL)

* Suetonius, *Caligula* 22, notes that Gaius would engage in conversation with Jupiter Capitolinus, alternately whispering and shouting angry threats. Gaius finally announced that Jupiter had persuaded him to live with him, and so he built a bridge connecting the imperial palace with the Capitol. Dio lix.4.2 remarks that though at first he forbade anyone to set up images of himself, he even went on to manufacture statues himself and to order temples to be erected and sacrifices offered to him as a god. Dio also (lix.28.5; similarly Suetonius, *Caligula* 22) notes that Gaius called himself Jupiter Latiaris, i.e. Jupiter of Latium, and remarks (lix.26.5) that he used to impersonate all the gods (LCL, p. 216 *ad loc.*).

Already in John 4:42 there is found a religious understanding of the ruler that was important in the first century CE, that of "Savior of the World" (esp. frequent as a title for Hadrian, but also for Nero: "Savior and Benefactor of the World"). Our text makes clear that for Jews of the first century the claim of deity was connected especially with the Roman emperor. The objection made against the Johannine Christ thus had political significance (competitive claim) and at the same time was offensive to Jews, or at least in need of interpretation. See nos. 219, 301, 389, 445, 472.

408. John 5:18

Philo, *Allegorical Interpretation of Genesis* 1:49 (15 BCE–50 CE)

. . . it is appropriate to God to plant and build virtues in the soul, but the mind shows itself to be without God *[atheos]* and full of self-love, when it deems itself as on a par with God [*isos*, the same word translated "equal" in NRSV]; and, whereas passivity is its true part, looks on itself as an agent. (LCL/adapted by MEB)

Philo's incidental comment shows that the phrase "equal to God" need not imply any metaphysical claim, but refers to the arrogance of human beings who attempt to do for themselves what they should passively receive from God.

409. John 5:19

Plutarch, *Moralia*, "On the Delays of the Divine Vengeance" 4 (45–125 CE)

[On the administration of justice:] And of this art [For that the cure of the soul, which goes by the name of chastisement and justice, is the greatest of all arts], Minos son of Zeus became a student [of Zeus], as Plato says, who suggests by this that it is impossible to succeed in questions of justice or to recognize success in another if one has not studied and mastered the science. (LCL)

As in John 5 the son is also a student of the father, who accomplishes his work on earth as a representative of and after the model of his father's work. Tradition concerning Moses on this point may be found for example in Philo, *Moses* 1:90, "Moses began to show the wonders which he had been previously taught to perform, thinking that the sight would convert them from the prevailing unbelief to belief in his words" (LCL). The text refers to Exodus 4. In 1:74 God's relation to Moses is portrayed as "the sender," just as the Father's relation to Jesus is described in the Fourth Gospel (Philo ὁ πέμψας, John ὁ πέμψας με).

410. John 5:21, 24

Joseph and Aseneth (a Hellenistic-Jewish "conversion novel") 8.10-11 (1 cent. CE)

> [The prayer of Joseph in 8:9-11:]
> Lord God of my father Israel,
> the Most High, the Powerful One of Jacob,
> who gave life to all [things]
> and called [them] from the darkness to the light,
> and from the error to the truth,
> and from the death to the life;
> you, Lord, bless this virgin,
> and renew her by your spirit,
> and form her anew by your hidden hand,
> and make her alive again by your life,
> and let her eat your bread of life,
> and drink your cup of blessing . . . (*OTP* 2:213)

Similarly in 15:5: "Behold, from today, you will be renewed and formed anew and made alive again, and you will eat blessed bread of life, and drink a blessed cup of immortality, and anoint yourself with blessed ointment of incorruptibility" (*OTP* 2:226). This text documents that for some streams of the Judaism contemporary with the New Testament not only was the experience of conversion/initiation sometimes understood as a rebirth (as in the contemporary mystery cults), but was formulated in a somewhat more biblical language and thought of as being created anew and being called into a new life, and is therefore at least analogous to being called "out of death into life." All this characterizes initiation not only as a decisive turning point, but represents it as an encounter with the God who, wherever one meets him, works exclusively as the one who gives new life to the dead. Cf. nos. 382 (on John 3:3-5), 843, 866.

411. John 5:22

Addition to *Testament of Levi* 2:3 (can be dated by its correspondence to Aramaic T. Levi from Qumran, 150–100 BCE)

Hear the cry of your servant Levi to be near you, and make him to be a participant in your words, so that he can exercise righteous judgment forever, I and my sons . . . (Text from M. de Jonge, *Testaments of the Twelve Patriarchs* [Leiden: E. J. Brill, 1978], 25. MEB/Berger, adapted to Greek text)

Analogies to the Gospel of John:
1) The one authorized by God has his authority by virtue of participation in God's word.

2) That means an authority granted by God to judge, without any temporal limitation (cf. Matt 16:19). But the difference: among the Levites it was a matter of institutionalized judgment within an existing community (cf. also *Jub.* 31:15: words of the Lord and making just decisions are related), in John 5 it is a matter of the consequences of one's decision and conduct for or against Jesus. With this is also to be compared the passage from the Mandean scriptures, *The True Ginza (Treasure)*:

"You are the chief of the Ganzibras,
to whom the Life gave dominion over all things.
The dead heard you and lived,
the sick heard you and became well.
You grant forgiveness to the elect and perfect,
in whose hearts kusta has settled.
Life is victorious, and victorious is the man [who has attained it]" (Foerster).
The text is an acrostic psalm of praise to Kusta (Truth/Justice).

412. John 5:27

Testament of Abraham (Hellenistic Jewish, from Egypt) Recension A 13:2-7 (1–3 cents. CE)

The Commander-in-chief [Michael] said, "Do you see, all-pious Abraham, the frightful man who is seated on the throne? This is the son of Adam, the first-formed, who is called Abel, whom Cain the wicked killed. And he sits here to judge the entire creation, examining both righteous and sinners. For God said, 'I do not judge you, but every man is judged by man.' On account of this he gave him judgment, to judge the world until his great and glorious Parousia. And then, righteous Abraham, there will be perfect judgment and recompense, eternal and unalterable, which no one can question. For every person has sprung from the first-formed, and on account of this they are first judged here by his son. And at the second Parousia they will be judged by the twelve tribes of Israel, both every breath and every creature. And, thirdly, they shall be judged by the Master God of all . . ." (*OTP* 1:889)

Abel is the "son of Adam" (Heb. ben Adam), and since this is also the Hebrew term for "Son of Man," we have here before us a conception of the last judgment with a particular Jewish stamp. As in the New Testament, the traditional figure of the judge has been identified with a concrete earthly human being (here with Abel, in early Christianity with Jesus, in *1 Enoch* [according to the general interpretation] with Enoch). The progressive stages of the acts of the last judgment result from a combining of different traditions and adjusting them to each other.

413. John 5:31-32

Cicero, *The Speech in Defense of Sextus Roscius of Ameria* 36.103 (106–43 BCE)

Africanus, who declares by his surname that he conquered a third part of the world, would nevertheless have refused to give evidence in a case in which his interests were at stake: for I do not venture to say in regard to such a man that, had he spoken, he would not have been believed. Consider now how everything has changed and altered for the worse. When it is a question of property and murder, a man is going to give evidence, one who is both a broker and an assassin, that is, he who is the purchaser and possessor of the very properties which are in question, and contrived the murder of the man whose death is the subject of investigation. (LCL)

This text illustrates how precarious it was to give testimony in one's own interest, a legal perspective also presupposed by John 5. The evangelist illustrates some familiarity with the forensic perspective of his own time.

414. John 5:46

Mekilta 14.31 (and Mekilta of R. Simon b. Jochai) (2 cent. CE from older traditions)

If they believed Moses *a fortiori* [How much more they believed] the Lord. (Smith)

See on no. 283 on Luke 6:40/ Matthew 10:24-25.

415. John 6:26-65

Philo, *Allegorical Interpretation* 3:173 (15 BCE–50 CE)

[Commenting on the "manna" (Heb. "what is it?" cf. Exod. 16:15):] The souls, therefore, that have indeed already had experience of the word, but are not able to answer the question, inquire one of another, "What is it?" . . . In the same way then the soul, when it has been gladdened, is often unable to say what the thing that gladdens it is. But it is taught by the hierophant and prophet Moses: he will tell it, "this bread is the food which God hath given to the soul, for it to feed on His own utterance and His own word; for this bread, which He hath given us to eat, is 'this word.'" (LCL)

Already for Philo, what the Israelites ate in the wilderness that gave them true life was the word of God that came down from heaven and gave life to the world. Philo, like John, considers the symbolic (for him, allegorical) meaning of the text the real meaning, and a concentration on the literal meaning to be an orientation to this material world rather than to the world of the Spirit.

416. John 6:31

2 Baruch 29:8 (ca. 100 CE)

And it will happen at that time that the treasury of manna will come down again from on high, and they will eat of it in those years because these are those who will have arrived at the consummation time. (*OTP* 1:630-31)

At the eschatological time when the Messiah appears, Behemoth and Leviathan will become the menu of the eschatological banquet, which will also have an extravagant abundance of wine—see on 2:1-11, no. 375. The manna was not only a symbol of God's past care for Israel in the wilderness. As the wilderness period was idealized (pre-idolatry, pre-Canaanization of Israelite religion), it was expected to reappear in the eschatological days. Not only the apocalyptic represented by *2 Baruch,* but rabbinic Judaism represented by e.g. Mek. Exod. 16:25 had this expectation: "R. Eleazar Hisma says, 'In this world you will not find it [the manna], but you will find it in the world to come'" (Neusner, *Mekhilta*). This general expectation was made concrete by the tradition that manna was one of the items kept in the ark of the covenant that had been lost when the first temple was destroyed, but which along with the ark had been preserved in heaven and would reappear in the eschatological time.

417. John 6:48, 51

Hymn of Isis (text is from a 1 or 2 cent. CE text found in Asia Minor, from an older inscription)

I am Isis, the mistress of every land, and I was taught by Hermes, and with Hermes I devised letters, both the sacred [hieroglyphs] and the Demotic, that all things might not be written with the same [letters].
I gave and ordained laws for men, which no one is able to change.
I am the eldest daughter of Kronos.
I am wife and sister of King Osiris.
I am she who findeth fruit for men.
I am mother of King Horus.
I am she that riseth in the dog star.
I am she that is called goddess by women.
For me was the city of Bubastis built.
I divided the earth from the heaven.
I showed the paths of the stars.
I ordered the course of the sun and the moon.
I devised business in the sea.
I made strong the right.
I brought together woman and man.
I appointed to women to bring their infants to birth in the tenth month.
I ordained that parents should be loved by children.
I laid punishment upon those disposed without natural affection toward their parents.
I made with my brother Osiris an end to the eating of men.
I revealed mysteries unto men.
I taught [men] to honor images of the gods.
I consecrated the precincts of the gods.
I broke down the governments of tyrants.
I made an end to murders.
I compelled women to be loved by men.
I made the right to be stronger than gold and silver.
I ordained that the true should be thought good.

I devised marriage contracts.

I assigned to Greeks and barbarians their languages.

I made the beautiful and the shameful to be distinguished by nature.

I ordained that nothing should be more feared than an oath.

I have delivered the plotter of evil against other men into the hands of the one he plotted against.

I establish penalties for those who practice injustice.

I decreed mercy to suppliants.

I protect [or honor] righteous guards.

With me the right prevails.

I am the queen of rivers and winds and sea.

No one is held in honor without my knowing it.

I am the Queen of war.

I am the Queen of the thunderbolt.

I stir up the sea and I calm it.

I am the rays of the sun.

I inspect the courses of the sun.

Whatever I please, this too shall come to an end.

With me everything is reasonable.

I set free those in bonds.

I am the Queen of seamanship.

I make the navigable unnavigable when it pleases me.

I created walls of cities.

I am called the Lawgiver [θεσμοφόρος, a classical epithet of Demeter].

I brought up islands out of the depths into the light.

I am Lord [κύριος, masculine form] of rainstorms.

I overcome Fate.

Fate hearkens to me.

Hail, O Egypt, that nourished me! (Grant)

This is the most complete of the Isis aretalogies, found in summarized or fragmentary form in several shorter recensions elsewhere. One may note:

1) The prevalence of the "I am" form. The Fourth Gospel makes contact not only, or even primarily, with the biblical tradition of Yahweh's self-predication (Exod 3:14, etc.), but with a widespread tradition of self-proclaimed aretalogies by the Hellenistic deities.

2) Similarities and differences to the sayings of the Johannine Jesus. Isis' self-predications are mainly aretalogical, declaring her mighty acts, not the metaphorical declarations of the Fourth Gospel. Though the Johannine form is reminiscent of the Isis form, there are significant formal differences as well. The Johannine ἐγώ εἰμι ὁ . . . ("I am the . . ." or "The . . ., it is I") does not occur. Here, the personal name "Isis" intervenes between "I" and the verb, giving not only a different effect, but by including the personal name, a different function and meaning as well.

Closer to the Johannine form is the Isis declaration in the *P. Lond.* 46:145-55, . . . ' Εγώ εἰμι ὁ ἀκέφαλος δαίμων, ἐγώ εἰμι ἡ ἀλήθεια . . . ἐγώ εἰμι ὁ γεννῶν καὶ ἀπογεννῶν, "I am the deity that had no beginning . . . I am the truth, I am the creator and the destroyer" (cf. John 14:6).

3) The aggressively syncretistic nature of Hellenistic religion is seen here. Isis claims the functions of many other gods, is a cosmic creator figure, not a local deity.

4) Social order and justice are claimed by her, not merely the rewarding of individuals.

In the New Testament, the formula "I am the . . ." (ἐγώ εἰμι ὁ ἡ τὸ) is found only in Matthew 22:32;

24:5; John 6:35, 41, 48, 51; 8:12; 10:7, 9, 11, 14; 11:25; 14:6; 15:1; Revelation 1:8, 17; 2:23; 22:16. Cf. also no. 360 above.

418. John 6:48, 51

Testament of Abraham Recension A 16:10-12 (1–2 cent. CE)

[An angelophany to Abraham, who asks the one who appears:] ". . . who are you and whence have you come?" Then Death said, "Most righteous Abraham, behold, I tell you the truth. I am the bitter cup of death." Abraham said to him, "No, rather you are the comeliness of the world, you are the glory and beauty of angels and of men . . ." (*OTP* 1:892)

The combination "I am" plus a metaphor is not found in the texts named by Rudolf Bultmann in his famous footnote on the subject in his commentary (*Gospel of John*, p. 225 n. 3). Nor is it found in later Mandean texts. But this combination is documented for Egypt in the time of the New Testament. This is seen not only in the *Testament of Abraham*, but already in the ancient Egyptian texts such as the speech of the god Re: "I am the steer of the eastern mountains, I am the lion of the western mountains" (from Chr. Kayatz, *Studien zu Proverbien* 1-9 [Neukirchen- Vluyn-Neukirchener, 1966], 88, 90). This is also seen in other texts, likewise from Egypt, such as the British Museum Papyrus 46, "I am the world maiden," and in the Isis texts, "I am the grace of the world" (*PGM* 1:149). Bultmann refers to the Isis text quoted from an inscription by Plutarch (*Moralia*, "Isis and Osiris," 9.354), "I am all that has been, and is, and shall be, and my robe no mortal has yet uncovered" (LCL).

Thus what was used prior to the New Testament as a name for the god is found in Judaism and the New Testament as a designation for God's messenger. For older Egyptian antecedents of this formula cf. J. Bergman, *Ich bin Isis. Studien zum memphitischen Hintergrund der griechischen Isisaretalogien* (Uppsala: Almquist & Wiksell, 1968), pp. 219-33, which attempts a derivation based on form criticism. (Cf. Berger, Formgeschichte §280.)

419. John 6:53

Poimandres (Corpus Hermeticum I), §29 (ca. 1 cent. CE)

. . . those who desired to be taught cast themselves at my feet. Having made them rise, I became guide to my race, teaching them the words—how to be saved and in what manner—and I sowed the words of wisdom among them, and they were nourished from the ambrosial water. When evening came and the sun's light began to disappear entirely, I commanded them to give thanks to god . . . (Copenhaver)

Analogies to the New Testament:
1) Teaching and feeding are closely related (not an unusual metaphor).
2) The twin ideas of solid food and liquid, of eating and drinking are found here as in John.
3) The content has to do with salvation/eternal life. In the Jewish realm one may especially note the formulation in *Joseph and Aseneth* 16:16: "And the man said to Aseneth, 'Behold, you have eaten

bread of life, and drunk a cup of immortality, and been anointed with ointment of incorruptibility'" and in 16:14: ". . . this is a comb of life, and everyone who eats of it will not die forever [and] ever" (*OTP* 2:229) (cf. no. 410). According to the text, Aseneth literally ate the honeycomb, but the bread and the cup were metaphorical expressions for initiation, as in the texts of the mystery cults.

For the I-saying in John 6:53, cf. in Judaism esp. Sir 24:19-22,

"Come to me, you who desire me,
and eat your fill of my fruits.
For the memory of me is sweeter than honey,
and the possession of me is sweeter than the honeycomb.
Those who eat of me will hunger for more,
and those who drink of me will thirst for more.
Whoever obeys me will not be put to shame,
and those who work with me will not sin." (NRSV)
See also John 6:35!

420. John 7:4

Kore Kosmou (Hermetica Tractate from Stobaeus, *Anthologium,* I) Fragments 23.55-56 (2–4 cents. CE)

[The elements of the world ask the creator; Fire speaks:] Master, and Fabricator of this new universe, thou whose name is revered among the gods and hidden from men, how long is it thy purpose to leave the life of mortals godless? These men do not let me render the services for which my nature fits me; they put a false and unmeet stamp on my imperishable being. I am polluted, Master, and by men's audacity I am forced to consume human flesh. Reveal thyself at once to the world that needs thee, and restrain that which is unbridled in life with thy peace. Give laws for life, oracles in the night, fill all with good hope . . . (adapted from trans. of Scott; MEB/Berger)

The theme of the hidden bringer of salvation, whose revelation humanity cannot expect, is treated in the *Kore Kosmou* and in the Gospels on different planes, the cosmological and the biographical respectively. Nevertheless, there is still a comparable problem, if one regards John 7:4 not only as an episode that can be looked at psychologically, but also sees therein a theological problem of the Johannine community: the relation of community and world, of relative hiddenness and complete revelation.

421. John 7:15

Life of Aesop G 37 (2 cent. CE)

But as they left, Zanthos said to the gardener, "I have a clever slave who lives with us. Go to him, and he will answer your question." The gardener responded, "And where is he?" Zanthos said, "See that ugly one there? He knows how to read and write" [lit.: "letters," i.e. elementary knowledge]. Aesop said to the gardener with a laugh, "So, too bad for you!" (MEB/adaptation of Berger's German, with reference to the Greek text of Perry)

In common with John 7: Contrary to all external appearances, the unlearned is wiser and more intelligent than others. The *Life of Aesop* is important for the evangelists, sharing with them a stringing together of scenes and episodes. The organizing principle is change of location and temporal succession. There are no complex or simultaneous actions. The narrative is told without details and circumstances, there is a limited number of persons, a schematic juxtaposition of good and evil, with a frequent structuring of episodes as chreiai. Especially, as in the scene reported here, the dialectic of external circumstances (bodily defects, ugliness, slave status) and the internal reality of the person's true being (wisdom, humor) makes the hiddenness of one's true being into a biographical motif. The discovery of the hidden identity of the other is at the same time the hearer/reader's own growth in wisdom. (Cf. also the challenge in chap. 25: "Don't judge by my external appearance, but rather examine the soul.")

422. John 7:27

Justin, *Dialogue with Trypho* 8:4 (ca. 165 CE)

[Trypho the Jew speaks:] But Christ—if He has indeed been born, and exists anywhere—is unknown, and does not even know Himself, and has no power until Elias come to anoint Him, and make Him manifest to all. And you, having accepted a groundless report, invent a Christ for yourselves, . . . (ANF)

Similarly in *Dialogue* 110:1; 49:1 (when the Messiah comes, he will be a human being among other human beings, and will be anointed by Elijah. Cf. no. 450). The puzzling text from the Oracula Leonis MPG 107.1148: In the first place the Messiah (Gk. ᾽ελειμενος), who is also called *Menachem* ("encourager"), will be unknown and disdained, but then his identity will be revealed by a sign from heaven, and he will be anointed with oil. A messenger proclaimed him for three days as the hoped-for one, while the people responded that they did not recognize him as the one who fulfilled their hopes. Finally he is led in a glorious procession to Zion. This is in a collection of Christian oracle literature which has adopted Jewish eschatological elements, as these are documented in Justin and which are also to be presupposed in the historical context of the Fourth Gospel. Although all these texts are later than John, they stand closer to the Jewish position presupposed in John than the earlier apocalyptic texts (and Targumim), which merely refer to the fact that the Messiah "will be revealed" (e.g. *2 Bar.* 29:3).

On the birth in Bethlehem and the previous anonymity of the Messiah, see also no. 15. (See also John 1:29-33.)

423. John 7:37-38

Odes of Solomon 30:1-7 (2 cent. [?] CE)

Fill for yourselves water from the living spring of the Lord,
because it has been opened for you.
And come all you thirsty and take a drink,
and rest beside the spring of the Lord.
Because it is pleasing and sparkling,

and perpetually pleases the self.
For more refreshing is its water than honey,
and the honeycomb of bees is not to be compared with it;
Because it flowed from the lips of the Lord,
and it named from the heart of the Lord.
And it came boundless and invisible,
and until it was set in the middle they knew it not.
Blessed are they who have drunk from it,
and have rested by it.
Hallelujah! (*OTP* 2:762)

We have here a speech inviting the hearers to a personification of revelation or the Wisdom of God, while in John 7 it is a matter of Jesus inviting the hearers to himself (cf. Berger, *Formgeschichte*, §§62, 72). One may readily compare this with the metaphorical language of "Joseph and Aseneth." (Cf. also nos. 398 and 410.)

424. John 7:37-38

The Canonical Prayer Book of the Mandeans, no. 45 (2–6 cents. CE)

Thy name, [O] Life, is excellent: its glory is great, its light abundant. Its goodness came over [or overflowed], inaugurating the First Mystery, life which proceeded from Life and Truth which existed before the beginning. This is a wellspring of life which sprang forth from the Place of Life: we drink thereof, of this Fount of Life which Life transmitted was established in the House of Life, which crossed worlds, came, cleft the heavens and was revealed.

Thou hast shown us that which the eye of man hath not seen, and caused us to hear that which human ear has not heard. Thou hast freed us from death and united us with life, released us from darkness and united us with light, led us out of evil and joined us to good. Thou hast shown us the Way of Life and hast guided our feet into the ways of truth and faith so that Life cometh and expelleth darkness and goodness cometh and casteth out evil.

[Like] the mingling of wine with water, so may Thy truth, thy righteousness and thy faith be added to those who love Thy name of Truth.

(This is the set prayer for the *mambuga* [sacramental drink]. Make the *pihta* and the *mambuha* and place them [ready for] the *masiqta*, and then make *the* myrtle wreath.) (Drower)

Note that the prayer is provided with the rubric, "This is the set prayer for the sacramental drink . . .," which contains instructions for the drink for the sacramental meal. As in John 7, it pertains to the revealer as the source of life. Revelation is understood as in 1 Corinthians 2:9 (cf. no. 626), just as in later Christian tradition the mixing of water and wine was understood as the union of deity and humanity. (Cf. the ancient Christmas prayer of the Roman mass, "Deus qui humanae substantiae . . .," "Let us through the mystery of this water and wine participate in the deity of the one who descended in order to participate in our humanity . . .") The reflection of biblical tradition is probably only in reference to Isaiah 52:15; 64:3 (1 Cor 2:9); the rest is more likely independently derived within the framework of a common religious-cultural basis.

425. John 7:43-46

Plutarch, *Parallel Lives*, "Life of Caius Marius" 44.3-4 (45–125 CE)

... the soldiers climbed the stairs and entered the room. But when they beheld Antonius, every man began to urge and push forward a companion to do the murder instead of himself. So indescribable, however, as it would seem, was the grace and charm of his words, that when Antonius began to speak and pray for his life, not a soldier had the hardihood to lay hands on him or even to look him in the face, but they all bent their heads down and wept. (LCL)

The widespread motif of the reluctance to attack a great man is here illustrated in the description of Marius' attempted assassination of the speaker Marcus Antonius.

426. John 7:53–8:11

b. Sanhedrin 6:1-4 (2 cent. CE?)

When sentence [of stoning] has been passed they take him forth to stone him. The place of stoning was outside [far away from] the court, as it is written, *Bring forth him that hath cursed outside the camp* [Lev. 24:14]. One man stands at the door of the court with a towel in his hand, and another, mounted on a horse, far away from him [but near enough] to see him. If [in the court] one said, "I have somewhat to argue in favor of my acquittal," they must bring him back, be it four times or five, provided that there is aught of substance in his words. If then they found him innocent they set him free; otherwise he goes forth to be stoned. A herald goes out before him [calling] "Such-a-one, the son of such-a-one, is going forth to be stoned for that he committed such or such an offense. Such-a-one and such-a-one are witnesses against him. If any man knoweth aught in favor of his acquittal let him come and plead it."

When he was about ten cubits from the place of stoning they used to say to him, "Make thy confession," for such is the way of them that have been condemned to death to make confession, for every one that makes his confession has a share in the world to come. For so have we found it with Achan. Joshua said to him, *My son, give, I pray thee, glory to the Lord, the God of Israel, and make confession unto him, and tell me now what thou hast done; hide it not from me. And Achan answered Joshua and said, Of a truth I have sinned against the Lord, the God of Israel, and thus have I done* [Joshua 7:19]. Whence do we learn that his confession made atonement for him? It is written, *And Joshua said, Why hast thou troubled us? The Lord shall trouble thee this day* [Joshua 7:25]—*this* day thou shalt be troubled, but in the world to come thou shalt not be troubled. ...

When he was four cubits from the place of stoning they stripped off his clothes. A man is kept covered in front, and a woman both in front and behind. So R. Judah. But the Sages say: A man is stoned naked but a woman is not stoned naked.

The place of stoning was twice the height of a man. One of the witnesses knocked him down on his loins; if he turned over on his heart the witness turned him over again on his loins. If he straightway died that sufficed; but if not, the second [witness] took the stone and dropped it on his heart. If he straightway died, that sufficed; but if not, he was stoned by all Israel, for it is written, *The hand of the witnesses shall be first upon him to put him to death and afterward the hand of all the people* [Deut. 17:7]. All that have been stoned must be hanged. So R. Eliezer. But the Sages say: None is hanged save the blasphemer and the idolater. A man is hanged with his face to the people and a woman with her face toward the gallows. So R. Eliezer. But the Sages say: A man is hanged but a woman is not hanged. . . . (Danby)

The past tenses and descriptive tone rather than prescriptive indicate that the material received its final form after the Jews lost their right of capital punishment, i.e. probably after the war of 70 CE. Hence the somewhat idealized portrayal. Yet one must notice how strong the safeguards are against executing an innocent person (see also the similar rules and perspective in *San.* 4–5). Stoning was official execution after careful trial, by appointed deputies of the court (who had also been witnesses against the accused), not mob action or the expression of a judgmental attitude eager to condemn. There was a concern that the condemned person, even if guilty, confess his wrong, so that he could be saved in the heavenly world. The stoning scenes in the New Testament are in contrast to this at every point (John 7:53–8:11; Acts 7:54-60; 14:19; 2 Cor 11:25).

427. John 8:12

The True Ginza (Treasure) 2:3 (7 cent. CE and much older; 7 cent. was the final redaction)

As I came, I, the One sent from the Light, the King, I who went forth from the King as Light, with community and splendor in my hand, with light and praise directed to me. . . . The Sent One from the Light am I, whom the Great One has sent into this world. The Legitimate Sent One am I, in whom there is no lie, in whom there is no lack or failure. The Sent One from Light am I; every one who breathes its fragrance receives life. Every one who receives his word . . . whose eyes are filled with the Light. . . . The Legitimate Sent One am I, in whom is no lie . . . a Vine we are, the Vine of Life, a Tree, in whom there is no lie . . . (MEB/from German trans. of Lidzbarski)

Analogies to the Fourth Gospel:

1) Self-description in the style of an I-am saying (cf. Berger, *Formgeschichte*, §72). In the above translation ". . . am I . . ." represents the Johannine "I am," expressing, as also is the case in the Fourth Gospel, that "I" is the predicate nominative, not the subject. In John, the meaning of Jesus' christological declarations is "The Light, it is I," "the true manna, it is I," etc. Cf. Bultmann, *Gospel of John*, 225.

2) The combination of self-presentation with comprehensive terms for salvation such as Light and Life (cf. John 11:25; 14:6).

3) The emphasis on sending and on being sent.

4) The picture of the vine for the community (cf. John 15:5).

The combination of the awareness of being sent and the idea of "aroma" is reminiscent of 2 Corinthians 2:14-16.

The value for the illumination of Johannine texts: the formation and development of the ancient Mandean texts is inconceivable apart from Judaism. Despite later pronounced anti-Jewish and anti-Christian tendencies (part of the process of self-definition), the ancient Mandean texts and the Gospel of John obviously share a common language and conceptuality. This is something different from merely having elements of common tradition. Nor is it a matter of Gnostic systems or myths, but of a semireligious, semiphilosophical form of thought within which "the world" (among the Mandeans, esp. "Life") is reflexively conceived in terms of general metaphors and abstractions, which include dualistic tendencies. There are also hymnic-poetic accents, a phenomenon that we might call "religious" or "sacralized philosophy," of the Imperial era, and which is not identical with "Gnosticism," but has this as part of its substructure. Among the Mandeans this is oriented more in the direction of folklore. (Cf. also nos. 461, 730, 830, 905, 906, 909.)

428. John 8:12

Plato, *The Republic*, Book 7.1-11, "Allegory of the Cave" (ca. 390 BCE)

And now, I said, let me show in a figure how far our nature is enlightened or unenlightened: Behold! human beings living in an underground den, which has a mouth open toward the light and reaching all along the den; here they have been from their childhood, and have their legs and necks chained so that they cannot move, and can only see before them, being prevented by the chains from turning round their heads. Above and behind them a fire is blazing at a distance, and between the fire and the prisoners there is a raised way; and you will see, if you look, a low wall built along the way, like the screen which marionette players have in front of them, over which they show the puppets.

I see.

And do you see, I said, men passing along the wall carrying all sorts of vessels, and statues and figures of animals made of wood and stone and various materials, which appear over the wall? Some of them are talking, others are silent.

You have shown me a strange image, and they are strange prisoners.

Like ourselves, I replied; and they see only their own shadows, or the shadows of one another, which the fire throws on the opposite wall of the cave?

True, he said; how could they see anything but the shadows if they were never allowed to move their heads?

And of the objects which are being carried in like manner they would only see the shadows?

Yes, he said.

And if they were able to converse with one another, would they not suppose that they were naming what was actually before them?

Very true.

. . . To them, I said, the truth would be literally nothing but the shadows of the images.

And now look again, and see what will naturally follow if the prisoners are released and disabused of their error. At first, when any of them is liberated and compelled suddenly to stand up and turn his neck round and walk and look toward the light, he will suffer sharp pains; the glare will distress him, and he will be unable to see the realities of which in his former state he had seen the shadows; and then conceive someone saying to him, that what he saw before was an illusion, when he is approaching nearer to being and his eye is turned toward more real existence, he has a clearer vision—what will be his reply? . . . Will he not fancy that the shadows which he formerly saw are truer than the objects which are now shown to him?

Far truer.

And if he is compelled to look straight at the light, will he not have a pain in his eyes which will make him turn away to take refuge in the objects of vision which he can see, and which he will conceive to be in reality clearer than the things which are now being shown to him? (Jowett)

This allegory was well known in Hellenistic times. In the subsequent discussion Plato explains that while most prefer to remain in the cave, when some break out of the cave into the sunlight they find the sunlight dazzling. At first they are disoriented, but after a while see things as they are, and realize that what they have been "seeing" in the darkness of the cave is unreality. "After an experience of ecstasy they return to the cave, because they have a duty to their fellow prisoners. As they return, they experience a second bewilderment. Accustomed to the light, they stumble in the darkness of the cave. Those who remained in the cave laugh at them and are so impatient with their stumbling that they may put them to death" (Ferguson, *Backgrounds*, 313-14).

As in the Allegory, so in the Fourth Gospel, ordinary human existence is seen as bondage, a life in darkness. But those in bondage suppose they see. When one who truly sees appears, they find him unbearable and put him to death. But there is an important difference between this myth and the soteriology of the Gospel of John. Jesus is not one of us who managed to get free and then return to deliver us. He does not "return" to the darkness of the world, but "comes" to it. His origin is in the eternal light, whence the saving initiative comes. Yet the general pattern and frame of reference are illuminating for the context of Johannine thought.

429. John 8:31-34

Cicero, *About the Ends of Goods and Evils* 3.75 (Praises of the Wise) (106–43 BCE)

Rightly will he be said to own all things, who alone knows how to use all things; rightly also will be styled beautiful, for the beauty of the soul is fairer than that of the body; rightly the one and only free man, as subject to no man's authority, and slave of no appetite; rightly unconquerable, for though his body be thrown into fetters, no bondage can enchain his soul. (LCL)

Similarly Stobaeus in his collection of *Hypothetica* (ed. Wachsmut, vol. 2, p. 101, lines 14-18): "The true riches, they say, is goodness, and evil is the real poverty. Goodness is the true freedom, and evil is the real slavery. This is why only the good are truly rich and free" (cf. also no. 576). So also concerning Abraham, and therefore relevant for John 8: Philo of Alexandria, *Sobriety* (he alone is king, "for he has received from the ruler of all the scepter of universal lordship, which none can dispute; sole freeman, for he is released from the most tyrannous of mistresses, vain opinion") (LCL). This philosophical conception stands behind the Johannine words of Jesus, while the misunderstanding from the Jewish side probably thinks in terms of the concrete political combination of *nobilitas* (of noble descent, here of Abraham) and *libertas*.

430. John 8:31-36

Epictetus, *Discourses* 4.1ff. (ca. 100 CE)

That man is free, who lives as he wishes, who is proof against compulsion and hindrance and violence, whose impulses are untrammeled, who gets what he wants to get and avoids what he wills to avoid.

Who then would live in error?

No one.

Who would live deceived, reckless, unjust, intemperate, querulous, abject?

No one.

No bad man then lives as he would, and so no bad man is free.

Who would live in a state of distress, fear, envy, pity, failing in the will to get and in the will to avoid.

No one.

Do we then find any bad man without distress or fear, above circumstance, free from failure?

None. Then we find none free.

If a man who has been twice consul hear this, he will forgive you if you add, "But *you* are wise, this does not concern you." But if you tell him the truth, saying, "You are just as much a slave yourself as those who have been thrice sold," what can you expect but a flogging?

"How can I be a slave?" he says; "my father is free, my mother is free, no one has bought me; nay, I am a senator, and a friend of Caesar, I have been consul and have many slaves." (LCL)

The same structure is present as in the Johannine discourse: those who think they are free are in fact slaves, and resent being told otherwise. But the content of "freedom" is different in Epictetus and in the New Testament, as is its source. For Epictetus, it was a matter of correct thinking; for the New Testament, it was the saving act of God. (See also Rom 6:15-23; Gal 5:1.)

431. John 8:44

Wisdom of Solomon 2:23-24 (150 BCE–50 CE)

. . . for God created us for incorruption
and made us in the image of his own eternity,
but through the devil's envy death entered the world,
and those who belong to his company experience it. (NRSV)

Already Wisdom of Solomon 1:13 had emphasized that it was not God who created death. "Envy" also plays an important role in Greek mythology. The function of envy that is here only hinted is developed in later Jewish texts: the favoritism given to Adam (made in the image of God and given dominion) was the reason for the revolt—from envy—of some of the angels (cf. also no. 596), who then fell from their previous estate (*LAE* §§14-16). These then brought about Adam's fall. It is different in John 8, which does not mention this motif. As in 1 John 3:10-12, the devil is described as resembling Cain.

432. John 8:44

Porphyry, *De Abstinentia* 2.42 (234–305 CE)

[On the evil demons:] . . . for these are full of all manner of deception and are able to lead people astray through their working of miracles. That is why evil demons deal in love potions and seductive devices. For all sorts of audacity and hopes for riches and glory come by their working. Their work is primarily deception, for the lie is their special tool. For they want to be gods, and their outstanding ability is that they can have the appearance of being the highest god themselves. (MEB/Berger)

For Judaism the deception of the serpent in Genesis 3:13 offered a point of contact for similar statements, which were then developed in the *Apocalypse of Moses* (chaps. 9, 15, 23, 30). Cf. also Romans 7:11.

433. John 9:1-7

Naroaoth 'anse ma'ase (rabbinic anthology) (CE, Middle Ages)

The following question was posed by the Roman emperor to the Master Joshua ben Korcha: "It is said of your God that all his ways are right. But can it be called right that there are so many deaf, dumb, blind and lame people, who came forth with these handicaps from their mother's womb, before anyone could know whether their life would be good or evil? Is that supposed to be an example of the righteousness of your God?"

To this Rabbi Joshua responded: "To the Lord, the deeds of human beings are already known, even before the idea had arisen to create them, as Daniel had already said: 'He uncovers what is deep and hidden, he knows what lies in the darkness [Dan 2:22].'" Then the emperor said, "Then does the evildoer have the opportunity to repent? May he turn and his eyesight be given back to him?" The sage answered: "If you please, I will illustrate by one example what one who has been born blind is really like inside; give me a thousand denarii and let me be accompanied by two trustworthy witnesses of your own company." The emperor gave him a thousand denarii and sent two of his dependable associates with him. Thereupon the sage went to a man who was blind from birth, and said to him: "The king has threatened me with death; so I will leave these thousand denarii with you. If I am killed, I will not need it, but if not, then I am counting on these thousand denarii that I am leaving with you." The blind man responded, "May it be so." Rabbi Joshua let three months pass. At the end of this period he came to the blind man and said to him, "Give me my thousand denarii back." The blind man asked, "What are you talking about?" Joshua answered, "I mean the thousand denarii which I gave you to keep for me." To this the blind man responded, "No such thing has ever occurred." Thereupon Joshua led the deceitful man before the emperor, and the two witnesses declared that he was the man who had received the money, while the blind man kept declaring that no such thing had ever happened. But while the case was still in process, someone came in and cried out, "Woe to this man here! I saw his wife joking with another man and heard her say, 'Now the starry-eyed guy is going to be killed, and we will live high on the thousand denarii.'" The blind man then immediately brought the money and laid it before the emperor. Then Joshua cried out, "You evildoer! Did I not say that you would steal the money entrusted to you? Righteous is the one who caused you to be born blind!" Then he turned to the emperor and said, "You wanted to accuse the Lord of injustice? What the Scripture says of him is true, that all his ways are just." Thereupon the emperor placed a string of pearls around the neck of the sage, and said to him, "Blessed is your God, and blessed are his people; blessed is the one who washes the dust from your feet." (MEB/Berger/bin Gorion)

Our comparison presupposes the following interpretation of John 9: the issue of past sins is completely pointless in view of the alternative offered by Jesus of being completely healed or of becoming a sinner. True sinners and blind are those who reject Jesus. The relation to this ancient rabbinic story is then as follows:

1) The case of the man born blind is linked to the question of sin.

2) Being born blind is understood as imposed by God (cf. John 9:33).

3) Both narratives hold fast to the connection between unrighteousness and blindness, though blindness is understood by John in the more comprehensive sense of hard-heartedness and impenitence that lead to death (9:39-41). Blindness seen as God's doing, if it is merely physical, can be undone by God's deed in Jesus.

4) Further differences. (a) In the rabbinic story, it is confirmed that God is just by the comprehensive foresight of God, who also saw the sin that would occur, so everything was determined in advance. But in John's story of Jesus everything is not predetermined: God's action at the beginning in allowing the man to be born blind is canceled by Jesus, so that who is blind and who is not is a matter to be decided wholly afresh. The advent of Jesus is therefore a fundamental turning point, and cancellation or transition to a new quality of blindness. (b) The rabbinic story is firmly fixed in the idea of physical blindness; John 9 operates with the concept of metaphorical blindness as in Isaiah 6:9.

434. John 9:6

Inscription, probably from the Asclepius temple on the island in the Tiber in Rome (138 CE)

To the blind soldier Valerius Aprus the god commanded by an oracle to come and take the blood of a white rooster, to mix it with honey and eye salve and to spread it on his eyes for three days. And he recovered his sight, and came and presented an offering of thanksgiving to the god. (MEB/from *SIG* no. 1173)

On the connection between healing and "magic" substances of a "disgusting" sort, cf. Mark 7:33; 8:23 (no. 237). Authority, magic, and medicine as healing are thought of here as a unity, complementing and strengthening each other. A "word" that works a miracle is no less "magic" than saliva or the following of a recipe. The decisive factor is the authority that stands behind it.

435. John 9:6

Suetonius, *Lives of the Caesars* 7, "The Deified Vespasian" (69–121 CE)

Vespasian as yet lacked prestige and a certain divinity, so to speak, since he was an unexpected and still new-made emperor; but these also were given him. A man of the people who was blind, and another who was lame, came to him together as he sat on the tribunal, begging for the help for their disorders which Serapis had promised in a dream; for the god declared that Vespasian would restore the eyes, if he would spit upon them, and give strength to the leg, if he would deign to touch it with his heel. Though he had hardly any faith that this could possibly succeed, and therefore shrank even from making the attempt, he was at last prevailed upon by his friends and tried both things in public before a large crowd; and with success. (LCL)

Cf. also Dio Cassius, *Roman History* 65.8. The "magical" *ex opere operato* potency of the saliva itself is emphasized in this story, since Vespasian himself is skeptical that it would work. His divine nature makes the saliva effective despite his lack of awareness and confidence in his divine identity. The point of contact with the Johannine story is the use of saliva; but it is the person of Jesus, who is fully aware of his being and power, that makes the act effective.

436. John 9:6

Tacitus, *Histories* 4.89 (ca. 110 CE)

During the months while Vespasian was waiting at Alexandria for the regular season of the summer winds and a settled sea, many marvels occurred to mark the favor of heaven and a certain partiality of the gods toward him. One of the common people of Alexandria, well known for his loss of sight, threw himself before Vespasian's knees, praying him with groans to cure his blindness, being so directed by the God Serapis, whom this most superstitious of nations worships before all others; and he besought the emperor to deign to moisten his cheeks and eyes with his spittle. Another, whose hand was useless, prompted by the same god, begged Caesar to step and trample on it. Vespasian at first ridiculed these appeals and treated them with scorn; then, when the men persisted, he began at one moment to fear the discredit of failure, at another to be inspired with hopes of success by the appeals of the suppliants and the flattery of his courtiers: finally, he directed the physicians to give their opinion as to whether such blindness and infirmity could be overcome by human aid. Their reply treated the two cases differently: they said that in the first the power of sight had not been completely eaten away and it would return if the obstacles were removed; in the other, the joints had slipped and become displaced, but they would be restored if a healing pressure were applied to them. Such perhaps was the wish of the gods, and it might be that the emperor had been chosen for this divine service; in any case, if a cure were obtained, the glory would be Caesar's, but in the event of failure, ridicule would fall only on the poor suppliants. So Vespasian, believing that his good fortune was capable of anything and that nothing was any longer incredible, with a smiling countenance and amid intense excitement on the part of the bystanders, did as he was asked to do. The hand was instantly restored to use, and the day again shone for the blind man. Both facts are told by eyewitnesses even now when falsehood brings no reward. (LCL)

This more "scientific" perspective may be compared with no. 434 above. Here, Vespasian is entirely human, skeptical, and politically calculating, and the "miracle" is made more credible by medical information in advance and disinterested eyewitness reports after the fact.

437. John 10:1-15

Themestios, *Speeches* I 9d-10d (317–388 CE)

When a flock has been alienated by its shepherd it becomes vulnerable to wolves. And it is unfortunate for goats to be placed in the care of one that hates them. Or if someone is placed in charge of a herd of cattle, then it is necessary that he loves these living creatures. For such people need to take satisfaction in their work like those who care for children, and not like those who are irritated by dealing with opponents. In the same way, it seems to me, a bad shepherd is one who is interested only in milking the flock often and filling up his milk pails, has no concern for the future of the flock and providing good pasture for them, and if it should happen that his flock is diminished by robbery, continues to fatten himself at the expense of the suffering of the animals. But such a shepherd can live the good life for only a limited time, since the flock will soon be gone. He himself will then become a hireling instead of a shepherd, or perhaps a porter or charcoal-burner, who will earn his meager living filled with trouble and weariness.

The good shepherd, on the other hand, has great advantages in his work. Even more, it is of mutual advantage for him and his flock that he keep wild animals away and to seek out good pasture for the flock. And the sheep will respond with love for the shepherd who loves them, just as the dog does for the hunter, a horse does to a friendly master, and the human flock to a benevolent king. (MEB/Berger)

The frequent connection that was made at least since Plato's *Republic* (343 ab/345cd) between the realm of shepherd/flock as a rich metaphorical source and the realm of statecraft (cf. also in the apocalyptic the talk of shepherds of the nations) lies also at the base of this text (a motif common enough to be trivial). But beyond the typical metaphor, at the base of this text, as in John 10, lie elements of a *Gattung* that could be called, from the point of view of form criticism, the "shepherd mirror" (cf. Berger, *Formgeschichte*, §41). As in John 10, the image of the good shepherd is juxtaposed to that of the hireling, and in both places the emotional and psychic elements in the relationship shepherd/flock are especially emphasized. In Judaism, the leadership role of the prophets was compared to that of the shepherd, as for example in 4 Ezra 5:18: "Rise therefore and eat some bread, so that you may not forsake us, like a shepherd who leaves his flock in the power of savage wolves" (*OTP* 1:532).

438. John 10:1-15

The Authoritative Teaching 6:31-33 (3 cent. CE)

But the soul—she who has tasted these things [knowledge]—realized that sweet passions are transitory. She had learned about evil: she went away from them and entered into a new conduct. Afterward she despises this life, because it is transitory. And she looks for those foods that will take her into life, and leaves behind her those deceitful foods. And she learns about her light, as she goes about stripping off this world, while her true garment clothes her within, [and] her bridal clothing is placed upon her in beauty of mind, not in pride of flesh. And she learns about her depth and runs into her fold, while her shepherd stands at the door. In return for all the shame and scorn, then, that she received in this world, she receives ten thousand times the grace and glory.

She gave the body to those who had given it to her, and they were ashamed, while the dealers in bodies sat down and wept because they were not able to do any business with that body, nor did they find any [other] merchandise except it. They endured great labors until they had shaped the body of this soul, wishing to strike down the invisible soul. They were therefore ashamed of their work; they suffered the loss of the one for whom they had endured labors. They did not realize that she has an invisible spiritual body, thinking, "We are her shepherd who feeds her." But they did not realize that she knows another way, which is hidden from them. This her true shepherd taught her in knowledge.

But these—the ones who are ignorant—do not seek after God. (NHL)

Analogies to John 10: the image of good/bad shepherds, the picture of the sheepfold with the shepherd at the door, the important function of the one good shepherd and his speech, the problem of to whom the sheep in the pasture truly belong.

Differences: John 10 is not oriented to a dualistic understanding of the relation of body and soul; its dualism is a "dualism of decision" oriented to the relation of human beings to God through Jesus or to the Johannine community. Nor is John 10 oriented to the one-to-one relationship of sheep and shepherd, but speaks always of "the sheep" in the plural, with ecclesiological aspects (10:16). Especially to be noted is the absence in the "Authoritative Teaching" of the idea that the shepherd sacrifices his life for the sheep. Precisely those items that were bothersome to the older Liberal theology (atoning death, doctrine of the church) are missing in this quasi-Gnostic text. (Cf. C. Colpe, "Heidnische, Jüdische und Christliche Überlieferung in den Schriften aus Nag Hammadi I," JbAC 15 [1972], 12-13.)

439. John 10:14

Odes of Solomon 9:12-14 (2 cent. CE)

And understand my knowledge, you who know me in truth;
love me with affection, you who love;
For I turn not my face from my own,
because I know them.
And before they had existed,
I recognized them;
and imprinted a seal on their faces.
(OTP 2:742)

In both texts the theme is the exclusive narrow relation between savior and saved. The knowledge of the saved in the Odes of Solomon, however, pertains to their own existence before they were born into this world. This concept of foreknowledge is lacking in the Fourth Gospel.

440. John 10:14, 27

A proverb in the *Corpus Paroemiographorum Graecorum*

I know Simon and Simon knows me. There were two guides, Nikon and Simon. But in deception, Simon was the stronger, so that he himself helped to give Nikon an inflated reputation. The proverb is said by people who recognize each other by their mean tricks. (MEB/Berger)

Similarly in Aristotle's *Rhetoric* A 1371 b: "All things akin and like are for the most part pleasant to each other, as man to man, horse to horse, youth to youth. This is the origin of the proverb: Beast knows beast" (LCL). More colloquially: "One animal knows another." Those of a similar nature "know" and "understand" each other. Cf. the American slang proverb "It takes one to know one." The language of the Fourth Gospel is thus here not mystical, but proverbial.

441. John 10:16

Zeno of Kition, according to Plutarch, *Moralia*, "On the Fortune or the Virtue of Alexander" 6 (333–262 BCE; Plutarch 45–125 CE)

Moreover, the much-admired Republic of Zeno, the founder of the Stoic sect, may be summed up in this one main principle: that all the inhabitants of this world of ours should not live differentiated by their respective rules of justice into separate cities and communities, but that we should consider all men to be of one community and one polity, and that we should have a common life and an order common to us all, even as a herd that feeds together and shares the pasturage of a common field. (LCL)

(For the continuation, see on Eph 2:12ff., no. 787.) Unity programs of this sort were very beloved in the Hellenistic world from the time of Alexander the Great onward, both philosophically and politically. (See no. 486.) Judaism gladly adopted them, since they could be used to emphasize the doctrine of the one and only God. In Christianity, Jesus became the grounder and basis of this unity (cf. on 1 Cor 8:6, nos. 672 and 604). Thus these unity formulae are found in abundance especially in Judaism and Christianity, which also concern unity within the perspective of human associations.

442. John 10:20

Plato, *Phaedrus* 249 cd (428–349 BCE)

And therefore it is just that the mind of the philosopher only has wings, for he is always, so far as he is able, in communion through memory with those things the communion with which causes God to be divine. Now a man who employs such memories rightly is always being initiated into perfect mysteries and he alone becomes truly perfect; but since he separates himself from human interests and turns his attention toward the divine, he is rebuked by the vulgar, who consider him mad and do not know that he is inspired. (LCL)

Similarly on the Sibyl in *Sib. Or.* 3:813-17 (responding to the charge of strangeness, as in John 8:48): "Throughout Greece mortals will say that I [the sibyl] am of another country, a shameless one, born of Erythrae. Some will say that I am Sibylla born of Circe as mother and Gnostos as father, a crazy liar. But when everything comes to pass, then you will remember me and no longer will anyone say that I am crazy, I who am a prophetess of the great God" (*OTP* 2:380).

In Wisdom of Solomon 5:4 the life of the righteous is considered madness (Gk. *mania*) by the unrighteous. That human bearers of divine revelation are charged with being frenzied or mad is a general characteristic known to the phenomenology and sociology of religion, which points to an actual ambiguity and ambivalence (inspired/mad). But without social isolation the *homo religiosus* does not have the possibility of functioning as a critical agent over against society. The context in each case is different. In John it is a matter of Jesus' death and resurrection, which are "misunderstood," while in Plato the issue is philosophical teaching and practice, and with the Sibyl it concerns prophetic pronouncements of judgment. (Cf. also nos. 235, 236, 897.)

443. John 11:1-44

Regina Inscription (ca. 100 CE)

Here lies Regina, covered by this grave. Her husband does this as an expression of his love. She spent twenty-one years and four months less eight days with him. She will live again and will return to the world of light, for she has the hope of resurrection into eternal life. That is the promise, and a matter of sincere faith to those who are worthy and pious. She has earned a place [lit., a seat, *sedem*] in the revered land [i.e. Palestine]. This will be yours because of the true religion you have practiced, because of your chaste life, your love for your people and obedience to the Law, your conducting yourself as a model wife in a marriage. You were always devoted to making this a praiseworthy marriage. Since you have lived this way, you may hope for the future, from which I, your mourning husband, receive comfort. (MEB/Berger from *CIJ* I, pp. 348-50 = Europa no. 476)

Here the following expressions are used as synonyms: return to the world of light, resurrection, live again, and to have a place in the holy land of Palestine (cf. the eschatological imagery of *1 Enoch* 89:40, "a land beautiful and glorious," "the beautiful land"). The emphasis on merit suggests Pharisaic influence. Since most Jewish grave inscriptions are brief, we have here one of the few witnesses to Jewish resurrection faith from Diaspora inscriptions (from Rome). Contrast no. 819! In John 11:25, on the other hand, the resurrection is so bound to Jesus that only a relationship to him grants one participation in the resurrection.

Cf. also Philo of Alexandria, "Flight," 55. "'In what other way,' I asked myself, 'does a man who dies come to his end save by death?' So I attended the lectures of a wise woman, whose name is 'Consideration,' and was rid of my questioning; for she taught me that some people are dead while living, and some alive while dead. She told me that bad people, prolonging their days to extreme old age, are dead men, deprived of the life in association with virtue, while good people, even if cut off from their partnership with the body, live forever, and are granted immortality" (LCL). Philo thus affirms a real life after death, and he has this begin in the present, similarly to how this is said in the Fourth Gospel (4:14). Concerning those who are already dead during the present life, cf. John 5:25!

444. John 11:39

Addition to the *Life of Adam and Eve* (9–10 cents. CE)

When a human being dies, the soul remains two days without being judged, and it travels around with an angel wherever it wants to go. One soul, because of the love that binds it to the body, returns to the body from which it has been separated. But the virtuous soul goes to that place where it had prayed to its redeemer [i.e., the church]. And on the third day the angel takes the soul to heaven. (MEB/Berger)

This text documents the widespread idea in the ancient Orient, that the soul hovered near the corpse for up to three days (cf. additional examples in Berger, *Auferstehung*, 370-71). Precisely for this reason the resurrection of Lazarus is all the more sensational, because the three-day period was already past.

445. John 11:50

Cassius Dio, *Roman History* 63.13 (200 CE)

[About Otho and his willingness to sacrifice himself, which he presented in a speech:] I love all Romans, even though they do not side with me. Let Vitellius be victor, since this has pleased the gods; and let the lives of his soldiers also be spared, since this pleases me. Surely it is far better and far more just that one should perish for all than many for one, and that I should refuse on account of one man alone to embroil the Roman people in civil war and cause so great a multitude of human beings to perish. For I certainly should prefer to be a Mucius, a Decius, a Curtius, a Regulus, rather than a Marius, a Cinna, or a Sulla—not to mention other names. Therefore do not force me to become one of these men that I hate, nor grudge me the privilege of imitating one of those that I commend. But as for you, be off to the victor and pay court to him; as for me, I shall free myself, that all men may learn from the event that you chose for your emperor one who would not give you up to save himself, but rather himself to save you. (LCL)

Cf. similarly Epictetus, *Discourses* 3.24.64 (55–135 CE) (concerning Diogenes): "Come, was there anybody that Diogenes did not love, a man who was so gentle and kind-hearted that he gladly took upon himself all those troubles and physical hardships for the sake of the common weal?" (LCL). In both cases the dominating ideal is "one for all"—again one of the behind-the-scenes messianic motifs of the Fourth Gospel (cf. nos. 389, 407).

In Dio Cassius §14 cited above, the soldiers respond: "Upon thee [Gk. ἐν σοὶ] our lives depend," they said, "and for thee we will all die" (LCL).

446. John 11:51

Josephus, *Jewish War* 1.68-69 concerning John Hyrcanus (37–100 CE)

. . . truly a blessed individual and one who left no ground for complaint against fortune as regards himself. He [John] was the only man to unite in his person three of the highest privileges: the supreme command of the nation, the high priesthood, and the gift of prophecy. For so closely was he in touch with the Deity, that he was never ignorant of the future; thus he foresaw and predicted that his two elder sons would not remain at the head of affairs. The story of their downfall is worth relating . . . (LCL)

The same fundamental point of view is expressed in Philo's exposition of Leviticus 10:9, in Philo "Special Laws," 4:192: ". . . the true priest is necessarily a prophet, advanced to the service of the truly Existent by virtue rather than by birth, and to a prophet nothing is unknown since he has within him a spiritual sun." (LCL)

In both Philo and John 11 only two of the three elements named by Josephus are bound together, namely priest and prophet. But see Philo, *Moses* 2, 1:2: "For it has been said, not without good reason, that states can only make progress in well-being if either kings are philosophers or philosophers are kings. But Moses will be found to have displayed, and more than displayed, combined in his single person, not only these two faculties—the kingly and the philosophical—but also three others, one of which is concerned with law-giving, the second with the high priest's office, and the last with prophecy" (LCL).

For the concept of unwitting prophecy, see further Philo, *Moses* 1.274, 277, 283, 286. For the High Priest as prophet, see further Philo, "Special Laws," 4.192; *t. Sota* 13:5-6; Josephus, *The Jewish War* 1.68-69; *Antiquities* 11.327; 13.299-300.

447. John 12:24

The report concerning Tammuz/Adonis in Origen's *Commentary on Ezekiel* 8:14 (185–253 CE)

Every year they observe public consecration services. First they hold a lamentation for him [sc. Tammuz/Adonis] as though he were dead. Then they celebrate for him as one would celebrate for one who has risen from the dead. Adonis is the patron saint of the fruits of the earth. They are lamented when they are sown in the earth, and when they grow [lit. "rise up"] they bring joy to the farmers. (MEB/Berger from MPG 15:800)

Origen here presents a Christian interpretation of certain annual rites of spring. These are oriented to the natural cycle of vegetation. In John 12:24, however, the destiny of Jesus (v. 23) and that of his disciples (vv. 25-26) are also linked to this natural annual cycle by an analogy. It may be intentional that this analogy appears precisely in the context where "Greeks" appear (12:20).

Additional documentation:

Theocritus (3 cent. BCE), *Idyls* 15 "Women at the Adonis Festival," describes the sequence of lamentation and joy. See further in G. Wagner, *Das religionsgeschichtliche Problem von Röm 6:1-11* (Zürich: Zwingli, 1962).

Besides Origen, in Christian church fathers the following references are found:

Cyril of Alexandria (+444 CE), *Commentary on Isaiah* 2:3 (*PG* 70:441) concerning Aphrodite:

"Because of the death of Adonis she mourned and lamented . . ., but when she comes out of Hades . . . she rejoices and leaps for joy" (MEB/Berger).

Jerome, *Exposition of Ezekiel* 3:8 (*PL* 25:82-83), explaining the name of the month "June": "It is so called, because according to the pagan myth it was in this month that Tammuz (= June) the lover of Venus, a very handsome youth was killed and then restored to life, in the very same month that bears his name. And they celebrate an annual festival for him, in which he is mourned by the women as though he were dead, and then is praised and hymns are sung to him as though he had come to life again . . . so that the death and resurrection of Adonis is accompanied by both lamentation and joy" (MEB/Berger).

Julius Firmicus Maternus (ca. 350 CE), in "On the Errors of the Pagan Religion," §3: ". . . they [the Phrygians] proceeded to consecrate with annual lamentations, the love affair of a rich woman, their queen, who chose to avenge in tyrannical fashion the haughty snub that she suffered from her young beloved. In order to satisfy the angry woman, or perhaps trying to find consolation for her after she repented, they advanced the claim that he whom they had buried a little while earlier had come to life again; and since the woman's heart burned unbearably with overweening love, they erected temples to the dead youth" (Forbes).

Cf. also no. 571. In the pagan texts, the emphasis was always on "dying." Among the reasons that early Christianity, in its liturgy and customs, was able to make contact with the idea of the "dying and rising god" was that Jesus' death in fact occurred in the spring. Cf. R. Wünsch, *Das Frühlingsfest der Insel Malta* (Leipzig, 1902).

448. John 12:29

Homer, *The Odyssey* 20.97-104 (prior to 7 cent. BCE)

"Father Zeus, if of your goodwill ye gods have brought me over land and sea to my own country, when ye had afflicted me sore, let some one of those who are awaking utter a word of omen for me within, and without let a sign from Zeus be shown besides."

So he spoke in prayer, and Zeus the counselor heard him. Straightway he thundered from gleaming Olympus, from on high from out the clouds; and goodly Odysseus was glad. (LCL)

The prayer of Jesus was followed by a heavenly response which the Greeks (12:20), consistent with their tradition, interpreted as thunder (cf. similarly Sir 46:16-17: "He called upon the Lord, the Mighty One, when his enemies pressed him on every side, and he offered in sacrifice a suckling lamb. Then the Lord thundered from heaven, and made his voice heard with a mighty sound" NRSV). In Jewish tradition too, thunder was understood as the voice of God, and was interpreted by specialists in the art. In revelatory scenes, thunder as the voice of God in response to prayer is probably best regarded as an element of particularly Greek tradition.

449. John 12:33

Heraclitus, according to Plutarch, "The Oracles at Delphi," 21 (Heraclitus, 6 cent. BCE; Plutarch, 45–125 CE)

. . . the Lord whose prophetic shrine is at Delphi neither tells nor conceals, but indicates. (LCL)

The Greek word here used for "indicates" (σημαίνειν, often translated "signify," the verbal form of the favorite Johannine word "sign") is also found in John 12:33. Jesus' passion prediction is thus here described with a term frequently used in describing Greek oracles. Here is one of the many elements in which the understanding of revelation in apocalyptic Judaism, Hellenistic Judaism, and early Christianity approaches that of manticism and invites comparison with it, a comparison that is facilitated by the actual choice of vocabulary.

450. John 12:34

Justin, *Dialogue with Trypho* 32:1 (ca. 150 CE)

And when I had ceased, Trypho said, "These and such like scriptures, sir, compel us to wait for Him who, as Son of man, receives from the Ancient of days the everlasting kingdom. But this so-called Christ of yours was dishonorable and inglorious, so much so that the last curse contained in the law of God fell on him, for he was crucified." (ANF)

As already with reference to John 7 (see no. 422), Justin documents the presence in his time of a Jewish messianic expectation in opposition to the Christian. In the Gospel of John too, the Christian understanding of Messiahship is confronted with a contrasting Jewish expectation. This expectation is also already seen in the second-century BCE *Sibylline Oracles* 3:46-50, 767-69:

"But when Rome will also rule over Egypt guiding it toward a single goal, then indeed the most great kingdom of the immortal king will become manifest over men. For a holy prince will come to gain sway over the scepters of the earth forever, as time presses on. . . .

And then, indeed, he will raise up a kingdom for all ages among men, he who once gave the holy Law to the pious" (*OTP* 1:363, 379).

In the Christian answers to the objections made to Christian appropriation and adaptation of these expectations, adjustments are made in terms of eternal life/resurrection in John and by distinguishing a first and second coming by Justin.

We may also mention here the messianic expectations of a personal origin as found in the Christian reception and interpretation of the Hystaspes oracle (documented since 160 BCE), as found in the fragment of Pauline apocrypha cited in Clement of Alexandria's *Stromata*, 6, 5; 43:1: "And taking Hystaspes, read, and you will find much more luminously and distinctly the Son of God described, and how many kings shall draw up their forces against Christ, hating Him and those that bear His name, and His faithful ones, and His patience, and His coming" (ANF). With reference to this same tradition Lactantius (240–320 CE) in his *Divine Institutions* 8:18 of the fact that during the siege Jupiter (!) would send his son, or a "great king" (7, 17:9). It is interesting that in Salomo of Bosra's "Bee Book," §§37-39, an obviously Christianized disciple of Zoroaster identifies the Christian messiah as the returned Zoroaster: "Zaradost [Zoroaster] answered him [namely, Hystaspes]: 'He [namely, the messiah] will come from my family. I am he, and he is I; he is in me, and I am in him. . . . At the beginning of his parousia, there will be mighty signs to be seen in heaven, and his light will outshine the sun'" (MEB/Berger). On the whole subject, cf. H. Windisch, *Die Orakel des Hystaspes* (Amsterdam: Koninklijke Akademie van Wetenschaggen, 1929), pp. 22ff., 34ff.; C. Colpe, *Kairos* 12 (1970), 81-112.

451. John 12:36

1QS 3:24–4:1 (2–1 cent. BCE)

. . . for all his [The Angel of Darkness] allotted spirits seek the overthrow of the sons of light.

But the God of Israel and His Angel of Truth will succor all the sons of light. For it is He who created the spirits of Light and Darkness and founded every action upon them and established every deed [upon] their [ways]. And He loves the one everlastingly and delights in its works for ever; but the counsel of the other He loathes and for ever hates its ways. (Vermes)

Cf. also the famous passage in 1:9-10: ". . . they may love all the sons of light . . . and hate all the sons of darkness, each according to his guilt in God's vengeance" (Vermes). The dualism of the Community Rule of Qumran corresponds to the reality of the angelic world. Since the angels rule the world, this means the whole creation apart from God. This is not the case in the Gospel of John. By means of its angelology the sect finds its place in the universe. This too is in contrast to the Fourth Gospel. In each case however, one's membership among the children of light (always plural) is obtained by joining the sect or the Johannine community (see John 3:19-21). The Gospel of John is less systematically consistent, and has no corresponding "children of darkness." This comes to expression most clearly in the different directions in which hatred is directed: in John, Jesus and his disciples are the objects of the world's hatred (15:18-19), while in 1QS the sect is called upon to hate all others. And for the Gospel of John, "light" and "darkness" are not realms already fixed in advance, but become reality in their confrontation with Jesus (3:19-21). The missionary dualism of a community experiencing persecution is in contrast to the fixed and cosmological dualism of the isolationist perspective of the Qumran sect that had fenced itself off from the rest of the world.

452. John 12:41

Targum Pseudo-Jonathan on Isaiah 6:1 and 6:5 (1 cent. BCE–3 cent. CE)

In the year that King Uzziah *was struck with it* [i.e. leprosy], *the prophet* said, I saw *the glory of* the LORD *resting* upon a throne, high and lifted up *in the heavens of the height;*

. . . for my eyes have seen *the glory of the Shekhinah of the eternal* king, the LORD of hosts! (Chilton)

The Masoretic Text reads: "I saw the Lord . . . my eyes have seen the king, the Lord of hosts." The Gospel of John thus follows the general tendency of the *Targum* to avoid the name of God, and especially never to make God an object. But in addition, the interpretation is christological. Already in Philo the Logos is the preexistent subject of the theophany reports of the Old Testament: *Dreams* 1:229-30: "Here he gives the title of 'God' to his chief Word [λόγος], not from any superstitious nicety in applying names, but with one aim before him, to use words to express facts. Thus in another place, when he had inquired whether He that is has any name, he came to know full well that He has no proper name, and that whatever name anyone may use of Him he will use by license of language; for it is not the nature of Him that is to be spoken of, but simply to be" (LCL).

John 1:1; on John 12:44-45, 13:20, cf. no. 84.

453. John 12:50

Epictetus, *Discourses* **3.1.36 (55–135 CE)**

But once you have heard these words go away and say to yourself, "It was not Epictetus who said these things to me; why, how could they have occurred to him? but it was some kindly god or other speaking through him. For it would not have occurred to Epictetus to say these things, because he is not in the habit of speaking to anyone. Come then, let us obey God, that we rest not under His wrath." (LCL)

Since the Cynic philosophers, like the New Testament preachers, understood themselves as God's messengers, they also had the same point of view regarding the inspiration of their words. Important for the evaluation of the relation between manticism and inspiration is the series of stages in the revelatory chain Zeus to Apollo to oracle giver, as they are seen in Aeschylus *Eumenides* 19 (prophet of Zeus, his father, where Loxias is identified with Apollo), and the scholiasts' interpretation ("obviously Apollo receives the oracle from Zeus"). But then in fact Apollo speaks through the human medium. For the messenger concept of the Fourth Gospel, cf. nos. 84, 135. For Epictetus, cf. no. 455.

454. John 13:15

Xenophon, *Memorabilia* **4.3.17-18 (d. 429 BCE)**

[On the relation to the gods:] And how can he please them better than by obeying them strictly? Thus by precept and by example alike he strove to increase in his companions Piety and Prudence. (LCL)

The inherent unity between word and deed was decisive for the philosophical teacher of antiquity—also the fundamental principle of the New Testament Gospels.

455. John 13:15

Epictetus, *Discourses* **4.8.30-31 (55–135 CE)**

"That you may see yourselves, O men, to be looking for happiness and serenity, not where it is, but where it is not, behold, God has sent me to you as an example; I have neither property, nor house, nor wife, nor children, no, not even so much as a bed, or a shirt, or a piece of furniture, and yet you see how healthy I am. Make trial of me, and if you see that I am free from turmoil, hear my remedies and the treatment which cured me." For this, at length, is an attitude both humane and noble. But see whose work it is; the work of Zeus, or of him whom Zeus deems worthy of this service . . . (LCL)

Point of comparison: the one sent from God is a model for his disciples. His life is a life of service, and exhibits freedom in regard to property, social status, and everything usually considered to make life pleasant. The difference: for Epictetus, it is a matter of personal happiness and internal serenity. In the Gospel of John, the present is a time of sorrow; joy comes later (John 16:20). (Though this is a matter of the Johannine story line; John affirms the presence of eschatological joy in his own, post-Easter time.) Still differently in Paul, where the charismatic gift of joy is the counterpart to the Stoic understanding of personal happiness, but is obviously not a matter of internal harmony and poise, but is the result of the ecstatic presence of the Spirit.

456. John 13:17

Hesiod, *Works and Days* 826-27 (7 cent. BCE)

That man is happy and lucky in them who knows all these things and does his work without offending the deathless gods, who discerns the omens of birds and avoids transgressions. (LCL)

Points of comparison: (1) the form of blessing for those who act according to what they know and have seen; (2) the commentarylike character at the conclusion of a passage, with a view to the reader's adopting the perspective commended in the story.

457. John 13:27

Testaments of the Twelve Patriarchs, "Testament of Simeon" 2:7 (ca. 160 BCE)

In the time of my youth I was jealous of Joseph, because my father loved him more than all the rest of us. I determined inwardly to destroy him, because the Prince of Error blinded my mind so that I did not consider him as a brother nor did I spare Jacob my father. (*OTP* 1:785)

The story in Genesis 37 of course knows nothing of a demonic power behind the evil deed of the brothers in selling Joseph into slavery. But by Maccabean times it was common to blame Satan for instigating human evil (cf. 2 Sam 24:1 and 1 Chr 21:1). As in the Johannine story, Satanic inspiration does not remove human responsibility.

458. John 13:35

Iamblichus, *Life of Pythagoras* 33:230 (4 cent. CE)

For all these instances taken together, then, there is one and the same word, that of "friendship," of which, by common consent, Pythagoras was the discoverer and legislator, and he taught such an admirable friendship to his friends, that even now many say of those who are unusually well-disposed to one another that they belong to the Pythagoreans. (Dillon and Hershbell)

There were other philosophical groups in the ancient world who distinguished themselves from their environment by their ideal of friendship, such as the Epicureans (cf. also no. 492). In the Gospel of John, this idea plays a greater role in the Jesus/disciples relationship than in the other New Testament documents (cf. 15:13-15). Also the famous expression of Tertullian, *Apology* 39, "See how they love one another" follows the same sociological model: the excluded group practices an ideal love with each other, is a model for human society as a whole.

459. John 14:1-6

The True Ginza (Treasure)
Book 11 (7 cent. CE final redaction)

[The Manda d'Haije speaks:] "I am going away, to direct Hibil to a place in the new abode, and then will come back quickly to you. Do not fear the sword of the planets, and let not fear and anxiety dwell in you. Afterward, be assured, I am coming to you. The eye of life is focused on you. I cover you with the garment of life, which it has loaned to you. Truly, I am with you. Every time you seek me, you will find me; every time you call me, I will answer you. I am not far from you." These words Manda d'Haije directed to Shitil. And Shitil extended Kushta to them [to the pious among the members of his own race]. Then Hibil spoke to Shitil, "Come quickly after me, and Anosh will come after you. Also the souls of people of proven righteousness, who acknowledged life and extended it, will go before and after you in the way which we are following, the way Manda d'Haije has prepared for us . . ." [more about Manda d'Haije and Shitil]. He led him forth on the way on which Hibil had gone, and let him dwell in the abode in which Hibil had lived, and where fellowship with the house of life had been prepared for the righteous souls, where there is no separation. (MEB/Berger)

Explanatory notes: Manda d'Haije ("Knowledge of Life") is providing for Shitil, Hibil, and the latter's brother or son, Anosh, so that they can escape the negative forces of the cosmos (planets, sword, fire). He is the mediator of salvation, who will not abandon those that belong to him. Through the ascent into heavenly dwelling places he preserves them from the sword (death) on earth. There is certainly no "dependence" of the Gospel of John on Mandean ideas here. The analogies are better explained as the result of a common basis: ethical dualism, the figure of a mediator, heavenly dwelling places for the righteous, a "way," the helpful support of a mediator. On "dwelling places" in Judaism, cf. *1 Enoch* 39:4; 41:2.

460. John 14:2

1 Enoch 39:3-4 (1 cent. BCE–1 cent. CE)

In those days, whirlwinds carried me off from the earth,
and set me down in the ultimate ends of the heavens.
There I saw other dwelling places of the holy ones and their resting places too.
(*OTP* 1:30)

Apocalyptic Judaism knew the idea of apartments or compartments in the heavenly world already prepared for the righteous. Cf. 41:2: "And there I saw the dwelling place of the sinners and the company of the holy ones . . . " Cf. also *2 Enoch* 61:2: "Many shelters have been prepared for people, good ones for the good, but bad ones for the bad, many without number" (*OTP* 1:186). In John, the "dwelling places" (NRSV) are closely related to the thematic word "abide" in Johannine thought (μονή/μένω), a relationship that could be captured by translating "abode" in 14:2. In *1* and *2 Enoch*, this aspect is lacking.

461. John 14:5-6

Epictetus, *Discourses* 1.4.23-30 (55–135 CE)

[An encomium to Chrysippus.] O the great good fortune! O the great benefactor who points the way! To Triptolemus, indeed, all men have established shrines and altars, because he gave us as food the fruits of cultivation, but to him who has discovered, and brought to light, and imparted to all men the truth which deals, not with mere life, but with a good life—who among you has for what set up an altar in his honor, or dedicated a temple or a statue, or bows down to God in gratitude for him? (LCL)

Precisely in comparison with the Mandean text in no. 459 above it becomes clear that the figure of the light bearer to humanity, the benefactor and savior figure from the heavenly world, was applied to the philosophers. What had remained at the level of reflection in the Mandean text appears here as philosophy. Here, too, the motif of "the way" is met. The mere existence of these elements in the Gospel of John is thus less surprising than the fact that this Gospel has stronger recourse to these general categories than the other New Testament writings. For a resolution of this problem see above no. 427. That the Gospel of John is more deeply rooted in that kind of sacralized popular philosophy of the imperial period that had become widespread especially in the East certainly has sociological conditions and implications. Cf. the model of the philosopher's circle of friends in no. 458 above.

462. John 14:15-16

Wisdom of Solomon 6:18-19 (150 BCE–50 CE)

. . . and love of her [wisdom] is the keeping of her laws
and giving heed to her laws is the assurance of immortality,
and immortality brings one near to God. (NRSV)

This is formally analogous to John, where love is the keeping of the divine commandment, and the result is fellowship with God, though the content is different. In Wisdom of Solomon it is wisdom instead of the (incarnate) Logos, immortality instead of resurrection/eternal life, and coming near to God rather than the Spirit of Truth coming near to the believer.

463. John 14:16-17

Philo, *On the Life of Moses* 2.134 (15 BCE–50 CE)

[Explaining that the garment of the high priest allegorically interpreted stands for the whole world:] For he who has been consecrated to the Father of the world must needs have that Father's Son [i.e. the cosmos] with all His fullness of excellence to plead his cause [lit. to function as a *paraclete*], that sins may be remembered no more and good gifts showered in rich abundance. (LCL)

What is meant here is the world as God's son and image. For Hellenistic Judaism the optimistic evaluation of the objective reality of the world as cosmos persisted, and thus he can serve as the *paraclete* before God. But this role of the advocate before God can be played by different figures. According to Philo's writing "Rewards" ¶166, this role can be played by the (personified) goodness of God's own heart, by the piety of the patriarchs who pray for their descendants, and by the reformation and improvement of humanity.

The origin of the idea of the counselor/advocate derives from the metaphorical conception of the relation between deity and humanity as a forensic situation: God presides as Judge in the heavenly court, like a ruler on his throne. The mercy of God in this situation consists in the fact that he appoints one especially close to him as the counsel for the defense, and responds positively to him. The metaphor "advocate/counselor" is thus a way of formulating the averting of God's wrath and its replacement by his compassion.

464. John 14:26

Plutarch, *Moralia*, "Dialogue on Love" 1 (45–125 CE)

[Autobulus is speaking.] My dear Flavian, why should my discourse need such preliminaries? The situation that gave rise to the debate merely wants a chorus to sympathize and lacks a stage, for no other element of drama is wanting. Only, let us pray to the Mother of the Muses [Gk., "memory"] to be graciously present and help me to resuscitate the story. A long time ago, before I was born . . . (LCL)

At the beginning of a narrative the goddess of memory is invoked to preserve the integrity of the transmission of the story by her protection. Cf. the following selection:

465. John 14:26

Plutarch, *Moralia*, "On the Delays of the Divine Vengeance" 33 (45–125 CE)

[At the conclusion of the trip to the underworld and the transformation of Thespesius (on which see no. 953:] Thus much he beheld. He was about to turn back, when he was driven frantic with terror, for a woman marvelously beautiful and tall took hold of him and said: "Come hither, sirrah, the better to remember everything," and was about to apply to him a red hot rod, such as painters use; but another woman interposed, and he was suddenly pulled away as by a cord and cast in a strong and violent gust of wind upon his body, opening his eyes again almost from his very grave. (LCL)

The appearance of the woman has the function of enabling Thespesius to appropriate and preserve what he had received in the "vision." Cf. the Jewish Christian variation of this theme in the following selection.

466. John 14:26

Shepherd of Hermas *Visions* 2:1:3-4 (ca. 120 CE? in Rome)

On rising from prayer, I see opposite me that old woman, whom I had seen the year before, walking and reading some book. And she said to me, "Can you carry a report of these things to the elect of God?" I say to her, "Lady, so much I cannot retain in my memory, but give me the book and I shall transcribe it." "Take it," says she, "and you will give it back to me." No sooner, however, had I finished the writing of the book, than all of a sudden it was snatched from my hands; but who the person was that snatched it, I saw not. (ANF)

As in the first two examples (nos. 464, 465 above), it is again a woman (here the Sibyl of Cumae) who guarantees by her help that what is reported corresponds to the truth. The text lets us see that the problem being dealt with is the integrity of Hermas' reports. The problem of legitimation is skillfully shifted: it is not the facticity itself that is problematical, but only the manner of transmission. Judaism too knows the topos, as is clear from the following example.

467. John 14:26

Jubilees 32:24-26 (2 cent. BCE)

"Do not fear, because just as you have seen and read, thus will everything come to pass. But you write down everything just as you have seen and read [it]." And Jacob said, "O Lord, how will I remember everything that I read and saw?" And he said to him, "I will cause you to remember everything." And he went up from him and he woke up from his sleep and he recalled everything that he had read and seen and he wrote down all of the matters which he had read and seen. (*OTP* 2:118)

Differently from Genesis 35: the angel gives Jacob seven tablets and shows him everything on it. Here an angel replaces the function of the women in the other examples. All the texts cited here (nos. 464-67) have the following in common:
1) It is in each case a matter of remembering particular items of content, namely sacred texts which must be preserved, the faithful preservation of which is facilitated by the help of a divine being.
2) It is in each case a matter of the dependability of the process of transmission, and the mistrust

of human memory as an adequate means. (It is important to note that this was perceived as a problem at all, in view of the emphasis conservative scholars often place on the absolute reliability of human memory in the transmission of oral tradition in the ancient world.)

3) It is in principle only through divine help that human memory can be considered a guarantor for the integrity of transmitted materials. That of course applies in the first place *eo ipso* to materials that were not written down (stories, visions), but is still highly significant (in every case it is a matter of revelation). In the Shepherd of Hermas the transition to a written text occurs already within the framework of the vision, but this is different in *Jubilees* 32. In John 14:26 the Paraclete takes the role of the "transcendent guarantor" of the tradition of Jesus' words, a role played elsewhere mostly by a woman or angelic figure.

468. John 15:5

Aelius Aristides, Speech 37.10 (117–187 CE)

The greatest benefit of all, which permeates every being and extends through all times and places, is that mankind has never erred under Athena's guidance, nor again will they ever do anything useful without Athena. (Behr)

"Nothing apart from God" is a hymnic topos (cf. Berger in "Hellenistische Gattungen," 1158-59), of course in the third-person style of hymnic predication. Formulated in the first-person style (or reformulated into an I-saying), the topos represents the highest claim.

469. John 15:15

Philo, *Migration of Abraham* 45 (15 BCE–50 CE)

You must not think that it [God's reprimand to Moses in Deut. 34:4] was said, as some unconsidering people suppose, to humiliate the all-wise leader; for indeed it is folly to suppose that the servants/slaves [*doulos*, as John 15:15] of God take precedence of His friends in receiving their portion in the land of virtue. (LCL)

Cf. *Sobriety* 55, where the wise person is God's friend rather than slave; *Sobriety* 56, where Philo substitutes "friend" for the LXX's "servant" in his citation of Genesis 18:17's description of Abraham; and *Cherubim* 49, where Moses is called "friend of God" (θεόφιλος) in association with his receiving mysteries. Wisdom of Solomon 7:27 declares that Wisdom makes people into friends of God and prophets, i.e. "friend of God" is a gift linked with the Spirit, as in John.

470. John 16:2

The Twelfth Benediction of the Eighteen Benedictions in the Jewish *Prayer Book* (1 cent. CE)

For the apostates let there be no hope, and let the arrogant government be speedily uprooted in our days. Let the Nazarenes [*nosrim* = Christians?] and the Minim be destroyed in a moment, and let them be blotted out of the Book of life and not be inscribed together with the righteous. (Martyn)

And for slanderers let there be no hope, and let all wickedness perish as in a moment; let all thine enemies be speedily cut off, and the dominion of arrogance do thou uproot and crush, cast down and humble speedily in our days. Blessed art thou, O Lord, who breakest the enemies and humblest the arrogant. (Singer)

Although the term ἀποσυνάγωγος ("cast out of the synagogue") is found only in John 9:22; 12:42; 16:2 in ancient literature, and thus may reflect a local or even peculiarly Johannine phenomenon, it is often generalized and related to the presumed promulgation of the 12th Benediction, *"Birkat Ha-Minim"* (the "blessing/curse against the heretics/separatists") in the late first century CE. This Benediction is part of the main synagogue prayer that came to be called the Eighteen Benedictions. The present form of the prayer represents modifications of many generations.

"No benediction has undergone as many textual variations as this one, some through the natural effect of changing times, and others through censorship. It is most doubtful that we will ever be in a position to recover its original text. Throughout the Middle Ages . . . its beginning is always cited as ולמשומדים, 'To the apostates.' This word has been preserved in only one prayer book still in use, that of Yemen; it is found also in the very rare edition of the Ashkenazic rite, Salonika, 1580, and in Romaniot, but is common in manuscripts. Further, the word מינים, 'sectarians,' from which the benediction's name derives, must also have appeared in it. From the church fathers, it may be conjectured that it also contained the word נוצרים, 'Christians' ['Nazoreans'], which in fact does occur in the Oxford manuscript of Amram. From the eulogy מכניע זדים, 'Who humbles the arrogant,' it may be assumed that similar language occurred also in the body of the petition, and in fact the Sulzberger manuscript of Amram, and Rome, Romaniot, and Yemenite read, 'and may the arrogant kingdom be speedily uprooted in our days, and may the Christians and sectarians instantly perish'" (Ismar Elbogen, *Jewish Liturgy: A Comprehensive History*, trans. Raymond P. Scheindlin, and the 1972 Hebrew edition ed. Joseph Heinemann et al. [Philadelphia & Jerusalem: Jewish Publication Society and Jewish Theological Seminary of America, 5753/1993], 45-46).

The following data may be considered a firm base for interpretation that illuminates New Testament documents:

1) The main structure of the 12th Benediction existed in the first century. It was apparently an addition to the traditional liturgy made during the time of Rabban Gamaliel II, the "Jamnia period" of ca. 80 CE, by Samuel the Small. This part of the liturgy became known as the Eighteen Benedictions.

2) Whether it originally contained the term נוצרים *"nosrim,"* and whether this term means "Nazareans" (Christians) is disputed. The term may have been added later. Even so, Jewish Christians could have readily been included in the מינים *minim.* But if so, the benediction was not directed exclusively at them.

3) Many scholars consider this key evidence for the sharp break between Judaism and Christianity which was supposed to have occurred about the end of the first century CE (e.g. W. D. Davies, *The Setting of the Sermon on the Mount* [Cambridge: Cambridge University Press, 1966], 256-77; J. Louis Martyn, *History and Theology in the Fourth Gospel* [Nashville: Abingdon, rev. ed., 1979], pp. 50-62).

4) The prayer probably reflects the tensions between synagogue and emerging church in the time and place of the Gospel of John and the Gospel of Matthew (not necessarily the same locale), but should not be generalized. "Jewish scholars in general deny not that Christians were here and there expelled from synagogues, but that the creation of this prayer reflected a universal, mandatory expulsion; such a conclusion exceeds the evidence" (Samuel Sandmel, *Judaism and Christian Beginnings* [Oxford: Oxford University Press, 1970], p. 438). (Cf. also John 9:22, 34.) Cf. P. W. van der Horst, "The Birkat ha-minim in Recent Research," *Expository Times* (1994), 363-68. Cf. further no. 304 above.

471. John 17:1, 5

Magical Papyrus *PGM* 7.500-504 (3 cent. CE)

Protect me, great and marvelous names of the great god [add the usual]. ASAO EIO NISAOTH. Lady Isis, Nemesis, Adrasteia, many-named, many-formed, glorify me, as I have glorified the name of your son Horus. (Betz)

On the identification of Isis, Nemesis, and Adrasteia, see Griffiths, *The Isis-Book* 153-54. Although the final sentence seems parallel to John 17:4-5, there is no Christian influence here (so Morton Smith, trans.).

It is not unusual in prayers (cf. Matt 6:12*b*) for the advance concessions or achievements to be brought forward as a means of commending oneself, in order that the deity might feel the need to respond in kind (cf. Berger, *Formgeschichte*, §§176-77; 265-66). Thus the balance of one's conduct and how one gets along is preserved. Similarly the connection of John 17:1 and 17:4. For service to God (as to Horus) the human being expects a share of God's power and might. On this mutual relation between the deity and humanity cf. also the different uses of the word "bless" in liturgical language. Human beings "bless" God by honoring and praising him, and God blesses human beings by allowing them to participate in his power.

The following text also concerns "magical" elements in John 17.

472. John 17:6

Magical Papyrus *PGM* 12.92-94 (ca. 300 CE)

I am the one whom you met at the foot of the holy mount and to whom you gave the knowledge of your most great [name], which knowledge will I even keep in sanctity, imparting it to no one save the very initiates into your own holy mysteries. IARBATHATRA MNEPSIBAO/CHNEMEOPS. Come! Submit to this service and be my assistant. (Betz)

Revelation of the secret name of divine beings was not only an element of biblical and Jewish tradition (e.g. Exod 3:13-15), but a common element of Hellenistic religion as well.

473. John 19:2-3

Philo, *Flaccus* 36-39 (50 CE)

There was a certain lunatic named Carabas, whose madness was not of the fierce and savage kind, which is dangerous both to the madmen themselves and those who approach them, but of the easy-going, gentler style. He spent day and night in the streets naked, shunning neither heat nor cold, made game of by the children and the lads who were idling about. The rioters drove the poor fellow into the gymnasium and set him up on high to be seen of all and put on his head a sheet of byblus spread out wide for a diadem, clothed the rest of his body with a rug for a royal robe, while someone who had noticed a piece of the native papyrus thrown away in the road gave it to him for his scepter. And when as in some theatrical farce he had received the insignia of kingship and had been tricked out as a king, young men carrying rods on their shoulders as spearmen stood on either side of him in imitation of a bodyguard. Then others approached him, some pretending to salute him, others to sue for justice, others to consult him on state affairs. Then from the multitudes standing round him there rang out a tremendous shout hailing him as Marin, which is said to be the name for "lord" in Syria. For they knew that Agrippa was both a Syrian by birth and had a great piece of Syria over which he was king. (LCL)

As in John and the other Gospels (Mark 15:17-20; Matt 27:28-31; cf. Luke 23:11), the mockery is not aimed at the victim alone, who is used to insult another. In the case of Philo, a Jewish insult to Agrippa; in the Gospels, a Roman insult to the Jews.

474. John 19:9

Maximus of Tyre, *Lectures* III, "Whether Socrates Did Right in Not Defending Himself" (125–185 CE)

. . . and when the eleven asked him, he proffered his body, for he was weaker than the bodies of many, but he did not offer his soul, for he was stronger than all the Athenians, nor was he angry at the servant, nor was he gloomy at the sight of the poison. Rather: the Athenians' action in condemning him was not the action of free men, but his own act in dying was the act of a free man. That it was an expression of his own freedom proves that, although it was possible for him to compensate for his offense with money and to flee, when he considered getting himself off the hook in some clandestine manner he preferred to die. . . . For what and on what grounds should Socrates have defended himself before those Athenians? Could he have done it before the judges? But they were unjust. Before intelligent people? But they were in fact unreasonable. Before good people? But they were corrupt. Before the "better" people? But they were even worse. Before those that were worse, then? But how can a good man ever defend himself before those worse than he is? . . . Who could stand to have Socrates stand before such a court—lowly and oppressed and dependent on others for his hope to live? For this would be his defense, in some form or other. Or if he were forced to speak, then it would not be anything humble as though he were subjected to others, but something free and worthy of philosophy. But then you are not talking about a defense, but an eruption of anger and passion . . . (MEB/Berger from Hobein, ed.)

Cf. also the brief note in Philostratus (beginning of 3 cent. CE), in *Life of Apollonius* 8.2: "I am sure that silence constitutes a fourth excellence much required in a law-court." Socrates too found it useful over against the Athenians to which it was responded, "And what good did it do him . . . seeing that he died just because he would say nothing?" (LCL). Thus in New Testament times there was a developed tradition of Socrates' silence before the court. The passages most often cited by commentaries on this passage do not refer explicitly to a forensic situation. Is there here an element of post-Socratic tradition? Does Jesus conduct himself like a philosopher, in the popular understanding? Would that be an additional argument for the age of the Johannine report and its internal writing style?

475. John 19:11

Ethiopian-Jewish Falasha writing *Te'ezaza Sanbat* (1–2 cent. CE)

Nimrod said to him [Abraham], "Come, let us worship this idol." Abraham refused [and said], "My God is in heaven. It is He who has created the sun, the moon, the heavens, and the earth. He who appoints thee king is in heaven." (Leslau)

In the confrontation with earthly powers Jewish and Christians regularly appeal to the overarching kingship of God. Monotheism here functions as a critical principle for dealing with authorities (cf. also 4 Macc 12:11, "You profane tyrant, most impious of all the wicked, since you have received good things and also your kingdom from God . . ." NRSV). (Cf. Berger, "Hellenistische Gattungen," 1251-55.)

476. John 19:10-11

Epictetus, *Discourses* 1.2.19-21 (55–135 CE)

[On the conflict between Helvidius and the emperor Vespasian:] When Vespasian sent him [Helvidius Priscus] word not to attend a meeting of the Senate, he answered, "It is in your power not to allow me to be a member of the Senate, but so long as I am one I must attend its meetings." "Very well then, but when you attend, hold your peace." "Do not ask for my opinion and I will hold my peace." "But I must ask for your opinion." "And I must answer what seems to me right." "But if you speak, I shall put you to death." "Well, when did I ever tell you that I was immortal? You will do your part and I mine. It is yours to put me to death, mine to die without a tremor; yours to banish, mine to leave without sorrow." (LCL)

For the Cynics, it is the uninhibited manner and evident freedom of Helvidius over against the emperor that is important about this tradition, and a model for their own ideal of conduct. A similar unselfconscious naturalness is also characteristic of Jesus' tone over against Pilate in 18:36-37; 19:10-11. In pagan texts and in the later acts of the martyrs, this tone is increased to a real impudence. (Cf. Berger, "Hellenistische Gattungen," 1251-55.)

477. John 19:35

Lucian, *A True Story* 1.4 (120–185 CE)

I am writing about things which I have neither seen or had to do with nor learned from others—which, in fact, do not exist at all and, in the nature of things, cannot exist. Therefore my readers should on no account believe in them. (LCL)

W. Ameling, "Evangelium Johannis 19, 35: Ein aretalogisches Motiv," ZPE 60 (1985), 25-34, has show that this text, as an ironic expression (Lucian writes stories that are lies!) can represent a traditional aretalogical motif, as is also present in John 19:35 (though Paul D. Duke, *Irony in the Fourth Gospel* [Atlanta: John Knox Press, 1985], does not treat this passage). He also refers to the conclusion of the Enosh Apocalypse in the Cologne Mani Codex (CMC 55:5-6): "For everything that he heard and saw he copied down and left behind for all those reborn of the Spirit of Truth" (MEB/Berger).

478. John 20:16

Plutarch, *Moralia*, "On the Sign of Socrates" 22 (45–125 CE)

[Timarch reports on the oracle of Trophonius; there are numerous formal elements of a visionary dialogue with the *angelus interpres* as the guide through the underworld.] When the voice [of the guide] ceased Timarchus desired to turn [he said] and see who the speaker was. But once more he felt a sharp pain in his head, as though it had been violently compressed, and he lost all recognition and awareness of what was going on about him; but he presently recovered . . . (LCL)

In John 20:16, Revelation 1:12, and in the Plutarch text (also no. 504), the coming to himself or herself of the receiver of the vision is the decisive act, which is to lead to the knowledge of the person with whom he or she speaks. Analogously, ancient art also frequently depicts that at the appearance of the god the human figure must turn. This aspect of the formation of the vision report is of Greek origin. According to Plutarch, *Life of Numa*, §14, Numa prescribed that when one prays to the gods, one should turn around and then be seated (with symbolic justification for this procedure). Demons prefer to attack from the rear (F. J. Dölger, *Ichthys* II [Münster: Aschendorf, 1922], p. 105).

479. John 20:19

Homeric Hymns, Hymn to Hermes 145-46 (prior to 7 cent. BCE)

Then Hermes, son of Zeus, bearer of boon, bowed his head, and entered the hall through the hole of the bolt, like mist on the breath of autumn. (Lang)

The Hermes-hymn attempts to make the event comprehensible, in contrast to John 20. The idea that the story could portray some kind of bodiless spirit then must be disposed of by the challenge in 20:27.

480. John 20:22

Wisdom of Solomon 15:11 (150 BCE–50 CE)

. . . because they failed to know the one who formed them and inspired them with active souls, and breathed a living spirit into them. (NRSV)

This is illuminating for the Johannine text in that it shows in Hellenistic Judaism the creative act of God's breathing the spirit/breath (both πνεῦμα and רוח mean both "spirit" and "breath" as well as "wind"; cf. John 3:3-5) into human beings at creation was associated with Σοφία = Λόγος. But in contrast to Wisdom of Solomon, the Fourth Gospel uses this vocabulary of Christ's regenerative act for believers, not the universal act of creation. In Wisdom of Solomon, Wisdom breathes (natural) life into all people, even the idolaters who do not recognize God's Wisdom. Thus though the vocabulary is similar, the theology is different. Cf. Philo, "Creation," 135: ". . . for that which He breathed in was nothing else than a Divine breath [πνευμα θειον]" (LCL), showing that the Holy Spirit and God's creative "breathing into" humanity were already related in Hellenistic Judaism.

481. John 20:28

Inscription from Egypt (24 BCE)

. . . the God and Lord Soknopaios . . . (MEB)

John's "My Lord and my God" directed to Jesus reflects the LXX, where it represents יהוה אלהים *Yahweh Elohim* and similar expressions, but also makes contact with an expression fairly common in pagan religion. (Cf. G. Deissmann, *Light from the Ancient East* [New York: George H. Doran, Co., 1927], pp. 366-67; Barrett, *Gospel According to St. John* 572; H. D. Betz, *Lukian von Samosata und das Neue Testament* [Leiden: E. J. Brill, 1961], p. 102.)

482. John 20:29

Plato, *Theaetetus* 155e (428–349 BCE)

[Socrates pictures the uninitiated.] The uninitiated are those who think nothing is except what they can grasp firmly with their hands, and who deny the existence of actions and generation and all that is invisible. (LCL)

Still more sharply, Corpus Hermeticum 4:9: "Visible things delight us, but the invisible cause mistrust. Bad things are the more open to sight, but the good is invisible to what can be seen" (Copenhaver). Bultmann, *Gospel of John*, 697, cites both passages for support of his exegesis of John 20:29, and attempts to interpret the passages in a Platonic sense. Meanwhile, he illustrates how exegesis in the idealistic tradition (Kant) can use older materials to support its point of view in a somewhat circular manner. Is this text really concerned to denigrate everything that is visible, including all the signs in the Fourth Gospel? Is Thomas really blamed? Is not his seeing a valuable and necessary witness for all who can no longer see for themselves? In short, one must ask whether the bringing in of analogies has not in fact blocked the view for an appropriate exegesis.

Cf. Jude 10, φυσικῶς, *physikos* (merely) on a natural basis, NRSV "by instinct."

483. John 20:30

Aelius Aristides, *Orations* 45, on the deeds of Serapis (117–187 CE)

It is he who has revealed the much sought after light of the sun to observers, whose sacred chests contain an infinite number of sacred books. The marketplaces are full, as they say, and the harbors, and the plazas of the cities with those who recount his individual acts. But if I shall try to tell them, an endless influx of days will find the catalog equally incomplete. For his deeds have not stopped, nor is their number what it was in the past, but every day and every night new ones are added. (Behr)

Similar conclusions to books are typical for laudatory presentations of great figures (on encomia, cf. Berger, *Formgeschichte,* §70:5) and have the function of making it appear impossible to do justice to the fame and number of deeds of the hero. Similarly 21:25. In terms of form criticism there is thus a certain similarity between encomium and Gospel on this point (cf. ibid., §§99-100).

484. John 21:25

Valerius Alexandria of Harpocration, *On the Powers of Nature* (2 cent. CE)

[At the conclusion of his essay on the vine:] If we were now to say all that could be said about this plant, an entire book would not be sufficient. (MEB/Berger)

This text documents that this kind of concluding expression was quite common in both Jewish and Greek literature (e.g. Exod. Rab. 30:22; Philo, *Cain.* 144; 1 Macc 9:22) and could find its way even into remote areas of epideictic literature (on the genre, cf. Berger, *Formgeschichte,* §§63-102). Cf. e.g. Porphyry, *Life of Pythagoras* 29 (234–305 CE) (after recounting a traditional list of the miracles connected with Pythagoras): "Ten thousand other things yet more marvelous and more divine are told about the man, and told uniformly in stories that agree with each other. To put it bluntly, about no one else have greater and more extraordinary things been believed" (Martin). Cf. also no. 483.

The Acts of the Apostles

485. Acts 1:9-11

Dio Cassius, *Roman History* Book 56.46 (end of 2, beginning of 3 cent. CE)

[About Augustus:] At the time they [these rumors] declared Augustus immortal, assigned to him priests and sacred rites, and made Livia, who was already called Julia and Augusta, his priestess; they also permitted her to employ a lictor when she exercised her sacred office. On her part, she bestowed a million sesterces upon a certain Numerius Atticus, a senator and ex-praetor, because he swore that he had seen Augustus ascending to heaven after the manner of which tradition tells concerning Proculus and Romulus. (LCL)

Cf. the reports of the ascensions of Romulus and Hercules in nos. 215, 217, 219. In stories of such ascensions, the clouds of heaven regularly play a role.

Witnesses to the ascension belong to the established ritual of the apotheosis of the Roman emperors. The question to be asked is, to what extent was Luke aware of Roman traditions and traditions about Hercules of this sort and wanted intentionally to juxtapose to them their Jewish-Christian counterparts (cf. also no. 407). (In the story of the ascent of Elijah, the presence of Elisha as witness is important [cf. 2 Kgs 2:10], but that is a relatively small element in the Jewish tradition as a whole.) Like its Roman counterparts, the Jewish-Christian picture too is associated with a universal empire (Acts 1:3*b*, 8).

Lucian of Samosata (120–185 CE) describes in ironic fashion the staged self-immolation of Peregrinus Proteus (ch. 39):

"I would thicken the plot a bit on my own account, saying that when the pyre was kindled and Proteus flung himself bodily in, a great earthquake first took place, accompanied by a bellowing of the ground, and then a vulture, flying up out of the midst of the flames, went off to Heaven, saying, in human speech, with a loud voice:

'I am through with the earth; to Olympus I fare.'

They were wonder-struck and blessed themselves with a shudder" (LCL).

486. Acts 2:6

Iranian eschatology according to Plutarch, *Moralia*, "Isis and Osiris" 47 (45–125 CE)

But a destined time shall come when it is decreed that Areimanius, engaged in bringing on pestilence and famine, shall by these be utterly annihilated and shall disappear; and then shall the earth become a level plain, and there shall be one manner of life and one form of government for a blessed people who shall all speak one tongue [ὁμόγλωσσος]. (LCL)

On the way in which it was precisely Alexander the Great who was the one who fulfilled these expectations, cf. on Ephesians 2, no. 787, as well as no. 441. On Ahriman, cf. no. 710 (at end).

In the Pentecost story, of course, a common language is not established, but still the Spirit gives the "guarantee" that everything is rightly understood. Neither is the glossalalia previously effected by the Spirit a universal language, since in any case it requires translation or miraculous understanding. Though the Pentecost narrative belongs within the series of portrayals of ideal beginnings in Acts, there are both similarities to and differences from the utopian novel of Jambulos (3 cent. BCE; in part preserved in Diodorus of Sinope 2.55-60). The similarity is that the novel deals with an island people in the East where utopian conditions prevail. Their tongues are able to articulate every sound and every language. "They can speak perfectly with each half of the tongue at the same time." The difference is that in the novel the ability is based on anatomy (while in Luke it is a special gift of the Spirit). Or has Plutarch (in the above reference) taken up features of that sort of utopian novel?

On Acts 2:9-11, cf. the lists of nations the Romans received into citizenship in Dionysius of Halicarnassus, *Roman Antiquities* 1.60.3 and 1.89.2-3, and cf. no. 528 at Acts 10:28 below.

487. Acts 2:11-13

Lucian of Samosata, *Alexander the False Prophet* 13 (120–185 CE)

[Alexander had secretly prepared a deception by depositing an egg in which he had placed a small snake at the base of a newly constructed temple, which he then "finds" and presents as the god Asclepius. Before doing this, he assembles a crowd and speaks of the imminent good fortune of the city that was about to receive the god in visible presence.] The assembly—for almost the whole city, including women, old men, and boys, had come running—marveled, prayed and made obeisance. Uttering a few meaningless words like Hebrew or Phoenician, he dazed the creatures, who did not know what he was saying save only that he everywhere brought in Apollo and Asclepius. (LCL)

Lucian's observation about prayers of magicians and prophets is confirmed by numerous prayer texts among the papyri: the language has a "Hebrew" ring, and is sometimes explicitly so labeled (cf. nos. 471, 472 above; Martyrdom of Paul, §5; Hennecke-Schneemelcher 2:267), the names of gods are preserved, since they of course have magical power. Hebraic elements are also preserved in Christian prayers (amen, halleluia), since this is the holy language by which one may approach God. So too, texts from the *Testament of Job* (see on 1 Cor 14, no. 701) could confirm the thesis that the glossalalia of early Christianity should not be interpreted in terms of the modern phenomenon, i.e. as though early Christians thought of them as untranslatable utterances that are elements of no language, earthly or heavenly. Rather, *Testament of Job* would suggest that while glossalalia were not human languages, they were regarded as the (translatable, "Hebraic") language of the angels (imitation of the Hebrew, as Indian is imitated in "abracadabra"?). Because this is the language by which one may approach God, glossalalia in Acts always has a kind of initiatory function, it is a kind of identity card or ticket which validates an entrance. In place of Hebrew, the same function could be exercised by Aramaic/Syriac (*Syr Treasury* [*Ginza*] 24:10-12).

488. Acts 2:11-13

Philo, *On the Decalogue*, 33, 46-47 (15 BCE–50 CE)

I should suppose that God wrought on this occasion a miracle of a truly holy kind by bidding an invisible sound to be created in the air more marvelous than all instruments and fitted with perfect harmonies, not soulless, nor yet composed of body and soul like a living creature, but a rational soul full of clearness and distinctness, which giving shape and tension to the air and changing it to flaming fire, sounded forth like the breath through a trumpet an articulate voice so loud that it appeared to be equally audible to the farthest as well as the nearest. . . . Then from the midst of the fire that streamed from heaven there sounded forth to their utter amazement a voice, for the flame became articulate speech in the language familiar to the audience, and so clearly and distinctly were the words formed by it that they seemed to see rather than hear them. What I say is vouched for by the law in which it is written, "All the people saw the voice . . ." [Exod 20:18]. (LCL)

In comparison to the Sinai theophany of Exodus 19, Philo's elaboration introduces new elements: (1) a connection between fire, spirit, and voice, (2) in which the "Spirit" is not the Spirit of God, but an independent being, a creature. (3) The passage represents an exposition of Exodus 20:18. Philo attempts to explain the amazing event in which a voice becomes visible.

Differently from Acts 2: (1) Neither is there a linguistic miracle in which people understand a language they have never learned, (2) nor are people "filled" with this phenomenon, (3) nor does it have to do with the Spirit of God (πνεῦμα also means "wind").

The passage does *not* permit us to infer that first-century Judaism celebrated Pentecost as a renewed Sinai event.

On seeing the heavenly voice, cf. Revelation 1:12.

489. Acts 2:23

Chrysippus, *Fragment* 625 (ca. 280–205 BCE)

The Stoics say that when the planets return, at certain fixed periods of time, to the same relative positions, in length and breadth, which they had at the beginning, when the cosmos was first constituted, this produces the conflagration and destruction of everything which exists. Then again the cosmos is restored anew in a precisely similar arrangement as before. The stars again move in their orbits, each performing its revolution in the former period, without any variation. Socrates and Plato and each individual man will live again, with the same friends and fellow citizens. They will go through the same experiences and the same activities. Every city and village and field will be restored, just as it was. And this restoration of the universe takes place not once but over and over again—indeed to all eternity without end. (Bevan)

This understanding of the cyclic view of cosmic history is the presupposition of the foreknowledge of the gods (see next quotation below).

490. Acts 2:23

Chrysippus, *Fragment* 1192 (ca. 280–205 BCE)

If there are gods and they do not declare to men beforehand future events, either (1) they do not love men, or (2) they are themselves ignorant of the future, or (3) they do not consider that it is to man's interest to have knowledge of the future, or (4) they do not think that it sorts with their dignity to foreshow the future to men, or (5) the gods themselves have not the power to do it. But (1) it is not the case that they do not love us, being beneficent and friends of mankind; (2) they cannot be ignorant of things which they themselves have instituted and ordained; (3) it *is* to our interest to know what is going to happen, for we shall act more prudently, if we know; (4) the gods cannot think such disclosure beneath their dignity, for nothing is of higher worth than to do good; and lastly (5) divination regarding the future cannot lie outside their power. To suppose, then, that there are gods and they do not give signs of the future, is impossible. But there are gods. Therefore they must give signs of the future. Further, if they give signs, it cannot be that they give us no means of reading the signs; for in that case they would give signs to no purpose. If they give us the means, we cannot deny the existence of divination. Therefore divination is a reality. (Bevan)

These texts illustrate that there was a broad stream of Hellenistic culture that affirmed that "all things are unfolding as they must," and that benevolent gods had revealed the future for the good of humanity. The New Testament's affirmations that all things are foreordained and foreknown by God, and that God has revealed these events through his prophets, would thus be not an alien idea to those to whom its mission was addressed. Yet this is far different from the New Testament idea of predestination, foreknowledge, and revelation. As C. K. Barrett remarks, this Stoic view that "all things have been predestined by the 'gods' is a popular way of saying [i.e. a way calculated to communicate to the unphilosophical masses] that all things happen in accordance with universal reason" (*New Testament Background,* 69). In Stoicism there is no redemptive plan and purpose executed by the gods, who know the future only because history is cyclical and they have already observed it. On the paradox of human responsibility and divine sovereignty affirmed by Luke, see no. 796 on Philippians 2:12-13, no. 792 on Ephesians 6:14-17, and no. 19 on Matthew 3:7. On the basis for the god's foreknowledge, see no. 490.

491. Acts 2:44

Josephus, *War* 2.122 after 119 (37–100 CE)

[Describing the Essenes:] Riches they despise, and their community of goods is truly admirable; you will not find one among them distinguished by greater opulence than another. They have a law that new members on admission to the sect shall confiscate their property to the order, with the result that you will nowhere see either abject poverty or inordinate wealth; the individual's possessions join the common stock and all, like brothers, enjoy a single patrimony. (LCL)

Josephus has great admiration for the Essenes, and perhaps somewhat idealizes them. He does not say that all of them live in Qumran-like communes. (Philo pictures [some of?] them as living in villages; see *Good Man* 75-80, no. 30 at Matt 5–7). Josephus does not mention the Essenes' repudiation of slavery.

492. Acts 2:44

Aristotle, *Nicomachean Ethics*, 8.9 (384–322 BCE)

The objects and the personal relationships with which friendship is concerned appear, as was said at the outset, to be the same as those which are the sphere of justice. For in every partnership we find mutual rights of some sort, and also friendly feeling: one notes that shipmates and fellow soldiers speak of each other as "my friend," and so in fact do the partners in any joint undertaking. But their friendship is limited to the extent of their association in their common business, for so also are their mutual rights as associates. Again, the proverb says "Friends' goods are common property," and this is correct, since community is the essence of friendship. Brothers have all things in common, and so do members of a comradeship; other friends hold special possessions in common, more or fewer in different cases, inasmuch as friendships vary in degree. (LCL)

The fundamental principle that friends have all things in common is found already in Plato, *Republic* 4.424a, in the context of the ideal state being founded on marriage, family, and the rearing of children. The differing orientation of Plato and Aristotle is seen precisely in their respective applications of this proverb. Aristotle describes the phenomenon of friendship, distinguishing it from other relationships by the use of this proverb, while Plato uses it in the most radical way possible. Luke uses the proverb with reference to possessions, without the concept "friend"; the "ideal" times (though in Luke's view not at all impractical!) lay at the beginning, to which the community already "looks back." Cf. also no. 458.

493. Acts 2:44

Lucian of Samosata, *The Passing of Peregrinus* 13 (120–185 CE)

[Peregrinus had joined the Christians, and they take care of him.] Indeed, people came even from the cities in Asia, sent by the Christians at their common expense, to succor and defend and encourage the hero. They show incredible speed whenever any such public action is taken; for in no time they lavish their all. So it was then in the case of Peregrinus; much money came to him from them by reason of his imprisonment, and he procured not a little revenue from it. The poor wretches have convinced themselves, first and foremost, that they are going to be immortal and live for all time, in consequence of which they despise death and even willingly give themselves into custody, most of them. Furthermore, their first lawgiver persuaded them that they are all brothers of one another after they have transgressed once for all by denying the Greek gods and by worshiping that crucified sophist himself and living under his laws. Therefore they despise all things indiscriminately and consider them common property, receiving such doctrines traditionally without any definite evidence. So if any charlatan and trickster, able to profit by occasions, comes among them, he quickly acquires sudden wealth by imposing upon simple folk. (LCL)

Lucian pictures the relationships among Christians—seen from Luke's perspective—as relatively intact in the late second century. Acts 2:45 likewise presents the community of goods not as a true communism, but as a fellowship in which no one is impoverished in time of need. Differently, Plutarch, *Sayings of Spartans:* Leon 1.

494. Acts 4:19; 5:29

Plato, *Apology* 29 C-D (428/27–349/48 BCE)

[Socrates to his Athenian judges:] . . . if you should say to me in reply to this: "Socrates, this time we will not do as Anytus says, but we will let you go, on this condition, however, that you no longer spend your time in this investigation or in philosophy, and if you are caught doing so again you shall die"; if you should let me go on this condition which I have mentioned, I should say to you, "Men of Athens, I respect and love you, but I shall obey the god rather than you, and while I live and am able to continue I shall never give up philosophy, or stop exhorting you and pointing out the truth to any one of you whom I may meet . . ." (LCL)

In another connection: Sophocles, *Antigone* 453-55:
Creon
"And yet wert bold enough to break the law?"
Antigone
"Yea, for these laws were not ordained of Zeus,
And she who sits enthroned with gods below,
Justice, enacted not these human laws.
Nor did I deem that thou, a mortal man,
Could'st by a breath annul and override
The immutable unwritten laws of Heaven" (LCL).
(Human laws must be just or they become a "species of violence.")
To the history of the effects of this passage from Plato *(Wirkungsgeschichte)* there belongs also the "Letter of Socrates" 1 (ca. 200 CE):
"God has appointed me to this task. I am then pretty well hated because of this, but he whom one must rather obey does not allow me to withdraw" (Malherbe).
Cf. also the "Letter of Diogenes" 34, §3 (free under Father Zeus, not afraid of any of the mighty rulers of this world); the Christian *Acta Acacii* 3.5 ("You are obligated to serve a human being . . . how much more am I obligated to serve the almighty God"). Cf. also Josephus, *Antiquities* 4.121-23 (Balaam). On Musonius, cf. above nos. 264, 325.
On Acts 5:37, cf. no. 160.

495. Acts 4:31

Virgil, *Aeneid* **3.84-89 (70–19 BCE)**

I was paying homage to the god's temple, . . . "Grant, father, an omen, and inspire our hearts!" Scarcely had I thus spoken, when suddenly it seemed all things trembled, the doors and laurels of the god; the whole hill shook round about and the tripod moaned as the shrine was thrown open. Prostrate we fall to earth, and a voice comes to our ears . . . (LCL)

Again the scene of the revelatory event itself, thus certainly the central core of the encounter with the deity, is portrayed with Hellenistic-pagan imagery, here in the series prayer-earthquake-hearing of the prayer.

496. Acts 5:1-11

1QS 6:24-25 (1 cent. BCE)

If one of them has lied deliberately in matters of property, he shall be excluded from the pure meal of the congregation for one year and shall do penance with respect to one quarter of his food. (Vermes)

The Lucan story not only reflects the biblical account of Joshua 7:1-26, using the same word for the offense (νοσφίζω, "misappropriate," "embezzle"), but the actual practice of the Qumran community. Cf. also the account of Diodorus Siculus 5.34.3 in which the Vaccaei, a Celtic community, imposed the death penalty on a member of the group who had held back some of the crops that had been declared common property. Luke's story differs from all of them, however, in that the fatal blow is struck by the deity rather than by human hands, even if at the divine command as in Joshua 7.

497. Acts 6:1

Testament of Job **10:1–11:4 (Hellenistic-Jewish; 1 cent. BCE–1 cent. CE)**

And I established in my house thirty tables spread at all hours, for strangers only. I also used to maintain twelve other tables set for the widows. When any stranger approached to ask alms, he was required to be fed at my table before he would receive his need. Neither did I allow anyone to go out of my door with an empty pocket.

I used to have 3,500 yoke of oxen. And I chose from them 500 yoke and designated them for plowing, which they could do in any field of those who would use them. And I marked off their produce for the poor, for their table. I also used to have fifty bakeries from which I arranged for the ministry of the table for the poor.

There were also certain strangers who saw my eagerness, and they too desired to assist in this service. And there were still others, at the time without resources and unable to invest a thing, who came and entreated me, saying, "We beg you, may we also engage in this service. We own nothing, however. Show mercy on us and lend us money so we may leave for distant cities on business and be able to do the poor a service. And afterward we shall repay you what is yours." (*OTP* 1:843)

This text not only proposes a program, but—especially with its ambitions in the realm of technical financial arrangements—presupposes a welfare program organized in a grand style, and experience with such arrangements. As in Acts 6 there are tables for widows, and as there the whole administration is called *diakonia*. In this text Job is a Gentile who has converted to Judaism, so in Luke's understanding would belong to the "Hellenists." Cf. also no. 346.

498. Acts 6:9

Inscription from Jerusalem (ca. 50 CE [?])

Theodotus, son of Vettenus, priest and archisynagogue [ἀρχισυνάγογος, "president of the synagogue"], son of an archisynagogue, and grandson of an archisynagogue ["presidents of synagogues"], built the synagogue for the reading of the Law and the teaching of the commandments, and the guest-house and the rooms and the water supplies as an inn for those who have need when they come from abroad; which [synagogue] his fathers founded and the elders and Simonides. (Lake and Jackson)

The inscription is not dated, but it is unlikely that such an inscription originated after the destruction of Jerusalem in 70 CE. Paleography seems to confirm a mid–first century CE date. That the founder and leader of the synagogue was a priest indicates that, though Pharisees, a lay movement, were the dominant synagogue leaders, priests also assumed leadership roles, and should not be restricted to the orbit of the temple.

That the inscription is in Greek shows the cosmopolitan nature of first-century Jerusalem (cf. John 19:20) and may indicate that this synagogue was founded for "Hellenists," Greek-speaking Diaspora Jews who had settled in Jerusalem. The attached guest-house was probably for the convenience of pilgrims from the Diaspora during the festivals.

The "president of the synagogue" is the same office mentioned in Mark 5:22 and elsewhere. Theodotus was a Greek name, indicating he was himself a Diaspora Jew, and the Latin Vettenus may indicate he was a freed slave, since slaves often took the name of their former masters. This inscription thus likely comes from the kind of synagogue described in Acts 6:9, if not from the very building. On one who builds a synagogue for the local population, see Luke 7:5.

499. Acts 7:48-49

Zeno of Citium, according to Clement of Alexandria, *Stromata* 5.11.76 (336–264 BCE)

Zeno, the founder of the Stoic sect, says in this book of the *Republic*, "that we ought to make neither temples nor images; for that no work is worthy of the gods." And he was not afraid to write in these very words: "There will be no need to build temples. For a temple is not worth much, and ought not to be regarded as holy. For nothing is worth much, and holy, which is the work of builders and mechanics." (ANF)

Cf. also Plutarch, *Moralia*, "Tranquillity of Mind," 20 (45–125 CE): "For the universe is a most holy temple and most worthy of a god; into it man is introduced through birth as a spectator, not of hand-made or immovable images, but of those sensible representations of knowable things that the divine mind, says Plato, has revealed, representations which have innate within themselves the beginnings of life and motion, sun and moon and stars, rivers which ever discharge fresh water, and earth which sends forth nourishment for plants and animals." (LCL)

500. Acts 7:48-50

Strabo, *Geography* 16.35, 37 (64/63 BCE–23 CE)

For he [Moses] said, and taught, that the Aegyptians were mistaken in representing the Divine being by the images of beasts and cattle, as were also the Libyans; and that the Greeks were also wrong in modeling gods in human form; for, according to him, God is this one thing alone that encompasses us all and encompasses land and sea—the thing which we call heaven, or universe, or the nature of all that exists.

His successors for some time abided by the same course, acting righteously and being truly pious toward God; but afterward, in the first place, superstitious men were appointed to the priesthood, and then tyrannical people; and from superstition arose abstinence from flesh, from which it is their custom to abstain even today, and circumcisions and excisions and other observances of the kind. And from the tyrannies arose the bands of robbers . . . (LCL)

Strabo develops here a theory of degeneration—possibly developed in Judaism itself—according to which visible rituals first emerged after Moses under the influence of superstition. Stephen advocates a very similar position with regard to the temple (cf. also Plato in part, according to nos. 368, 401). Acts 7:49 advocates a position regarding Moses similar even in vocabulary to that of Strabo regarding idols. Neither the rejection of the temple by Stephen nor the rejection of rituals by Strabo is a violation of the letter of the Law. Cf. also M. Klinghardt, *Das Gesetz in der Theologie des Lukas* (Tübingen: J. C. B. Mohr [Paul Siebeck], 1986).

501. Acts 7:48-50

Pseudo-Philo, *Liber Antiquitatum Biblicarum* 22:5-6 (1 cent. BCE–1 cent. CE)

And Joshua said, "Is not the Lord the King more powerful than a thousand sacrifices? And why have you not taught your sons the words of the Lord that you heard from us? For if your sons had been meditating upon the Law of the Lord, their mind would not have been led astray after an altar made by hand. Or do you not know that when the people were left alone for a while in the wilderness, when Moses went up to receive the tablets, their mind was led astray and they made idols for themselves. And so now, go and dig up the altars that you have built for yourselves, and teach your sons the Law and have them *meditate on it day and night.*" (*OTP* 2:331)

From Joshua 22 comes a text against the temple, because it is made by human hands. As in Acts 7:41 this is illustrated with material from the story of the golden calf. As in Acts 7:53 (cf. differently vv. 51-52), a contrast is drawn between cult and keeping the Law. Only the latter is really important. This text from Pseudo-Philo is therefore an example from contemporary Judaism that stands near the position of the Lucan Hellenists.

502. Acts 8:9-10

Inscription from Lydia (1–3 cent. CE)

The great God of Heaven is one. The heavenly Mēn [Μήν] is the great Power of the immortal God. (MEB/from E. Lane, *Corpus Monumentorum Religionis Dei Menis* [Leiden: E. J. Brill, 1971], 55)

Mēn is, as the name indicates, a moon god, at first widely accepted in Anatolia, then also in Greece, a god of slaves; often found together with the "mother" goddess of the city. The inscription is both an acclamation intended to pay homage to the deity, and an invocation at the same time. Formally, it is similar to 1 Corinthians 8:6 (Father God and κύριος, Lord), in that alongside the first-named deity a second figure of lesser rank is named, who represents him and reveals him. Like Mēn, so Simon Magus is also called "the Great Power." Thereby nothing other is claimed for himself than what is affirmed about Jesus with the *kurios* title, the claim to be representative and exclusive revealer of God. Cf. H. G. Kippenberg, *Garizim und Synagogue* (Berlin: de Gruyter, 1971), pp. 328-49. See also Lane, *Corpus Monumentorum,* 17-38, 76-79, 95.

503. Acts 8:26-40

Wisdom of Solomon 3:14 (150 BCE–50 CE)

Blessed also is the eunuch whose hands have done no lawless deed,
and who has not devised wicked things against the Lord;
for special favor will be shown him for his faithfulness,
and a place of great delight in the temple of the Lord. (NRSV)

The Mosaic legislation prohibited those who had been castrated from participation in the covenant life of Israel (Deut 23:1). The postexilic prophet III Isaiah had promised that in the time of eschatological salvation, eunuchs would be welcomed in the house of God (Isa 56:3-5). Wisdom of Solomon here reaffirms this an eschatological promise. In Luke's story, a pious Gentile eunuch, excluded from the empirical temple in Jerusalem but nevertheless visiting its precincts and reading the Hebrew Scriptures as he returns, is welcomed into the eschatological community in which the promises are fulfilled. The story stands in the tradition of III Isaiah and Wisdom of Solomon.

504. Acts 9:1-9

Letter of Hippocrates 15 (1 cent. BCE)

In that night . . . I had a dream, from which, I believe, nothing dangerous will come. But I woke up terrified, for I thought I saw Asclepius himself, and he came near to me. . . . But Asclepius did not look as he usually does in pictures, gentle and mild, but his gestures were wild and quite terrible to behold. Dragons followed behind him . . . but the god stretched out his hand to me, and I took it and asked him to heal me and not to leave me. However, he said, "At the moment you need nothing from me, but this goddess . . . will lead you. . . ." So I turned around and saw a large woman, with a simple hairdo, splendidly clothed. Pure light streamed forth from the pupils of her eyes, like lightning from stars. And the god withdrew from me, but the woman grasped my hand. . . . As she then turned around, I said, "Please tell me who you are and how I should address you." She replied, "'Truth' . . . which you see appearing: 'shine.' . . ." (MEB/Berger from Herscher, 296)

This text illustrates that a variety of NT vision reports are constructed on a base of widespread traditional material. (On the genre, cf. Berger, *Formgeschichte*, §75; Berger, *Auferstehung*, 153-70.) Here the following traits are important: (1) One vision fades into another, with the turning oneself around standing between them and linking them (cf. John 20:14). (2) The question "Who are you? . . . I am" corresponds to Acts 9:5 (cf. also Philostratus in no. 7 and 418; Berger, *Auferstehung*, 439-44). (3) The portrayal of the appearance of the manifestation corresponds to Acts 16:9, just as does the nocturnal dream vision. Cf. in addition esp. the beginning of the *Shepherd of Hermas* with this text; see also nos. 464-65.

505. Acts 9:7; 22:9

Targum of Pseudo-Jonathan on Genesis 22:10 (1 cent. BCE–3 cent. CE)

The eyes of Abraham were looking at the eyes of Isaac, and the eyes of Isaac were looking at the angels on high. Isaac saw them but Abraham did not see them. (Maher)

As in the Bible (e.g. Num 22:22-35), the Jewish tradition knows of visionary phenomena that are visible or audible to some but not to others. The categories "subjective" and "objective" would be anachronistic.

506. Acts 9:12

Inscription from Epidaurus (late 4 cent. CE)

XXI. Arate of Laconia, dropsy. For this, her mother slept, while she herself was in Lakadaimon, and had a dream: it seemed to her that the god cut off her daughter's head in order to hang the body upside down. After much liquid had drained out, he returned the body to the upright position and restored the head to its place. After she had seen the dream, she returned to Lakadaimon and found her daughter well. The daughter had seen the same dream. (MEB/from Leipold and Grundmann)

In the New Testament too (but only in Acts, cf. 10:9-22; 11:5-14), the divine origin of the event is authenticated by the corroboration of dream or vision testimony given independently to two different persons. The content of the Epidaurus text and the Acts texts is very different; the pattern and presuppositions are the same.

507. Acts 10:2; 13:16, 26

Inscription from Aphrodisias (ca. 200 CE)

Emmonius, a Godfearer (θεοσεβής)
Antoninus, a Godfearer
Samuel son of Politanus
Joseph son of Eusebius, a proselyte. (MEB)

At Aphrodisias, in the Roman province of Asia about 30 miles west of Colossae, two stone tablets have recently been found, erected early in the third century CE apparently as a memorial to those who had helped the community during a period of distress. Since the meaning of the opening lines of the inscription is disputed, no translation of the whole inscription is attempted here. The list distinguishes Jews, proselytes, and "Godfearers" (θεοσεβείς). While the interpretation is not clear, the latter group apparently corresponds to the σεβόμενοι of Acts, i.e. to interested and supportive Gentiles who formed a penumbra around the synagogue community without becoming Jewish proselytes. See L. H. Feldman, "Proselytes and 'Sympathizers' in the Light of the New Inscriptions from Aphrodisia," *REJ* 148 (1989), 265-305. For the complete Greek text and discussion, see J. Reynolds and R. Tannenbaum, *Jews and Godfearers at Aphrodisias: Greek Inscriptions with Commentary* (Cambridge: Cambridge University Press, 1987).

508. Acts 10:28

Dionysius of Halicarnassus, *Roman Antiquities* 1.89.1-90.1 (taught 30–38 CE in Rome)

. . . it is at once the most hospitable and friendly of all cities, and when he bears in mind that the Aborigines were Oenotrians, and these in turn Arcadians, and remembers those who joined with them in their settlement, the Pelasgians who were Argives by descent and came into Italy from Thessaly; and recalls, moreover, the arrival of Evander and of the Arcadians, who settled round the Palatine hill, after the Aborigines had granted the place to them; and also the Peloponnesians, who, coming along with Hercules, settled upon the Saturnian hill; and, last of all, those who left the Troad and were intermixed with the earlier settlers. For one will find no nation that is more ancient or more Greek than these. But the admixtures of the barbarians with the Romans, by which the city forgot many of its ancient institutions, happened at a later time. And it may well seem a cause of wonder to many who reflect on the natural course of events that Rome did not become entirely the Samnites, the Tyrrhenians, the Bruttians and many thousands of Umbrians, Ligurians, Iberians and Gauls, besides innumerable other nations, some of whom came from Italy itself and some from other regions and differed from one another both in their language and habits; for their very ways of life, diverse as they were and thrown into turmoil by such dissonance, might have been expected to cause many innovations in the ancient order of the city. For many others by living among barbarians have in a short time forgotten all their Greek heritage, so that they neither speak the Greek language nor observe the customs of the Greeks nor acknowledge the same gods nor have the same equitable laws (by which most of all the spirit of the Greeks differs from that of the barbarians) nor agree with them in anything else whatever that relates to the ordinary intercourse of life. Those Achaeans who are settled near the Euxine sea are a sufficient proof of my contention; for, though originally Eleans, of a nation the most Greek of any, they are now the most savage of all barbarians. (LCL)

"Mixing" of peoples is a positive value in Dionysius, who reflects the Roman point of view: the Empire's power presided over something of a melting-pot that was inherent in the Roman ideology. They ruled by "mixing." But "mixing" with other races was a violation of the Jewish understanding of their mission to be a "peculiar people." Cf. 1 Esdras 8:70-71, 86-87: "For they and their descendants have married the daughters of these people, and the holy race has been mixed with the alien peoples of the land; and from the beginning of this matter the leaders and the nobles have been sharing in this iniquity. 71 As soon as I heard these things I tore my garments and my holy mantle, and pulled out hair from my head and beard, and sat down in anxiety and grief. . . . 86 And all that has happened to us has come about because of our evil deeds and our great sins. For you, O Lord, lifted the burden of our sins 87 and gave us such a root as this; but we turned back again to transgress your law by mixing with the uncleanness of the peoples of the land," and 2 Maccabees 14:3, 37-38: "Now a certain Alcimus, who had formerly been high priest but had willfully defiled himself in the times of mixing [reading the alternate text from the NRSV] . . . 37 A certain Razis, one of the elders of Jerusalem, was denounced to Nicanor as a man who loved his compatriots and was very well thought of and for his goodwill was called father of the Jews. 38 In former times, when there was no mingling with the Gentiles, he [Razis, a Jerusalem elder in contrast to the wicked Alcimus] had been accused of Judaism, and he had most zealously risked body and life for Judaism" (NRSV). Dionysius the Roman and the Jewish 1 Esdras and 2 Maccabees discuss the same subject using the same vocabulary, but Acts stands with the Roman point of view against the Jewish perspective: it is God's will to mix with the ἀλλόφυλοι (allophuloi, "those of other races"). Cf. no. 543 below.

509. Acts 10:9-35

Plutarch, *Parallel Lives*, "Brutus" 20 (45–125 CE)

These men [Caesar's slayers], indeed, having previously barricaded themselves well, repelled the danger; but there was a certain Cinna, a poet, who had no share in the crime, but was actually a friend of Caesar's. This man dreamed that he was invited to supper by Caesar and declined to go, but that Caesar besought and constrained him, and finally took him by the hand and led him into a yawning and darksome place, whither he followed unwillingly and bewildered. After having this vision, he fell into a fever which lasted all night; but in the morning, nevertheless, when the funeral rites were held over Caesar's body, he was ashamed not to be present, and went out into the crowd when it was already becoming savage. He was seen, however, and being thought to be, not the Cinna that he really was, but the one who had recently reviled Caesar before the assembled people, he was torn in pieces. (LCL)

Cf. also "Cicero" 44. In both cases, the point of contact with Acts 10 is the phenomenon of revelatory dreams that become meaningful only in retrospect. This is in contrast to the New Testament in general, where revelation through dreams is straightforward and immediately clear. Luke-Acts, however, is nearer to the pagan idea than any other New Testament document (cf. Berger on "vision reports," no. 937 on Rev 1:9-20).

510. Acts 14:11-13

Ovid, *Metamorphoses* 8.610-700 (43 BCE–17 CE)

"These are but fairy tales you tell, Acheloüs," Pirithoüs said, "and you concede too much power to the gods, if they give and take away the forms of things." All the rest were shocked and disapproved such words, and especially Lelex, ripe both in mind and years, who replied: "The power of heaven is indeed immeasurable and has no bounds; and whatever the gods decree is done. And, that you may believe it, there stands in the Phrygian hill-country an oak and a linden tree side by side, surrounded by a low wall. I have myself seen the spot; for Pittheus sent me to Phrygia, where his father once ruled. Not far from the place I speak of is a marsh, once a habitable land, but now water, the haunt of divers and coots. Hither came Jupiter in the guise of a mortal, and with his father came Atlas' grandson, he that bears the caduceus, his wings laid aside. To a thousand homes they came, seeking a place for rest; a thousand homes were barred against them. Still one house received them, humble indeed, thatched with straw and reeds from the marsh; but pious old Baucis and Philemon, of equal age, were in that cottage wedded in their youth, and in that cottage had grown old together; there they made their poverty light by owning it, and by bearing it in a contented spirit. It was of no use to ask for masters or for servants in that house; they two were the whole household, together they served and ruled. And so when the heavenly ones came to this humble home and, stooping, entered in at the lowly door, the old man set out a bench and bade them rest their limbs, while over this bench busy Baucis threw a rough covering. Then she raked aside the warm ashes on the hearth and fanned yesterday's coals to life, which she fed with leaves and dry bark, blowing them into flame with the breath of her old body. Then she took down from the roof some fine-split wood and dry twigs, broke them up and placed them under the little copper kettle. And she took the cabbage which her husband had brought in from the well-watered garden and lopped off the outside leaves. Meanwhile the old man with a forked stick reached down a chine of smoked bacon, which was hanging from a blackened beam and, cutting off a little piece of the long-cherished pork, he put it to cook in the boiling water. . . . The gods reclined. The old woman, with her skirts tucked up, with trembling hands set out the table. [The description continues in detail of their careful preparation of the modest meal.] Meanwhile they saw that the mixing bowl, as often as it was drained, kept filling of its own accord, and that the wine welled up of itself. . . . They had one goose, the guardian of their tiny estate; and him the hosts were preparing to kill for their divine guests. But the goose was swift of wing, and quite wore the old couple out in their efforts to catch him. . . . Then the gods told them not to kill the goose. 'We are gods,' they said, 'and this wicked neighborhood shall be punished as it deserves; but to you shall be given exemption from this punishment. Leave now your dwelling and come with us to that tall mountain yonder.' They both obeyed, and, propped on their staves, they struggled up the long slope. When they were a bowshot distant from the top, they looked back and saw the whole countryside covered with water, only their own house remaining. And, while they wondered at this, while they wept for the fate of their neighbors, that old house of theirs, which had been small even for its two occupants, was changed into a temple." (LCL)

The motif of the incognito god appears here in a charming and entertaining form. Jupiter and Mercury correspond to Zeus and Hermes. Lycaonia and Phrygia are neighboring lands in the interior of Asia Minor. The names of Zeus and Hermes are also documented in (later) inscriptions in this region, for example in Ak-Kilise, about 30 km south of Lystra. One can therefore suppose that Acts 14 rests in part on this same Phrygian tradition from which Ovid drew his own narrative. Such texts as Hebrews 3:12 reflect not only the biblical tradition (Gen 18), but also a motif widespread in pagan literature (the *Neuer Wettstein* gives numerous examples at Heb 13:12). Cf. nos. 221, 749. While Hebrews uses the motif in a positive manner, Luke is concerned to picture it as a pagan misunderstanding of the Christian missionaries.

511. Acts 15:19-21

b. Sanhedrin 56A

Our Rabbis have taught on Tannaite authority:
Concerning seven religious requirements were the children of Noah commanded: setting up courts of justice, idolatry, blasphemy [cursing the Name of God], fornication, bloodshed, thievery, and cutting a limb from a living beast. (Neusner, *Talmud*)

The "Apostolic Decree" is often understood as reaffirming the Jewish view that Gentiles were obligated to live by certain minimum rules, the "Noachic covenant" (cf. Gen 9:1-17). The Jewish elaboration of the stipulations of the Noachic covenant do not fit the Apostolic Decree very closely, however, so that it may be better to see it as derived from Leviticus 18:6-18, 26, where rules are given for both Israelites and outsiders living in Israel.

512. Acts 15:28

Inscription *IG* 12.3, 178 from Astypalaia (3 cent. CE)

The following appears right to the priest Ophelion from Enation and the [local] president Syros from Viettos, along with the goddess Atargatis and the Council of the Association of the Ancestral Gods: [then follows the decree of the gods]. (MEB/Berger)

The usual formula for decisions for the popular assembly is: "The following appeared right to the Council and the People/People's Assembly," then follows the decree. (Cf. the summary in Berger, "Volksversammlung und Gemeinde Gottes," *ZTK* 73 [1976], 182 n. 83.) The inscription from Astypalaia shows, along with further texts in Dittenberger, *SIG* 3 [4th ed.], no. 997 Ad 1, that it was possible to transfer this formula to gods and divine beings. In K. Latte, *Heiliges Recht* (1920), p. 46, no. 22, a decision is determined together by a deity and a prophet, or by a deity and a human judge.

On Acts 17:6-8, see no. 200.

513. Acts 16:9

Strabo, *Geography* 4.1.4 (64/63 BCE–23 CE)

Now the goddess [the Ephesian Artemis], in a dream, it is said, had stood beside Aristarcha, one of the women held in very high honor, and commanded her to sail away with the Phocaeans, taking with her a certain reproduction which was among the sacred images; this done and the colony finally settled, they not only established the temple but also did Aristarcha the exceptional honor of appointing her priestess; further, in the colonial cities the people everywhere do this goddess honors of the first rank, and they preserve the artistic design of the "xoanon" the same, and all the other usages precisely the same as is customary in the mother-city. (LCL)

This story, very similar to the stories from the Egyptian cults, is somewhat analogous to the account of Paul's vision at Troas. In the Hellenistic world, however, it was not the representatives of religions that were "evangelistic," but philosophers. See also no. 504.

514. Acts 16:13, 16

Inscription of Schedia (Egypt) (246–221 BCE)

For King Ptolemy and Queen Berenike, his sister and wife, and for their children, the Jews built the synagogue. (Horsley, *New Documents*, 4)

This inscription clearly refers to a building erected by the Jews as the place of prayer, i.e. a synagogue, yet it is called ἡ προσευχή, "The [Place of] Prayer." It is the earliest extant such reference. For several other such references, cf. Horsley, *New Documents* 4:201. It is thus quite possible that Acts 16:13, 16 refers to a synagogue building, elsewhere called by Luke συναγωγή "synagogue," as in the inscription from Corinth, [ΣΥΝ]ΑΓΩΓΗ ΕΒΡ[ΑΙΩΝ] (dated 200–100 BCE).

515. Acts 16:21

Cotta in Cicero, *On the Nature of the Gods* 3.2.5 (1 cent. BCE)

. . . I ought to uphold the beliefs about the immortal gods which have come down to us from our ancestors, and the rites and ceremonies and duties of religion. For my part I always shall uphold them . . ., and no eloquence . . . shall ever dislodge me from the belief as to the worship of the immortal gods which I have inherited from our forefathers. . . . The religion of the Roman people comprises ritual, auspices, and the third additional division consisting of all such prophetic warnings as the interpreters of the Sibyl or the soothsayers have derived from portents and prodigies. Well, I have always thought that none of these departments of religion was to be despised, and I have held the conviction that Romulus by his auspices and Numa by his establishment of our ritual laid the foundations of our state, which assuredly could never have been as great as it is had not the fullest measure of divine favor been obtained for it. (LCL)

The importance of religion in the general life of the person and the state is expressed in this quotation from a person otherwise pictured as quite skeptical. The traditional and external nature of religious commitment does not diminish its importance in the life of the state. In encountering such religious attitudes, Christianity was up against an appreciation for the state and its cultural history and contribution, not merely religion conceived in a more narrow, if more personal, manner as in Judaism and Christianity.

516. Acts 17:18

Diogenes, an Epicurean (ca. 200 CE)

Nothing to fear in God;
Nothing to feel in Death;
Good can be attained;
Evil can be endured.
(Murray)

"Epicurean" in the ancient world did not connote the selfish, exuberant hedonism it often suggests today. Already Epicurus himself had to combat this misunderstanding (Epistle to Menoeceus 132): "When, therefore, we maintain that pleasure is the end, we do not mean the pleasures of profligates and those that consist in sensuality, as is supposed by some who are either ignorant or disagree with us or do not understand, but freedom from pain in the body and from trouble in the mind. For it is not continuous drinkings and revelings, nor the satisfaction of lusts, nor the enjoyment of fish and other luxuries of the wealthy table, which produce a pleasant life, but sober reasoning, searching out the motives of all choice and avoidance, and banishing mere opinions, to which are due the greatest disturbance of the spirit" (Bailey). The Epicureans rejected traditional Greek religion with its fear of gods and the afterlife. But their philosophy that "nothing exists but atoms and the void" (Democritus) removed the fear of capricious gods, demons, and spirits. They advocated a quiet, somewhat withdrawn, uninvolved life, indifferent to externals, symbolized by their meeting place, "the Garden."

"Christians and Epicureans were sometimes lumped together by pagan observers because of their common rejection of traditional religion ("atheists") and separation of their communities from ordinary life (1 Thess 4:9-12 employs words used by Epicureans to describe a life of quietness withdrawn from public affairs)" (E. Ferguson, *Backgrounds* 355). Of course, in the Pauline churches the basis for such a life was not primarily a philosophical perspective, but their eschatological expectation.

517. Acts 17:22

Polybius, *Histories* 6.56 (2 cent. BCE)

The quality in which the Roman commonwealth is the most distinctly superior is in my opinion the nature of their religious convictions. I believe that it is the very thing which among other peoples is an object of reproach, I mean superstition [δεισιδαιμονία], which maintains the cohesions of the Roman state. (LCL)

In one quotation we see both the positive way *deisidaimonia* was evaluated (by Polybius himself, a Roman citizen who considered it the main factor in the success of the Roman Empire), and the way it was disdained by others (cf. Plutarch's *Superstition*, and Acts 25:19, the only other NT use of the term. Adjective in 17:22, noun in 25:19). Cf. Cicero, *Soothsayers,* 9.19: "We have excelled neither Spain in population, nor Gaul in vigor, nor Carthage in versatility, nor Greece in art, nor indeed Italy and Latium itself in the innate sensibility characteristic of this land and its peoples, but in piety, in devotion to religion, . . . we have excelled every race and every nation" (LCL).

518. Acts 17:22-31

Cleanthes, "Hymn to Zeus" (3 cent. BCE)

Thou, O Zeus, art praised above all gods:
many are thy names and thine is all power for ever.
The beginning of the world was from thee:
and with law thou rulest over all things.
Unto thee may all flesh speak: for we are thy offspring.
Therefore I will raise a hymn unto thee:
and will sing of thy power.
The whole order of the heavens obeyeth thy
word: as it moveth around the earth:
With little and great lights mixed together:
how great thou art, King above all forever.
Nor is anything done upon earth apart from thee: nor in the firmament, nor in the seas:
Save that which the wicked do: by their own folly.
But thine is the skill to set even the crooked straight: what is without fashion is fashioned
and the alien akin before thee.
Thus hast thou fitted together all things into one: the good with the evil:
That thy word should be one in all things: abiding for ever.
Let folly be dispersed from our souls: that we may repay thee the honor, wherewith thou
has honored us:
Singing praise of thy works forever. (Bevan)

This is a Stoic prayer that addresses Zeus in personal terms as the inclusive term for that Divine Reason that rules the universe by Law. One may note not only Luke's direct reference to this text in 17:28, but the idea that the deity is one, though addressed by many names, that human beings are the children of God, and that they can and should address God in prayer and praise. Such a religion is hardly "cold" and "sterile," even if in conceptual terms it is hesitant to think of the deity as personal. But Zeus is far different here from the old Greek myths, having become a symbol of the benevolent unifying and ruling principle of the cosmos.

Another sample of the fervent religious feeling that could be expressed in Stoicism is given in Epictetus, *Discourses* 16.25-30:

"If we had sense we ought to do nothing else, in public and in private, than praise and bless God and pay him due thanks. Ought we not, as we dig and plough and eat, to sing the hymn to God? 'Great is God that he gave us these instruments wherewith we shall till the earth. Great is God that he has given us hands, and power to swallow, and a belly, and the power to grow without knowing it, and to draw our breath in sleep.' At every moment we ought to sing these praises and above all the greatest and divinest praise, that God gave us the faculty to comprehend these gifts and to use the way of reason" (LCL).

For additional samples of authentic religious fervor in prayer and praise, see the Hermetic "Sacrifice of Praise and Thanksgiving" at Romans 12:1-2.

519. Acts 17:22-31

Apuleius, *Metamorphoses* 11.4 (2 cent. CE)

[Isis speaks:] Behold, Lucius, I am come; thy weeping and prayer hath moved me to succor thee. I am she that is the natural mother of all things, mistress and governess of all the elements, the initial progeny of worlds, chief of the powers divine, queen of all that are in hell; the principal of them that dwell in heaven, manifested alone and under one form of all the gods and goddesses. At my will the planets of the sky, the wholesome winds of the seas, and the lamentable silences of hell be disposed; my name, my divinity is adored throughout all the world, in divers manners, in variable customs, and by many names. For the Phrygians that are the first of all men call me the Mother of the gods of Pessinus; the Athenians, which are sprung from their own soil, Cecropian Minerva; the Cyprians, which are girt about the sea, Paphian Venus; the Cretans which bear arrows, Dictynnian Diana; the Sicilians, which speak three tongues, infernal Proserpine; the Eleusians their ancient goddess Ceres; some Juno, others Bellona, others Hecate, others Rhamnusia, and principally both sort of the Ethiopians which dwell in the Orient and are enlightened by the morning rays of the sun, and the Egyptians, which are excellent in all kind of ancient doctrine, and by their proper ceremonies accustom to worship me, do call me by my true name, Queen Isis. (LCL)

As in Acts 17, there is only one God, and all who worship God worship this one God, though they mistakenly call her by other names and worship her by different rites. This text also shares Luke's view that the common denominator between all the gods is not some general divine principle, but a particular deity with a particular name, who is in fact the only real God. In both texts, the revelation of the identity of the one God worshiped by many names is saving good news.

520. Acts 17:28

Aratus of Soli in Cilicia (b. ca. 315–305), cited in Aristobulus (middle of 2 cent. BCE; Hellenistic-Jewish author). Fragment 4 of Eusebius, *The Preparation for the Gospel*

And Aratus also speaks about the same things thus:

"Let us begin with God [Zeus], whom men never leave unspoken; full of God are the streets, and all the marketplaces of humanity, and full the sea and the harbors; and we are all in need of God everywhere. We are all his children; and he gently to humanity gives good omens, and rouses people to work, reminding [them] of sustenance; and he tells when the soil is best for cattle and for pickaxes, and he tells when seasons are favorable both for planting trees and for sowing all seeds. I believe it has been clearly shown how the power of God is throughout all things. And we have given the true sense, as one must, by removing the [name] Zeus throughout the verses. For their [the verses] intention refers to God, therefore it was so expressed by us. We have presented these things therefore in a way not unsuited to the things being discussed." (*OTP* 2:842)

In Aratus this is part of the introduction to a grand astrological poem that deals mainly with constellations and signs in the heavens. This is clear from the opening verses cited, for the function of the deity consists essentially in providing the right signs for the execution of human tasks. Aristobulus, however, is not interested in this function. The point is the universal activity of the one God, which he finds confirmed by a pagan.

For the Lucan Paul of Acts 17, the point is something different again. He brings God and human life close together, emphasizing the similarity of human beings to God, in order to polemicize against idols (cf. v. 29). They are much more unlike the true God than are human beings themselves. An echo of the original function in Aratus is found in the reference to the "signs" etc. in 17:26. See also Philo, "Husbandry," §47. For Paul himself, cf. no. 604. Since the works of Aratus in general and this poem in particular were a part of every curriculum and known by everyone who had attended school, the citation does not necessarily picture the Lucan Paul as steeped in Hellenistic literature, nor indicate that Luke was.

521. Acts 18:2

Claudius' Decree (49 CE; reported in Suetonius, *Lives of the Caesars*, "Claudius" 25, early 2 cent. CE)

He allowed the people of Ilium perpetual exemption from tribute, on the ground that they were the founders of the Roman race. . . . Since the Jews constantly made disturbances at the instigation of Chrestus *[impulsore Christo]*, he expelled them from Rome. He allowed the envoys of the Germans to sit in the orchestra, led by their naive self-confidence. . . . He utterly abolished the cruel and inhuman religion of the Druids among the Gauls, which under Augustus had merely been prohibited to Roman citizens; on the other hand he even attempted to transfer the Eleusinian rites from Attica to Rome, and had the temple of

Venus Erycina in Sicily, which had fallen to ruin through age, restored at the expense of the treasury of the Roman people. (LCL)

It is often thought that the Chrestus referred to is Suetonius' (or his source's) misunderstanding of the word "Christ," and that the reference is to disturbances that occurred in the Jewish synagogues in response to the preaching of Jesus as the Christ by Christians. The context (of which only a section is quoted here) shows Claudius' act was not particularly anti-Jewish. Suetonius reports similarly about Tiberius ("Tiberius" 36) more than two decades previously: "Foreign religions, the Egyptian and Jewish religious rites, he suppressed, and compelled those who were engaged in that superstition to burn their religious vestments with all their apparatus. The Jewish youth he dispersed, under pretense of military service, into provinces of unhealthy climate; the rest of that race, and those who adopted similar opinions, he expelled from the city, on pain of perpetual slavery if they did not obey. He also banished the astrologers . . ." (LCL).

522. Acts 18:12-17

Delphi Inscription of Gallio (1 cent. CE)

Tiberius Claudius Caesar Augustus Germanicus Pontifex Maximus, in his tribunician power year 12, acclaimed emperor the 26th time, father of the country . . . sends greetings to the city of Delphi. I have long been zealous for the city of Delphi and favorable to it from the beginning, and I have always observed the cult of the Pythian Apollo, but with regard to the present stories, and those quarrels of the citizens of which a report has been made by Lucius Junio Gallio, my friend and proconsul of Achaia . . . will still hold the previous settlement. (Lake and Jackson)

Much of the relative chronology of Paul's ministry can be inferred from material in his letters, but they provide no data that fixes the absolute chronology of his life, and thus for other events in early Christianity. In all of Paul's letters, he refers to public history external to the life of the church only once (2 Cor 11:32, Aretas as king of Arabia). The Gallio inscription is thus helpful in providing a fixed point in "external" history to which the relative chronology derived from the "interior" history in Paul's letters can be related. Claudius' reign began in 41 CE, so the "twelfth year" would be between 25 January, 52 CE and 24 January, 53 CE. If the following probabilities are accepted, the New Testament chronology may be made even more precise: (1) Claudius' twenty-sixth acclamation occurred between the end of 51 CE and August 1, 52. (2) Gallio followed the normal pattern of provincial governors of entering their term of service about July 1 and served for one year. (3) Acts 18:11 is accurate in reporting Paul's stay in Corinth as eighteen months. (4) Acts 18:18 is to be understood as meaning that Paul left Corinth some time after the Gallio incident, and the report is accurate. All these are very probable, with (1) virtually certain. This would place Paul's arrival in Corinth early in 50, and his departure late in 51, and would give the one fixed date in Pauline chronology.

The purpose of the inscription was not, of course, to provide chronological data for future historians, but to place a conspicuous inscription at Delphi, visited by crowds from all over the world, illustrating the emperor's support of and connection with the popular oracle (and incidentally to settle a local dispute reported by the new governor; a public inscription would not have been necessary for this, however).

523. Acts 19:13-20

Plutarch, *Parallel Lives*, "Life of Alexander" 2.7-8 (45–125 CE)

[Discussing the miraculous birth of Alexander:] But concerning these matters there is another story to this effect: all the women of these parts were addicted to the Orphic rites and the orgies of Dionysus from very ancient times . . . and imitated in many ways the practices of the Edonian women and the Thracian women about Mount Haemus, from whom, as it would seem, the word "threskeuein" [θρησκεύειν] came to be applied to the celebration of extravagant and superstitious [περίεργοις] ceremonies. (LCL)

Περίεργα (superstitious) can be used more generally, but in Plutarch as in Acts it refers to the practice of magic. Cf. also text nos. 60-64 above, which illustrate the combination of popular magic, superstition, and Jewish-Christian religious ideas that appears also in Acts 19:13-20. Luke takes pains to distance Christian faith from these.

524. Acts 19:19

Suetonius, *Lives of the Caesars*, "The Deified Augustus" 31.1-1-4 (early 2 cent. CE)

After he finally had assumed the office of pontifex maximus on the death of Lepidus (for he could not make up his mind to deprive him of the honor while he lived), he collected whatever prophetic writings of Greek or Latin origin were in circulation anonymously or under the names of authors of little repute, and burned more than two thousand of them, retaining only the Sibylline books and making a choice even among those; and he deposited them in two gilded cases under the pedestal of the Palatine Apollo. Inasmuch as the calendar, which had been set in order by the Deified Julius, had later been confused and disordered through negligence, he restored it to its former system; and in making this arrangement he called the month Sextilis by his own surname, rather than his birth-month September, because in the former he had won his first consulship and his most brilliant victories. He increased the number and importance of the priests, and also their allowances and privileges, in particular those of the Vestal virgins. Moreover, when there was occasion to choose another vestal in place of one who had died, and many used all their influence to avoid submitting their daughters to the hazard of the lot, he solemnly swore that if anyone of his granddaughters were of eligible age, he would have proposed her name. He also revived some of the ancient rites which had gradually fallen into disuse, such as the augury of Safety, the office of Flamen Dialis, the ceremonies of the Lupercalia, the Secular Games, and the festival of the Compitalia. At the Lupercalia he forbade beardless youths to join in the running, and at the Secular Games he would not allow young people of either sex to attend any entertainment by night except in company with some adult relative. (LCL)

Suetonius presents Octavian, the emperor at the time of Jesus' birth (29 BCE–14 CE), as the restorer of Roman religion who purifies it from alien and superstitious accretions, and therefore as reestablishing the older Roman ideals and morals. So also Horace, in the song composed for the celebration of the Secular Games: "Already Faith and Peace and Honor and ancient Modesty and neglected Virtue have courage to come back, and blessed Plenty with her full horn is seen" (*Carmen Saeculare* lines 38-40 [LCL]). The burning of inferior religious and superstitious books is one of a number of things mentioned to support this picture of Octavian's role. Suetonius also presents Tiberias (emperor 14–37) as taking measures against astrology and other superstitions, and burning their religious paraphernalia (those of Jews were included; cf. "Tiberius" 36 as well as Tacitus, *Annals* 2.85).

The point of contact with Luke's narrative is that the arrival or restoration of the true religion means the destruction of the books of the false religion, equated with magic and superstition. Luke's picture of the success of the gospel in Ephesus is resonant with descriptions of Octavian's restoration of Roman religious practices. In each case, the true, good, and old prevails over later perverse accretions. There is also a certain analogy in the connection of religion and morals, and in the revering of the true writings (*Sibylline Oracles;* the Jewish Scriptures) while destroying the old. The difference: Octavian imposed the new regime by force, while the Ephesian converts spontaneously rejected their old ways and destroyed their books.

The text also illustrates the prevalence of oracles and prophecies, and the necessity of discriminating among them (cf. 1 Cor 14:1-40). Cf. also no. 771.

525. Acts 19:19

Greek Magical Papyri 3.1-164

[Take a] cat, and [make] it into an *Esies* [by submerging] its body in water. While you are drowning it, speak [the formula] to its back.

The formula during the drowning [is as follows]:

"Come hither to me, you who are in control of the form of Helios, you the cat-faced god, and behold your form being mistreated by [your] opponents, [them] NN, so that you may revenge yourself on them, and accomplish the NN deed, because I am calling upon you, O sacred spirit. Take on strength and vigor against your enemies, them, NN, because I am conjuring you by your names BARBATHIAO BAINCHOOOCH NIABOAITHABRAB SESENGENBARPHARARGES . . . PHREIMI; raise yourself up for me, O cat-faced god, and perform the NN deed" [add the usual].

Take the cat, and make [three] lamellae, one for its anus, one for . . ., and one for its throat; and write the formula [concerning the] deed on a clean sheet of papyrus, with cinnabar [ink] and [then the names of] the chariots and charioteers, and the chariot boards and the racehorses. Wind this around the body of the cat and bury it. Light seven lamps upon [seven] unbaked bricks, and make an offering, fumigating storax gum to it, and be of good cheer. Take its body and preserve it by immuring it either in a tomb or in a burial place . . . with colors, . . . bury . . . looking toward the sunrise, pour out [?] . . . saying:

'Angel, . . . [SEMEA], chthonic . . . lord [?] grant [safety?], . . . O chthonic one, in [the] horse race, IAKTORE; hold . . . restrain . . ., PHOKENSEPSEUARE [KTATHOUMI-SONKTAI], for me, the spirit . . . the daimon of [the] place . . . and may the [NN deed] come about for me immediately, immediately; quickly, quickly, because I conjure you, at this place and at this time, by the implacable god . . . THACHOCHA EIN CHOUCHEOCH, and by the great chthonic god, ARIOR EUOR, and by the names that apply to you; perform the NN deed [add the usual].'

Then take up the water in which the drowning took place, and sprinkle it [on] the stadium or in the place where you are performing [the rite].

The formula to be spoken, while you are sprinkling the drowning water, is as follows, 'I call upon you, Mother of all men, you who have brought together the limbs of Meliouchos, even Meliouchos himself, OROBASTRIA NEBOU-TOSOUALETH, Entraper, Mistress of corpses, Hermes, Hekate, [Hermes?], Her-mekate, LETH AMOUMAMOUTERMYOR; I conjure you, the daimon that has been aroused in this place, and you, the daimon of the cat that has been endowed with spirit; come to me on this very day and from this very moment, and perform for the NN deed [add the usual, whatever you wish], CHYCHBACHYCH BACHACHYCH BACHAXICHYCH BAZABACHYCH BAIACHACHYCH BAZETOPHOTH BAINCHOOOCH ANIBOOO CHOCHE . . . PHIOCHEN GEBROCHTHO MYSA-GAOTH CHEOO . . . O SABAOTH EULAMOSI EELAXIMA . . . [. . . THACHOCH] AXIN CHOUCHEOCH.'

On the [1st and 3rd leaves of metal] which you are to use for the conjuration, there should be this: 'IAEO' . . . [there follows lengthy formulae including the drawing of symbolic pictures, the whole ritual taking two pages of fine print to reproduce].

This is the ritual of the cat, [suitable] for every ritual purpose: A charm to restrain charioteers in a race, a charm for sending dreams, a binding love charm, and a charm to cause separation and enmity." (NN in the trans. is the translator's indication that the appropriate name or act was to be inserted into the formula at this point.) (Betz)

"'The Greek magical papyri' is a name given by scholars to a body of papyri from Greco-Roman Egypt containing a variety of magical spells and formulae, hymns and rituals. The extant texts are mainly from the second century B.C. to the fifth century A.D." (Betz, "Introduction," *Greek Magical Papyri*, xli). Only a fraction of what was available has been preserved, most having disappeared not only because they were written on perishable material (hence most of the surviving fragments are from the dry sands of Egypt), but because they were systematically destroyed by secular officials (see no. 524 on Acts 19:19) and later by Christian leaders. The most complete collection of those that have survived is found in Betz, *Greek Magical Papyri*, which contains 553 magic spells and formulae in 131 papyri. The modern distinction between "religion" and "magic" was rarely made by the populace of the Hellenistic world, so that the magical papyri give glimpses into the everyday religious life of many people in the Hellenistic world who also participated in other forms of religious expression. They included not only many exorcism formulae (cf. no. 60 on Mark 5:1-20 and no. 636 on 1 Cor 5:1-13), but spells to do such things as improve one's memory, forecast the future, detect thieves, cure colds, bring success in love, athletics, or business, as well as more directly religious spells such as for revelation and divination. The elaborate spell, a portion of which is printed above, is prescribed for a number of purposes, mostly malicious, but was written with special reference to a chariot race. This and the other examples of magical papyri mentioned here give a small sample of the kind of thing Luke pictures as being rejected when the Christian faith was accepted in Ephesus.

526. Acts 21:27-36

Jerusalem Temple Inscription, OGIS 598 (1 cent. CE; now in Rockefeller Museum, Jerusalem)

No foreigner is to enter within the fence and enclosure surrounding the sanctuary. Whoever is caught so doing will himself be the cause of his ensuing death. (MEB)

A dividing wall about five feet high separated the Court of the Gentiles, into which all could enter, from the Court of Israel, which could be entered only by Jews. Josephus, *War* 5.193-94 describes it as follows: "Proceeding across this [the Court of the Gentiles] toward the second court of the temple, one found it surrounded by a stone balustrade, three cubits high and of exquisite workmanship; in this at regular intervals stood slabs giving warning, some in Greek, others in Latin characters, of the law of purification, to wit that no foreigner was permitted to enter the holy place, for so the second enclosure of the temple was called" (LCL).

527. Acts 23:6-10

Josephus, *Jewish War* 2.162-65 (37–100 CE)

Of the two first-named schools, the Pharisees, who are considered the most accurate interpreters of the laws, and hold the position of the leading sect, attribute everything to Fate and God; they hold that to act rightly or otherwise rests, indeed, for the most part with men, but that in each action Fate cooperates. Every soul, they maintain, is imperishable, but the soul of the good alone passes into another body, while the souls of the wicked suffer eternal punishment.

The Sadducees, the second of the orders, do away with Fate altogether, and remove God beyond, not merely the commission, but the very sight, of evil. They maintain that man has the free choice of good or evil, and that it rests with each man's will whether he follows the one or the other. As for the persistence of the soul after death, penalties in the underworld, and rewards, they will have none of them. (LCL)

Though Josephus claims to belong to the Pharisees, he here describes their views rather objectively (though in the next paragraph he does describe their conduct, "even among themselves," as "rather boorish"). His terminology is chosen to communicate to his Hellenistic readers. Though Josephus became rather Hellenized himself, it is unclear whether he distinguished between the Greek concept of immortality of the soul and the Hebrew-biblical concept of resurrection.

Cf. also Mark 12:18-27. On Acts 27:21-37, see nos. 53-57.

528. Acts 28:1-6

Mekilta According to Rabbi Ishmael, "Kaspa" 3.78.12 (2 cent. CE)

Judah b. Tabbai came into a ruin and found the slain man writhing, with the sword dripping blood from the hand of the slayer. Said to him Judah b. Tabbai, "My such-and-so come upon me, if either you or I have killed this man. But what am I going to do? For the Torah has said, 'At the testimony of two witnesses . . . shall a matter be established'" [Dt. 19:15].

"But the One who knows and the Master of all intentions is the one who will exact punishment from that man."

The man had barely left the place before a snake bit him and he died. (Smith, *Tannaitic Parallels*)

Though a typical Hellenistic idea, the above text shows that the idea that divine justice prevails in punishing evildoers when human justice fails is also a Jewish idea. In the rabbinic text, however, the story illustrates not only the overruling sovereignty of divine justice, but that the Torah (requiring two witnesses) must be respected even when it seems to thwart justice.

529. Acts 28:1-6

b. *Berakoth* 33a (1 cent. CE tradition, written down much later)

There was the case concerning a certain place in which a lizard was going around and biting people. They came and told R. Hanina b. Dosa.

He said to them, "Show me its hole."

They showed him its hole. He put his heel over the mouth of the hole. The lizard came out and bit him and died.

He took it on his shoulder and brought it to the school house. He said to them, "See, my sons, it is not the lizard that kills but sin that kills."

At that moment they said, "Woe to the man who meets a lizard, and woe to the lizard that meets up with R. Hanina b. Dosa." (Neusner, *Talmud*)

As in the New Testament story, by divine protection the man of God is immune to snakebite, and the snake ends up dead.

The Letters of Paul

530. Romans 1:1-7

Papyrus BGU 27 (2 cent. CE)

Irenaeus to Apollinarius his dearest brother many greetings. I pray continually for your health, and I myself am well. I wish you to know that I reached land on the 5th of the month Epeiph and we unloaded our cargo on the 18th of the same month. I went up to Rome on the 25th of the same month and the place welcomed us as the god willed, and we are daily expecting our discharge, it so being that up till today nobody in the corn fleet has been released. Many salutations to your wife and to Serenus and to all who love you, each by name. Good-bye. Mesore 9. (LCL)

The prescripts of the undisputed Pauline letters have the same distinctive form (cf. 1 Cor 1:1-3; 2 Cor 1:1-2; Gal 1:1-5; Phil 1:1-2; 1 Thess 1:1; Phlm 1-3), his own distinctive adaptation of the standard prescript of a Hellenistic letter. The basic form of the Greek letter remained constant for many centuries, from the fourth century BCE to the fourth century CE. The letter regularly began with the greeting "A to B, greetings" (cf. Acts 15:23; Jas 1:1). Normally, the greeting was followed immediately with a prayer or thanksgiving. Its omission in a brief personal letter was not unusual, as in Papyrus BGU 37 (50 CE):

"Mystarion to his own Stotoetis, many greetings! I have sent you my Blastus to get forked sticks for my olive gardens. See that he does not loiter; for you know how I need him every single hour. Farewell" (cf. ἔρρωσθε, Acts 15:29).

The brevity, rigidly stereotyped forms, and lack of personal chattiness were characteristic, and did not indicate unfriendliness. To make it a vehicle of community instruction, Paul expanded the Hellenistic form in the direction of the literary public letters used by philosophers and teachers, but Paul's letters remained real letters to particular addressees. Both the greeting and the thanksgiving, which had become conventional forms, were developed by Paul into pregnant theological affirmations. In particular, transforming the colorless greeting form χαίρειν with the distinctive combination χάρις ὑμῖν καὶ εἰρήνη ("grace to you and peace"; the word for "grace" is similar to the conventional "greetings"). See William G. Doty, *Letters in Primitive Christianity* (Philadelphia: Fortress Press, 1973); Stanley K. Stowers, *Letter Writing in Greco-Roman Antiquity* (Philadelphia: Westminster, 1986); John L. White, *Light from Ancient Letters* (Philadelphia: Fortress Press, 1986).

531. Romans 1:3

4QpsDan Aa = 4Q 246 (2–1 cent. BCE)

He shall be called son of God, and they shall designate him son of the Most High. Like the appearance of comets, so shall be their kingdom. For [brief] years they shall reign over the earth and shall trample on all; one people shall trample on another and one province on another . . . until the people of God shall rise and all shall rest from the sword. (Vermes)

The conferral of the name is formulated as in Luke 1:32 ("he will be called Son of the Most High") and 1:35 (. . . "will be called Son of God . . ."), the names being placed in parallel as here. This could be the only pre–New Testament text in which the Jewish Messiah is named "Son of God." Hesitation is called for, however, since the text fades quickly from singular into the plural ("people of God"), since the people collectively could also be named "Son of God." Then when the text switches back quickly to the third person singular, it is not clear whether it refers to people or Messiah, if two figures are in fact spoken of at all. Finally, it could also be the case that in the whole passage up to the place in which the people of God is spoken of for the first time, that an opposing anti-kingdom has been spoken of, whose people or ruler has falsely been called Son of God. Then the subject would be either perverted Jewish Messianic expectation or—more likely—an attack against pagan divine kingship ideology (cf. Plutarch on Alexander the Great, nos. 120, 122; cf. also 2 Thess 2:8-12).

532. Romans 1:16

Egyptian Papyrus praising Imouthes-Asclepius P. Oxy. 1381 (2 cent. CE)

Assemble hither, ye kindly and good men; avaunt ye malignant and impious! . . . Assemble, all ye . . ., who by serving the god have been cured of diseases, ye who practice the healing art, ye who will labor as zealous followers of virtue, ye who have been blessed by great abundance of benefits, ye who have been saved from the dangers of the sea! For every place has been penetrated by the saving power of the god.

I now purpose to recount his miraculous manifestations, the greatness of his power, the gifts of his benefits. The history is this. (Grenfell and Hunt)

The text is the introduction to a typical aretalogy (report of the wonderful deed[s] of a god; cf. Berger, *Formgeschichte*, 239-40; 347-48). The linguistic field overlaps Romans 1:16 (power, deliverance/salvation), and in both cases is oriented toward universal proclamation. To this extent the Egyptian text contributes to understanding Romans 1:16: saving power is the act of God. On the competition Asclepius/Christianity, cf. nos. 405, 504.

533. Romans 1:17

Community Rule (1QS) 11:2-22 (1 cent. CE)

As for me,
    my justification is with God.
In his hand are the perfection of my way
    and the uprightness of my heart.
He will wipe out my transgression
    through his righteousness
. . . for the rock of my steps is the truth of God
    and His might is the support of my right hand.
From the source of His righteousness [צדקתו]
    is my justification . . .
As for me,

I belong to wicked mankind,
   to the company of ungodly flesh.
My iniquities, rebellions, and sins,
   together with the perversity of my heart,
belong to the company of worms
   and to those who walk in darkness.
For mankind has no way,
   and man is unable to justify his steps
since justification is with God
   and perfection of way is out of His hand.
. . . As for me,
   if I stumble, the mercies of God
   shall be my eternal salvation.
If I stagger because of the sin of flesh,
   my justification shall be
   by the righteousness of God which endures forever.
. . . He will draw me near by His grace,
   and by His mercy will He bring my justification.
He will judge me in the righteousness of His truth
   and in the greatness of His goodness
   He will pardon all my sins.
Through His righteousness he will cleanse me
   of the uncleanness of man
   and of the sins of the children of men,
That I may confess to God His righteousness,
   and His majesty to the Most High. (Vermes)

While vocabulary is not precisely the same as Paul's (מֹשְׁפֹט used more than צדקה), the basic similarity in thought and feeling is clear. Cf. also Hodayoth 1QH 6.30, 40:
"Righteousness, I know, is not of man,
   nor is perfection of way of the son of man:
To the Most High God belong all righteous deeds.
. . . for thou wilt pardon iniquity,
   and through thy righteousness
   thou wilt purify man of his sin.
Not for his sake wilt Thou do it,
   [but for the sake of thy glory]" (Vermes).
Cf. esp. 1QH 14.15-16:
"For thou art righteous, and all Thine elect are truth.
Thou wilt blot out all wickedness [and s]in for ever,
and Thy righteousness shall be revealed before the eyes of all Thy creatures" (Vermes).
At Qumran, the biblical phrase (Isa 56:1) is taken to mean the eschatological salvation that will appear before the whole world, vindicating God's purpose and God's people. In this light, Paul's meaning is that the eschatological salvation and vindication expected for the eschatological future has already appeared and is revealed in the gospel.
Cf. also no. 759 on Galatians 3:11.

534. Romans 1:17

Plutarch, *Moralia*, "The Dinner of the Seven Wise Men" 18 (45–125 CE)

[One who had survived shipwreck tells:] . . . There came into his [Arion] thoughts, as he said, not so much a feeling of fear in the face of death, or a desire to live, as a proud longing to be saved that he might be shown to be a man loved by the gods, and that he might gain a sure opinion regarding them. At the same time, observing that the sky was dotted with stars, and the moon was rising bright and clear, while the sea everywhere was without a wave as if a path were being opened for their course, he bethought himself that the eye of Justice is not a single eye only, but through all these eyes of hers God watches in every direction the deeds that are done here and there both on land and on the sea. By these reflections, he said, the weariness and heaviness which he was already beginning to feel in his body were relieved . . . (LCL)

In "Obsolescence of Oracles" 24, Plutarch also says that God not only created a single world, "For He, being consummately good, is lacking in none of the virtues, and least of all in those which concern justice [δικαιοσύνη, 'righteousness' in Rom 1:17] and friendliness [φιλία]," but God also has virtues expressed in relationship with others, "For not in relation with Himself nor with any part of Himself is there any exercise of justice [δικαιοσύνη] or benevolence [χάρις] or kindness, but only in relation with others" (LCL).

In both texts the righteousness of God has a strictly positive function in terms of its content. In the first text it means rescue, it is the proof of something almost like "election," it is the benevolent providence. Of course, in the background stands the idea that God's *"Diké"* (already in early times personified as "God's daughter," Hesiod, *Works* 5.256) balances everything out justly and lets no one who is innocent perish. This balanced judgment is given with the world itself. It is this just balancing of things that stands behind most of the texts cited in Berger, "Neues Material zur 'Gerechtigkeit Gottes,' " *ZNW* 68 (1977), pp. 266-75.

In the second text however, "righteousness" stands beside "grace" and is evaluated as an inner-community virtue. This meaning corresponds clearly to the Hebrew צֶדֶק *tsedeq*. Still, it is hardly to be equated with "love"; it is rather a fundamental mode of behavior in community relationships. In this light, Romans 1:17 and 3:21 affirm: God restores relationships with humanity on his own initiative. The carrying out of the office of *Diké* mentioned above would be only a marginal meaning in this case.

535. Romans 1:19-21

Pseudo-Aristotle, *On the Cosmos* 399b (3 cent. BCE)

It is a similar idea that we must have of the universe: by a single inclination all things are spurred to action and perform their peculiar functions—and this single agent is unseen and invisible. Its invisibility is no impediment either to its own action or to our belief in it; for the soul, whereby we live and build households and cities, though it is invisible is perceived through its deeds: for all the conduct of life is discovered, arranged and maintained by the soul—the ploughing and sowing of land, the inventions of art, the use of laws, the order of a city's government, the activities of people in their own country, and war and peace with foreign nations. This is what we must also believe about God, who is mightiest in power, outstanding in beauty, immortal in life, and supreme in excellence, because though he is invisible to every mortal thing he is seen through his deeds. For it would be true to say that all the phenomena of the air, the land and the water are the works of the God who rules the cosmos. (LCL)

The text presents not only the contrast "invisible"/"seen" as in Romans 1:20, but also the unusual Greek construction with ἀπο ([to see and infer something] "from"). One can thus assume that this text stands in a more or less direct literary relationship to Romans 1. The text cited more frequently in this connection from the Corpus Hermeticum 5.2, "Only understanding, because it, too, is invisible, sees the invisible . . ." (Copenhaver), at first glance seems to stand in opposition to Paul's view, since the visible works of creation constitute his point of departure. To be sure, they are perceived by the νοῦς, mind (v. 20), so that it forms an intermediate stage in the process of seeing and understanding. The difference is that in Pseudo-Aristotle the point is not made that those who see are therefore without excuse.

536. Romans 1:26-27

Philo, *On the Special Laws* 3.37-39, 42 (15 BCE–50 CE)

Much graver than the above is another evil, which has ramped its way into the cities, namely pederasty [τὸ παιδεραστεῖν]. In former days the very mention of it was a great disgrace, but now it is a matter of boasting not only to the active but to the passive partners who habituate themselves to endure the disease of effemination, let both body and soul run to waste, and leave no ember of their male sex-nature to smolder. Mark how conspicuously they braid and adorn the hair of their heads, and how they scrub and paint their faces with cosmetics and pigments and the like, and smother themselves with fragrant unguents. For of all such embellishments, used by all who deck themselves out to wear a comely appearance, fragrance is the most seductive. In fact the transformation of the male nature to the female [τὴν ἄρρηνα φύσιν . . . εἰς θήλειαν μεταβάλλειν] is practiced by them as an art and does not raise a blush. These persons are rightly judged worthy of death by those who obey the law, which ordains that the man-woman [ἀνδρόγυνον] who debases the sterling coin of nature [το φύσεως νόμισμα παρακόπτοντα] should perish unavenged, suffered not to live for a day or even an hour, as a disgrace to himself, his house, his native land and the whole human race. And the lover of such may be assured that he is subject to the same penalty. He pursues an unnatural pleasure and does his best to render cities desolate and uninhabited by destroying the means of procreation. Furthermore he sees no harm in becoming an instructor in the grievous vices of unmanliness and effeminacy by prolonging the bloom of the young and emasculating the flower of their prime, which should rightly be trained to strength and robustness. Finally, like a bad husbandman he lets the deep-soiled and fruitful fields lie sterile, by taking steps to keep them from bearing, while he spends his labor night and day on soil from which no growth at all can be expected. The reason is, I think, to be found in the prizes awarded in many nations to licentiousness and effeminacy. Certainly you may see these hybrids of man and woman continually strutting about through the thick of the market, heading the processions at the feasts, appointed to serve as unholy ministers of holy things, leading the mysteries and initiations and celebrating the rites of Demeter. (LCL)

Philo offers his exposition of the laws against fornication and sexual perversion (cf. Lev 18:22; 20:13; Deut 23:18), and allows us to see how the sexual practices in Hellenistic cities appeared from the point of view of a Hellenistic Jew. Cf. also Abraham 135, 136; "Contemplative Life" 59-62, the latter following a sharp critique of Plato's Symposium. The texts in Philo present verbal similarities to Paul, and both are concerned with homosexuality as "against nature." Unlike Paul, Philo elaborates reasons for rejecting such practices as evil. Paul simply assumes this, but Philo permits us to see the kind of reasoning in the background of the Pauline position. The relation of homosexuality to "nature" was a topos in the Hellenistic discussion of the subject. Further:

537. Romans 1:26-27

Pseudo-Lucian, *Affairs of the Heart* 19-20

. . . females are not coy and do not cloak their desires with deceits or trickeries or denials; nor do the males, driven on by the sting of mad lust, purchase the act of procreation by money or toil or servitude. No! Both parties celebrate at the proper time a love without deceit or hire, a love which in the season of spring awakens, like the burgeoning of plants and trees, the desire of animals, and then immediately extinguishes it. Neither does the female continue to receive the male after she has conceived, nor does the male attempt her. So slight and feeble is the regard we have for pleasure: our whole concern is with Nature. Whence it comes about that to this very day the desires of beasts have encompassed no homosexual mating. But you have a fair amount of such trafficking among your high and mighty nobility, to say nothing of the baser sort. Agamemnon came to Boeotia hunting for Argynnus, who tried to elude him, and slandering the sea and winds . . . then he gave his noble self a noble bath in Lake Copaïs to drown his passion there and get rid of his desire. Just so Heracles, pursuing a beardless lad, lagged behind the other heroes and deserted the expedition. On the Rotunda of Ptoian Apollo one of your men secretly inscribed Fair is Achilles—when Achilles already had a son. And I hear that the inscription is still in place. But a cock that mounts another for the lack of a female is burned alive because some prophet or seer declares that such an event is an important and terrible omen. On this basis even men themselves acknowledge that beasts have a better claim to temperance and the nonviolation of nature in their pleasures. Not even Nature, with Law for her ally, can keep within bounds the unchastened vice of your hearts; but as though swept by the current of their lusts beyond the barrier at many points, men do such deeds as wantonly outrage Nature, upset her order, and confuse her distinctions. (LCL)

As in Paul, heterosexual love is considered "natural," and homosexual acts "contrary to nature." The text also illustrates that homosexuality was both widespread and widely condemned in the ancient world. The view that homosexuality was a violation of nature was widespread in antiquity (cf. e.g. Aeschines, *Speeches,* "Timarch" 185; Plutarch, *Moralia,* "De placitis Philosophorum" 990 D-F; "Dialogue on Love" 751 C-D; Galen, *De Propiorum Animi . . . Affectum* 6.9; Ovid, *Metamorphoses* 9.715-48).

538. Romans 1:26-27

Plato, *Laws* 836 A-C (428/27–349/48 BCE)

But when we come to the amorous passions of children of both sexes and of men for women and women for men—passions which have been the cause of countless woes both to individuals and to whole States—how is one to guard against these, or what remedy can one apply so as to find a way of escape in all such cases from a danger such as this? It is extremely difficult, Clinias. For whereas, in regard to other matters not a few, Crete generally and Lacedaemon furnish us (and rightly) with no little assistance in the framing of laws which differ from those in common use—in regard to the passions of sex (for we are not alone by ourselves) they contradict us absolutely. If we were to follow in nature's steps and enact that law which held good before the days of Laïus, declaring that it is right to refrain from indulging in the same kind of intercourse with men and boys as with women, and adducing as evidence thereof the nature of wild beasts, and pointing out how male does not touch male for this purpose, since it is unnatural—in all this we would probably be using an argument neither convincing nor in any way consonant with your States. Moreover, that object which, as we affirm, the lawgiver ought always to have in view does not agree with these practices. For the inquiry we always make is this—which of the proposed laws tends toward virtue and which not. Come then, suppose we grant that this practice is now legalized, and that it is noble and in no way ignoble, how far would it promote virtue? Will it engender in the soul of him who is seduced a courageous character, or the soul of the seducer the quality of temperance? Nobody would ever believe this . . . (LCL)

While Plato regards the argument by analogy from the animal world as unconvincing (contrast no. 537), like Paul, he regards same-sex relationships as contrary to nature (as clearly in *Phaedrus* 251 A; *Laws* 1.636 B-D; *Laws* 8.841 D-E). For Plato, the "unnatural" quality of homosexuality does not make homosexuality as such immoral. The immoral element is the "seduction" of one person by another. If homosexuality were legalized, the ethical question would be not its "naturalness," but whether it produced temperance, courage, and nobility of soul, which, he says, no one would affirm.

539. Romans 1:28-32

Wisdom of Solomon 14:21-27 (150 BCE–50 CE)

And this became a hidden trap for humankind, because people, in bondage to misfortune or to royal authority, bestowed on objects of stone or wood the name that ought not to be shared. 22 Then it was not enough for them to err about the knowledge of God, but though living in great strife due to ignorance, they call such great evils peace. 23 For whether they kill children in their initiations, or celebrate secret mysteries, or hold frenzied revels with strange customs, 24 they no longer keep either their lives or their marriages pure, but they either treacherously kill one another, or grieve one another by adultery, 25 and all is a raging riot of blood and murder, theft and deceit, corruption, faithlessness, tumult, perjury, 26 confusion over what is good, forgetfulness of favors, defiling of souls, sexual perversion, disorder in marriages, adultery, and debauchery. 27 For the worship of idols not to be named is the beginning and cause and end of every evil. (NRSV)

In common with Paul is not only the common view of Hellenistic Judaism that idolatry is the source of immorality, but also the form of a vice catalog in which several of the same items appear. Paul appears to have been deeply influenced by the thought world reflected in the Wisdom of Solomon, and probably by the text itself (cf. e.g. Anders Nygren, *Commentary on Romans,* trans. Carl C. Rasmussen [Philadelphia: Muhlenberg Press, 1949]).

540. Romans 2:12-15

Aristotle, *Rhetoric* 1.15.3-8 (384–322 BCE)

Let us first then speak of the laws, and state what use should be made of them when exhorting or dissuading, accusing or defending. For it is evident that, if the written law is counter to our case, we must have recourse to the general law and equity, as more in accordance with justice; and we must argue that, when the dicast takes an oath to decide to the best of his judgment, he means that he will not abide rigorously by the written laws; that equity is ever constant and never changes, even as the general law, which is based on nature, whereas the written laws often vary (this is why Antigone in Sophocles justifies herself for having buried Polynices contrary to the law of Creon, but not contrary to the unwritten law):
For this law is not of now or yesterday, but is eternal . . .
this I was not likely [to infringe through fear of the pride]
of any man;
and further, that justice is really an expedient, but not that which only appears just; nor the written law either, because it does not do the work of the law; that the judge is like an assayer of silver, whose duty is to distinguish spurious from genuine justice; that it is the part of a better man to make use of and abide by the unwritten rather than the written law. (LCL)

Here Paul seems to reflect the Greek concept of the unwritten law of nature, not "unwritten Law" in the Jewish sense of oral Torah. Cf. also *Nicomachean Ethics* 5.7.18-24; Galen, citing the writing of Hippocrates, "On Human Nature" 43, that "according to the law" and "according to nature" are one and the same (κατὰ νόμον /κατὰ φύσιν); Hermogenes, "On Ideas," 1.221; Dio Chrysostom, *Discourse* 36.23.

541. Romans 2:14

Aristotle, *Nicomachean Ethics* 4.8.8-10 (384–322 BCE)

. . . we feel that deeds which a man permits to be ascribed to him he would not stop at actually doing. Hence a man will draw the line at some jokes; for raillery is a sort of vilification, and some forms of vilification are forbidden by law; perhaps some forms of raillery ought to be prohibited also. The cultivated gentleman will therefore regulate his wit, and will be as it were *a law to himself*. Such then is the middle character, whether he be called "tactful" or "witty." (LCL)

People who achieve the Aristotelian ideal of the "golden mean" can differentiate and regulate their own conduct just as if a lawgiver had made rules for it which they are obeying. At least they perceive intuitively that which lawgivers have in other places actually legislated. By the principle of the "mean," Aristotle thus attempts to give a kind of meta-norm.

Similarly, in *Politics* 3.13 (1284a), Aristotle deals with people who when measured by the categories of virtue are truly outstanding, for whom the law does not really apply because they transcend it, so that they are themselves the law, and whoever would attempt to give them laws would only be laughable (cf. no. 828).

In the seventh letter of Heraclitus (*First-century Cynicism in the Epistles of Heraclitus*, ed. H. W. Attridge [Missoula, Mont.: Scholars Press, 1976]) (1 cent. BCE–2 cent. CE), Heraclitus laments his fate of being banned from the city. He had done nothing wrong, but those who banned him made the city worse by their own evil act. He could make the city better, but they did not want this. "But I want it, and am a law for others."

These texts should be distinguished from those Stoic documents which speak of the meta-norm as the *natural law* directly available to the reason. Aristotle of course knows an unwritten law as a general law "according to nature" (*Rhetoric* 10 [1368b]), in addition to which habit and custom form unwritten laws. The general laws of nature (e.g. the command to take care of one's parents) are in any case from God. Paul avoids the all too optimistic idea, based on their outstanding righteousness, that the Gentiles had themselves embodied the law (νόμος ἔμψυχος). In its place, in v. 15 he presents the uncommon idea that God has written it in their hearts, thus strictly preserving God's own authority. The *Neuer Wettstein* presents a series of 32 texts on the relation of written law and "natural," unwritten law.

542. Romans 2:15

Seneca, *Epistles to Lucilius*, 3.28.10, "On Travel as a Cure for Discontent" (4–65 CE)

Some boast of their faults. Do you think that the man has any thought of mending his ways who counts over his vices as if they were virtues? Therefore, as far as possible, prove yourself guilty, hunt up charges against yourself; play the part, first of accuser, then of judge, last of intercessor. At times be harsh with yourself. (LCL)

Similarly, "On Wrath" 3.26.1: One must ask daily about one's own weaknesses and one's progress, anger must "appear every day before its judge." The soul becomes observer of itself and a secret censor; nothing of one's own action or thought is concealed from oneself. Paul thinks like Seneca about the independence of the capacity to judge found in human beings, and the impossibility of bribing or fooling it (though Seneca does not name it "conscience"). In Seneca it is more like a voluntary subjecting of oneself to one's own better judgment, while in Paul one hardly has to exert oneself in order to hear the verdict of conscience. Cf. no. 717.

In addition, cf. the article *"Gewissen"* (conscience) by H. Chadwick in *RAC* 10 (1025-1107; on Seneca, 1049f.).

543. Romans 2:17

2 Baruch (1 cent. CE)

In you we have put our trust, because, behold, your Law is with us, and we know that we do not fall as long as we keep your statutes. We shall always be blessed; at least, we did not mingle with the nations. For we are all a people of the Name; we, who received one Law from the One. And that Law that is among us will help us, and that excellent wisdom which is in us will support us. (*OTP* 1:636)

God's response then of course lets there be no doubt that judgment and law demand righteous living, and that Israel will be punished because of their bad conduct. The uncontested distinction that Israel has in the possession of the Law is here, just as in Paul, no soft cushion on which Israel may rest. Paul is not here arguing against "the" Jewish point of view, but adopts a standpoint also present in Judaism and adapts it to his own argument. Cf. also no. 508 above.

544. Romans 2:17-24

Plutarch, *Moralia*, "How to Profit By One's Enemies" 4-5 (45–125 CE)

And if you are led into reviling, remove yourself as far as possible from the things for which you revile him. Enter within the portals of your own soul, look about to see if there be any rottenness there, lest some vice lurking somewhere within whisper to you the words of the tragedian: Wouldst thou heal others, full of sores thyself? . . .

For there is nothing more disgraceful or painful than evil-speaking that recoils upon its author. So reflected light appears to be the more troublesome in cases of weak eyesight, and the same is true of censures that by the truth are brought back upon the very persons who are responsible for them. For as surely the north-east wind brings the clouds, so surely does a bad life bring revilings upon itself. . . .

Do not therefore ever revile an adulterer when you yourself are given to unnatural lust, nor a profligate when you yourself are stingy. . . . "Know thyself" . . . (LCL)

This text shows that Paul here adopts a widespread topos of ancient pedagogic (in Plutarch it is practically already quoted as an accepted gnome). While the motivation in Plutarch is to avoid making oneself laughable (pain and shame) and rather to know oneself, in Paul the motivation is the honoring of God's name (2:23-24). Further:

545. Romans 2:17-22

Seneca, *On Anger* 2.28.5-8 (4–65 CE)

It will be said that someone spoke ill of you; consider whether you spoke ill of him first, consider how many there are of whom you speak ill. Let us consider, I say, that some are not doing us an injury but repaying one, that others are acting for our good, that some are acting under compulsion, others in ignorance, that even those acting intentionally and willingly do not, while injuring us, aim only at the injury; one slipped into it allured by his wit, another did something, not to obstruct us, but because he could not reach his own goal without pushing us back; often adulation, while it flatters, offends. If anyone will recall how often he himself has fallen under undeserved suspicion, how many of his good services chance has clothed with the appearance of injury, how many persons whom once he hated he learned to love, he will be able to avoid all hasty anger, particularly if as each offense occurs he will first say to himself in silence: "I myself have also been guilty of this." But where will you find a judge so just? The man who covets everybody's wife and considers the mere fact that she belongs to another an ample and just excuse for loving her—this same man will not have his own wife looked at; the strictest enforcer of loyalty is the traitor, the punisher of falsehood is himself a perjurer, and the trickster lawyer deeply resents an indictment being brought against himself; the man who has no regard for his own chastity will permit no tampering with that of his slaves. The vices of others we keep before our eyes, our own behind our back; hence it happens that a father who is even worse than his son rebukes his son's untimely revels, that a man does not pardon another's excesses who sets no bound to his own, that the murderer stirs a tyrant's wrath, and the temple robber punishes theft. It is not with the sins but with the sinners that most men are angry. We shall become more tolerant from self-inspection if we cause ourselves to consider: "Have we ourselves never been guilty of such an act? Have we never made the same mistake? Is it expedient for us to condemn such conduct?" (LCL)

Seneca, a contemporary of Paul, commends the noble view of being understanding toward the faults of others and being more critical of oneself than is typically the case. In the course of his exhortation there are striking parallels to Paul's own rhetoric, even to the point of using "temple robbers" as an illustration—but the point is entirely different. While they have in common the view that by acknowledging oneself to be an imperfect person among other imperfect people, one will be more tolerant, understanding, and caring, Paul is on the way to building a case that all human beings are sinful and stand under the wrath of God, and are thus in need of God's grace, while Seneca's perspective is altogether on the interpersonal and introspective level.

546. Romans 2:23

Testaments of the Twelve Patriarchs, "Testament of Naphtali" 8:4, 6 (2–1 cent. BCE)

If you achieve the good, my children, men and angels will bless you; and God will be glorified through you among the gentiles. The devil will flee from you; wild animals will be afraid of you, and the angels will stand by you.

The one who does not do the good,
men and angels will curse,
and God will be dishonored among the gentiles because of him;
the devil will inhabit him as his own instrument.
Every wild animal will dominate him,
and the Lord will hate him. (*OTP* 1:813)

The text from "Testament of Naphtali" stands at an important juncture within the broad wake of the history of interpretation of Isaiah 52:5. The stages in the development of this interpretative tradition may be outlined as follows: (1) God is reviled: Isaiah 52:5 MT: the Gentile rulers boast about Israel's fate. The way out of this situation is Israel's repentance 52:5. LXX: the Gentiles blaspheme the name of God because of Israel. (2) In this stage the text is thoroughly reinterpreted in terms of ethics. It is no longer Israel's fate, but through current failures that causes God to be blasphemed: Romans 2:24; Titus 2:5 (without Gentiles). (3) The fork in the road: alongside blaspheming, the *positive alternative* emerges, and both are named together ("T. Naph." 8, honor/dishonor); *2 Clement* 13 (blaspheme/admire). (4) In the missionary context, only honoring and glorifying are spoken of (Matt 5:16; 1 Pet 2:10 [both times with "good works"]; Hermas, *Mandates* 3:1-5). Then the references to "glorifying" can drop out, leaving only conversion on the basis of conduct: Ignatius, *Ephesians* 10 (conversion, works). These "stages" are not, of course, necessarily a chronological progression.

547. Romans 2:28

Archytas of Tarentum, "On Law and Righteousness" (a Pythagorian, 4 cent. BCE)

I say now that every society consists of ruler and ruled, the third element being the laws. Among these laws, however, there is the living law represented by the king [lit. ἔμψυχος "ensouled," "with a soul"], and the lifeless law of the letter [lit. ἄψυχος "without a soul"]. The law is in the first place, for the king faithful to the law abides in it, the ruler who follows it, those who are ruled are free, and the whole society is happy. (MEB/Stobaeus, *Anthologium* vol. 4.1.135)

The law is the all-encompassing entity. The king as its living manifestation is only another materialization alongside the written law. In view of Romans 7:12, 14, one could defend the thesis that this analogy is no different for Paul—for the one who is redeemed. Paul, to be sure, emphasizes more strongly the contrast between the form of the law as letter and the form as living reality. Still, that does not conflict with the Hellenistic distinction, since, as was shown in no. 540 above, people who are completely righteous are themselves a living law. As justified people, the Christians themselves are such. That which could not be affirmed in Romans 2:14-15 is appropriate here. The status here contrasted to the letter of the law is precisely the νόμος ἔμψυχος of Greek tradition (cf. also no. 614). The difference consists in the fact that in these cases the Greeks do not speak of the Spirit of God. That, however, is the Jewish–Old Testament "component" of the composite concept. Cf. the gift of the Spirit according to Ezekiel 36:26-27 and Jubilees 1:23-24 (gift of the Spirit from God, plus fulfilling of the commandments). Cf. also Romans 8:2.

548. Romans 2:28

Philo, *Questions and Answers on Exodus* 2.2 (15 BCE–50 CE)

. . . the sojourner is one who circumcises not his uncircumcision but his desires and sensual pleasures and the other passions of the soul. (LCL)

The contrast not this/but that in regard to the criteria for being a true Jew agrees with Paul, as does the content, in contrasting the visible mark of circumcision with the invisible realities of the soul. Again, the difference lies in the gift of the Spirit of God. See also no. 659.

549. Romans 3:4

1QH 1:26 (2–1 cent. BCE)

> For thine, O God of knowledge,
> are all righteous deeds
> and the counsel of truth;
> but to the sons of men is the work of iniquity
> and deeds of deceit. (Vermes)

Similarly 1QH 9:14-15. As in Paul, truth is confronted with falsehood. But in 1QH it is a matter of a hymnic predication directed to God, which first occurs in Paul in the Scripture quotation. In Paul, however, the dominant context is argumentative, with the result that the critical question can be added in 3:5, whether the righteousness of God is not enhanced by human unrighteousness. Paul thus makes a critical use of an idea widespread in Judaism, but rejects it in 3:6. Cf. also no. 601.

550. Romans 3:9-25

1QH 9.14-15 (2–1 cents. BCE)

> For I know there is hope in Thy grace and expectation in Thy great power.
> For no man can be just in Thy judgment or [righteous in] Thy trial. (Vermes)

As in Paul, the pronouncement of universal sinfulness is not part of an abstract pessimistic doctrine of human nature, but serves as the ground for the declaration of the universal need of grace, by which alone God's salvation comes. This sentiment is often found at Qumran, especially in the Hodayot. Thus e.g. 1QH 13:16-17, "By Thy goodness alone is man righteous" (Vermes). While "grace *alone*" is implicit in the Pauline argument, it is explicit at Qumran. Cf. H.-W. Kuhn, "The Impact of the Qumran Scrolls on the Understanding of Paul," in Devorah Dimant and Uriel Rappaport, eds., *The Dead Sea Scrolls: Forty Years of Research* [Leiden: E. J. Brill, 1992], 333-34.

551. Romans 3:20

Seneca, *On Anger* 2.28.1-4 (4–65 CE)

If we are willing in all matters to play the just judge, let us convince ourselves first of this—that no one of us is free from fault. For most of our indignation arises from our saying, "I am not to blame," "I have done nothing wrong." Say, rather, that you admit no wrong! We chafe against the censure of some reprimand or chastisement although at the very time we are at fault because we are adding to wrongdoing arrogance and obstinacy. What man is there who can claim that in the eyes of every law he is innocent? But assuming that this may be, how limited is the innocence whose standard of virtue is the law! How much more comprehensive is the principle of duty than that of law! How many are the demands laid upon us by the sense of duty, humanity, generosity, justice, integrity—all of which lie outside the statute books! But even under that other exceedingly narrow definition of innocence we cannot vouch for our claim. Some sins we have committed, some we have contemplated, some we have desired, some we have encouraged; in the case of some we are innocent only because we did not succeed. Bearing this in mind, let us be more just to transgressors, more heedful to those who rebuke us (for who will escape if we are to be angry even with the good?), and least of all with the gods. For it is not by their power, but by the terms of our mortality, that we are forced to suffer whatever ill befalls. "But," you say, "sickness and pain assail us." At any rate there must be an ending some time, seeing that we have been given a crumbling tenement! (LCL)

The Pauline declaration of universal human sinfulness may be seen in its Hellenistic context as illustrated by Seneca. Here a good man confesses his own faults, and the declaration that there is no human being who is without fault. As in Paul, the declaration comes in a context dealing with the propensity to condemn others and justify ourselves (cf. Rom 2:1-11). Seneca also illustrates the Pauline affirmation that those without the Torah nevertheless have a law "written on their hearts" to which they are responsible (cf. Rom 1:12-16). Here too, the undefensive acknowledgment of one's own faults is the prescription for proper relations with others. Missing is Paul's radical understanding of sin as transgression against the holiness of God. Seneca brings in "the gods" only superficially at the end, in order to emphasize that the whole discussion is in a "natural" framework.

552. Romans 3:21-24, 29

Plutarch, *Moralia*, "On the Fortune of the Romans" 9-10 (45–125 CE)

[On the time under Numa:] For they relate that no famine nor pestilence nor failure of crops nor any unseasonable occurrence in either summer or winter vexed Rome during that time, as if it were not wise human counsel, but divine Fortune that was Rome's guardian during those crucial days.

And Servius Tullius, the man who of all the kings most increased the power of his people, and introduced a well-regulated government and imposed order upon both the holding of elections and military procedure, and became the first censor and overseer of the lives and decorum of the citizens, and held the highest repute for courage and wisdom, of his own initiative attached himself to Fortune and bound his sovereignty fast to her, with the result that it was even thought that Fortune consorted with him, descending into his chamber through a certain window. (LCL)

Similarly in §11, ". . . the progress of Rome's sovereignty was not brought about by the handiwork and urging of human beings, but was speeded on its way by divine escort and the fair wind of Fortune" (LCL). This whole tractate of Plutarch's is in fact a discussion of grace and works, if one identifies "grace" with the "fortune" sent by the gods, and describes human virtue and accomplishment as "works." Of course, Paul discusses this relationship less as a matter of anthropology than as a theology of history, and Plutarch too is much more interested in history than anthropology. Further:

553. Romans 3:21-24, 29

Philo, *Who Is the Heir of Divine Things* 6 (15 BCE–50 CE)

For who was I, that Thou shouldst impart speech to me, that Thou shouldst promise me something which stood higher in the scale of goods than "gift" or grace, even a "reward." Am I not a wanderer from my country, an outcast from my kinsfolk, an alien from my father's house? Do not all men call me excommunicate, exile, desolate, disfranchised? But Thou, Master, art my country, my kinsfolk, my paternal hearth, my franchise, my free speech, my great and glorious and inalienable wealth. Why then shall I not take courage to say what I feel? Why shall I not inquire of Thee and claim to learn something more? Yet I, who proclaim my confidence, confess in turn my fear and consternation, and still the fear and the confidence are not at war within me in separate camps, as one might suppose, but are blended in a harmony. I find then a feast which does not cloy in this blending, which has schooled my speech to be neither bold without caution, nor cautious without boldness. For I have learnt to measure my own nothingness, and to gaze with wonder on the transcendent heights of Thy loving-kindnesses. And when I perceive that I am earth and cinders or whatever is still more worthless, it is just then that I have confidence to come before Thee, when I am humbled, cast down to the clay, reduced to such an elemental state, as seems not even to exist. (LCL)

Similarly on "Special Laws" 1.264-65: "Now the substance of which our body consists is earth and water, and of this he reminds us in the rite of purging. For he holds that the most profitable form of purification is just this, that a man should know himself and the nature of the elements of which he is composed, ashes and water, so little worthy of esteem. For if he recognizes this, he will straightway turn away from the insidious enemy, self-conceit, and abasing his pride become well-pleasing to God and claim the aid of His gracious power Who hates arrogance. For that is a good text which tells us that he who sets his hand to words and deeds of pride 'provokes' not only men, but also 'God,' the author of equality and all that is most excellent" (LCL).

Human nothingness before God and the divine sovereignty as alone responsible for all goodness is clearly formulated by Philo, and is not to be explained away in terms of some hidden works-righteousness (contra H. Braun, *Wie man über Gott nicht denken soll* [Tübingen: J. C. B. Mohr, 1971]). God is not only the creator of good, God is the one who continues to create all that is good ("Plant" 31). This is seen also in God's act of election (see below under Rom 9, no. 600). The difference from Paul consists rather in the following: That which is widely attributed to Paul by modern exegetes, namely what may be described anthropologically as a relationship between God and humanity that is valid for all times, is in fact Philo's understanding. For Philo the point has to do with the contrast between divine and human action as such, and his way of stating it is: human activity amounts to nothing, all comes from God. In particular, boasting is excluded. On the other hand, for Paul this contrast is replaced by a different, all-encompassing, but precisely not timeless contrast, the contrast between life under the law (under Jewish presuppositions, without Christ and the Spirit), and life in Christ (grace, Spirit). Here is where the line is to be drawn. Unwholesome human boasting is oriented to works of law done under the law to the extent that Jews (and e.g. his opponents in

Galatia) do not perceive the new way of God and by appealing to the old way exclude themselves from the new.

554. Romans 3:21–4:25

Community Rule (1QS) 11 (1 cent. BCE)

As for me,
my justification is with God.
In His hand are the perfection of my way
and the uprightness of my heart.
He will wipe out my transgression
through His righteousness. . . .
From the source of His righteousness
is my justification,
and from His marvelous mysteries
is the light in my heart.
My eyes have gazed
on that which is eternal,
on wisdom concealed from men,
on knowledge and wise design
[hidden] from the sons of men;
on a fountain of righteousness
and on a storehouse of power,
on a spring of glory
[hidden] from the assembly of flesh. . . .
As for me,
I belong to wicked mankind,
to the company of ungodly flesh. . . .
For mankind has no way,
and man is unable to establish His steps
since justification is with God
and perfection of way is out of His hand. . . .
As for me,
if I stumble, the mercies of God
shall be my eternal salvation.
If I stagger because of the sin of flesh,
my justification shall be
by the righteousness of God which endures forever. . . .
He will draw me near by His grace,
and by His mercy will he bring my justification. . . .
Through His righteousness he will cleanse me
of the uncleanness of man
and of the sins of the children of men,
that I may confess to God His righteousness,

and His majesty to the Most High.
Blessed art thou, my God,
who openest the heart of thy servant to knowledge!
Establish all his deeds in righteousness . . .
(Vermes)

The points of contact with Paul's doctrine of justification are both structural and terminological. Humanity is universally sinful and condemned, including the author (presumably the Teacher of Righteousness, the founder and first leader of the Qumran community). Salvation is by God's grace. Righteousness is not a human achievement but a gift of God. The human response is gratitude and good works. The mood is grateful, joyful worship. The key word "righteousness" is sometimes משפט, which could be translated "judgment" rather than "justification," but צדקה is also used, which is closer to Paul's own terminology. This understanding of justification-from-God is found not only in the Community Rule, but in the Hymns, e.g. 1QH 4:39-40:

"I lean on Thy grace
and on the multitude of Thy mercies,
for Thou wilt pardon iniquity
and through Thy righteousness
[Thou wilt purify man] of his sin.
Not for his sake wilt Thou do it,
[but for the sake of Thy glory]" (Vermes).

555. Romans 3:21-24*a*

Corpus Hermeticum 13.9-10 (2–4 cent. CE)

[Hermes speaks by revelation to his son Tat; §§1-3 speak of rebirth; cf. no. 129; §§6-8 speak of the *grace* of God that has come down to humanity, in several 'powers.' Hermes has already spoken of four powers: Knowledge, Joy, Continence, Endurance:] This next level, my child, is the seat of justice. See how she has expelled injustice, without a judgment. With injustice gone, my child, we have been made just. . . . My child, you have come to know the means of rebirth. (Copenhaver)

This section is preceded by declarations about the positive Powers whose advent drives out the negative elements from human beings: ignorance driven out by Knowledge, sadness by Joy, lack of self-discipline by Continence, sensual appetites by Endurance. Thus those attributes that come down to human beings here at rebirth are very similar to the "imputed virtues" of later Christian dogmatics.

Important similarities in comparison with Paul: (1) Righteousness is given to human beings (by grace). (2) This happens in connection with initiation. (3) The setting aside of unrighteousness happens without condemnation (cf. also Rom 3:25*b*; 8:1).

The primary difference (apart from the manner of mediation through faith in Jesus' death in Paul) is that in Paul, the human being standing before God lacks just one thing, righteousness/justification. This ethical/forensic aspect is in CH 13 ranked as only one item on a list. But Paul is first of all a Pharisee and oriented above all to righteousness. Still, in Paul too one should not underrate the role of knowledge (of the one God) and joy (as a charismatic phenomenon)—so that CH 13 could even provide a kind of "corrective function" in our perception of Paul.

Cf. also no. 590.

556. Romans 3:23

Apocalypse of Moses 21 (1 cent. BCE)

[Eve speaks:] And then I quickly persuaded him, and he ate, and his eyes were opened, and he recognized his nakedness, and said to me, "O wicked woman, what have you done to us. You have made me an alien to the glory of God." (MEB/from K. Tischendorf edition cited by Berger)

In Romans Paul often uses material from Jewish interpretations of the paradise story, without explicitly quoting them (cf. 5:12; 7:7-10). The Greek verb ἀπαλλοτριόω of the *Apocalypse of Moses* corresponds to the verb ὑστερέω used by Paul in 3:23. The first verb describes the beginning, the second one the lasting results. That is, now, as a result of the fall brought about by Adam and Eve, all human beings lack the glory of God (which Adam still had at first, cf. below no. 713).

557. Romans 3:25

Plutarch, *Moralia*, "Isis and Osiris" 73 (45–125 CE)

If there befall a great and severe drought that brings on in excess either fatal diseases or other unwonted and extraordinary calamities, the priests, under cover of darkness, in silence and stealth, lead away some of the animals that are held in honor; and at first they but threaten and terrify the animals, but if the drought still persists, they consecrate and sacrifice them, as if, forsooth, this were a means of punishing the deity, or at least a mighty rite of purification in matters of the highest importance! The fact is that in the city of Eileithyia they used to burn men alive, as Manetho has recorded; they called them Typhonians, and by means of winnowing fans they dissipated and scattered their ashes. But this was performed publicly and at a special time in the dog-days. The consecrations of the animals held in honor, however, were secret. . . . (LCL)

In "Roman Questions" 83, Plutarch points out that the Romans did not punish the leaders of the Bletonesier who had sacrificed a human being to the gods. "Did they think it impious to sacrifice men to the gods, but necessary to sacrifice them to the spirits?" The answer is no, since there was a case among the Romans in which sacred Virgins had been violated, the *Sibylline Oracles* were consulted, and they commanded that ". . . to avert the impending disaster, they should offer as a sacrifice to certain strange and alien spirits two Greeks and two Gauls, buried alive on the spot" (LCL).

Both texts show that while human sacrifice was rare, it was not unknown. The function is clear: to avert catastrophe (which could also be described as the wrath of the gods). Cf. no. 154. So also the Maccabean martyrs were regarded as sin offerings, despite the rejection of human sacrifice in the Old Testament. Esp. important for Romans 3:24-25 is 4 Maccabees 17:21, since it refers to the "atoning death" (ἰλαστήριος θάνατος), and since the use of ἰλαστήριος as an adjective also opens up the possibility of understanding ἰλαστήριον in Romans 3:25 adjectivally. Second Maccabees 7:38 speaks of "bringing an end to the wrath of God" through the death of the martyrs. That in Paul God has designated Jesus to play that role at least has analogies in the pagan texts that command human sacrifice, and there too it is the gods who institute the practice. Does the special purity and charismatic righteousness of Jesus (i.e. on the basis of his sonship to God) really constitute a fundamental difference to these ancient analogies? Or is it rather the case that through his charismatic righteousness Jesus' sacrifice has the eschatological power lacking in both the Maccabean martyrs and the human sacrifices among the pagans? It is a matter of the ἅπαξ, once-for-all character of Jesus' death. See also no. 564.

558. Romans 3:25

Inscription in the Santa Prisca Mithraeum in Rome (3 [?] cent. CE)

You saved us by shedding the eternal blood. (Ferguson, *Backgrounds*)

This ascription of praise to Mithras could seem to be analogous to early Christian affirmations of salvation by Jesus' blood (see also Matt 26:28; Acts 20:28; Rom 5:9; Eph 1:7; 2:13; Col 1:20; Heb 9:12-22; 10:19; 13:12; 1 Pet 1:19; 1 John 1:7; Rev 1:5). But here the blood is not Mithras' own, but that of the bull-slaying that was Mithras' greatest feat, portrayed as the foundational myth of the cult in the typical Mithraic sculpture (not to be confused with the Taurobolium of the cult of Cybele and Attis, see no. 386 on John 3:3-5). The wild cosmic bull represents not only chaotic power, but life and vigor. The bull-slaying was a creative and salvific act, that released the life and power inherent in its blood for the benefit not only of human beings, but of nature, which was made fertile by this act.

Mithraism, once thought to offer solid parallels to New Testament theology, is now seen to be quite distant. The sources are too late to be of direct value for the study of Christian origins. New Testament blood imagery is drawn from the sacrificial cultus of the Hebrew Bible.

On Romans 3:27 (boasting), see no. 342.

559. Romans 4:3

Pseudo-Philo (Armenean), *On Samson* §25

If he [Samson] therefore had received the gifts of the Spirit, then he would also have had to prove himself to be a sinless human being. But if he had [only] received one drop from the great spring of grace, yea the great sea of grace, then how could he, to whom [only] one of [many] parts belongs, have command over the whole? [Examples] Our ancestor Abraham received the Spirit of righteousness. [This Spirit] apparently let him be full of goodness, for he believed on the Living One. Joseph received the Spirit of self-control, and when the woman offered her body to him, he overcame fleshly desire. Simeon and Levi received the Spirit of zeal . . . Judah received the Spirit of right judgment. . . . (MEB/Berger)

Within the history of interpretation of Genesis 15:6 (cf. e.g. 1 Macc 2:52), this text has a special position: (1) Abraham's righteousness is thought of as conferred by God's Spirit, like the *charismata* of 1 Corinthians 12. The connection between righteousness and Spirit that is indirect in Pauline theology (Rom 8:1-12) is here directly made. (2) The question that is raised again and again in

Pauline theology, whether faith is a kind of "work," perhaps the only "work" required of human beings to be acceptable to God, is here skillfully avoided: Abraham could believe, because he already had the Spirit of righteousness. Faith is therefore the expression of the previously given righteousness, and its appropriate demonstration. Righteousness itself is the gift of God. As in the text from CH 13 discussed in no. 555, righteousness is only one of the gifts of the Spirit. Cf. no. 758, and 1 Corinthians 12:12-31; Romans 12:4-8.

On grace/works, cf. no. 600.

560. Romans 4:3

Jubilees 31:21-25 (145–140 BCE)

And turning, he kissed him again and embraced him and rejoiced greatly because he had seen the sons of Jacob, his own true son. And he withdrew from his embrace and fell down and bowed down to him. And he blessed them. And he rested there near Isaac, his father, during that night. And they ate and drank joyfully. And he made the two sons of Jacob sleep, one on his right hand and one on his left, and it was counted to him [as] righteousness. And Jacob told his father everything during the night, how the Lord had shown him great mercy, and how he had made all his affairs prosper and protected him from all evil. And Isaac blessed the God of his father, Abraham, who did not withhold his mercy and his righteousness from the son of his servant Isaac. (*OTP* 2:116)

Cf. also Galatians 3:6. The Genesis 15:6 text understood as an example of "imputed righteousness" already had a history of interpretation before being adopted by Paul in this sense. The application to Isaac is in contrast to Paul's view of the "justification of the ungodly," however, since Isaac is understood as a righteous and saintly figure. Though a rather pale figure in the Hebrew Bible, Isaac was understood in first-century Jewish tradition to be the example of self-giving obedience to God, one greatly blessed and endowed with divine power. In *Jubilees*, Isaac was a model of righteousness, "And a spirit of prophecy came down upon his mouth" (31:12). The *Targum Pseudo-Jonathan* 22:1-19 (7 cent. CE, containing early material) retells the Genesis story in such a way that Isaac is the willing victim in obedience to God's will:

"After these events, after Isaac and Ishmael had quarreled, Ishmael said, 'It is right that I should be my father's heir, since I am his first-born son.' But Isaac said, 'It is right that I should be my father's heir, because I am the son of Sarah his wife, while you are the son of Hagar, my mother's maidservant.' Ishmael answered and said, 'I am more worthy than you, because I was circumcised at the age of thirteen. And if I had wished to refuse, I would not have handed myself over to be circumcised. But you were circumcised at the age of eight days. If you had been aware, perhaps you would not have handed yourself over to be circumcised.' Isaac answered and said, 'Behold, today I am thirty-seven years old, and if the Holy One, blessed be He, were to ask all my members I would not refuse.' These words were immediately heard before the Lord of the world, and at once the Memra of the Lord tested Abraham and said to him, 'Abraham!' and he said to him, 'Here I am.' He said, 'Take your son, your only one, Isaac whom you love, and go to the land of worship, and offer him there as a burnt offering on one of the mountains of which I will tell you.' Abraham rose early in the morning and saddled his ass and took with him his two servant boys Eleazer and Ishmael and his son Isaac. He cut wood of the olive tree, the fig tree, and the palm tree, which are suitable for the burnt offering, and he rose and went to the place of which the Lord had told him. On the third day Abraham lifted up his eyes and saw the cloud of Glory enveloping the mountain, and he recognized it from afar. And Abraham said to his servants, 'Wait here with the ass, while the lad and

I betake ourselves over there to find out if that which was announced to me—"so shall your children be"—will be fulfilled. We will bow down to the Lord of the world, and we will return to you.' Abraham took the wood for the burnt offering and placed [it] on Isaac his son, and he took the fire and the knife in his own hand; and the two of them went together. Isaac spoke to his father Abraham, and said, 'Father!' And he said, 'Here I am [my son].' He said, 'Behold the fire and the wood; but where is the lamb for the burnt offering?' Abraham said, 'The Lord will choose for himself the lamb for the burnt offering, my son.' And the two of them went together with a perfect heart. They came to the place of which the Lord had told him, and there Abraham [re]built the altar which Adam had built and [which] had been demolished by the waters of the Flood. Noah rebuilt it, but it was demolished in the generation of the Division. He arranged the wood upon it, and tied Isaac his son and placed him on the altar, on top of the wood. Abraham put forth his hand and took the knife to slaughter his son. Isaac spoke up and said to his father: 'Tie me well lest I struggle because of the anguish of my soul, with the result that a blemish will be found in your offering, and I will be thrust into the pit of destruction.' The eyes of Abraham were looking at the eyes of Isaac, and the eyes of Isaac were looking at the angels on high. Isaac saw them but Abraham did not see them. The angels on high exclaimed: 'Come, see two unique ones who are in the world; one is slaughtering, and one is being slaughtered; the one who slaughters does not hesitate, and the one who is being slaughtered stretches forth his neck.' But the angel of the Lord called to him from heaven and said to him: 'Abraham, Abraham!' and he said 'Here I am.' And he said, 'Do not put forth your hand against the boy, and do not do him any harm, for it is now manifest before me that you fear the Lord, since you have not withheld your son, your only one, from me.' Abraham lifted up his eyes and saw one ram—[the one] that had been created at twilight when the world was completed—caught by its horns in the dense branches of a tree. Abraham went and took it and offered it as a burnt offering instead of his son. Abraham gave thanks and prayed there in that place, and said: 'I beseech, by the mercy from before you, O Lord! It is manifest before you that there was no deviousness in my heart, and that I sought to perform your decree with joy. Therefore, when the children of Isaac my son enter into a time of distress, remember them, and answer them, and redeem them. All these generations to come will say, "On this mountain Abraham tied his son Isaac, and there the Shekinah of the Lord was revealed to him!"' The angel of the Lord called to Abraham a second time from heaven and said, 'By my Memra I have sworn, says the Lord, because you have done this thing and have not refused your son, your only one, I will bless you abundantly and multiply your children as the stars of heaven and as the sand that is on the seashore, and your children shall inherit the cities of those who hate them. All the peoples of the earth shall be blessed because of the merits of your children, because you obeyed my word.' The angels on high took Isaac and brought him to the schoolhouse of Shem the Great, and he was there three years. On that day Abraham returned to his servants, and they arose and went together to Beer-sheba. And Abraham dwelt in Beer-sheba" (Maher). On Romans 4:4-5 (faith/works), cf. no. 822. On Romans 4:13, cf. no. 758.

561. Romans 4:17

Wisdom of Solomon 11:17 (150 BCE–50 CE)

For your all-powerful hand,
    which created the world out of formless matter . . . (NRSV)

Here, the Jewish author adopts the Platonic view of creation, with Wisdom playing the role of the Demiurge that shapes preexisting matter according to the heavenly Ideas. This is in contrast to 2 Maccabees 7:28: "I beg of you, my child, to look at the heaven and the earth and see everything that is in them, and recognize that God did not make them out of things that existed" (or: "that God made them out of things that did not exist") (NRSV).

Though Paul is influenced by the ideas found in Wisdom of Solomon (see Ancient Author Index), his understanding of creation is that of 2 Maccabees rather than that of Wisdom of Solomon. The point, however, is not *creatio ex nihilo* as a doctrine, which Paul simply assumes as a powerful illustrative analog to his doctrine of justification.

Cf. also 2 Maccabees 7:23: "Therefore the Creator of the world, who shaped the beginning of humankind and devised the origin of all things, will in his mercy give life and breath back to you again, since you now forget yourselves for the sake of his laws" (NRSV). As in Paul, resurrection is related to and based on creation: the Creator God does not need preexistent material to "work with," but creates out of nothing and raises the dead.

562. Romans 5:1-10

Plutarch, *Parallel Lives*, "Life of Themistocles" 28 (45–125 CE)

But when he [Themistocles] was led into the presence of the King and had made him obeisance, and was standing in silence, the King ordered the interpreter to ask him who he was, and, on the interpreter's asking, he said: "I who thus come to thee, O King, am Themistocles the Athenian, an exile, pursued by the Hellenes. . . . Now, therefore, I may look for any sequel to my present calamities, and I come prepared to receive the favor [χάρις] of one who benevolently offers reconciliation [διαλλάττω], or to deprecate the anger [ὀργή] of one who cherishes the remembrance of injuries. But do thou take my foes to witness for the good I wrought the Persians, and now use my misfortunes for the display of thy virtue [ἀρετή] rather than for the satisfaction of thine anger [ὀργή]. For it is a suppliant of thine whom thou wilt save [σώζω] . . . (LCL)

All the basic concepts of Romans 5:1-11 are contained in this text: grace, reconciliation, salvation, wrath; also enemies. Not only so, the scene itself, metaphorically considered, is analogous to Romans 5, since the access to the one who can bestow grace is in the Pauline text none other than access to God's throne (similar imagery and vocabulary in Hebrews 4:16). The pagan application of the verbal root ἀλλαττ- (= NT ἀλλασσ-) is rarely documented with reference to the relation to God; Paul obviously makes direct contact with the throne metaphor in its political context, and is himself responsible for the application to the divine-human relationship. Cf. no. 787.

563. Romans 5:1-11

Apuleius, *Metamorphoses* 11.6, 24-25 (2 cent. CE)

[Lucius had, by recklessly fooling around with magic, transformed himself into a donkey, i.e. had lost his true human self. Isis appears to Lucius in a dream, directs him to follow an Isis procession and eat the garland of roses carried by the priest, and speaks of the salvation he is to receive:] . . . and know thou this of certainty, that the residue of thy life until the hour of death shall be bound and subject to me; and think it not an injury to be always serviceable toward me whilst thou shalt live, since as by my mean and benefit thou shalt return again to be a man. Thou shalt live blessed in this world, thou shalt live glorious by my guide and protection, and when after thine allotted space of life thou descendest to hell [i.e. Hades, the world of the dead, not a place of punishment], there thou shalt see me in that subterranean firmament shining (as thou seest me now) in the darkness of Acheron, and reigning in the deep profundity of Styx, and thou shalt worship me as one that hath been favorable to thee. And if I perceive that thou art obedient to my commandment and addict to my religion, meriting by thy constant chastity my divine grace, know thou that I alone may prolong thy days above the time that the fates have appointed and ordained. . . .

[After following Isis' instructions and being transformed back into his human self, Lucius accepts the priest's invitation to be initiated. After his initiation he is full of joy:] Now when I had continued there some days, conceiving a marvelous pleasure and consolation in beholding ordinarily the image of the goddess, because of the benefits, beyond all esteem or reward, which she had brought me, at length she admonished me to depart homeward, not without rendering of thanks, which although they were not sufficient, yet they were according to my power. Howbeit I could hardly be persuaded to break the chains of my most earnest devotion and to depart, before I had fallen prostrate before the face of the goddess and wiped her feet with my face, whereby I began so greatly to weep and sigh that my words were interrupted, and as devouring my prayer I began to say in this sort: "O holy and blessed dame, the perpetual comfort of humankind, who by thy bounty and grace nourishest all the world, and bearest a great affection to the adversities of the miserable as a loving mother, thou takest no rest night or day, neither art thou idle at any time in giving benefits and succoring all men as well on land as sea; thou art she that puttest away all storm and dangers from men's life by stretching forth thy right hand, whereby likewise thou doest unweave even the inextricable and entangled web of fate, and appeasest the great tempests of fortune, and keepest back the harmful course of the stars. The gods supernal do honor thee; the gods infernal have thee in reverence; thou doest make all the earth to turn, thou givest light to the sun, thou governest the world, thou treadest down the power of hell [the realm of the dead]. By thy mean the stars give answer, the seasons return, the gods rejoice, the elements serve: at thy commandment the winds do blow, the clouds nourisheth the earth, the seeds prosper, and the fruits do grow. The birds of the air, the beasts of the hill, the serpents of the den, and the fishes of the sea do tremble at thy majesty: but my spirit is not able to give thee sufficient praise, my patrimony is unable to satisfy thy sacrifices; my voice has no power to utter that which I think of thy majesty, no, not if I had a thousand mouths and so many tongues and were able to continue forever. Howbeit as a good religious person, and according to my poor estate, I will do what I may: I will always keep thy divine appearance in remembrance, and close the imagination of thy most holy godhead within my breast." (LCL)

The story of the bungled attempt at magic resulting in losing his true self and being transformed into a donkey, followed after some time by the appearance of Isis who restores him to his true self and promises him eternal life, is only a thinly disguised allegory of passing from the state of being "lost" to the state of salvation by the gracious gift of the goddess. The authentic religious fervor is unmistakable; Lucius (= Apuleius himself) believes that he has been given new life by the deity, a blessed life in the present and joy in the presence of the deity in the transcendent world after death.

The similarities to the Pauline doctrine of salvation are clear: (1) Salvation is by the grace of the god, the initiative being entirely from the divine side. (2) Salvation restores the believer to the true estate for which humans were created but lost by their own sin. (3) Salvation is both present and future, beginning in this world and continuing beyond this life, being consummated in the presence of the deity. (4) The hallmark of salvation is joy and praise.

Three of several significant differences: (1) The savior in Apuleius is the deity, who remains deity without anything like incarnation. (2) The saving act is the communication of saving information from the deity, not a this-worldly act of love; there is and can be nothing like suffering and dying in the Isis story. (3) Even though Lucius is initiated, the saving act remains individual; for Paul, the community of the redeemed is an essential aspect of the saving event.

564. Romans 5:7

Aristotle, *Nicomachean Ethics* 8.9 (384–322 BCE)

But it is also true that the virtuous man's conduct is often guided by the interests of his friends and of his country, and that he will if necessary lay down his life in their behalf [ὑπεραποθνήσκω]. For he will surrender wealth and power and all the goods that men struggle to win, if he can secure nobility for himself. . . . (LCL)

In secular thought (differently from no. 557), the concept of dying for another person is most at home in the ethic of friendship. Cf. also Seneca, "On Philosophy and Friendship," Epistle 9.10: "For what purpose, then, do I make a man my friend? In order to have someone for whom I may die, whom I may follow into exile, against whose death I may stake my own life, and pay the pledge, too" (LCL). Seneca distinguishes friendship from that which is merely useful and practical. But according to Romans 5:7-8 God transcends even such love as is found in friendship, in that he gave Christ over to die not for his friends (so explicitly in v. 10), but for sinners. Paul thus seeks to demonstrate the greatness of God's saving act in contrast to pagan ethics. We have therefore taken "good" in v. 7*b* in the personal sense in contrast to "sinner" of v. 8.

On Romans 5:9 cf. no. 813. On Romans 5:10 (universal reconciliation), cf. no. 787. On Romans 5:12ff. (Christ/Adam), cf. on 1 Corinthians 15 (no. 713).

565. Romans 5:12

Krantor in Plutarch, *A Letter to Apollonius* 6 (340/35–275 BCE)

To Hippocles upon the death of his children, [Crantor] says: "All our ancient philosophy states this and urges it upon us; and though there be therein other things which we do not accept, yet at any rate the statement that life is oftentimes toilsome and hard is only too true. For even if it is not so by nature, yet through our own selves it has reached this state of corruption. From a distant time, yes from the beginning, this uncertain fortune has attended us and to no good end, and even at our birth there is conjoined with us a portion of evil in everything. For the very seed of our life, since it is mortal, participates in this causation, and from this there steals upon us defectiveness of soul, diseases of body, loss of friends by death, and the common portion of mortals." (LCL)

This is different from Paul in that the beginning with a first human being is lacking.
Agreements: (1) Human beings themselves bear the responsibility for the misery of their

existence. (2) Sin and death have a common origin. (3) This misery is for every person from the beginning on (in Paul not specifically, but clear through 14*a*). (4) The cause of the misery is not inherent in the ultimate beginning (Krantor: it is not a matter of nature; Paul would say: God is not responsible for it). In Krantor as in Plutarch, the passage is found in a comforting letter. So too in Paul, the theme of "death" stands in the foreground.

566. Romans 5:12

4 Ezra 3:6-8 (late 1 cent. CE)

And you led him into the garden that your right hand had planted before the earth appeared. And you laid upon him one commandment of yours; but he transgressed it, and immediately you appointed death for him and for his descendants. From him there sprang nations and tribes, peoples and clans, without number. And every nation walked in your sight and rejected your commands . . . (NRSV)

New, in contrast to Genesis, but in agreement with Paul: (1) Death was really inflicted on Adam, not only threatened. (2) Death applies to Adam and all his descendants. Thus although Romans 5 is not about original sin in the Augustinian sense, it is about the sentence of death that every human receives as an inheritance from Adam. (3) It is emphasized that all sinned, not only Adam (cf. also *2 Bar.* 48:38: every individual). Differently: no. 431.

567. Romans 5:12-21

Corpus Hermeticum 1.12-15 (2–4 cents. CE)

[Mind, the father of all, who is life and light, gave birth to a man like himself whom he loved as his own child. The man was most fair: he had the father's image; and god, who was really in love with his own form, bestowed on him all his craftworks. And after the man had observed what the craftsman [or: demiurge] had created with the father's help, he also wished to make some craftwork, and the father agreed to this. Entering the craftsman's sphere, where he was to have all authority, the man observed his brother's craftworks; the governors loved the man, and each gave a share of his own order. Learning well their essence and sharing in their nature, the man wished to break through the circumference of the circles to observe the rule of the one given power over the fire.

Having all authority over the cosmos of mortals and unreasoning animals, the man broke through the vault and stooped to look through the cosmic framework, thus displaying to lower nature the fair form of god. Nature smiled for love when she saw him whose fairness brings no surfeit [and] who holds in himself all the energy of the governors and the form of god, for in the water she saw the shape of the man's fairest form and upon the earth its shadow. When the man saw in the water the form like himself as it was in nature, he loved it and wished to inhabit it; wish and action came in the same moment, and he inhabited the unreasoning form. Nature took hold of her beloved, hugged him all about and embraced him, for they were lovers.

Because of this, unlike any other living thing on earth, mankind is twofold—in the body mortal but immortal in the essential man. Even though he is immortal and has authority over all things, mankind is affected by mortality because he is subject to fate; thus, although man is above the cosmic framework, he became a slave within it. He is androgyne because he comes from an androgyne father, and he never sleeps because he comes from one who is sleepless. [Yet love and sleep are his] masters. (Copenhaver)

Gnosticism was exercised by the problem of evil: if there is one supreme God who is perfectly good and almighty, how did an evil world ever come into being? There are numerous variations of myths of preworld events within the heavenly world that give sophisticated explanations, one of the best-known being the Valentinian myth of Sophia and the Pleroma. Hermes "Man" is not the this-worldly Adam, but the cosmic figure, the perfect creation of God. As God can love only that which is perfect, Man is loved by God. Such a perfect creation can love only that which is perfect, and thus loves his own reflection in watery Nature. Thus the myth is not the story of sinful pride and Narcissism, but explains how a perfect being could become entangled in an imperfect world. Such a brief excerpt and comments as are here given should not be taken as doing justice to the myth, which is elaborate and profound. Such theosophical explanations for "the way things are" was a key element in the "knowledge" that gave the Gnostic movement its name.

The Bible is not oriented toward giving mythological, behind-the-scenes, before-creation mythological explanations, but is oriented to this world and history. The Adam story of Genesis 1–3, elements of which are taken into the Hermetic myth, occurs under the dome of heaven, in this world, after the creation. Though Paul is much oriented to the biblical perspective and to the problem of human sin rather than the problem of cosmic evil, his picture of a suprapersonal Adam whose original act has fateful consequences for us all may both draw from and provide material for such gnosticizing speculations.

568. Romans 5:12-21

4 Ezra 7:46-50; 116-20 (late 1 cent. CE)

I answered and said, "This is my first and last comment: it would have been better if the earth had not produced Adam, or else, when it had produced him, had restrained him from sinning. 117 [7:47] For what good is it to all that they live in sorrow now and expect punishment after death? 118 [7:48] O Adam, what have you done? For though it was you who sinned, the fall was not yours alone, but ours also who are your descendants. 119 [7:49] For what good is it to us, if an immortal time has been promised to us, but we have done deeds that bring death? 120 [7:50] And what good is it that an everlasting hope has been promised to us, but we have miserably failed?" (NRSV)

Like Paul, 4 Ezra understands the human condition to be already so conditioned by our descent from Adam that none of us begins with a blank slate, but with the evil tendency already firmly planted within us. Also like Paul, "Ezra" does not understand this to obviate individual responsibility. He is less a dialectical thinker than Paul, however, and does not deal with this as a paradox. Thus the ultimately disastrous effects of sin are not quite universal: "For an evil heart has grown up in us, which has alienated us from God, and has brought us into corruption and the ways of death, and has shown us the paths of perdition and removed us far from life—and that not merely for a few but for almost all who have been created" (7:48 NRSV). Rather than Paul's all/all dialectic (cf. Rom

11:32), he has a coherent many/few. He is thus burdened by the fate of the many, and unable to join in Paul's doxology (Rom 11:33-36).

569. Romans 6:1

Sirach 5:4-6 (ca. 180 BCE)

Do not say, "I sinned, yet what has happened to me?"
for the Lord is slow to anger.
Do not be so confident of forgiveness
that you add sin to sin.
Do not say, "His mercy is great,
he will forgive the multitude of my sins,"
for both mercy and wrath are with him
and his anger will rest on sinners. (NRSV)

Judaism too knew the affirmation of the radical grace of God for sinners, and the danger that presumption on such grace entailed, and attempted to warn against misunderstanding God's mercy as "cheap grace."

570. Romans 6:1-10

Lucius Apuleius, *The Golden Ass*, "Metamorphoses" 11.21-24 (125 CE)

[Initiation into the Isis mysteries:] . . . it was in her [Isis'] power both to damn and to save all persons, and that the taking of such orders was like to a voluntary death and a difficult recovery to health: and if anywhere there were any at the point of death and at the end and limit of their life, so that they were capable to receive the dread secrets of the goddess, it was in her power by divine providence to make them as it were new-born and to reduce them to the path of health. Finally he said that I must therefore attend and wait for the celestial precept . . .

Then he brought me, when he found that the time was at hand, to the next baths, accompanied with all the religious sort, and demanding pardon of the gods, washed me and purified my body according to the custom: after this, when two parts of the day was gone, he brought me back again to the temple and presented me before the feet of the goddess, giving me a charge of certain secret things unlawful to be uttered, and commanding me generally before all the rest to fast by the space of ten continual days, without eating of any beast or drinking any wine: which things I observed with a marvelous continency. Then behold the day approached when as the sacrifice of dedication should be done; and when the sun declined and evening came, there arrived on every coast a great multitude of priests, who according to their ancient order offered me many presents and gifts. Then was all the laity and profane people commanded to depart, and when they had put on my back a new linen robe, the priest took my hand and brought me to the most secret and sacred place of the temple.

Thou shalt understand that I approached near unto hell, even to the gates of Proserpine, and after that I was ravished throughout all the elements, I returned to my proper place: about midnight I saw the sun brightly shine, I saw likewise the gods celestial and the gods infernal, before whom I presented myself and worshiped them.

When morning came and that the solemnities were finished, I came forth sanctified with twelve stoles and in a religious habit.

There I was commanded to stand upon a pulpit of wood which stood in the middle of the temple, before the figure and remembrance of the goddess.

Then they began to solemnize the feast, the nativity of my holy order, with sumptuous banquets and pleasant meats: the third day was likewise celebrated with like ceremonies, with a religious dinner, and with all the consummation of the adept order. (LCL)

This text was often regarded by the older history-of-religions school as evidence for the coupling of baptism and death in the mystery religions. But in this text they are separated by an interval of ten days, and contact with the boundary of death is unrelated to the preliminary purifying bath that allowed one to participate in the ritual. It is important, however, to note the way in which the "trip through the world of the gods" is concretely conceived. We might venture the following possibilities: (1) As in the mystery cults, it is a matter of encounter with symbolic objects, perhaps in a kind of "horror tunnel." (2) It involves an ecstatic state, and what is experienced corresponds to the tradition of heavenly tours, but here applied to a tour of the *underworld* (cf. W. Bousset, *Die Himmelsreise der Seele,* repr. Darmstadt, 1960; in particular, cf. nos. 464-67, 953). Indications of this are the encounter with the sun, which is in the underworld during its absence during the day, and with the higher and lower gods. The heavenly tours also sometimes included visions of heavenly bodies, "Hell" and "Heaven." Most important in this regard is of course the contact with the realm of the dead. Obviously belonging to this realm or becoming personally aware of it shows that after death one does not simply vanish into nothingness.

By initiation, one is not only inoculated against death, one is placed in subjection to Isis, so that one can no longer be harmed by anything. Both fear of death and the objective threat posed by death are removed by the initiation. Theologically, the "new birth" *(renatus)* means a symbolic return from the realm of the dead, then the reawakening from ecstasy is pictured as analogous to a resurrection (some texts picture this concretely as the return of the soul to the body, cf. no. 953), and finally being filled with the (eschatological) power which overcomes death.

Analogies to Paul: the initiation represents such a radical break with the previous life that it is understood as death, with a new existence that follows it. This analogy is merely formal, however, so that one should see here no real "dependence" by Paul on this understanding from the mystery cults.

Differences to Paul: In Paul, it is a matter of dying "with" the Crucified One, in which one's death to the old sinful self ("body of sin") is the decisive thing, that is the giving up of the entanglement with sin. This must of course prove itself in a new manner of life, before one can talk about a resurrection (Paul's "eschatological reservation"). In the mystery cults, however, the experienced encounter with the world of the dead is itself decisive. Cf. also nos. 382, 410, 843.

571. Romans 6:1-10

Firmicus Maternus, *The Error of the Pagan Religions* 22.1, 3 (4 cent. CE)

On a certain night a statue is laid flat on its back on a bier, where it is bemoaned in cadenced plaints. Then when the worshipers have had their fill of feigned lamentation, a light is brought in. Next a priest anoints the throats of all who were mourning, and once that is done he whispers in a low murmur: "Rejoice, O mystai! Lo, our god appears as saved! And we shall find salvation, springing from our woes."

You bury an idol, you lament an idol, you bring forth from its sepulture an idol, and having done this, unfortunate wretch, you rejoice. You rescue your god, you put together the stony limbs that lie there, you set in position an insensible stone. Your god should thank you . . .

So you should die as he dies, and you should live as he lives! (Forbes)

The text belongs to the cultic tradition of the "dying and rising gods" of the annual agricultural cycle (esp. Osiris), here probably referring to Attis; cf. no. 447. It is cited here because the pattern in which the fate of the deity and that of human beings is linked together (the god: dead/saved from death; human beings: distress/delivered from distress) is also found in Romans 6. The rite here portrayed also has many analogies with the Christian Easter vigil, which was also, of course, the time when candidates were baptized. (A similar pattern was associated with the cult of the divine mother: cf. Photius, *Bibliotheca* 242 [ed. Bekker 345a] = *Vita Isidori*, "Tale of Damascus": ". . . which made clear that we had received deliverance from Hades.")

To be sure, this text is concerned neither with initiation nor with ethics, but it becomes clear what an enormous significance the relation to the religions of antiquity had for the existence of the Christian year as such. In this case, do the Christian and pagan statements stand to each other in an implicitly competitive relationship? (Cf. Original Introduction to the German Edition, §3.A.IV.) That is, could it be that the statements of Romans 6—and all the more, the later theoretical and liturgical statements from Christian authors on baptism and the Easter vigil—represent a kind of "de-paganized mystery cult"? Or is it a matter of a new kind of Christian mystery, for which the pagan statements do not form the "background," but which they repaganize? (Cf. also the commentary to the inscription cited in no. 572.) Cf. C. Colpe, "Zur mythologischen Struktur der Adonis-, Attis- und Osiris Überlieferungen," in W. Röllig, ed., *Lisan mithurti* (Festschrift W. von Soden) (Neukirchen-Vluyn: Neukirchener, 1969), pp. 23-44. Further:

572. Romans 6:1-10

Prudentius, *Persistephanon* §10 (348 CE)

[Discourse of the Martyr St. Romanus Against the Pagans:]
Your high priest verily goes down into a trench,
Dug deep beneath the earth, to there be sanctified,
Above the trench they build a platform made of planks
Laid side by side, with ample crevices between,
And then by cutting or by boring through the floor
In many places with an auger or a saw,
They make a score of little openings in the wood.
Then to the place is led a bull of monstrous size,
With shaggy, threatening brow.
Above the trench the beast of sacrifice is placed.
With consecrated spear they open wide his heart,
And from the wound a stream of hot blood gushes out,
Which falls upon the bridge of wooden planks below

And spreads out over it, a heated billowing flood.
Then through the many channels of a thousand chinks
It filters in a gory shower of fetid rain
That falls upon the high priest in the pit below.
He holds his abject head to catch the dripping blood
That stains his robe and all his body with its filth.
And leaning back, he lifts his cheeks to meet the spray,
Beneath it hold his ears, his nostrils and his lips,
His very eyes subjecting to the laving stream,
And overlooking not the palate or the tongue,
Until his body wholly drinks the somber gore.
When all the blood is spent, the flamens drag away
The bullock's rigid carcass from the bridge of planks,
And frightful to behold, the pontiff then comes forth,
With dripping head and beard all matted by the clots,
His fillets sodden and his vestments drenched with blood.
This man defiled by such impurity and filth,
Bespattered with the gore of recent sacrifice,
The crowd with reverential awe salutes and glorifies,
Because they think a dead ox's blood has hallowed him
As he was crouching in that dreadful cave below. (Eagan)

This "taurobolium" mediates the living power of the bull, and at the same time signifies rebirth (cf. the 376 CE inscription *CIL* VI 510, "Reborn for eternity by the taurobolium and the sacrifice of a ram"), whose previously unparalleled statement, like that of Firmicus Maternus (above, no. 571), could have been influenced by circumstances implying competition with Christianity. As in baptism, this happens through participation in the death of the deity's representative. But here there is no symbolic death of the "baptized," and the ethical aspect is lacking. Nor is there any reference to blood in Romans 6. Further:

573. Romans 6:1-10

Plutarch, *A Letter of Condolence to Apollonius* 13 (45–125 CE)

If death indeed resembles a journey, even so it is not an evil. On the contrary, it may even be a good. For to pass one's time unenslaved by the flesh and its emotions, by which the mind is distracted and tainted with human folly, would be a blessed piece of good fortune.

For if it is impossible in company with the body to have any pure knowledge, then one of two things is true: either it is not possible to attain knowledge anywhere, or else only after death. For then the soul will be quite by itself, separate from the body, but before that time never. And so, while we live, we shall, as it appears, be nearest to knowledge if, as far as possible, we have no association or communion with the body, except such as absolute necessity requires, and if we do not taint ourselves with its nature, but keep ourselves pure of it until such time as God himself shall release us. (LCL)

Points of contact with Paul: (1) For both authors, the death of the body as here understood is necessary for salvation. Thus both authors connect the death of the body with God's liberating act of salvation. Salvation consists in the new mode of being given by God after death.

(2) By Plutarch it is explicitly said, and Paul comes near to it by his keyword "baptism," that the new state for which one strives is purity, while the old is impurity, an impurity given with the present body.

(3) Plutarch thinks anthropologically and in terms of general principles (cf. analogously Philo in no. 553 above), while Paul is rather oriented to the history of salvation. In Plutarch, it is a matter of getting the soul separated from the body as such, while for Paul it has to do with the death of the body marred by sin; Paul is horrified at the thought of some sort of bodiless existence (cf. 2 Cor 5:3).

(4) For both Plutarch and Paul, death, which brings freedom from all that is negative and impure, is conceived in a thoroughly physical fashion. Paul, however, hardly thinks of the body merely as a given material object, but rather as the whole complex of external relationships of a person, that is, the person himself or herself regarded from the point of view of relationship to other beings. Thus the death of the body is the radical dying away from all old relationships and entanglements. (Cf. Rudolf Bultmann, *Theology of the New Testament* [New York: Scribners, 1951/1955], 1:192-203, esp. 195-96.)

574. Romans 6:7

Epitaph for a slave

I am Zosime who was formerly a slave only with my body; now I have found freedom for my body as well. (MEB)

Two common Hellenistic motifs meet in this epitaph: even the slaves can be free in their innermost selves even during their lifetime, and death as the great liberator that grants freedom for all. On the first, see the several citations from Epictetus in this volume, and e.g. Sophocles, Fragment 940, εἰ σῶμα δοῦλον, ἀλλ' ὁ νοῦς ἐλεύθερος, "Even if the body is enslaved, the mind is still free." Paul adapts this general sentiment connected with the universal reality of death, and relates it to the liberating death of Jesus, and the believer's being liberated by being united, already during life, to this death.

575. Romans 6:10

Philo, *That the Worse Is Wont to Attack the Better* 49 (15 BCE–50 CE)

. . . the wise man, when seeming to die to the corruptible life, is alive to the incorruptible; but the worthless man, while alive to the life of wickedness, is dead to the happy life. (LCL, which reverses the last two words)

Philo, *Who Is the Heir of Divine Things* 82

[Commenting on "He led him out outside":] Would you not agree that the high priest whose heart is not perfect is both inside and outside, when he is performing the ancestral rites in the inmost shrine; inside in his visible body, outside in his wandering vagrant, soul; and on the contrary that one who loves and is loved by God, even if he is not of the consecrated line, though he stands outside the sacred limits abides right inside them? For he holds all his life in the body to be a sojourning in a foreign land, but when he can live in the soul alone, he feels that he is a dweller in his fatherland. (LCL)

[So also §111:] For God has permitted the mind to comprehend of itself the world of the mind, but the visible world only through sense. Oh! if one can live with all the parts of his being to God rather than to himself, using the eye of sense to penetrate into the objects of sense and thus discover the truth, using the soul to study the higher verities of mental things and real existences, using the organ of his voice to laud both the world and its Maker, he will live a happy and blessed life. (LCL)

[So also in *Special Laws*, 1.345:] The Law tells us that all who "cleave to God live," and herein it lays down a vital doctrine fraught with much wisdom. For in very truth the godless are dead in soul, but those who have taken service in the ranks of the God Who only Is are alive, and that life can never die. (LCL)

In all these texts, as in Romans 6, life and death are not thought of as absolute qualities or realities in themselves, but are related to another reality, which determines life also qualitatively. At the same time, there is a certain dualism in the thought: whoever lives for the one is dead for the other. So criteria are sought for what is truly life and what is really death. Cf. also no. 757.

576. Romans 6:12-23

Dio Chrysostom, *Discourses* 14.17-18 (40–120 CE)

[On slavery and freedom:] Therefore, the wise are permitted to do anything whatsoever they wish, while the foolish attempt to do what they wish although it is not permissible; so that it follows of necessity that while the wise are free and are allowed to act as they wish, the ignorant are slaves and do that which is not allowable for them?

Perhaps we are therefore forced to define freedom as the knowledge of what is allowable and what is forbidden, and slavery as ignorance of what is allowed and what is not. According to this definition there is nothing to prevent the Great King, while wearing a very tall tiara upon his head, from being a slave and not being allowed to do anything that he does; for every act that he performs will bring a penalty and be unprofitable. But some other man who is regarded as a slave and is so called, who has not once but often, if it so chance, been sold, and if it should so happen, wears very heavy fetters, will be more free than the Great King. (LCL)

On this text: (1) As is typical for Hellenistic philosophy, freedom and slavery are conceived independently of given social realities, and even contrary to them (cf. nos. 429, 660). (2) Freedom is by no means a purely theoretical knowledge, but a kind of "practical consciousness" about what is advisable and useful, as also in Seneca, Epistle 94. This consciousness is the basis for inner autonomy. Accordingly, the issue here dealt with is autonomy versus heteronomy. For Paul, this problem is bound up with another, with the freedom from evil desire and sin (see on no. 578), for the situation of being "under" the law is at the same time slavery to desire and sin. The reason for this combination is given by Paul in Romans 7:7-11: there is a cooperative working relationship between the law and sin.

577. Romans 6:12-23

Plutarch, *Moralia*, "On Superstition" §4 (45–125 CE)

A despot much feared in Samos was Polycrates, as was Periander in Corinth, but nobody feared these men after he had removed to a free State governed by its own people. But as for the man who fears the rule of the gods as a sullen and inexorable despotism, where can he remove himself, where can he flee, what country can he find without gods, or what sea? Into what part of the universe shall you steal away and hide yourself, poor wretch, and believe that you have escaped God? There is a law even for slaves who have given up all hope of freedom, that they may demand a sale, and thus exchange their present master for one more mild. But superstition grants no such exchange; and to find a god whom he shall not fear is impossible for him who fears the gods of his fathers and his kin, who shudders at his saviors [σωτῆρας], and trembles with terror at those gentle gods . . .

These are the very things that most inspire a shuddering fear and dread in the superstitious man, and yet it is in them that those who are in fear of the most dreadful fate place their hopes. (LCL)

Quite apart from its association with Augustine's *Confessions* 1.1-3; 10, this text is an illuminating contrast to Romans 6.

1) The text documents the possibility that slaves could voluntarily change their masters. A bad master can be changed for a better one. Precisely this picture is what is used by Paul. Romans 6:19 is a reflection on the new status of the Christian, which also is to be described as slavery; the picture is appropriate because of human weakness that continues into the new life in Christ. The relation to the new master results not in death but in life. Plutarch, however, explicitly denies the possibility that such a change of masters can take place in the realm of religion.

2) In Paul too, of course, it is not a matter of a change of gods, but a change from law to grace, even if grace is understood within the pattern of apostolic teaching (v. 17). But the condition under the law has all the marks of what Plutarch describes as the condition of superstition of people with regard to their gods: the hopeless inescapability because of the impossibility of being able to satisfy such masters. (Also in his description of those "weak" Christians in Pauline churches who were still loyal to the law are to be found a number of points of contact with ancient views of superstition; cf. nos. 674, 677.)

3) In contrast to the picture described by Plutarch, the possibility of a change of masters declared by Paul is fascinating.

578. Romans 6:12-23

Plutarch, *Moralia*, "Advice About Keeping Well" 7 (45–125 CE)

But when the case is reversed, and the desires descend from the mind to the body and force it to be subservient to the mind's emotions, and to join in their excitements, there is no way to prevent their leaving as a residue the most violent and serious injuries as the aftermath of feeble and evanescent pleasures. (LCL)

Similarly Plutarch, *Moralia*, "Love of Wealth" 5: "Asked if he was able to enjoy a woman, Sophocles replied: 'Hush fellow, I am now a free man, delivered by old age from a set of mad and cruel masters.' For it is a happy thing that when pleasures fail desires should fail as well. . . . But it is otherwise with avarice . . ." (LCL). Numerous such passages could be listed from the whole range of contemporary philosophical literature.

The comparison with Paul: (1) The relation to evil desire is regarded as a kind of slavery, to which the body and its members is delivered over. (2) This slavery proceeds from the inner self of a person. Plutarch calls this the "soul." For Paul it is the self of those who are addressed in 6:13. (3) The distress brought about by this slavery is described in sharper terms by Paul, as death. (4) The way to freedom is different: in Plutarch it is a matter of reasonable instruction, while for Paul it is a matter of being united with Christ through the concrete bodily redemption from the entanglements of sin (baptism as dying to the old life).

579. Romans 6:17

Iamblichus, *Life of Pythagoras* (4 cent. CE)

Cf. the document "Basic Form of Instruction" (τύπος τῆς διδασκαλίας) above, no. 98. Cf. also no. 780.

580. Romans 7:7-23

Ovid, *Amores* 3.4.17 (43–17 BCE)

We're all rebels against restriction—in love with the illicit. (Lee)

Cf. also Euripides, Fragment 1063 (1295) (485/84–406 BCE): "A smart man will never restrict his wife too much to staying at home, for the eyes love the enjoyment that can be seen outside. If she can move about without restrictions and can let her eyes drink their fill, then she will not be subject to evil temptations. Men too are always lusting after what they are not permitted to see" (MEB/Berger). According to this rule of popular psychology, human beings are so weak that evil desires are provoked and encouraged by the mere fact of prohibition. Is it also Paul's view that the law incites to evil? No, Paul is to be evaluated differently. Cf. 581.

581. Romans 7:7-11

4 Maccabees 2:1-6 (1 cent. CE)

And why is it amazing that the desires of the mind for the enjoyment of beauty are rendered powerless? 2 It is for this reason, certainly, that the temperate Joseph is praised, because by mental effort he overcame sexual desire. 3 For when he was young and in his prime for intercourse, by his reason he nullified the frenzy of the passions. 4 Not only is reason proved to rule over the frenzied urge of sexual desire, but also over every desire. 5 Thus the law says, "You shall not covet your neighbor's wife or anything that is your neighbor's." 6 In fact, since the law has told us not to covet, I could prove to you all the more that reason is able to control desires. (NRSV)

Both 4 Maccabees and Paul honor the Law as God's gift for curbing sinful passions, as holy, just, and good. Both 4 Maccabees and Paul hit upon the last command of the Decalogue as the focus of their argument, since it deals with inner desire and not only with overt acts. But 4 Maccabees takes the existence of this law as proof for the thesis of his whole book, that "devout reason is sovereign over the emotions" (1:1 and repeatedly), the argument being that since God commanded it, it must be possible. Paul, on the other hand, finds that precisely this command shows the difficulty in keeping the Law—not because of any defect in the Law or its Giver, but because in the human situation the good Law has been commandeered by an evil power, Sin, that turns even good to evil.

582. Romans 7:7

Philo, *On the Special Laws*, 4.84-85 (15 BCE–50 CE)

So great then and transcendent an evil is desire, or rather it may be truly said, the fountain of all evils. For plunderings and robberies and repudiations of debts and false accusations and outrages, also seductions, adulteries, murders and all wrongful actions, whether private or public, whether in things sacred or things profane, from what other source do they flow? For the passion to which the name of originator of evil can truly be given is desire . . . (LCL)

The passage is found in Philo's exposition of the tenth commandment of the Decalogue (from 4.79 onward). On the basis of its key position at the conclusion, Philo makes the first two words of this commandment ("You shall not have evil desire") the essence of the Decalogue and thus of all of God's commandments. Thus it is not the commandment that brings forth evil desire. Rather, sin has an opponent in the world, and that is God's command. And because this commandment forbids evil desire, it is precisely the business of sin to call forth evil desire in human beings. So it is not the commandment that produces evil desire, but rather sin (in contrast to the general pagan view of no. 580).

On this subject, *Targum Neofiti I* (1 cent. CE?) on Genesis 2:15 points out that the law existed in humanity's prefallen state in Eden: "And the Lord God took Adam and had him dwell in the garden of Eden to toil in the Law and to observe its commandments" (McNamara). Cf. Martha Craven Nussbaum, *The Therapy of Desire: Theory and Practice in Hellenistic Ethics* (Princeton: Princeton University Press, 1994).

583. Romans 7:7-13

Sifre to Deuteronomy 82b (3 cent. CE)

. . . words of Torah are compared to a lifegiving medicine.

The matter may be compared to the case of a king who grew angry with his son and gave him a severe blow, but then put a salve on the wound and said to him, "My son, so long as this bandage is on the wound, eat whatever you like, drink whatever you like, and wash in either warm or cold water, and nothing will do you injury. But if you remove the bandage, the sore will immediately begin to produce ulcers."

So the Holy One, blessed be he, said to Israel, "My children, I have created in you an impulse to do evil, than which nothing is more evil.

"Sin crouches at the door and to you is its desire [Gen. 4:7]."

"Keep yourselves occupied with teachings of the Torah, and [sin] will not control you." (Neusner, *Sifre Deuteronomy*)

The image of the Torah as a medicinal "plaster" is derived as a pun on Deuteronomy 11:18, which it intends to evoke. Here, in contrast to Paul, the Law is seen as a divinely given means of subduing the sinful impulse in human beings, rather than inciting to sin. That this good purpose of the Law could be subverted by an alien power, so that it functions contrary to God's purpose, does not come within the purview of this text.

584. Romans 7:11

Plato, *Laws* 9.863b, §7 (428/27–349/48 BCE)

. . . we distinguish "pleasure" from passion, and we assert that its mastering power is of an opposite kind, since it effects all that its intention desires by a mixture of persuasion and deceit. (LCL)

Similarly, Dio Chrysostom, *Discourses* 8.20-21ff. (40–ca. 120 CE) ". . . there is another battle more terrible and a struggle not slight but much greater than this and fraught with greater danger, I mean the fight against pleasure. . . . pleasure uses no open force but deceives and casts a spell with baneful drugs, just as Homer says Circe drugged the comrades of Odysseus, and some forthwith became swine, some wolves, and some other kinds of beasts. Yes, such is this thing pleasure, that hatches no single plot but all kinds of plots, and aims to undo men through sight, sound, smell, taste, and touch, with food too, and drink and carnal lust, tempting the waking and the sleeping alike" (LCL).

For Paul, the deceitfulness of sinful pleasure as found in pagan tradition corresponds to the deceitfulness of the serpent of Genesis 3:13. Thus Paul omits the role of the serpent, just as he does the role of Eve in this story. Contemporary Judaism had already represented the role of the serpent as that of the devil (*Apocalypse of Moses* 9, 15, 23, 30, 39): "The adversary deceived us," or simply "we were deceived" (cf. no. 432).

585. Romans 7:14

Plutarch, *Moralia*, "On the Delays of the Divine Vengeance" 27 (45–125 CE)

[Instruction to Thespesius, on which see also nos. 465, 953.] . . . the intelligent part of the soul is dissolved away and liquefied by pleasure, while the irrational and carnal part is fed by its flow and puts on flesh and thus induces memory of the body; and that from such memory arises a yearning and desire that draws the soul toward birth [γένεσις] . . . (LCL)

The text is an indication of Hellenistic anthropology: the spirit (thinking) stands over against the elements body (σῶμα) and flesh (σάρξ) in human being. Both are delivered over to lust, yearning, and craving. Paul superimposes his own categories of Spirit and flesh on these, so that the "Spirit" is that which comes from God, the new life of the eschatological age, while "flesh" is the sinful human being subjected to death, i.e. human existence as a whole, "spirit" and "flesh" in the sense of Plutarch.

586. Romans 7:17-18, 20

Greek aphorism

It is impossible for one who thinks rightly and lives rightly to fall victim to disgraceful offenses or demonic deception. Just as a worm eats the wood at its point of entrance, so also sin remains in that one who has done it. (MEB/from G. Röhser's German trans. in J. F. Boissonade, *Anecdota Graeca I* [Paris, 1829], 125-26)

Analogies to Paul: having one's existence involved in something with disastrous consequences; the action on one's life of something that dwells parasitically within it; the existence and method of working remains externally unobservable (on all these points cf. G. Röhser, *Metaphorik und Personifikation der Sünde* [Tübingen: J. C. B. Mohr (Paul Siebeck), 1987], 169-72).

587. Romans 7:15, 19-21

Epictetus, *Discourses*, 2.26.1, 4 (55–135 CE)

Every error involves a contradiction. For since he who is in error does not wish to err, but to be right, it is clear that he is not doing what he wishes. For what does the thief wish to achieve? His own interest. Therefore, if thievery is against his interest, he is not doing what he wishes. Now every rational soul is by nature offended by contradiction. . . . He, then, who can show to each man the contradiction which causes him to err, and can clearly bring home to him how he is not doing what he wishes, and is doing what he does not wish, is strong in argument, and at the same time effective both in encouragement and refutation. (LCL)

As above (no. 576), sin consists of ignorance of what is truly in one's self-interest. The opposition is thus not within the person, as in Paul (between the understanding and the members of the body), but is between what the person intends and the real result. (Translator's note: some scholars would also understand this latter contrast to be Paul's own view.) According to Epictetus the sinners act falsely because they operate on the basis of false ideas about the relationship between deed and its results.

The Pauline understanding is engaged better by the text from Seneca in no. 588.

588. Romans 7:15, 19-21

Seneca, *Epistles*, "Epistle to Lucilius" 51.13 (4–65 CE)

If any vice rend your heart, cast it away from you; and if you cannot be rid of it in any other way, pluck out your heart also. Above all, drive pleasures from your sight. Hate them beyond all other things, for they are like the bandits whom the Egyptians call "lovers," who embrace us only to garrote us. (LCL)

As in Paul, the battle is here within the person. Also, the violent aspect of evil desire which robs one of freedom is expressed here. The difference to Paul is of course that here the struggle is within the soul, not between the heart and the body's members. This is also confirmed by Epistle 52.1: "What is it that wrestles with our spirit, and does not allow us to desire anything once for all?" (LCL).

589. Romans 7:22

Plato, *Republic* 9, 12 (588D-589B) (428/27–349/48 BCE)

[Within the human person there lurks a lion, a human being, and a many-headed beast:] "It was, I believe, averred that injustice is profitable to the completely unjust man who is reputed just. Was not that the proposition?" "Yes, that." "Let us, then, reason with its proponent now that we have agreed on the essential nature of injustice and just conduct." "How?" he said. "By fashioning in our discourse a symbolic image of the soul . . ."

. . . "Mold, then, a single shape of a manifold and many-headed beast that has a ring of heads of tame and wild beasts and can change them and cause to spring forth from itself all such growths."

"Then fashion one other form of a lion and one of a man . . ."

"Join the three in one, then, so as in some sort to grow together."

"Then mold about them outside the likeness of one, that of the man, so that to anyone who is unable to look within but who can see only the external sheath it appears to be one living creature, the man."

"Let us then say to the speaker who avers that it pays this man to be unjust, and that to do justice is not for his advantage, that he is affirming nothing else than that it profits him to feast and make strong the multifarious beast and the lion and all that pertains to the lion, but to starve the man and so enfeeble him that he can be pulled about whithersoever either of the others drag him, and not to familiarize or reconcile with one another the two creatures but suffer them to bite and fight and devour one another."

"And on the other hand he who says that justice is the more profitable affirms that all our actions and words should tend to give the man within us complete domination over the entire man and make him take charge of the many-headed beast—like a farmer who cherishes and trains the cultivated plants but checks the growth of the wild—and he will make an ally of the lion's nature, and caring for all the beasts alike will first make them friendly to one another and to himself, and so foster their growth." (LCL)

The point here is obviously that within the human being there are different sorts of powers, whose balance and cooperation is the goal of the formation of a truly human life. The lion stands for the instincts and carnal appetites, the "inner self" (ὁ ἐντὸς ἄνθρωπος) is the most noble part that is threatened by ignoble actions, in 589D described as "the divine element" in human being, in 590D as that which is divine and reasonable. The popularity of this tradition originated by Plato is documented not only by Philo, but by the *Gospel of Thomas* (logion 7). Further:

590. Romans 7:22

Corpus Hermeticum 13.7 (2–4 cent. CE)

[Hermes speaks by revelation to his son Tat.] Am I without the power, then, father?

May it not be so, my child. Draw it to you, and it will come. Wish it, and it happens. Leave the senses of the body idle, and the birth of divinity will begin. Cleanse yourself of the irrational torments of matter.

Do I have the tormenters in me, father?

More than a few, my child; they are many and frightful.

I am ignorant of them, father.

This ignorance, my child, is the first torment; the second is grief; the third is incontinence; the fourth, lust; the fifth, injustice; the sixth, greed; the seventh, deceit; the eighth, envy; the ninth, treachery; the tenth, anger; the eleventh, recklessness; the twelfth, malice. These are twelve in number, but under them are many more besides, my child, and they use the prison of the body to torture the inward person with the sufferings of sense. Yet they withdraw (if not all at once) from one to whom the god has shown mercy, and this is the basis of rebirth, the means and the method. (Copenhaver)

As in Plato, so also here, the "inner self" is described as under duress, but conversion/rebirth creates a fundamental change. In Romans 7 too the inner self is in distress, though there it is more a matter of not being able to fulfill one's good intentions. This text in CH could make a contribution to the debate as to whether Paul describes a Christian or a pre-Christian experience, from a history-of-religions perspective. In CH too the decisive change happens at rebirth, even though remnants of the old life endure. Cf. nos. 380-88 above.

591. Romans 7:22

Plutarch, *Moralia*, "That a Philosopher Ought to Converse Especially with Men in Power" 2 (45–125 CE)

. . . the aim and end of both the speech in the mind and the speech in the utterance is friendship, toward oneself and toward one's neighbor respectively; for the former, ending through philosophy in virtue, makes a man harmonious with himself, free from blame from himself, and full of peace and friendliness toward himself.

"Faction is not, nor is ill-starred strife, to be found in his members," there is no passion disobedient to reason, no strife of impulse with impulse, no opposition of argument to argument, there is no rough tumult and pleasure on the border-line, as it were, between desire and repentance . . . (LCL)

The citation "Faction is not . . ." is ascribed to Empedocles (cf. Diels-Kranz I 324 = Fragment 27a). Along with this citation it includes, this text is the only one known to us which documents a struggle that is fought not only in the soul, but between the inner self and the members of the body, as is the case in Romans 7. In Paul's sense, this text would picture the redeemed person.

592. Romans 7:24

Epictetus, *Discourses* 1.3.3, 5 (55–135 CE)

. . . inasmuch as these two elements were commingled in our begetting, on the one hand the body, which we have in common with the brutes, and, on the other, reason and intelligence, which we have in common with the gods, some of us incline toward the former relationship, which is unblessed by fortune and is mortal, and only a few toward that which is divine and blessed.

"For what am I? A miserable, paltry man," say they, and, "Lo, my wretched, paltry flesh!" Wretched indeed, but you have also something better than your paltry flesh. Why then abandon that and cleave to this? (LCL)

Cf. further Epictetus, *Discourses:* "Wail, then, and groan, as you deserve to do. For what greater penalty can befall the man who is uninstructed and disobedient to the divine injunctions than to grieve, to sorrow, to envy, in a word to have no good fortune but only misfortune? Do you not wish to free yourself from all this? And how shall I free myself?—Have you not heard over and over that you ought to eradicate desire utterly, direct your aversion toward the things that lie within the sphere of moral purpose, and those things only" (LCL). Like Paul, Epictetus describes a division in human nature. The cry of anguish is the same in both cases (ταλαίπωρος!), and for the same reason, that human existence is bound to the weakness of the body. The way of salvation is different. According to Epictetus, each person should orient himself or herself to the higher part of his or her nature, while in Paul deliverance comes from God. Of course, in Epictetus the help that comes "from outside" is the instruction of philosophers. So also the text in the Corpus Hermeticum ("Kore Kosmou" 22.35) belongs to the genre of lamentation: "What have we unfortunates done so wrong? How many sins await us unfortunates [i.e. to be paid off]? What will we all do as a result of bad hopes [lit. 'because of bad things of hope'], so that we can provide this watery and soon to be dissolved body with the things it needs?" (MEB/Berger).

A. Bonhoeffer, *Epiktet und das Neue Testament* (Religionsgeschichtliche Versuche und Vorarbeiten 10. Giessen, 1910) has a more negative view of the connections between the thought world of Epictetus and that of the New Testament.

On Romans 8:1, cf. no. 395.

593. Romans 8:10

Corpus Hermeticum, 1.15 (1 cent. CE)

Because of this, unlike any other living thing on earth, mankind is twofold—in the body mortal but immortal in the essential man. Even though he is immortal and has authority over all things, mankind is affected by mortality because he is subject to fate; thus, although man is above the cosmic framework, he became a slave within it. (Copenhaver)

As in Paul, human existence is divided, and its mortality is grounded in its bodilyness. The "essential" or "substantial" element in human being is for CH the "inner self" (cf. nos. 589, 590), which is also the way Paul would designate it (2 Cor 4:16; Rom 7). For Paul, however, the inner self is still in need of renewal through the Spirit of God, and does not have freedom and kinship with God in and of itself. For Paul, the inner self is the place where the new redemptive life happens and begins, in order then to become the condition for the new redeemed body.

594. Romans 8:12

Philo, *Moralia*, "Who Is the Heir of Divine Things" 57 (15 BCE–50 CE)

[Exposition of Lev 17:14 and Gen 2:7:] So we have two kinds of men, one that of those who live by [Gk. dative] reason, the divine inbreathing, the other of those who live by [Gk. dative] blood and the pleasure of the flesh. This last is a molded clod of earth, the other is the faithful impress of the divine image. (LCL)

The Greek dative, here translated "by," can also be translated "for," i.e. it can be "by the power of," "by means of," and "toward the goal of" all at once. The function is thus the same as the "according to" (κατα) of Romans 8:12. The text in Philo deals with two groups of people; the Pauline text deals with two possibilities for the way the same person lives his or her life. The statements are not, however, to be taken as a statement of fundamental theological principles, but as conditioned by their genre (an ethical tract, or in Paul's case, a letter). Still, in contrast to Philo, for Paul life according to the Spirit of God is only possible for the person who in Christ has come to participate in the renewal/fulfillment of creation.

On the contrast earthly image/divine image, cf. the very similar 1 Corinthians 15:47-49.

595. Romans 8:14-17

Sifre to Numbers, Shelah 115, 35a (3 cent. CE)

Another matter: Why make mention of the Exodus from Egypt in the setting of discourse on each and every one of the religious duties?

The matter may be compared to the case of a king whose ally was taken captive. When the king paid the ransom [and so redeemed him], he did not redeem him as a free man but as a slave, so that if the king made a decree and the other did not accept it, he might say to him, "You are my slave."

When he came into a city, he said to him, "Tie my shoe-latch, carry my clothing before me and bring them to the bath house." [Doing these services marks a man as the slave of the one for whom he does them.]

The son began to complain. The king produced the bond and said to him, "You are my slave."

So when the Holy One, blessed be he, redeemed the seed of Abraham, his ally, he redeemed them not as sons but as slaves. When he makes a decree and they do not accept it, he may say to them, "You are my slaves."

When the people had gone forth to the wilderness, he began to make decrees for them involving part of the lesser religious duties as well as part of the more stringent religious duties, for example, the Sabbath, the prohibition against consanguineous marriages, the fringes, and the requirement to don *tefillin*. The Israelites began to complain. He said to them, "You are my slaves. It was on that stipulation that I redeemed you, on the condition that I may make a decree and you must carry it out." (Neusner, *Sifre Numbers*)

Paul's language of slaves and children (υἱοί, lit., "sons") participates in a rabbinic discussion. Superficial contrasts should be avoided: just as the rabbis were aware of the Bible's son-language for Israelites (Exod 4:22; Hos 11:1), so Paul can use slave-language of Christians, as he has in this same letter (Rom 6:15-23). The rabbis, like Paul, were aware of the value and limitations of metaphorical language, and in the above passage are careful to point out their awareness that neither metaphorical language (nor any other human language) refers in one to one terms to deity.

596. Romans 8:38

3 Enoch 4.6-9 (final redaction 4 cent. CE)

[God has exalted Metatron, identified as Enoch, who reports on his experience.] Then three of the ministering angels, 'Uzzah, 'Azzah, and 'Aza'el, came and laid charges against me in the heavenly height. They said before the Holy One, blessed be he, "Lord of the Universe, did not the primeval ones give good advice when they said, Do not create man!" The Holy One, blessed be he, replied, "I have made and will sustain him; I will carry and deliver him." When they saw me they said before him, "Lord of the Universe, what right has this one to ascend to the height of heights? Is he not descended from those who perished in the waters of the Flood? What right has he to be in heaven [the Firmament]?" Again the Holy One, blessed be he, replied, and said to them, "What right have you to interrupt me? I have chosen this one in preference to all of you, to be a prince and a ruler over you in the heavenly heights." At once they all arose and went to meet me and prostrated themselves before me, saying "Happy are you, and happy your parents, because your Creator has favored you." (*OTP* 1:258-59)

Agreements: (1) Angelic powers attempt to separate a human being from God. The context in *3 Enoch* shows that they are the protectors of the majesty of God and emphasize the unworthiness of human beings at every point (cf. the Satan in Job 1), since they are "over" humanity, between human beings and God (cf. P. Schäfer, *Rivalität zwischen Engeln und Menschen* [Berlin: de Gruyter, 1975], p. 98).

(2) This attempt fails in both cases. In *3 Enoch*, God is "well disposed" toward his "elect"; in Paul, because God "loves" us in Jesus Christ (on the synonymous usage cf. "elect" in Rom 8:33). In both cases, God's love for humanity is stronger than the resistance of his angelic princes. Paul here doubtless participates in the tradition of the "mystical" Judaism as it is later formulated in the dramatic scenes of *3 Enoch*. The texts from Qumran also already document acquaintance with "mystical" traditions of a similar sort.

Difference: In Paul a whole community is united with Jesus, while *3 Enoch* deals only with an individual figure. Early Christianity has made enormous changes by "democratizing" Jewish traditions of this sort.

597. Romans 9:1-2

4 Ezra 7:47-61 (late 1 cent. CE)

[Ezra speaks to the revealing Angel, who is transparent to God:] "And now I see that the world to come will bring delight to few, but torments to many. 48 For an evil heart has grown up in us, which has alienated us from God, and has brought us into corruption and the ways of death, and has shown us the paths of perdition and removed us far from life—and that not merely for a few but for almost all who have been created."

49 He answered me and said, "Listen to me, Ezra, and I will instruct you, and will admonish you once more. 50 For this reason the Most High has made not one world but two. 51 Inasmuch as you have said that the righteous are not many but few, while the ungodly abound, hear the explanation for this.

52 "If you have just a few precious stones, will you add to them lead and clay?" 53 I said, "Lord, how could that be?" 54 And he said to me, "Not only that, but ask the earth and she will tell you; defer to her, and she will declare it to you. 55 Say to her, 'You produce gold and silver and bronze, and also iron and lead and clay; 56 but silver is more abundant than gold, and bronze than silver, and iron than bronze, and lead than iron, and clay than lead.' 57 Judge therefore which things are precious and desirable, those that are abundant or those that are rare?"

58 I said, "O sovereign Lord, what is plentiful is of less worth, for what is more rare is more precious."

59 He answered me and said, "Consider within yourself what you have thought, for the person who has what is hard to get rejoices more than the person who has what is plentiful. 60 So also will be the judgment that I have promised; for I will rejoice over the few who shall be saved, because it is they who have made my glory to prevail now, and through them my name has now been honored. 61 I will not grieve over the great number of those who perish; for it is they who are now like a mist, and are similar to a flame and smoke—they are set on fire and burn hotly, and are extinguished." (NRSV)

"Ezra" accepts the apocalyptic dogma that most of humanity is damned, and, like Paul, laments it. Ezra dares to be somewhat heretical himself, questioning the justice of the apocalyptic schema, but does not dare to believe that God could question this schema (cf. no. 948 on Rev 6:9-10, no. 965 on Rev 14:10-11, and no. 974 on Rev 21:1–22:5).

598. Romans 9:3

Plutarch, *Parallel Lives*, "Antony" 44.2-5 (45–125 CE)

Then Antony, wishing to harangue his soldiers, called for a dark robe, that he might be more pitiful in their eyes. But his friends opposed him in this, and he therefore came forward in the purple robe of a general and made his harangue, praising those who had been victorious and reproaching those who had fled. The former exhorted him to be of good courage, and the latter, by way of apology for their conduct, offered themselves to him for decimation, if he wished, or for any other kind of punishment; only they begged him to cease being distressed and vexed. In reply, Antony lifted up his hands and prayed the gods that if, then, any retribution were to follow his former successes, it might fall upon him alone, and that the rest of the army might be granted victory and safety [σωτηρία]. (LCL)

On the return from the unsuccessful siege of the city of Phraata in 36 BCE, Antony and his troops are constantly harassed by attacks and threats from the Parthians. After one such attack in which many Roman soldiers died, Antony addresses his troops. Both Antony and Paul are willing to suffer the wrath of the deity in behalf of their comrades. Both use the language of salvation. The similarities are more apparent than real: salvation for Paul is eschatological, and he is not attempting to atone for his own past mistake.

599. Romans 9:6

1 Maccabees 1:53 (2–1 cents. BCE)

Many of the people, everyone who forsook the law, joined them, and they did evil in the land; they drove Israel into hiding in every place of refuge they had. (NRSV)

Cf. also 7:5, 9: "Then there came to him [the Seleucid king Demetrius] all the renegade and godless men of Israel; they were led by Alcimus, who wanted to be high priest. . . . 9 He [Demetrius] sent him [Bacchides, a royal counselor], and with him he sent the ungodly Alcimus, whom he made high priest; and he commanded him to take vengeance on the Israelites." These texts illustrate how unselfconsciously a loyal Jewish author can use "Israel" in both senses of empirical Israel, the nation as such (7:5) and of those who are faithful to the covenant, the "true" Israel (1:53; 7:9). Both Paul and the author of 1 Maccabees belong to the long tradition beginning in the Hebrew Bible that regarded belonging to Israel as more than a matter of physical circumcision, but "circumcision of the heart" (cf. Deut 10:16; Jer 4:4; 9:26; Ezek 44:7; Rom 3:28-29).

600. Romans 9:7-13

Philo, *Allegorical Interpretation of Genesis* 3.75-88 (15 BCE–50 CE)

And if thou wilt consider, my friend, thou wilt find that God has made in the soul some natures faulty and blameworthy of themselves, and others in all respects excellent and praiseworthy, just as is the case with plants and animals. Seest thou not that among the plants the Creator has made some repaying cultivation and useful and wholesome, and others wild and injurious and productive of disease and destruction . . .

Exactly, then, as God has conceived a hatred for pleasure and the body without giving reasons, so too has he promoted goodly natures apart from any manifest reason, pronouncing no action of theirs acceptable before bestowing his praises upon them. For should anyone ask why the prophet says [Gk.: φησί] that Noah found grace in the sight of the Lord God [Gen. vi. 8] when as yet he had, so far as our knowledge goes, done no fair deed, we shall give a suitable answer to the effect that he is shown to be of an excellent nature from his birth, for Noah means [rest] or [righteous]. But it cannot but be that he who rests from sinful and unrighteous acts and rests upon what is noble and lives in fellowship with righteousness, should find favor with God.

The righteous man exploring the nature of existences makes a surprising find, in this one discovery, that all things are a grace of God, and that creation has no gift of grace to bestow, for neither has it any possession, since all things are God's possession, and for this reason grace too belongs to Him alone as a thing that is His very own. Thus to those who ask what the origin of creation is the right answer would be, that it is the goodness and grace of God, which He bestowed on the race that stands next after Him. For all things in the world and the world itself is a free gift and act of kindness and grace on God's part.

Melchizedek, too, has God made both king of peace, for that is the meaning of "Salem," and His own priest [Gen. xiv. 18]. He has not fashioned beforehand any deed of his, but produces him to begin with as such a king, peaceable and worthy of His own priesthood.

What good thing had Abram already done, that he bids him estrange himself from fatherland and kindred there and dwell in whatever land God Himself may give him? [Gen. xii. 1].

Some even before their birth God endows with a goodly form and equipment, and has determined that they shall have a most excellent portion. Dost thou not see what He says concerning Isaac to Abraham when unable to trust that he shall ever become the father of such an offspring, nay when he actually laughed at the promise and said, "Shall it come to pass to him that is a hundred years old, and shall Sarah who is ninety years old bear a child?" [Gen. xvii. 17].

Once again, of Jacob and Esau, when still in the womb, God declares that the one is a ruler and leader and master, but that Esau is a subject and a slave. For God the Maker of living beings knoweth well the different pieces of his own handiwork, even before He has thoroughly chiseled and consummated them, and the faculties which they are to display at a later time, in a word their deeds and experiences. (LCL)

Analogies: (1) As in Romans 9 a series of examples is drawn from the same period of history as Isaac and Jacob/Esau. (2) Both series of examples illustrate the fundamental principle of the free gracious choice of God before anything good or evil had been done by the human beings concerned. (3) Philo emphasizes God as creator; Paul will do it in the following passage 9:14-23.

Differences: In Philo the point is that one has been created either good or evil (so also the circumstances of one's birth and life), thus the discussion of the praiseworthy qualities and potential, or the "good" works. This is definitely not Paul's understanding, for when he speaks of God's "loving" Jacob and "hating" Esau (i.e. choosing the former and not choosing the latter), he is assigning them specific roles in the saving plan of God. Salvation history, not personal qualities—even if given by divine grace—is Paul's point.

601. Romans 9:19

Oenomaus, Cynic philosopher, quoted in Eusebius, *The Preparation for the Gospel* 6, 7.36 (Oenomaus, 2 cent. CE; Eusebius, 4 cent. CE)

[Addressing the gods:] And why are we mortals to blame, and not that necessity of yours? Thou doest not justice, O Apollo, nor art right in laying the punishment upon us who do no wrong.

And this Zeus of yours, I mean the necessity of your necessity, why does he take vengeance upon us, and not upon himself [if he must punish someone], for having shown the necessity to be of such a character? And why too does he threaten us? Or why, as if we were the masters of this event, do we suffer famine for it? (Gifford)

The rationalistic philosopher poses the paradoxical problem that results when one (artificially) attempts to bring within one systematic understanding the concept of "necessity" (ἀνάγκη) with human free will, responsibility, and capacity for guilt. Paul too dares to venture into this area of critical religious ideas (cf. no. 549 above), only instead of "fate" or "necessity" he speaks of the "will of God." Eusebius discusses the problem as found in a variety of ancient authors.

On Romans 11:15*a* (reconciliation), see nos. 562, 787.

602. Romans 11:26

Oracle of Hystaspes, as cited in Lactantius, *The Divine Institutes* 7, 17.9; 18.1 (Hystaspes, 2 cent. BCE ?; Lactantius, 4 cent. CE)

. . . another king shall arise out of Syria, born from an evil spirit, the overthrower and destroyer of the human race, who shall destroy that which is left by the former evil, together with himself. . . . When these things shall so happen, then the righteous and the followers of truth shall separate themselves from the wicked, and flee into solitude. And when he hears of this, the impious king, inflamed with anger, will come with a great army, and bringing up all his forces, will surround all the mountain in which the righteous shall be situated, that he may seize them. But they, when they shall see themselves to be shut in on all sides and besieged, will call upon God with a loud voice, and implore the aid of heaven; and God shall hear them, and send from heaven a great king to rescue and free them and destroy all the wicked with fire and sword.

Hystaspes says that the pious and faithful, being separated from the wicked, will stretch forth their hands to heaven with weeping and mourning, and will implore the protection of Jupiter: that Jupiter will look to the earth, and hear the voices of men, and will destroy the wicked.

. . . the Son of God would then be sent, who, having destroyed all the wicked, would set at liberty the pious. (ANF)

In the Iranian eschatology of this time, not only is the deliverer sent from heaven important, but also the mountain as the central location of the final events. In Jewish eschatology that developed in the Persian period, this corresponds to the centrality of Zion in the theology of Deutero- and Trito-Isaiah. In §18 the report and commentary by Lactantius is perhaps expressed in Christian terminology (C. Colpe, *RAC* IX. 1976, 596-97). (Cf. nos. 966-67.) Cf. Revelation 20:7-10.

603. Romans 11:26

4 Ezra 13:3-8, 35-37 (late 1 cent. CE)

As I kept looking the wind made something like the figure of a man come up out of the heart of the sea. And I saw that this man flew with the clouds of heaven; and wherever he turned his face to look, everything under his gaze trembled, and whenever his voice issued from his mouth, all who heard his voice melted as wax melts when it feels the fire. After this I looked and saw that an innumerable multitude of people were gathered together from the four winds of heaven to make war against the man who came up out of the sea. And I looked and saw that he carved out for himself a great mountain, and flew up on to it. And I tried to see the region or place from which the mountain was carved, but I could not. After this I looked and saw that all who had gathered together against him, to wage war with him, were filled with fear, and yet they dared to fight. . . . But he shall stand on the top of Mount Zion. And Zion shall come and be made manifest to all people, prepared and built, as you saw the mountain carved out without hands. Then he, my Son, will reprove the assembled nations for their ungodliness (this was symbolized by the storm) . . . (NRSV)

Fourth Ezra 13 and the Hystaspes text (no. 602) are independent witnesses (cf. the time of the coming of the Son, and his origin from the sea/from heaven). Yet they give evidence of an eschatological conception structured in the same way: a besieged mountain, righteous and un-righteous, a deliverer from God called the Son of God. It is thus no coincidence that Paul cites a text from Isaiah 59. This text itself represents an early stage of development of such an eschatological concept, a development that was still going on in the first century. If the "redeemer" who comes from Zion is for Paul the returning Jesus (he is the deliverer, cf. 1 Thess 1:10), then there is a special affinity with 4 Ezra 13. That would mean that when Paul is concerned to discuss the future destiny of Israel, Paul adopts conceptions at home in the nationalistic Jewish eschatology. The difference: while the theme Jews/Gentiles is common to Paul and 4 Ezra, in Paul the Gentiles are not destroyed but redeemed (cf. 4 Ezra 13:29, "will deliver those who are on the earth").

604. Romans 11:36

Marcus Aurelius, *Meditations* 4.23 (121–180 CE)

Everything is fitting for me, my universe, which fits thy purpose. Nothing in thy good time is too early or too late for me; everything is fruit for me which thy seasons, nature, bear; from thee, in thee are all things. (Farquharson)

For related formulae, cf. E. Norden, *Agnostos Theos* (1913, repr. Darmstadt, 1956), pp. 240-50, who speaks of a kind of "creedal formulation of Stoic theology." For its lingering aftereffects, cf. also the ring inscription from an old alchemy manuscript on p. 249, "The One is the All, and through it is the All, and to it is the All." Jews and Christians, as well as disciples of Isis then applied this impersonal formula of the Stoics to personal deities. Paul too stands in this tradition (cf. no. 672). Luke also ascribes such ideas to Paul; cf. Acts 17:28 (no. 520).

605. Romans 12:1

Josephus, *Against Apion* 170-71 (37–100 CE)

[Discussing Israel's life under the constitution of the "theocracy" as revealed through Moses:] The cause of his success was that the very nature of his legislation made it [always] far more useful than any other; for he did not make religion a department of virtue, but the various virtues—I mean, justice, temperance, fortitude, and mutual harmony in all things between the members of the community—departments of religion. (LCL)

The basic structure of Paul's ethic is indicative/imperative, the imperative of human responsibility always being based on the prior act of God. In Romans this comes to expression as twelve chapters of theological affirmation, then the "therefore" that introduces the ethical precepts of the Christian community (cf. Gal 1–4, 5–6).

606. Romans 12:1

Mekilta on Exodus 20:2 (2 cent. CE with older materials)

[And God spoke all these words, saying,] "I am the Lord your God, [who brought you out of the land of Egypt, out of the house of bondage]":

How come the Ten Commandments were not stated at the very beginning of the Torah?

The matter may be compared to the case of a king who came into a city. He said to the people, "May I rule over you?"

They said to him, "Have you done us any good, that you should rule over us?"

What did he then do? He built a wall for them, brought water for them, fought their battles.

Then he said to them, "May I rule over you?"

They said to him, "Yes, indeed."

So the Omnipresent brought the Israelites out of Egypt, divided the sea for them, brought manna down for them, brought up the well for them, provided the quail for them, made war for them against Amalek.

Then he said to them, "May I rule over you?"

They said to him, "Yes, indeed."

Rabbi says, "This serves to express the praise that is coming to the Israelites.

For when all of them stood before Mount Sinai to receive the Torah, they were unanimous in receiving the dominion of God with a whole heart."

R. Nathan says, "In this connection we find a refutation of the *minim*, who maintain that there are two dominions (two powers)."

"When the Holy One, blessed be He, went and said, 'I am the Lord your God, [who brought you out of the land of Egypt, out of the house of bondage],' who went and opposed him?" (Neusner, *Mekhilta*)

Like the preceding citation from Josephus, this rabbinic text illustrates the theological perspective of the Hebrew Bible and Judaism that God's gracious act of salvation precedes the ethical demand, but also requires it. Neither theological affirmations of the saving acts of God nor ethical demands calling for human responsibility can stand alone; each requires the other. What is true of the parenesis of the Epistles is also true of the ethical instruction of the Gospels. The Sermon on the Mount, for instance, does not stand alone but is embedded in the narrative of God's saving act in Jesus.

607. Romans 12:1-2

Corpus Hermeticum 1.30-32 (2–4 cents. CE)

Within myself I recorded the kindness of Poimandres, and I was deeply happy because I was filled with what I wished, for the sleep of my body became sobriety of soul, the closing of my eyes became true vision, my silence became pregnant with good, and the birthing of the world became a progeny of goods. This happened to me because I was receptive of mind—of Poimandres, that is the word of sovereignty. I have arrived, inspired with the divine breath of truth. Therefore, I give praise to god the father from my soul and with all my might:
Holy is god, the father of all;
Holy is god, whose counsel is done by his own powers;
Holy is god, who wishes to be known and is known by his own people;
Holy are you, who by the word have constituted all things that are;
Holy are you, from whom all nature was born as image;
Holy are you, of whom nature has not made a like figure;
Holy are you, who are stronger than every power;
Holy are you, who surpass every excellence;
Holy are you, mightier than praises.
You whom we address in silence, the unspeakable, the unsayable, accept pure speech offerings [λογικὰς θυσίας] from a heart and soul that reach up to you. Grant my request not to fail in the knowledge that befits our essence; give me power; and with this gift I shall enlighten those who are in ignorance, brothers of my race, but your sons. Thus I believe and I bear witness; I advance to life and light. Blessed are you, father. He who is your man wishes to join you in the work of sanctification since you have provided him all authority. (Copenhaver)

Cf. further Corpus Hermeticum 1.30-32. Here is the sense of the holiness of the Deity, grateful praise for the revelation, a replacement of material sacrifices with spiritual and rational devotion (λογικὰς θυσίας), and a conviction that the revelation must be shared with others, all of which have points of resonance with Paul and other New Testament texts (1 Pet 2:2, 5; Heb 13:15).

The idea of "spiritual sacrifices" in place of or alongside of animal sacrifice was widespread in the ancient world in both Jewish and pagan circles. Cf. Philo, "Special Laws" 1.269-72; 277, 290; *Testament of Levi* 3.4-6; Isocrates 2.20; Hierocles, *In Aureum Phythagoreorum Carmen Commentarius* 1.18; Porphyry, cited in Eusebius, *Preparation for the Gospel* 4.14d: "But when a young man has learned that gods delight in costliness, and, as is said, in feasts upon kine and other animals, when would he ever choose to be thrifty and temperate? And if he believes that these offerings are pleasing to the gods, how can he avoid thinking that he has license to do wrong, being sure to buy off his sin by his sacrifices? But if he be persuaded that the gods have no need of these sacrifices, but look to the moral disposition of those who approach them, receiving as the greatest offering the right judgment concerning themselves and their affairs, how can he fail to be prudent, and just, and holy? The best sacrifice to the gods is a pure mind and a soul free from passions" (Gifford). On Romans 12:4-5, cf. nos. 694-96.

608. Romans 12:17-20

1QS 10.17-21 (1 cent. BCE)

I will pay to no man the reward of evil [Paul: Repay no one evil for evil].

I will pursue him with goodness [Paul: Take thought for what is good in the sight of all men].

For judgment of all the living is with God, and it is He who will render to man his reward [Paul: Leave it to the wrath of God; for it is written, "Vengeance is mine, I will repay," says the Lord].

I will not grapple with the men of perdition [Paul: Live at peace with all men]. (Vermes)

The similarities between the Qumran text and Paul's composition are clear in both order and content. "In the fifth parallel Qumran and Paul diverge. While Qumran speaks of hate against all who do not join the Community, Paul speaks of enemy love, citing Proverbs 25:21-22. Qumran says: 'My wrath shall not turn from the men of falsehood . . .; I will have no pity on all who depart from the way.' I will offer no comfort to the smitten until their way becomes perfect' [Vermes]. Whereas in Paul we find: 'No, "if your enemy is hungry, feed him; if he is thirsty, give him to drink"'" (Kuhn, "Impact of the Qumran Scrolls," 334).

609. Romans 12:(19-)21

Plutarch, *Moralia*, "On Compliancy" 13 (45–125 CE)

For he who said [Epicharmus, Fragment 275], "A handy arm with knave is knavery," recommends to us the bad habit of resisting vice by resorting to it; whereas to rid ourselves of brazen and unabashed suitors by being unabashed ourselves, and not, by giving to shame, to render shameful favors to the shameless, is what is rightly and justly done by men of sense. (LCL)

Plutarch fundamentally disputes that it makes sense to fight evil with evil. We are in the exceptional situation of being able to reconstruct a complete history of the development of this statement: (1) Do not reward good with evil (Jer 18:20; Prov 17:13). (2) Do not repay evil with evil (Prov 20:22; Sir 28:1-6; *Jos. Asen.* 28:10, 14; 29:3; Rom 12:17; 1 Pet 3:9; *2 Enoch* [cf. no. 273]); outside the biblical tradition, the Plutarch passage above. (3) Do not respond with evil under any circumstances because of the law of retribution, (*1 Enoch* 95:5 ["Woe unto you who reward evil to your neighbors!" *OTP* 1:76]; Matt 7:2). Repaying evil with evil is also rejected in the *Mid. Genesis Rabbah* 38:3 on Genesis 11:1: "Said R. Simeon b. Abba, 'It is not the end of the matter that he who repays evil for good [will suffer], but even as to him who repays evil for evil, evil shall not depart from his house either'" (Neusner, *Gen. Rab.*). (4) First in relatively late texts, still not reduced to the short formula "repay evil with good" (Rom 12:20-21; cf. also 1 Pet 3:9 and *Jos. Asen.* 29:3, "It does not befit a man who worships God to repay evil for evil" [*OTP* 2:246] [cf. context!]), and with hesitation, *Testament of Joseph* 18:2. First found explicitly in *Mid. Exodus Rabbah* 26:2 (on 17:8), "God said: 'Resemble Me; just as I repay good for evil so do thou also repay good for evil,' as it says, *Who is a God like unto Thee, that pardoneth the iniquity, and passeth by the transgression* [Mic 7:18]" (Lehrman), and later the *Midrash* on the Psalms *Tehillim* 41:11 (on Ps 8), "I will requite them good for evil" (Braude).

The positive view of overcoming evil through good as a programmatic statement is thus a relatively late "achievement." So too in the pagan realm this form developed only late, in Polyaenus (Rome, ca. 150 CE, *Strategica* 5.12, "I have not warded off evil with evil, but evil with good") (MEB/Berger).

610. Romans 13:1-7

Suetonius, *Lives of the Caesars*, "Nero" 19 (early 2 cent. CE)

I have brought together these acts of his, some of which are beyond criticism, while others are even deserving of no slight praise, to separate them from his shameful and criminal deeds, of which I shall proceed now to give an account. (LCL)

Romans was written ca. 56, during the reign of Nero. Since Nero is primarily remembered in history for his cruel and megalomaniacal acts, including the first persecution of Christians (see no. 961 from Tacitus at Rev 13:1-18), Paul's instructions to Roman Christians to obey the "powers that be" as established by God for their good is difficult to understand. The first five years of Nero's rule, 54-59, were good years, however, the so-called *Quinquennium Neronis* during which the government was virtually in the hands of the noble Seneca. Suetonius notes the difference in the two periods of Nero's reign, describes the former period in some detail, and summarizes them in the above quote. It is doubtful that Paul could have written Romans 13:1-7 the same way after the fire of 64 CE for which Nero blamed the Christians, had many of them arrested, and put them to terrible deaths.

611. Romans 13:1-5

Dio Chrysostom, *The First Discourse on Kingship* 45-46 (40–120 CE)

[The relationship between a king and those who stand by him is determined by their similarity.] ... so too among kings, since they, I ween, derive their powers and their stewardship from Zeus, the one who, keeping his eyes upon Zeus, orders and governs his people with justice and equity in accordance with the law and ordinances of Zeus, enjoys a happy lot and a fortunate end, while he who goes astray and dishonors him who entrusted him with stewardship or gave him this gift, receives no other reward from his great authority and power than merely this: that he has shown himself to all men of his own time and to posterity to be a wicked and undisciplined man . . . (LCL)

Analogy to Paul: (1) The authority is conferred by God. (2) In Paul too, the context has to do with the fulfilling of God's law (13:8, but also the whole thematic of "good"/"evil" from 12:17 on) which is closely related to the preservation of "order" in the world.

The difference: In Paul the directive is addressed to the Romans, for whom it is possible to fail in regard to this directive. They, not the rulers, are addressed. Paul says nothing about the possibility of their damaging the established order of the world itself, and thus nothing about God's judgment of them. It is the opposite with Dio Chrysostom: his speech addresses the Emperor, is a "diatribe" for him (cf. Berger, *Formgeschichte,* §33). Thus the possible misconduct of the ruler comes within his purview, as it does not for Paul. Cf. also no. 831.

The view that kingship was from the gods was not merely the self-serving propaganda of the rulers themselves, but was widely shared by the populace of the Hellenistic world, Jewish and Gentile. Cf. Josephus, *The Jewish War* 1.390; 2.139-41; Homer, *Iliad* 2.196-97; 203-5; Hesiod, *Theogony* 81-96; Suetonius, *Lives of the Caesars,* "The Deified Julius," 6.1.

612. Romans 13:1-7

Hierocles the Stoic, *On Duties*, "How to Conduct Oneself Toward One's Fatherland" (3.730, 17-734, 10 Hense) (wrote 117–138 CE)

After discussing the gods, it is most reasonable to set forth how to conduct oneself toward one's fatherland [πατρίς]. For, by Zeus, it is as it were some second god, and our first and greatest parent. Hence he who gave it a name did not do so inappropriately; he formed a derivative [from "father"], but gave it a feminine ending so that it might be a sort of mixture of "father" and "mother." This word also dictates that we honor our one fatherland equally with our two parents, that we prefer it to either of our two parents separately, and that we not honor the two together more than it, but that we respect them equally. There is still another reason which exhorts us to honor it more than our two parents together, and not only them, but together with them, to honor it more than our wives, children and friends, in short, more than all other things.

Let us then sum up, that we should not separate what is publicly profitable from what is privately profitable, but to consider them one and the same. For what is profitable to the fatherland is common to each of its parts, since the whole without its parts is nothing. And what is profitable to the citizen is also fitting to the city, if indeed it is taken to be profitable to the citizen. (Malherbe, *Moral Exhortation*)

Also in the Stoic "Mirror of Duties" (cf. Berger, *Formgeschichte,* §41) it is usual to name the Fatherland immediately after the gods. Of course, in contrast to Paul, the status of one's country is not here grounded theologically, but on the principle of usefulness, and thus empirically and logically, but with the same consequences as for Paul. (But Roman patriotism has consequences that go far beyond what Paul would allow [MEB].) Similarly Plutarch, "Precepts of Statecraft" 21, ". . . it is a most excellent and useful thing to learn to obey those in authority, even if they happen to be deficient in power and reputation" (LCL).

613. Romans 13:1-7

Sirach 10:4 (ca. 180 BCE)

The government of the earth is in the hand of the Lord, and over it he will raise up the right leader for the right time. (NRSV)

A long Hebrew and Jewish tradition affirmed that all sovereigns rule only at God's behest. Sirach's teaching may refer obliquely to the Hellenistic kings to which Judea was subject in his day, reminding his students that the final sovereignty belonged to God, and thus had a different thrust than Paul's teaching to Christians, which is calculated to promote cooperation with the Roman authorities rather than to encourage distance and inner resistance.

A similar-sounding statement is Sirach 17:17: "He appointed a ruler for every nation, but Israel is the Lord's own portion." Though this is a reflection of Deuteronomy 32:8-9, so that "ruler" refers not to earthly kings but to heavenly angels, in the first century the verse could be understood as declaring that the earthly "powers that be" are ordained of God.

614. Romans 13:3

Plutarch, *Moralia*, "To an Uneducated Ruler" 3 (45–125 CE)

Who, then, shall rule the ruler?
"The Law, the king of all,
Both mortals and immortals,"
as Pindar says—not law written outside him in books or on wooden tablets or the like, but reason endowed with life within him, always abiding with him and watching over him and never leaving his soul without its leadership. For example, the King of the Persians had one of his chamberlains assigned to the special duty of entering his chamber in the morning and saying to him: "Arise, O King, and consider matters which the great Oromasdes wished you to consider." But the educated and wise ruler has within him the voice which always thus speaks to him and exhorts him. Indeed Polemo said that love was "the service of the gods for the care and preservation of the young"; one might more truly say that rulers serve god for the care and preservation of men, in order that of the glorious gifts which the gods give to men they may distribute some and safeguard others.

. . . these gifts and blessings, so excellent and so great, which the gods bestow cannot be rightly enjoyed nor used without law and justice and a ruler. (LCL)

Analogies to Paul: (1) The binding connection between ruler and law (cf. above no. 547). (2) The king rules according to the will of God and as his servant. As in Paul, a soteriological function is attributed to him. (3) (Important for other Pauline texts:) The distinction between that which is written, externally visible (the Persian king's servant commanded to admonish him daily), and that which is internal and invisible (for the Persian king, reason). For Paul, this difference is described as letter/Spirit; cf. e.g. 2 Corinthians 3:3, 6.

Additional important analogies to Romans 13 in Plutarch: On Romans 13:3, in "Praising Inoffensively," §17 (the responsible political leader must reject praise for actions that are in fact bad). In "Delays Divine Vengeance," §7 (God provides peoples who need discipline and punishment with the bitterness of tyrants and stern rulers).

Important parallel texts from the inscriptions are found in A. Ströbel, "Zum Verständnis von Röm 13" in *ZNW* 47 (1956), 67-93.

615. Romans 13:12*b*-14

Plutarch, *Moralia*, "Precepts of Statecraft" 26 (45–125 CE)

When entering some sanctuaries men leave their gold outside; but iron, one may say, they do not at all carry into any sanctuary. And since the orators' platform is a sanctuary common to Zeus the Counselor and the Protector of Cities, to Themis and to Justice, do you strip off all love of wealth and of money, as you would iron full of rust and a disease of the soul, cast them straightway at the beginning into the marketplace of hucksters and money-lenders . . . (LCL)

These texts help us to understand the New Testament's metaphors of "taking off" and "putting on," especially in the context of conversion to the Christian faith. This text specifically mentions the realm from which the metaphor is taken, which is simply assumed in the New Testament texts, and which inhibits their understanding for people today: on entering a holy place, certain items of clothing and equipment were always removed. Plutarch also uses this metaphorical field in his writing "Listening" 1-2: "And just as Herodotus says that women put off their modesty along with their undergarments, so some of our young men, as soon as they lay aside the garb of childhood, lay aside also their sense of modesty and fear, and, undoing the habit that invests them, straightway become full of unruliness. . . . Philosophy, which alone can array young men in the manly and truly perfect adornment that comes from reason" (LCL).

On Romans 14:1–15:13 (strong and weak), cf. nos. 673-75, 784.

616. Romans 14:2, 6, 14, 21

Testaments of the Twelve Partiarchs, "Testament of Reuben" 1.8-10 (2–1 cent. BCE)

For I was thirty years old when I committed this evil deed in the sight of the Lord, and for seven months I was an invalid on the brink of death. And after this, with determination of soul, for seven years I repented before the Lord: I did not drink wine or liquor; meat did not enter my mouth, and I did not eat any pleasurable food. Rather, I was mourning over my sin, since it was so great. (*OTP* 1:782)

Analogies are also presented by the peculiar diet of John the Baptist (cf. Mark 1:6*b;* Luke 1:15; nos. 18, 952). His role as a preacher of repentance also corresponds to the penitential basis of Reuben's diet. Also, Jewish Christians in Rome could have adopted dietary rules as an indication that they had repented, i.e. joined the Christian movement (cf. also Nebuchadnezzar, Dan 4:33*a* LXX). The visible sign of repentance was in part formed from the Nazarite tradition, so that it is probably no accident that James the brother of Jesus is represented as a Nazarite, and that Paul is pictured as participating in the Nazarite rituals of early Jerusalem Christians (Acts 23:23-24, 26). In Acts Luke describes the Christians consistently as "Nazarenes." For bibliography, cf. B. Gärtner, *Die rätselhaften Termini Nazoräer und Iskariot* (Uppsala: Appelbergs Boktryckeri, 1957). Here we meet an early form of the Christian penitential movement.

On asceticism cf. also no. 570.

617. Romans 14:2, 6, 14, 21

Philo, *On Providence* 2.69-70 (15 BCE–50 CE)

The various kinds of fishes, birds, and land-animals do not give grounds for charging Nature of inviting us to pleasure, but they constitute a severe censure on our want of restraint. For to secure the completeness of the universe and that the cosmic order should exist in every part it was necessary that the different kinds of living animals should arise, but it was not necessary that man the creature most akin to wisdom should be impelled to feast upon them and so change himself into the savagery of wild beasts. And therefore to this day those who have thought for self-restraint abstain from every one of them and take green vegetables and the fruits of trees as a relish to their bread with the utmost enjoyment. And those who hold that feasting on these animals is natural have had placed over them teachers, censors, and lawgivers who in the different cities make it their business to restrain the intemperance of their appetites by refusing to allow all people to use them all without restriction. (LCL)

A variety of types of people and groups avoided meat and wine. In addition to the Philonic fragment transmitted by Eusebius, *Preparation for the Gospel* 8.14.69-70, cf. no. 616, and Plutarch, *Parallel Lives,* "Life of Cato the Elder," 23.5-6; Seneca, *Epistles* 108.14-23.

618. 1 Corinthians 1:18-25

Plato, *Apology* 20 DE, 23A (428/27–349/48 BCE)

[Socrates speaks at his trial:] The fact is, men of Athens, that I have acquired this reputation on account of nothing else than a sort of wisdom. What kind of wisdom is this? Just that which is perhaps human wisdom. For perhaps I really am wise in this wisdom; and these men, perhaps, of whom I was just speaking, might be wise in some wisdom greater than human, or I don't know what to say . . .

For of my wisdom—if it is wisdom at all—and of its nature, I will offer you the god of Delphi as a witness.

. . . the fact is, gentlemen, it is likely that the god is really wise and by his oracle means this: "Human wisdom is of little or no value . . ." (LCL)

As in Paul, the mantic wisdom of the gods, divine wisdom, theological wisdom, is made into a critical principle over against human wisdom. Like Paul against his opponents, so Socrates places himself on the side of the former.

619. 1 Corinthians 1:19–2:7

Plutarch, *Moralia*, "Isis and Osiris" 1-2 (45–125 CE)

All good things, my dear Clea, sensible men must ask from the gods; and especially do we pray that from those mighty gods we may, in our quest, gain a knowledge of themselves, so far as such a thing is attainable by men. For we believe that there is nothing more important for man to receive, or more ennobling for God of His grace to grant, than the truth. God gives to men the other thing for which they express a desire, but of sense and intelligence He grants them only a share, inasmuch as these are His especial possessions and His sphere of activity. For the Deity is not blessed by reason of his possession of gold and silver, nor strong because of thunder and lightning, but through knowledge and intelligence.

. . . the primacy of Zeus is nobler since it is elder in knowledge and in wisdom.

Therefore the effort to arrive at the Truth, and especially the truth about the gods, is a longing for the divine. [In what follows, "Isis" is related etymologically to the word for "knowledge."] (LCL)

As in Paul, wisdom/knowledge consists above all in knowledge of God, and as in Paul, they are given by God himself and signify participation in the divine life. Paul's emphasis on the contrast between human and divine wisdom is missing here, however. Still, true wisdom comes only from God.

620. 1 Corinthians 1:19–2:7

Plutarch, *Moralia*, "On the Delays of the Divine Vengeance" 20 (45–125 CE)

There is another matter, however, no longer within Hesiod's capacity, nor a task for human wisdom, but rather for God: to discriminate and distinguish between similar and dissimilar propensities before the actual passions bring them to light by involving them in great acts of wrong. (LCL)

The capacity to know the human heart and its secrets is also in biblical tradition a specific indication that one is dealing with the deity or his direct representative. Plutarch here clearly knows the contrast between human and divine wisdom. The only distinction from Paul is that the paradoxical juxtaposition of opposites is lacking.

621. 1 Corinthians 1:19–2:7

Plutarch, *Moralia*, "How the Young Man Should Study Poetry" 11 (45–125 CE)

Yet was Zeus the earlier born and his knowledge was wider.

For he declares understanding to be a most divine and kingly thing, to which he ascribes the very great superiority of Zeus, inasmuch as he believes that all the other virtues follow upon this one.

. . . and Aeschylus sets it down as a point of good sense not to be puffed up with fame, nor to be excited and elated by popular praise . . . (LCL)

Understanding and wisdom are here synonyms. As in Paul, wisdom means freedom from the standards of normal cultural pressures for social prestige (cf. no. 882). The presuppositions for these similar conclusions are of course different in each case. For Paul, the point is that it is God's electing grace that is here at work, so one can only boast "in the Lord." For Plutarch on the other hand, it is a matter of showing that all right conduct is dependent on wisdom and therefore can be learned. To be sure Plutarch too has the Pauline view that praise does not belong to human beings but to God, though he does not relate this to wisdom.

622. 1 Corinthians 1:19–2:7

Plutarch, *Moralia*, "On Praising Oneself Inoffensively" 11 (45–125 CE)

But those who are forced to speak in their own praise are made more endurable by another procedure as well: not to lay claim to everything, but to disburden themselves, as it were, of honor, letting part of it rest with chance, and part with God.

Noticing that some persons were jealous and disaffected he [Python of Aenos] came forward and said: "This, men of Athens, was the doing of some god; I did but lend my arm."

Thus the code of Zaleucus found favor with the Locrians not least, it is said, because he asserted that Athena had constantly appeared to him and had in each case guided and instructed him in his legislation, and that nothing he proposed was of his own invention or devising. (LCL)

Plutarch reports here as the clever, statesmanlike act of invoking religious legitimation for authoritative measures something not very different from what Paul does in his response to the Corinthians: his gospel is legitimated by the fact that it comes from God, so that he has renounced any sort of self-praise, not to speak of participation in the party strife at Corinth. The model for this is the earthly fate of Jesus Christ. This aspect of personal self-abnegation even to the point of crucifixion is lacking in Plutarch.

In §12 of this writing Plutarch takes his stand against those who let themselves be designated as "wise" or "sons of God."

On Paul's conduct in relation to the party strife in 1 Corinthians 1, cf. also Plutarch, "Precepts of Statecraft" 10 (do not join any party, but conduct one's affairs without party spirit, and with word and deed work toward unity).

623. 1 Corinthians 1:26-31

Celsus, *True Doctrine* (3 cent. CE, cited from Origen, *Against Celsus* 3.44, 59, 64)

Their injunctions are like this. "Let no one educated, no one wise, no one sensible draw near. For these abilities are thought by us to be evils. But as for anyone ignorant, anyone stupid, anyone uneducated, anyone who is a child, let him come boldly." By the fact that they themselves admit that these people are worthy of their God, they show that they want and are able to convince only the foolish, dishonorable and stupid, and only slaves, women, and little children.

Those who summon people to the other mysteries make this preliminary proclamation: "Whosoever has pure hands and wise tongue." And again, others say: "Whosoever is pure from all defilement, and whose soul knows nothing of evil, and who has lived well and righteously." Such are the preliminary exhortations of those who promise purification from sins. But let us hear what folk these Christians call. "Whoever is a sinner," they say, "whosoever is unwise, whosoever is a child, and in a word, whosoever is a wretch, the kingdom of God will receive him." (Chadwick)

This quotation, though much later than Paul, illustrates the disdain, not to say dismay, of the cultivated educated class in the Hellenistic world at the message of Christianity and the type of people to whom it mostly appealed. But that there was an appeal to some of the educated, see Wayne Meeks, *The First Urban Christians: The Social World of the Apostle Paul* (New Haven: Yale University Press, 1983), and Abraham J. Malherbe, *Social Aspects of Early Christianity* (Philadelphia: Fortress Press, 1983).

624. 1 Corinthians 2:1-6

b. *Hagigah* 2.1 (233)

The [subject of] forbidden relations may not be expounded in the presence of three, nor the work of creation in the presence of two, nor [the work of] the chariot in the presence of one, unless he is a sage and understands his own knowledge. (Soncino)

The view that some teachings were dangerous and to be explained only to the initiated was not only a Hellenistic view advocated among the mysteries and gnosticizing groups, but had its counterpart in Judaism. Morton Smith (*Tannaitic Parallels*, 156) points out the interesting parallel between חכם מבין מדעתו "wise in the Law and of good understanding" and τέλειος "mature," among whom "wisdom" may be discussed in 1 Corinthians 2:6.

On 1 Corinthians 2:5-6, cf. no. 443.

625. 1 Corinthians 2:9

Empedocles, *Fragments* 1.2 (5 cent. BCE)

For scant means of acquiring knowledge are scattered among the members of the body; and many are the evils that break in to blunt the edge of studious thought. And gazing on a little portion of life that is not life, swift to meet their fate, they rise and are borne away like smoke, persuaded only of that on which each one chances as he is driven this way and that, but the whole he vainly boasts he has found. Thus these things are neither seen nor heard distinctly by men, nor comprehended by the mind. And thou, now that thou hast withdrawn hither, shalt learn no more than what mortal mind has seen. (Nahm)

The text Paul cites with the customary formula for Scripture (γέγραπται) has not been identified. Origen claimed it was from the lost *Apocalypse of Elijah*. Similar ideas and vocabulary are present in the fragment from Empedocles, but there is no direct citation.

626. 1 Corinthians 2:9

Pseudo-Philo, *Liber Antiquitatum Biblicarum* 26.13 (1 cent. CE, probably pre-70)

[Concerning the eschatological time:] And when the sins of my people have reached full measure and enemies begin to have power over my house, I will take those stones and the former stones along with the tablets, and I will store them in the place from which they were taken in the beginning. And they will be there until I remember the world and visit those inhabiting the earth. And then I will take those and many others better than they are from where eye has not seen nor has ear heard and it has not entered into the heart of man, until the like should come to pass in the world. And the just will not lack the brilliance of the sun or the moon, for the light of those most precious stones will be their light. (*OTP* 2:338-39)

For the author of this Jewish Midrash, the history of Israel is the history of its symbolic stones (cf. also Rev 21!). The place from which the glorious luminous stones of the consummation of history are taken is described with the same expression used by Paul to describe the divine mystery. On the basis of a whole series of parallel texts in Jewish literature and early Christian apocalypses (cf. Berger, "Zur Diskussion über die Herkunft von I Kor. II.9," *NTS* 24 [1977], 271-83, and no. 424 above), one can show that these words were in fact used with regard to the future reward of the righteous (and in part with reference to the punishment of sinners) to designate the hidden mystery that no human being had seen, except possibly by the seer on his heavenly tour. In the literature known to us (including the ancient Christian apocalypses), only Paul uses the expression christologically and in a certain sense of the present reality: the Christian community has received insight into this mystery (2:10). That Christ himself is the mystery is indicated by 2:8-9.

627. 1 Corinthians 2:10-14

Plutarch, *Moralia*, "How the Young Man Should Study Poetry" 11 (45–125 CE)

And by the line, "Glad was Athena because of the man that was prudent and honest," the poet permits us to draw a similar conclusion in that he represents the goddess as taking delight, not in some rich man or in the one who is physically handsome or strong, but in one who is wise and honest. And again when she says that she does not overlook Odysseus, much less desert him, "Since he is courteous and clever of mind and prudent," her words indicate that the only one of our attributes that is dear to the gods and divine is a virtuous mind, if it be true that it is the nature of like to delight in like. (LCL)

Analogous to Paul: Only that in humankind which is like the gods is befitting and pleasing to them (for Paul: God's Spirit). Plutarch is here making theological use of an old statement of the principle of the ethics of friendship, to which Aristotle's statement may be compared: ". . . like is the friend of like" (*Nic. Eth.* 9 3.3); cf. under no. 764 below. Cf. also C. W. Müller, *Gleiches zu Gleichem. Ein Prinzip frühgriechischen Denkens* (Wiesbaden: Otto Harrassewitz, 1965).

628. 1 Corinthians 2:14

Posidonius, cited by Galen, *De Hippocratis et Platonis Decretis* 4.7 (Posidonius 135–51 BCE)

The cause of the passions—the cause, that is, of disharmony and of the unhappy life—is that men do not follow absolutely the daemon that is in them, which is akin to, and has a like nature with, the Power governing the whole cosmos, but turn aside after the lower animal principle, and let it run away with them. Those who fail to see this neither thereby set the cause of the passions in any better light, nor hold the right belief regarding happiness and concord. They do not perceive that the very first point in happiness is to be led in nothing by the irrational, unhappy, godless element in the soul. (Barrett)

The anthropological dualism of the ancient world was expressed in many forms, and cannot be reduced to a simple soul/body dualism in which "soul" represents the good, eternal element in humanity and "body" the evil, material element. Posidonius represents one of many variations, presenting the Stoic view that the good power within each human being is the "daemon," the seminal reason (λόγος σπερματικός) that is akin to the divine Reason permeating the universe, while other elements in the soul (not just in the material body) represent the lower nature of humanity. This is not Paul's anthropology, but the point of contact is that "soul" for Paul here is the "*un*spiritual" dimension of human being (ψύχικος). Cf. also 15:44, 46; James 3:15; and Jude 19, where ψύχικοι is explicitly equated with "not having the Spirit."

629. 1 Corinthians 3:13-15

Oracle of Hystaspes, as cited in Lactantius, *The Divine Institutes* 7, 21.3-6 (Hystaspes, 2 cent. BCE ?; Lactantius, 4 cent. CE)

[On the eternal flame:] But that divine fire always lives by itself, and flourishes without any nourishment; nor has it any smoke mixed with it, but it is pure and liquid, and fluid, after the manner of water. For it is not urged upward by any force, as our fire, which the taint of the earthly body, by which it is held, and smoke intermingled, compels to leap forth, and to fly upward to the nature of heaven, with a tremulous movement.

The same divine fire, therefore, with one and the same force and power, will both burn the wicked and will form them again,

But when He shall have judged the righteous, He will also try them with fire. Then they whose sins shall exceed either in weight or in number, shall be scorched by the fire and burnt: but they whom full justice and maturity of virtue has imbued will not perceive the fire for they have something of God in themselves which repels and rejects the violence of the flame. (ANF)

Analogous to Paul: the "righteous" too come in contact with the divine fire of judgment, even if they are saved. That which is burned up of those who are not completely righteous doubtless refers to their evil works which are destroyed. Similarly:

630. 1 Corinthians 3:13-15

Testament of Abraham 13 (1–3 cent. CE)

And the fiery and merciless angel, who holds the fire in his hand, this is the archangel Purouel, who has authority over fire, and he tests the work of men through fire. And if the fire burns up the work of anyone, immediately the angel of judgment takes him and carries him away to the place of sinners, a most bitter place of punishment. But if the fire tests the work of anyone and does not touch it, this person is justified and the angel of righteousness takes him and carries him up to be saved in the lot of the righteous. And thus, most righteous Abraham, all things in all people are tested by fire and balance. (*OTP* 1:890)

As in Paul, this text pictures the fire attacking the works of a person, and if they are bad, they (the works) are burned up. In distinction from Paul however, the judgment is pictured in strictly dualistic terms, that is without a middle category of those who are not completely righteous.

631. 1 Corinthians 3:16-17; 6:19-20

Epictetus, *Discourses* 2.8.9-14 (55–135 CE)

Will you not, therefore, seek the true nature of the good in that quality the lack of which in all creatures other than man prevents you from using the term "good" of any of these?
But what then? Are not these creatures also works of God?
They are, but they are not of primary importance, nor portions of Divinity. But you are a being of primary importance; you are a fragment of God; you have within you a part of Him. Why, then, are you ignorant of your own kinship? Why do you not know the source from which you are sprung? Will you not bear in mind, whenever you eat, who you are that eat, and whom you are nourishing? Whenever you indulge in intercourse with women, who you are who do this? Whenever you mix in society, whenever you take physical exercise, or engage in conversation, do you not know that it is God you are nourishing and training? You bear God about with you, poor wretch, and know it not. Do you think I speak of some external god of silver or gold? No, you bear him about within you, and are unaware that you are defiling him with unclean thoughts and foul actions. If an image of God were present, you would not dare to do any of the things you do; yet when God himself is present within you and sees and hears all things, you are not ashamed of thinking and acting thus: O slow to understand your nature, and estranged from God! (LCL)

Points of contact: (1) The deity is not merely an external object, but an invisible, spiritual, inner reality. (2) This has ethical implications. Those who are aware that God resides within them will avoid defiling God's temple by participation in evil, which is not only overt external acts, including sexual misconduct, but unclean thoughts.

Differences: (1) Neither Paul nor any first-century Jew could speak of human beings as "fragments of God." (2) Epictetus and Stoicism explain what all human beings are by nature, and challenge them to realize and live by their true nature that they already possess by birth. Paul understands the indwelling divine Spirit not as a natural element of human being, but the eschatological gift to the holy community of faith. (3) For Paul the temple of God is first the holy community (as in 3:16-17) and then its individual members (as 6:19-20). For Stoicism the community is the human race at large, but the application is understood individualistically. There is no Stoic community corresponding to the church.

632. 1 Corinthians 3:16-17

1QS 8.5-9 (1 cent. BCE)

When these are in Israel, the Council of the Community shall be established in truth. It shall be an Everlasting Plantation, a House of Holiness for Israel, an Assembly of Supreme Holiness for Aaron. They shall be witnesses to the truth at the Judgment, and shall be the elect of Goodwill who shall atone for the Land and pay to the wicked their reward. It shall be that tried wall, that precious cornerstone, whose foundations shall neither rock nor sway in their place (Isa. xxviii, 16). It shall be a Most Holy Dwelling for Aaron, with everlasting knowledge of the Covenant of justice, and shall offer up sweet fragrance. It shall be a House of Perfection and Truth in Israel that they may establish a Covenant according to the everlasting precepts. (Vermes)

The temple is still standing in Jerusalem as Paul writes 1 Corinthians, but Paul considers the Christian community as God's true temple. So also at Qumran, an alienated group within Israel that saw itself as the eschatological community comes to consider the community itself as the true temple. In the Hellenistic period or earlier, there is no evidence of any other group except the Qumran community and the early church that considered the group to be the temple. (See Kuhn, "Impact of the Qumran Scrolls," 331.) Paul may be (indirectly) dependent on Qumran. The similar idea in 1 Peter 2:4-5 is probably a development of this Christian tradition represented by Paul rather than evidence for 1 Peter's own contact with Qumran.

633. 1 Corinthians 5–10

Plutarch, *Moralia*, "How a Man May Become Aware of His Progress in Virtue" 12 (45–125 CE)

"It [a naturally despotic soul] attempts incest," and feels a sudden hunger for a great variety of food, acting in lawless fashion, and giving loose rein to the desires . . . (LCL)

Similarly in "Virtues and Vices," §2 (getting sexually involved with one's mother, eating forbidden foods, restraining oneself from no vice). The repeated naming of this series by Plutarch (in the second passage with an allusion to Plato) shows that the series of topics treated by Paul may possibly have a pagan tradition as its model. In each author the leading theme is "complete lack of restraint and thoroughgoing lawlessness."

634. 1 Corinthians 5:1

Josephus, *Antiquities*, 3.274 (37–100 CE)

[Concerning purity, God through Moses decreed:] . . . concerning wedlock that it was to the interest alike of the state and the family that children should be legitimate. Again, to have intercourse with one's mother is condemned by the law as the grossest of sins; likewise union with a stepmother, an aunt, a sister, or the wife of one's child is viewed with abhorrence as an outrageous crime. (LCL)

In his paraphrase of biblical history and Moses' laws, Josephus interprets Leviticus 18:8. He is concerned to show that the moral standards of Israel were at least as high as those of surrounding nations, and thus does not make the point that Gentiles also forbade these practices. Paul's point is that Corinthian conduct is [not only against the Torah and Jewish standards, but is] considered sacrilege by Gentiles. Cf. Philo, "Special Laws" 3.14, 20; Sophocles, *Oedipus Tyrannus* 1403-9; Cicero, *Cluentius Habitus* 14-15; Aelius Spartianus, *Life of the Emperor Antoninus Caracalla* 10.1-4.

635. 1 Corinthians 5:1-13

1QS 2.4b-10 (1 cent. BCE)

And the Levites shall curse all the men of the lot of Satan, saying: "Be cursed because of all your guilty wickedness! May He deliver you up for torture at the hands of the vengeful Avengers! May He visit you with destruction by the hand of all the Wreakers of Revenge! Be cursed without mercy because of the darkness of your deeds! Be damned in the shadowy place of everlasting fire! May God not heed when you call on Him, nor pardon you by blotting out your sin! May He raise His angry face toward you for vengeance! May there be no 'Peace' for you in the mouth of those who hold fast to the Fathers!" And after the blessing and the cursing, all those entering the Covenant shall say, "Amen, Amen!"

And the priests and Levites shall continue saying, "Cursed be the man who enters this Covenant while walking among the idols of his heart . . ." (Vermes)

Analogous to 1 Corinthians 5: A congregational cursing of other (evil) people by the congregational leaders (here, Levites) and the congregation itself (confirming the curse by their "Amen, Amen").

The difference from Paul: Here the curse is obviously directed against outsiders (but cf. 2:11-18, where those are cursed who have become members of the community while retaining "the gods of their hearts," and who become apostate). Another difference is that in 1QS no ultimate salvation is provided for—though in Corinth the curse itself will not have contained this. Paul himself is probably here interpreting a curse formula (cf. Berger, *Formgeschichte*, 181). All this is a different world from the magical curses against individuals, often written on lead tablets and pierced with a nail, e.g., "I curse Tretia Maria and her life and mind and memory and liver and lungs mixed up together, and her words, thoughts, and memory/thus may she be unable to speak what things are concealed nor be able . . ." (*PGM*). Cf. also no. 309 at Luke 11:42, Matt 23:23. Further:

636. 1 Corinthians 5:1-13

Magical Papyrus *PGM* 4.1227-64 (4 cent. CE)

Excellent rite for driving out daimons: Formula to be spoken over his head: Place olive branches before him, / and stand behind him and say:

"Hail, God of Abraham; hail, God of Isaac; hail, God of Jacob; Jesus Chrestos, the Holy Spirit, the Son of the Father, who is above the Seven, / who is within the Seven. Bring Iao Sabaoth; may your power issue forth from him, NN, until you drive away this unclean daimon Satan, who is in him. I conjure you, daimon, / whoever you are, by this god. SABARBARBATHIOTH SABARBARBATHIOUTH SABARBARBATHIONETH SABAR-BARBAPHAI. Come out, daimon, whoever you are, and stay away from him, NN, / now, now; immediately, immediately. Come out, daimon, since I bind you with unbreakable adamantine fetters, and I deliver you into the black chaos in perdition." (Betz)

(NN in the trans. is the translator's indication that the appropriate name or act was to be inserted into the formula at this point.)

Analogous to 1 Corinthians 5: By a curse formula, "someone" is "delivered over" to destruction (cf. 1 Cor 5:5). The difference: in this text, it is the demon who is "delivered over," while in Paul it is the sinful person himself, in the flesh. On "delivering over" cf. also additional examples from Qumran, e.g. CD 19:13 (?). On the dispatch with which this is done, cf. no. 949.

On 1 Corinthians 5:6-11, cf. no. 771. On 1 Corinthians 5:11, cf. no. 755.

637. 1 Corinthians 6:1-11

Epictetus, *Discourses* 3.22.55-56 (55–135 CE)

[On the true Cynic:] This too is a very pleasant strand woven into the Cynic's pattern of life; he must needs be flogged like an ass, and while he is being flogged, he must love the men who flog him, as though he were the father or brother of them all. But that is not your way. If someone flog you, go stand in the midst and shout, "O Caesar, what do I have to suffer under your peaceful rule? Let us go before the Proconsul." But what to a Cynic is Caesar, or a Proconsul, or anyone other than He who has sent him into the world and whom he serves, that is Zeus? Does he call upon anyone but Zeus? And is he not persuaded that whatever of these hardships he suffers, it is Zeus that is exercising him? (LCL)

Instead of a legal battle before the Proconsul, it is recommended that the true Cynic only make a scene, for God is the only court of appeal of the Cynic, who voluntarily suffers (cf. 1 Cor 6:6, 7). The difference from Paul: a "congregation" does not come within the Cynic perspective, and thus no internal disciplinary means by the community. (There are also points of contact with the Synoptic missionary discourse [cf. Matt 10:17-25; Mark 13:9-13; Luke 12:11-12] as well as the challenge to voluntary suffering in 1 Pet 2:13-17; 3:13; 4:12-19.) For loving those who inflict punishment, cf. Matthew 5:43-44; Luke 6:27-28. For suffering at the hands of the state as God's will, cf. the Gospels' passion story Matthew 26–27; Mark 14–15; Luke 22–23, esp. Matthew 26:39; Mark 14:35-36; Luke 22:41-42. Further:

638. 1 Corinthians 6:1-11

Musonius Rufus, *Will the Philosopher Prosecute Anyone for Personal Injury?* 10.15-23 (30–100 CE)

He said that he himself would never prosecute anyone for personal injury nor recommend it to anyone else who claimed to be a philosopher. For actually none of the things which people fancy they suffer as personal injuries are an injury or a disgrace to those who experience them, such as being reviled or struck or spit upon. Of these the hardest to bear are blows. That there is nothing shameful or insulting about them however is clear from the fact that Lacedaemonian boys are whipped publicly, and they exult in it. If, then, the philosopher cannot despise blows and insults, when he ought obviously to despise even death, what good would he be?

For what does the man who submits to insult do that is wrong? It is the doer of wrong who forthwith puts himself to shame, while the sufferer, who does nothing but submit, has no reason whatever to feel shame or disgrace. Therefore the sensible man would not go to law nor bring indictments, since he would not even consider that he had been insulted. (Lutz)

As with Epictetus (cf. no. 637), so also here court action is to be absolutely avoided. As in 1 Corinthians 6:7, doing evil is contrasted with suffering evil, and the latter is recommended (cf. also Plato, *Gorgias* 469c). The difference from Paul, however, is that for Paul this conduct is grounded in the corporate life of the community (holiness of the congregation) and in eschatology (judging angels), and above all in soteriology.

In the philosophical field related to Cynicism, the avoidance of court battles is also recommended by Plutarch, "Sufferings" 4 (anger, quarrelsomeness, selfish desire as causes). Plutarch's "Precepts of Statecraft" 19: (Out of greed and their desire always to be right, prominent upper-class types avoid local courts and oppress the little people. They appeal to the higher courts, because they don't want to give in to local citizens. The statesman must therefore attempt to keep the trials in the local jurisdiction of the city. But instead of this, people take their cases to orators and advocates, in order not to have to give in to one's local fellow citizens.) This text shows once again (cf. nos. 619-22, final part of no. 693) how Paul can make use of "political" reason.

639. 1 Corinthians 6:2

Philo, "On Dreams That They Are God-Sent" 130-32 (15 BCE–50 CE)

[Concerning an Egyptian official who wanted to abolish the Jewish customs and who compares himself with the forces of nature that shake established institutions:] Would he delay to utter blasphemies against the sun, moon and the other stars, if what he hoped for at each season of the year did not happen at all or only grudgingly, if the summer visited him with scorching heat or the winter with a terrible frost, if the spring failed in its fruit-bearing or the autumn showed fertility in breeding disease? Nay, he will loose every reef of his unbridled mouth and scurrilous tongue and accuse the stars of not paying their regular tribute . . . (LCL)

These kinds of complaints—in his eyes meaningless—are according to Philo raised by godless people against Providence, the "Divine Natures" or the "Olympian Beings" that regulate the course of the world (cf. K. Berger, "Streit um Gottes vorsehung. Zur position der Gegner im 2 Petrusbrief," in Festschrift for J. Lebram [Leiden: E. J. Brill, 1986], 121-35). In the tradition represented by Paul, the holy community of the elect will as God's servants participate in the Last Judgment of the whole world. That which appears in the Philonic tradition as presumptuous arrogance becomes in the Pauline tradition, where people are understood to participate in God's Spirit (but of course only with this condition) an eschatological mark of distinction. In connection with 1 Corinthians 6:3 commentators often think of the fallen angels of Genesis 6 and their judgment as described in the Enoch literature. But these angels are already condemned (*1 Enoch* 13–16). While the Epistle of Jude disputes that the church has this right in the present, at any rate (cf. Jude 8-9, 19-20), Paul declares it to be an eschatological function of the church.

On 1 Corinthians 6:2 cf. no. 772 (holiness), and no. 916 (judging).

640. 1 Corinthians 6:9

Juvenal, *Satire* 2.36 (100–110 CE)

[Sarcastic response to a general criticism of women's morals:] Laronia could not contain herself when one of these sour-faced worthies cried out, "What of your Julian Law? Has it gone to sleep?" To which she answered smilingly, "O happy times to have you as a censor of our morals! Once more may Rome regain her modesty; a third Cato has come down to us from the skies! But tell me, where did you buy that balsam juice that exhales from your hairy neck? Don't be ashamed to point out to me the shopman! If laws and statutes are to be raked up, you should cite first of all the Scantinian: inquire first into the things that are done by men; men do more wicked things than we do, but they are protected by their numbers, and the tight-locked shields of their phalanx. Male effeminates agree wonderfully well among themselves; never in our sex will you find such loathsome examples of evil." (LCL)

The Julian Law was passed to encourage marriage (*Lex Iulia de maritandis ordinibus*). The Scantinian law (*Lex Scantinia*, 149 BCE) was against homosexual practices. The interchange illustrates that homosexuality was not uncommon, that it was considered evil by some, and that laws were promulgated to regulate it. As in Paul, here homosexual practices are placed in the same category as sexual sins such as adultery.

So also in Martial, *Epigrams* 1.90, "In that I never saw you, Bassa, intimate with men, and that no scandal assigned you a lover, but every office a throng of your own sex round you performed without the approach of a man—you seemed to me, I confess, a Lucretia; yet, Bassa—O, monstrous!—you are, it seems, a nondescript. You dare things unspeakable, and your portentous lust imitates man.

You have invented a prodigy worthy of the Theban riddle, that here, where no man is, should be adultery!" (LCL).

On the varying opinions on the relation of homosexuality to "nature," cf. nos. 536-38 on Romans 1:26-27.

641. 1 Corinthians 6:9

Seneca, *Epistles* 95.23-24 (4–65 CE)

[Lamenting the general decline of morals and culture:] All intellectual interests are in abeyance; those who follow culture lecture to empty rooms, in out-of-the-way places. The halls of the professors and the philosophers are deserted; but what a crowd there is in the cafés! How many young fellows besiege the kitchens of their gluttonous friends! I shall not mention the troops of luckless boys who must put up with other shameful treatment after the banquet is over. I shall not mention the troops of catamites [castrated males], rated according to nation and color, who must all have the same smooth skin, and the same amount of youthful down on their cheeks, and the same way of dressing their hair, so that no boy with straight locks may get among the curly-heads. (LCL)

Such condemnations do not address the issue of homosexuality as such, but the abuse of boys and castration of males as examples of licentious conduct in general. So also in Suetonius, *Lives of the Caesars,* "Nero," 28-29, illustrating Nero's immorality:

"Besides abusing freeborn boys and seducing married women, he debauched the vestal virgin Rubria. The freedwoman Acte he all but made his lawful wife, after bribing some ex-consuls to perjure themselves by swearing that she was of royal birth. He castrated the boy Sporus and actually tried to make a woman of him; and he married him with all the usual ceremonies, including a dowry and a bridal veil, took him to his house attended by a great throng, and treated him as his wife. And the witty jest that someone made is still current, that it would have been well for the world if Nero's father Domitius had had that kind of wife. This Sporus, decked out with the finery of the empresses and riding in a litter, he took with him to the assizes and marts of Greece, and later at Rome through the Street of the Images, fondly kissing him from time to time" (LCL).

642. 1 Corinthians 6:9

Plato, *Laws* 841 D-E (428/27–349/48 BCE)

Possibly, should God so grant, we might forcibly effect one of two things in this matter of sex-relations—either that no one should venture to touch any of the noble and freeborn save his own wedded wife, nor sow any unholy and bastard seed in fornication, nor any unnatural and barren seed in sodomy—or else we should entirely abolish love for males, and in regard to that for women, if we enact a law that any man who has intercourse with any women save those who have been brought to his house under the sanction of Heaven and holy marriage, whether purchased or otherwise acquired, if detected in such intercourse by any man or woman, shall be disqualified from any civic commendation, as being really an alien—probably such a law would be approved as right. So let this law—whether we ought to call it one law or two—be laid down concerning sexual commerce and love affairs in general, as regards right and wrong conduct in our mutual intercourse due to these desires. (LCL)

This is part of a dialogue constructed by Plato, in which other views are presented, illustrating the view of those who considered homosexuality immoral and to be regulated by the state. That there were varying views on the issue is seen from the following selection. Plato's own views are more clearly presented in no. 538 above on Romans 1:26-27.

643. 1 Corinthians 6:9

Sextus Empiricus, *Outlines of Pyrrhonism* 3.198-200 (ca. 200 CE)

And perhaps it may not be amiss, in addition to what has been said, to dwell more in detail, though briefly, on the notions concerning things shameful and not shameful, unholy and not so, laws and customs, piety toward the gods, reverence for the departed, and the like. For thus we shall discover a great variety of belief concerning what ought or ought not to be done.

For example, amongst us sodomy is regarded as shameful or rather illegal, but by the Germani [probably a Persian tribe, not the Germans of north Europe], they say, it is not looked on as shameful but as a customary thing. It is said, too, that in Thebes long ago this practice was not held to be shameful, and they say that Meriones the Cretan was so called by way of indicating the Cretans' custom, and some refer to this the burning love of Achilles for Patroclus. And what wonder, when both the adherents of the Cynic philosophy and followers of Zeno of Citium, Cleanthes and Chrysippus, declare that this practice is indifferent? (LCL)

Sextus Empiricus treats the varying judgments on the morality of homosexual relations as an illustration of the conventions of what is considered acceptable that vary from place to place, such as tattooing and whether men may wear earrings. On the relativity and conventional nature of how homosexuality was perceived, see also Xenophon, *The Lacedaemonians* 2:12-14:

"I think I ought to say something also about intimacy with boys, since this matter also has a bearing on education. In other Greek states, for instance among the Boeotians, man and boy live together, like married people; elsewhere, among the Eleians, for example, consent is won by means of favors. Some, on the other hand, entirely forbid suitors to talk with boys.

The customs instituted by Lycurgus were opposed to all of these. If someone, being himself an honest man, admired a boy's soul and tried to make of him an ideal friend without reproach and to associate with him, he approved, and believed in the excellence of this kind of training. But if it was clear that the attraction lay in the boy's outward beauty, he banned the connection as an abomination (αἴσχιστον); and thus he purged the relationship of all impurity, so that in Lacedaemon it resembled parental and brotherly love.

I am not surprised, however, that people refuse to believe this. For in many states the laws are not opposed to the indulgence of these appetites" (LCL).

Plutarch, *Moralia* 12 A, uses almost the same words with regard to homosexuality as does Paul in Romans 14:5 with regard to the observance of special days and the enjoyment of wine or abstinence from it: "Let each be persuaded according to his own convictions."

For the view that homosexuality is a violation of nature, see nos. 536-38 on Romans 1:26-27.

644. 1 Corinthians 6:12; 10:23

Plutarch, *Moralia*, "Various Sayings of Spartans to Fame Unknown" 65 (45–125 CE)

Another, on going to Athens, saw that the Athenians were hawking salt fish and dainties, collecting taxes, keeping public brothels, and following other unseemly pursuits, and holding none of them to be shameful. When he returned to his own country, his fellow-citizens asked how things were in Athens, and he said, "Everything fair and lovely," speaking sarcastically and conveying the idea that among the Athenians everything is considered fair and lovely, and nothing shameful. (LCL)

The Spartan who had been reared in the strict atmosphere of his native town was scandalized by the loose-living Athenians. This is the way the whole Hellenistic world must have appeared to Jews who had been reared in the atmosphere of strict Torah piety. In both places the contrasting lifestyle is described as permitting "everything," including traffic with prostitutes. In each case it is simply stated without explicit criticism. It is possible, however, that this formula also had a positive meaning for Paul, and was even a part of his own proclamation before it was misunderstood in the above sense by the Corinthians.

645. 1 Corinthians 6:12; 10:23

Epictetus, *Discourses* 4.4.1 (55–135 CE)

He is free who lives as He wills, who is subject neither to compulsion, nor hindrance, nor force, whose choices are unhampered, whose desires attain their end, whose aversions do not fall into what they would avoid. (LCL)

The inference is then immediately drawn: no evil person lives as he or she really intends, and thus no evil person is really free. Therefore virtuous living and doing right are the presuppositions of freedom. First Timothy 1:9 and the tradition that stands behind it point in the same direction (e.g. Antiphanes, see under no. 828). The statement can thus express the consequence of freedom from external law or at least an inference from the abolition of the ritual laws that hamper freedom of conduct (cf. no. 541).

646. 1 Corinthians 6:12-20

Strabo, *Geography* 8.20-21, 23 (64/63 BCE–23 CE)

Corinth is called "wealthy" because of its commerce, since it is situated on the Isthmus and is master of two harbors, of which the one leads straight to Asia, and the other to Italy; and it makes easy the exchange of merchandise from both countries that are so far distant from each other. . . . And also the duties of what by land was exported from the Peloponnesus and what was imported to it fell to those who held the keys. And to later times this remained ever so. But to the Corinthians of later times still greater advantages were added, for also the Isthmian Games, which were celebrated there, were wont to draw crowds of people. . . . And the temple of Aphrodite was so rich that it owned more than a thousand temple-slaves, courtesans, whom both men and women had dedicated to the goddess. And therefore it was also on account of these women that the city was crowded with people and grew rich. . . . (LCL)

This often-cited text from Strabo has been used to illustrate the low moral level of public ethics in Paul's day. No doubt the problem of loose sexual ethics in Corinth, and the lack of connection between religion and ethics in much Hellenistic religion, did pose a problem for the struggling new Christian community. But Corinth was probably no worse than other large Hellenistic cities. The famous reference to "1000 cultic prostitutes" is an exaggerated slander intended to demean the reputation of the city, fueled in part by Athens' commercial rivalry with Corinth. In any case, Strabo's description refers to the early days of the city, not to its character in Paul's time. Cf. Hans Conzelmann, *Korinth und die Mädchen der Aphrodite* (Göttingen: Vandenhoeck & Ruprecht, 1967), who argues Corinth was never a center of cultic prostitution.

647. 1 Corinthians 6:12-20

Musonius Rufus, *On Sexual Indulgence* (30–100 CE)

Not the least significant part of the life of luxury and self-indulgence lies also in sexual excess; for example those who lead such a life crave a variety of loves not only lawful but unlawful ones as well, not women alone but also men; sometimes they pursue one love and sometimes another, and not being satisfied with those which are available, pursue those which are rare and inaccessible, and invent shameful intimacies, all of which constitute a grave indictment of manhood. Men who are not wantons or immoral are bound to consider sexual intercourse justified only when it occurs in marriage and indulged in for the purpose of begetting children, since that is lawful, but unjust and unlawful when it is mere pleasure-seeking, even in marriage. But of all sexual relations those involving adultery are most unlawful, and no more tolerable are those of men with men, because it is a monstrous thing and contrary to nature. But, furthermore, leaving out of consideration adultery, all intercourse with women which is without lawful character is shameful and is practiced from lack of self-restraint. So no one with any self-control would think of having relations with a courtesan or a free woman apart from marriage, no, nor even with his own maid-servant. The fact that these relationships are not lawful or seemly makes them a disgrace and a reproach to those seeking them; whence it is that no one dares to do any of these things openly, not even if he has all but lost the ability to blush, and those who are not completely degenerate dare to do these things only in hiding and in secret. And yet to attempt to cover up what one is doing is equivalent to a confession of guilt. "That's all very well," you say, "but unlike the adulterer who wrongs the husband of the woman he corrupts, the man who has relations with a courtesan or a woman who has no husband wrongs no one for he does not destroy anyone's hope of children." I continue to maintain that everyone who sins and does wrong, even if it affects none of the people about him, yet immediately reveals himself as a worse and a less honorable person; for the wrongdoer by the very fact of doing wrong is worse and less honorable. Not to mention the injustice of the thing, there must be sheer wantonness in anyone yielding to the temptation of shameful pleasure and like swine rejoicing in his own vileness. In this category belongs the man who has relations with his own slave-maid, a thing which some people consider quite without blame, since every master is held to have it in his power to use his slave as he wishes. In reply to this I have just one thing to say: if it seems neither shameful nor out of place for a master to have relations with his own slave, particularly if she happens to be unmarried, let him consider how he would like it if his wife had relations with a male slave. Would it not seem completely intolerable not only if the woman who had a lawful husband had relations with a slave, but even if a woman without a husband should have? And yet surely one will not expect men to be less moral than women, nor less capable of disciplining their desires, thereby revealing the stronger in judgment inferior to the weaker, the rulers to the ruled. In fact, it behooves men to be much better if they expect to be superior to women, for surely if they appear to be less self-controlled they will also be baser characters. What need is there to say that it is an act of licentiousness and nothing less for a master to have relations with a slave? Everyone knows that. (Lutz)

Analogies: (1) The context deals with unlawful sexual conduct. Musonius regards as moral sexual activity only that which has the procreation of children as its goal, and is opposed to all purely sensual pleasure.

(2) Sexual relations of a man with a prostitute or with an unmarried woman is presented as a sin against oneself.

(3) Homosexual acts are condemned as unnatural. (See nos. 536-38 on Rom 1:27.)

(4) Both Paul and Musonius are combating the more popular view that sexual activity is only the innocent satisfying of a natural appetite, so that the question of ethics does not arise.

(5) There is an analogous combination of affirming the equal rights of women (on which see Musonius, no. 651, explicitly rejecting the double standard, with the assumption of some of the perspectives of the patriarchal society in which they live.

Differences: (1) "One's body" against which one sins is according to Paul in reality the Lord's body. One's identity is thus determined christologically and pneumatologically, rather than being thought of autonomously as in Musonius. (2) "Sin" for Musonius is primarily the loss of personal honor, of being subject to one's own senses and revealing oneself to be a less honorable person. For Paul the transgression is against Christ. (3) Nor does Paul regard procreation as the purpose of marital sexual activity. See further no. 771.

648. 1 Corinthians 6:20

t. Berakoth 4:1 (600 CE)

A. One must not taste anything until he has [first] recited a benediction [over it],

B. as Scripture states, *The earth is the Lord's and all that it contains* [Ps. 24:1].

C. One who derives benefit from this world [by eating its produce] without first having recited a benediction has committed sacrilege [viz., it is as if he ate sanctified Temple produce, thereby misappropriating God's property],

D. until he has fulfilled all the obligations which permit him [to use the produce; viz., until he has recited the proper benediction].

E. One should make use of his face, his hands, and his feet only for the honor of his creator,

F. as Scripture states, *The Lord has made everything for its purpose* [Prov. 16:4, read as "Everything that God has made (should be used) for his sake, for his glory"]. (Neusner, *Tosefta*)

As in 1 Corinthians 6, here it is a matter of respecting God's property, and in both cases the temple analogy is used. The conclusion is also the same: God's property may only be used to his glory.

The difference: According to 1 Corinthians 6, the body belongs to God by virtue of the indwelling Spirit of God, while the Tosefta passage makes it a matter of creation. In Paul, regarding the Christian as not only God's creation but as one who has received the Spirit intensifies the motivation. Thus the consequence is also different in each case: in the Tosefta, the honoring of God occurs through the recitation of the benediction, i.e. liturgically, while for Paul it is a matter of ethics and a sign of the distinctive way of life of the holy community to shun disruptive social relationships such as trafficking with prostitutes.

649. 1 Corinthians 7:1-40; 14:1-40

Philo, *Life of Moses* 2.13.68 (15 BCE–50 CE)

But first he [Moses] had to be clean, as in soul so also in body, to have no dealings with any passion, purifying himself from all the calls of mortal nature, food and drink and intercourse with women. This last he had disdained for many a day, almost from the time when, possessed by the spirit, he entered on his work as prophet, since he held it fitting to hold himself always in readiness to receive the oracular messages. (LCL)

The connection between sexual asceticism and ecstatic prophecy was widespread in the Hellenistic world, especially in Judaism (see Boring, *Continuing Voice*, pp. 134-37). There may have been a connection between the Corinthians' interest in ecstatic spiritual phenomena and in sexual asceticism.

650. 1 Corinthians 7:1-40

Epictetus, *Discourses* 3.22.69-70 (55–135 CE)

But in such an order of things as the present, which is like that of a battlefield, it is a question, perhaps, if the Cynic ought not to be free from distraction, wholly devoted to the service of God, free to go about among men, not tied down by the private duties of men, nor involved in relationships which he cannot violate and still maintain his role as a good and excellent man, whereas, on the other hand, if he observes them, he will destroy the messenger, the scout, the herald [κῆρυξ] of the gods that he is. (LCL)

Both Epictetus and Paul discourage marriage for the special situation to which they speak, without forbidding it in principle. Both use military imagery. Only Paul does it on the basis of eschatological theology, understood in the context of the religious community. Cf. no. 753 on Galatians 1:1.

651. 1 Corinthians 7:1-40

Musonius Rufus, *That Women Too Should Study Philosophy* (30–100 CE)

When someone asked him if women too should study philosophy, he began to discourse on the theme that they should, in somewhat the following manner. Women as well as men, he said, have received from the gods the gift of reason, which we use in our dealings with one another and by which we judge whether a thing is good or bad, right or wrong. Likewise, the female has the same senses as the male; namely sight, hearing, smell, and the others. Also both have the same parts of the body, and one has nothing more than the other. Moreover, not men alone, but women too have a natural inclination toward virtue and the capacity for acquiring it, and it is the nature of women no less than men to be pleased by good and just acts and to reject the opposite of these. If this is true, by what reasoning would it ever be appropriate for men to search out and consider how they may lead good lives, which is exactly the study of philosophy, but inappropriate for women? Could it be that it is fitting for men to be good, but not for women? Let us examine in detail the qualities which are suitable for a woman who would lead a good life, for it will appear that each one of them would accrue to her most readily from the study of philosophy. In the first place, a woman must be a good housekeeper; that is a careful accountant of all that pertains to the welfare of her house and capable of directing the household slaves. It is my contention that they are the very qualities which would be present particularly in the woman who studies philosophy, since obviously each of them is a part of life, and philosophy is nothing other than knowledge about life, and the philosopher, as Socrates said, quoting Homer, is constantly engaged in investigating precisely this: "Whatsoever of good and of evil is wrought in thy halls." But above all a woman must be chaste and self-controlled; she must, I mean, be pure in respect of unlawful love, exercise restraint in other pleasures, not be a slave to desire, not be contentious, not lavish in expense, nor extravagant in dress. Such are the works of a virtuous woman, and to them I would add yet these: to control her temper, not to be overcome by grief, and to be superior to uncontrolled emotion of every kind. Now these are things which the teaching of philosophy transmits, and the person who has learned them and practices them would seem to me to have become a well-ordered and seemly character, whether man or woman. Well then, so much for self-control. As for justice, would not the woman who studies philosophy be just, would she not be a blameless life-partner, would she not be a sympathetic help-mate, would she not be an untiring defender of husband and children, and would she not be entirely free of greed and arrogance? And who better than the woman trained in philosophy—and she certainly of necessity if she has really acquired philosophy—would be disposed to look upon doing a wrong as worse than suffering one (as much worse as it is the baser), and to regard being worsted as better than gaining an unjust advantage? Moreover, who better than she would love her children more than life itself? What woman would be more just than such a one? Now as for courage, certainly it is to be expected that the educated woman will be more courageous than the uneducated, and one who has studied philosophy than one who has not; and she will not therefore submit to anything shameful because of fear of death or unwillingness to face hardship, and she will not be intimidated by anyone because he is of noble birth, or powerful, or wealthy, no, not even if he be the tyrant of her city. For in fact she has schooled herself to be high-minded and to think of death not as an evil and life not as a good, and likewise not to shun hardship and never for a moment to seek ease and indolence. So it is that such a woman is likely to be energetic, strong to endure pain, prepared to nourish her children at her own breast, and to serve her husband with her own hands, and willing to do things which some would consider no better than slaves' work. Would not such a woman be a great help to the man who married her, an ornament to her relatives, and a good example for all who know her? Yes, but I assure you, some will say, that women who associate with philosophers are bound to be arrogant for the most part and presumptuous, in that abandoning their own households and turning to the company of men they practice speeches, talk like sophists, and analyze syllogisms, when they ought to be sitting at home spinning. I should not expect the women who study philosophy to shun their appointed tasks for mere talk any more than men, but I maintain that their discussions should be conducted for the sake of their practical application. For as there is no merit in the science of medicine unless it conduces to the healing of a man's body, so if a philosopher has or teaches reason, it is of no use if it does not contribute to the virtue of man's soul. Above all, we ought to examine the doctrine which we think women who study philosophy ought to follow; we ought to see if the study which presents modesty as the greatest good can make them presumptuous, if the study which is a guide to the greatest self-restraint accustoms them to live heedlessly, if what sets forth intemperance as the greatest evil does not teach self-control, if what represents the management of a household as a virtue does not impel them to manage well their homes. Finally, the teachings of philosophy exhort the woman to be content with her lot and to work with her own hands. (Lutz)

Like Paul's discussions of marriage, domestic issues, and male-female relations, this passage from a Roman Stoic contemporary of Paul manifests a surprising affirmation of the equality of the sexes, while retaining many of the patriarchal cultural presuppositions, including slavery. Cf. similar affirmations of the equality of male and female in his *Should Daughters Receive the Same Educations as Sons*, which gives an extensive argument for the affirmative, though like Paul recognizing that it is against the cultural mainstream (excerpt in no. 895 below).

652. 1 Corinthians 7:1

Letter of Diogenes 47 (1 cent. BCE–3 cent. CE)

To Zeno, do well.
One should not wed nor raise children, since our race is weak and marriage and children burden human weakness with troubles. Therefore, those who move toward wedlock and the rearing of children on account of the support these promise, later experience a change of heart when they come to know that they are characterized by even greater hardships. But it is possible to escape right from the start. Now the person insensitive to passion, who considers his own possessions to be sufficient for patient endurance, declines to marry and produce children. (Malherbe)

The burden of which Pseudo-Diogenes speaks refers to the impossibility of being "wise" under the conditions of marriage and family. In view of the concern with "wisdom" in Corinth, and the affinity between early Christian charismatics and Cynics otherwise attested (cf. nos. 144, 148, 296, 298, and Subject Index, s. v. "Cynic"), this text could be evidence that the Corinthian statements about marriage might not be unrelated to their fascination with "wisdom." On this see esp. no. 667.

For Jewish contact, see Wisdom of Solomon 3:13-14. Further:

653. 1 Corinthians 7:1

Inscription from Pergamon for the cult of Athene Nikephoros (1 cent. BCE)

Those citizens may enter the temple of the goddess who have not engaged in sex with their own wives or husbands on that day, or with anyone else for two days, and who have bathed themselves. (MEB/Berger)

This text from *SIG* III 982 is only one documentation for the widespread conviction that sexuality and ritual purity cannot be combined (cf. E. Fehrle, *Die kultische Keuscheit im Altertum* [Berlin: A. Töpelman, 1910]). In the OT, cf. Exodus 19:15; Leviticus 15:18; in Judaism, cf. Josephus, *Apion* 2.203, and esp. Philo, *Moses* 2.68 (Moses had no relations with women from his call to be a prophet, in order to always be prepared for a revelation from God). On permanent celibacy, cf. Ignatius, *Letter to Polycarp* 5:2.

On 1 Corinthians 7:1ff. (the place of women): nos. 443, 772, 790, 811.

654. 1 Corinthians 7:4

Musonius Rufus, *What Is the Chief End of Marriage?* (30–100 CE)

The husband and wife, he used to say, should come together for the purpose of making a life in common and of procreating children, and furthermore of regarding all things in common between them, and nothing peculiar or private to one or the other, not even their own bodies. . . . But in marriage there must be above all perfect companionship and mutual love of husband and wife, both in health and in sickness and under all conditions, since it was with desire for this as well as for having children that both entered upon marriage. (Lutz)

Similarly Hierocles (Stoic from Hadrian's time, 117–138 CE), according to Stobaeus 4.22: ". . . whereby they agree with one another to such an extent and have everything in common even to the point of their own bodies—even more, their own souls themselves" (MEB/Berger and from *Stobaeus, Anthologium,* vol. 4).

In Judaism, the idea that each partner has the rights over the other's body is not documented in precisely this way. The term for "have authority over" (ἐξουσιάζω) is however found in Sir 47:19 (cf. 1 Cor 6:12). In contrast to the Stoic philosopher, it is not the general sharing of life involved in marriage in which Paul is interested, but on the particular point of parity between the partners in their sexual relations.

655. 1 Corinthians 7:5

Testaments of the Twelve Patriarchs, "Testament of Naphtali" 8:7-9 (1 cent. BCE)

The commandments of the Lord [the law] are double, and they are to be fulfilled with regularity. There is a time for having intercourse with one's wife, and a time to abstain for the purpose of prayer.

And there are the two commandments: Unless they are performed in proper sequence they leave one open to the greatest sin. (*OTP* 1:814)

The text is intended as a contribution to the inner-Pharisee discussion of perfect fulfillment of the Law. "Testament of Naphtali" 8:10 expresses the general point: "So be wise in the Lord and discerning, knowing the order of his commandments, what is ordained for every act, so that the Lord will love you." Similarly the concern for "order" in "Testament of Naphtali" 3:2-4. Paul participates in the cultic discussion, as well as in the narrower Pharisaic discussion.

656. 1 Corinthians 7:5

m. Ketuboth 5:6 (200 CE)

A. He who takes a vow not to have sexual relations with his wife—

B. the House of Shammai say, "[He may allow this situation to continue] for two weeks."

C. And the House of Hillel say, "For one week."

D. Disciples go forth for Torah study without [the wife's] consent for thirty days.

E. Workers go out for one week.

F. "The sexual duty of which the Torah speaks [Ex. 21:10]: (1) those without work [of independent means]—every day; (2) workers—twice a week; (3) ass drivers—once a week; (4) camel drivers—once in thirty days; (5) sailors—once in six months," the words of R. Eliezer. (Neusner, *Mishnah*)

As in Paul, "marital duty" is here understood as regulated by rules. In distinction from him, the criterion for a period of abstinence from sex is not a cultic act, but the man's vocation.

657. 1 Corinthians 7:7

Letter of Aristeas 236-38 (2 cent. BCE)

On the following day the arrangements for the banquet were the same as before, and when it seemed suitable to the king he began to question the guests . . .

"What makes the greatest contribution to health?" He [the second guest] replied, "Self-control, which it is impossible to achieve unless God disposes the heart and mind toward it." [The king] congratulated this guest . . . (*OTP* 2:28)

Similarly, Wisdom 8:21: ". . . except when God gives it." As with Paul, sexual abstinence is not a natural ability, but a special gift of God.

658. 1 Corinthians 7:12-16

Plutarch, *Moralia*, "Advice to Bride and Groom" 19 (45–125 CE)

A wife ought not to make friends of her own, but to enjoy her husband's friends in common with him. The gods are the first and most important friends. Wherefore it is becoming for a wife to worship and to know only the gods that her husband believes in, and to shut the front door tight upon all queer rituals and outlandish superstitions. For with no god do stealthy and secret rites performed by a woman find any favor. (LCL)

Greeks and Romans thought that women in particular needed to be warned against foreign cults. Elements of Judaism and early Christianity (e.g. the false teachers of the Pastoral Letters), appealed especially to wealthy married women and drew many of their disciples from these circles. With reference to foreign cults, "mixed marriages" are also not a pagan ideal.

659. 1 Corinthians 7:19

Josephus, *Jewish Antiquities* 20.41 (37–100 CE)

[With reference to king Izates:] "The king could," he [Ananias] said, "worship God even without being circumcised if indeed he had fully decided to be a devoted adherent of Judaism, for it was this that counted more than circumcision." (LCL)

The text deals with King Izates of Adiabene, who at first intended to convert to this form of Judaism without being circumcised, but then after all decided to be circumcised as a result of the objections of the Galilean Jewish teacher Eleazar. Paul refers here as similarly in no. 548 to an issue that nevertheless continued to be discussed. Within the framework of Pauline pneumatology, fulfillment of the Law without circumcision is also the right way (cf. Rom 8:4; Gal 5:14).

660. 1 Corinthians 7:21-23

Letter of Crates to Metrocles 34 (1–2 cent. CE)

[Diogenes speaks to his fellow prisoners, with whom he is to be sold:] . . . "Won't you stop feigning ignorance and crying over your imminent slavery, as if you were really free before you fell into the hands of pirates and were not slaves even to worse masters?"
[The buyers, looking over the slaves, are amazed at his freedom from emotion, and ask whether he is skilled at anything.] And he said that he was skilled at ruling men. "So, if any of you needs a master, let him come forward and strike a bargain with the sellers." But they laughed at him and said, "And who is there who, since he is free, needs a master?" "All,"

he said, "who are base and who honor pleasure and despise toil, the greatest incitements to evils." (Malherbe)

The text follows the classical dialectical pattern of freedom/slavery that extends to Hegel and Marx (cf. nos. 429, 576): the one sold as slave is master and free, while the masters are really slaves. Epictetus, *Discourses* 1.19.9 is also important (the philosopher speaks to the tyrant): "Zeus has set me free. Or do you really think that he was likely to let his own son be made a slave? You are, however, master of my dead body, take it" (LCL). Paul inserts a third element into the dialectic of slave/master relationships, that of slaves who have been freed. They too are "in the Lord" and belong to the Lord. Thus the choice of illustrative material prepares for the Pauline point.

Similarly also Bion (3 cent. BCE): "Slaves who are morally good are free; masters who are morally evil are slaves of their desires" (MEB/Berger from Stobaeus, *Anthologium*, vol. 3 187.5).

For Philo's description of the Essenes as a community that repudiated slavery, see no. 30 on Matthew 5–7.

661. 1 Corinthians 7:21-23

Apocryphal Jewish Biographies (1–3 cent. CE)

[On the relation of Joshua to Moses:] because of the service [ὑποταγή] with which he served [ὑποτάσσειν] Moses as disciple—for he differed not at all from a servant—he was worthy too that the Lord should be with him as his master, for he was not a slave in his race [γένος]: but he used [χρῆσθαι] the servitude, knowing him whose servant he was . . . he loved one who was God's servant, and was his servant of his own choice [προαίρεσις]. (Winstedt)

This text is the first documentation for a use of the expression "make use of" (μᾶλλον χρῆσαι) independently of Paul, and as a religious text leads us beyond previous exegetical alternatives (Paul admonishes to remain a slave/Paul admonishes to strive for freedom). The text describes the voluntary servitude of a man for whom it is "not necessary" because he is really free, and precisely from religious motivations. On "make use of," cf. also Epictetus, *Discourses* 2.5.6-8 (on the "use" of external things, which is either "good" or "bad," in contrast to things that happen to one not under one's control).

According to Musonius Rufus (30–100 CE) ("That Women Too Should Study Philosophy," 3.10), women should nourish children at their own breast, and serve their husbands with their own hands, ". . . which some would consider no better than slaves' work." Here too the point is voluntary slave work from philosophical reasons (Lutz).

For Philo's description of the Essenes as a community that repudiated slavery, see no. 30 on Matthew 5–7.

On 1 Corinthians 7:25-31, see no. 177 on Mark 13:14-20.

662. 1 Corinthians 7:27

Teles the Cynic 10-11 (240 BCE)

. . . one should not try to change circumstances, but rather to prepare oneself for them as they are. . . . You have grown old: do not seek the things of a young man. Again, you have become weak: do not seek to carry and submit your neck to the loads of a strong man. . . . Again, you have become destitute: do not seek the rich man's way of life . . . (O'Neil)

Similarly Epictetus, *Discourses* 3.21.5: "Do something of the same sort yourself too; eat as a man, drink as a man, adorn yourself, marry, get children, be active as a citizen; endure revilings, bear with an unreasonable brother, father, son, neighbor, fellow traveler. Show us that you can do these things, for us to see that in all truth you have learned something of the philosophers" (LCL). Putting up with everyday problems corresponds to Paul's instruction to remain in the state in which one finds oneself as a Christian. When Paul here speaks of being "called," he intends this as the testing ground of one's call.

663. 1 Corinthians 7:29-31

6 Ezra 16:40-46 (1–2 cent. CE)

Hear my words, O my people; prepare for battle, and in the midst of the calamities be like strangers on the earth. Let the one who sells be like one who will flee; let the one who buys be like one who will lose; let the one who does business be like one who will not make a profit; and let the one who builds a house be like one who will not live in it; let the one who sows be like one who will not reap; so also the one who prunes the vines, like one who will not gather the grapes; those who marry, like those who will have no children; and them that do not marry, like those that are widowed. Because of this those who labor, labor in vain; for strangers shall gather their fruits, and plunder their goods, and overthrow their houses, and take their children captive; for in captivity and famine they will produce their children. (NRSV)

The intensity of the coming sufferings is pictured. The text is hortatory only at the beginning ("prepare . . ."); the point of the rest, however, is to consider the possibility that everything begun might turn out to be unsuccessful. All activity directed toward the future will be meaningless; no hopes will be fulfilled. Compare with this text also W. Schrage, "Die Stellung zur Welt bei Paulus, Epiktet und in der Apokalyptic," in *ZTK* 61 (1964) 125ff. The closely related text in the Ethiopic Apocalypse of Elijah is without any eschatological aspect and only teaches how quickly the things of this world pass away: before one has a chance to look around, everything has already melted away. Further:

664. 1 Corinthians 7:29-31

Epictetus, *Discourses* 2.16.28 (55–135 CE)

And what is the law of God? To guard what is his own, not to lay claim to what is not his own, but to make use of what is given him, and not to yearn for what has not been given; when something is taken away, to give it up readily and without delay, being grateful for the time in which he had the use of it—all this if you do not wish to be crying for your nurse and your mammy! (LCL)

The various aspects of "remaining in the state in which you were called" discussed by Paul in 1 Corinthians 7:17-27 and the attitude of freedom even within those binding relationships one has

(1 Cor 7:29-31) are here brought together, of course without Paul's eschatological perspective, but also not without a temporal aspect. Further:

665. 1 Corinthians 7:29-31

Epictetus, *Discourses* 3.24.4-5 (55–135 CE)

God made all mankind to be happy, to be serene. To this end He gave them resources, giving each man some things for his own, and others not for his own.

"But I have parted from So-and-so, and he is stricken with grief." Yes, but why did he regard what was not his own as his own? Why, when he was glad to see you, did he not reflect that you are mortal, and likely to go on a journey? And therefore he is paying the penalty for his own folly. But why are you bewailing yourself, and to what end? Or did you also neglect to study this matter, but, like worthless women, did you enjoy everything in which you took delight as though you were to enjoy it forever, your surroundings, human beings, your ways of life? (LCL)

As in Paul, this text deals with one's attitude toward worldly goods that pass away. While in Paul this is followed by the age to come that will not pass away, Epictetus deals only with conduct appropriate to temporal goods. (According to David L. Balch, Paul and the Stoics do not value human relationships in the same way. Paul puts great weight on "loving one's neighbor," but for Stoics these "external" relationships were finally ethically "indifferent." Cf. no. 876.) Further:

666. 1 Corinthians 7:29-31

Epictetus, *Discourses* 3.24.59-60 (55–135 CE)

How, then, shall I become affectionate? . . .

And what keeps you from loving a person as one subject to death, as one who may leave you? Did not Socrates love his own children? But in a free spirit, as one who remembers that it is his first duty to be a friend to the gods. (LCL)

Similarly, 4, 1.159: ". . . take Socrates and observe a man who had a wife and little children, but regarded them as not his own, who had a country, as far as it was his duty, and in the way in which it was his duty, and friends, and kinsmen, one and all subject to the law and to obedience to the law" (LCL). Different from Paul, here it is the moral obligation to the gods understood as law that is the basis of freedom from relationships. In contrast, Paul argues on the basis of the passing away of this age.

667. 1 Corinthians 7:32-35

Epictetus, *Discourses* 3.22.69-71 (55–135 CE)

But in such an order of thing as the present, which is like that of a battlefield, it is a question, perhaps, if the Cynic ought not to be free from distraction, wholly devoted to the service of God, free to go about among men, and not tied down by the private duties of men, nor involved in relationships which he cannot violate and still maintain his role as a good and excellent man, whereas, on the other hand, if he observes them, he will destroy the messenger, the scout, the herald of the god, that he is. For see, he must show certain services to his father-in-law, to the rest of his wife's relatives, to his wife herself; finally, he is driven from his profession, to act as a nurse in his own family and to provide for them. To make a long story short, he must get a kettle to heat water for the baby, for washing it in a bath-tub; wool for his wife when she has had a child, oil, a cot, a cup (the vessels get more and more numerous); not to speak of the rest of his business, and his distraction. (LCL)

The context: only where all are wise would the Cynic need not renounce marriage. As in Paul,* the point is being free from the distractions of marriage (the same word as in 1 Cor 7:35, ἀπερίσπαστον/ἀπερισπάστως). But while the Cynic who gets married must give up his vocation as messenger, scout, and herald of the gods, Paul permits—with hesitation, to be sure—a compromise, allowing a certain division in one's interests. Differently: no. 811, text 2.

Plutarch uses the verb corresponding to the adverb "unhindered(ly)" in 1 Corinthians 7:35, in the "Seven Sages," in order to describe the possibility of the soul's freedom from service to the body. See no. 652.

*Rather, according to David L. Balch, in Paul the point is freedom from distraction, but marriage distracts some, celibacy distracts others. Paul does not formulate a general rule for all, but each is to make up his or her own mind.

668. 1 Corinthians 7:32

Posidippus (2 cent. CE)

You have a marriage; you will not live without cares. You do not marry; you will live a lonely life. (MEB/Berger and Stobaeus, *Anthologium*, vol. 4)

Cf. similarly Menander (343–292 BCE) according to Stobaeus, *Anthologium* 4.22, #44: "To have a wife and to be father to children, my Parmenon, brings many cares into one's life" (MEB/Berger). The texts belong to the classic texts on "cares": making a living and/or family. Paul can here make use of gnomic tradition (cf. Berger, *Formgeschichte*, §19).

On 1 Cor 7:36, cf. no. 824 (at end).

669. 1 Corinthians 7:37

Pseudo-Phocylides, *Sentences* 215-17 (2 cent. BCE)

Guard a virgin in firmly locked rooms, and do not let her be seen before the house until her wedding day. The beauty of children is hard for their parents to guard. (*OTP* 2:581)

Josephus, *Antiquities* 3.277 also deals with the guarding of virgins: "As for the high-priest, he would not suffer him to take even a woman whose husband was dead, though he concedes this to the other priests: none but a virgin may he wed and withal one of his own tribe" (LCL). The "guarding" of virgins is here, as in Paul, both a social and religious ideal, though it is doubtful that Paul would have supported the restriction of women to the women's quarters of a house.

On 1 Corinthians 8:1-3 ("having knowledge"), cf. no. 382.

670. 1 Corinthians 8–14

Statutes of Society of Iobacchi, Inscription from Attica (178 CE)

No one may be an Iobacchus unless he first lodge with the priest the usual notice of candidature and be approved by a vote of the Iobacchi as being clearly a worthy and suitable member of the Bacchic society. The entrance fee shall be fifty denarii. . . . The Iobacchi shall meet on the ninth of each month and on the anniversary of the foundation and on the festivals of Bacchus and on any extraordinary feast of the god, and each member shall take part in word or act or honorable deed, paying the fixed monthly contribution for the wine. If he fail to pay, he shall be excluded from the gathering. . . . When anyone has lodged his application and has been approved by vote, the priest shall hand him a letter stating that he is an Iobacchus, but not until he has first paid the priest the entrance fee, and in the letter the priest shall cause to be entered the sums paid under one head or another. No one may either sing or create a disturbance or applaud at the gatherings, but each shall say and act his allotted part with all good order and quietness under the direction of the priest or the arch-bacchus. No Iobacchus who has not paid his contributions for the monthly and anniversary meetings shall enter the meeting until the priests have decided either that he must pay or that he may be admitted. If any one start a fight or be found acting disorderly or occupying the seat of another member or using insulting or abusive language to anyone, the person so abused or insulted shall produce two of the Iobacchi to state upon oath that they heard him insulted or abused, and he who was guilty of the insult or abuse shall pay to the Society twenty-five light drachmas. . . . And if anyone come to blows, he who has been struck shall lodge a written statement with the priest or the vice-priest, and he shall without fail convene a general meeting, and the Iobacchi shall decide the question by vote under the presidency of the priest, and the penalty shall be exclusion for a period to be determined and a fine not exceeding twenty-five silver denarii. And the same punishment shall be imposed also on one who, having been struck, fails to seek redress with the priest or the arch-bacchus but has brought a charge before the public courts. And the same punishment shall be imposed upon the orderly officer if he failed to eject those who were fighting. . . . And no one shall deliver a speech without the leave of the priest or the vice-priest on pain of being liable to a fine of thirty light drachmas to the Society. The priest shall perform the customary services at the meeting and the anniversary in proper style, and shall set before the meeting the drink-offering for the return of Bacchus and pronounce the sermon. . . . And the arch-bacchus shall offer the sacrifice to the god and shall set forth the drink-offering on each tenth day of the month Elaphabolion. And when portions are distributed, let them be taken by the priest, vice-priest, arch-bacchus, treasurer, bucolicus, Dionysus, Core,

Palaemon, Aphrodite, Preteurythmus; and let these names be apportioned by lot among all the members. And if any Iobacchus receive any legacy or honor or appointment, he shall set before the Iobacchi a drink-offering corresponding to the appointment . . . The orderly officer shall be chosen by lot or appointed by the priest, and he shall bear thyrsus of the god to him who is disorderly or creates a disturbance. And anyone beside whom the thyrsus is laid shall, with the approval of the priest or of the arch-bacchus, leave the banqueting-hall; but if he disobey, the "horses" who shall be appointed by the priests shall take him up and put him outside the front door and he shall be liable to the punishment inflicted upon those who fight. The Iobacchi shall elect a treasurer by ballot for a term of two years, and he shall take over all the property of the Bacchic Society in accordance with an inventory, and he shall likewise hand it over to his successor as treasurer. And he shall provide out of his own pocket the oil for the lights on each ninth day of the month and on the anniversary and at the assembly and on the customary days of the god. . . . And he shall be allowed the treasurer's drink-offering and shall be free from the payment of subscriptions for the two years. And if any Iobacchus die, a wreath shall be provided in his honor not exceeding five denarii in value, and a single jar of wine shall be set before those who have attended the funeral. (Tod)

In the first-century Roman Empire, voluntary associations were permitted but since they were thought to pose a potential political danger, they had to be licensed and were observed rather closely. Many assumed the form of a burial society, or a club that met regularly in the name of a god. Christian groups that were too large to meet at the home of a patron would readily assume such a form, and would easily be so categorized by their neighbors and the authorities. To some extent some members of the Christian communities themselves will have continued to think of themselves in such terms, despite the differences.

Some points of contact between the picture of church life reflected in 1 Corinthians and the portrayal of club life given in this inscription:

1) There was a tendency toward disorder with a consequent emphasis on "decency and order" (cf. 1 Cor 11:17-22; 14:23-24, 40).

2) There was general participation by the whole group in the regular meetings, rather than being spectators as the leaders performed the significant acts (1 Cor 14:26).

3) Disputes could break out between members, but these should be settled internally by authorized members of the group rather than going to the public authorities (cf. 1 Cor 6:1-8).

4) The group meets in honor of a god, food and wine is distributed (1 Cor 11:17-34), money is collected, disbursed, and accounted for (cf. 1 Cor 16:1-4), membership is clarified (there are definite insiders and outsiders, and people can be expelled against their will; cf. 1 Cor 5:3-5).

5) The existence of many such clubs and social organizations alongside the church, all of which were under the auspices of various gods and goddesses (1 Cor 8:5) created a severe problem for the new Christians, a much deeper problem than that of personal ethics, i.e. whether they could in good conscience eat of meat that had been "sacrificed to an idol." Such texts as the one printed above give the modern reader a glimpse of how thoroughly the social and business life of the Hellenistic world was permeated by religious connections and practices that could only be considered idolatrous by Christians. Did becoming a Christian mean that the new convert must simply drop out or withdraw from the social and business life of the community? These were the kinds of questions both Paul and the Corinthians were struggling with.

These points of contact were real, but often superficial. There were of course profound differences between the church and such clubs meeting under the sponsorship of a god, including a different structure (Paul had no officials to whom he could appeal to establish order, as in the above citation) and a profoundly different theology and self-understanding.

Cf. further on nos. 189-96, 676, 687.

671. 1 Corinthians 8:4

Plutarch, *Moralia*, "The Obsolescence of Oracles" 19 (45–125 CE)

[Speech of Cleombrotus:] . . . "Yet we know," he continued, "that the Stoics entertain the opinion that I mention, not only against the demigods, but they also hold that among the gods, who are so very numerous, there is only one who is eternal and immortal, and the others they believe have come into being, and will suffer dissolution." (LCL)

As in Paul, here a distinction is made between the one supreme God and the multiplicity of other heavenly beings, here named by Paul "gods" and "lords" (the existence of which he never doubts) and called "demons" in 10:19-20. Paul could have found a model for the relation between the one God and the many gods in Stoicism.

In §14 of the same writing by Plutarch, it is said of certain offensive rites of the mystery cults that ". . . these acts [the eating of raw flesh, rending of victims, fasting, and beating of breasts, and again in many places scurrilous language at the shrines] are not performed for any god, but are soothing and appeasing rites for the averting of evil spirits" (LCL). In Plutarch, *Moralia*, "Isis and Osiris" 67, Plutarch himself obviously adopts the Stoic idea named above: as sun, earth, and sea are common to all human beings, though they are called by different names in different places, so there is only one Logos that orders all things, and one Providence to which all forces and powers are subject, "which are set over all things," though they are named and honored differently in different parts of the world.

672. 1 Corinthians 8:6

Plutarch, *Moralia*, "Obsolescence of Oracles" 436 (45–125 CE)

[On the origin of all things from a single cause:] Zeus the beginning, Zeus in the midst, and from Zeus comes all being. (LCL)

Cf. also Oppianus, 2–3 cent. CE, "Father Zeus, everything goes to you and everything receives its roots from you."

Similarly Philo, *Special Laws* 1. 208: the cutting up of the sacrificial animal, interpreted allegorically, teaches ". . . either that all things are one or that they come from and return to one . . ." (LCL).

All these formulae continue the tradition of the pre-Socratic explanation of the world's origin from a single element. This formulaic summary achieved wide popularity during the period of the flowering of pop-Stoicism and Hellenistic Judaism. First Corinthians 8:6 stands out from this formula by the use of "we" in contrast to "all," and by the special role played by the mediator (in contrast to the "one"). Cf. the similar conception in Ephesians 1:4-5.

Cf no. 604 above from Marcus Aurelius and esp. nos. 502, 802.

673. 1 Corinthians 8:7-13; 10:23-33

Galen, *On the Teaching of Hippocrates and Plato* 4.6.1-2 (129–199 CE)

[On Chrysippus, 281/77–208/04 BCE:] Chrysippus declares not once or twice, but very often, that something besides one's reasonable powers are the causes of the passions in human souls. This can be seen from those passages in which he gives as the reason for wrong actions a "relaxing" or "weakness" [ἀσθένεια] of the soul. This is what he calls them, just as he designates their opposites "stiffening" and "strength" [ἰσχύς] of the soul. For when people do not act properly, he traces it back either to poor judgment or to a relaxing and weakness of the soul. (MEB/Berger)

All nonrational, emotional judgments and actions are therefore "weak," and lie outside the realm of right knowledge. In view of 1 Corinthians 8:1-2 one might especially consider whether the "weak" are not such who are characterized by the lack of rational knowledge and thus are too much swayed by their emotions (regarded by Chrysippus and others as too fearful). This would then be the philosophical correlation to those texts in which "weakness" means "superstition." From the philosophical perspective, all this is nonrational behavior, guided by emotions, especially fear (and thus also difficult to communicate).

So also no. 784. Further:

674. 1 Corinthians 8:7-13; 10:23-33

Horace, *Satires* 1, 9.60-72 (8.12.65 BCE–27.11.8 CE)

[Horace meets a friend, whom he claims he must speak to, in order to disengage from the unwanted person who accompanies him.] While he is thus running on, lo! there comes up Aristius Fuscus, a dear friend of mine, who knew the fellow right well. We halt. "Whence come you? Whither go you?" he asks and answers. I begin to twitch his cloak and squeeze his arms—they were quite unfeeling—nodding and winking hard for him to save me. The cruel joker laughed, pretending not to understand. I grew hot with anger. "Surely you said there was something you wanted to tell me in private."

"I mind it well, but I'll tell you at a better time. Today is the thirtieth Sabbath. Would you affront the circumcised Jews?"

"I have no scruples," say I.

"But I have. I'm a somewhat weaker brother, one of the many. You will pardon me; I'll talk another day." (LCL)

Cf. also Romans 14:1–15:6. The one whom Horace meets declines to have a conversation on the basis that it is the Sabbath of the New Moon, and one should not offend the people of the circumcision by profaning this day. According to the context, those with such hesitations have *religio*, and he describes himself in the same breath as "weak" and as influenced by the opinions of others. It is remarkable that "weakness" is spoken of precisely in connection with Jewish religious practices. "Weakness" is thus almost the same as Oriental superstition, hesitation about holy times, which Gentiles can have with regard to Jewish institutions.

In a series of comparable texts the predicate "weak" and its synonyms have the following functions:

1) The superstitious person (cf. no. 577) is in fact inclined to be an atheist, but is too weak to think about the gods in the way he or she would really like to do (Plutarch, "Superstition," §11). He is not free and driven by irrational fear.

2) The gods give oracles to the wise in the form of riddles, but to the weak in a shorter form (Plutarch, "Pythian Dialogues," §25). Here it is a matter of "education" and level of culture.

3) "Weak" (really "unmanly") are those people without education and with prejudices (Plutarch, "Vice Causes Unhappiness," §4).

4) In Epictetus, *Discourses* 1.8.8, "weak" and "uneducated" (ἀπαίδευτος) stand side by side as synonyms.

5) Finally, Plutarch, "Table Talk" 4, 4.4; 5.1, illustrates that the Jewish prohibition of pork involves putting up with mockery and misunderstanding at banquets.

675. 1 Corinthians 8:7-13; 10:23-33

4 Maccabees 6:12-19 (50–150 CE)

At that point, partly out of pity for his old age, 13 partly out of sympathy from their acquaintance with him, partly out of admiration for his endurance, some of the king's retinue came to him and said, 14 "Eleazar, why are you so irrationally destroying yourself through these evil things? 15 We will set before you some cooked meat; save yourself by pretending to eat pork." 16 But Eleazar, as though more bitterly tormented by this counsel, cried out: 17 "Never may we, the children of Abraham, think so basely that out of cowardice we feign a role unbecoming to us! 18 For it would be irrational if having lived in accordance with truth up to old age and having maintained in accordance with law the reputation of such a life, we should now change our course 19 and ourselves become a pattern of impiety to the young by setting them an example in the eating of defiling food." (NRSV)

Both in 4 Maccabees and in Paul, in order not to mislead others one renounces the eating of what would in itself be permitted. The difference is that what is a conflict of interpretations in Paul over a matter of principle is in 4 Maccabees a matter of deceit. Nonetheless, the crucial issue in each case is the manner in which one's actions affect the religious decisions others must make, and not merely what is "right" for the individual.

676. 1 Corinthians 8:10

Invitation to a banquet, P. Oxy. 1.110 (2 cent. CE)

Chaeremon requests your company at dinner at the table of the lord Sarapis in the Serapaeum tomorrow, the 15th, at 9 o'clock. (Grenfell and Hunt)

Here is exactly the situation pictured in 1 Corinthians 8:10, an invitation to a banquet in an "idol temple." Here too the god is named κύριος, "Lord," as is presupposed in 1 Corinthians 8:5-6. The title "Lord" is either the model for or an analogical formation for the Greek title for God in LXX. Cf. similarly the invitation from the second century CE in P. Oxy. 3.523 ("at the table of the Lord

Serapis," but here in a private house, that of Claudius Serapion). Cf. the extensive discussion at no. 191 above.

677. 1 Corinthians 9:9-10

Philo, *On the Special Laws* 1.260 (15 BCE–50 CE)

[Commenting on the detailed descriptions for animal sacrifice in Leviticus:] For you will find that all this careful scrutiny of the animal is a symbol representing in a figure the reformation of your own conduct, for the law does not prescribe for unreasoning creatures, but for those that have mind and reason. It is anxious not that the victims should be without flaw but that those who offer them should not suffer from any corroding passion. (LCL)

Like Philo, Paul does not use the rabbinic *qal va-homer* ("light and heavy," arguing from the lesser to the greater). Contrast the Jesus of the Gospels (e.g. Matt 6:30).

678. 1 Corinthians 9:19-23

Plutarch, *Moralia*, "Table-Talk" 1.1.3 (45–125 CE)

In just such a manner a philosopher too, when with drinking companions who are unwilling to listen to his homilies, will change his role, fall in with their mood, and not object to their activity so long as it does not transgress propriety. For he knows that, while men practice oratory only when they talk, they practice philosophy when they are silent, when they jest, even, by Zeus, when they are the butt of jokes and when they make fun of others. Indeed, not only is it true that "the worst injustice is to seem just when one is not," as Plato says, but also the height of sagacity is to talk philosophy without seeming to do so, and in jesting to accomplish all that those in earnest could. (LCL)

In the example of father and sons, in the conduct of the philosopher, and in Paul's procedure in 1 Corinthians 9, the "missionary" effect directed to "outsiders" is the only criterion for the form of the message and of one's conduct. On the critical later reception of this Pauline procedure cf. the text from the Arabic *Apocalypse of Peter* (A. Mingana, *The Apocalypse of Peter* [Woodbrooke Studies III 2, Cambridge: Cambridge University Press, 1951] 382): Paul is discovered praying to idols in a pagan temple.

679. 1 Corinthians 10:4

Targum of Pseudo-Jonathan on Numbers 21:16-18, "Song to the Well" (1–3 cent.)

The well that Abraham, Isaac, and Jacob, the princes of the world, saw at the beginning, was also seen by the wise of the world, the Sanhedrin, the seventy wise men. Moses and

Aaron, Israel's writers, found it in their staffs, and it was given to them as a gift in the wilderness. And then it was given to them in Mattanah: it turned and went out with them to the high mountains, and from there it went down to the hills that surrounded the whole camp of Israel and gave them to drink, each at the door of his tent. From the high mountains it descended to the lower hills. But it was hidden from them at the boundary of Moab, at the peak of the mountain that looks in the direction of Beth Jeshimon, because they despised the words of the Law. (Bowker)

The statement of Numbers 21:18, "from the wilderness to Mattanah" was not understood as (following a parenthesis) the continuation of v. 16 ("From there they continued to Beer . . ."), but connected with the immediately preceding subject (the well). The first author to understand the well as wandering with Israel through the wilderness was Pseudo-Philo (1 cent. BCE or CE): "Now he [Moses] led his people out into the wilderness; for forty years he [God] rained down for them bread from heaven and brought quail to them from the sea and brought forth a well of water to follow them" (*OTP* 2:317). Then the well was pictured as a huge wandering cliff-rock, since water also comes forth from such rocky cliffs. Thus it could happen that Philo of Alexandria ("Allegorical Interpretation" 2.86) could identify this well with the allegorically interpreted rock of Deuteronomy 8:15-16 ("For the flinty rock is the wisdom of God, which He marked off highest and chiefest from His powers, and from which He satisfies the thirsty souls that love God.") (LCL). That also happens not only here in Paul, but also in *t. Sukk.* 3.11 ("And so the well which was with the Israelites in the wilderness was a rock, the size of a large round vessel, surging and gurgling upward, as from the mouth of this little flask, rising with them up onto the mountains, and going down with them into the valleys. Wherever the Israelites would encamp, it made camp with them, on a high place, opposite the entry of the Tent of Meeting. The princes of Israel come and surround it with their staffs, and they sing a song concerning it: Spring up, O well! Sing to it [the well] which the princes dug, which the nobles of the people delved with the scepter and with their staves [Num 21:17-18]" [Neusner, *Tosefta*]). Philo is thus important in this connection, because he interprets the rock as the preexistent Wisdom, and Paul here incorporates a fragment of older Logos/Wisdom Christology (as often elsewhere in 1 Cor; cf. no. 681). Cf. also Pseudo-Clementine *Recognitions* 1, 35.3 (manna, drinking from the rock that followed them).

680. 1 Corinthians 11:3

Corpus Hermeticum 11:15 (2–4 cent. CE)

Eternity, therefore, is an image of God; the cosmos is an image of eternity; and the sun is an image of the cosmos. The human is an image of the sun. (Copenhaver)

The "image of God" is in biblical writings always exclusively the figure who in a particular aspect stands closest to God. These figures (Adam; Christ in 1 Cor) are thus distinguished with great honor. Where it has become a matter of several such images, then a cosmological scheme has grown out of the original image. On the Greek parallels which speak of "sonship" in this connection, cf. no. 364 above. On Christ as "head," cf. nos. 802, 803.

681. 1 Corinthians 11:4-16

Plutarch, *Moralia*, "The Roman Questions" 10 (45–125 CE)

But if there is anything else to be said, consider whether it be not true that there is only one matter that needs investigation: why men cover their heads when they worship the gods; and the other follows from this. For they uncover their heads in the presence of men more influential than they: it is not to invest these men with additional honor, but rather to avert from them the jealousy of the gods, that these men may not seem to demand the same honors as the gods, nor to tolerate an attention like that bestowed on the gods, nor to rejoice therein. But they thus worshiped the gods, either humbling themselves by concealing the head, or rather by pulling the toga over their ears as a precaution lest any ill-omened and baleful sound from without should reach them while they were praying. That they were mightily vigilant in this matter is obvious from the fact that when they went forth for purposes of divination, they surrounded themselves with the clashing of bronze.

Or, as Castor states when he is trying to bring Roman customs into relation with Pythagorean doctrines: the Spirit within us entreats and supplicates the gods without, and thus he symbolizes by the covering of the head the covering and concealment of the soul by the body. (LCL)

This text is interesting for the following reasons:

1) Plutarch's discussion shows that the issue of head covering in worship was not considered a triviality, but a matter of serious philosophical discussion, and also one with cultural overtones: the Romans worshiped with the head covered, the Greeks bare-headed. Cf. also Plutarch, *Moralia,* "The Roman Questions" 267 A-C; Plautus, *Curc.* 389-90; Lucretius, *De rerum natura* 5.1196-1203; Virgil, *Aeneid* 3.543-47; Ovid, *Fasti* 3.363-66; Macrobius, *Saturnalia* 1.8.2; 10.22.

2) "Humbling oneself" here doubtless has a positive religious meaning (contra Grundmann, "ταπεινός," *TDNT* 8:5, 27-28).

3) Despite his rationalistic explanation, Plutarch lets the apotropaic meaning of covering the head remain clear. This is important, since veils (and such) had this function in the ancient world and even today (cf. bridal veils).

4) After all, Corinth was (re-)founded by Rome. Paul's instruction was thus easily understandable precisely by Christians in Corinth.

Difference: In Plutarch, nothing in particular is said about women. For Paul, the issue deals with the function of the veil in warding off angels who, according to ideas derived from Jewish mysticism, attempt to leave their own assigned domain and enter the divine realm or the human world. This means of repelling evil angels was considered all the more important in the case of women. Cf. above no. 596.

682. 1 Corinthians 11:10

4Q 403 1 1.30-46, the Seventh Sabbath Song (2–1 cent. BCE)

For the Master Song of the holocaust of the seventh Sabbath on the sixteenth of the month.

Praise the most high God, O you high among all the gods of knowledge.

Let the holy ones of the "gods" sanctify the King of glory, who sanctifies by his holiness all his holy ones.

Princes of the praises of all the "gods," praise the God of majestic praises,

For in the splendor of praises is the glory of his kingship.

In it are [contained] the praises of all the "gods" together with the splendor of all [his] king[ship].

Exalt his exaltation on high, O "gods," above the gods on high, and his glorious divinity above all the highest heights.

For he [is the God of gods], of all the Princes on high, and the King of king[s] of all the eternal councils.

By a discerning good-will [expressed by] the words of his mouth a[ll the gods on high] come into being,

at the opening of his lips all the eternal spirits, by his discerning good-will, all his creatures in their undertakings.

Exult O you who exult [in his knowledge with] an exultation among the wonderful "gods";

utter his glory with the tongue of all who utter knowledge; may his wonderful exultation be in the mouth of all who utter [his knowledge].

[For he] is the God of all who exult in everlasting knowledge, and the Judge through his might of all the spirits of understanding.

Celebrate all celebrating gods the King of majesty, for all the gods of knowledge celebrate his glory,

and all the spirits of righteousness celebrate his truth, and seek acceptance of their knowledge by the judgments of his mouth, and of their celebrations when his mighty hand executes [?] judgments of reward.

Sing to the God of power with an offering of the princely spirit, a song of divine joy,

and a jubilation among all the holy, a wonderful song for eter[nal] rejoicing.

With these shall praise all the f[oundations of the hol]y of holies,

the pillars bearing the highest abode, and all the corners of its structure.

Sing to the Go[d who is a]wesome in strength . . .

to extol together the splendid firmament, the supreme purity of [his] holy sanctuary.

[Praise] him, divine spirits, prai[sing for ever and] ever the firmament of the highest heavens,

all . . . and its walls, a[l]l its [struc]ture, its shape.

[The spi]rits of the hol[y] of holies, the living "gods," [the spir]its of [et]ernal holiness above all the holy [ones];

. . . marvelous marvel, majesty and beauty and marvel.

[Gl]ory is in the perfect light of knowledge . . . in all the marvelous sanctuaries.

The divine spirits surround the dwelling of the King of truth and righteousness; all its walls . . . (Vermes)

The meaning of Paul's "because of the angels" is disputed. The probability that it expresses Paul's belief that the worship of the early Christian communities was carried out in the presence of angels is strengthened by the fact that in the ancient world the idea was widespread that in worship and cultic activities human beings are in the presence of, or are watched over and supervised by, heavenly beings. The Qumran community believed that they joined with the angels in worship, experiencing communion with them as they along with the angels worshiped God. Each of the Qumran Sabbath songs begins with a call to the angels to join in the worship of God. This could become not only worship with, but of, angelic beings (cf. Col 2:18; Heb 1:4-14). For variations of this general idea in Hellenistic Judaism and in pagan piety, see nos. 683 and 684 below.

683. 1 Corinthians 11:10

Philo, *On the Virtues* 73-74 (15 BCE–50 CE)

He convoked a divine assemblage of the elements of all existence and the chiefest parts of the universe, earth and heaven, one the home of mortals, the other the house of immortals. With these around him he sang his canticles with every kind of harmony and sweet music in the ears of both mankind and ministering angels: of men that as disciples they should learn from him the lesson of like thankfulness of heart: of angels as watchers, observing, as themselves masters of melody, whether the song had any discordant note, and scarce able to credit that any man imprisoned in a corruptible body could like the sun and moon and the most sacred choir of the other stars attune his soul to harmony with God's instrument, the heaven and the whole universe. (LCL)

Moses is a model of love for the neighbor, as expressed in the song at the close of his life, a song heard not only by human beings, but by angels, who are observers of human worship.

684. 1 Corinthians 11:10

Plutarch, *Moralia*, "The Obsolescence of Oracles" 417 A-B (45–125 CE)

But as for us, let us not listen to any who say that there are some oracles not divinely inspired, or religious ceremonies and mystic rites which are disregarded by the gods; and on the other hand let us not imagine that the god goes in and out and is present at these ceremonies and helps in conducting them; but let us commit these matters to those ministers of the gods [λειτουγροῖς θεῶν] to whom it is right to commit them, as to servants and clerks, and let us believe that demigods are guardians of sacred rites of the gods [ἐπισκό-πους θεῶν] and prompters in the Mysteries, while others go about as avengers of arrogant and grievous cases of injustice. (LCL)

"Demons" (δαίμονες) are here heavenly beings who are more exalted than mortals, but who are not themselves gods. As in nos. 682 and 683 above, heavenly beings take an active interest in earthly worship, and those who participate in such worship had better not do it casually. (Cf. 1 Cor 11:30-31 for a different expression of this perspective.)

685. 1 Corinthians 11:14

Musonius Rufus, *On Cutting the Hair* (30–100 CE)

He used to say that a man should cut the hair from the head for the same reason that we prune a vine, that is merely to remove what is useless. [But just as the eyebrows or eyelashes which perform a service in protecting the eyes should not be cut, so] neither should the beard be cut from the chin [for it is not superfluous], but it too has been provided us by nature as a kind of cover or protection. Moreover, the beard is nature's symbol of the male just as the crest of the cock and the mane of the lion; so one ought to remove the growth of hair that becomes burdensome, but nothing of the beard; for the beard is no burden so long as the body is healthy and not afflicted with any disease for which it is necessary to cut the hair from the chin. The remark of Zeno was well made that it is quite as natural to cut the hair as it is to let it grow long, in order not to be burdened by too much of it nor hampered for any activity. For nature plainly keeps a more careful guard against deficiency than against excess, in both plants and animals, since the removal of excess is much easier and simpler than the addition of what is lacking. In both cases man's common sense ought to assist nature. . . . (Lutz)

This is only part of a more extensive discussion, illustrating that hair length was a topic of philosophical discussion under the heading of what is "natural." (Cf. e.g. Dio Chrysostom, *Discourses* 35.11-12; Pseudo-Phocylides, *Sentences* 210-12; a scholion in Aristophanes, "The Acharnians," 911 declares: "To wear long hair was the sign of a free citizen.") Paul, of course, is just as far from entering into the philosophical discussion on the issue of what is "natural" as is Musonius from discussing the cultic and Christian theological concerns of Paul. The text from Musonius illustrates, however, that Paul's tangential reference to what "nature itself" teaches about hair length was not an ad hoc argument, but made contact with a more sophisticated philosophical discussion. The fact that Musonius considers nature to teach that men should wear long hair (and beards), cutting it only when it becomes burdensome, while the Pauline passage (sometimes considered an interpolation) understands "nature itself" to "teach" that men should wear their hair shorter than women, illustrates the lack of clear distinction between "nature" and social convention.

686. 1 Corinthians 11:14

Epictetus, *Discourses* (55–135 CE)

Come, let us leave the chief works of nature, and consider merely what she does in passing. Can anything be more useless than the hairs on a chin? Well, what then? Has not nature used even these in the most suitable way possible? Has she not by these means distinguished between the male and the female? Does not the nature of each one among us cry aloud forthwith from afar, "I am a man; on this understanding approach me, on this understanding talk with me; ask for nothing further; behold the signs"? . . . Wherefore, we ought to preserve the signs which God has given; we ought not to throw them away; we ought not, so far as in us lies, to confuse the sexes which have been distinguished in this fashion. (LCL)

Among Paul's several arguments for women's maintaining the appearance and decorum that had become conventional is the argument from "nature." Epictetus, for whom the all-pervasive divine Reason is identical with nature, has only this one argument. Epictetus' is in fact the more cogent argument, since the presence or absence of a beard is a natural distinction between men and women, while hair length is purely conventional.

687. 1 Corinthians 11:17-34

Statutes of the Association of the Worshipers of Diana and Antinous, *Inscr. Lat.* sel. 7212 (2 cent. CE)

§8 So it is decreed: Everyone who for one year according to the order of the membership list is "Master" for the arrangements of the meal but does not fulfill his duty, must pay 30 sesterces into the treasury. . . .

§9 The order for the festival meals: on the 8th before the Ides of March, the birth of Caesennius' father . . ., on the 5th before the Calends of December, the birth of Antinous, on the Ides of August the birth of Diana and the founding of the Association, on the 13th before the Calends of September the birth of Silvanus, the brother of Caesennius, on the 1st before the Nones . . . the birth of the mother Cornelia Procula, on the 19th before the Calends of January the birth of the founder and patron Caesennius Rufus.

§10 The Master for the meals, who are appointed according to the order of the membership list, four in number, must deliver: several amphoras of good wine, in addition for each person, one loaf of bread, four anchovies, a dining cushion, warm water, and service. . . .

§13 So it is decreed: If anyone wishes to register a complaint or conduct business, then it is to be introduced into the assembly, not at the meals, so that we can enjoy the banquets on the festival days. (MEB/from Leipoldt-Grundmann)

Similar is the list of statutes for the Association "Andreius" (inscription in Picenum, according to Dessau, *Inscr. Lat.* sel. 7215: a yearly banquet on the birthday; a three-day assembly in the temple of the muse; prescriptions for the financing of the festival meals; all decisions by majority vote from which there is no appeal; selection of the Epissophus [executive secretary] and Keeper of the Archives). The regulations are oriented to the regular meals of the Association. The closest formal analogy in early Christianity is found in §§49-52 of the church order of Hippolytus, but there the financial aspect recedes, and its place is taken by an emphasis on the hierarchy (significance of the bishop).

These texts from ancient religious associations are important for understanding NT eucharistic texts for the following reasons: (1) The common meal, which has a religious character, is constitutive for the association (at least in the drink contribution before the first cup). (2) The organizational regulations revolve around the meal itself (who presides; membership; financial arrangements; frequency of meeting of the association). (3) The detailed casuistic discussions presuppose that arguments of all kinds had occurred in the context of the meal, which are now to be controlled by these regulations. (4) The sociological phenomenon of institutionalization allows us to observe regarding the relation of 1 Corinthians 11 to these association bylaws that both the festival meals of the associations and the eucharistic meals of early Christianity became institutionalized, an observation that applies despite the difference in their regulations.

Analogies to 1 Corinthians 11: (1) An association founded on religious beliefs meets regularly to celebrate festive meals, which form the center of the organization's life. (2) These festive meals require casuistic regulation; §13 above presupposes that there had been arguments at the meals. (3) The festive meals serve as memorials to important events in the lives of honored figures in the life and history of the group.

Cf. in addition nos. 189-96, 670, 676, 688-89. Additional literature: H.-J. Klauck, *Herrenmahl und hellenistischer Kult* (Münster: Aschendorff, 1982). Further:

688. 1 Corinthians 11:17-34

Lucian, *Saturnalia Letters* 3, 32 (120–185 CE)

O yes, the dinners and their dining with you—they asked me to add this to my letter, that at present you gorge alone behind locked doors, and, if ever at long intervals you are willing to entertain any of them, there is more annoyance than good cheer in the dinner, and most of what happens is done to hurt them—that business of not drinking the same wine as you, for instance—goodness, how ungenerous that is! . . .

The rest is so disgraceful that I hesitate to mention their complaints of the way the meat is apportioned and how the servants stand beside you until you are full to bursting, but run past them. There are many more like complaints of meanness, complaints that bring little credit to gentlemen. In fact the pleasantest thing, more in keeping with conviviality, is equality, and a controller of the feast presides over your banquets just so that all can have an equal share. (LCL)

Lucian's *Saturnalia Letters* are a treasure trove of religiously motivated social critique (cf. no. 292), for the Saturnalia was for Lucian not only a folk festival, but a reflection of the saturnaliac empire and its ideal state. In Corinth the deplorable state of affairs consisted in the poorer members of the community being shamed by the differences in the meal provided before the celebration of the eucharistic meal, while for Lucian the bad situation was the result of discrimination by those who served the tables.

That the issue of rank and social prestige was often present in meals outside the family is documented especially by Plutarch's "Table Talk." He affirms that when one becomes an annoyance to others, the god Dionysus is offended (I, 1.5); that equality should be preserved, in that without pride or compulsion the rich should dine beside the poor (I, 2.3); that the "best" place is even to sit beside an unknown stranger (I, 2.4); that the task of the master of ceremonies is to preserve concord and unity (I, 4.2). In response to the question, "Whether people of old did better with portions served to each, or people of today, who dine from a common supply . . .?" he gives the answer, "we invite each other not for the sake of eating and drinking, but for drinking together and eating together, and this division of meat into shares kills sociability and makes many dinners and many diners with nobody anybody's dinner-companion when each takes his share by weight as from a butcher's counter and puts it before himself" (2.10.1) (LCL).

See also no. 670 at 1 Corinthians 8–14 and the references given there.

689. 1 Corinthians 11:17-34

Plutarch, *Moralia*, "Sayings of Spartans: Lycurgus" 6-7 (45–125 CE)

He [Lycurgus] took care that none should be allowed to dine at home and then come to the common meal stuffed with other kinds of food and drink. The rest of the company used to berate the man who did not drink or eat with them, because they felt that he was lacking in self-control, and was too soft for the common way of living. Moreover, a fine was laid upon the man who was detected.

The well-to-do citizens resented legislation of this type, and, banding together, they denounced him and pelted him, wishing to stone him to death. (LCL)

According to §4 the Sissites (meals in common) were founded explicitly to establish equality. Lycurgus took steps diametrically opposite those of Paul, and the text makes clear that Paul obviously did not decide in favor of the wealthy.

690. 1 Corinthians 11:25

CD 1-8 selections (2 cent. CE)

None of the men who enter the New Covenant in the land of Damascus, (B I) and who again betray it and depart from the fountain of living waters, shall be reckoned with the Council of the people or inscribed in its Book from the day of the gathering in (B II) of the Teacher of the Community until the coming of the Messiah out of Aaron and Israel. . . .

For they have spoken wrongly against the precepts of righteousness, and have despised the Covenant and the Pact—the New Covenant—which they made in the land of Damascus. (Vermes)

The *Damascus Document* several times refers to the renewed covenant made by God with the members of the author's community "in the land of Damascus" (cf. 2:2; 8:11). The meaning of "Damascus" is unclear, but it can hardly be literal. The New Covenant also seems to be referred to in 1QpHab 2.3 and 1Q34 2.6. The Qumran community understood itself as the community of the New Covenant, i.e. the eschatologically renewed covenant, which, in contrast to Paul and much of early Christianity, it did not understand in contrast to the covenant with Israel at Sinai. Cf. also 2 Corinthians 3:6. "New" covenant is also found in Luke 22:20, Mark 14:24, and Matthew 26:28, all of which have textual uncertainties. "New" in all these references does not mean "new and improved" in the sense of modern Western culture, but "eschatologically renewed" as the fulfillment of Jeremiah 31:31.

691. 1 Corinthians 11:27-29

Epictetus, *Discourses* 3.21.14 (55–135 CE)

The worshiper "ought to come with sacrifice and with prayers, and after a preliminary purification, and with his mind disposed to the idea that he will be approaching holy rites." (LCL)

There were doubtless pagan and Jewish worshipers who merely went through the motions with their mind on other things, as there have been many such Christian worshipers. The text from Epictetus shows there were also those who considered the appropriate mental attitude to be a part of authentic worship.

692. 1 Corinthians 11:30-32

Hierocles the Stoic, "How to Conduct Oneself Toward Gods" 54 (2 cent. CE)

We should certainly not neglect noting that, even though the gods are not the causes of evil, they attach some evils to certain people and surround those who deserve corporal punishment and loss of their property. They do this not because of malice, thinking that man of necessity must live in distress, but for the sake of punishment. For just as pestilence and drought, and also deluges of rain, earthquakes, and everything of this kind are for the most part produced by certain other physical causes, but at times are caused by the gods when it is critical that the sins of the masses be punished publicly and generally, so also in the same way the gods sometimes afflict an individual's body or cause him to lose his property in order to punish him and to turn others and make them choose what is better. (Malherbe)

According to Hierocles both the person being disciplined and others who observe it understand the chastening action of the gods as a pedagogical act in the interest of improving the person disciplined. Both Paul and Hierocles understand the chastening to be directed to individuals. Jewish parallels, on the other hand, always speak of the people of Israel as a whole and its being chastened or judged by God. What Paul does have in common with Jewish texts is the final goal that by such chastening, those who are thus disciplined will escape condemnation in the great eschatological judgment of the world (so also in 2 Macc 6:14-15).

693. 1 Corinthians 12:4-6

Philo, *On the Cherubim* 9.1 (15 BCE–50 CE)

But there is a higher thought than these. It comes from a voice in my own soul, which oftentimes is God-possessed and divines where it does not know. This thought I will record in words if I can. The voice told me that while God is indeed one, His highest and chiefest powers are two, even goodness and sovereignty. Through His goodness He begat all that is, through His sovereignty He rules what He has begotten. And in the midst between the two there is a third which unites them, Reason, for it is through reason that God is both ruler and good. Of these two potencies, sovereignty and goodness, the Cherubim are symbols . . . (LCL)

For Philo as for Paul and the New Testament generally, monotheism is axiomatic. Yet within this affirmation of the unity of the one God some Jews found room for discussion of a plurality of "powers" within the one God. Philo orients his thought to Greek patterns, without becoming too speculative. Other speculations concerning "two powers in heaven" were considered dangerous (cf. the citations at no. 848 on Heb 1:1, and *Mek. Exodus* 20:2, "Rabbi Nathan says: 'From this one can cite a refutation of the heretics who say: There are two Powers. For when the Holy One, blessed be He, stood up and exclaimed: I AM THE LORD THY GOD was there any one who stood up to protest against Him? . . .'").
Though Paul stands firmly in the Jewish tradition of absolute monotheism (cf. e.g. Rom 3:30;

1 Thess 1:9), he too can use pluralistic language of the deity. Unlike Philo's moderate ontological speculation, Paul's terminology is entirely functional and dynamic. For additional "nascent trinitarian" passages in the New Testament, cf. Matthew 28:20; 1 Peter 1:2.

On 1 Corinthians 12:8-10 (the variety of spiritual gifts), cf. no. 559.

694. 1 Corinthians 12:12-27

Livy, *History of Rome* 2.32.9-12 (59 BCE–17 CE)

In the days when man's members did not all agree amongst themselves, as is now the case, but had each its own ideas and a voice of its own, the other parts thought it unfair that they should have the worry and the trouble and the labor of providing everything for the belly, while the belly remained quietly in their midst with nothing to do but to enjoy the good things which they bestowed upon it; they therefore conspired together that the hands should carry no food to the mouth, nor the mouth accept anything that was given it, nor the teeth grind up what they received. While they sought in this angry spirit to starve the belly into submission, the members themselves and the whole body were reduced to the utmost weakness. Hence it had become clear that even the belly had no idle task to perform, and was no more nourished than it nourished the rest, by giving out to all parts of the body that by which we live and thrive, when it has been divided equally amongst the veins and is enriched with digested food—that is, the blood. (LCL)

Menius Agrippa soothed the angry masses in Rome with this fable in their protests against the patricians, and caused them to change their minds. The fable thus stabilized the existing rule of the patricians.

Analogies to 1 Corinthians 12: Comparison of a community with a body, and the relations of the members to each other; the problem of seemingly unimportant members who are likely to be neglected; so too in Paul there is imagined protest of some members of the body against the others (12:15-16, 21); the solution by demonstrating the necessity of all the members of the body.

Differences: In Paul, the figure concentrates on "less honorable" parts of the body and their being given more honor by means of clothing. Whereas in Menius Agrippa the point has to do with confirming the status quo of different degrees of power within the community, Paul intends a revaluation: those parts of the body thought to be of lesser honor receive more respect, and this is the way God has ordered the Christian community (thus vv. 28-31; as an apostle, Paul is not particularly honored; cf. e.g. 4:9-10). In Livy the emphasis on the one body is lacking, and in contrast to Paul, apart from the stomach the individual functions of the body's various organs are not distinguished. In Livy, the point has to do with the rulership of an individual member.

The picture is used by Chrysippus (v. Arnim, SVF II 367) with regard to an ἐκκλησία: "Often a single body consists of many separate bodies like an ἐκκλησία and an army and a choir, from which still life, thought, and learning comes to each individual" (MEB/Berger).

The metaphor of the body is also often met in the resolution of political problems: Plutarch, *Life of Agis* 2 (Fable of the Snake: the tail argues with the head and wants to have its turn at going first. The attempt is ruined by its inexperience); "Brotherly Love" 7 (a united body, once split, can hardly come back together again); Plutarch, "Precepts of Statecraft" 32 (in a riot among the people: in sick bodies, too, healing does not proceed from those parts that are suffering together, but the mixture of healthy parts must gain the upper hand).

On the significance of political reason in Paul, cf. nos. 619-22, 638. Further:

695. 1 Corinthians 12:12-27

Marcus Aurelius, *Meditations* 12.35-36 (121–180 CE)

Thou hast seen a hand cut off or a foot, or a head severed from the trunk, and lying at some distance from the rest of the body. Just so does the man treat himself, as far as he may, who wills not what befalls and severs himself from mankind or acts unsocially. Say thou hast been torn away in some sort from the unity of Nature; for by the law of thy birth thou was a part; but now thou hast cut thyself off. Yet here comes in that exquisite provision that thou canst return again to thy unity. To no other part has God granted this, to come together again, when once separated and cleft asunder. Aye, behold his goodness, where-with he hath glorified man! For he hath let it rest with a man that he be never rent away from the Whole, and if he do rend himself away, to return again and grow onto the rest and take up his position again as part. (LCL)

Cf. *Meditations* 6.54: "That which is not in the interests of the hive cannot be in the interests of the bee" (LCL).

Similar ideas are at work here, but what Marcus Aurelius understands in terms of the human race as a whole Paul understands in terms of the church. Thus for Paul the unity of the body is not something given by nature that applies to all human beings, but the eschatological gift of God through the Spirit that unifies the holy community. Marcus Aurelius emphasizes the given unity of the body, but not the value of its variety. While there were certainly selfless interests in pagan religion, and Christian ethics and proclamation sometimes appealed to the believer's own self-interest, the orientation toward enlightened self-interest sounded here is missing from the Christian kerygma and ethics (cf. the texts at Matt 25:31-46), and Paul's concern for actions that are good for the body as a whole is absent from the picture given by Marcus Aurelius.

696. 1 Corinthians 12:12-27

Plato, *Republic* 5.10 (428/27–349/48 BCE)

"And the city [is best ordered] whose state is most like that of an individual man. For example, if the finger of one of us is wounded, the entire community of bodily connections stretching to the soul for 'integration' with the dominant part is made aware, and all of it feels the pain as a whole, though it is a part that suffers, and that is how we come to say that the man has a pain in his finger. And for any other member of the man the same statement holds, alike for a part that labors in pain or is eased by pleasure." "The same," he said, "and, to return to your question, the best governed state most nearly resembles such an organism." "That is the kind of a state, then, I presume, that, when anyone of the citizens suffers aught of good or evil, will be most likely to speak of the part that suffers as its own and will share the pleasure or the pain as a whole." "Inevitably," he said, "if it is well governed." (LCL)

The picture used by Paul in 1 Corinthians 12:26 of sympathy [lit., "feeling-with," "suffering-with"] thus has connotations of the political use of the body-metaphor tradition. Paul has made an innovation in this tradition in that alongside suffering he also speaks of glorification and thereby introduces a term from the early Christian vocabulary with a particular set of meanings. In Hierocles the Stoic (2 cent. CE) the matter is then formulated unmetaphorically: there is no whole without its parts; what is useful to the citizen is also beneficial to the state. (*On Duties*, "How to Conduct Oneself Toward One's Fatherland." Stobaeus, *Anthologium*, 39:36 = III 733-34).

On the more general application of the body metaphor, cf. Seneca, "On the Usefulness of Basic Principles," 52: ". . . all that you behold, that which comprises both god and man, is one—we are the parts of one great body. Nature produced us related to one another, since she created us from the same source and to the same end" (LCL).

Cf. also nos. 276, 802, 803.

697. 1 Corinthians 12:23

Musonius Rufus, *On Clothing and Shelter* 19-29 (30–100 CE)

. . . the garment which is most useful for the body is best—for the covering should at once render the thing covered better and stronger than its natural condition, rather than weaker and worse.

. . . those who strengthen and invigorate the body by the clothing they wear, those, I say, are the only ones who benefit the parts of the body so covered. (Lutz)

For Judaism, cf. *Jubilees* 3:30: "But from all the beasts and all the cattle he granted to Adam alone that he might cover his shame. Therefore it is commanded in the heavenly tablets to all who will know the judgment of the Law that they should cover their shame and they should not be uncovered as the gentiles are uncovered" (*OTP* 2:60). Here the difference between human beings and animals is that humans cover their nakedness. As in Paul, such covering is related to honor and dishonor (similarly *Apoc. Mos.* 20).

698. 1 Corinthians 13:1-13

Plato, *Symposium* 197 A-E (428/27–349/48 BCE)

And who, let me ask, will gainsay that the composing of all forms of life is Love's own craft, whereby all creatures are begotten and produced? Again, in artificial manufacture, do we not know that a man who has this god for a teacher turns out a brilliant success, whereas he on whom Love has laid no hold is obscure? If Apollo invented archery and medicine and divination, it was under the guidance of Desire [ἐπιθυμία] and love [ἔρως], so that he too may be deemed a disciple of Love, as likewise may the Muses in music, Hephaestus in metal work, Athene in weaving and Zeus "in pilotage of gods and men." Hence also these dealings of the gods were contrived by Love—clearly love of beauty—astir in them, for Love has no concern with ugliness; though aforetime, as I began by saying, there were many strange doings among the gods, as legend tells, because of the dominion of Necessity. But since this god [love ,Ἔρως] arose, the loving of beautiful things has brought all kinds of benefits both to gods and to men.

Thus I conceive, Phaedrus, that Love was originally of surpassing beauty and goodness, and is latterly the cause of similar excellencies in others. And now I am moved to summon the aid of verse, and tell how it is he who makes

Peace among men, and a windless waveless main;
Repose for winds, and slumber in our pain.

He it is who casts alienation out, draws intimacy in; politeness contriving, moroseness outdriving; kind giver of amity, giving no enmity; gracious, superb; a marvel to the wise, a delight to the gods; coveted of such as share him not, treasured of such as good share have not; father of luxury, tenderness, elegance, graces and longing and yearning; careful of the good, careless of the bad; in toil and fear, in drink and discourse, our trustiest helmsman, boatswain, champion deliverer; ornament of all gods and men; leader fairest and best, whom every one should follow, joining tunefully in the burthen of his song wherewith he enchants the thought of every god and man.

"There Phaedrus," he said, "is the speech I would offer at his shrine: I have done my best to mingle amusement with a decent gravity." (LCL)

Analogies to Paul: Both adopt the same genre to express their point (encomium, cf. Berger, *Formgeschichte*, §99), characterized by describing a series of attributes and elevated comparison (*syncrisis*, cf. *Formgeschichte*, §64) with all other goods and virtues, and a listing of the effects and fruits of love. After Plato it was customary to connect the theme "in praise of love" to the literary genre of the symposium (cf. *Formgeschichte*, p. 256). Cf. especially 1 Esdras 4:13-41 and Plutarch, "Table Talk" 1, 5.1 (love has power, courage, and initiative to confer on everyone; it enables the silent to speak, the hesitant to be zealous, the superficial to be more caring, the frugal and stingy more open and giving, affectionate and lovable). There seems to be no distinction between ἔρως, ἀγάπη, and other words for love. Cf. Maximus of Tyre, *Dissertations* 20.2 a-c and no. 721 on 2 Corinthians 2:17–3:9.

699. 1 Corinthians 13:8-13

Plutarch, *Moralia*, "The Education of Children" 8 (45–125 CE)

Good birth is a fine thing, but it is an advantage which must be credited to one's ancestors. Wealth is held in esteem, but it is a chattel of fortune.

Beauty is highly prized, but short-lived. Health is a valued possession, but inconstant. Strength is much admired, but it falls an easy prey to disease and old age.

But learning, of all things in this world, is alone immortal and divine. Two elements in man's nature are supreme over all—mind and reason. The mind exercises control over reason, and reason is the servant of the mind, unassailable by fortune, impregnable to calumny, uncorrupted by disease, unimpaired by old age. For the mind alone grows young with increase of years, and time, which takes away all things else, but adds wisdom to old age. (LCL)

As in Paul, the literary form is that of a *priamel* (cf. Berger, *Formgeschichte*, 212-13), i.e. that which is most to be valued is measured against other, lesser candidates. As in Paul, the primary criterion is the temporary or abiding nature of the quality examined. Paul had learned such forms as part of his rhetorical education.

700. 1 Corinthians 13:12

4 Ezra 7:33-34 (late 1 cent. CE)

The Most High shall be revealed on the seat of judgment, and compassion shall pass away, and patience shall be withdrawn. 34 Only judgment shall remain, truth shall stand, and faithfulness shall grow strong. (NRSV)

Both 4 Ezra and Paul write within an eschatological perspective. In response to the implied question "What shall endure into the age to come," 4 Ezra understands patience and compassion to be temporary aspects of God's dealing with creation and judgment to be the ultimate quality that remains as the determinative factor in the eternal world. Paul regards love as the ultimate characteristic of God, which shall not pass away at the eschaton, and draws ethical inferences from this in a way that 4 Ezra does not. The author of 4 Ezra finds himself being more merciful than he can believe God to be, that his own inclinations to compassion are out of step with what is eternally lasting. For Paul, acts of love cohere with the ultimate nature of God, their source. (See on no. 597 at Rom 9:1-2.)

701. 1 Corinthians 14:1

Testament of Job 48-50 (1 cent. CE)

Thus, when the one called Hemera arose, she wrapped around her own string just as her father said. And she took on another heart—no longer minded toward earthly things—but she spoke ecstatically in the angelic dialect, sending up a hymn to God in accord with the hymnic style of the angels. And as she spoke ecstatically, she allowed "The Spirit" to be inscribed on her garment.

Then Kasia bound hers on and had her heart changed so that she no longer regarded worldly things. And her mouth took on the dialect of the archons and she praised God for the creation of the heights. So, if anyone wishes to know "The Creation of the Heavens," he will be able to find it in "The Hymns of Kasia."

Then the other one also, named Amaltheia's Horn, bound on her cord. And her mouth spoke ecstatically in the dialect of those on high, since her heart also was changed, keeping aloof from worldly things. For she spoke in the dialect of the cherubim, glorifying the Master of virtues by exhibiting their splendor. (*OTP* 1:865-66)

As was the case with Elijah (2 Kgs 2:10) and Jesus (Acts 1), so also here when God's elect one is taken out of the world, the event is testified to by the occurrence of ecstatic phenomena (the spirit of Elijah falls on Elisha; the Spirit of Jesus falls on the disciples in the form of glossalalia and the linguistic miracle; the language of the angels is granted to Job's daughters). The language of the angels is here understood not as other-worldly jibberish, but as cultic hymns written on columns (Hebrew hymns for the Diaspora communities?); cf. no. 487. An extensive description of contemporary pagan charismatic phenomena is found in Plutarch, "Pythian Oracles," §21 (external and internal movements). Cf. also Strabo, *Geography* 10.3.7-23.

702. 1 Corinthians 14:26-28

Philo, *Life of Moses* 2.35.191 (15 BCE–50 CE)

[Discussing the three kinds of prophecies delivered by Moses:] Besides, they [the first type of prophetic oracles given directly to the prophet by God] are delivered through an interpreter, and interpretation and prophecy are not the same thing.

Cf. 1 Corinthians 12:27-30. Both Philo and Paul list "interpretation" among the divine gifts. Paul links it to glossalalia, which is unintelligible without an interpreter, while prophecy is edifying speech understandable by all. Philo, on the other hand, says nothing specifically about glossalalia, but considers interpretation as a gift related to a particular kind of prophecy, namely those "spoken by God in his own person" (as distinct from inspired speech in which the prophet speaks with his own ego). Cf. Plato, *Timaeus* 71, for whom prophets are interpreters of the divine oracles: "God gave unto man's foolishness the gift of divination [μαντικήν] . . . no man achieves true and inspired [ἐνθεου] divination when in his rational mind [ἐννοί], but only when the power of his intelligence is fettered in sleep or when it is distraught by disease or by reason of some divine inspiration [ἐνθυσιασμόν]. . . . It is not the task of him who has been in a state of frenzy, and still continues therein, to judge the apparitions and voices seen or uttered by himself. . . . Wherefore also it is customary to set the tribe of prophets [τῶν προφητῶν γένος] to pass judgment upon these inspired divinations; and they, indeed, themselves are named 'diviners' [μαύτεις] by certain who are wholly ignorant of the truth that they are not diviners but interpreters of the mysterious voice and apparition, for whom the most fitting name would be 'prophets of things divined' [προφῆται μαντευομένων]" (LCL).

703. 1 Corinthians 14:34

Plutarch, *Moralia*, "Advice to Bride and Groom" 31-32 (45–125 CE)

[Women should remain at home.] Theano, in putting her cloak about her, exposed her arm. Somebody exclaimed, "A lovely arm." "But not for the public," said she. Not only the arm of the virtuous woman, but her speech as well, ought to be not for the public, and she ought to be modest and guarded about saying anything in the hearing of outsiders, since it is an exposure of herself; for in her talk can be seen her feelings, character, and disposition.

Pheidias made the Aphrodite of the Eleans with one foot on a tortoise, to typify for womankind keeping at home and keeping silence. For a woman ought to do her talking either to her husband or through her husband, and she should not feel aggrieved if, like the flute-player, she makes a more impressive sound through a tongue not her own. (LCL)

Cf. Democritus, *Fragment* 110-11 (460–380 BCE) (Diels-Kranz II, p. 164): "A woman must not practice argument; this is dreadful.

111 To be ruled by a woman is the ultimate outrage for a man" (Freeman).

Cf. Philo, "On the Animals," 5-7 (1 cent. CE) on the silence of the learner as well as his own role as interpreter:

"PHILO: Since I know that you are interested, indeed that you are always eager to hear new things,

I shall begin to speak if you will keep quiet and not always interrupt my speech by making forceful remarks on the same matter.

6 LYSIMACHUS: Such a restrictive order is unreasonable. But since it is expedient to seek and to ask for instruction, your order must be complied with. So here I sit quietly, modestly, and with restored humility as is proper for a student; and here you are seated in front of me on a platform looking dignified, respectable, and erudite, ready to begin to teach your teachings.

7 PHILO: I shall begin to interpret, but I will not teach, since I am an interpreter and not a teacher. Those who teach impart their own knowledge to others, but those who interpret present through accurate recall the things heard from others. And they do not do this just to a few Alexandrians and Romans—the eminent or the excellent, the privileged, the elite of the upper class, and those distinguished in music and other learning—gathered at a given place" (Terian).

For further illustrations of the expectation that women be silent as a Hellenistic rule or convention, cf. Aeschylus, *Seven Against Thebes* 230-32; Democritus, *Fragments* 274; Sophocles, *Ajax* 292-93 ("O Woman, woman's best jewel is silence!" with the scholion "For as leaves decorate trees, wool is the beauty of sheep, the mane the glory of horses, and the beard the pride of man, so silence is the jewel of women"); Euripides, *Heracles* 474-77; *Phoenician Maidens*, 198-201; *Daughters of Troy* 651-56.

704. 1 Corinthians 15

Common inscription on tombs (Hellenistic age)

I was not, I was, I am not, I care not. (MEB/Berger)

This formula was common enough in Latin that it could be represented by the letters NFFNSNC in many inscriptions *(non fui, fui, non sum, non curo)*. An interesting variant is found among the Roman tomb inscriptions of the Imperial period: οὐκ ἤμην, ἐγενόμην, ἤμην, οὐκ εἰμί τοσαῦτα, "I did not exist, I was born; I existed, I do not exist; so much for that," the last word showing how trite but obligatory the sentiment had become (Horsley, *New Documents* 4). Contrast no. 443.

705. 1 Corinthians 15

Sophocles, Fragment 837 (5 cent. BCE)

Thrice-blessed are those mortals, who after viewing these sacred things descend into Hades. To them alone life is allotted there; for all others only calamity awaits. (MEB)

Cf. also Pindar, Fragment 121 (5 cent. BCE): "Blessed is the one who has seen that, and then goes under the earth. That one knows the end of life, but also knows its divinely given new beginning" (MEB). Each fragment refers to "seeing" the sacred objects during the rite of initiation into the mystery religion. Neither here nor in Paul do we have a general affirmation of human immortality, but the gift of life beyond the grave to a select group that has been converted. The Sophocles fragment also has postmortem punishment for those not initiated, an element missing from the eschatology of the undisputed Pauline letters. On the differences between the mystery cults and Pauline Christianity on this point, see nos. 570-71, 671, 770, 832, 847, and the Subject Index.

706. 1 Corinthians 15:24-26

Theopompus in Plutarch, *Moralia*, "Isis and Osiris" 47, reports on Iranian eschatology (Theopompus, 4 cent. BCE; Plutarch, 45–125 CE)

Theopompus says that, according to the sages, one god is to overpower, and the other to be overpowered, each in turn for the space of three thousand years, and afterward for another three thousand years they shall fight and war, and the ones shall undo the works of the other, and finally Hades shall pass away; then shall the people be happy, and neither shall they need to have food nor shall they cast any shadow. And the god, who has contrived to bring about all these things, shall then have quiet and shall repose for a time . . . (LCL)

Analogies to Paul: (1) An apocalyptic "timetable" is given. (2) The time before the end is characterized by struggle against the cosmic opponent. (3) The End consists in the abolition of Death, immediately followed by a new happy existence of humanity under radically changed bodily conditions. (4) God as "all in all" means for Paul too a kind of rest.

Differences: Paul does not picture the struggle of two gods of equal rank, and the arrival of the End is something different from the (in principle repeatable) apocalyptic season of a universal year. (Cf. also C. Colpe, "Eschatologie" in *Altiranische und zoroastrische Mythologie* [Wörterbuch der Mythologie IV, 1986], 333-40.) The explanation for the similarities between Pauline and Iranian apocalyptic is the simultaneous development of structural dualistic eschatologies.

707. 1 Corinthians 15:28

Corpus Hermeticum 13.2 (2–4 cent. CE)

[Dialogue between Tat and Hermes on one who has been reborn.] And what manner of man is he that is brought into being by the Rebirth? He that is born by that birth is another; he is a god, and son of God. He is the All, and is in all [τὸ πᾶν ἐν παντί]; for he has no part in corporeal substance; he partakes of the substance of things intelligible, being wholly composed of Powers of God. (Scott)

Cf. also on John 3:3-5.

The text begins as a description of God, but then the description modulates into a description of those who are reborn, since the nature of deity is also expressed in them: God is All and is in all things, that is, he constitutes them completely as what they are by his own being, filling them completely with himself so that they are filled with his fullness (cf. Eph 3:19; 4:10). Reality is this indwelling of God in all things through the divine power (δύναμις), in that he constitutes their substance. Thus there is a reconciliation between God and world. Those who are reborn are incorporated into this all-embracing unity.

It is thus interesting that 1 Corinthians 15:24-26 speaks of these powers, of which Death is the last. But they must first be brought into subjection, and God becomes "all in all" only after this. That which CH 13 speaks of as existing reality into which those who are reborn can be incorporated, is still a matter of the eschatological future for 1 Corinthians 15. In both Paul and CH however, the

God who is "all in all" is bound up with the fact that the "powers" stand at his disposal, that his own being is realized in this, that he is present to everything through them. Against the background of the worldview of CH 13, 1 Corinthians 15 means that so long as there are powers that resist the divine rule, God is not "all in all." CH 13 is not only the earliest documented "parallel" to 1 Corinthians 15:28c, but also the most clear. This also shows that this half-verse is not to be read in isolation, but that from v. 24 it deals with a coherent conceptual world already available in Paul's time.

708. 1 Corinthians 15:29

2 Maccabees 12:38-45 (1 cent. BCE)

Then Judas assembled his army and went to the city of Adullam. As the seventh day was coming on, they purified themselves according to the custom, and kept the Sabbath there. 39 On the next day, as had now become necessary, Judas and his men went to take up the bodies of the fallen and to bring them back to lie with their kindred in the sepulchers of their ancestors. 40 Then under the tunic of each one of the dead they found sacred tokens of the idols of Jamnia, which the law forbids the Jews to wear. And it became clear to all that this was the reason these men had fallen. 41 So they all blessed the ways of the Lord, the righteous judge, who reveals the things that are hidden; 42 and they turned to supplication, praying that the sin that had been committed might be wholly blotted out. The noble Judas exhorted the people to keep themselves free from sin, for they had seen with their own eyes what had happened as the result of the sin of those who had fallen. 43 He also took up a collection, man by man, to the amount of two thousand drachmas of silver, and sent it to Jerusalem to provide for a sin offering. In doing this he acted very well and honorably, taking account of the resurrection. 44 For if he were not expecting that those who had fallen would rise again, it would have been superfluous and foolish to pray for the dead. 45 But if he was looking to the splendid reward that is laid up for those who fall asleep in godliness, it was a holy and pious thought. Therefore he made atonement for the dead, so that they might be delivered from their sin. (NRSV)

The significant "parallel" is that in each case the author is contending for the doctrine of the resurrection of the dead, and appeals to events and practices in the experience of the readers as a basis for inference. In neither 2 Maccabees nor 1 Corinthians is the point to establish a doctrine of praying for the dead. In each case, practices otherwise unexplained but assumed to be true provide support for the point at issue, the doctrine of the resurrection.

709. 1 Corinthians 15:33

Inscription from Aphrodisia (undated; from time of the Empire) (MAMA 8.569)

As long as you are alive, be happy, eat, drink, live high, embrace others. For this was the End. (MEB/Berger)

Paul cites not only Isaiah 22:13 LXX, for the comparison with Luke 12:19*c* (independent of Isaiah) but points rather to the fact that Paul is citing an inscription common on tombs and widely known in the Hellenistic world. The clause "For this was the End" refers to the death of the one buried beneath the above inscription. Cf. the useful collection by W. Ameling, "Φαγώμεν καὶ Πίωμεν" in *ZPE* 60 (1985), 35-43.

710. 1 Corinthians 15:23-24, 35-44

Bundahisn 30:4-30 (so-called Indian Version = Iranian Version 34:4-30; a composition from the 9 cent. CE from older sources; no Christian influence)

After the arrival of Sosyans they prepare [for] the resurrection of the dead, as it is said, that Zarathustra asked Ormazd, "How can the body be reconstituted, if it has been carried off by wind or water, and how can the resurrection happen?" Ormazd answered, "If I created the distant sky, shining like polished steel though as a spiritual reality without supporting pillars, and if the earth came into being through me . . ., if through me sun, moon, and the stars in the firmament move about as illuminating heavenly bodies, and if through me the grain has been created so that it is sown in the earth and multiplies, and if I have generated different colors in the plants, and have placed fire in plants and other things without burning them up, if through me the child is conceived in the womb and grows, the skin, nails, blood and so on receiving their special form. . . . Then each of these, as it was created by me, was more difficult than a resurrection, since at the resurrection I am already aided by the fact that materials are present to work with, but the creation was made out of nothing. . . . At first the bones of Gayomard will rise, then those of Masya and Masyoi [the names of the first human pair, the Iranian "Adam and Eve"], then the rest of the human race. All human beings will rise, righteous and godless, each human being will rise from the spot where they died. . . . Only one class will be attributed to them [i.e. there will be no class distinctions in the resurrection life]. Then the righteous will be separated from the godless. The righteous will proceed to Paradise, while the godless will be thrown back into hell. . . . They [the resurrected ones] will live as they do now in the world, but there will be no more begetting of children. Then at the command of Ormazd will Sosyans [and his helpers] give to each one the reward deserved according to their deeds. This means: Whoever has offered no sacrifice and has done no Getikharid [an eight-day "mass"-like service] and has given no clothing as a gift of piety, will be naked in that day. And he will bring an offering to Ormazd, and the heavenly angels will bring him a garment. Then Ormazd will strike Ahriman . . . and he will fall back into the darkness of hell from which he forced his way into heaven." (MEB/Berger/Geldner)

Analogies with Christian eschatology, in particular with Pauline eschatology, extend even to details (e.g. the line of argument involving the existing creation in response to the question of "how?"; damnation understood as nakedness [cf. 2 Cor 5:3] and resurrection as being "not unclothed but further clothed"; an ordered progression in the resurrection, in which the "prototype" is first). On the other hand, the differences are so great that there can be no thought of any sort of direct dependence in either direction. It is a matter of structural similarities in the apocalyptic outline (common firm data: a mediator of salvation and the resurrection of the dead). The analogies emerge through a similar posing of the problem. Cf. C. Colpe, "Auferstehung," in H.-W. Haussig, ed., *Wörterbuch der Mythologie* IV (1986), 299-300.

On resurrection, cf. no. 443. On resurrected ones not marrying and begetting or bearing children, cf. Matthew 22:23-33; Mark 12:18-27; Luke 20:27-40.

711. 1 Corinthians 15:35-54

Euripides, Fragment 839, quoted in Plutarch, *Physics*, "Teachings of the Philosophers" 5.19 (Euripides, 485/84–406 BCE; Plutarch, 45–125 CE)

The Epicureans, according to whom [the world] is uncreated, think that living beings originated from the transmutation of different forms of matter, so they are all simply parts of the world. So too Anaxagoras and Euripides: none of the existent things utterly perish, but separate into their component parts and recombine into different forms. (MEB/Berger)

The whole world process is here understood as a constant transformation of its elements, so that even death is only such a transformation. This last idea is thus found especially in comforting speeches on the occasion of someone's death (cf. Berger in "Hellenistische Gattungen," 1200-1201).

Analogy to Paul: Death is understood as a transformation, with which Pseudo-Philo *LAB* (1 cent. BCE or CE) 19:16 may be compared, as he comments on the death of Moses: "And his form was changed into glory." Yet for Paul, it is not death that works the transformation, but that which follows, the event of the resurrection initiated by Christ. If the Greek ideas of transformation emphasized the aspect of continuity even to the point of identity, for Paul the point is an unexpected, miraculous victory over death. Nevertheless, he makes use of the conceptuality of transformation, in order to respond to the Corinthians' question "How?"

712. 1 Corinthians 15:35-57

Philo, *Life of Moses* 2.51.288 (15 BCE–50 CE)

Afterward the time came when he had to make his pilgrimage from earth to heaven, and leave this mortal life for immortality, summoned thither by the Father, Who resolved his twofold nature of soul and body into a single entity, transforming his whole being into mind, pure as the sunlight. (LCL)

Like Paul, Philo does not regard the future life as a matter of flesh and blood. Unlike Paul, he does not here speak of resurrection, but of immortality (though cf. Paul's v. 53). The life of the eternal world is not for Philo the "putting on" of a resurrection "body," but the transformation of all that is bodily into incorporeal mind such as now already inhabits our mortal bodies, an immaterial form of being similar to light.

713. 1 Corinthians 15:45-49

1QS 4.20-23 (1 cent. BCE)

God will then purify every deed of man with his truth; He will refine for Himself the human frame by rooting out all spirit of falsehood from the bounds of his flesh. He will cleanse him of all wicked deeds with the spirit of holiness; like purifying waters He will shed upon him the spirit of truth . . . For God has chosen them for an everlasting Covenant and all the glory of Adam shall be theirs. (Vermes)

Similarly, the Qumran texts speak of the (eschatologically realized) glory of Adam in 1QH 17:15: "Thou wilt cast away all their sins. Thou wilt cause them to inherit all the glory of Adam and abundance of days" (Vermes).

And in CD 3:20: "Those who hold fast to it are destined to live forever and all the glory of Adam shall be theirs" (Vermes). For similar expressions on the glory of Adam, cf. also 1QS 4:7-8; *Apocalypse of Moses* 20 ("clothed with glory"); and no. 556.

If this interpretation is correct, this means that the Qumran people expected the eschatological restoration of the glory of Adam as a collective reality for the righteous, without needing to think of an individual mediator figure as the "Last Adam," as is the case with Paul. The logic of the matter does not necessarily require a second Adam—just as in no. 710 there is no second Gayomard. Paul introduces this figure into the traditional imagery, which was perhaps more simple than Paul's own concept (15:49).

On 1 Corinthians 15:45-47, cf. no. 594.

714. 1 Corinthians 15:45-49

Philo, *On the Account of the World's Creation Given by Moses* 134 (15 BCE–50 CE)

After this he [Moses] says that "God formed man by taking clay from the earth, and breathed into his face the breath of life" [Gen ii 7]. By this also he shows very clearly that there is a vast difference between the man thus formed and the man that came into existence earlier after the image of God: for the man so formed is an object of sense-perception, partaking already of such or such quality, consisting of body and soul, man or woman, by nature mortal; while he that was after the [Divine] image was an idea or type or seal, an object of thought [only], incorporeal, neither male nor female, by nature incorruptible. (LCL)

There have been numerous attempts to relate the two Adam-figures of 1 Corinthians 15:45-46 with this passage in Philo. They have in common: On the basis of the creation stories in Genesis 1 and 2, two different Adam-figures are understood. In Philo there is the ideal Human (according to Gen 1) and the real material Human (of Gen 2). In Paul there is a physical (ψυχικός) Human in Genesis 2 and a spiritual (πνευματικός), which one must then take as the eschatologically understood Human of Genesis 1. In this view, Paul would have understood the Adam of Genesis 1 not protologically, but eschatologically, the true Human first entering the world with Christ. This would then explain the emphasis on the reversed order in 15:46. Paul would then be directing his own theology against an idealistic theory of degeneration: the original ideal Human degenerated into the historical human beings we see about us. The objection to be raised is whether we may really postulate this kind of idealism against which Paul is presumed to argue as the understanding of human existence at Corinth. What has Christ in common with such an ideal Humanity?

Thus there is another suggestion:

715. 1 Corinthians 15:45-49

Philo, *Allegorical Interpretation of Genesis* 1.31-32 (15 BCE–50 CE)

"And God formed the man by taking clay from the earth, and breathed into his face a breath of life, and the man became a living soul" [Gen. ii. 7]. There are two types of men; the one a heavenly man, the other an earthly. The heavenly man, being made after the image of God, is altogether without part or lot in corruptible and terrestrial substance; but the earthly one was compacted out of the matter scattered here and there, which Moses calls "clay." For this reason he says that the heavenly man was not molded, but was stamped with the image of God; while the earthly is a molded work of the Artificer, but not His offspring. We must account the man made out of the earth to be mind mingling with, but not yet blended with, body. But this earthlike mind is in reality also corruptible, were not God to breathe into it a power of real life; when He does so, it does not any more undergo molding, but becomes a soul, not an inefficient and imperfectly formed soul, but one endowed with mind and actually alive; for he says, "man became a living soul." (LCL)

Here are pictured two types of existing human beings, the heavenly one is no longer, as in the preceding text, the ideal human, but is made according to this ideal (cf. G. Sellin, *Der Streit um die Auferstehung der Toten. Eine religionsgeschichtliche und exegetische Untersuchung von 1 Kor 15* [Göttingen: Vandenhoeck & Ruprecht, 1986], 102ff.). Both are named Νοῦς, "mind." This νοῦς would remain earthly and corruptible, if God did not breathe into it the breath of true life. This means that Philo is not speaking of a general act of creation in the past, but of the ever-present possibility of inspiration: human being is potentially immortal, as a pneumatic. The soul as natural νοῦς is mortal. The pneumatics incorporate the heavenly Human Being. If Paul found such a position before him, or argues against it, then his move would have been to relate this πνεῦμα exclusively to Christ.

So too, the statements about transformation in the context of 1 Corinthians 15 (e.g. 15:51) are to be understood against the background of the world of ideas illustrated by Philo's statements about transformation by inspiration. Cf. e.g. Philo's "Questions and Answers on Exodus," Book 2.29: ". . . having given up and left behind all mortal kind, he [the one who is resolved into the nature of unity] is changed into the divine, so that such men become kin to God and truly divine" (LCL). Cf. also 2 Peter 1:4.

716. 2 Corinthians 1:3-11

Letter of the soldier Apion to his father (BGU 423) (2 cent. CE)

Apion to Epimachus his father and lord, many greetings. I pray above all that you are healthy and strong, and that things are going well with you, as well as with my brother and my sister and her daughter. I give thanks to the Lord Serapis that he saved me when I was in danger on the sea. (MEB/Berger)

Analogy to Paul: beginning the letter with thanksgiving for deliverance from a life-threatening danger. Form critical analogy: a report of his own prayer for the addressees and those mentioned in the letter (cf. Berger, *Formgeschichte*, 246).

Difference: Paul includes the congregation in his prayer of thanksgiving; it stands only at the beginning of a letter, and the deliverance for which he gives thanks has a legitimating function.

On 1:8-10, cf. no. 534, first part.

717. 2 Corinthians 1:12

Periander, in *Gnomologium Vaticanum* 450 (660–560 BCE)

The wise Periander was asked what freedom is, and he responded: "A good conscience." (MEB/Berger)

As a rule, examples of the phrase "good conscience" are found in pagan literature only from the second century CE on (previously in Judaism, only in Philo and Josephus). The text is mentioned here because the Pauline idea of freedom is closely related to his concept of "conscience" (cf. M. Wolter, "Gewissen" II, *TRE* 13:213-18). Cf. no. 542.

718. 2 Corinthians 2:14-16

Testament of Abraham 16:7-8; 17:16-18 (1–3 cent. CE)

Now the righteous Abraham [had] come out of his room and [was] seated under the trees of Mamre, holding his chin in his hand and waiting for the arrival of the archangel Michael. And behold a sweet odor came to him and a radiance of light. And Abraham turned around and saw Death coming toward him in great glory and youthful beauty. . . . And he [the angel] showed him [Abraham] another face, of a fierce, storm-tossed sea and a fierce, turbulent river and a frightening three-headed dragon and a mixed cup of poisons; and in a word, he showed him great ferocity and unbearable disease as of the odor of death. And from the great bitterness and ferocity, male and female servants, numbering about seven thousand [some editions: 318], died. (*OTP* 1:892-93)

Analogies to Paul: (1) Along with the divine messenger, a pervasive pleasant odor comes to the addressee of the message. This fragrance is not only a subjective quality of the messenger, but he mediates it. (2) This odor which accompanies the divine messenger is ambivalent: for the righteous, it is a pleasant fragrance; for others, it is the stench of death. The activity of the messenger himself recedes behind this olfactory form of the message. The odor is similarly active in the Tree of Fragrance in *1 Enoch* 25:4-6: it is forbidden for anyone to touch it now, but after the Day of Judgment

"Then they shall be glad and rejoice in gladness,
and they shall enter into the holy [place];
its fragrance shall [penetrate] their bones,
long life they will live on earth,

such as their fathers lived in their days" (*OTP* 1:26).

In this text too, being permeated by the fragrance results in the gift of life. Cf. also no. 427.

Further: B. Kötting, "Wohlgeruch der Heiligkeit," *Jenseitsvorstellungen in Antike und Christentum* (JAC Supplementary Vol. 9; Memorial Volume to A. Stuiber) (Münster: Aschendorff, 1982), 168-75, which refers to the important passage in Philo, "Dreams," 1.178: "For just as the exhalations from aromatic herbs fill those who come near them with a sweet fragrance, in the same way those who belong to the circle and neighborhood of a wise man, drinking in the atmosphere which spreads far and wide around him, are improved in character" (LCL).

Older material (but without the idea of the *mediator* of the fragrance important for 2 Cor 2) is found in E. Lohmeyer, *Vom göttlichen Wohlgeruch* (Heidelberg: C. Winter, 1919).

719. 2 Corinthians 2:15

b. Ta'anith 7a (date of the tradition uncertain)

R. Banna'ah used to say: "Whosoever occupies himself with the Torah for its own sake his learning becomes an elixir of life to him, for it is said, *It is a tree of life to them that grasp it;* and it is further said, *It shall be as health to thy navel;* and it is also said, *For whoso findeth me findeth life.* But, whosoever occupies himself with the Torah not for its own sake, it becomes to him a deadly poison." (Soncino)

Here the Torah stands in place of the apostle. In each case, the encounter with the divine representative has two possible effects, contrasted with each other as life and death. Which effect it has depends on the human response.

720. 2 Corinthians 2:17

Lucian, *Hermotimus, or Concerning the Sects* 59 (120–185 CE)

[Lycinus to Hermotimus:] I certainly cannot say how in your view philosophy and wine are comparable, except perhaps at this one point that philosophers sell their lessons as wine-merchants their wines—most of them adulterating and cheating and giving false measure. (LCL)

The statement belongs to the tradition of polemic against the Sophists common since Plato (*Protagoras* 5; *Sophists* 19), charging the Sophists with engaging in the practice of philosophy for money. Paul adapts imagery from this tradition in his dispute with the Corinthians about his renunciation of financial support from them.

721. 2 Corinthians 2:17–3:9

Epictetus, *Discourses* 3.24.64-65 (55–135 CE)

A. [Discussing whether Diogenes loved anyone:] But what was the manner of his loving [ἀλλ ἐφίλει πῶς]? As became a servant of Zeus, caring for men indeed, but at the same time subject unto God. That is why for him alone the whole world, and no special place, was his fatherland; and when he had been taken prisoner he did not hanker for Athens nor his acquaintances and friends there, but he got on good terms with the pirates and tried to reform them. (LCL)

B. Further: *Discourses* 3.26.28: Does God so neglect His own creatures, His servants, His witnesses, whom alone He uses as examples to the uninstructed, to prove that He both is, and governs the universe well, and does not neglect the affairs of men, and that no evil befalls a good man either in life or in death? (LCL)

C. Further: *Discourses* 4.7.20: . . . always I wish rather the thing which takes place. For I regard God's will as better than my will. I shall attach myself to Him as a servant and follower, my choice is one with His, my desire one with His, in a word, my will is one with His will. (LCL)

Analogies to the Pauline concept of apostleship: (1) The expression διάκονος (cf. 1 Cor 11:23) or διακονία; cf. also "follower" (ἀκόλουθος), although "following" is not found in Paul. (2) The servant of God is a mediator between God and human beings. He practices "pastoral care." (3) As the messenger of God among human beings he radically conforms his own will to God's, and is completely given over to God's service as a homeless wandering preacher (cf. nos. 144, 148, 296, 298).

Cf. 1 Corinthians 13 and nature of ἀγαπη, φιλία, and other words for "love."

722. 2 Corinthians 3:3

Thucydides, *History of the Peloponnesian War* 2.43.2 (460–400 BCE)

[Funeral address for Pericles.] For the whole world is the sepulcher of famous men, and it is not the epitaph upon monuments set up in their own land that alone commemorates them, but also in lands not their own there abides in each breast an unwritten memorial of them, planted in the heart rather than graven on stone. (LCL)

This text is a more appropriate analogy to 2 Corinthians 3:3 than texts usually cited about the unwritten law, since here it is a matter of people's names being "written" on the hearts of other persons.

723. 2 Corinthians 3:6

Dio Chrysostom, *The Seventy-Sixth Discourse* (40–120 CE)

. . . while laws are preserved on tablets of wood or of stone, each custom is preserved within our own hearts. And this sort of preservation is surer and better. Furthermore, the written law is harsh and stern, whereas nothing is more pleasant than custom. Then too, our laws we learn from others, but our customs we all know perfectly. (LCL)

On the theory of "unwritten law" cf. above nos. 547, 614.

724. 2 Corinthians 3:7*b*

Pseudo-Philo, *Liber Antiquitatum Biblicarum* 12:1
(1 cent. CE, probably pre-70)

And Moses came down. And when he had been bathed with invisible light, he went down to the place where the light of the sun and the moon are; and the light of his face surpassed the splendor of the sun and the moon, and he did not even know this. And when he came down to the sons of Israel, they saw him but did not recognize him. But when he spoke, then they recognized him. And this was like what happened in Egypt when Joseph recognized his brothers but they did not recognize him. And afterward, when Moses realized that his face had become glorious, he made a veil for himself with which to cover his face. (*OTP* 2:319)

Further:

725. 2 Corinthians 3:7*b*

Philo, *On the Life of Moses* 2.70 (15 BCE–50 CE)

Then, after the said forty days had passed, he descended with a countenance far more beautiful than when he ascended, so that those who saw him were filled with awe and amazement; nor even could their eyes continue to stand the dazzling brightness that flashed from him like the rays of the sun. (LCL)

In comparison with the OT text, the two later Jewish interpretations provide important preliminary developments for 2 Cor 3. Especially to be noted in the Pseudo-Philo text (no. 724) is something that does not happen in the OT, namely the linking of Exodus 34:29-30 (radiant face) with 34:33*b* (preparation of a veil). The Philo text above speaks, contrary to the OT, of the people's inability to continue looking at Moses' face, and so prepares the way for 2 Corinthians 3:7. Both texts give a more extensive description of the splendor of Moses' face.

726. 2 Corinthians 3:17

Hermetic Sentences (2–4 cent. CE)

Everything in heaven is unchangeable; everything on earth is changeable. Nothing in heaven is enslaved; nothing on the earth is free. Nothing is unknown in heaven; nothing is known on the earth. The heavenly realities do not participate in the things on the earth; the things on the earth do not participate in the heavenly realities. Everything in heaven is flawless; everything on earth is flawed. (MEB/from Stobaeus, *Anthologium,* vol. 1, no. 41)

Cf. Philo, "Husbandry," §68: Only the heavenly realm has been made by the creator free from necessity, and whoever disdains the earthly world has attained to that realm.

Again in 3:17 Paul takes up the key word πνεῦμα, which has previously stood in contrast to the letter of the Law, and the freedom here corresponds to the "boldness" of 3:12. Here freedom means having direct access to the Lord, and freedom from hardening and temporality, the fate of Israel, in contrast to the new covenant. Whereas Paul thinks in terms of salvation history, the hermetic text (and Philo) are more oriented to cosmological thought.

727. 2 Corinthians 3:18

Hierocles of Alexandria, *Commentary* to the *Carmen Aureum* of Pythagoras (d. 431 CE)

For just as it is not possible for a running eye that has not been healed to see even brilliant illumination, so it is also impossible for a soul that possesses no virtue to see the beauty of truth. (MEB/from *Mullachius*)

Analogies to Paul: (1) Use of the verb stem -οπτριζ-, by Paul with κατ-, here with ἐν-, in both cases with the meaning "see" (this meaning is also possible for Paul, cf. vv. 7 and 13, in addition to the fact that Paul discusses "seeing oneself in a mirror"). (2) This qualified "seeing" is the presupposition for further salvific existence that follows from it, for it is directed in a particular, predetermined way to the goal of "becoming."

728. 2 Corinthians 3:18

Philo, *On the Life of Moses* 2.69 (15 BCE–50 CE)

As for eating and drinking, he had no thought of them for forty successive days, doubtless because he had the better food of contemplation, through whose inspiration, sent from heaven above, he grew in grace, first of mind, then of body also through the soul, and in both so advanced in strength and well-being that those who saw him afterward could not believe their eyes. (LCL)

Through "seeing," as in Paul, the whole person is gradually involved, leading even to a transformation of the body. As in a central passage in the Gospels (cf. nos. 125-29 above on Matt 17:1-9; Mark 9:2-10; Luke 9:28-36), the transfiguration motif is here met, again in connection with Moses. To be noted is that this event does not remain limited to Moses, but embraces Christ (Mark 9 par.) and Christians (2 Cor 3), and is here thought of as the decisive saving event. Moses' encounter with God becomes the soteriological model. On the "forty days" cf. Matthew 4:2; Mark 1:13; Luke 4:2.

729. 2 Corinthians 4:2

Epictetus, *Discourses* 3.22.13-15 (55–135 CE)

. . . you must feel no anger, no rage, no envy, no pity; no wench must look fine to you, no petty reputation, no boy-favorite, no little sweet-cake. For this you ought to know: Other men have the protection of their walls and their houses and darkness, when they do anything of that sort, and they have many things to hide them.

But the Cynic, instead of all these defenses, has to make his self-respect his protection; if he does not, he will be disgracing himself naked and out of doors. (LCL)

Renunciation of the protection afforded by normal privacy is inherent in the vocation of the wandering Cynic philosopher-preacher, who sets forth what he preaches in his own life. Among the numerous points of contact with the New Testament's understandings of apostleship, cf. above no. 721.

730. 2 Corinthians 4:4, 6

Corpus Hermeticum 7:2-3 (2–4 cent. CE)

[Hermes speaks by revelation to his son Tat:] . . . Then seek a guide to take you by the hand and lead you to the portals of knowledge. There shines the light cleansed of darkness. There no one is drunk. All are sober and gaze with the heart toward one who wishes to be seen, who is neither heard nor spoken of, who is seen not with the eyes but with the mind and heart. But first you must rip off the tunic that you wear, the garment of ignorance, the foundation of vice, the bonds of corruption, the dark cage, the living death, the sentient corpse, the portable tomb, the resident thief, the one who hates through what he loves and envies through what he hates.

Such is the odious tunic you have put on. It strangles you and drags you down with it so that you will not hate its viciousness, not look up and see the fair vision of truth and good that lies within. . . . (Copenhaver)

Second Corinthians 4:4 and CH 7:2 manifest widespread agreement in the philosophical-religious terminology used (darkness, light, knowledge, hindrance, perception, "that you do not . . ."; on the "garment," cf. 5.1-4). In CH these terms are understood anthropologically and metaphysically, by Paul theistically and personally (God of this world/God and Jesus Christ). The common background can be seen in the more extensive treatment in CH.

731. 2 Corinthians 4:5

Dio Chrysostom, *Discourse* 13.11-12 (40–120 CE)

And the men whom I met, on catching sight of me, would sometimes call me a tramp and sometimes a beggar, though some did call me a philosopher. From this it came about gradually and without any planning or any self-conceit on my part that I acquired this name. Now the great majority of those styled philosophers proclaim themselves such, just as the Olympian heralds proclaim the victors; but in my case, when the other folk applied this name to me, I was not able always and in all instances to have the matter out with them. (LCL)

In the immediate context (§§9-10) Dio consulted an oracle and was challenged by the deity to action with great zeal ("until thou comest to the uttermost parts of the earth"). On the analogy to Socrates, cf. no. 618. As in the case of Paul, "preaching oneself" gets in the way of one's mission. Dio is responding to the critique of Cynics made by Sophists, whereas Paul responds to a different understanding of the early Christian apostolic office.

732. 2 Corinthians 4:8

Epictetus, *Discourses* 2.24.24 (55–135 CE)

[Responding to the question, what is a Stoic?:] Show me a man who though sick is happy, though in danger is happy, though dying is happy, though condemned to exile is happy, though in disrepute is happy. Show him! By the gods, I would fain see a Stoic. (LCL)

On the form of the peristasis catalog (listing of negative experiences), cf. Berger, *Formgeschichte*, §66. In Paul as in Epictetus, the point is that in every single case the negative is overruled by a positive. In Stoicism this is by the inward resolution to conquer suffering; in Paul this is by the constant saving intervention of God (cf. 1:9-10).

733. 2 Corinthians 4:10-12

Plato, *Phaedo* 66DE, 67E (428/17–349/48 BCE)

. . . if we are ever to know anything absolutely, we must be free from the body and must behold the actual realities with the eye of the soul alone. And then, as our argument shows, when we are dead we are likely to possess the wisdom which we desire and claim to be enamored of, but not while we live.

. . . but keep ourselves pure from it [the body] until God himself sets us free. . . .

"In fact, then, Simmias," said he, "the true philosophers practice dying, and death is less terrible to them than to any other men." (LCL)

Paul, like Plato's philosopher, lives with death constantly in view. For Plato, the point is the necessary philosophical distance from the body as the precondition for knowledge; the body hinders pure perception, and so is to that extent impure itself. For Paul, on the other hand, the constantly real danger of bodily harm and death becomes to him a demonstration of the God who delivers from death and brings life out of death. Similarly Philo, "Giants," 14. The idea had continuing effects in the ancient church, as illustrated in the liturgical song "Constant Reflection on Death."

734. 2 Corinthians 4:16

Seneca, *Epistle* 24.19-20, "On Despising Death" (4–65 CE)

I remember one day you were handling the well-known commonplace—that we do not suddenly fall on death, but advance toward it by slight degrees; we die every day. For every day a little of our life is taken from us; even when we are growing, our life is on the wane.

We lose our childhood, then our boyhood, and then our youth. Counting even yesterday, all past time is lost time; the very day which we are now spending is shared between ourselves and death. It is not the last drop that empties the water-clock, but all that which has previously flowed out; similarly, the final hour when we cease to exist does not of itself bring death; it merely of itself completes the death-process. (LCL)

Paul has the first half of v. 16 completely in common with Seneca, but in the second half he inserts the new, different element that derives from his own theology. The daily experience of renewed life corresponds to the daily experience of dying. Each day is not a repeated experience of receiving a wholly new life, but a continuous process of being renewed.

On 2 Corinthians 4:16 ("the inner person"), cf. nos. 589, 590, 593.

735. 2 Corinthians 4:17

Seneca, *Moral Essays*, "On Tranquillity of Mind" 16.4 (4–65 CE)

I shall weep for no one who is happy, for no one who weeps; the one with his own hand has wiped away my tears, the other by his tears has made himself unworthy of having any of mine. Should I weep for Hercules because he was burned alive? or for Regulus because he was pierced by so many nails? or for Cato because he wounded his own wounds? All these by a slight sacrifice of time found out how they might become eternal, and by dying reached immortality. (LCL)

Hans Windisch, *Der Zweite Korintherbrief* (Göttingen: Vandenhoeck & Ruprecht, 1924), 155, comments on this text, "Seneca never comes so near to Paul as in the view expressed here." This idea also plays a role in the later martyrologies: it is a favorable exchange made by the martyrs, for after a brief moment of suffering they enter into eternal blessedness. In Hellenistic tradition Hercules plays an especially important role for the idea that glory follows upon suffering.

736. 2 Corinthians 4:17

Asclepius Hymn in *P. Oxy.* 11, 1381.191ff. (2 cent. CE)

For every gift of a votive offering or sacrifice lasts only for the immediate [παραυτίκα] moment, and presently perishes, while a written record is an undying deed of gratitude, from time to time renewing its youth in the memory. (Grenfell and Hunt)

A critical reflection on cultic practice, emphasizing what is temporary and what is permanent. What Paul relates to human destiny is here applied in the context of Hellenistic religion to cultic acts.

737. 2 Corinthians 5:1-8

Pseudo-Plato, *Axiochus* 365 E–366 A (428/27–349/48 BCE)

Consider this: once the connection [between body and soul] is dissolved and the soul [ψυχη] reaches its place in the heavens, then the body [σῶμα] that is left behind—earthly and without reason [ἄλογος]—is not the real person [ὁ ἄνθρωπος]. For we are souls, immortal living beings, enclosed in a fleshly dungeon. Nature enclosed us in a tent [σκῆνος] to our disadvantage . . . therefore being released from life is a change from something bad to something good. (MEB/Souilhé, *Complètes*)

Analogies: Homeland and foreign country; the picture of the tent (σκῆνος); death as the end of exile from our homeland, i.e. the leaving/dissolution of our earthly body.

Differences: Paul expects a new body, and it is important not to be "naked" (5:2-3). Paul is thus not fundamentally hostile to bodily existence as such; heavenly existence is in a qualitatively different body. Paul would say to the Platonic doctrine: to exist merely as a naked soul is no life at all, but existence as a ghost. The Platonic position is a development of the familiar σῶμα/σῆμα idea (wordplay *sōma/sema* = "body/tomb") in which the body is a tomb in which the soul is buried, as e.g. in *Cratylus* 400C.

738. 2 Corinthians 5:1-5

Philo, *On the Virtues* 12:76 (15 BCE–50 CE)

When he [Moses] had ended his anthems [cf. Deut 32–34], a blend, we may call them of religion and humanity, he began to pass over from mortal existence to life immortal and gradually became conscious of the disuniting of the elements of which he was composed. The body, the shell-like growth which encased him, was being stripped away and the soul laid bare and yearning for its natural removal hence. (LCL)

Here Philo has adapted his thought more completely than Paul to the Greek dualistic anthropology. "The body" is only the shell that encases the true self, and is discarded at death. The somewhat gradual process is also reminiscent of Paul's expression in 2 Corinthians 3:18.

739. 2 Corinthians 5:2-4

Corpus Hermeticum 10.17-18 (2–4 cent. CE)

. . . the mind cannot seat itself alone and naked in an earthly body. The earthly body cannot support so great an immortality, nor can so great a dignity endure defiling contact with a body subject to passion. Mind, therefore, has taken the soul as a shroud, and the soul, which is itself something divine, uses the spirit as a sort of armoring-servant. The spirit governs the living being.

Then, when the mind has got free of the earthly body, it immediately puts on its own tunic, a tunic of fire, in which it could not stay when in the earthly body. (For earth cannot bear fire; the whole thing burns even from a little spark; this is why water has spread all around the earth guarding like a fence or a wall against the burning of the fire.) (Copenhaver) [The νοῦς in human beings is naked, without fire, and cannot be active as a demiurge.]

In contrast to the previous text, here we have an explicit discussion of a specific heavenly garment for the spiritual self of the person, a garment which the spiritual self receives when it is free from the body. Paul, of course, in place of reflections on "soul" and "mind," speaks of the "I" that would like to be "at home" with the Lord. One can also say that the orientation of Paul's thought to the God of Israel and Jesus Christ has such a high degree of speculative potency that it can commandeer this thought world (which has many metaphorical and mythical elements) and at least in part reorganize it about this new center. Cf. also no. 710.

On the content, cf. J. Z. Smith, "The Garments of Shame," in *Map Is Not Territory* (Leiden: E. J. Brill, 1978), 1-23 (on *Gos. Thom.* 37, etc.).

740. 2 Corinthians 5:3

Hierocles of Alexandria, *Commentary on Pythagoras' "Carmen Aureum"* 26 (d. 431 CE)

This is the goal of the Pythagorean method, that everyone be empowered to receive the divine goodness, so that when the moment of death comes they may leave behind on earth this mortal body and take off [ἀποδύω] its nature, and that those who have fought the good fight of philosophy will be well-girded for the heavenly way . . . then they will become participants in the divine nature themselves [καὶ θεοποιεῖσθαι, ὅσον οἷον τε ἀνθρώποις θεοὺς γενέσθαι]. (MEB/from Mullachius)

Further:

741. 2 Corinthians 5:3

Corpus Hermeticum 1.24-26 (1 cent. CE)

To this Poimandres said: "First in releasing the material body you give the body itself over to alteration, and the form that you used to have vanishes. To the demon you give over your temperament, now inactive. The body's senses rise up and flow back to their particular sources, becoming separate parts and mingling again with the energies. And feeling and longing go on toward irrational nature. Thence the human being rushes up through the cosmic framework, at the first zone surrendering the energy of increase and decrease, at the second evil machination, a device now inactive; at the third the illusion of longing, now inactive; at the fourth the ruler's arrogance, now freed of excess; at the fifth unholy presumption and daring recklessness; at the sixth the evil impulses that come from wealth, now inactive; and at the seventh zone the deceit that lies in ambush. And then, stripped of the effects of the cosmic framework, the human enters the realm of the ogdoad; he has his own proper power, and along with the blessed he hymns the father." (Copenhaver)

Analogies to Paul: (1) The dissolution/letting-return of the human body at the time of the individual's death is described. (2) The person loses all that does not correspond to the heavenly realm, so that one can speak of being "unclothed" ("take off" in Hierocles; "unclothed" in CH; both in Paul). (3) In both Hierocles and CH, that which remains is that which is appropriate to the heavenly world or is the precondition to divination. More forcefully than in Hierocles, Paul emphasizes that the heavenly gift ("our heavenly dwelling") effects the new existence.

742. 2 Corinthians 5:10

Plato, *Phaedrus* 249AB (428/27–349/48 BCE)

[The souls of philosophers can return to earth after three thousand years:] . . . the rest, when they have finished their first life, receive judgment, and after the judgment some go to the places of correction under the earth and pay their penalty, while the others, made light and raised up into a heavenly place by justice, live in a manner worthy of the life they led in human form. But in the thousandth year both come to draw lots and choose their second life . . . (LCL)

Cf. Hierocles of Alexandria (d. 431 CE), commentary on Pythagoras' "Carmen Aureum": "After the destruction of the body the human soul continues to exist and attains to justice and judgment, receiving a worthy reward for good deeds done in life" (MEB/from Mullach).

Each of the above texts, separated by about eight centuries, with 2 Corinthians 5 about halfway between them, points to an individual postmortem judgment in which repayment is made for deeds done during the earthly life. Cf. L. Ruhl, *De mortuorum iudicio* (RGVV II 2) (Berlin: A. Töpelman, 1903). Paul knows of the same idea of a general judgment, which he adapts to Jewish concepts of salvation history. Cf. also Lucian, "Dialogues on Death," 10:13: "the life of each person will be thoroughly examined." Cf. also no. 710. On the three-decker universe "heaven," "earth," "under the earth," cf. Philippians 2:5-11; Revelation 5:13.

743. 2 Corinthians 5:17

Polybius, *The Histories* 4.2.4-5 (200–120 BCE)

[Polybius gives his reasons for beginning the new volume with Philip of Macedon:] But my chief reason for beginning at this date, was that Fortune had then so to speak rebuilt [καινοποιέω] the world [οἰκουμένη]. For Philip, son of Demetrius, being still quite a boy, had inherited the throne of Macedonia . . . (LCL)

According to Polybius, the principle by which the whole of history is to be "explained" is Tyche [Τύχη], thought of less as a personified Power and more as only "luck" or "accident." Here, the renewing of the whole world is the fundamentally new ordering of political and economic relations. Similarly, Jewish texts understand renewal as introducing a new order, especially by the Law (*Jub.* 19:25; *Targ. 1 Chron.* 4:23) with reference to the calendar (*2 Enoch* 65; *Jub.* 1:29). "New creation" is here a transformation, even if thoroughgoing, not a new creation "from the ground up." This idea was related to the "new creation" only relatively late (passing away of heavens and earth, *1 Enoch* 91:15; Rev 20:11; 21:1; 2 Pet 3).

On 2 Corinthians 5:18-21 (reconciliation), see nos. 562, 787.

744. 2 Corinthians 6:10

Letter of Crates 7, "To the Wealthy" (1 cent. BCE–3 cent. CE)

[The rich are troubled and commit crimes to hold on to their wealth.] But as for us, we observe complete peace since we have been freed from every evil by Diogenes of Sinope, and although we possess nothing, we have everything, but you, though you have everything, really have nothing because of your rivalry, jealousy, fear, and conceit. (Malherbe)

The text manifests extensive similarities extending even to vocabulary between Paul's understanding of apostleship and the Cynic wandering philosophers (cf. no. 721). How Paul grounds Christian freedom christologically can be seen in 1 Corinthians 3:22-23. Concretely, "possessing everything" probably means an attitude of leaving things alone without making use of them.

745. 2 Corinthians 6:14–7:1

4QMMT 6.7-8, 13-16, Letter of "Teacher of Righteousness" (?) (2 cent. BCE)

[And it is] written [in the book of Moses] that you should [not] bring any abomination [into your home, since]
7 abomination is a hateful thing. [And you know that] we have separated ourselves (פרשנו) from the multitude of the people [and from all their impurity]
8 and from being involved with these matters and from participating with [them] in these things.

And it is written
13 "and it shall come to pass, when
14 all these things [be]fall you," at the end of days (באחרית הימים), the blessings
15 and the curses, ["then you will take] it to hea[rt] and you will return unto Him with all your heart
16 and with all your soul," at the end (באחרית) [of time, so that you may live . . .]

The six fragments designated 4QMMT may be from the letter mentioned in 4QpPs37 4.6-8, written by the "Teacher of Righteousness" to the "Wicked Priest" (perhaps the Hasmonean king Jonathan (d. 143/142). If so, it is truly remarkable that we have a contemporary copy of a letter preserved by the sender, something that we have from no New Testament or early Christian figure. The beginning of the letter is still missing. The extant fragments contain a calendar (only partially preserved), a list of Qumranic Halakhot, and the conclusion of the letter. Twelve lines of the concluding fragment are cited here.

Second Corinthians 6:14–7:1 has often been considered an un-Pauline (e.g. Joseph Fitzmyer) or even anti-Pauline (so H. D. Betz, *Galatians: A Commentary on Paul's Letter to the Churches in Galatia. Hermeneia—A Critical and Historical Commentary on the Bible* [Philadelphia: Fortress Press, 1979], 329-30) fragment, and connections between this section and the Qumran documents have often been noticed (cf. e.g. no. 747 below).

Illuminating for the New Testament documents is the awareness of being the eschatological community, the struggle with the eschatological enemy Belial, and the feeling of separateness over against "main-stream" Judaism expressed by the declaration that "we have separated ourselves from the multitude of the people" (cf. line 7 of the final fragment above). The latter expression is particularly important in that it is the first documented instance of פרש (*parash*, the root of the word "Pharisee") being used to indicate separation from the main body of Jews, and supports the view that such "separated ones" had made a voluntary separation, rather than being excluded (as is suggested by the fact that the term "Pharisee" is based on the passive form of the verb).

Cf. E. Qimron and J. Strugnell, "An Unpublished Halakhic Letter from Qumran," *The Israel Museum Journal* IV [1985], 9-12; the complete Hebrew text with English translation is published in *Discoveries in the Judean Desert*, vol. 10, ed. Elisha Qimron and John Strugnell (New York and London: Oxford University Press, 1994).

746. 2 Corinthians 6:15

Sentence of Epictetus (55–135 CE)

For neither does evil have any agreement with virtue, nor does freedom have any agreement with slavery. (MEB/Berger)

Cf. a fragment from Philo (from the *Sacra Parallel. des Joh. v. Damaskus*, ed. C. E. Richter, *Philonis Iudaei Opera* = Tauchnitz VI, pp. 229-30): "It is impossible that love for the world can agree with love for God, just as it is impossible that light and darkness exist together in agreement" (MEB).

Cf. also no. 337.

747. 2 Corinthians 6:15

1QM 1:1 (2–1 cent. BCE)

The Rule of War on the unleashing of the attack of the sons of light against the company of the sons of darkness, the army of Satan [Belial]: against the band of Edom, Moab, and the sons of Ammon . . .
The sons of Levi, Judah, and Benjamin,
shall battle against them . . . (Vermes)

In common with Paul: The opposition between God (Christ) and Belial, between light and darkness.

Difference: For Paul the point is that these pairs cannot be united, i.e. he has a parenetic intention. In 1QM it is a narrative of a future event in which this dualism will be overcome.

748. 2 Corinthians 8:9

Plutarch, *Moralia*, "Isis and Osiris" 57 (45–125 CE)

The subject seems in some wise to call up the myth of Plato, which Socrates in the *Symposium* gives at some length in regard to the birth of Love, saying that Poverty, wishing for children, insinuated herself beside Plenty while he was asleep, and having become pregnant by him, gave birth to Love ['Έρως], who is of a mixed and utterly variable nature, inasmuch as he is the son of a father who is good and wise and self-sufficient in all things, but of a mother who is helpless and without means and because of want always clinging close to another and always importunate over another. For Plenty is none other than the first beloved and desired, the perfect and self-sufficient; and Plato calls raw material Poverty, utterly lacking of herself in the good, but being filled from him and always yearning for him and sharing with him. The World, or Horus, which is born of these . . . (LCL)

The analogy to the Pauline passage is seen in the way the deity and creation are linked by the combination of riches and poverty. God is on the side of riches, the creature on the poverty side. The link materializes by the fact that creation participates in these riches. Both think of the event in the imagery of a mythical event: Plato using the imagery of begetting and generation, in which Love is produced, while Paul uses the imagery of the majestic expression of power (the ruler shares the lot of the subjects, in order to help them and bring them to salvation, cf. e.g. Dio Cassius concerning Caesar). Paul describes the process as χάρις, ruling grace, the grace of the ruler. Previously, as he shifts to the perspective of the community in 8:8, Paul has spoken of love (ἀγάπη), using it as a synonym for the Platonic ἔρως. For Plato Eros is participation in the divine and longing for it, thus thought of in erotic-genealogical terms. For Paul ἀγάπη is the unselfish giving of the higher one on behalf of the lower. Another difference: Paul exhorts and warns (parenesis), while Plato describes (etiological myth).

749. 2 Corinthians 11:14

Life of Adam and Eve 9 (3 cent. CE)

[The second temptation of Eve.] Then Satan was angry and transformed himself into the brightness of angels and went away to the Tigris River to Eve and said to her, "Step out of the river and cry no more. . . . all we angels have entreated for you and interceded with the Lord." (OTP 2:260)

It is presupposed that all beings of higher rank than earthly humans can change into whatever form they choose. For a pagan example, see Porphyry, "On Abstinence," 2.40, 42. This is extensively illustrated in Pseudo-Clementine, Homilies 9.13. Cf. here nos. 221, 510. This transformation serves to deceive human beings, who accept the message as legitimate on the basis of the appearance of the messenger. On "angel of light" see also no. 866.

750. 2 Corinthians 12:1-10

Philo, On the Migration of Abraham 34-35 (15 BCE–50 CE)

I feel no shame in recording my own experience, a thing I know from its having happened to me a thousand times. On some occasions, after making up my mind to follow the usual course of writing on philosophical tenets, and knowing definitely the substance of what I was to set down, I have found my understanding incapable of giving birth to a single idea, and have given it up without accomplishing anything, reviling my understanding for its self-conceit, and filled with amazement at the might of Him that IS to Whom is due the opening and closing of the soul-wombs. On other occasions, I have approached my work empty and suddenly become full, the ideas falling in a shower from above and being sown invisibly, so that under the influence of the Divine possession I have been filled with corybantic frenzy and been unconscious of anything, place, persons present, myself, words spoken, lines written. For I obtained language, ideas, an enjoyment of light, keenest vision, pellucid distinctness of objects, such as might be received through the eyes as the result of clearest showing. (LCL)

Many writers would testify to something like Philo's experience—though one approaches the writing desk (or computer) well prepared, the ideas do not flow and nothing is accomplished, but sometimes when one comes to the task seemingly empty of one's own study and reflection, ideas and words are given. Yet Philo's description goes far beyond the customary "wooing the muse" of the typical author. His talk of divine inspiration is intended seriously, and the "corybantic frenzy" in which he was "unconscious of anything" is not too distant from Paul's "whether in the body or out of the body I do not know." Other points of contact and contrast: (1) Whether one should speak of the experience or not is an issue to be decided. (2) Philo has experienced this "thousands" of times; for an impressive vision, Paul must go back fourteen years, but he also claimed the effective presence of God's Spirit when composing his "ordinary" letters (cf. e.g. 1 Cor 7:40; 14:37-38). Yet it is clear that Philo claims to experience inspiration more often than Paul. (3) The experience gives Philo clarity of vision and ability to communicate; Paul cannot share what he has experienced in the special vision referred to in 2 Corinthians 12 (cf. next no. 752).

751. 2 Corinthians 12:1-10

m. Hagigah 2.1 (2–3 cents. CE?)

The forbidden degrees may not be expounded before three persons, nor the Story of Creation before two, nor the chapter of the Chariot before one alone, unless he is a sage that understands of his own knowledge. Whoever gives his mind to four things it were better for him had he not come into the world—what is above? what is beneath? what was beforetime? and what will be hereafter? And whoever takes no thought for the honor of his Maker, it were better for him if he had not come into the world. (Danby)

Mystical experience is common to all religions, but some religions value and cultivate it, while others regard it as a real, but dangerous experience to be discouraged and strictly controlled. Rabbinic Judaism belongs to the latter category (in contrast to Philo). The Merkabah mysticism associated with Ezekiel and his vision of the wheels (Merkabah = chariot) that became prominent later, already had roots in the first century. Some were hesitant to admit Ezekiel to the canon because of the danger it posed of luring the unwary into mystical speculation. Though Paul experienced charismatic gifts and "mystical" experiences, he was wary of them, and hesitated to speak of them. He belonged to that stream of Judaism that acknowledged the validity of trips to paradise, but was very reserved about them, and did not encourage them among others. Contrast the extensive and detailed reports of visions and trips to heaven in Jewish apocalyptic documents such as *1 Enoch*, nos. 934, 944-48 on Revelation.

Cf. *t. Hagigah* 2.3, 4: "Four entered the garden [Paradise]: Ben 'Azzai, Ben Zoma, the Other [Elisha], and 'Aqiba.

One gazed and perished, one gazed and was smitten, one gazed and cut down sprouts, and one went up whole and came down whole.

Ben 'Azzai gazed and perished.

Concerning him Scripture says, *Precious in the sight of the Lord is the death of his saints* [Ps. 116:15].

Ben Zoma gazed and was smitten.

Concerning him Scripture says, *If you have found honey, eat only enough for you, lest you be sated with it and vomit* [Prov. 25:16].

Elisha gazed and cut down sprouts.

Concerning him Scripture says, *Let not your mouth lead you into sin* [Qoh. 5:5].

A. R. 'Aqiba went up whole and came down whole.

Concerning him Scripture says, *Draw me after you, let us make haste*" (Neusner, *Tosefta*).

The rabbi Elisha ben Abuhah's "cutting the plants" is explained in the Talmud as his inhibiting the children's study of the Torah by his speculations about the heavenly world.

752. 2 Corinthians 12:10

Epictetus, *Discourses* 1.6.40 (55–135 CE)

And yet God has not merely given us these faculties, to enable us to bear all that happens without being degraded or crushed thereby, but—as became a good king and in very truth a father—He has given them to us free from all restraint, compulsion, hindrance; without reserving even for Himself any power to prevent or hinder. (LCL)

Analogy to Paul: from God, precisely in adverse circumstances, comes unrestrained and unlimited power (δύναμις) to bear them. The sentence "our weakness is our strength" occurs verbatim in Philo, *Moses* 1.67-69 (the burning bush shows that those who are suffering unjustly cannot be destroyed by their attackers).

753. Galatians 1:1

Epictetus, *Discourses* 3.22.23 (55–135 CE)

. . . the true cynic . . . must know that he has been sent by Zeus to men, partly as a messenger [ἄγγελος ἀπὸ τοῦ Διὸς ἀπέσταλται], in order to show them that in questions of good and evil they have gone astray, and are seeking the true nature of the good and the evil where it is not, but where it is they never think; and partly, in the words of Diogenes, when he was taken off to Philip, after the battle of Chaeroneia, as a scout [κατάσκοπος].

The true apostle is not sent by other human beings, but is sent by God to humanity. The verbal form of "apostle" is used here (ἀποστέλλω; ἀπόστολος). In both pagan literature and the LXX, the verb form is common, the noun quite rare. For Paul, the apostle's message is not general instruction about the nature of good and evil, as it was for the Cynic, but the kerygma (κήρυγμα), the gospel (εὐαγγέλιον) of God's saving act in Christ.

754. Galatians 1:1

Plato, *Ion* 534 E (428/27–349/48 BCE)

For the god, as it seems to me [Socrates], intended him to be a sign to us that we should not waver or doubt that these fine poems are not human or the work of men, but divine and the work of god; and that the poets are merely the interpreters of the gods, according as each is possessed by one of the heavenly powers. (LCL)

Similarly Dio Chrysostom (40–ca. 120 CE), *Discourses* 77/78 §1, about Hesiod (not with human art, but by association with the Muses and as their student). Paul thus here formulates completely in accord with ancient ideas of inspiration, which also of course embraces the whole realm of poetic inspiration by the Muses, not only the sphere of cultic oracles and religious speech.

On Galatians 2:12*a* objection from outsiders, cf. no. 659.

755. Galatians 2:12

Jubilees 22:16 (140 BCE)

[Abraham's blessing over Jacob.] And you also, my son, Jacob, remember my words, and keep the commandments of Abraham, your father. Separate yourself from the gentiles, and do not eat with them, and do not perform deeds like theirs. And do not become associates of theirs. Because their deeds are defiled, and all of their ways are contaminated, and despicable, and abominable. (*OTP* 2:98)

On the avoidance of table fellowship as a means of community self-definition, cf. besides Josephus, *Antiquities* 11.346 (κοινοφαγία alongside profaning the Sabbath as the main cultic offenses that required punishment and occasioned flight to Samaria!), *Jos. Asen.* 7:1 (Joseph maintained his own table, and "never ate with the Egyptians, for this was an abomination to him"), and Paul himself in 1 Corinthians 5:11 and no. 815.

As in the genealogy of Matthew 1:2-17, "son of" does not mean direct descendant.

756. Galatians 2:13

Epictetus, *Discourses* 2.9.19-22 (55–135 CE)

Why, then, do you call yourself a Stoic, why do you deceive the multitude, why do you act the part of a Jew, when you are a Greek? Do you not see in what sense men are severally called Jew, Syrian, or Egyptian? For example, whenever we see a man halting between two faiths, we are in the habit of saying, "He is not a Jew, he is only acting the part [ὑποκρίνεται].” But when he adopts the attitude of mind of the man who has been baptized and has made his choice, then he both is a Jew in fact and is also called one. So we also are counterfeit “baptists” [παραβαπτισταί], ostensibly Jews, but in reality something else, not in sympathy with our own reason, far from applying the principles which we profess, yet priding ourselves upon them as being men who know them. So, although we are unable even to fulfill the profession of man, we take on the additional profession of the philosopher . . . (LCL)

Regarding text criticism: The above translation represents a textual emendation according to the context, since manuscripts for the second question read “Why do you act the part of a Greek when you are a Jew?” The above translation follows the context, not the MSS, for “counterfeit ‘baptists’” according to the context refer to “ostensible Jews,” since in this text being baptized is identical with being a Jew, perhaps because in this time (baptized) Christians were still confused with Jews. (But in this text it is clear that Epictetus presupposes the possibility of becoming a proselyte to Judaism. Thus it is more likely that the reference is to Jews throughout, and that this text from Epictetus is evidence for proselyte baptism. Cf. no. 269.)

“A man halting between two faiths” is literally limping on both legs, i.e. swaying back and forth between two commitments (cf. 1 Kgs 18:21; is a Jewish metaphor here adopted?). Such people are not authentic Jews, but only pretenders. This classification presupposes that one who deserves the designation “Jew” is a sincere person who does not play the hypocrite. “Jews” or “baptized” are precisely models of those who practice what they preach, whose words and deeds agree. Their religion stands for authenticity. Hypocrisy is specifically not on their program. This makes hypocritical Jews all the worse. This inclination and way of looking at things is here applied to philosophers, from whom it is correspondingly demanded that their words and deeds form a coherent whole.

The meaning for Galatians 2:13: the setting aside of the discrepancy between inner and outer is a special concern of Pharisaism, and thus also of Paul (cf. Matt 23:25-26 etc.). It is precisely the anti-Pharisee polemic in the Gospels that shows that here one strikes a nerve. The Pauline understanding of justification/righteousness signifies a new level in the Pharisees’ discussion of the relation of inner/outer.

757. Galatians 2:19

Sentences of Sextus, “The Pythagorean Sentences” 30 (2 cent. CE)

In the same way, the self-sufficient one [ὁ αὐτάρκης], the one without possessions, the philosopher, truly lives for God. He considers it the greatest riches to be in need of nothing, not even the most necessary, for the accumulation of goods never satisfies the lust for more. The self-sufficient ones have what is needed to live well: they do no injustice. (MEB/from Chadwick, *Sentences*)

Cf. above no. 574.

Cf. *Sentences of Sextus* 201: “Hold as the goal of your life to live for God” (MEB). In this gnomic tradition (for the genre, cf. Berger, *Formgeschichte*, §19), to “live for God” is identified with freedom from all things. In contrast, for Paul the point is freedom from the Law on the one hand, and on the other it is freedom from the old “I,” the old self being replaced by “Christ who lives within me.” This is more radical, but not without the danger of spiritualizing.

758. Galatians 3:6-14

Mekilta Beshallah 7.25-27 (2 cent. CE)

Great is faith before the One who spoke and brought the world into being.

For as a reward for the act of faith that the Israelites made in the Lord, the Holy Spirit rested upon them and they sang the song, as it is said, "and they believed in the Lord and in his servant Moses." Then Moses and the people of Israel sang this song [to the Lord, saying, "I will sing to the Lord, for he has triumphed gloriously; the horse and his rider he has thrown into the sea"].

R. Nehemiah says, "How do you know that whoever takes upon himself the obligation to carry out a single religious duty in faith is worth that the Holy Spirit should rest upon him?"

For so we find in the case of our ancestors that as a reward for the act of faith that they made, they achieved merit, so that the Holy Spirit rested on them as it is said, "and they believed in the Lord and in his servant Moses."

. . . So you find that Abraham our father inherited this world and the world to come only as a reward for the faith that he believed, as it is said, "And he believed in the Lord [Gen 15:6]." (Neusner, *Mekhilta Rabbi Ishmael*)

Differently from Paul, faith is here understood as one commandment beside others. But like Paul, faith and the gift of the Holy Spirit are connected (Gal 3:6, 9, 14; cf. also no. 559). The song of the Israelites is understood as a gift of the Spirit, as are New Testament hymns (cf. Col 3:16; Eph 5:19; Luke 1:67ff.).

759. Galatians 3:11

1 QpHab 7:17–8:3 (1 cent. BCE)

[Interpreting the same text, Hab 2:4:] *But the righteous shall live by his faith* [ii, 4b].

Interpreted, this concerns all those who observe the law in the House of Judah, whom God will deliver from the House of Judgment because of their suffering and because of their faith in the Teacher of Righteousness. (Vermes)

At first glance the interpretation of Habakkuk 2:4 at Qumran is contrasted with the Pauline understanding, for the doing of the Law is here the precondition for righteousness. "Faith" is here understood as "faithfulness, loyalty." For all that, however, this "loyalty" is here directed to the Teacher of Righteousness, who is understood as the initiator of this new way of righteousness. There is no doubt that his advent forms the framework and condition for the new Torah obedience. The exposition of this passage at Qumran thus corresponds somewhat to the perspective regarding the person of Jesus in the Synoptic Gospels. (Cf. also H.-W. Kuhn's comment that "the impact of the Habakkuk Commentary VIII 1-3 in deepening our understanding of Paul cannot be overestimated," in "Impact of the Qumran Scrolls," 330.)

760. Galatians 3:13

Inscription from Delphi (200–199 BCE)

Apollo the Pythian
bought from Sosibius
of Amphissa for freedom
a female slave, whose name
is Nicaea, by race a Roman, with a price
of three minae of silver and
a half-mina. Former seller according to
the law: Eumnastus
of Amphissa. The price he hath received.
The purchase, however
Nicaea hath committed unto Apollo
for freedom. (Deissmann)

Cf. also the 162 BCE inscription (CII 710, from Leipold-Grundmann 241) documenting the release of a Jewish slave:

"Under the ruler Eumenidas, son of Kallios, in the month Apellaios. Kleon, son of Kleudamos, in joint action with Xenophania, the mother of Kleudamos, [sold] to the Pythian Apollo a male slave by the name of Judaios, of the Jewish people, for the price of four silver minas, so that he is to be free and unmolested by all his whole life long. Since Judaios has entrusted the purchase price to the god, he is free to do what he wants. Witnesses: Amyntas and Tarantinos priests of Apollo, and the rulers Aristion, Asandros, Aristomachos; as private citizens Sodamidas, Theophrastos, Teison, Glaukos, son of Xenon, and Menes" (MEB).

A. Deissmann (*Light from the Ancient East* [New York: George H. Doran, 1927], 271-77) understood these texts as instances of sacral redemption of slaves. The slave first paid the price into the temple treasury, since as a slave he or she could not negotiate legal contracts. By a benevolent legal fiction, the god or goddess then purchased the slave, who became the deity's property and must serve him, but this service is in fact freedom. The appropriateness of this practice as a soteriological metaphor that could be adopted by Christians is apparent: the slave is powerless, but the deity does what the slave cannot do. After being redeemed, the slave belongs to the god, "whose service is perfect freedom." At a crucial point, of course, the practice was in contrast to the salvific reality posited by the Christian proclamation: the slave in fact must purchase his or her own freedom, and the "redemption" was only a legal fiction to facilitate this.

This Deismannian interpretation both of the ancient practice and of its metaphorical use in the New Testament has been widely accepted, but recent discussion has questioned whether it is correct. There are relatively few such texts, and the key word ἐξαγοράζω is not found. It is disputed that the slave was purchased by the god, and argued instead that the god served as an intermediary, arranging the sale which the slave could not do, a function that could in fact have been performed by others, such as a relative or friend. See esp. F. Bömer, *Untersuchungen über die Religion der Sklaven in Griechenland und Rom*, II, *Die sogenannte sakrale Freilassung in Griechenland und die δοῦλοι ἱεροί* (1960). The verb is used for purchasing the freedom of slaves, e.g. in Diodorus Siculus (1 cent. BCE) 15.7.1 (Plato was purchased out of slavery). For a discussion of the recent evidence, see Horsley, *New Documents* 6:70-81.

As an instance of the later effects of this interpretation, cf. the Cologne *Mani-Codex* (4–5 cent. CE) 69:9ff.: "Again he [Mani] said, 'When my father took delight in me, had compassion and care for me, he sent from there my companion, who is very reliable, the whole fruit of immortality, that this one should purchase my freedom and redeem me from this error of those who belong to the Law [namely, the Elkasites]. Coming to me, he brought me the best hope . . .'" (MEB/Berger).

Although the Jews also performed rituals of manumission at their sacred places, as indicated in the following inscription found at Panticapaeum in the Crimea, it is only the pagan practice that provides a suitable metaphor.

(*CIJ* 683; *CIG* 2114 bb) "In the reign of king Tiberius Julius Rhescuporis, friend of Caesar and friend of Rome, the pious; in the year 377, in the month Penitius, the 20th [or 23rd], I Chreste, formerly wife of Nicias, son of Sotas, release at the house of prayer [προσευχή] my slave Heraclas to be completely free according to my vow. He is not to be retained or disturbed by any heir of mine, but to go wherever he wishes, without let or hindrance according to my vow, except for the house of prayer which is for worship and meeting. Assent is given to this also by my heirs, Pericleides and Heliconias. Joint oversight will be taken also by the synagogue of the Jews" (Barrett).

761. Galatians 3:13

4Q 169 psNah 1.17-18 (1 cent. BCE–1 cent. CE)

[And chokes prey for its lionesses; and it fills] its caves [with prey] and its dens with victims [ii, 12a-b].

Interpreted, this concerns the furious young lion [who executes revenge] on those who seek smooth things and hangs men alive . . . formerly in Israel. Because of a man hanged alive on [the] tree, He proclaims, "Behold I am against [you, says the Lord of Hosts]." (Vermes)

The Qumran commentary on Nahum, in referring to Alexander Janneus' crucifixion of 800 of his enemies, who were also Jews, about 90 BCE in Jerusalem, alludes to the text of Deuteronomy 21:23, thus proving that prior to Paul's time Jews had already interpreted this text in terms of crucifixion. The Qumran text also shows that Jews did not first discover the Deuteronomy 23 reference as an element of their anti-Christian polemic. Paul is here dependent on this Jewish tradition, a tradition he probably learned as a Jew before he became a Christian. (See also no. 763 on Gal 3:10-13, and H.-W. Kuhn, "Impact of the Qumran Scrolls," 329.)

762. Galatians 3:13

Apocryphon of James 13:19-25 (2–3 cent. CE)

Do not be proud because of the light that illumines, but be to yourselves as I myself am to you. For your sakes I have placed myself under the curse, that you may be saved. (NHL)

Cf. the saying of Jesus (?) in the *Second Apocalypse of James*, ". . . they have already proclaimed through these [words]: He shall be judged with the [unrighteous]. He who lived [without] blasphemy died by means of [blasphemy]. He who was cast out they [. . .]." Neither text shows any dependence on Galatians 3:13 and they are thus possibly Jewish Christian texts that independently of Paul provide evidence for the understanding of a crucified one as being cursed.

763. Galatians 3:10-13

11Q Temple, The *Temple Scroll* from Qumran 64:6-13 (2–1 cent. BCE)

If a man slanders his people and delivers his people to a foreign nation and does evil to his people, you shall hang him on a tree and he shall die. If a man is guilty of a capital crime and flees [abroad] to the nations, and curses his people, the children of Israel, you shall hang him also on the tree, and he shall die. . . . But his body shall not stay overnight on the tree. Indeed you shall bury him on the same day. For he who is hanged on the tree is accursed of God and men. You shall not pollute the ground which I give you to inherit. (Vermes)

Deuteronomy 21:22-23 is here more precisely focused on the betrayal of one's own people and country, perhaps in the light of the experiences of the second century CE (and the application of Lev 19:16?). The crucified one is cursed not only by God (Deut 21:23), but by both God and human beings. Another new element is the introduction of witnesses (Deut 19:15ff.). To be noticed is the specification of the crime as anti-Israelite activity among Gentiles.

764. Galatians 3:19–4:5

Hippias of Elis, according to Plato, *Protagoras* 26 (5 cent. BCE)

All you men who are present, I believe that you are all relatives, members of the same family, and [fellow] citizens by nature and not by the law. For like is related to like by nature, but the law is a tyrant that compels much that is contrary to nature. (LCL)

Talk of the law as tyrant could be a transformation of the old maxim of the law as king (so H.-D. Betz, *Galatians*, 164-66). This is found for instance in Pindar, Fragment 169, who speaks of "The Law, the lord of all, mortals and immortals carrieth everything with a high hand, justifying the extreme of violence" (LCL).

Philo is remarkably critical of the law that the masses follow blindly (Philo, "Sobriety," §198): "Now I for my part do not wonder that the chaotic and promiscuous multitude who are bound in inglorious slavery to usages and customs introduced anyhow, and who are indoctrinated from the cradle with the lesson of obedience to them, as to masters and despots, with their souls buffeted into subjection and incapable of entertaining any high or generous feeling, should give credence to traditions delivered once for all, and leaving their minds unexercised, should give vent to affirmations and negations without inquiry or examination" (LCL).

According to Josephus, *Antiquities* 4.145-49, the apostate Zambrias judged the Law to be tyrannical and Jewish life as life under tyranny.

For Paul, one could say that so long as one is under the power of sin, the Law has a tyrannical function. Cf. no. 877. On Galatians 3:19, cf. no. 500.

765. Galatians 3:22

Polybius, *Histories* 3.63.3-4 (200–120 BCE)

[Hannibal speaks to his troops after he has paraded prisoners of war in front of them:] "Fortune," he said, "has brought you to a like pass, she has shut you in on a like listed field of combat, and the prizes and prospects she offers you are the same. For either you must conquer, or die, or fall alive into the hands of your foes." (LCL)

Similarly also Diodorus Siculus (1 cent. BCE) *Library of History* 15.63.1: the Lacedaemonians were "restricted by the blows of fortune to but few citizen soldiers . . ." (LCL), i.e. fate had brought them into a situation of having only a few. The restricting act of Fortune thus brings one into a stressful situation in which only a little operating room is left and one's options are few. The unwholesome power of the Law is comparable to the way Fortune works, prior to the sending and advent of Jesus Christ.

766. Galatians 3:24

Xenophon, *Constitution of the Lacedaemonians* 3.1 (429 BCE)

When a boy ceases to be a child, and begins to be a lad, others release him from his moral tutor and his schoolmaster: he is then no longer under a ruler and is allowed to go his own way. (LCL)

This text exactly reproduces the realm from which the metaphor for Paul's argument is taken.

767. Galatians 3:27

Athenaeus, *Deipnosophistae* 12.537 (200 CE)

Ephippus, again, says that Alexander also wore the sacred vestments at his dinner-parties, at one time putting on the purple robe of Ammon, and thin slippers and horns just like the god's, at another time the costume of Artemis, which he often wore even in his chariot, wearing the Persian garb and showing above the shoulders the bow and hunting-spear of the goddess, while at still other times he was garbed into the costume of Hermes; . . . yet often, again, he bore the lion's skin and club in imitation of Heracles. (LCL)

Similarly as in Apuleius (see above no. 570), the divine garment is a material symbol for unity with the god. It is to be noted that Paul himself uses this symbol only metaphorically, i.e. linguistically, not with actual symbolic garments.

768. Galatians 3:28

Plato, *Symposium* 189 DE (428/27–349/48 BCE)

For our original nature was by no means the same as it is now. In the first place, there were three kinds of human beings, not merely the two sexes, male and female, as at present: there was a third kind as well, which had equal shares of the other two, and whose name survives though the thing itself has vanished. For "man-woman" was then a unity in form no less than name, composed of both sexes and sharing equally in male and female. (LCL)

The myth to which this text belongs then reports the division of this being by the gods, and the longing for the reunification of the two halves (eros). The sexual differentiation of the two is now and then overcome by love in a new, re-won unity. Perhaps this idea stands at the beginning of the long tradition of the later widespread conception that redemption consists of "the two becoming one" (list of instances in K. Berger, "Gnosis" I, *TRE* 13:527-28). This is of course no longer a matter of sexual union, but in the rule is an eschatological event involving a new kind of bodily existence. Only in Galatians 3, Colossians 2, and Ephesians 2 is it not the case that the unity is first attained at the eschaton, but is already present, charismatically caused. Further:

769. Galatians 3:28

Aristotle, *Politics* 1, 2.3 (384–322 BCE)

Others however [namely, the Sophists] maintain that for one man to be another man's master is contrary to nature, because it is only convention that makes the one a slave and the other a freeman and there is no difference between them by nature, and that therefore it is unjust, for it is based on force. (LCL)

Can one say that Paul comes to the same conclusion: with the abolition of the Law's power over Christians they are restored to the "natural" state? There are also other indications that the nullification of the letter of the Law means the same as the restoration of the—said in Jewish terms—original will of God in creation. Cf. above no. 540.

On slavery as only a secondary phenomenon, cf. also Alcidamas (4 cent. BCE), Fragment 1, "God let all be free, nature has made none slaves" (MEB/Berger). Cf. also Philo, "Special Laws" 2.68. Further:

770. Galatians 3:28

Inscription about Zeus Panamaros (2 cent. CE)

God invites all human beings to a banquet, and sets the table for all in common and equally, no matter where they come from. (MEB/Berger)

The mystery cults, like the Hellenistic clubs and associations particularly emphasize the equality of all their members (cf. nos. 687 and 772, and the inscription SEG 4 308.8, 303.8: foreigners and slaves are included in the invitation). Further:

771. Galatians 3:28; 5:13–6:10

Inscription from Philadelphia in Asia Minor (Lydia) (late 2 cent. or early 1 cent. BCE)

To good fortune! Written for the health and common good and best regards: the prescriptions given to Dionysus in his sleep, who grants free access to his house for men and women, free and slaves. For altars are built within for Zeus Eumenes and Hestia, his companion, and the other saving gods, for Prosperity and Wealth, Virtue, Health, good Fortune, the good Daemon, Remembrance, the Charities, and Nike [Victory]. To this one (i.e. Dionysus) Zeus gave prescriptions for the performance of healings, purifications, and mysteries according to the customs of the ancestors, as they are now written.

When they enter this house, men and women, free and slaves should swear by all the gods that they bear no lies against man or woman, perform no poison or evil curses against others, that they neither participate themselves nor advise others to participate in love potions, abortions, contraception, nor anything else that kills children, and that they are not accomplices in such. All who enter must swear that they are well-intentioned toward this house, and that if they are aware of any of the above offenses either being done or planned, that they will neither permit them or be silent about them, but will make them public and defend against them.

Except for sexual relations with his own wife, a man must not defile a foreign woman whom a man has, whether slave or free, and a man must not defile a boy or a virgin, nor commend these actions to others. If one is aware of such conduct in others, one should not keep silent about it, but make it public. A woman or man who violates these prescriptions may not enter this house. For great gods have constructed it, and they have an eye on such things, and will not tolerate that these prescriptions be transgressed.

A free woman must keep herself holy and not know anyone except her own husband. If she nevertheless knows another man, then this woman is not holy, but defiled, and filled with disgrace for the group to which she belongs, and unworthy to worship the god whose holy things are here set forth, to be present at the sacrifices, to knock [meaning of word unclear] at the healings and purifications, and to see how the sacred mysteries are performed. If she nevertheless does any of these things, from the time when these prescriptions were inscribed onward, she will suffer evil curses from the gods, who watch over these regulations. For it is against the will of the god that any of these things happen. God wants rather that people follow. The gods will be gracious to those who follow, and will always give them the good things that gods give to people whom they love. But they will hate transgressors, and place severe punishments upon them.

These prescriptions are set forth by Agdistis, the very holy Supervisor and Lady of this house. May they make good hearts for men and women, free and slaves, that they will follow what is here prescribed. And in the monthly and yearly sacrifices, the men and women who are confident are to touch this inscription in which the commandments of the gods are written, so that it may become clear who follows these prescriptions and who does not. Zeus Savior, graciously accept the touch of Dionysus, and grant to him and his family success, health, prosperity, peace, security on land and water. (MEB/from Berger's German trans. of F. Sokolowski, *Lois sacrées de l'Asie Mineure* [1955], 53-58, #20)

The inscription is here given in full, since it has not previously been translated into English, and since in several aspects it is significant for New Testament interpretation. The place itself is addressed in a letter in Revelation 3:7-13 and by Ignatius of Antioch. Some important analogies to the New Testament:

1) Equality of women and men, slaves and free is emphasized.

2) A house congregation and the importance of hospitality.

3) The voluntary character of belonging to the community, and the private individual initiative in its founding.

4) The congregation as a morally elite group claiming superiority to the culture at large, in a time when official institutions no longer provide such high moral leadership.

5) The significance of charismatic elements (revelation in a dream; cf. esp. Acts, e.g. 16:9; 18:9).

6) Cultic assemblies in a house as the focus of group activities; regular meetings on special days.

7) The anti-magical character also in early Christianity (Acts 8; 13:8-12; 19:18-19; Rev 9:21).

8) Belonging to the cultic community excludes certain activities, that are set forth in catalog style. Cf. in particular the agreement with Didache 2:6 and Barnabas 19:3. The orientation of the moral life to the initiation rite invites comparison with the New Testament's post-conversion admonitions in the Epistles (cf. Berger, *Formgeschichte,* §40).

9) A strict code of sexual ethics, bound to the concept of "holiness," so that one's personal sin is also a defiling of the congregation (cf. 1 Cor 5:6-11; 6:1-20).

10) An oath at the time of initiation (cf. Pliny, *Letters to Trajan* 10, 96.7: Christians band themselves together by a solemn oath not to engage in any crime, but to abstain from all thievery, assault, and adultery, not to break their word once they have given it, and not to refuse to pay their legal debts).

11) To love God is the summary of the commands. God is thought of as the giver of grace.

12) The presence of the god in the cult (cf. Matt 18:20).

13) Neither group is hierarchically structured, but both are cooperative and egalitarian. Further:

772. Galatians 3:28

Philostratus, *The Life of Apollonius of Tyana*, Letter 67 (d. 97 CE)

To those of the Ephesians who frequented the temple of Artemis:
Your temple is thrown open to all who would sacrifice, or offer prayers, or sing hymns, to suppliants, to Hellenes, barbarians, free men, to slaves. (LCL)

Further:

773. Galatians 3:28

Diogenes Laertius, *Lives of Eminent Philosophers*, "Thales" 1.33 (3 cent. CE)

Hermippus in his *Lives* refers to Thales the story which is told by some of Socrates, namely, that he used to say there were three blessings for which he was grateful to Fortune:

"first, that I was born a human being and not one of the brutes; next, that I was born a man and not a woman; thirdly, a Greek and not a barbarian." (LCL)

Similarly, Plutarch, *Life of Marius* 46 (about Plato: a human being, a Greek and not a barbarian, not an unreasoning animal of nature). The origin of this proverb is possibly Persian; cf. J. Darmesteter, *Une Prière Judéo-Persane* (Paris, 1891): Thanksgiving to Ormazd (as Iranian, in the right religion, as free and not slave, as man and not woman). Adopted into the Jewish morning prayer (not as Gentile, ignorant, slave, woman). Further:

774. Galatians 3:28

Plutarch, *Moralia*, "A Letter of Condolence to Apollonius" 112-13 (45–125 CE)

They say that the lawgiver of the Lycians ordered his citizens, whenever they mourned, to clothe themselves first in women's garments and then to mourn, wishing to make it clear that mourning is womanish and unbecoming to decorous men who lay claim to the education of the free-born. Yes, mourning is verily feminine, and weak, and ignoble, since women are more given to it than men, and barbarians more than Greeks, and inferior men more than better men; and of the barbarians themselves, not the most noble, Celts and Galatians, and all who by nature are filled with a more manly spirit, but rather, if such there are, the Egyptians and Syrians and Lydians and all those who are like them. (LCL)

The capacity not to mourn clearly increases as one goes up the social scale. The list is a precise catalog of the social ranking in the eastern Mediterranean of that time.

775. Galatians 3:28

Plutarch, *Moralia*, "The Bravery of Women" 242F (45–125 CE)

. . . and now, as you [Clea] desired, I have also written out for you the remainder of what I would have said on the topic that man's virtues and woman's virtues are one and the same. This includes a good deal of historical exposition . . . [Then follows reference to the oracle of the Sibyl and that of Bacis; despite their different formation there are no differences in the kind of virtues found in men and women, e.g. courage, etc.] (LCL)

Cf. the opinion of Anacharsis in Plutarch's "Seven Sages," §11: that democracy is best in which all are equal, only virtue is ranked higher and only vice is ranked lower. Further:

776. Galatians 3:28

Crates, *Letters to Hipparchia* 28-29 (1 cent. BCE–3 cent. CE)

Women are not by nature worse than men. The Amazons, at any rate, who have accomplished such great feats, have not fallen short of men in anything. . . .

Stand fast, therefore, and live the cynic life with us (for you are not by nature inferior to us, for female dogs are not by nature inferior to male dogs), in order that you might be freed even from nature, since we are all slaves either by law or through wickedness. (Malherbe)

The contrast between nature and human law is here no longer regarded as a key to salvation. The concern here is rather to be freed from nature too, and in view of the fact that nature makes slaves of us all, social distinctions are meaningless. Further:

777. Galatians 3:28

The Tripartite Tractate 132:16-29 (2–3 cent. CE)

For when we confessed the kingdom which is in Christ, [we] escaped from the whole multiplicity of forms and from inequality and change. For the end will receive a unitary existence just as the beginning is unitary, where there is no male nor female, nor slave and free, nor circumcision and uncircumcision, neither angel nor man, but Christ is all in all. (NHL)

This text is included in order to see the later history of the effects *(Wirkungsgeschichte)* of the ideas behind Galatians 3:28.

Here, as in the tradition discussed in no. 768, the abolition of all differences is regarded protologically and eschatologically, but not ecclesiologically as in Paul. Cf. similarly concerning the eternal heavenly reality in Hippolytus, *Refutation of all Heresies* 5.7.15, on the Naasenes (Attis, castrated, enters into heaven. The reality above is neither male nor female, but is a new creation, a new humanity, which is male-female).

778. Galatians 4:9/Colossians 2:20

Corpus Hermeticum, "Letter of Hermes" excerpt 29 (2–4 cent. CE)

There are seven wandering stars which circle at the threshold of Olympus, and among them ever revolves unending Time. The seven are these; night-shining Moon, and sullen Kronos, and glad Sun, and the . . . Lady of Paphos, and bold Ares, and swift-winged Hermes, and Zeus, first author of all births, from whom Nature has sprung. To those same stars is assigned the race of men; and we have in us Moon, Zeus, Ares, the Lady of Paphos, Kronos, Sun, and Hermes. Wherefore it is our lot to draw in from the ethereal life-breath tears, laughter, wrath, birth, desire.

. . . birth is Zeus; . . . the Moon is sleep; . . . the Sun is laughter . . . (Scott)

The correspondence between the macrocosmos and the microcosmos is the presupposition for every form of determinism (and astrology). Many exegetes think that the kind of worldview expressed in this text played a role in the opponents troubling the churches in Galatia and Colossae, since they speak of "elements" and astral cults. Cf. also no. 805.

On Galatians 5:2-12 (circumcision) cf. no. 659. On Galatians 5:13–6:10, cf. no. 771.

779. Galatians 5:2-3

Midrash Sifre on Numbers 112 (2 cent. CE)

The soul shall be utterly cut off. "Cut off" means ceasing to be [total annihilation is implied].
From among his people. But the people will be at peace [the whole people is not responsible for the *intentional* idolatry of the individual].

Because he has despised the word of the Lord and has broken His Commandment. "Despised the word of the Lord" refers to a Sadducee; "and has broken His Commandment"—to an Epicurean. Another explanation: *Because he has despised the Word of the Lord*—is he who treats Torah irreverently; "And hath broken His Commandment" is he who breaks the covenant of the flesh [i.e. who opposes circumcision]. Hence R. El'azar of Modi'im says: "He who profanes the holy things [the sanctuary], and despises the *festivals,* and breaks the covenant of Abraham our father *[circumcision]*, even if he has in his hand many other good deeds, is worthy to be thrust out of the world [i.e. the world to come]." If he says: "I accept the whole torah, with the exception of *this* word," of him it is said: "For he despised the word of the Lord." If he says, "The whole torah was spoken by the mouth of Holiness, and this word Moses himself said," he despises the word of the Lord. (Neusner, *Sifre*)

Paul's argument fits the Jewish context in which circumcision as the mark of the covenant represents keeping the whole Law.

780. Galatians 5:15

Plutarch, *Moralia,* "Reply to Colotes" 30 (45–125 CE)

[Opposing Colotes' opinion that the abolition of the law would result in reducing human behavior to that of animals that devour each other:] . . . For this is Colotes' public declaration in his own words, and it is dishonest and untrue. For if someone takes away the laws, but leaves us with the teaching of Parmenides, Socrates, Heracleitus and Plato, we shall be very far from devouring one another and living the life of wild beasts; for we shall fear all that is shameful and shall honor justice for its intrinsic worth, holding that in the gods we have good governors . . . (LCL)

People would act on the basis of reason, and do voluntarily what the law now compels people to do. Paul has just spoken of the fulfillment of the Law. Its fulfillment through love, without observance of the letter of the law, stands in a clear analogical relation to Plutarch's understanding of the law being fulfilled through reason, oriented to the teaching of the philosophers (cf. Rom 6:17b: after the abolition of the Law as the norm for conduct, this role is played by apostolic teaching). The Pauline resolution of the question of Law thus stands clearly within the horizon of the Hellenistic discussion of the law. Cf. nos. 540, 547, 770, 787.

On Galatians 5:17, cf. nos. 585, 587, 588, 591.

781. Galatians 5:19-23

Corpus Hermeticum 9.3-4 (2 cent. CE)

Mind conceives every mental product: both the good, when mind receives seeds from god, as well as the contrary kind, when the seeds come from some demonic being. [Unless it is illuminated by god,] no part of the cosmos is without a demon that steals into the mind to sow the seed of its own energy, and what has been sown the mind conceives—adulteries, murders, assaults on one's father, acts of sacrilege and irreverence, suicides by hanging or falling from a cliff, and all other such works of demons.

Few seeds come from god, but they are potent and beautiful and good—virtue, moderation and reverence. Reverence is knowledge of god, and one who has come to know god, filled with all good things, has thoughts that are divine and not like those of the multitude. (Copenhaver)

As in Paul, the impulse to both good and evil is exterior to human beings, and both are expressed in terms of lists (cf. nos. 782-83). For Paul, however, these external powers are not eternal cosmic principles. The good impulse that generates the "fruits of the Spirit" is the eschatological Holy Spirit, given at the climax of the history of salvation; the evil impulse is the unredeemed human nature, the "flesh," which is nonetheless personified and thought of as a cosmic power dominating all human existence. Paul knows of cosmic demons who have enslaved humanity, so that human existence as such is slavery to them, but does not connect individual evil acts with them directly.

782. Galatians 5:19-23

Diogenes Laertius, *Lives of Eminent Philosophers*, "Zeno" 7 (3 cent. CE)

This is why Zeno was the first [in his treatise *On the Nature of Man*] to designate as the end "life in agreement with nature" . . . which is the same as a virtuous life, virtue being the goal toward which nature guides us. [So too Cleanthes, Posidonius, Hecato, and Chrysippus] . . . for our individual natures are parts of the nature of the whole universe. And this is why the end may be defined as life in accordance with nature, or, in other words, in accordance with our own human nature as well as that of the universe, a life in which we refrain from every action forbidden by the law common to all things, that is to say, the right reason which pervades all things, and is identical with this Zeus.

Amongst the virtues some are primary, some are subordinate to these. The following are the primary: wisdom, courage, justice, temperance. Particular virtues are magnanimity, continence, endurance, presence of mind, good counsel. And wisdom they define as the knowledge of things good and evil and of what is neither good nor evil; courage as knowledge of what we ought to choose, what we ought to beware of, and what is indifferent; justice . . .; magnanimity as the knowledge or habit of mind which makes one superior to anything that happens, whether good or evil equally; continence as a disposition never overcome in that which concerns right reason, or a habit which no pleasures can get the better of; endurance as as knowledge or habit prompt to find out what is meet to be done at any moment; good counsel as knowledge by which we see what to do and how to do it if we would consult our own interests.

Similarly, of vices some are primary, others subordinate: e.g. folly, cowardice, injustice, profligacy are accounted primary; but incontinence, stupidity, ill-advisedness subordinate. Further, they hold that the vices are forms of ignorance of those things whereof the corresponding virtues are the knowledge.

Good in general is that from which some advantage comes, and more particularly what is either identical with or not distinct from benefit. . . . Another particular definition of good which they give is "the natural perfection of a rational being *qua* rational." To this answers virtue and, as being partakers in virtue, virtuous acts and good men; as also its supervening accessories, joy and gladness and the like. So with evils: either they are vices, folly, cowardice, injustice, and the like; or things which partake of vice, including vicious acts and wicked persons as well as their accompaniments, despair, moroseness, and the like.

All good [they say] is expedient, binding, profitable, useful, serviceable, beautiful, beneficial, desirable, and just or right. It is expedient, because it brings about things of such a kind that by their occurrence we are benefited. It is binding, because it causes unity where unity is needed; profitable, because it defrays what is expended on the transaction. It is useful, because it secures the use of benefit; it is serviceable, because the utility it affords is worthy of all praise. It is beautiful, because the good is proportionate to the use made of it; beneficial, because by its inherent nature it benefits; choiceworthy, because it is such that to choose it is reasonable. It is also just or right, inasmuch as it is in harmony with law and tends to draw men together. . . .

And grief or pain they hold to be an irrational mental contraction. Its species are pity, envy, jealousy, rivalry, heaviness, annoyance, distress, anguish, distraction. Pity is a grief felt at undeserved suffering; envy, grief at others' prosperity; jealousy, grief at the possession by another of that which one desires for oneself; rivalry, pain at the possession by another of what one has oneself. Heaviness or vexation is grief which weighs us down . . . (LCL)

As early Christianity developed its ethical discourse, it was influenced by the terminology and forms, and to some extent the ideals of the Hellenistic ethicists, especially by the Cynic-Stoic synthesis of popular philosophy. There is some similarity to the virtue and vice lists of the New Testament (Rom 1:29-31; Mark 7:21-22 par.; 1 Cor 5:10-11; 6:9-10; 13:4-7; 2 Cor 12:20; Gal 5:19-23; Eph 4:31; 5:3-5; Phil 4:8-9; Col 3:5, 8; 1 Tim 1:9-10; 6:4-5; 2 Tim 3:3-4; Titus 3:3; 1 Pet 4:3; Rev 9:21; 21:8; 22:15). In Stoicism, however, such lists are embedded in a theoretical, rational argument about the nature of human being and cosmic reality, while for Paul and the New Testament, ethics derive from a conviction about the eschatological act of God. This generates a corresponding difference in some elements of content: cf. the differing treatments of joy and love in Stoicism and the NT. David L. Balch points out that Stoic ethics stress the virtue of the individual; Christian ethics emphasize the relationship with the neighbor/enemy.

783. Galatians 5:19-23

1QS 4.2-6, 9-11 (1 cent. BCE)

These are their ways in the world for the enlightenment of the heart of man, and that all the paths of true righteousness may be made straight before him, and that the fear of the laws of God may be instilled in his heart: a spirit of humility, patience, abundant charity, unending goodness, understanding, and intelligence; (a spirit of) mighty wisdom which trusts in all the deeds of God and leans on His great loving kindness; a spirit of discernment in every purpose, of zeal for just laws, of holy intent with steadfastness of heart, of great charity towards all the sons of truth, of admirable purity which detests all unclean idols, of humble conduct sprung from an understanding of all things, and of faithful concealment of the mysteries of truth. These are the counsels of the spirit to the sons of truth in this world.

And as for the visitation of all who walk in this spirit, it shall be healing, great peace in a long life, and fruitfulness, together with every everlasting blessing and eternal joy in life without end, a crown of glory and a garment of majesty in unending light.

But the ways of the spirit of falsehood are these: greed, and slackness in the search for righteousness, wickedness and lies, haughtiness and pride, falseness and deceit, cruelty and abundant evil, ill-temper and much folly and brazen insolence, abominable deeds (committed) in a spirit of lust, and ways of lewdness in the service of uncleanness, a blaspheming tongue, blindness of eye and dullness of ear, stiffness of neck and heaviness of heart, so that man walks in all the ways of darkness and guile. (Vermes)

As in Paul, here we have a double catalog of virtues and vices within a dualistic and eschatological framework (3.13–4.26) (Kuhn, "Impact of the Qumran Scrolls," 330). When one considers that in Romans 13:12 Paul introduces a catalog of vices with the contrasting pair works of darkness and armor of light, the Qumran connection becomes the clearer and more likely. Cf. also no. 823 on 1 Thessalonians 5:4-9.

784. Galatians 5:24

Plutarch, *Moralia*, "Whether Vice Be Sufficient to Cause Unhappiness?" 3-4 (45–125 CE)

Or will you reduce a man from splendid wealth and house and table and lavish living to a threadbare cloak and wallet and begging of his daily bread? These things were the beginning of happiness for Diogenes, of freedom and repute for Crates. But will you nail him to a cross or impale him on a stake? And what does Theodorus care whether he rots above ground or beneath? Among the Scythians such is the manner of happy burial; . . . Whom, then, do these things make wretched? The unmanly and irrational . . . (LCL)

For the people of wisdom, even crucifixion itself is no disgrace. The conventional cultural values of avoiding pain and achieving fame are not accepted by them. They are free from such standards. In comparison with this, "Crucifixion of the flesh with its passions and desires" is a shade more radical, because it is active; crucifixion becomes a metaphor for the expulsion and destruction of that which afflicts one. So also here: the overturning of conventional values and striving for freedom from them. Literally and metaphorically, "crucifixion" is the expression of an ultimate disdain and separation. The philosopher is free from them; Christians apply the metaphor to themselves. For both, the cross is the sign of radical separation.

Cf. also Philo, "Dreams," 2.213: "Thus the mind stripped of the creations of its art will be found as it were a headless corpse, with severed neck nailed like the crucified to the tree of helpless and poverty-stricken indiscipline" (LCL). Here the comparison with crucifixion serves to illustrate the punishment of the godless and false mind. The texts of both Plutarch and Philo make clear that in the Hellenistic world the crucifixion metaphor was applied to ethical concerns independently of its connection with the crucifixion of Jesus and Christian theology developed therefrom.

785. Ephesians 1:4

Damascus Document CD 2 (2 cent. BCE with later additions)

Wisdom and understanding He has set before Him, and prudence and knowledge serve Him. Patience and much forgiveness are with Him toward those who turn from transgression; but power, might, and great flaming wrath by the hand of all the Angels of Destruction toward those who depart from the way and abhor the Precept. They shall have no remnant or survivor. For from the beginning God chose them not; He knew their deeds before ever they were created and He hated their generations, and He hid His face from the Land until they were consumed. For He knew the years of their coming and the length and exact duration of their times for all ages to come and throughout eternity. (Vermes)

As in Ephesians, God chooses before the foundation of the world. Unlike Ephesians, the conviction is expressed negatively, but has the same positive meaning: God did choose us before the foundation of the world, our membership in the redeemed community is God's grace, not our own doing. Thus in both the Qumran text and the New Testament, such statements function as confessions of faith, in the mode of praise to God, not objectifying claims about the status of outsiders.

786. Ephesians 2:2

Plutarch, *Moralia*, "Isis and Osiris" 26 (45–125 CE)

Xenocrates also is of the opinion that such days as are days of ill omen, and such festivals as have associated with them either beatings or lamentations or fastings or scurrilous language or ribald jests have no relation to the honors paid to the gods or to worthy demigods, but he believes that there exist in the space about us certain great and powerful natures, obdurate, however, and morose, which take pleasure in such things as these, and, if they succeed in obtaining them, resort to nothing worse. (LCL)

In his "Life of Aemilius Paulus" he cites Democritus, Fragment 166, according to which evil can strike us from the surrounding atmosphere. Cf. C. Zintzen, "Geister (Daemonen)" B.III.c. Hellenistische und kaiserzeitliche Philosophie, in *RAC* 9 (640-68), e.g. 642 (Augustine, *City of God* 7.6: from Poseidonius?).

787. Ephesians 2:14-17

Plutarch, *Moralia*, "On the Fortune or the Virtue of Alexander" 6 (45–125 CE)

Moreover, the much-admired *Republic* of Zeno, the founder of the Stoic sect, may be summed up in this one main principle: that all the inhabitants of this world of ours should not live differentiated by their respective rules of justice into separate cities and communities, but that we should consider all men to be of one community and one polity, and that we should have a common life and an order [κόσμος] common to us all, even as a herd that feeds together and shares the pasturage of a common field/law [a word-play: νόμος means both "field" and "law"].

But, as he believed that he came as a heaven-sent governor to all, and as a mediator [διαλλακτής] for the whole world, those whom he could not persuade to unite with him, he conquered by force of arms, and he brought together into one body all men everywhere, uniting and mixing in one great loving-cup, as it were, men's lives, their characters, their marriages, their very habits of life. He bade them all consider as their fatherland the whole inhabited earth, as their stronghold and protection his camp, as akin to them all good men, and as foreigners only the wicked. . . . (LCL)

Cf. no. 441 above. Analogies:

1) Using the same verbal root *(ἀλλασσ-)*, both texts speak of a mediator/reconciler (cf. no. 562).

2) Both texts are concerned with the unification of ethnically different groups into one human community. The abolition of the boundary between Greek and barbarian corresponds to the abolition of the distinction between Jew and Greek in Ephesians 2.

3) The differences that previously prevailed are traced back primarily to differences created by laws.

4) Regarding each other as foreigners is replaced by regarding each other as fellow citizens. Distinctions are swallowed up in a greater unity. This borders on Plutarch's metaphor of the one body, a step promptly taken by the translator J. C. F. Bahr, who reproduces it with "who sought to unite all in one and the same body." Also oriented toward the problem resolved by Alexander was Philo's *Joseph* 29-30. Here too it becomes clear that for Ephesians too the question of the Law is integral to the Hellenistic discussion of particular laws and the universal law (cf. no. 781).

788. Ephesians 2:14

See no. 526 on Acts 21:27-36 for Jerusalem temple inscription.

789. Ephesians 3:9-10

Addition to Proverbs 8:21 in LXX (2–1 cent. BCE)

[Wisdom speaks:] If I declare to you what happens day by day [through me], then I will also remember to recount the things that happened in days of old. (MEB)

In terms of content, Wisdom is oriented in two directions: she is related to the present creation, illuminates and permeates it—and she gives information about the beginnings. How that can be is then clarified by the following verses 8:22-30: she was already there at the beginning. The subject of Ephesians 3:9-10 is wisdom, and at the same time the mystery hidden from the eons; both are obviously identical, but have a new content over against Judaism: the unity of all humanity (of Jews and Gentiles) in the one universal mediator Jesus Christ.

On Ephesians 3:19; 4:10, cf. no. 707.

790. Ephesians 5:22-23

Hierocles the Stoic, "On Marriage" (2 cent. CE)

It would make this discussion too long to go through all the details one after the other and describe how capable she is at festivals when she takes joint charge of sacrifices and offerings; how capable during her husband's travels abroad when she keeps the household stable and does not leave it entirely without someone in charge; how capable in taking care of servants; how capable a helper in times of illness. . . . I also think that a married life is beautiful. For what else could be such an adornment as the association between a husband and wife? . . . the beauty of a household consists in the yoking together of a husband and wife who are united to each other by fate, are consecrated to the gods who preside over weddings, births, and houses, agree with each other and have all things in common, including their bodies, or rather their souls, and who exercise appropriate rule over their household and servants, take care in rearing their children, and pay an attention to the necessities of life which is neither intense nor slack, but moderate and fitting. . . . For a wife, by Zeus, is not a burden or a load, as they think, but on the contrary, she is something light and easily borne, or rather, she has the ability to relieve her husband of things that are truly annoying and burdensome. (Malherbe)

Hierocles the Stoic's understanding of marriage suggests both a partnership of equals and a perspective in which the wife is nonetheless subordinate. The marriage is not merely a secular contract, but a physical and spiritual union blessed by the gods. The defensive tone indicates his argument is against the stream. Cf. also no. 811 below.

791. Ephesians 6:14-17

Menog i Xrad 43.5-13 (middle-Persian author of the wisdom document Pahlavi-Literature, ca. 600 CE. This or similar writings were probably current among the magicians of the Parthian period, 3 cent. BCE to 3 cent. CE)

[One can overcome Ahriman and the Devs and escape from hell, in order to obtain Ohrmazd, the Amesa Spentas, and paradise] if one makes the spirit of wisdom the armor for the waist and puts on the spirit of satisfaction as armor for the body and makes the spirit of truth one's shield and the spirit of gratitude one's club, the spirit of perfection one's bow, the spirit of liberality one's arrow, the spirit of moderation one's lance, and the spirit of endeavor one's hand guard, and the spirit of predestination one's secure refuge. (MEB/from Widengren)

According to G. Widengren (*Iranisch-semitische Kulturbegegnung in parthischer Zeit* [Köln/Opladen, 1960], 39), this analogy had its origin in military circles of the Parthian period "in which the life of the warrior was the ideal life." The allegory then "migrated from Parthian culture westward . . . finally to emerge in Eph 6:11-13, where the character is just as eschatological as it was in the Menog i Xrad text." The process is probably more complex, since there are corresponding analogies in Isaiah 11:5;

59:17; Judges 6:34 LXX; and Pseudo-Philo, *LAB* 36:2, as well as esp. Wisdom 5:17-22 and finally 1 Thessalonians 5:8, as well as in Mandean writings. The allegorization of military equipment is therefore a general phenomenon of at least a rather large cultural expanse. The presupposition is always the impressive presence of military (foreign?) power. Cf. also A. Oepke, "πανοπλία," TDNT V, 297-99; C. Colpe, *Wörterbuch der Mythologie* IV (1986) 239-40; 261-66; 316-19; 475-78.

792. Philippians 1:21

Plato, *Apology* 40 CD (428/27–349/48 BCE)

[Discussing the nature of death:] And if it is unconsciousness, like a sleep in which the sleeper does not even dream, death would be a wonderful gain. For I think if any one were to pick out that night in which he slept a dreamless sleep and, comparing with it the other nights and days of his life, were to say, after due consideration, how many days and nights in his life had passed more pleasantly than that night—I believe that not only any private person, but even the great King of Persia himself would find that they were few in comparison with the other days and nights. So if such is the nature of death, I count it a gain; for in that case, all time seems to be no longer than one night. (LCL)

Cf. further Aeschylus (525-65), *Prometheus* 747, 750-51 (the reaction of Io): "What gain is to me to go on living? Should I not quickly throw myself from this rough cliff, in order to be catapulted to the ground, free from all care? For it is better to die once, than to suffer every day" (LCL). Sophocles (497–406 BCE), *Antigone* 463-64: "For who that lives in many troubles such as I would not gain by having death take him out of them?" (LCL). For Aeschylus and Sophocles death is gain because life is filled with suffering. It is different for Socrates: Death could be like a dreamless sleep, and then it is a gain not merely as escape, but has positive value in itself. For Paul however, dying is the precondition to unity with Christ. Thus in the history of a "figure of speech" a fundamental change in the understanding of death becomes visible.

793. Philippians 2:6-11

Letter of Hippocrates (1 cent. BCE)

According to his family identification he was a Dor from the city of Cos, his father is Heraclides, the son of Hippocrates, the son of. . . . He was endowed with a divine nature, and developed the art of healing from small and limited beginnings to something that was truly a great art. The divine Hippocrates is now the ninth from King Crisamis, the eighteenth from Asclepius, the twentieth from Zeus. His mother was Praxithea, the daughter of Phainarete from the house of the Heraclides. He thus inherited the divine nature from both sides of his family, an Asclepiad on his father's side and a Heraclide on his mother's side. He learned the art of healing from his father . . . but he, endowed with the divine nature, himself taught others the whole art. He purified much land and sea not from animals, but from wild, animal-like diseases [comparison with Hercules]. . . . Thus he has rightly been honored in many places on earth with divine honors; he was counted worthy by the Athenians to receive the same gifts as Hercules and Asclepius. (MEB/Berger)

The structure of this encomium (for the form cf. Berger, *Formgeschichte*, §99) follows the same form as Philippians 2:6-11: portrayal of the divine nature, report of saving activity on earth, account of his receiving divine honors. The schema is widespread in such encomia. Further:

794. Philippians 2:6-11

Corpus Hermeticum 1.12-15 (1 cent. CE)

Mind, the father of all, who is life and light, gave birth to a man like [ἴσον] himself whom he loved as his own child. The man was most fair: he had the father's image; and god, who was really in love with his own form [μορφή], bestowed on him all his craftworks. And after the man had observed what the craftsman [or: demiurge] had created with the father's help, he also wished to make some craftwork, and the father agreed to this. Entering the craftsman's sphere, where he was to have all authority, the man observed his brother's craftworks; the governors loved the man, and each gave a share of his own order. Learning well their essence and sharing in their nature, the man wished to break through the circumference of the circles to observe the rule of the one given power over the fire.

Having all authority over the cosmos of mortals and unreasoning animals, the man broke through the vault and stooped to look through the cosmic framework, thus displaying to lower nature the fair form [μορφή] of god. Nature smiled for love when she saw him whose fairness brings no surfeit [and] who holds in himself all the energy of the governors and the form of god [μορφὴ τοῦ θεοῦ], for in the water she saw the shape of the man's fairest form and upon the earth its shadow. When the man saw in the water the form like himself as it was in nature, he loved it and wished to inhabit it; wish and action came in the same moment, and he inhabited the unreasoning form. Nature took hold of her beloved, hugged him all about and embraced him, for they were lovers.

Because of this, unlike any other living thing on earth, mankind is twofold—in the body mortal but immortal in the essential man. Even though he is immortal and has authority over all things, mankind is affected by mortality because he is subject to fate; thus, although man is above the cosmic framework, he became a slave within it. He is androgyne because he comes from an androgyne father, and he never sleeps because he comes from one who is sleepless. [Yet love and sleep are his] masters. (Copenhaver)

The text contains important concepts also found in Philippians 2 (form of God; slave; equal to God; mortality). The theme in CH is the origin and explanation of the prototypical Anthropos. Despite the similarity in terminology, only those will see this text as directly related to Philippians 2 who were already convinced of the significance of the Hellenistic Anthropos speculation for the development of Christology. Further:

795. Philippians 2:6-11

Ascension of Isaiah, Greek recension 2:33-36 (1 cent. BCE–1 cent. CE)

[Dialogue between God and Isaiah, after Isaiah had arrived in heaven at the throne of God; God speaks:] "Now turn back, Isaiah, in the garment of your flesh, for you must complete the time of your life in the perishable world." And I besought Him saying, "Lord, send me not back into that world of nothingness." But again he answered and said, "Return, for the time of your life there is not yet fulfilled." And I fell at his feet and prayed that he would not send me back into the world. And the Lord spoke again and said, "Why are you crying, Isaiah? See, your place! See, your throne! See, your crown! See, all your garments that I have prepared for you! For you must fulfill your testimony on the allotted wood, and then ascend here. For the godless will saw you in two with a wooden saw. . . ." (MEB/Berger)

Here the chronology is: revelatory trip to heaven/martyrdom/ascent to heavenly glory. The critical phase is that before the martyrdom, as Isaiah is already present with God and has received the corresponding heavenly body (cf. preceding context), and now does not want to return to the earth. Here it becomes a matter of obedience. This schema is also documented elsewhere (the contrast between being elected and the fate of death), and, if applied to Philippians 2, would throw new light on this text and its presumed doctrine of preexistence, which could also be illuminated from Mark 9:2-13 (cf. nos. 125-29). Cf. Berger, "Hellenistische Gattungen," 1184-86, n. 159.

796. Philippians 2:12-13

Aboth 3.16 (2–3 cents. CE)

All is foreseen, but freedom of choice is given; and the world is judged by grace, yet all is according to the excess of works. (Danby)

When Paul unselfconsciously combines human responsibility and the sovereignty of divine grace, he is operating from his Pharisaic background. The rabbis were aware of the tensions inherent in religious discourse, and utilized paradoxical statements and especially narratives to express religious truths that logically are in tension. Josephus, somewhat adapting his vocabulary to current Hellenistic terminology, described the Jewish religious parties as "philosophical schools" who were concerned with the relationship of divine sovereignty and human free will. His description moderates the sharpness of the rabbinic and New Testament paradox of full human responsibility and full divine sovereignty: "The Pharisees . . . attribute everything to Fate and to God; they hold that to act rightly or otherwise rests, indeed, for the most part with men, but that in each action Fate cooperates. . . . The Sadducees . . . do away with Fate altogether, and remove God beyond the commission, but the very sight, of evil. They maintain that man has the free choice of good or evil, and that it rests with each man's will whether he follows the one or the other" (LCL). (*Wars* 2.162-65; cf. also *Antiquities* 13.5.9 [171-72]). Cf. also on Acts 2:23.

797. Philippians 3:5

Philo, *On the Life of Moses* 2.32 (15 BCE–50 CE)

The High Priest was naturally pleased, and, thinking that God's guiding care must have led the king to busy himself with such an undertaking, sought out such Hebrews as he had of the highest reputation, who had received an education in Greek as well as in their native lore . . . (LCL)

As in Philippians 3:5 and Acts 6:1, "Hebrew" when used of a Jew is a linguistic term, referring to Jews who knew the Hebrew language, even if this was not their only language. Second and Four Maccabees also use the term in this way (2 Macc 7:31; 11:13; 15:37; 4 Macc 4:11; 5:2; 8:2; 9:6, 18; 12:7; 16:15; 17:9).

798. Philippians 3:20 (cf. also 1:27)

Letter of Heraclitus to Amphidamas, Nr. 5 (1 cent. BCE)

But if my body should become water-logged before I heal it, it will sink into what is fated for it. Yet my soul will not sink, but, since it is a thing immortal, it will fly on high into heaven. The ethereal dwellings will receive me and I shall prosecute the Ephesians. I shall be a citizen, not among men, but among the gods. I shall not erect altars for others, but others will erect them for me. (Malherbe)

Analogy: Human beings as citizens of heaven in parallel to their earthly citizenship, and in a certain competition with it for the person's loyalty. Difference: What is here not expected until after death is by Paul already a present reality. That is a typical difference between New Testament texts and their environment. The material ground for this is the exaltation of Jesus and the charismatic experience of the community.

799. Philippians 4:11-13

Vettius Valens, *Anthologies* 5.9.2 (2 cent. CE)

Whoever takes the trouble to learn about the future and to know the truth will possess his soul in freedom from this servitude, disregarding Chance [Τύχη] and assigning no importance to Hope, not fearing death and living without distraction, having disciplined his soul to courage, and neither rejoicing over good fortune nor depressed by misfortune, but giving himself contentedly to the present. Since he does not long for things beyond his reach, he bears what is decreed for him with self-discipline and, renouncing both pleasures and penalties, becomes a good soldier of Fate. For it is impossible by means of prayer or sacrifice to overcome the destiny fixed from the beginning. . . . What has been assigned to us will happen without our praying for it, what is not fated will not happen for all our prayers. So we too must don the masks and play as Fate requires of us, and accept the parts which time's conjunctions bring about, even when they do not suit us. If anyone refuses, "he does badly, but he must nevertheless submit." (Grant)

The concluding quotation is from Cleanthes, Fragment 527.
Points of contact with the New Testament:
1) Stoic outlook vs. personal God. Valens has the philosophers' disdain of popular religion that understands prayer as a technique for getting things from the deity. The tone is a noble acknowledgment of one's own sense of dependence and of fitting in with destiny, not resignation or despair. From a personal theistic point of view, Paul's words in Philippians 4:11 are somewhat similar: "I have learned in whatever state I am to be content." Cf. Plutarch, "Virtues and Vices" 4, "If you become a

philosopher, you will not live unpleasantly, but you will learn to subsist pleasantly anywhere and with any resources" (LCL). But neither Valens nor Plutarch could add a philosophical equivalent to "I can do all things through Christ who strengthens me."

2) Yet from this point of view there could be no prayer, not even a willing "thy will be done," for it was inevitable.

3) This quotation shows that reverence for the cosmic powers, the στοιχηεῖα, need not always have been in terms of cultic worship of personal angelic beings, but could be the religious feeling of dependence on the order of the universe that to which one willingly submits (μοῖρα, *moira;* αἱμαρμένη, *hairarmene;* τύχη, *tuche,* three words for the divinized "fate"; none are in the NT). Those against whom Galatians 4:3 and Colossians 2:8 were written would still be considered slaves by Paul and the author of Colossians, and would regard the attitude expressed in the above quotation as a kind of slavery from which the Christian is set free.

800. Colossians 1:15

Plutarch, *Moralia,* "The Dialogue on Love" 13 (45–125 CE)

This is the reason why Parmenides declares that Eros is the most ancient work of Aphrodite; his words in the *Cosmogony* are
"And first of all the gods she framed was Love."
But Hesiod, in my opinion, was more scientific when he depicted Eros as the firstborn [προγενέστατον] of them all, in order to make him indispensable for the generation of all things. (LCL)

As Proverbs 8:22 speaks of Wisdom as the first one created by God, Colossians 1 and in the text from Plutarch have to do with the birth of the firstborn. Thus unavoidable and wide-ranging consequences depend on whether one grants the primacy to logos/wisdom (as in the Hellenistic Judaism in the background of Colossians 1, cf. nos. 354, 358), or Eros (as in Plutarch, cf. also nos. 698, 748), or to Jesus Christ as the image of God.

801. Colossians 1:15-17

Wisdom of Solomon 7:22, 24-27a; 8:1, 4-5; 9:1-2 (150 BCE–50 CE)

[Solomon speaks:] I learned both what is secret and what is manifest,
for wisdom, the fashioner of all things, taught me. . . .
For wisdom is more mobile than any motion;
because of her pureness she pervades and penetrates all things.
For she is a breath of the power of God,
and a pure emanation of the glory of the Almighty;
therefore nothing defiled gains entrance into her.
For she is a reflection [ἀπαύγασμα, *apaugasma*] of eternal light,
a spotless mirror of the working of God,
and an image of his goodness.
Although she is but one, she can do all things,

and while remaining in herself,
she renews all things; . . .
She reaches mightily from one end of the earth to the other,
and she orders all things well.
She is an initiate in the knowledge of God,
and an associate in his works.
If riches are a desirable possession in life,
what is richer than wisdom, the active cause of all things? . . .
O God of my ancestors and Lord of mercy,
who have made all things by your word,
and by your wisdom have formed humankind . . . (NRSV)

Wisdom is identified with λόγος (*logos*, "word"), with the Spirit of God (1:7: ". . . the spirit of the Lord has filled the world, and that which holds all things together knows what is said"), and with God himself. The act of God in both creating and sustaining the creation is attributed to Wisdom, who is ("the active cause of all things"; "that which holds all things together"), who is both identified with God and a distinct figure (9:4, "the Wisdom that sits by your throne"). This conceptuality is in the background of the first strophe of the Colossian hymn, as it is for the Johannine prologue (see on John 1:1-18).

802. Colossians 1:18/ Ephesians 1:22

Orphic Hymn quoted in Eusebius, *Praeparatio Evangelica* 3, 9.2 (*date?*)

Zeus was the first, Zeus last, the lightning's lord,
Zeus head, Zeus center, all things are from Zeus.
Zeus born a male, Zeus virgin undefiled;
Zeus the firm base of earth and starry heaven;
Zeus sovereign, Zeus alone first cause of all:
One power, divine, great ruler of the world,
One kingly form, encircling all things here,
Fire, water, earth, and ether, night and day;
Wisdom, first parent, and delightful Love:
For in Zeus' mighty body these all lie.
His head and beauteous face the radiant heaven
Reveals, and round him float in shining waves
The golden tresses of the twinkling stars
On either side bulls' horns of gold are seen
Sunrise and sunset, footpaths of the gods.
His eyes the sun, the Moon's responsive light;
His mind immortal ether, sovereign truth,
Hears and considers all; nor any speech,
Nor cry, nor noise, nor ominous voice escapes
The ear of Zeus, great Kronos' mightier son:
Such his immortal head, and such his thought.
His radiant body, boundless, undisturbed
In strength of mighty limbs was formed thus: . . . (Gifford)

Zeus is here in a certain way "identical" with the universe. Everything is his body and in his body. A number of exegetes explain Colossians 1:18*c* "the church" unhesitatingly as an addition and regard the source commented on by the author of Colossians as a "hymn" (on determination of the genre cf. Berger, *Formgeschichte*, 240, 345, 367-68) that in a similar way regarded the cosmos as the body of Christ, with Christ as its head. The hypothesis hovers in the background that the "cosmic" ideas of the original hymn were "corrected" by church theology. Since the body metaphor is also found for the "church" (cf. above no. 694), it is not surprising that the head metaphor was also met in the political realm (Plutarch, "Precepts of Statecraft" 17: the statesman is head of the state like a queen bee in a beehive), as already 2 Kings 22:44 (head of the nations) and in Philo, "Rewards," 125 (humanity as body, the nobility as head by whom all are beloved).

The conception of Zeus presented above is already found applied to the logos by Philo, "Questions Exodus," 2.117: "The head of all things is the eternal Logos of the eternal God, under which, as if it were his feet or other limbs, is placed the whole world, over which He passes and firmly stands. . . . for its perfect fullness the world is in need of the care and superintendence of the best ordered dispensation, and for its own complete piety, of the Divine Logos, just as living creatures [need] a head, without which it is impossible to live" (LCL).

This text has received Christian interpolations, eliminated in the section printed above. The conception as a whole is not foreign to Philo's thought elsewhere: In *Dreams* 1.128 he speaks of the Logos as the head (!) of the body (!), the divine Logos being head over the immortal souls. In this connection texts are often discussed in which the "world" is regarded as a "body" (e.g. Philo, *Noah's Work* 7), but an unprejudiced view can hardly see any connection between them and Colossians 1. (For a different view, cf. Eduard Schweizer, "σῶμα" *TDNT*, 7:1051-56, 1066.) Further:

803. Colossians 1:18

Philo, "On Rewards and Punishments" 125 (15 BCE–50 CE)

. . . For as in an animal the head is the first and best part and the tail the last and meanest, and in fact not a part which helps to complete the list of members, but a means of swishing off the winged creatures which settle on it, so too he means that the virtuous one, whether single man or people, will be the head of the human race and all the others like the limbs of a body which draw their life from the forces in the head and at the top. (LCL)

Philo attributes a similar function to the head in "Questions Genesis," 2.9 (the human being is a kind of head among the living creatures; when humanity goes wrong, the other creatures go wrong too; sympathy between head and body).

On Colossians 1:19, Ephesians 1:23 (Fullness), cf. nos. 870, 911.

804. Colossians 2:6-19

Inscription from Giaur-Köi in Asia Minor (2 cent. CE)

In Amisos, the free, autonomous city contractually related to Rome. Under the rule of Apollo . . . there came—in order to seek a revelation from the gods—Crispus Tryphon and Poplius Pupius Callacles, who underwent an initiation and walked within the inner holy place [μυηθέντες ἐνεβάτευσαν]. (MEB/from Dittenberger, Ed., *Orientis Graeci: Inscriptiones Selectae* [Hildesheim: Georg Olms–Verlagsbuchhandlung, 1960], 192-94)

The portrayal of the Colossian opponent's position culminates in 2:18, which speaks of angel worship in the context of visionary experiences and the key word ἐμβατεύω is named. One can attempt to interpret this word in terms of the material given here, and then will arrive at the conclusion that the opponents in Colossae advocated a kind of Jewish mysticism (cf. in K. Berger, "Die implitizen Gegner," *Kirche*. Ed. D. Lührmann and G. Strecker [Tübingen: J. C. B. Mohr (Paul Siebeck)], 1984, 390-91):

In order to clarify this passage Dittenberger refers to Tacitus, *Annals* 2.54: Germanicus inquires of the oracle of Apollo Clarius: A priest climbs down into a cave, draws water from the holy spring, and gives the oracle. Dittenberger thinks of a cave as the setting for what is described in this inscription.

Martin Dibelius interpreted the verb ἐμβατεύω as "walking in the inner holy place [of the temple] under divine protection." The word is found elsewhere in initiation exercises into the mysteries.

It is also possible—and the references to angels in the context would point to this—that the passage deals with entrance into the heavenly holy place; cf. *3 Enoch* 43:2: "He bore me up with him, and taking me by his hand, he led me to the throne of glory and showed me those souls which have already been created and have returned" (*OTP* 1:294).

Cf. also M. Dibelius, "Die Isis-Weihe bei Apuleius und verwandte Riten," in *Botschaft und Geschichte* II (Tübingen: J. C. B. Mohr, 1956), 56-62.

805. Colossians 2:6-19

Kerygma Petrou according to Clement of Alexandria, *Stromata* 6.5.41 (2–3 cent. CE)

Neither worship as the Jews; for they, thinking that they only know God, do not know Him, adoring [λατρεύω] as they do angels and archangels, the month and the moon. And if the moon be not visible, they do not hold the Sabbath, which is called the first; nor do they hold the new moon, nor the feast of unleavened bread, nor the feast, nor the great day. (ANF)

The special focus of some Jewish groups on the calendar as illustrated in *Jubilees* and *1 Enoch* (cf. K. Berger, "Einleitung" *Das Buch der Jubiläen* JSHRZ II 3 [Gütersloh: Gerd Mohn, 1981], 283-84, 296) leads to the charge that they worship astral deities. The *Kerygma Petrou*, identifies this (probably only in part correctly) with the significance attributed to doctrines of angels and the invocation of the names of angels. Following Judges 13:17, revelatory angels were often asked about their names, so that they could be cultically venerated (Josephus, *Antiquities* 5.281: thanksgiving and gift; *T. Levi* 5.5-6; *Jos. Asen.* 15:12: praise and honor). On the other hand, angels frequently refuse such praise (e.g. Rev 19:10; 22:8). Obviously the idea of cultic worship of angels was in the atmosphere in Asia Minor, and was a disputed point (cf. A. R. R. Sheppard, "Pagan Cults of Angels in Roman Asia Minor," *Talanta* 12-13 [1980-81], 77-101). The dispute had to do with the status of the messenger (the Christology of the Fourth Gospel is related to this dispute), and the issue was, "Is God present in the messenger in such a way that God can be worshiped through the messenger?" The connection with the calendar comes about through the idea that angels had been made responsible for the regular functioning of the world (cf. no. 639).

One could imagine that angel worship was based on yet another idea: Plutarch, "Isis and Osiris,"

76: one can worship the divine through the beings of nature gifted with souls, not that they themselves are gods, but they are the most natural and appropriate mirrors and agents of the divine reality that orders the universe.

On Colossians 2:8, cf. no. 799 on Philippians 4:11-13. On Colossians 2:12, cf. nos. 382, 410, 843. On Colossians 2:16, cf. no. 500. On Colossians 2:16, 20, cf. no. 778.

806. Colossians 2:18

Inscriptions from Claros (2 cent. CE)

Two delegates, having been initiated and having entered, consulted the oracle.
Two others came who, having been initiated, entered [ἐμβατεύω].
A delegate completed the mystery.
A delegate completed the mystery.
A delegate completed the mystery.
Certain delegates [who were ini]tiated and ent[ered, (ἐμβατεύω)
consulted . . .] . . . the oracle
Another delegate, having received the mystery, entered [ἐμβατεύω].
Those present with a delegate were initiated, he being initiated with them. (Francis)

The translation and meaning of the key phrase in Colossians is disputed. Ἁ ἑόρακεν ἐμβατεύων could mean "things he saw when he was initiated," i.e. visionary experiences during mystery rites (so e.g. Eduard Lohse, *A Commentary on the Epistles to the Colossians and to Philemon* [Hermeneia. Philadelphia: Fortress, 1971], 118-21). ἐμβατεύω is indeed found in this context in the sanctuary of Apollo at Claros. This interpretation is also disputed (cf. e.g. Fred O. Francis, "Humility and Angelic Worship in Col. 2:18," *ST* 16 [1962], 109-34; "The Background of *embateuein* [Col 2:18] in legal papyri and oracle inscriptions," in Francis and Meeks, eds., *Conflict at Colossae: A Problem in the Interpretation of Early Christianity Illustrated by Selected Modern Studies* [Sources for Biblical Study 4. Missoula, Mont.: Society of Biblical Literature, 1973], 197-208).

807. Colossians 2:18

Plutarch, *Moralia*, "The Roman Questions" 10 (45–125 CE)

. . . But they thus worshiped the gods, either humbling [ταπεινοῦντες] themselves by concealing the head, or rather by pulling the toga over their ears as a precaution lest any ill-omened and baleful sound from without should reach them while they were praying.

. . . the Spirit within us entreats and supplicates the god without, and thus he symbolizes by the covering of the head the covering and concealment of the soul by the body. (LCL)

Cf. no. 681 above.

One way to understand Paul's discussion of the Christian's relation to angels in 1 Corinthians 11 (in regard to prayer and prophecy) could be understood in the context of invoking angels in worship as self-abasement before them. Thus Colossians 2 rejects in general what Paul commends for the particular case of 1 Corinthians 11. On Colossians 3:11, cf. no. 774.

808. Colossians 3:16/ Ephesians 5:19

Corpus Hermeticum 13:15 (2–4 cent. CE)

[Dialogue between Tat and Hermes:] *Tat:* "Father, I would like to hear the praise in the hymn which you said I should hear from the powers once I had entered the ogdoad, just as Poimandres foretold of the ogdoad."

Hermes: "That you hasten to strike the tent is good, child, for you have been purified. Poimandres, the mind of sovereignty, has transmitted to me no more than has been written down, knowing that on my own I would be able to understand everything, to hear what I want and to see everything, and he entrusted it to me to make something beautiful of it. Thus, the powers within me sing in all things as well." (Copenhaver)

The beginning emphasizes that the song of praise is not from Poimandres, but it is rather Hermes Trismegistes himself through whom the powers that dwell in him are mediated. The elements "through" which the man calls out are the organs of his own body.

Cf. further, no. 701 above.

809. Colossians 3:18–4:1

Aristotle, *Politics* 1.2.1-4 (384–322 BCE)

And now that it is clear what are the component parts of the state, we have first of all to discuss household management; for every state is composed of households. Household management falls into departments corresponding to the parts of which the household in its turn is composed; and the household in its perfect form consists of slaves and freemen. The investigation of everything should begin with its smallest parts, and the primary and smallest parts of the household are master and slave, husband and wife, father and children; we ought therefore to examine the proper constitution and character of each of these three relationships, I mean that of mastership, that of marriage (there is no exact term denoting the relation uniting wife and husband), and thirdly the progenitive relationship (this too has not been designated by a special name). Let us then accept these three relationships that we have mentioned. There is also a department which some people consider the same as household management and others the most important part of it, and the true position of which we shall have to consider: I mean what is called the art of getting wealth.

Let us begin by discussing the relation of master and slave, in order to observe the facts that have a bearing on practical utility, and also in the hope that we may be able to obtain something better than the notions at present entertained, with a view to the theoretic knowledge of the subject. For some thinkers hold the function of the master to be a definite science, and moreover think that household management, mastership, and statesmanship and monarchy are the same thing, as we said at the beginning of the treatise; others however maintain that for one man to be another man's master is contrary to nature, because it is only convention that makes the one a slave and the other a freeman and there is no difference between them by nature, and that therefore it is unjust, for it is based on force.

Since therefore property is a part of a household and the art of acquiring property a part of household management (for without the necessities even life, as well as the good life, is impossible), and since, just as for the definite arts it would be necessary for the proper tools to be forthcoming if their work is to be accomplished, so also the management of a household must have his tools and of tools some are lifeless and others living (for example, for a helmsman the rudder is a lifeless tool and the look-out man a live tool—for an assistant in the arts belongs to the class of tools), so also an article of property is a tool for the purpose of life, and property generally is a collection of tools, and a slave is a live article of property. (LCL)

This text from Aristotle is fundamental for consideration of thinking about household codes in the Hellenistic world, especially illuminating on the spectrum of views on slavery. For Philo's description of the Essenes as a community that repudiated slavery, see no. 30 on Matthew 5–7.

On the status of women in the household hierarchy, cf. Livy, *History* 34.1.12 (59 or 64 BCE–12 or 17 CE): "Never, while their men survive, is feminine subjection shaken off; and they themselves abhor the freedom which the loss of husbands and fathers produces" (LCL).

This was one expression of the Roman ideal, from one (male) point of view. While "subjection" would be a typical characterization of woman's status in society (cf. Rom 7:2, where "married" translates ὕπανδρος, lit. "subject to [her] man"), generalizations about the status of women in the New Testament era should be avoided. A spectrum of conditions and attitudes on the role of women in the family existed. Apollodorus (ca. 350 BCE) represents an earlier Greek view still represented in some first-century situations: "We have courtesans [ἑταῖραι] for pleasure, handmaidens for the day-to-day care of the body, wives to bear legitimate children and to be a trusted guardian of things in the house" (quoted in Pseudo-Demosthenes 59.122). The Roman period and tradition brought a generally higher status to women, who gradually attained more and more liberty, influence, and legal status during the time of earliest Christianity (C. T. Seltman, *Women in Antiquity* [New York: St. Martin's Press, 1956], 174). The Jewish tradition, which generally located the status of women between those indicated by Apollodorus and Livy, was also a factor in the development of women's role in the church.

For additional Hellenistic texts related to household codes, see nos. 890-95 on 1 Peter 2:13–3:7.

810. Colossians 3:18–4:1

P. Oxy. 744 (1 cent. BCE)

I beg and entreat you, take care of the little one, and as soon as we receive our pay I will send it up to you. If by chance you bear a child, if it is a boy, let it be, if it is a girl, expose it. (LCL)

This brief note from Hilarion, absent on military duty in Alexandria, to his wife Alis in the interior of Egypt, illustrates the authority of the father over both wife and children, as well as the higher value placed on sons. The former is reflected in the New Testament, but not the latter. This text, which seems exceedingly cruel to us, reflects a different perspective on the disputed issue of when new life is considered to be a person, a human being. Whereas in our culture the debate has centered on the options of the moment of conception, or when the fetus is able to live outside the womb, or the moment of birth, the Hellenistic world extended the time to the moment of being accepted into society, which happened when the father acknowledged the child as his own and formally received it into the family. Exposure of unwanted infants was not regarded as murder because the baby was not yet considered a person. The decision lay in the hands of the father. Judaism opposed both abortion and exposure of infants; the Hellenistic world generally accepted both.

811. Colossians 3:18/ Ephesians 5:22-33

Musonius Rufus, "What Is the Chief End of Marriage?" 10-20 (30–100 CE)

[That the primary end of marriage is community of life with a view to the procreation of children] The husband and wife, he used to say, should come together for the purpose of making a life in common and of procreating children, and furthermore of regarding all things in common between them, and nothing peculiar or private to one or the other, not even their own bodies.·

. . . in marriage there must be above all perfect companionship and mutual love of husband and wife, both in health and in sickness and under all conditions, since it was with desire for this as well as for having children that both entered upon marriage. (Lutz)

[So also Musonius Rufus, "Is Marriage a Handicap for the Pursuit of Philosophy?" 1-9:] One could find no other association more necessary nor more pleasant than that of men and women. For what man is so devoted to his friend as a loving wife is to her husband? What brother to a brother? What son to his parents? Who is so longed for when absent as a husband by his wife, or a wife by her husband? Whose presence would do more to lighten grief or increase joy or remedy misfortune? To whom is everything judged to be common, body, soul, and possessions, except man and wife? For these reasons all men consider the love of man and wife to be the highest form of love. . . . (Lutz)

In view of Ephesians 5:28-29, 33, it is striking how often contemporary tractates emphasize the communion of souls between husbands and wives. In Ephesians the manner of expression is less developed and refined, interest being focused more on the theological picture. On tendencies toward the equality of women and men in the imperial period, cf. K. Thraede, "Zum historischen Hintergrund der 'Haustafeln' des NT," in *Pietas*, Festschrift for B. Kötting, *JAC* Supplementary vol. 8 (Munich: Aschendorff, 1980), 359-68. Cf. also the Regina inscription, no. 443 above. Further: no. 772.

812. 1 Thessalonians 1:6

Plutarch, *Moralia*, "How a Man May Become Aware of His Progress in Virtue" 14 (45–125 CE)

Furthermore, as has already been said, the translating of our judgments into deeds, and not allowing our word to remain mere words, but to make them into actions, is, above all else, a specific mark of progress. An indication of this is, in the first place, the desire to emulate what we commend, eagerness to do what we admire, and, on the other hand, unwillingness to do, or even to tolerate, what we censure.

We must therefore believe we are making but little progress so long as the admiration which we feel for successful men remains inert within us and does not of its own self stir us to imitation.

. . . the man who is truly making progress . . . is ready in the words of Simonides
"To run like a weanling colt beside its dam,"
so great is his craving all but to merge his own identity in that of the good man. (LCL)

The Hellenistic ethic is largely oriented to the imitation of human examples. In a different manner this orientation is also a common denominator of the Gospels and the Letters of Paul. This concept is foreign to the Old Testament, and is especially true with regard to the idea of imitating God. This picture is unchanged until the intertestamental literature.

813. 1 Thessalonians 1:10

Sibylline Oracles 3.555-62 (140 BCE)

But when the wrath of the great God comes [lit. "is"] upon you, then indeed you will recognize the face of the great God. All the souls of men will groan mightily and stretch out their hands straight to broad heaven and begin to call on the deliverer [ῥυστήρ] from great wrath. (*OTP* 1:374)

The subject of both texts is deliverance from the coming wrath of God by God himself, i.e. the deliverance comes from heaven (cf. also Rom 5:9-10). What according to *Sib. Or.* 3 human beings can only hope and pray for, is for Paul already a matter of certainty through the Resurrected One and his call. This is the classic difference between Judaism and Christianity.

Comparable with *Sib. Or.* 3 is the Oracle of Hystaspes as reported by Lactantius (beginning of 4 cent. CE), *Divine Institutions* 7.18: "For Hystaspes, whom I have named above, having described the iniquity of this last time, says that the pious and faithful, being separated from the wicked, will stretch forth their hands to heaven with weeping and mourning, and will implore the protection of Jupiter: that Jupiter will look to the earth, and hear the voices of men, and will destroy the wicked. All which things are true except one, that he attributed to Jupiter those things which God will do. But that also was withdrawn from the account, not without fraud on the part of the demons, viz., that the son of God would then be sent, who having destroyed all the wicked, would set at liberty the pious." (ANF)

814. 1 Thessalonians 2:5-6

Aelius Aristides, *Discourses* 4 (117–187 CE)

[Description of a hypocritical Cynic:] For these are the men who believe that shame-lessness is freedom, that to be hated is to speak freely, and that to take is to be generous. They have achieved such wisdom, that they do not exact money, but they know how to take gifts which are the equivalent of money. And if ever someone appears to have sent too little, they always remain firm in their resolve. But if the wallet appears rather heavy to them, Perseus always conquers the Gorgon (through an even more grim look), until a greater sum is forced upon them. (Behr)

Cf. also Lucian on Christian cheats, no. 230 above.

Contrast the picture of the true Cynic in the letter of Diogenes, §38: "Because of this some gave me money, others things worth money, and many invited me to dinner. But I took from moderate people what was suitable to nature, but from the worthless I accepted nothing. And from those who felt gratitude toward me for accepting the first time, I accepted again as well; but never again from those who did not feel thankful" (Malherbe).

815. 1 Thessalonians 2:15

Tacitus, *Histories*, 5.5 (55–120 CE)

. . . again, the Jews are extremely loyal toward one another, and always ready to show compassion, but toward every other people they feel only hate and enmity. They sit apart at meals, and they sleep apart, and although as a race, they are prone to lust, they abstain from intercourse with foreign women; yet among themselves nothing is unlawful. They adopted circumcision to distinguish themselves from other peoples by this difference. Those who are converted to their ways follow the same practice, and the earliest lesson they receive is to despise the gods, to disown their country, and to regard their parents, children, and brothers as of little account. (LCL)

Somewhat similarly Philostratus, *Life of Apollonius*, 5.33: "For the Jews have long been in revolt not only against the Romans, but against humanity; and a race that has made its own a life apart and irreconcilable, that cannot share with the rest of mankind in the pleasures of the table nor join in their libations or prayers or sacrifices, are separated from ourselves by a greater gulf than divides us from Susa or Bactra or the more distant Indies" (LCL). Cf. also Josephus, *Apion* 2.121, 148, refuting the charges of Apollonius Molon and Apion that Jews are as a race hostile to the rest of humanity; Diodorus Siculus 34.1, *Universal History;* Libanius of Antioch, *Epistles* 998.2, 1007.2; Tacitus, *History* 5.5.1-2.

The Jews are frequently described as "unholy" (ἀνόσιος). Paul is thus here adopting traditional elements of ancient anti-Jewish polemic. (So Berger; Colpe considers the passage a non-Pauline interpolation.) It might be asked to what extent something analogous is found elsewhere as the prophetic style. Cf. also no. 755. On ancient anti-Semitism cf. also M. Stern, *Greek and Latin Authors on Jews and Judaism* I-III (Jerusalem: Israel Academy of Sciences and Humanities, 1976–1984); C. Colpe, "Antisemitismus" in *Der Kleine Pauly* I (München: GmbH, 1979), cols. 400-402; and Hans Conzelmann, *Gentiles/Jews/Christians: Polemics and Apologetics in the Greco-Roman Era* (Minneapolis: Fortress Press, 1992).

On 1 Thessalonians 2:19 (parousia), cf. no. 338. On 1 Thessalonians 4:5-7, cf. no. 730.

816. 1 Thessalonians 2:15-16

1QM 4.2 (1 cent. BCE)

On the standard of the Thousand they shall write, *The Wrath of God* is kindled against Satan and against the Men of his Company, leaving no Remnant, together with the name of the chief of the Thousand and the names of the leaders of its Hundreds. (Vermes)

This is one of several instances in the Dead Sea Scrolls (cf. 1QM 4.1-2; 1QS 2.15-17; 4.13-14; 5.12-13) in which a Jewish community that saw itself as the renewed eschatological Israel declared that the wrath of God has come upon other Jews not in the eschatological remnant, and that this wrath is "to the uttermost" (עד כלותם, also translated "without remainder," "completely," or "forever"). For several reasons, 1 Thessalonians 2:15-16 has sometimes been taken to be a later interpolation. Two of these have now been eliminated by the Qumran texts: (1) The verb in 1QM 3.9 is in the perfect tense, though the expectation is for the eschatological future (the "prophetic perfect"). Thus the ἔφθασεν of 1 Thessalonians need not point or look back to the Jewish war and the destruction of Jerusalem. (2) It can no longer be claimed that 1 Thessalonians 2:15-16 must have been written by a Gentile, for the Qumran texts show that the pronouncing of the ultimate wrath of God upon (other) Jews can be a purely Jewish dictum. (See H.-W. Kuhn, "Die Bedeutung der Qumrantexte für das Verständnis des Ersten Thessalonicherbriefes," in *The Madrid Qumran Congress: Proceedings of the International Congress on the Dead Sea Scrolls Madrid 18-21 March, 1991* [Leiden: E. J. Brill, 1992], 344-46).

817. 1 Thessalonians 4:6*b*

Letter of Diogenes 45 (1 cent. BCE–3 cent. CE)

[To Perdiccas:] Be ashamed at the threats you wrote me. . . . You threaten to kill me—the threat of an insect! Nor are you aware that if you do this you in turn will suffer. For there is someone who cares about you, and he exacts equal satisfaction for such deeds from those who initiate unjust actions. From the living it's a single penalty, but from the dead tenfold. I write this not out of fear of your threats, but wishing that you not do anything wrong on my account. (Malherbe)

The horizon of this concept of retribution is possibly the doctrine of providence (πρόνοια). As in early Judaism, retribution is in the hand of a personal God. As in Mark 10:29-30, there is double retribution (see above no. 147), in the present life and in the life after death. What is lacking here is an eschatological conception.

818. 1 Thessalonians 4:9

Homer, *Iliad* 304-8 (prior to 7 cent. BCE)

And his father drew nigh and gave counsel to him for his profit—a wise man to one that himself had knowledge. "Antilochus, for all thou art young, yet have Zeus and Poseidon loved thee and taught thee all manner of horsemanship; wherefore to teach thee is no great need, for thou knowest well how to wheel about the turnpost." (LCL)

Achilles had offered a prize for the best driver in a chariot race. Antilochus is encouraged by his father with words that may have been current in the Hellenistic world, echoed by Paul, and recognized by his readers—though of course communicating a different content. The idea that one is taught by the deity is also found in Homer, *Odyssey* 22.343-49: "By thy knees I beseech thee, Odysseus, and do thou respect me and have pity; on thine own self shall sorrow come hereafter, if thou slayest the minstrel, even me, who sing to gods and men. Self-taught am I, and the god has planted in my heart all manner of lays, and worthy am I to sing to thee as to a god . . ." (LCL). The latter passage is cited and elaborated by Aelius Aristides, "To Plato, in Defense of Oratory," 2.92.

819. 1 Thessalonians 4:13

Tomb Inscription from Thessalonica *CIG* 1973

. . . for this woman had this surname/nickname, while she was still among the living. Because of her special disposition and good sense [σωφροσύνη] her devoted husband Eutropos created this tomb for her and also for himself, in order that later he would have a place to rest together with his dear wife, when he looks upon the end of life that has been spun out for him by the indissoluble threads of the Fates. (MEB/from Augustus Boeckhius, ed., *Corpus Inscriptionum Graecarum* [Hildesheim and New York: Georg Olms Verlag, 1977], 56)

This inscription is one of many from Thessalonica (!) that illustrate how little expectation for a life after death existed among the Gentile population. Being together with one's partner in marriage in the grave is the final expectation, which for Paul was replaced by being together with other resurrected ones with Christ. Differently, no. 443.

820. 1 Thessalonians 4:13-18

Letter of Irene, an Egyptian woman, to a grieving family, P. Oxy. 1. no. 115 (2 cent. CE)

Irene to Taonnophris and Philo good comfort.

I am as sorry and weep over the departed one as I wept for Didymas. And all things, whatsoever were fitting, I have done, and all mine, Epaphroditus and Thermuthion and Philion and Apollonius and Plantas. But, nevertheless, against such things one can do nothing. Therefore comfort ye one another. Fare ye well. Athyr 1. (= October 28) (Deissmann)

Deissmann comments: "Personal suffering had made her more sympathetic for the troubles of others. . . . But after these painfully written lines full of names, her true feeling breaks through, that of hopeless resignation, that speaks of unavoidable fate. And then illogically, in conclusion the request, 'comfort each other.' Who could deny sympathy to this helpless woman, whose own feelings are certainly genuine?" (p. 176). For a discussion of ancient consolation literature and 1 Thessalonians, see Juan Chapa, "Is First Thessalonians a Letter of Consolation?" *NTS* 40 (1994) 150-60, with bibliography.

821. 1 Thessalonians 4:13-18

4 Ezra 5:41-42 (late 1 cent. CE)

I said, "Yet, O Lord, you have charge of those who are alive at the end, but what will those do who lived before me, or we, ourselves, or those who come after us?"

He said to me, "I shall liken my judgment to a circle, just as for those who are last there is no slowness, so for those who are first there is no haste." (NRSV)

The meaning here is that no one will be first and no one will be the last to be named, for the judgment strikes all equally. As in a circle every point is equidistant from the center, none being further away and none being nearer, so in the context of the Last Judgment whether one lived one's life early or late in the world's history plays no role. The author of 4 Ezra handles the same problem as Paul in 1 Thessalonians 4, but uses other means. In both authors, the issue is the possible advantage that those of the last generation may have. Both dispute that they have any such advantage, the author of 4 Ezra using the image of a circle, while Paul is using the schema of the resurrection preceding the common exaltation to heaven with those of the last generation still alive at the parousia. Paul thinks concretely, while 4 Ezra argues in terms of abstract principle. On the manner in which this is realized, see no. 896. Further:

822. 1 Thessalonians 4:13-18

4 Ezra 13:16-24 (late 1 cent. CE)

Then I woke up in great terror, and prayed to the Most High, and said, "From the beginning you have shown your servant these wonders, and have deemed me worthy to have my prayer heard by you; now show me the interpretation of this dream also. For as I consider it in my mind, alas for those who will be left in those days! And still more, alas for those who are not left! For those who are not left will be sad because they understand the things that are reserved for the last days, but cannot attain them. But alas for those also who are left, and for that very reason! For they shall see great dangers and much distress, as these dreams show. Yet it is better to come into these things, though incurring peril, than to pass from the world like a cloud, and not to see what will happen in the last days." He answered me and said, "I will tell you the interpretation of the vision, and I will also explain to you the things that you have mentioned. As for what you said about those who survive, and concerning those who do not survive, this is the interpretation: The one who brings the peril at that time will protect those who fall into peril, who have works and faith toward the Almighty. Understand therefore that those who are left are more blessed than those who have died." (NRSV)

The problems of the church in Thessalonica with the question of what will happen to those who had already died could have originated as a response to Paul's preaching, if it had been something like: "The Messiah has come. We are the Messianic generation. He is coming back soon." For the Messianic generation—in our text "those who are left," the same word used by Paul—is in many texts regarded as the specially favored generation.
Cf. *Psalms of Solomon* 17:44; 18:5-6
"Blessed are those born in those days
to see the good fortune of Israel
which God will bring to pass in the assembly of the tribes."
"May God cleanse Israel for the day of mercy in blessing,
for the appointed day when his Messiah will reign.
Blessed are those born in those days,
to see the good things of the Lord

which he will do for the coming generation" (*OTP* 2:669).

Sirach 48:11: "Happy are those who will live in those days and who will be permitted to see the salvation of the Lord." (MEB/Berger; cf. NRSV, "Happy are those who saw you and were adorned with your love! For we also shall surely live," with note that text and meaning are uncertain.)

Sibylline Oracles 4.187-92: "But as many as are pious, they will live on earth again when God gives spirit and life and favor to these pious ones. Then they will all see themselves beholding the delightful and pleasant light of the sun. Oh most blessed, whatever man will live to that time" (*OTP* 1:389).

823. 1 Thessalonians 5:4-9

1QS 3.13-15, 20-21; 4:18-19, 22-23 (1 cent. BCE)

The Master shall instruct all the sons of light and shall teach them the nature of all the children of men according to the kind of spirit which they possess, the signs identifying their works during their lifetime, their visitation for chastisement, and the time of their reward . . .

He has created man to govern the world, and has appointed for him two spirits in which to walk until the time of His visitation: the spirits of truth and falsehood. Those born of truth spring from a fountain of light, but those born of falsehood spring from a source of darkness. All the children of righteousness are ruled by the Prince of Light and walk in the ways of light, but all the children of falsehood are ruled by the Angel of Darkness and walk in the ways of darkness. (Vermes)

The expression "children of light" is not found in the Hebrew Bible, and is practically nonexistent in the literature of early Judaism except for the Qumran MSS, where it occurs several times as a self-description of the members of the sect. Paul not only uses "children of light" as a description for Christians, he also places the whole discussion within the dualistic light/darkness framework as at Qumran, and speaks in this passage of a divine predestination of believers and of an arming of Christians for the eschatological spiritual battle, both of which are Qumran themes. Thus Hans-Wolfgang Kuhn, who is preparing a commentary on the New Testament as illuminated by the Qumran texts, considers this number one in his "top ten" examples of a Qumran "parallel" to a Pauline passage (in "Impact of the Qumran Scrolls," 328-29). "Children/son of light" is also found in the New Testament in John 12:35-36; Ephesians 5:8; Luke 16:8. Kuhn does not posit any direct connection between Qumran and the NT authors, but in view of the numerous striking parallels, argues that it is clear there were indirect points of contact and influence.

824. 2 Thessalonians 2:2

Hippolytus of Rome, *Commentary on Daniel 4*, 19 (235 CE)

There was a similar story about a person in Pontus, who also was a leader in the church, a pious and humble man, but did not hold strictly to the Scriptures, believing more in the visions that he himself had seen. For after he had received a first, second, and third dream-vision, he began to address the brothers and sisters in the congregation as though he were a prophet: "Here is what I saw, and here is what will happen." He once made a clearly erroneous prophecy, when he announced "Recognize it, brothers and sisters, that the Judgment will happen in one more year." They heard him as he said that the Day of the Lord is near [ἐνέστηκεν ἡ ἡμέρα τοῦ κυρίου], and prayed to the Lord day and night with crying and lamentation, always having the coming judgment before their eyes. So he led the brothers and sisters to such great anxiety and fearfulness that they let their farms and fields lie idle, and most sold their possessions. He then said to them, "If what I have predicted does not happen, then do not believe the Scriptures any longer, but each of you do as you wish." They were in expectation of what was to come. As a year went by, and none of the things predicted in fact came to pass, he himself was ashamed that he had lied, but the Scriptures had turned out to be true. Those members of the church who had believed him were angry, but they returned to their normal lives, their virgins getting married and their men returning to work in the fields. But those who had vainly sold their possessions were found to be beggars for their daily bread. (MEB/Berger)

The key sentence is almost identical with 2 Thessalonians 2:2, just as the bad circumstances of 3:10-11 are pictured here in a similar fashion. Yet 2 Thessalonians 2 reports nothing of disappointed expectations, as Hippolytus does. The text is one of several examples of intensified near expectation of the End in the second century. By its concreteness, it illustrates what is only hinted at in 2 Thessalonians. In place of the fictive letter of Paul, here we have the appeal to visions, which were apparently authentic apocalyptic experiences.

825. 2 Thessalonians 2:3-4

Ascension of Isaiah 4:2-3 (1 cent. CE)

Beliar . . . the king of the world . . . will come down from his firmament in the form of a man, a lawless king, who murders his mother, who himself, this king, will persecute the plant that the twelve apostles of the Beloved have planted. And one of the twelve will be delivered into his hand. (Schneemelcher)

The "king" is transparently Nero. "One of the twelve" is Peter, here understood to have perished in the Neronian persecution. That Nero is identified as the "lawless one" and the incarnation of Beliar (Satan) interprets him as the eschatological opponent of God, as in Revelation 13 and passim.

826. 2 Thessalonians 2:4

Josephus, *Jewish Wars* 2.184-86, 192-97 (37-100 CE)

The insolence with which the emperor Gaius defied fortune surpassed all bounds: he wished to be considered a god and to be hailed as such, he cut off the flower of the nobility of his country, and his impiety extended even to Judea. In fact, he sent Petronius with an army to Jerusalem to install in the sanctuary statues of himself; in the event of the Jews refusing to admit them, his orders were to put the recalcitrants to death and to reduce the whole nation to slavery. But these orders, as the sequel shows, were under God's care.

Petronius accordingly with three legions and a large contingent of Syrian auxiliaries, left Antioch on the march for Judea. . . . alarm soon became universal . . .

The Jews assembled with their wives and children in the plain of Ptolemais and implored Petronius to have regard first for the laws of their fathers, and next for themselves. Yielding so far to this vast multitude and their entreaties, he left the statues and his troops at Ptolemais and advanced into Galilee, where he summoned the people, with all persons of distinction, to Tiberias. . . . The Jews replied that they offered sacrifice twice daily for Caesar and the Roman people, but that if he wished to set up these statues, he must first sacrifice the entire Jewish nation; and that they presented themselves, their wives and their children, ready for the slaughter. (LCL)

As Josephus is happy to report, Caligula's opportune death lifted the threat and resolved the situation. The text illustrates both an emperor's taking his own deity seriously and the depth of Jewish revulsion at the idea of a representation of a pagan god being set up in their temple. This image imprinted itself on the Jewish consciousness, and may have influenced the traditions behind 2 Thessalonians 2, Mark 13, and other apocalyptic traditions.

For further vivid descriptions of the impact Gaius' decree had for Jews, cf. Philo, *Embassy to Gaius* 186-89, and 263-68.

827. 2 Thessalonians 2:6-7

1Q 27:1, *The Triumph of Righteousness* (2 cent. BCE)

. . . the mysteries of sin. . . . They know not the mystery to come, nor do they understand the things of the past. They know not that which shall befall them, nor do they save their soul from the mystery to come.

And this shall be the sign for you that these things shall come to pass.

When the breed of iniquity is shut up, wickedness shall then be banished by righteousness as darkness is banished by the light. As smoke clears and is no more, so shall wickedness perish for ever and righteousness be revealed like a sun governing the world. All who cleave to the mysteries of sin shall be no more; knowledge shall fill the world and folly shall exist no longer.

This word shall surely come to pass; this prophecy is true. And by this may it be known to you that it shall not be taken back. (Vermes)

In 1Q 27 the evil people hold back the decrease of evil, while in 2 Thessalonians 2 someone or something holds back the revelation of evil that is now already at work. In 2 Thessalonians the subject is not the hindering of evil itself, but rather the hindering of its revelation, for according to 2 Thessalonians the evil at work at present does not yet have anything to do with the temple in Jerusalem. The background is thus formed by the understanding of the structure of the predetermined temporal phases: so long as one phase lasts, it hinders the advent of the next phase. In both texts the "restrainer" is obviously a "strong" ("compact") figure.

Also in 4 Ezra 4:38-39 there is the unexpressed idea of the restraining power. In the background there certainly stands the idea of the fixed number of the righteous which must be completed if the End is to come. Thus Ezra ponders whether it might be because of the sins of the present generation that the harvest of the righteous must be postponed.

Pseudo-Philo, *LAB* 51:5 is also concerned with this issue (1 cent. BCE or CE):

"And when the wicked have died, then they will perish.
And when the just go to sleep, then they will be freed.
Now so will every judgment endure,
until he who restrains will be revealed"
(*OTP* 2:366).
Is the subject here, in contrast to 2 Thessalonians, the revelation of God himself? Will God confirm the present judgments?
On 2 Thessalonians 2:8-12, cf. nos. 175, 400, 531, 912-15, 958.

828. 1 Timothy 1:9

Sentence of Antiphanes (408/405–334/331 BCE)

The one who does no wrong is in no need of law. (MEB/from Stobaeus, *Anthologium* vol. 3)

Cf. similarly no. 540; Menander of Carchedon, "Wherever good is found, it is better than the law" (MEB/from Stobaeus, *Anthologium* vol. 3); and Philo, "Allegorical Interpretation" 1.94: "There is no need, then, to give injunctions or prohibitions or exhortations to the perfect man formed after the [Divine] image, for none of these does the perfect man require" (LCL).

829. 1 Timothy 1:10; 6:3/ 2 Timothy 4:3/ Titus 1:9; 2:1-8

Maximus of Tyre, *Discourses* 16:3 (125–185 CE)

[Anaxagoras speaks:] Truth and healthy understanding and morality and knowledge of the law and right cannot be acquired in any other way than by actually doing them, just as one can never learn the craft of shoemaking unless one actually works at it. (MEB/Berger)

In the Pastoral Letters, truth is also synonymous with spiritual health. Maximus of Tyre here and elsewhere points to the practical, everyday dimension of "philosophy," for which he chooses appropriate metaphors. On the value of *practice* at practical matters, cf. e.g. 1 Timothy 4:7-8.

830. 1 Timothy 1:17

Diogenes Laertius, *Lives of Eminent Philosophers*, "Epicurus" 10.123 (342–271 BCE)

First believe that God is a living being immortal and blessed, according to the notion of a god indicated by the common sense of mankind; and so believing, thou shalt not affirm of him aught that is foreign to his immortality or that agrees not with blessedness, but shalt believe about him whatever may uphold both his blessedness and his immortality. (LCL)

Predicates of the deity of this sort are of Hellenistic origin and are found in Jewish circles only after the LXX translation became current. Does the above represent a fixed liturgical language? This kind of language for the deity could be used at the same time in the sphere of the cult, in mysticism, and by philosophers.

831. 1 Timothy 2:1-2

Aelius Aristides, *Discourses* 46, "The Isthmian Oration: Regarding Poseidon" 42 (117–187 CE)

It remains for each of us to go to our respective duties after a prayer to Poseidon, Amphitrite, Leucothea, Palaemon, the Nereids, and all the gods and goddesses of the sea, to grant safety and preservation on land and sea to the great Emperor, to his whole family, and to the Greek race, and to us to thrive in oratory and in other respects as well. (Behr)

In Judaism the custom of praying for the emperor was adapted from Persian models. Cf. Herodotus, *The Histories*, Book 1, 132: "To pray for blessings for himself alone is not lawful for the sacrificer; rather he prays that it may be well with the king and all the Persians" (LCL).

Cf. LXX, Ezra 6:9-10. For Egyptian Jews cf. the stone from Schedia (ca. 250 BCE): "For the king Ptolemy and the queen Bernice, his sister and wife, and the children, this house of prayer [was built]" (MEB/Berger).

On 1 Timothy 2:8, cf. no. 118.

832. 1 Timothy 2:8-11

Statutes of Society of Iobacchi, Inscription from Attica (178 CE)

No one may either sing or create a disturbance or applaud at the gatherings, but each shall say and act his allotted part with all good order and quietness under the direction of the priest or the arch-bacchus. No Iobacchus who has not paid his contributions for the monthly and anniversary meetings shall enter the meeting until the priests have decided either that he must pay or that he may be admitted. . . . And no one shall deliver a speech without the leave of the priest or the vice-priest on pain of being liable to a fine of thirty light drachmas to the Society. The priest shall perform the customary services at the meeting and the anniversary in proper style, and shall set before the meeting the drink-offering for the return of Bacchus and pronounce the sermon. (Ferguson)

This is a brief excerpt from an Athenian inscription giving a long list of rules governing the conduct of the assembly of an Athenian mystery cult whose members are called Jobakchoi (cf. no. 670 at 1 Corinthians 8-14). The other rules deal with compulsory attendance, the paying of dues, and the like. The ecstatic experiences and enthusiasm of the earlier days of the cult seem to have completely receded, though vaguely remembered and memorialized, and have been replaced by an emphasis on tradition, order, and ritual. An analogous development took place in the Pauline communities. Cf. 1 Corinthians 12:1–14:40, esp. 14:26-40, representing the early days of the Pauline churches in which women participated freely and there was no set order or structure, the excesses of which Paul already perceived as a danger.

833. 1 Timothy 2:12

Philo, *Life of Moses* 1.32.180 (15 BCE–50 CE)

This great and marvelous work [the Exodus] struck the Hebrews with amazement, and, finding themselves unexpectedly victorious in a bloodless conflict, and seeing their enemies, one and all, destroyed in a moment, they set up two choirs, one of men and one of women, on the beach, and sang hymns of thanksgiving to God. Over these choirs Moses and his sister presided, and led the hymns, the former for the men and the latter for the women. (LCL)

Cf. Exodus 15:1-21, which Philo rewrites from the perspective of the contemporary Jewish understanding that was very hesitant to have women exercise authority over men, even in choral conducting. Even sophisticated Hellenistic Jews assumed that it had also been so in the biblical stories.

834. 1 Timothy 3:4-5

Isocrates, *To Demonicus* 35 (3–2 cent. BCE)

Whenever you purpose to consult with any one about your affairs, first observe how he has managed his own; for he who has shown poor judgment in conducting his own business will never give wise counsel about the business of others. (LCL)

This gnomic rule (for the form, cf. Berger, *Formgeschichte,* §19.41) is applied in 1 Timothy to the relationship between home and congregation, while in Isocrates it is the relation between two individual persons that stands in the foreground.

835. 1 Timothy 3:16

Virgil, *Eclogues* 4:15-17 (29 BCE)

[Concerning the prophesied son:] He shall have the gift of divine life, shall see heroes mingled with gods, and shall himself be seen of them, and shall sway a world to which his father's virtues have brought peace. (LCL)

Presupposing that lines 3 and 4 of the encomium in 1 Timothy 3:16 are to be translated "he appeared to angels" (rather than "he appeared to the messengers," i.e. the apostles, which is more likely the correct meaning), one can compare these two texts. Whoever in this way appears to deities and semidivine beings belongs to the same status as they, belongs in their company. Mutual seeing is what is presupposed. (Does that cast a different light on Jesus in the company of Moses and Elijah in Mark 9? Is he not then "one of them"? Cf. no. 127.) What happens in 1 Timothy 3 at the exaltation is in Virgil (and in Mark 9) thought of as the initiation for the successor to the throne which is already granted to the earthly figure.

836. 1 Timothy 4:12

Inscription of Antiochus I of Commagene (1 cent. BCE)

[Near the end of a list of cultic laws:] piety is a sacred obligation to the gods and to the ancestors. I have made myself a model [τύπος] of such piety [εὐσέβεια] for my children and grandchildren by many things, especially through this [list of cultic laws], in the faith that they will have a good model to imitate and will constantly increase the related honor of the family and also show such honor to me for the decoration of the house in the flourishing of my own times. (MEB/from Dittenberger, *Orientis Graeci Inscriptiones Selectae*, and Berger's German)

Here as in 1 Timothy the focus is on being a model in things religious, expressed in the word τύπος. The difference is not so much in the fact that here it is straightforward edification, while 1 Timothy is paradoxical, but rather that in 1 Timothy individual items of content are lacking (cf. above no. 812).

837. 1 Timothy 5:24

6 Ezra 16:64-66 (chaps. 15-16 are a Christian addition to the first-century Jewish apocalypse, known as 6 Ezra)

The Lord will strictly examine all your works, and will make a public spectacle of all of you. You shall be put to shame when your sins come out before others, and your own iniquities shall stand as your accusers on that day. What will you do? Or how will you hide your sins before the Lord and his glory? (NRSV)

Similarly, Revelation 14:13*c* (their works follow them). In these texts, sins are pictured as personified individual beings (cf. *Acts of Thomas* 58: "And you also, if you do not turn to this God whom I preach, and desist from your former works and from the deeds which you wrought without knowledge, shall have your end in these punishments. Believe therefore in Christ Jesus, and he forgives you the sins committed before this and will cleanse you from all your bodily desires which remain on the earth, and will heal you from the trespasses which follow you and depart with you and are found before you" (Hennecke Schneemelcher).

This metaphor is taken from one scene extracted from the course of a trial. The accused proceeds into the courtroom along with the witnesses for the prosecution (and at the conclusion they emerge again). At this entrance into the law court, the accused is visible to all. What is important is, who accompanies him as witnesses against him.

On accusers before God, cf. John 5:45; Revelation 12:10.

838. 1 Timothy 6:10

Bion (itinerant preacher and philosopher), from Stobaeus, *Anthologium* 3, 417 (= III 10, 37) (3 cent. BCE)

Bion the sophist said, "The love of money [φιλαργυρίαν] is the mother city [μετρόπολις, *metropolis*] of all evils." (MEB/from Hense, Stobaeus, *Anthologium*, vol. 3)

The picture of the metropolis with many daughter cities brings the same thing to expression as the picture of the root, from which plants and fruits spring forth. Genealogical imagery (mother/daughter) or fraternal imagery (brother/brother) was a favorite way of formulating the relation of one vice or one virtue to a whole series (cf. Berger, *Formgeschichte*, 97, 148-49, 151, 156).

839. 1 Timothy 6:14

Diodorus of Sicily, *Library of History* 4.3.1-4; 3.62.10 (1 cent. BCE)

Then he [Dionysus] made a campaign into India, whence he returned to Boeotia in the third year, bringing with him a notable quantity of booty, and he was the first man ever to celebrate a triumph seated on an Indian elephant. And the Boeotians and other Greeks and the Thracians, in memory of the campaign in India, have established sacrifices every other year to Dionysus, and believe that at that time the god reveals himself to human beings. Consequently in many Greek cities every other year Bacchic bands of women gather. . . .

[3.62.10] Furthermore, the tradition that Dionysus was born twice of Zeus arises from the belief that these fruits also perished in common with all other plants in the flood at the time of Deucalion, and that when they sprang up again after the Deluge it was as if there had been a second epiphany of the god among men, and so the myth was created that the god had been born again from the thigh of Zeus. (LCL)

The Pastoral letters too know of a repeated epiphany of Jesus: 2 Timothy 1:10 refers to the first appearing of Jesus, while Titus 2:13 to the appearing that is still expected (as does 1 Tim 6:14). The ancient concept of epiphany lived from the tension between the visible and the invisible, between the experienced, visible working of a deity and his or her invisible existence. The effected change becomes transparent to that which causes it, and this is the epiphany. Thus "epiphany" did not necessarily mean appearing in the sense of becoming visible in a way that could be photographed, as it is used today, but still "epiphany" and "glory" (δόξα) are often used together. The visible effects are signs of the presence of the deity himself (cf. Josephus, *Antiquities* 18.118-19: all watch how the fire consumes the sacrifice, to which Josephus comments, "As this epiphany occurred. . . ."). This presence is focused in one point, is temporally limited, directed toward human beings, is an initiating event, even when the effects continue. Cf. no. 859.

On 2 Timothy 3:6, cf. no. 658.

840. 2 Timothy 3:8

Numenius of Apamea (Platonic-Pythagorean philosopher, 2 cent. CE, as cited in Eusebius, *Preparation for the Gospel* 9, 8)

And next in order came Jannes and Jambres, Egyptian sacred scribes, men judged to have no superiors in the practice of magic, at the time when the Jews were being driven out of Egypt. (Gifford)

The names of the two magicians are not from the OT. They are found in expositions of Exodus 7:11, 22. The first name occurs for the first time in the *Damascus Document* CD 5:17-19: "For [already] in ancient times God visited their deeds and His anger was kindled against their works; *for it is a people of no discernment [Isa. xxvii, 11], it is a nation void of counsel inasmuch as there is not discernment in them* [Deut. 32:28]. For in ancient times, Moses and Aaron arose by the hand of the Prince of Lights and Satan in his cunning raised up Jannes and his brother when Israel was first delivered" (Vermes).

Jannes is also documented in Pliny, *Natural History* 30.2.11, alongside Moses as a magician (1 cent. CE), as also in the *Apologia* of Apuleius (2 cent. CE), §90. The Apuleius named above is the first pagan author in whom both names occur. Cf. also J. Bidez and F. Cumont, *Les Mages hellénisés* (Paris: Société d'editions "Les Belles Lettres," 1938), pp. 11ff. Obviously it was the case that the names of famous magicians were early and consistently placed in association with Moses by Jewish apologetic, with the result that they are found together in secondary appropriation by pagan authors. The interest in miraculous powers was of great significance for the (Jewish-) Hellenistic transmission and reception of the picture of Moses (as it was for the authors of the Christian Gospels).

841. 2 Timothy 3:16

Philo, *Life of Moses* 2.36-40 (15 BCE–50 CE)

[After recounting Ptolemy's initiative in securing the translators from Jerusalem, their grand reception in Egypt, and their choosing the island of Pharos for their work:] Judging this to be the most suitable place in the district, where they might find peace and tranquillity and the soul could commune with the laws with none to disturb its privacy, they fixed their abode there; and, taking the sacred books, stretched them out toward heaven with the hands that held them, asking of God that they might not fail in their purpose. And He assented to their prayers, to the end that the greater part, or even the whole, of the human race might be profited and led to a better life by continuing to observe such wise and truly admirable ordinances.

Sitting here in seclusion with none present save the elements of nature, earth, water, air, heaven, and the genesis of which was to be the first theme of their sacred revelation, for the laws begin with the story of the world's creation, they became as it were possessed, and under inspiration, wrote, not each several scribe something different, but the same word for word, as though dictated to each by an invisible prompter. Yet who does not know that every language, and Greek especially, abounds in terms, and that the same thought can be put in many shapes by changing single words and whole phrases and suiting the expression to the occasion? This was not the case, we are told, with this law of ours, but the

Greek words used corresponded literally with the Chaldean [Hebrew], exactly suited to the things indicated. For, just as in geometry and logic, so it seems to me, the sense indicated does not admit of variety in the expression which remains unchanged in its original form, so these writers, as it clearly appears, arrived at a wording which corresponded with the matter, and alone, or better than any other, would bring out clearly what was meant. The clearest proof of this is that, if Chaldeans have learned Greek, or Greeks Chaldean, and read both versions, the Chaldean and the translation, they regard them with awe and reverence as sisters, or rather one and the same, both in matter and words, and speak of the authors not as translators but as prophets and priests of the mysteries, whose sincerity and singleness of thought has enabled them to go hand in hand with the purest of spirits, the spirit of Moses. (LCL)

Judaism became more a religion of a book than did the Christianity of New Testament times. Yet in the later NT documents, esp. those concerned to establish orthodoxy against the threat of growing heresy, a focus on the sacred text becomes more prominent (cf. not only 2 Tim 3:16 but 2 Pet 1:20; 3:14-16). With the increased concentration on normative sacred texts, it is more necessary to guarantee the validity of these texts by a doctrine of inspiration. There are tendencies in this direction in the late New Testament period, but do not reach the explicitness of Philo, who affirms a kind of verbal inspiration and dictation theory that makes every word of the LXX the infallible word of God, and a proper subject for his elaborate kind of allegorical exegesis.

A later rabbinic account (*Meg* 1.8) agrees with Philo that the translation of the LXX was a divine miracle, without using Philo's vocabulary of inspiration and prophetism: "King Ptolemy brought together seventy-two elders, whom he led into seventy-two closets, without telling them for what purpose he had assembled them. He then went into each and said to them, 'Write out for me the Law of Moses your teacher.' God gave each one counsel in his heart, so that all agreed on every point" (Soncino).

These are developments beyond that of the earlier *Epistle of Aristeas* 301-2 (140–100 BCE): "Three days afterward, Demetrius took the men with him, traversed the mile-long jetty into the sea toward the island, crossed the bridge, and went in the direction of the north. There he assembled them in a house which had been duly furnished near the shore—a magnificent building in a very quiet situation—and invited the men to carry out the work of translation, all that they would require being handsomely provided. They set to completing their several tasks, reaching agreement among themselves on each by comparing versions. The result of their agreement was made into a fair copy by Demetrius" (*OTP* 2:32-33). Here, their translation is according to their own competence and insight, and after drafts are made by individual members of the committee, agreement is reached by plenary discussion—much as in the production of modern translations.

842. 2 Timothy 3:16

4 Ezra 14:23-26, 37-48 (late 1 cent. CE)

[After the sacred books had all been destroyed in the Babylonian invasion, God addresses Ezra:] Go and gather the people, and tell them not to seek you for forty days. But prepare for yourself many writing tablets, and take with you Sarea, Dabria, Selemia, Ethanus, and Asiel—these five, who are trained to write rapidly; and you shall come here, and I will light in your heart the lamp of understanding, which shall not be put out until what you are about to write is finished. And when you have finished, some things you shall make public, and some you shall deliver in secret to the wise; tomorrow at this hour you shall begin to write. . . .

So I took the five men, as he commanded me, and we proceeded to the field, and remained there. And on the next day a voice called me, saying, "Ezra, open your mouth and drink what I give you to drink." So I opened my mouth, and a full cup was offered to me; it was full of something like water, but its color was like fire. I took it and drank; and when I had drunk it, my heart poured forth understanding, and wisdom increased in my breast, for my spirit retained its memory, and my mouth was opened and no longer closed. Moreover, the Most High gave understanding to the five men, and by turns they wrote what was dictated, using characters that they did not know. They sat forty days; they wrote during the daytime, and ate their bread at night. But as for me, I spoke in the daytime and was not silent at night. So during the forty days, ninety-four books were written. And when the forty days were ended, the Most High spoke to me, saying, "Make public the twenty-four books that you wrote first, and let the worthy and the unworthy read them; but keep the seventy that were written last, in order to give them to the wise among your people. For in them is the spring of understanding, the fountain of wisdom, and the river of knowledge." (NRSV)

The ninety-four books are the twenty-four of the Hebrew canon, intended for public use by all, and seventy apocryphal books considered equally divinely inspired and authoritative, but not intended for all. This contrast is unknown in the New Testament. Likewise, this understanding of inspiration, in which the historical development of the canonical corpus over a long period is leveled out into a once-for-all giving of a single inspired text from heaven, stands in contrast with any understanding of inspiration found in the NT. This text, like the rabbinic and Philonic texts above, illustrates that "inspiration" was understood in a variety of ways in the Hellenistic world. It is thus meaningless to pose the question of inspiration in yes/no terms; the understanding of inspiration at work in such affirmations must first be probed.

843. Titus 3:5

Mithras-Inscription of Santa Prisca in Rome (220 CE)

. . . the one well-pleasing to god who is reborn [Latin: *renatum*] and re-created [Latin: *creatum*] through sweet things . . . (MEB/Berger)

Cf. M. J. Vermaseren/van Essen, *The Excavations in the Mithraeum of the Church of Santa Prisca in Rome* (Leiden: E. J. Brill, 1965), #6; and H. D. Betz, "The Mithras Inscriptions of Santa Prisca and the New Testament," in *NT* 10 (1987): 62-80. This is from graffiti written by participants in the cult (the next one reads "Poultry liver [pâté de foie gras] is sweet, but grief and worry reigns"). The key word "sweet" is found here too. On rebirth through "sweetness," cf. *Jos. Asen.*, chap. 16 (being fed honeycomb by the angel). The text is important as a parallel, since it deals with an initiation (into Judaism conceived as a mystery cult?), and in 8.9 conversion is spoken of as new creation. According to Porphyry (Antr. Nymph 15), honey has a purifying function, and thus in this regard is also appropriate to initiation. On the character of Mithraism as a mystery religion, cf. C. Colpe, "Mithra-Verehrung, Mithras-Kult und die Existenz iranischer Mysterien," in J. Hinnels (ed.), *Mithraic Studies* II (Manchester: Manchester University Press, 1975), pp. 378-405. On new creation at baptism, cf. also *Barnabas* 6:11. Further above under nos. 382, 410, 570 (!).

844. Philemon

Inscription from Necropolis of Nikaia (1 cent. CE)

In this place Chrestos buried aged Italos; he wept for his faithful slave when he died. In return for [Italos'] good life and industrious servitude [Chrestos] fulfilled these sacred rites for him as a favor. (Horsley, *New Documents* 3)

The inscription is one of several such grave inscriptions that show that humane relations could prevail between master and slave. Chrestos' name indicates that he had previously been a slave, so the text also illustrates that freed slaves could become wealthy enough to own their own slaves.

845. Philemon

Papyrus Colon. 7921 (3 cent. CE)

To Aurelius Protarchos, also called Heron, *strategos* of the Oxyrhynchite [nome], from Aurelia Sarapias, also called Dionysarion, daughter of Apollophanes, also called Sarapammon, former *exegetes* of Antinoopolis, acting without guardian according to the *ius trium liberorum*.

I have a slave, who formerly belonged to my father, by the name of Sarapion, and I considered that he had done no base deed whatsoever as he was part of my inheritance and had been entrusted by me with our household. [Nevertheless] he, I know not how, at the instigation of certain folk, disdaining the honor afforded him by me and the provision of the necessities for life, [and] purloining some items of clothing from our household with which I had provided him and even other items which he also took possession of for himself from our household has secretly run away. Having heard that he resides in the hamlet of the Nome with Chairemon, I asked . . . (Horsley, *New Documents* 6)

Since the remainder of the papyrus is missing, exactly what Aurelia was asking the *strategos* to do is unclear, but there can be no doubt that she was asking official help in having the slave returned, and perhaps prosecution for those whom she supposed instigated the escape and who now shelter the runaway. A slave represented a considerable investment, usually second only to the price paid for land and home. Cf. the papyrus contract preserved in the same volume, 48-49, for the sale of a ten-year-old slave girl in good health for 280 denarii, almost a year's generous wage. References to runaway slaves are rather frequent in the papyri (see additional recently published examples in Horsley, *New Documents* 6:58-59, 101-3).

846. Philemon

Philo, *Every Good Man Is Free* 79 (15 BCE–50 CE)

[Describing the Essenes] Not a single slave is to be found among them, but all are free, exchanging services with each other, and they denounce the owners of slaves, not merely for their injustice in outraging the law of equality, but also for their impiety in annulling the statute of Nature, who mother-like has born and reared all men alike, and created them genuine brothers, not in mere name, but in very reality, though this kinship has been put to confusion by the triumph of malignant covetousness, which has wrought estrangement instead of affinity and enmity instead of friendship. (LCL)

For the context of this citation in Philo's admiring discussion of the high ethical standard of the Essenes, see on no. 30 above.

847. Philemon 10

Genesis Rabbah 39

One who brings a foreigner near and makes a proselyte of him is as if he created him. *(Talmudic Anthology)*

Cf. also *b. Yeb.* 48B: "Rabbi Jose ben Halafta said: 'A proselyte who embraces Judaism is like a new-born child.'" Such statements show that Paul's references to himself as "father" to his converts need not be understood only in terms of Gentile practice (e.g. those who sponsored initiates in the mystery cults were known as their "fathers"), but also represents an extension of Jewish understanding into Christian usage. Cf. also 1 Corinthians 4:15; 2 Corinthians 5:17.

The Letter to the Hebrews

848. Hebrews 1:1

3 Enoch 11, 12, 16 (5 cent. CE, with older traditions)

R. Ishmael said: The angel Metatron, Prince of the Divine Presence, said to me:
The Holy One, blessed be he, revealed to me from that time onward all the mysteries of wisdom, all the depths of the perfect Torah and all the thoughts of men's hearts. All the mysteries of the world and all the orders of nature stand revealed before me as they stand revealed before the Creator. From that time onward I looked and beheld deep secrets and wonderful mysteries. Before a man thinks in secret, I see his thought; before he acts, I see his act. There is nothing in heaven above or deep within the earth concealed from me.

[12] R. Ishmael said: Metatron, Prince of the Divine Presence, said to me:
Out of the love which he had for me, more than for all the denizens of the heights, the Holy One, blessed be he, fashioned for me a majestic robe, in which all kinds of luminaries were set, and he clothed me in it. He fashioned for me a glorious cloak in which brightness, brilliance, splendor, and luster of every kind were fixed, and he wrapped me in it. He fashioned for me a kingly crown in which 49 refulgent stones were placed, each like the sun's orb, and its brilliance shone into the four quarters of the heaven of 'Arabot, into the seven heavens, and into the four quarters of the world. He set it upon my head and he called me, "The lesser YHWH" in the presence of his whole household in the height, as it is written, "My name is in him."

[16] R. Ishmael said: The angel Metatron, Prince of the Divine Presence, the glory of highest heaven, said to me:
At first I sat upon a great throne at the door of the seventh palace, and I judged all the denizens of the heights on the authority of the Holy One, blessed be he. I assigned greatness, royalty, rank, sovereignty, glory, praise, diadem, crown, and honor to all the princes of kingdoms, when I sat in the heavenly court. The princes of kingdoms stood beside me, to my right and to my left, by authority of the Holy One, blessed be he. But when 'Aher came to behold the vision of the chariot and set eyes upon me, he was afraid and trembled before me. His soul was alarmed to the point of leaving him because of his fear, dread, and terror of me, when he saw me seated upon a throne like a king, with ministering angels standing beside me as servants and all the princes of kingdoms crowned with crowns surrounding me. Then he opened his mouth and said, "There are indeed two powers in heaven!" Immediately a divine voice came out from the presence of the Shekinah and said, "Come back to me, apostate sons—apart from 'Aher!" Then 'Anapie'el YHWH, the honored, glorified, beloved, wonderful, terrible, and dreadful Prince, came at the command of the Holy One, blessed be he, and struck me with sixty lashes of fire and made me stand to my feet. (*OTP* 1:264-65, 268)

These texts, though late, contain earlier materials, and may illumine the kind of angel speculation going on in some Jewish circles in New Testament times. Not only does the author of Hebrews both utilize such conceptuality—that there is a divine being distinct from YHWH of whom God-language may appropriately be used—he also engages in a polemic against placing the exalted Christ in the category of "angels." Cf. also, on the one hand, Philippians 2:9-10, where the exalted Christ is given a name above every other name, and, on the other hand, the warning against "worship of angels" in Colossians 2:18.

849. Hebrews 1:1-4

Wisdom of Solomon 7:21-27 (150 BCE–50 CE)

I [Solomon] learned both what is secret and what is manifest, for Wisdom, the fashioner of all things, taught me. . . . For Wisdom is more mobile than any motion; because of her pureness she pervades and penetrates all things. For she is a breath of the power of God, and a pure emanation of the glory of the Almighty; therefore nothing defiled gains entrance into her. For she is a reflection [ἀπαύγασμα] of eternal light, a spotless mirror of the working of God, and an image of his goodness. Although she is but one, she can do all things, and while remaining herself, she renews all things; in every generation she passes into holy souls and makes them friends of God, and prophets. (NRSV; "Wisdom" is capitalized since she is personified. Cf. NRSV's "she" instead of "it".)

As in Hebrews, there is a divine being through whom God made the worlds, who permeates the world, and who has been at work in the line of Israel's revelatory prophets. The same rare word as in Hebrews 1:3 (ἀπαύγασμα) is used. While Wisdom of Solomon deals more with personification than hypostatization, Hebrews goes on to virtually identify this figure with God, engaging in a polemic against seeing him merely as an angel (1:4-14) and using explicit God-language of him (1:8). On the other hand, that this divine figure became human (2:5-18) and offered himself as a sacrifice for sins (1:3) is an impossible idea for the author of the Wisdom of Solomon.

850. Hebrews 1:2

Philo, *On the Confusion of Tongues* 146 (15 BCE–50 CE)

But if there be any as yet unfit to be called a Son of God, let him press to take his place under God's Firstborn, the Word, who holds the eldership among the angels, their ruler as it were. And many names are his, for he is called, "the Beginning," and the Name of God, and His Word, and the Man after His image, and "he that sees," that is Israel. (LCL)

So too in Philo, *Dreams* 1.215, the Logos is called the "Firstborn" (Son) and High Priest (!). In the passage above, his relative rank above the angels is worthy of note. In the context it becomes the more clear: If human beings may not call themselves "children of God," then at least they may call themselves sons of "a man," his eternal image and most holy Logos. The essential element in the equating of Jesus with the Logos of Hellenistic Judaism that is presupposed in Hebrews 1 was probably the concept of the "only Sent One" and bearer of the divine name, which also plays a role in the above quotation ("many names are his"; "Lord"). As in Hebrews (cf. 2:10), so the relation between the many sons of God to the Logos plays a role, even if in a different way. Cf. nos. 364, 800.

851. Hebrews 1:4-14

Hekhaloth-Text (3–6 cent. CE)

[God speaks:] And I have entrusted to him [Enoch/Metatron] all the servants above and all the servants below. And I set everything in order for him at the beginning [of creation]. And I named his name "the little Adonai [LORD]." The numerical value of his name is 71. And I gave him wisdom and insight superior to all the angels, and I gave him power superior to all the ministering angels. (MEB/from Berger's citation of P. Schäfer, *Synopse zur Hekhalot-Literatur* [Tübingen: J. C. B. Mohr, 1981], pp. 131, 133, §295 [= H. Odeberg, *3 Enoch* (Cambridge: Cambridge University Press, 1928) 48 C 9 and 7 according to K; the German trans. of H. Hofmann was corrected according to Schäfer's Synopsis])

The man chosen and exalted by God is placed above all the angels and receives God's name (Adonai [LORD]). In Hebrews, Jesus is given this function by designating him "Son," but Philippians 2:11 also knows of the conferral of God's name on Jesus. Cf. Schäfer, *Rivalität Zwischen Engeln und Menschen* Berlin: de Gruyter, 1975). As the exalted one, Enoch has the name/function of "Metatron" (from μετὰ τὸν τύραννον?), the "throne assistant" of God.

852. Hebrews 1:6

Plato, *Statesman* 271D, 272E (4 cent. BCE)

The life about which you ask, when all the fruits of the earth sprang up of their own accord for men, did not belong at all to the present period of revolution, but this also belonged to the previous one. For then, in the beginning, God ruled and supervised the whole revolution, and so again, in the same way, all the parts of the universe were divided by regions among gods who ruled them, and, moreover, the animals were distributed by species and flocks among inferior deities as divine shepherds, each of whom was in all respects the independent guardian of the creatures under his own care, so that no creature was wild, nor did they eat one another, and there was no war among them, nor any strife whatsoever. (LCL)

Cf. also, *Phaedo* 107D; *Republic* 617D. Plato speaks familiarly of a companion daimon or spirit that accompanies one somewhat like a guardian angel. He pictures Socrates as having a personal angel/daimon. There were both good and bad daimons (cf. Ferguson, *Backgrounds* 220-22). While the immediate background of the New Testament's ideas of angels is the Hebrew Bible and Jewish tradition, the idea of divine spiritual beings sent forth by the supreme God to be an accompanying guide and protector for individuals was also well known in the Hellenistic world independently of the biblical tradition.

853. Hebrews 1:9

Epictetus, *Discourses* 2.16.44 (55–135 CE)

If Heracles had sat about at home, what would he have amounted to? He would have been Eurystheus and no Heracles. Come, how many acquaintances and friends did he have with him as he went up and down through the whole world? Nay, he had no dearer friend than God. That is why he was believed to be a son of God, and was. It was therefore in obedience to His will that he went about clearing away wickedness and lawlessness. (LCL)

Important points of contact with Hebrews 1 are sonship, righteousness, lawlessness, love, and the suffering of the son (Heb 2:10). In the environment of the New Testament, Hercules is in a similar way the prototype of the pattern "per aspera ad astra" ("to the stars through difficulties"). As in NT Christology, this way is especially associated with the title "Son of God."

854. Hebrews 2:10

Corpus Hermeticum 1.26 (1 cent. CE)

This is the final good for those who have received knowledge: to be made god. Why do you still delay? Having learned all this, should you not become guide to the worthy so that through you the human race might be saved by god? (Copenhaver)

The Greek "guide" (καθοδηγός) is a synonym for the "leader/scout/pioneer" (ἀρχηγός) of Hebrews 2:10. The point of both texts is the salvation of humanity through the One who has already reached the heavenly goal. The difference: the way of Christ and those that follow him leads through suffering to God (cf. Heb 13:3-9), and the "pioneer" Christ purifies human beings so that they can approach God's throne.

855. Hebrews 3:1-6

Memar Marqah 4.6; 3.6 (Samaritan document, 4 cent. CE)

4.6 Where is there the like of Moses and who can compare with Moses the servant of God, the faithful one of His House, who dwelt among the angels in the Sanctuary of the Unseen? They all honored him when he abode with them.
3.6 Where is there the like of Moses whom the Lord sent, a righteous apostle, faithful in the unseen and in the seen? (MacDonald)

In Hebrews as in Memar Marqah, Numbers 12:7 diverges from the MT by developing the attribute "faithful" (as in the LXX). In the Samaritan text precisely the predicates are attributed to Moses that in Hebrews are given to Jesus: the title "apostle" (Heb 3:1) and exaltation over the angels (Heb 1), as well as residence in the heavenly holy place (Heb 8–9). It is possible that Hebrews takes over considerable elements of Jewish or Samaritan traditions about Moses and reworks them christologically. Cf. no. 71.

856. Hebrews 4:4

Pirqe Rabbi Eliezer 18 (9d) (old material; final redaction 9 cent. CE ?)

The Holy One, blessed be He, created seven eons, and of them all He chose the seventh eon only; the six eons are for the going in and coming out [of God's creatures] for war and peace. The seventh eon is entirely Sabbath and rest in the life everlasting. (Friedlander)

Cf. similarly *Abot R. Nat.* 1c: "*the Sabbath day* [Ps 92:1]. It is a day that is wholly a Sabbath, on which there is no eating, drinking, or conducting of business, but the righteous are seated in retinue with their crowns on their heads and derive sustenance from the splendor of God's presence" (Neusner, *Rabbi Nathan*).

In all cases the seventh day is associated with the seventh eon of world history. The tendency already observable in *Jubilees* to interpret the whole history of Israel according to the seven-day schema is here developed eschatologically (similarly in *Barnabas* 15), arriving at the concept of a single world-week. Concerns for the calendar and for a theology of history are here very close together. Cf. already 1QH 7:15 ("perpetual Sabbath").

857. Hebrews 4:14–10:18

Plato, *Laws* 290 (4 cent. BCE)

There is also the priestly class, who, as the law declares, know how to give the gods gifts from men in the form of sacrifices which are acceptable to them, and to ask on our behalf blessings in return from them. (LCL)

Although qualifications and particular duties of priests varied from setting to setting, this statement of Plato illustrates the two general functions of priests throughout the Hellenistic period: sacrifice and intercession. The Roman word for priest, "pontifex," means "mediator" or "bridge," and sums up the function of the priest in reuniting humanity and the offended deity. Such quotations show that the Hellenistic world, and not only the Hebrew Scriptures, form the setting for the argument regarding priesthood as a christological category in the Letter to the Hebrews.

858. Hebrews 4:16

Corpus Hermeticum, fragment from Stobaeus (2–4 cent. CE)

[Prayer of the souls before being enclosed in the body:] This is what the souls attained who said this, my son Horus. For the Monarch who was also present, sitting on the throne of truth, said to those who had besought him, as follows . . . (MEB/from Stobaeus, *Anthologium*, vol. 1)

Cf. also no. 562.

In a completely different context from that provided by Hebrews, a scene involving a heavenly throne is portrayed, a throne provided with genitive attributes ("throne of truth"). The text documents the widespread phenomenon of imagery in which the foundation of the metaphorical process reflects the political context: monarchial relationships in political life provide the metaphors for expressing the religious experience of divine power. This is said explicitly in Pseudo-Aristotle, "On the World," §6 (God enthroned at the apex of the whole heavenly structure. His administration of the universe must be conceived like that of the Persian emperor. The ruler is enthroned in a magnificent palace. The king is addressed as "Lord" and "God." He has spies, so that he hears and sees everything. Only God needs no service from others, for the glory of the emperor is still small in comparison with that of the all-ruling God).

859. Hebrews 5:7

3 Maccabees 5:7-9 (1 cent. CE [?])

For to the Gentiles it appeared that the Jews were left without aid, because in their bonds they were forcibly confined on every side. But with tears [μετὰ δακρύων] and a voice [βοή] hard to silence they all called upon the Almighty Lord and Ruler of all power, their merciful God and Father, praying that he avert with vengeance the evil plot against them and in a glorious manifestation rescue them from the fate now prepared for them. So their entreaty ascended fervently to heaven. (NRSV)

Crying and tears in association with sacrificial metaphors for prayer belong to the imagery of contemporary prayer (cf. also 3 Macc 1:16; 5:25; Philo, "Questions on Genesis" 4:233: Esau cried out with tears). Thus it follows that it is not necessary to think of a specific connection between Hebrews 5:7 and the Gethsemane tradition. It is more likely that the author of Hebrews adopts the general tradition that pictures Jesus as a man of prayer, adopted especially by Luke.

On Hebrews 5:10, cf. nos. 864-66 on Hebrews 7:1-28.

860. Hebrews 5:8

Philo, *On Dreams* 2.107-8 (15 BCE–50 CE)

. . . when he claims the goods of his kinsmen and father from which he seemed to have been disinherited and holds it his duty to recover that portion of virtue which falls to his lot; when he passes step by step from betterment to betterment and, established firmly as it were on the crowning heights and consummation of his life, utters aloud the lesson which experience had taught him so fully, "I belong to God" [Gen. 50.19], and not any longer to any sense object that has been created, then his brethren will make with him covenants of reconciliation, changing their hatred to friendship, their ill-will to goodwill, and I, their follower and their servant, who have learnt to obey them as masters, will not fail to praise him for his repentance. (LCL)

The motif of "learning by suffering" is common to Philo's Joseph and Hebrew's Christology. The contrast is evident: Joseph's suffering eventuates in this-worldly vindication, while in Hebrew's Christology the suffering of the human Jesus was an element in the divine plan of salvation "for all who obey him."

861. Hebrews 6:4

b. Baba Batra 15b-16a (undatable tradition)

What is the meaning of "the oxen were ploughing and the asses were feeding beside them" [Job 1:14]? [= here interpreted as a miracle: fodder already sprouts as the oxen are plowing.]

Said R. Yohanan, "This teaches that the Holy One, blessed be He, gave Job a taste of the world to come."

[Similarly 16b-17a:] There were three persons whom the Holy One, blessed be He, gave a foretaste in this world of the life of the world to come: Abraham, Isaac, and Jacob [because of the "all" in Gen 24:1; 27:33; 33:11]. (Neusner, *Talmud*)

The text has to do with "tasting the powers of the age to come." On "tasting" cf. also Psalm 34:9. Jewish exegesis was concerned to verify eschatological expectations among great and small biblical characters. For Hebrews this is assumed in general without supporting it with particular stories.

On the impossibility of a second repentance in Hebrews 6:4, cf. 1QS 7:1-2, 16-17, 22-24.

862. Hebrews 7:1-9

Inscription from Nottinghamshire

To the god Jupiter optimus maximus there is given that he may hound . . . through his mind, through his memory, his inner parts [?], his intestines, his heart, his marrow, his veins . . . whoever it was, whether man or woman, who stole away the denarii of Canius [?] Dignus that in his own person in a short time he may balance the account. There is given to the god above named a tenth part of the money when he has [repaid it]. (Turner cited in Ferguson, *Backgrounds*)

Giving the deity a tenth of one's gains was not only the Hebrew-Jewish tradition, but had Hellenistic backgrounds. It was customary to give the deity a tenth of the spoils of war, i.e. to present them to a shrine such as Delphi.

863. Hebrews 7:2

Thucydides, *History of the Peloponnesian War* 3.50.1-2 (460–400 BCE)

The rest of the men, however whom Paches had sent to Athens as chief authors of the revolt, numbering somewhat more than a thousand, were put to death by the Athenians on the motion of Cleon. They also pulled down the walls of Mytilene and took possession of the Mytilenaean fleet. Afterward, instead of imposing a tribute upon the Lesbians, they divided all the land except that of the Methymnaeans into three thousand allotments, and reserving three hundred of these as sacred to the gods they sent out Athenian colonists, chosen by lot, to occupy the rest. (LCL)

This text from the fifth century BCE is one of several that documents the custom of devoting a tenth of the spoils to the deity, a practice that continued to be widespread in the later world. Cf. from the second century CE Pausanias, *Description of Greece*, "Elis" 1.10.4:

"At Olympia a gilt cauldron stands on each end of the roof, and a Victory, also gilt, is set in about the middle of the pediment. Under the image of Victory has been dedicated a golden shield, with Medusa the Gorgon in relief. The inscription on the shield declares who dedicated it and the reason why they did so. It runs thus:

The temple has a golden shield; from Tanagra
The Lacedaemonians and their allies dedicated it,
A gift taken from the Argives, Athenians, and
Ionians,
The tithe [δεκάταν] offered for victory in war" (LCL).

The *Neuer Wettstein* offers several other examples from both Greek and Latin authors: Nicolaus of Damascus, Fragment 16; Diodorus Siculus, *History* 11.62.2-3; Plutarch, *Parallel Lives,* "Camillus," 7.6-7; Florus, *Sketch of all the Wars in the 700 Years* (of Roman history) 1.12.9-10; Justinus, *Historiae Phillippicae* 18.7.7; 20.3.1-3; Macrobius, *Saturnalia* 1.7.28, 30. Apart from such references, the exegete is likely to think only of the biblical story of Genesis 14:17-20 to which Hebrews explicitly refers, and to miss the contacts of this familiar pagan practice of tithing in the Hellenistic world.

864. Hebrews 7:1-28

1QS 9 (2–1 cent. BCE)

As for the property of the men of holiness who walk in perfection, it shall not be merged with that of the men of falsehood who have not purified their life by separating themselves from iniquity and walking in the way of perfection. They shall depart from none of the counsels of the Law to walk in the stubbornness of their hearts, but shall be ruled by the primitive precepts in which the men of the Community were first instructed until there shall come the Prophet and the Messiahs of Aaron and Israel. (Vermes)

4Q 175 A Messianic Anthology

He took up his discourse and said:
Oracle of Balaam son of Beor. Oracle of the man whose eye is penetrating. Oracle of him who has heard the words of God, who knows the wisdom of the Most High and sees the vision of the Almighty, who falls and his eyes are opened. I see him but not now. I behold him but not near. A star shall come out of Jacob and a sceptre shall rise out of Israel; he shall crush the temples of Moab and destroy all the children of Sheth [Num. xxiv, 15-17].
And of Levi he said:
Give Thy Tummim to Levi, and Thy Urim to Thy pious one whom Thou didst test at Massah, and with whom Thou didst quarrel at the waters of Meribah; who said to his father and mother, "I know you not," and who did not acknowledge his brother, or know his sons. For they observed Thy word and kept Thy Covenant. They shall cause Thy precepts to shine before Jacob and Thy Law before Israel. They shall send up incense toward Thy nostrils and place a burnt offering upon Thine altar. Bless his power, O Lord, and delight in the work of his hands. Smite the loins of his adversaries and let his enemies rise no more [Deut. xxxiii, 8-11]. (Vermes)

1QSa 2 (2–1 cent. BCE)

([This shall be the ass]embly of the men of renown [called] to the meeting of the Council of the Community when [the Priest-] Messiah shall summon them.)

He shall come [at] the head of the whole congregation of Israel with all [his brethren, the sons] of Aaron the Priests, [those called] to the assembly, the men of renown; and they shall sit [before him, each man] in the order of his dignity. And then [the Mess]iah of Israel shall [come], and the chiefs of the [clans of Israel] shall sit before him, [each] in the order of his dignity, according to [his place] in their camps and marches. And before them shall sit all the heads of [family of the congreg]ation, and the wise men of [the holy congregation,] each in the order of his dignity.

And [when] they shall gather for the common [tab]le, to eat and [to drink] new wine, when the common table shall be set for eating and the new wine [poured] for drinking, let no man extend his hand over the first-fruits of bread and wine before the Priest; for [it is he] who shall bless the first-fruits of bread and wine, and shall be the first [to extend] his hand over the bread. Thereafter, the Messiah of Israel shall extend his hand over the bread, [and] all the congregation of the Community [shall utter a] blessing, [each man in the order] of his dignity. (Vermes)

Testaments of the Twelve Patriarchs, "Testament of Levi" 18:1-14 (2 cent. BCE–1 cent. CE)

[Describing the eschatological priest from the tribe of Levi:]

(1) When vengeance will have come upon them from the Lord, the priesthood will lapse.

(2) And then the Lord will raise up a new priest
to whom all the words of the Lord will be revealed.
He shall effect the judgment of truth over the earth for many days.

(3) And his star shall rise in heaven like a king;
kindling the light of knowledge as day is illumined by the sun.
And he shall be extolled by the whole inhabited world.

(4) This one will shine forth like the sun in the earth;
he shall take away all darkness from under heaven,
and there shall be peace in all the earth.

(5) The heavens shall greatly rejoice in his days
and the earth shall be glad;
the clouds will be filled with joy
and the knowledge of the Lord will be poured out on the earth like the water of the seas.
And the angels of glory of the Lord's presence will be made glad by him.

(6) The heavens will be opened,
and from the temple of glory sanctification will come upon him,
with a fatherly voice, as from Abraham to Isaac.

(7) And the glory of the Most High shall burst forth upon him.
And the spirit of understanding and sanctification
shall rest upon him [in the water].*

(8) For he shall give the majesty of the Lord to those who are his sons in truth forever.
And there shall be no successor for him from generation to generation forever.

(9) And in his priesthood the nations shall be multiplied in knowledge on the earth,

and they shall be illumined by the grace of the Lord,
but Israel shall be diminished by her ignorance
and darkened by her grief.
In his priesthood sin shall cease
and lawless men shall rest from their evil deeds,
and righteous men shall find rest in him.
(10) And he shall open the gates of paradise;
he shall remove the sword that has threatened since Adam,
(11) and he will grant to the saints to eat of the tree of life.
The spirit of holiness shall be upon them.
(12) And Beliar shall be bound by him.
And he shall grant his children the authority to trample on wicked spirits.
*"In the water" is apparently an interpolation based on Jesus' having received the spirit at baptism (Mark 1:9-11), which is also linked with a heavenly voice. (H. C. Kee's footnote in *OTP*) (*OTP* 1:794-95)

During the Maccabean period there was a tendency to reinterpret the hopes for a future Messiah from the Davidic royal imagery into Levitical priestly imagery, since the Hasmoneans were not Davidides but priests of the tribe of Levi. Thus the *T. Judah* 21:1 pictures Judah (from whom David and the kings were descended) as saying, "And now, my children, I command you, love Levi," ordering the royal family to cooperate with the priestly family of Levi. By the first century some groups (such as the covenanters of Qumran) believed that the present priesthood was illegitimate and corrupt, and the true Priest would appear only at the eschaton.

865. Hebrews 7:1-28

11 Q Melchizedek 1-26 (1 cent. BCE–1 cent. CE)

(2) . . . and concerning that which He said, In [this] year of Jubilee [each of you shall return to his property (Lev. xxv, 13); and likewise, And this is the manner of release:] every creditor shall release that which he has lent [to his neighbor. He shall not exact it of his neighbor and his brother], for God's release [has been proclaimed] [Deut. xv, 2]. [And it will be proclaimed at] the end of days concerning the captives as [He said, To proclaim liberty to the captives (Isa. lxi, 1). Its interpretation is that He] will assign them to the Sons of Heaven and to (5) the inheritance of Melchizedek; f[or He will cast] their [lot] amid the po[rtions of Melchize]dek, who will return them there and will proclaim to them liberty, forgiving them [the wrongdoings] of all their iniquities.

And this thing will [occur] in the first week of the Jubilee that follows the nine Jubilees. And the Day of Atonement is the e[nd of the] tenth [Ju]bilee, (8) when all the Sons of [Light] and the men of the lot of Mel[chi]zedek will be atoned for, [And] a statute concerns them [to prov]ide them with their rewards. For this is the moment of the Year of Grace for Melchizedek. [And h]e will, by his strength, judge the holy ones of God, executing judgment as it is written concerning him in the Songs of David, who said ELOHIM has taken his place in the divine council; in the midst of the gods he holds judgment [Ps.lxxxii, 1]. And it was concerning him that he said [Let the assembly of the peoples] return to the height above them; EL [god] will judge the peoples [Ps. vii, 7-8]. As for that which he s[aid, How long will you] judge unjustly and show partiality to the wicked? Selah [Ps. lxxxii, 1], its interpretation concerns Satan and the spirits of his lot [who] rebelled by turning away from the precepts of God to . . . and Melchizedek will avenge the vengeance of the judgments of God . . . and he will drag [them from the hand of] Satan and from the hand of all the sp[irits of] his [lot]. And all the "gods [of Justice"] will come to his aid [to] attend to the de[struction] of Satan. And the height is . . . all the sons of God. . . . This is the day of [Peace/Salvation] concerning which [God] spoke [through Isa]iah the prophet, who said, [How] beautiful upon the mountains are the feet of the messenger who proclaims peace, who brings good news, who proclaims salvation, who says to Zion: Your ELOHIM [reigns] [Isa. lii. 7]. Its interpretation: the mountains are the prophets . . . and the messenger is the Anointed one of the spirit, concerning whom Dan[iel] said, [Until an anointed one, a prince (Dan. ix, 25)] . . . [And he who brings] good [news], who proclaims [salvation]: it is concerning him that it is written . . . [To comfort all who mourn, to grant to those who mourn in Zion] [Isa. lxi, 2-3]. To comfort [those who mourn: its interpretation], to make them understand all the ages of t[ime]. . . . In truth . . . will turn away from Satan . . . by the judgment[s] of God, as it is written concerning him, [who says to Zion] your ELOHIM reigns. Zion is . . ., those who uphold the Covenant, who turn from walking [in] the way of the people. And your ELOHIM is [Melchizedek, who will save them from] the hand of Satan.

As for that which He said, Then you shall send abroad [the loud] trump[et] in the [seventh] m[on]th [Lev. xxv, 9]. (Vermes)

Significance of the text for the New Testament:

1) The text documents an eschatological interpretation of Melchizedek without appealing to Genesis 14 or Psalm 110:4, and possibly independently of them.

2) In contrast to Hebrews, Melchizedek is here not at all represented as a priestly figure, and thus points to another stream of Jewish eschatology. Melchizedek is here the opponent of Belial and the spirits of his lot, and he brings freedom as the executor of God's judgment. It is not clear that the atonement of line 8 refers to Melchizedek.

3) Melchizedek is associated with an eschatological proclaimer of good news. Isaiah 52:7 is interpreted in terms of this messenger, as also in the NT (Acts 10:36; Rom 10:15). This one is also called, if the textual reconstruction is correct, the "anointed one of the Spirit" (analogous to CD 2:12 and interpreting Isa 61:1). Alongside Melchizedek, who is thought of in political terms, an eschatological authority conceived in prophetic terms is here discernible.

4) Lines 9-13 suggest that Melchizedek is thought of as an Elohim-being who qualitatively belongs to the heavenly world and heavenly law. That fits Hebrews 7:3, where Melchizedek is thought of as belonging to the category "Son of God." Melchizedek is repeatedly regarded as a heavenly being in the expositions of later centuries (Logos; Angel and Power; advocate in the heavens; a heavenly being superior to the Christ; the Holy Spirit).

Cf. also no. 5.

866. Hebrews 7:1-28

Melchizedek, Tractate from Nag Hammadi IX, 1.14-20 (2 cent. CE)

And [immediately I] arose, [I, Melchizedek], and I began to [. . .] God [. . .] that I should [rejoice . . .] while he [is acting . . .] living [. . . I said], "I [. . . and I] will not cease, from [now on for ever], O Father of the [All, because] you have had pity on me, and 15 [you have sent the] angel of light [. . .] from your [eons . . . to] reveal [. . .] when he came he caused me [to be raised up] from ignorance and [from] fructification of death to life. For I have a name, I am Melchizedek, the Priest of [God] Most High; I [know] that it is I who am truly [the image of] the true High-Priest [of] God Most High, and [. . .] the world. For it is not [a] small [thing that] God [. . .] with [. . .] while he [. . .]. And [. . . the angels that dwell upon the] earth [. . .] is the [sacrifice] of [. . .] whom Death deceived. When he [died] he bound them with the natures which are [leading them astray]. Yet he offered up 16 offerings [. . .] cattle [. . .] I gave them to [Death and the angels] and the [. . .] demons [. . .] living offering [. . .] I have offered up myself to you as an offering, together with those that are mine, to you yourself, [O] Father of the All, and those whom you love, who have come forth from you who are holy [and] [living]. And [according to] the [perfect] laws I shall pronounce my name as I receive baptism [now] [and] forever, [as a name] among the living [and] holy [names], and [now] in the [waters], Amen.

19 "They gave [. . .] their words [. . .] and they said to me, [. . . Melchizedek, Priest] of God [Most High . . . they] spoke as though [. . . their] mouths [. . .] in the All [. . .] lead astray 20 [. . .]with his [. . .] worship [and . . .] faith [and . . .] his prayers, And [. . .] those that [are his . . .] first [. . .]. They did not care that [the priesthood] which you perform, [which] is from [. . . in the] counsels of [. . .] Satan [. . .] the sacrifice [. . .] his doctrines [. . .]. (NHL)

As near as we can tell, Melchizedek is here conceived to be an angel of light with revelation (conversion), and is baptized. (On the I-saying form of address, cf. Berger, *Formgeschichte*, §72.) In the last section Melchizedek is obviously addressed in connection with the eschatological battle, in which he will play a special role. This was also referred to in 11QMelch, line 13. It is not clear that this text presupposes the NT letter to the Hebrews. Rather, Melchizedek here stands alongside Jesus, and is thought of as a priest who makes the sin offering.

Melchizedek also figures in Pistis Sophia, as one of the five powers subordinate to Jeu, the Father of Jesus' Father. For literature, see C. Colpe, "Heidnische, jüdische und christliche Überlieferung in den Schriften aus Nag Hammadi IX," JAC 23 (1980), 109-21.

On Hebrews 7:25, cf. no. 369.

867. Hebrews 9:7

Heraclitus, Fragment 5 (6 cent. BCE)

They purify themselves by staining themselves with other blood, as if one were to step into mud in order to wash off mud. But a man would be thought mad if any of his fellow-men should perceive him acting thus. Moreover, they talk to these statues *[of theirs]* as if one were to hold conversation with houses, in his ignorance of the nature of both gods and heroes. (Freeman)

The text cited here refers to the remarkable state of affairs formulated in Hebrews 9:7 and elsewhere, that blood is used as a cultic means of purification, although it itself is a taboo substance and is in reality or potentially "unclean." Cf. Plutarch, "Superstition" 12, who speaks of "unclean purifications," and also the scholion on Pseudo-Plato, *Minos* in H. Braun, *Der Hebräerbrief* (HNT 14) (Tübingen: J. C. B. Mohr, 1984), 256: "All women who purify the guilty, pour with the blood of the sacrificial animal" (315 C). Cf. also R. Parker, *Miasma. Pollution and Purification in Early Greek Religion* (Oxford: Clarendon, 1983).

Purification with blood, which already in the citation from Heraclitus is thinking critically about religious matters, is no longer understood. From the point of view of the phenomenology of religion, the basic principle here is that only items of equal value can offer satisfaction ("life for life"), and certainly not just any offering, but only that which qualifies: only the innocent, the right, the sacrificial animal without blemish. Only they can be presented for the exchange that in any case is no longer equal.

868. Hebrews 9:13; 10:4

Diogenes Laertius, *Lives of Eminent Philosophers* (3 cent. CE)
"Diogenes," 6.42 (5–4 cent. BCE)

Seeing someone perform religious purification, he [Diogenes of Sinope] said, "Unhappy man, don't you know that you can no more get rid of errors of conduct by sprinklings than you can of mistakes in grammar?" (LCL)

Here is a piece of ancient rationalistic critical reflection on religion. Hebrews takes it over, but unites in a unique way the purification of the conscience with the purification of the heavenly sanctuary (9:14, 23). On merely external purification, cf. Philo, "Cherubim," 95: "Furthermore they cleanse their bodies with lustrations and purifications, but they neither wish nor practice to wash off from their souls the passions by which life is defiled. They are zealous to go to the temples white-robed, attired in spotless raiment, but with a spotted heart they pass into the inmost sanctuary and are not ashamed" (LCL).

869. Hebrews 9:23

3 Baruch 8:4-5 (3 cent. CE)

"When the day is completed, 4 angels take the crown of the sun and carry it to heaven and renew it because it and its rays are defiled upon earth. And every day it is renewed."
And I Baruch said, "Lord, by what are its rays defiled upon earth?" And the angel said to me, "By the sight of the lawlessness and unrighteousness of men committing fornication, adultery, theft, robbery, . . . which are unacceptable to God. By means of these it is defiled, and because of this it is renewed." (*OTP* 1:671-73)

It is conceivable that Hebrews understands heaven (the heavenly holy place) is defiled and must be purified because human beings defile heaven by their unrighteousness, as in the text cited above the sun is defiled by the sight of human beings and must be purified. Similarly nos. 49, 962.

870. Hebrews 10:20

Clement of Alexandria, *Excerpta ex Theodoto* 38:1 (150 CE)

A river of fire comes forth from beneath the throne of The Place and flows into the emptiness of what has been created, which is the pit of hell [Γέεννα] that has not been filled since the river of fire has been created. And also The Place itself is fiery. That is why there is a curtain, so that the Spirits are not destroyed by looking in. The archangel alone goes in to it. It is on this model that the High Priest alone goes only once a year into the Holy of Holies. (MEB/from Greek text in François Signard, *Clement D'Alexandrie: Extraits De Théodote* [Paris: Les Éditions Du Cerf, 1970], 140)

The text reflects Jewish mystical thought. The "Place" is a circumlocution for the name of God, as also in *3 Enoch* 45:1: "Come and I will show you the curtain of Ha- Maqom [The Place]. . . ." On protection for the angels, cf. *Targum of Job* 26:9, "[God] holds fast to the darkness that surrounds the divine throne, so that the angels do not see him, extending around and over himself the cloud of his own glory like a curtain [Aramaic *pargoda*]" (MEB/Berger). The penetration through the barrier of this curtain is consequently the final and decisive problem on the way to God.

871. Hebrews 10:22

Philo, *Concerning Noah's Work as a Planter* 162 (1 cent. CE)

[On the "ancients":] For after having first prayed and presented sacrifice and implored the favor of the Deity, when they had cleansed their bodies by ablutions and their souls by streams of holy ordinances and instructions in the right way, radiant and gladsome they turned to relaxation and enjoyment . . . (LCL)

Hebrews 10:22*b* also knows the double purification of heart and body, which may be surprising in view of the texts presented in no. 868, but is here applied to the visible act of baptism and its invisible effect. The author of Hebrews can here do without neither of these two elements. So with regard to the Old Testament cult he thinks platonistically, but not with regard to Christian baptism, for here he must accept and affirm both visible and invisible. In his report of John the Baptist Josephus too emphasizes purification of both body and soul (*Antiquities* 18:117).

On Hebrews 12:29, cf. no. 393.

872. Hebrews 13:2

Plutarch, *Moralia,* "Greek and Roman Parallel Stories" 9 (45–125 CE)

The Story of Icarius who entertained Dionysus: Eratosthenes in his Erigonê. Saturn, when once he was entertained by a farmer who had a fair daughter named Entoria, seduced her and begat Janus, Hymnus, Faustus, and Felix. He then taught Icarius the use of wine and viniculture . . . (LCL)

Offering hospitality to angels in the OT-Jewish tradition (cf. esp. Gen 18:1-16) corresponds to the entertainment of gods in human form in the pagan realm. Cf. also no. 510. Cf. D. Flückiger-Guggenheim, *Göttliche Gäste: Die Einkehr von Göttern und Heroen in der griechischen Mythologie,* 1984.

The Letter of James

873. James 1:2-4, 12-14

Plutarch, *Moralia*, "How a Man May Become Aware of His Progress in Virtue" 5 (45–125 CE)

. . . The way [of progress] is no longer uphill, nor very steep, but easy and smooth and readily accomplished, as though it were made smooth by practice, and as though it brought on a light, which is to be found in the study of philosophy, and an illumination succeeding upon perplexity, errant thought, and much vacillation, which students of philosophy encounter at the outset, like persons who have left behind the land which they know and are not yet in sight of the land to which they are sailing. For having given up the common and familiar things before gaining knowledge and possession of the better, they are carried hither and thither in the earth to lie upon. (LCL)

In the Hellenistic-Jewish and early Christian thought world, the experience of a new religious beginning or the life of a hero (call/initiation) is regularly followed by temptations that test the authenticity of the call or initiation. Thus especially the discussion of the testing of Abraham, the prototype of the proselyte (cf. no. 878), as well as the reinterpretation of the sufferings of Job in this sense in the *T. Job*. The text of Plutarch cited above shows that there were analogical structures in the thought of Cynic philosophy, where "conversion" was followed by the phase of preliminary difficulties testing whether the candidate would persevere or return to the old life.

874. James 1:25

Epictetus, *Discourses* 4.1.158 (55–135 CE)

[About Diogenes: He was permitted to speak candidly even to kings.] Why, then someone asks, are you permitted? "Because I do not regard my paltry body as my own; because I need nothing; because the law, and nothing else, is everything to me." This it was which allowed him to be a free man. (LCL)

In §159, Socrates too is pictured as a man who subjected everything to the law, and thus was a completely free man. The expression "the law of liberty" thus means against this background: there is an indispensable link between freedom from everything inessential and obedience to the law.

875. James 1:25; 2:12

m. Aboth 6.2 b (2–3 cent. CE)

R. Joshua B. Levi said: "And it is written, *And the tables were the work of God, and the writing was the writing of God, graven [haruth] upon the tables.* Read not *haruth* but *heruth* [freedom], for thou findest no freeman excepting him that occupies himself in the study of the Law; and he that occupies himself in the study of the Law shall be exalted." (Danby)

This text is a witness for the rabbinic striving to actualize in terms of Torah-obedience the Hellenistic theory that the good and righteous alone are truly free. The same happens with the expression "law of liberty" in James.

876. James 1:27

Marcus Aurelius, *Meditations* 2.13.2 (121–180 CE)

Nothing is more wretched than the man who goes round and round everything, and, as Pindar says, "searches the bowels of the earth," and seeks by conjecture to sound the minds of his neighbors, but fails to perceive that it is enough to abide with the Divinity that is within himself and to do Him genuine service. Now that service is to keep Him unsullied by passion, trifling, and discontent with what comes from God or men. (Farquharson)

In Marcus Aurelius the reference to one's needy fellow human beings is lacking. He is concerned only with the preservation of the divine element in oneself (the "Divinity") by distancing oneself from the world. James too is concerned to keep oneself pure, but this is not identified with a divine element in oneself. Because God is extra-individual, transcendent, other human beings come within his perspective. Cf. also Corpus Hermeticum 12.23 (honoring God means only one thing: not to be malicious).

877. James 2:8

Pseudo-Plato, Letter 8 C (3 cent. BCE)

For the Law as Lord is king over human beings, rather than human beings tyrants over the law. (MEB/from Joseph Souilhé, *Platon: Oeuvres Complètes* [Paris: Sociéte d'Édition "Les Belles Lettres," 1949], 354)

This is the reason given for the lasting effects of the work of Lycurgus. The context speaks of "royal power" (βασιλικὴ ἀρχή) and discusses the difference between royalty and tyranny. The "royal" law would then be a law that one would follow as one follows a good king (rather than a tyrant). (See no. 764; on James 2:12, no. 875.)

878. James 2:20-23

Vulgate of Judith 8:22 (4 cent. CE)

Our fathers were tempted, in that they were put to the test of whether they would truly worship their God . . . mindful of how our father Abraham was tempted and tried by many troubles became the friend of God . . . all who have pleased God have persevered as faithful [Lat. *fideles*] through many afflictions . . . (MEB/Berger)

Analogies: (1) Connection by the "friend of God" motif. (2) "Worship of God" and "faithfulness" *(fidelis)* describe the semantic elements of "faith" in James. Thus it becomes clear that in James faith has something to do with faithfulness in both this Vulgate text and in James. James speaks of "works" where the Vulgate text speaks of "troubles," or rather of faithfulness in them. The latter is in fact more appropriate to the example of Abraham and the Abraham tradition. James' contrast between "faith" and "works" has been introduced secondarily by the author from someplace outside this tradition. On this issue cf. no. 600.

879. James 2:23

1 Maccabees 2:51-60 (2–1 cents. BCE)

Remember the deeds of the ancestors, which they did in their generations; and you will receive great honor and an everlasting name. 52 *Was not Abraham found faithful when tested, and it was reckoned to him as righteousness?* 53 Joseph in the time of his distress kept the commandment, and became lord of Egypt. 54 Phinehas our ancestor, because he was deeply zealous, received the covenant of everlasting priesthood. 55 Joshua, because he fulfilled the command, became a judge in Israel. 56 Caleb, because he testified in the assembly, received an inheritance in the land. 57 David, because he was merciful, inherited the throne of the kingdom forever. 58 Elijah, because of great zeal for the law, was taken up into heaven. 59 Hananiah, Azariah, and Mishael believed and were saved from the flame. 60 Daniel, because of his innocence, was delivered from the mouth of the lions. (NRSV)

As in James and Paul (cf. Rom 4:3; Gal 3:6), Abraham is cited as an example of one whose faith/faithfulness was reckoned to him as righteousness. The context in 1 Maccabees makes it clear that the Pauline understanding of justification by faith is not in the author's mind. It was Abraham's faithful deeds, like those of the other biblical men of action named, that caused him to be counted righteous. Thus the interpretation in James is not merely a reaction to the Pauline understanding, but the appropriation of an interpretation of Genesis 15:6 long current in Judaism. Cf. also the understanding of this text at Qumran, 533.

880. James 3:6

Empedocles, Fragment 17, 5.13, 27-29 (483/1–423 BCE)

[On the idea of the cycle of the elements in the continual process of the world's becoming:] thus insofar as they have the power to grow into One out of Many, and again, when the One grows apart and Many are formed, in this sense they come into being and have no stable life; but insofar as they never cease their continuous exchange, in this sense they remain always unmoved [unaltered] as they follow the cyclic process.

All these [elements] are equal and of the same age in their creation; but each presides over its own office, and each has its own character, and they prevail in turn in the course of Time. (Freeman)

Empedocles combines Heraclitic and Eleatic philosophy. On the one hand everything is traced back to unchanging elements, and on the other hand everything comes into being by mixture and separation of these elements, through their friendship and quarrel. There is no absolute dissolution of anything into nothing.

The text pictures with the key word "cycle" or "course of Time" a concept that was originally behind James 3:6. In the ancient world this cycle of becoming and dissolution was for Stoics also frequently associated with the idea of the periodic world conflagration (cf. no. 901), so that James would also make contact with this picture, somewhat as follows: the tongue, when it does evil, effects the dissolution and conflagration of the world. Still, these ideas only hover faintly in the background of James 3:6, for the author hardly thinks specifically on a cyclic view of being or on a cyclic conflagration, at least not in the sense of pagan cosmologies. The point in James has to do with the damaging consequences for personal existence in the present.

The expression used by James is also found in the context of the cycle of personal existence in Simplicius' (ca. 550 CE) commentary on Aristotle (on "On the Heavens" II, 1, ed. J. L. Heiberg [1984], p. 377): Zeus had Ixion, who falsely bragged that he had embraced Hera, bound to a wheel on which he has ever since been whirled through the air. This is then explained: "The creator god, who gives to everyone what he deserves, bound him to the wheel of destiny and becoming. Zeus had charged certain gods to free human souls from the cycle of evil, but Orpheus could not get them to be gracious." (MEB/Berger)

881. James 3:9

2 Enoch 44:1 (1 cent. CE)

The Lord with his own two hands created mankind; in a facsimile of his own face, both small and great, the Lord created them. And whoever insults a person's face, insults the face of a king, and treats the face of the Lord with repugnance. He who treats with contempt the face of any person treats the face of the Lord with contempt. (*OTP* 1:171)

While usually declarations about being made in the image of God are expressions of human dignity in their own right, here this image is used to express the substitutionary role of human beings (cf. Berger, *Formgeschichte*, 184-85). Since human beings are made in the image of God, an offense against them is an offense against God himself.

882. James 3:15

Plato, *Philebus* 49 A (428/27–349/48 BCE)

And of all the virtues, is not wisdom the one to which people in general lay claim, thereby filling themselves with strife and false conceit of wisdom? (LCL)

The text reflects the experience that strife is a marked characteristic of philosophers (cf. e.g. the anti-Sophist polemic; cf. Luke T. Johnson, "The New Testament's Anti-Jewish Slander and the

Conventions of Ancient Polemic," *JBL* 108 [1989]: 419-41). This is also presupposed in James 3 and 1 Corinthians 1 (cf. nos. 619-22). In James and Paul however, the answer is sought in a superior wisdom that comes from God, which cannot be a matter of selfish strife.

883. James 4:14

Pseudo-Phocylides, *Sentences* 116-17 (1 cent. CE)

Nobody knows what will be after tomorrow or after an hour.
Death is heedless of mortals, and the future is uncertain. (*OTP* 2:578)

Here the saying is the motivation for the following admonition, "Do not let evils dismay you nor therefore exult in success." In James 4 the saying grounds the concluding admonition addressed to social relationships of 4:13.

884. James 5:12

Diogenes Laertius, *Lives of Eminent Philosophers*, "Pythagoras" 8.22 (3 cent. CE)

He is said to have advised his disciples as follows [in a gnomic catalog of duties:] "Not to call the gods to witness, man's duty being rather to strive to make his own word carry conviction." (LCL)

Cf. also Iamblichus (4 cent. CE), "Life of Pythagoras" 47: "The council members *[Sanhedrin!]* should not misuse the gods' [names] in an oath, but indulge only in such statements as would be trustworthy even without oaths" (Dillon and Hershbell).

The "Delphic Precepts" (7–6 cent BCE): "Use no oaths" (Dittenberger, *Sylloge* III, 1268, left column line 8).

Finally Epictetus (55–135 CE), "Encheiridion" 33: "Refuse, if you can, to take an oath at all, but if that is impossible, refuse as far as circumstances allow" (LCL). Cf. nos. 36, 394.

The prohibition of oaths thus comes from gnomic tradition and was adopted especially in Pythagorean circles. In contrast, the reference from Epictetus is understandable from the context.

885. James 5:20

Pistis Sophia 3, 104 (2–3 cent. CE)

. . . he who will give life to one soul and save it, apart from the glory which he has in the Kingdom of the Light, he will receive further glory in return for the soul which he has saved. (MacDermot)

The text reflects a whole parenetic tradition of early Christianity on deliverance and salvation, adapted to the specific concerns and point of view of this document. Cf. further *2 Clement* 17:2; 19:1; *Epistula Apostolorum* 39.

The First Letter of Peter

886. 1 Peter 1:1

Philo, *On the Cherubim,* 120-21 (15 BCE–50 CE)

In relation to each other all created beings rank as men of longest descent and highest birth; all enjoy equal honor and equal rights, but to God they are aliens and sojourners. For each of us has come into this world as into a foreign city, in which before our birth we had no part, and in this city he does but sojourn, until he has exhausted his appointed span of life. And there is another lesson of wisdom that he teaches in these words, even this—God alone is in the true sense a citizen, and all created being is a sojourner and alien, and those whom we call citizens are so called only by a license of language. But to the wise it is a sufficient bounty, if when ranged beside God, the only citizen, they are counted as aliens and sojourners, since the fool can in no wise hold such a rank in the city of God, but we see him an outcast from it and nothing more. (LCL)

The explicit identification of Christian believers as "foreigners" in this world is found explicitly only in 1 Peter, where it is a major theme. (Indirect identification is made in Acts 7:6, 29 and Heb 11:9, 13, where the Christian life is compared to that of the ancestors of Israel, who lived as foreigners in Egypt.) Philo too understands the people of God to be foreigners in this world, but he has here adopted the Hellenistic dualism of soul and body (cf. nos. 232, 438, 488, 536, 712, 714, 737, 889), and understands this as the separation of the soul from its heavenly homeland. This understanding, though it later became common in Gnostic Christianity, is in contrast to that of 1 Peter, where not a hint of it is found. For 1 Peter, Christians are "foreigners" because they represent the continuing people of God in this world, and so, like Israel, have been elected and called by God to be a people distinct from the nations. "Christians are foreigners among their fellow human beings, even among relatives and acquaintances, because their existence has been established on a wholly new basis. They are 'elected' or—as is said subsequently in 1:3—'born anew to a living hope through Jesus Christ's resurrection from the dead' " (Leonhard Goppelt, *A Commentary on 1 Peter,* trans. and augmented by John E. Alsup [Grand Rapids: Eerdmans, 1993], 67).

887. 1 Peter 1:12

11QPsa Hymn to the Creator 26.4-5

He divides light from obscurity; he establishes the dawn by the knowledge of his heart.
    When all his angels saw it, they sang, for he showed them that which they had not known. (Vermes)

Cf. also perhaps 1QH 13:11. In the text cited, the angels are surprised at the presentation of the previously hidden plan of God for the creation. The surprise indicates that here is something new and amazing. Similarly at the suffering and glory of Christ. Here of course is the additional element of the tension between "you," the addressees and the angels, who would love to know what you know. Only those addressed are designated for special favor.

On 1 Peter 2:11, cf. nos. 585, 587, 588, 591.

888. 1 Peter 2:5, 9

CD 3:21–4:6 (2 cent. BCE)

As God ordained for them by the hand of the Prophet Ezekiel, saying, "The Priests, the Levites, and the sons of Zadok who kept the charge of my sanctuary when the children of Israel strayed from me, they shall offer me fat and blood" [Ezek xliv, 15].

The *Priests* are the converts of Israel who departed from the land of Judah, and [the *Levites* are] those who joined them. The sons of *Zadok* are the elect of Israel, the men called by name who shall stand at the end of the days. Behold the exact list of their names according to their generations, and the time when they lived, and the number of their trials, and the years of their sojourn, and the exact list of their deeds . . . (Vermes)

Cf. further CD 6:4-5: "The *Well* is the Law, and those who dug it were the converts of Israel who went out of the land of Judah to sojourn in the land of Damascus." Here the Qumran community interprets the scriptural declarations about priests in terms of themselves. All Israel had been called to be a priestly nation (Exod 19:6), but empirical Israel had failed, and the true Israel continues as the Qumran community. "Damascus" is not geography, but the symbolic name representing exile. Not only those who stand in the priestly line genealogically, but all who choose to follow the Qumran group into its voluntary exile, belong to the community of priests. Both 1 Peter and the Qumran community understand the promises to Israel to apply now to them, and regard themselves as strangers and exiles. First Peter uses the Hellenistic Jewish term "Diaspora," rather than the Hebrew-Qumranic "exile," to correspond to its understanding of its mission as representing the scattered people of God *in* society rather than withdrawn from it as at Qumran.

889. 1 Peter 2:12

Plutarch, *Moralia*, "On Exile" 17 (45–125 CE)

But "exile" is a term of reproach. Yes, among fools, who make terms of abuse out of "pauper," "bald," "short," and indeed "foreigner" [ξένος] and "immigrant" [μέτοικος]. But those who are not carried away by such considerations admire good men, even if they are poor or foreigners or exiles.

But it is truest to say that the soul is an exile and a wanderer, driven forth by divine decrees and laws; and then, as on an island buffeted by the seas, imprisoned within the body "like an oyster in its shell," as Plato says, because it does not remember or recall "what honor and what high felicity" it has left, not leaving Sardis for Athens or Corinth for Lemnos or Scyros, but Heaven and the Moon for earth and life on earth . . . (LCL)

Both Plutarch and 1 Peter are concerned with coming to terms with analogous situations: with exile and social marginalization within the framework of Asia Minor society. Plutarch's answer: the real criterion is morality, and the real situation of all human beings is that of exile. In 1 Peter on the other hand, the isolation of being a foreigner is something to be affirmed, to be deepened as an aspect of Christian ethics, and to be transformed into a missionary opportunity. David Aune has pointed out to me the connection between this type of thought and the Hellenistic idea of the hierarchy of being: some things are more real than others. Just as God is more real than the world, the soul is more real than the body.

890. 1 Peter 2:13–3:7

Arius Didymus in Stobaeus, *Anthologium* 148-51 (1 cent. CE)

A primary kind of association [πολιτεία] is the legal union of a man and a woman for begetting children and for sharing life. This is called a household and is the source for a city, concerning which it is also necessary to speak. For the household is like any small city, if, at least as is intended, the marriage flourishes, and the children mature and are paired with one another; another household is founded, and thus a third and a fourth, and out of these a village and a city. After many villages come to be, a city is produced. So just as the household yields for the city the seeds of its formation, thus also it yields the constitution [πολιτεία].

Connected with the house is a pattern of monarchy, of aristocracy and of democracy. The relationship of parents to children is monarchic, of husbands to wives aristocratic, of children to one another democratic. For the male is to unite with the female in accordance with a desire for begetting children and for continuing the race. For each of the two is to aim at producing children. When they come together and take for themselves a helper of the partnership—either a slave by nature (strong in body for service, but stupid and unable to live by himself, for whom slavery is beneficial) or a slave by law—a household is organized by the union of the ones added together and by the forethought of all for one thing that is profitable.

The man has the rule of this household by nature. For the deliberative faculty of the woman is inferior, in children it does not yet exist, and in the case of slaves it is completely absent. Economic prudence, which is the controlling both of a household itself and of those things related to the household, is naturally fitting for a man. Belonging to this are the arts of fatherhood, marriage, being a master, and moneymaking. . . . For clearly this division [moneymaking] of household management is the most important. . . . There is a better and a worse kind of moneymaking. The better kind is engaged in according to nature and the worst through trade. And these things are sufficient concerning "household management."

"Concerning politics" these might be the headings. First, cities were organized both because the human being is social by nature and because it is useful. Next, the most perfect partnership is a city, and a citizen is one who has a claim to civic office. A city is the population composed of enough people for a self-sufficient life. The population is limited to the degree that the city is neither unfeeling nor contemptible, but is equipped both to live without want and to take care of those who set upon it from the outside. Now household management, lawgiving, politics and making war are various kinds of prudence.

Necessarily, either one, a few or all persons rule cities. Each of these is either good or bad. It is good when the rulers aim at benefiting the public and bad when they aim at their personal interest. The bad is a deviation from the good. Monarchy, then, and aristocracy and democracy aim at the good, but tyranny, oligarchy and mob-rule aim at the bad. The best constitution is some mixture of the good forms.

Seditions in cities occur either rationally or emotionally. They occur rationally whenever those with equal rights are compelled to be unequal, or when those who are unequal have equality. (Balch in Aune)

It is debated whether the household codes (*Haustafeln*) adopted and adapted by second- and third-generation Christianity derive from the Stoic (Dibelius), Oriental and Hellenistic Jewish (Weidegger, Crouch) or Aristotelian (Lührmann, Thraede, Balch) traditions. The above text is evidence for the view that "the primary source for the form of the code is neither Stoicism nor Oriental or Hellenistic Judaism. Instead, the NT codes are derived from the Hellenistic discussion 'concerning household management' [περὶ οἰκονομίας], especially as outlined by Aristotle, *Politics* I 1253b 1-14. This Aristotelian text outlines relationships between a) three pairs of social classes b) which are related reciprocally, and c) it argues that one social class in each of the three pairs is to 'be ruled'" (David L. Balch, "Household Codes," in David E. Aune, ed., *Greco-Roman Literature and the New Testament*, SBL Sources for Biblical Study 21 [Atlanta: Scholars Press, 1988]). This text is esp. important for the interpretation of the household code in 1 Peter, since both relate the structure of the household to that of the state, a further development in the direction of the Aristotelian tradition from the household codes in Colossians 3:18–4:1 and Ephesians 5:21–6:9.

891. 1 Peter 2:14

Plutarch, *Moralia*, "Sayings of Kings and Commanders: Nicostratus" 1 (45–125 CE)

Nicostratus, the general of the Argives, was urged by Archidamus to betray a certain stronghold, his reward to be a large sum of money and marriage with any Spartan woman he wished, save only the royal family; but his reply was that Archidamus was not descended from Heracles, for Heracles, as he went about, punished the bad men, but Archidamus made the good men bad. (LCL)

The text, a chreia, presents a piece of contemporary interpretation of the role of rulers, oriented theologically to Hercules. His deeds were understood as a model for the responsibility of rulers to punish evil. (Cf. also Plutarch, "Life of Theseus.")

On 1 Peter 2:21-25, cf. no. 68. On 1 Peter 3:1-7, cf. no. 771.

892. 1 Peter 3:1-6

Pythagorean Letter of Melissa to Clearete (3 cent. BCE–2 cent. CE)

Melissa to Clearete, greetings.

Of your own desire, it seems to me, you possess most of what is good. For your zealous [wish] to listen to the topic of [women's adornment] offers fair hope [that you intend] to perfect yourself in virtue. [It is necessary then] for the moderate and liberal woman to live [with] [her lawful] husband [adorned] with quietness, white and clean in her dress, plain and [not costly], simple and not elaborate [or excessive]. For she must reject [. . .], and garments shot with purpose of gold. For these are used by call-girls in [soliciting] the generality of men, but if she is to be [attractive] to one man, her own, a woman's ornament is her manners and not her clothing. And a liberal and moderate woman must seem good-looking to her own husband, but not to the man next door, having on her cheeks the blush of modesty rather than of rouge and powder, and good bearing and decency and moderation rather than gold and emerald. For it is not in expenditure on dress and looks that the moderate woman should express her love of the good but in the management and maintenance of her household, and pleasing her own husband, given that he is a moderate man, by fulfilling his wishes. For the husband's will ought to be engraved as law on a decent wife's mind, and she must live by it. And she must consider that the dowry she has brought with her that is best and greatest of all is her good order. And she must believe in the beauty and wealth of the soul rather than in that of money and appearance. As for money and looks, time, envy, illness and fortune take them away. But adornment of soul lasts till death with women who possess it. (Horsley, *New Documents* 6)

The text printed is a 3 cent. CE paraphrase of a letter from the traditional corpus of Pythagorean letters (for a trans. of the originals, cf. Malherbe). It is debated whether the originals were pseudepigraphical or were real letters written by and to women within the Pythagorean school. The (probably majority) view that the letters are pseudepigraphical products of the conservative Pythor- agean school is assumed by Balch, "Household Codes," in Aune, *Greco-Roman Literature and the New Testament*, 30-31. Among others, Sarah B. Pomeroy, *Women in Hellenistic Egypt from Alexandra to Cleopatra* (New York: Schocken, 1984), 64, argues the letters are authentic compositions by the persons to whom they are ascribed. In either case, they point out the virtues considered appropriate to women in the Pythagorean tradition and in many other streams of Hellenistic life. While there is much similarity to the ideal virtues for women taught in the New Testament Haustafel (cf. also Col 3:18–4:1; Eph 5:22–6:9; Titus 2:1-10; 1 Tim 2–3), here the NT note of reciprocity and community is lacking, the emphasis being on the cultivation of individual virtue. Also, the conservative Pythago- rean tradition lagged somewhat behind the actual possibilities for equality as seen in Musonius Rufus and Plutarch (cf. Balch, "Household Codes," 26-30), but Balch points out there are also Neopythagorean texts in which the wife has governing authority: the prudent and modest wife "will not only benefit her husband, but also her children, her kindred, her slaves, and the whole of her family. . . . For, from the possession of these virtues, she will act worthily when she becomes a wife, toward herself, her husband, her children and her household [οἶκον]. Frequently, also, such a woman will act beautifully toward cities, if she happens to rule over cities or nations, as we see is (sometimes) the case in a kingdom [Perictione, *On the Harmony of a Woman* 142, 21-143; 144]." Cf. also David Balch, "Neopythagorean Moralists and the New Testament Household Codes," *ANRW* 26.1, 380-411.

893. 1 Peter 3:1-6

Corpus Inscriptionum Latinarum 6.10230 (early 1 cent. CE)

My dearest mother deserved greater praise than all the others, since in modesty, propriety, chastity, obedience, woolworking, industry, and honor she was on an equal level with other good women, nor did she take second place to any woman in virtue, work, and wisdom in times of danger. (Lefkowitz and Fant)

First Peter's ideal of the virtuous woman corresponds not only to biblical models (cf. Prov 31), but especially to the Hellenistic ideal as documented in this eulogy inscribed by a son in honor of his mother.

894. 1 Peter 3:1-7

Callicratidas, *On the Happiness of a Household*, 106.1-10

Since therefore the husband rules over the wife, he either rules with a despotic or with a guardian, or in the last place, with a political power: But he does not rule over her with a despotic power, for he is diligently attentive to her welfare. Nor is his government of her entirely of a guardian nature; for this is itself a part of the communion [between man and wife]. It remains therefore that he rules over her with a political power, according to which both the governor and the thing governed establish the common advantage. Hence, also, wedlock is established with a view to the communion of life. (Balch in Aune)

As in 1 Peter, the assumed patriarchal structure of the household also admonishes the husband not to abuse his authority, but to show consideration to the wife as a partner. As in 1 Peter, the connection is made between the political structure of the state and the governance of the household. On the woman as the "weaker sex," see no. 890 above on 1 Peter 2:13–3:7.

895. 1 Peter 3:7

Musonius Rufus, *Should Daughters Receive the Same Educations as Sons?* (30–100 CE)

[In the context of affirming the equality of the sexes, arguing especially that girls should receive an education equal to boys:] "Come now," I suppose someone will say, "do you expect that men should learn spinning the same as women, and that women should take part in gymnastic exercises the same as men?" No, that I should not demand. But I do say that, since in the human race man's constitution is stronger and woman's weaker, tasks should be assigned which are suited to the nature of each; that is the heavier tasks should be given to the stronger and lighter ones to the weaker. Thus spinning and indoor work should be more fitting for women than for men, while gymnastics and outdoor work would be more suitable for men. Occasionally, however, some men might more fittingly handle certain of the lighter tasks and what is generally considered women's work, and again, women might do heavier tasks which seem more appropriate for men whenever conditions of strength, need, or circumstance warranted. For all human tasks, I am inclined to believe, are a common obligation and are common for men and women, and none is appointed for either one exclusively, but some pursuits are more suited to the nature of one, some to the other, and for this reason some are called men's work and some women's. But whatever things have reference to virtue, these one would properly say are equally appropriate to the nature of both, inasmuch as we agree that virtues are in no respect more fitting for the one than the other. (Lutz)

As in no. 651 on 1 Corinthians 7:1-40, Musonius (a Roman Stoic contemporary with the author of 1 Peter) manifests an interesting combination of affirmations of the equality of the sexes and cultural presuppositions. He spells out and qualifies, as 1 Peter does not, what he means by the reference to women as the "weaker sex," but it is likely that 1 Peter would explicate the phrase in a similar way.

896. 1 Peter 3:19; 4:6

Pseudo-Jeremiah Agraphon in Justin, *Dialogue with Trypho* 72 (165 CE)

And again, from the sayings of the same Jeremiah these have been cut out: "The Lord God remembered His dead people of Israel who lay in the graves; and He descended to preach [εὐαγγελίσασθαι] to them His own salvation." (ANF)

A conception such as is represented in this text (Irenaeus also offers five versions) could also have provided the common background for 1 Peter 3:18 and 1 Thessalonians 4:14-17, which could then have been elaborated in two different directions: the saving eschatological descent of God to the dead; the decisive turning point in their lot through this message. The development of this pattern in 1 Thessalonians 4: the Lord Jesus descends (4:16), the resurrection of the dead through Christ; the "good news" would then be the command to rise from the grave, or the "command" of 4:16. The development of this pattern in 1 Peter 3: the dead are preserved in an intermediate place of safekeeping, Christ descends to them after his death (a particular interpretation of the "descent of the Lord"); 4:6 speaks explicitly of the preaching of the gospel. In both cases what had been originally said of God in the pseudo-Jeremiah quotation is now applied to Christ.

897. 1 Peter 3:18-20

1 Enoch 15:2-4 (2 cent. BCE)

[God speaks to Enoch:] and go and tell [πορεύθητι] the Watchers of heaven on whose behalf you have been sent to intercede [namely, the unrighteous angels]: "It is meet [for you] that you intercede on behalf of man, and not man on your behalf. For what reason have you abandoned the high, holy, and eternal heaven: and slept with women and defiled yourselves with the daughters of the people, taking wives, acting like children of the earth, and begetting giant sons? Surely you, you [used to be] holy, spiritual, the living ones." (*OTP* 1:21)

According to *1 Enoch* 21:10 these angels (cf. Gen 6:1-6) are held in a "prison" (δεσμωτήριον). This is analogous to going to the spirits kept in the place of safekeeping. Enoch, of course, had ultimately bad news to report. Is Christ pictured here as a "new Enoch"? But why would this tradition be applied to him, and where does the interest in fallen angels come from, angels that in any case have already been condemned?

A more reasonable explanation would thus be to think of Noah here as a type, in support of which one could call on the tradition that developed between the testaments that pictured Noah as a preacher of repentance to his fellow human beings who refused to listen to him. According to *Sibylline Oracles* 1.129, Noah was commissioned to preach (κηρύσσειν) "... so that all may be saved." Noah's preaching is then reported in 1.150-70. The response: "When they heard him they sneered at him, each one, calling him demented, a man gone mad" (171-72). Then follows his second preaching mission. According to 1.199, the result: "... he had spoken these things in vain to a lawless generation ..." (*OTP* 1:338-39).

Something similar is transmitted in the Latin "Vision of Paul" (Noah was laughed to scorn when he preached repentance to his generation), and in the Syrian Homilies (ed. A. Bensley et al., *Fragments of Ancient Homilies* [Oxford, 1896], p. 81): Noah is to plant cedars for the Arche, and the time it takes them to grow is the time of God's patience; cf. 1 Peter 3:20! If 1 Peter presents Jesus as outdoing Noah, this would be an exemplary and impressive extension of the message of salvation into the past.

898. 1 Peter 3:21

Josephus, *Antiquities* 18.117 (37–100 CE)

[Describing John the Baptist:] ... was a good man and commanded the Jews to practice virtue, by exercising virtue toward one another and piety toward God, and to come together to baptism. For the baptism would be acceptable to God if they used it, not for the putting away of certain sins, but for the purification of the body, the soul having previously been cleansed by righteousness. (LCL)

Both Josephus and 1 Peter are concerned to relate the bodily washing aspect of baptism to spiritual renewal, though they do it in contrasting ways.

899. 1 Peter 4:4

Aramaic Testament of Levi 90-92 (from the Cairo Geniza) (2 cent. BCE–1 cent. CE)

Look, my sons, on Joseph, my brother, who gave instruction in the Scripture and directions in wisdom [lacuna] (91) He is not like a foreigner among you and not like an outsider ... for all honor him, and all want to learn from his wisdom. (92) His friends are numerous, and those who greet him are important people. They seat him in a place of honor, in order to learn wisdom from him ... (MEB/from Jürgen Becker, *Die Testamente der Zwölf Patriarchen. Unterweisung in lehrhafter Form* III.1 [Gütersloher: Gerd Mohn, 1980], 146)

In wide realms of postexilic and intertestamental Judaism Joseph was regarded as the model of the Jew who had attained respect in the surrounding non-Jewish world. This text presents the important key words for the social background "foreigner," "outsider," which are contrasted with "friend," "place of honor." Wisdom is the means to overcoming this sense of being regarded as an outsider, for our text makes clear that wisdom, which is accepted by others, is the instrument of con-socialization. First Peter 4:4, where to a certain degree the external situation is described, stands in contrast to this. The means of overcoming the prejudice against outsiders is not "wisdom," but through the exemplary lifestyle of Christians (e.g. 2:12).

On 1 Peter 4:17, cf. no. 171.

The Second Letter of Peter

900. 2 Peter 1:5

m. Sotah 9.15 (2 cent. CE)

R. Phineas b. Jair says: Heedfulness leads to cleanliness, and cleanliness leads to purity, and purity leads to abstinence, and abstinence leads to holiness, and holiness leads to humility, and humility leads to the shunning of sin, and the shunning of sin leads to saintliness, and saintliness leads to [the gift of] the Holy Spirit, and the Holy Spirit leads to the resurrection of the dead. And the resurrection of the dead shall come through Elijah of blessed memory. (Danby)

The rabbinic text has a chain of virtues analogous to that of 2 Peter. In contrast to 2 Peter, however, the chain that begins as personal characteristics modulates into historical and eschatological events that precede the advent of the Messiah (see on no. 176 at Mark 13:12). On 2 Peter 2:10-12, cf. no. 639.

901. 2 Peter 3:5-7

Berosos, according to Seneca, *Natural Questions* 3.29 (4–3 cent. BCE)

[On the great year:] Berosos, says that these catastrophes occur with the movements of the planets. Indeed, he is so certain that he assigns a date for the conflagration and the deluge. For earthly things will burn, he contends, when all the planets which now maintain different orbits come together in the sign of Cancer.

The deluge will occur when the same group of planets meets in the sign of Capricorn. (LCL)

Against such opinions, cf. Origen, *Contra Celsum* 4.12 (neither the flood nor the final conflagration is to be attributed to a cycle of the times, but to the sins of the human race). In this connection the view expressed in 2 Peter 3:5 is important, the world consists of water. For Heraclitus, Fragment 30, in the context of a discussion of cyclical world renewal expresses the theory that the world is a shimmering and extinguishable fire. Here later speculation has added the supplement in the sense of a world that consists of water. That judgment by water and judgment by fire are juxtaposed in 2 Peter 3 at all is a reflective image that could well have been evoked by the analogies named here.

902. 2 Peter 3:5-7

Zeno, Fragment 98 (ca. 336–263 BCE)

The element of all the things which exist is Fire, and the origins of this fire are Stuff [ὕλη, matter] and God. Both of these are bodily substances: God, the active substance, and

Matter the passive substance. At certain destined periods of time the whole universe is turned into fire; then it is once more constituted an ordered manifold world. But the primal fire subsists in it like a kind of seminal fluid, containing in itself the formulas and causes of all the things which have been and are and shall be; the concatenation and sequence of these things is Destiny or Understanding or Truth, an inevitable and ineluctable Law of things. (Bevan)

This is the later Stoic elaboration of the ancient idea of Heraclitus that fire is [one of the] primal element[s]. For Stoicism the law of periodic renewal of the cosmos by burning (ἐκπύρωσις) was an internal law of nature that started the cycle of history over again. Cf. Chrysippus, *Fragment* 625: "The Stoics say that when the planets return, at certain fixed periods of time, to the same relative positions, in length and breadth, which they had at the beginning, when the cosmos was first constituted, this produces the conflagration and destruction of everything which exists. Then again the cosmos is restored anew in a precisely similar arrangement as before. . . . And this restoration of the universe takes place not once but over and over again—indeed to all eternity without end" (Bevan).

The author of 2 Peter certainly does not share this view, but affirms the unilinear view of biblical history from creation to eschaton. Yet his picture of the eschaton as the eruption of fire stored up in the universe itself is not derived from the Bible, but is reminiscent of the Stoic imagery. Although their view of history and its meaning was very different, there were already people in the Hellenistic world who looked forward to a fiery renewal of the universe. The author of 2 Peter borrows imagery from this world of ideas, imagery that would be recognized in the Hellenistic world.

903. 2 Peter 3:8

Plutarch, *Moralia*, "On the Delays of the Divine Vengeance" 5-6, 9 (45–125 CE)

. . . it is far more likely that when we see that God, who knows no fear or regret in anything, yet reserves his penalties for the future and awaits the lapse of time, we should become cautious in such matters, and hold the gentleness and magnanimity displayed by God a part of virtue that is divine, which by punishment amends a few.

. . . whereas God, we must presume, distinguishes whether the passions of the sick soul to which he administers his justice will in any way yield and make room for repentance [μετάνοια], and for those in whose nature vice is not unrelieved or intractable, he fixes a period of grace.

So likewise those of the wicked who appear to have escaped the immediate blow, pay not after, but during, a longer period a penalty more lasting, not more delayed, and have not been punished on growing old, but have grown old in punishment. When I speak of a long period I mean it relatively to ourselves, as for the gods any length of human life is but nothing, and to put the evildoer on the rack or hang him now, and not thirty years ago, is like doing it in the evening and not in the morning, especially as he is shut up in his life as in a prison-house affording no removal or escape . . . (LCL)

Analogies:
1) Common to 2 Peter and this whole composition of Plutarch is the problem of the delayed reaction of God (for Plutarch, the delay of punishment; for 2 Pet esp. related to God's promises).

2) Common to both is the view that the interim period is to be used for repentance.

3) Common to both is the argument that deity operates on a different temporal scale. Second Peter utilizes Psalm 90:4; Plutarch operates with the length of a human life. A corresponding distinction is found in the manner in which Plutarch is concerned with retribution for the individual during his lifetime, while 2 Peter deals with apocalyptic eschatology. Both are responding to the objection that God or the gods are unconcerned with what goes on in this world. Cf. Berger, in the Festschrift for J. Lebram ([Leiden: E. J. Brill, 1986), pp. 121-35. On the problem cf. also nos. 100, 267.

904. 2 Peter 3:9, 15

4 Ezra 7:74 (late 1 cent. CE)

How long the Most High has been patient with those who inhabit the world!—and not for their sake, but because of the times that he has foreordained. (NRSV)

The author of 4 Ezra is also concerned with the theological and existential problem of the delay of the eschaton, but not, as in 1 Peter, due to the jibes of outsiders. Rather, for him it is a personal problem: if God will ultimately demolish evil and establish righteousness, then why delay? Cf. 5:43-45:

"Then I answered and said, 'Could you not have created at one time those who have been and those who are and those who will be, so that you might show your judgment the sooner?' He replied to me and said, 'The creation cannot move faster than the Creator, nor can the world hold at one time those who have been created in it.' I said, 'How have you said to your servant that you will certainly give life at one time to your creation? If therefore all creatures will live at one time and the creation will sustain them, it might even now be able to support all of them present at one time'" (NRSV).

The author believes there is a rational explanation for the delay of the eschaton, and wishes to understand it. In contrast to 2 Peter, the answer is not in the divine mercy, but in the preexistent divine timetable, which once established must be respected even by its Author (cf. Mark 13:20, and no. 948 on Rev 6:9-11).

The Letters of John

905. 1 John 1:5

Pseudo-Asclepius, *Logos Teleios* (4 cent. CE)

We rejoice because you have revealed yourself to us, we rejoice that, while we were still in (bodily) form, you deified us by your knowledge. . . . We have recognized, O life of human life, we have recognized, O mother of all knowledge [Reitzenstein read "O greatest light of all knowledge"]. (MEB/Berger)

Cf. the commentary of R. Reitzenstein, *Poimandres. Studien zur griechisch-ägyptischen und frühchristlichen Literatur* (Leipzig: B. G. Teubner, 1904; repr. Darmstadt: Wissenschaftliche Buchgesellschaft, 1966), pp. 147ff. In both texts the subject—within the horizon of the philosophical religiosity of the Empire period—is divine knowledge, joy in this knowledge, life and fellowship among human beings and with God, with which reflection on the human body is explicitly associated.

The difference: In 1 John, the knowledge is mediated through witnesses—thus ecclesiological—and the body is the instrument of this mediation, not the great obstacle to it.

906. 1 John 1:5-7*a*

Corpus Hermeticum 13.9 (2–4 cent. CE)

[Hermes speaks by revelation to his son Tat:] and when greed has departed, I summon another, truth, who puts deceit to flight. And truth arrives. See how the good has been fulfilled, my child, when truth arrives. For envy has withdrawn from us, but the good, together with life and light has followed after truth, and no torment any longer attacks from the darkness. Vanquished, they have flown away in a flapping of wings. (Copenhaver)

The common comprehensive abstractions are light, life, truth. The difference is that in 1 John there is emphasis on fellowship with one another and the reference, completely alien to the atmosphere of Corpus Hermeticum, to the blood of Jesus in vol. 1:7b.

907. 1 John 1:9

Pesiqta de Rab Kahana 24, Rabbi Simon and Rabbi Jehoshua ben Levi in the name of Rabbi Shimon ben Chalaphta (2 cent. CE)

Conceal your faults and you will not prosper; [confess and give them up and you will find mercy] [Prov. 28:13]: . . .

The matter may be compared to the case of a mugger on trial before a magistrate. So long as he denies the crime, he is flogged. Once he confesses, he receives the decree.

But the Holy One, blessed be He, is not that way. But before one confesses, he gives out the decree. Once one confesses, he provides forgiveness. (Neusner, *Pesiqta*)

The rabbinic text explicitly explains that the connection between confession and forgiveness that seems obvious to us was at least for ancient hearers not in the least obvious as an analogy from everyday life.

908. 1 John 2:9

Inscription, *CIL* 6.377

Valerius Crescentius, Father for all gods, and Aurelius Exuperantius, priest of Silvanus, have dedicated [this] with the brothers and sisters. (MEB/Berger)

The title "Father" (Lat. *Pater*) indicates the Mithras cult, though the addition of "sisters" is unusual, since elsewhere there is nothing known of women participating in this cult. In general, however, "brother" is the usual mutual designation of members among mystery-type cultic associations. That points to the fact that here, as in early Christianity, the model on which the association was based was that of the family. For additional material, cf. K. H. Schelke, "Bruder," 2:631-35, *RAC*. Very often the "brother" relationship among the members presupposes a "Father" relation between the cult/association members and the sponsoring deity.

909. 1 John 2:11

Odes of Solomon 18:6-7 (2 cent. CE)

Let not light be conquered by darkness,
nor let truth flee from falsehood.
Let your right hand set our salvation to victory,
and let it receive from every region,
and preserve [it] on the side of everyone who is besieged by evils. (*OTP* 2:751)

The imagery corresponds to much of the philosophical religiosity of the imperial period. First John stands out from this background by being more concrete in the realm of ethics, ecclesiology (and, in other passages, Christology).

910. 1 John 2:16

Plutarch, *Moralia*, "That Epicurus Actually Makes A Pleasant Life Impossible" 1096 (Epicurus, 342–271 BCE; Plutarch, 45–125 CE)

Instead they lay the contemplative part of the soul flat in the body and use the appetites of the flesh as leaden weights to hold it down. In this they are no better than stable hands or shepherds, who serve their charges with hay or straw or grass of one kind or the other as the proper food for them to crop and chew. Do they not in similar fashion play swineherd to the soul, feeding it only on this swill of the bodily pleasures, permitting it to delight only in the hope or experience or recollection of some carnal thing, and forbidding it to take or seek from itself any pleasure or gratification of its own? (LCL)

In protesting against the Epicureans here the lusts of the flesh are contrasted with the nobility of intellectual potential, while in 1 John the contrast is with the love of God. This is the typical reception schema in early Christian letters when dealing with pagan materials: in place of the orientation to anthropology, an orientation that becomes theological only at the point of a doctrine of creation, the role of the higher good is taken by an orientation toward the personal God, his new act of salvation and his charismatic gift.

911. 1 John 2:15-17

Corpus Hermeticum 6.4 (2–4 cent. CE)

[Hermes, once an Egyptian sage but now himself deified and belonging to the divine world, speaks by revelation to Asclepius:] As for me, I give thanks to god for what he has put in my mind, even to know of the good that it is impossible for it to exist in the cosmos. For the cosmos is a plenitude [πλήρωμα] of vice, as god is a plenitude of the good . . . (Copenhaver)

CH here concentrates on picturing redemption, 1 John on ethics. Both have in common a God/world dualism (cf. nos. 362-63). Nevertheless, it is inconceivable that statements such as this from CH could appear in 1 John, for here it can be said that God loves the world (John 3:16). This would be impossible in CH. It is out of the question, however, that Johannine believers should love the world. On "fullness, mass" (πλήρωμα), cf. no. 870.

912. 1 John 2:18

2 Baruch 36:7-11 (end of 1 cent. CE)

And I saw, and behold, that vine opened its mouth and spoke and said to the cedar, "Are you not that cedar which remained of the forest of wickedness? Because of you, wickedness remained and has been during all these years, but never goodness. And you possessed power over that which did not belong to you; you did not even show compassion to that which did belong to you. And you extended your power over those who were living far from you, and you keep those who are close to you in the nets of your wickedness, and you uplift your soul always like one who could not be uprooted. But now your time has hastened and your hour has come. Therefore O cedar, follow the forest which has departed before you and become ashes with it, and let your earth be mixed together. And now, sleep in distress and rest in pain until your last time comes in which you will return to be tormented even more." (OTP 1:632)

Cf. under no. 962, the "Potter's Oracle."

The picture then continues with the burning of the cedar, while the vine grows. It is here not possible to maintain a strict separation between the respective people and its representative. In later texts the invective (*Scheltrede,* cf. Berger, *Formgeschichte,* §53) against the Anti-Christ becomes a fixed topos; cf. above, no. 131. The subject here is the final Adversary. This text deals with the political line of expectation. Further:

913. 1 John 2:18

1QpHab 10:5b-13 (1 cent. BCE?)

[On Hab 2:12-13:] Woe to him who builds a city with blood and founds a town upon falsehood! Behold, is it not from the Lord of Hosts that the peoples shall labor for fire and the nations shall strive for naught? [ii, 12-13].

Interpreted, this concerns the Spouter of Lies who led many astray that he might build his city of vanity with blood and raise a congregation on deceit, causing many thereby to perform a service of vanity for the sake of its glory, and to be pregnant with [works] of deceit, that their labor might be for nothing and that they might be punished with fire who vilified and outraged the elect of God. (Vermes)

Here there is a nameless eschatological prophetic adversary who "leads into error" and has won numerous followers. Also in 1 John 2:18 it is presupposed that in the course of the apocalyptic events there will be an individual Adversary. As in Qumran, he is connected with lies (2:21). This text deals with the prophetic line of expectation. Further:

914. 1 John 2:18

Didache 16:2-5 (1 cent. CE; closer dating not possible)

But be frequently gathered together seeking the things which are profitable for your souls, for the whole time of your faith shall not profit you except ye be found perfect at the last time; 3. for in the last days the false prophets and the corrupters shall be multiplied, and the sheep shall be turned into wolves, and love shall change to hate; 4. for as lawlessness increaseth they shall hate one another and persecute and betray, and then shall appear the deceiver of the world as a Son of God, and shall do signs and wonders and the earth shall be given over into his hands and he shall commit iniquities which have never been since the world began. 5. Then shall the creation of mankind come to the fiery trial and "many shall be offended" and be lost, but, "they who endure" in their faith "shall be saved by the curse itself." (LCL)

Didache 16:3 speaks like Mark 13:22 of many false prophets and corrupters who will come in the last days, and 16:4 beyond this of the expected final "deceiver." In contrast, in 1 John 2:18 the many and the one are essentially identified. It is notable that in 1 John there is no reference to miraculous signs. Further:

915. 1 John 2:18

Ethiopic *Apocalypse of Peter*, §2 (4–5 cent. CE ?)

And the Master answered and said unto me, "Dost thou not understand that the fig tree is the house of Israel? Even as a man hath planted a fig tree in his garden and it brought forth no fruit, and he sought its fruit for many years. When he found it not, he said to the keeper of his garden, 'Uproot the fig tree that our land may not be unfruitful for us.' And the gardener said to God, 'We thy servants [?] wish to clear it [of weeds] and to dig the ground around it and to water it. If it does not then bear fruit, we will immediately remove its roots from the garden and plant another one in its place.' Hast thou not grasped that the fig tree is the house of Israel? Verily I say to you, when its boughs have sprouted at the end, then shall deceiving Christs come, and awaken hope [with the words]: 'I am the Christ, who am [now] come into the world.' And they shall see the wickedness of their deeds [even of the false Christs], and they shall turn away after them and deny him to whom their fathers gave praise [?], the first Christ whom they crucified and thereby sinned exceedingly. But this deceiver is not the Christ. And when they reject him, he will kill with the sword [dagger] and there shall be many martyrs." (Schneemelcher)

Here the prophetic and the political are combined (similarly as in Rev 13, there too associated with martyrdom). In the following verses Enoch and Elijah appear, in order to instruct people "that this is the Deceiver, who must come into the world and do signs and wonders, in order to deceive. . . ."

On the figure of the Anti-Christ see further nos. 175, 531, 962.

916. 1 John 3:1

Pesiqta Rabbati 11 (46b) (3–4 cent.)

In this world, Israel cleave unto the Holy One, blessed be He, as is said *But ye that did cleave unto the Lord* (Deut 4:4). But in the time-to-come they will become like [the Lord]. As the Holy One, blessed be He, is a fire consuming fire, as is written *For the Lord is a devouring fire* (Deut 4:24), so shall they be a devouring fire, as is written *And the light of Israel shall be for a fire, and his Holy One for a flame* [Isa 10:17]. (Braude)

Analogy: two phases, in the second of which human beings do become like God. The Pesiqta passage is also a documentation of the view that the righteous shall function as judges (cf. 1 Cor 6:2-3; Matt 19:28; Rev 3:21). The Jewish background of 1 John needs more extensive attention.

917. 1 John 3:1

Orphic gold tablet from the necropolis of Thurioi (southern Italy), lines 8-9 (dating of grave 4 cent. BCE)

Happy and blessed, you will be a god instead of a mortal; like a young kid I have fallen down for milk. (MEB/Berger taken from H. Lloyd-Jonas, *Pindar and the After-Life*, Entretiens Foundation Hardt 31 [1984], 245-79, p. 272)

Parallels are found in A. Dieterich, *Nekyia* 85:2: The one initiated into the mysteries lives, with regard to death, under an expectation completely contrary to the "normal" perspective: for that person, real happiness is still to come.

918. 1 John 4:6

1QS 3 (2–1 cents. BCE)

He has created man to govern the world, and has appointed for him two spirits in which to walk until the time of His visitation: the spirits of truth and falsehood.

All the children of righteousness are ruled by the Prince of Light and walk in the ways of light, but all the children of falsehood are ruled by the Angel of Darkness and walk in the ways of darkness.

The Angel of Darkness leads all the children of righteousness astray; and until his end, all their sin, iniquities, wickedness, and all their unlawful deeds are caused by his dominion in accordance with the mysteries of God.

But the God of Israel and His Angel of Truth will succor all the sons of light. For it is He who created the spirits of Light and Darkness and founded every action upon them and established every deed [upon] their [ways]. (Vermes)

Prior to the discovery of the Dead Sea Scrolls, the dualism of the Johannine literature was often thought to be late and "Greek," i.e. non-Jewish. The Qumran MSS let us see that a kind of dualism had penetrated into very Jewish settings, though the citation illustrates that this was a penultimate dualism: the one God is creator of all, both the good and evil spirits, a temporary arrangement with an eschatological termination. Though expressed in a different idiom, the two spirits are somewhat like the two yetzers ("impulses") of the rabbinic literature. For Qumran, the spirit of truth is dominant within the community, and the spirit of error outside it; for 1 John, the two spirits characterize a conflict within the community.

The Letter of Jude

On Jude 6, cf. no. 137.

919. Jude 8-9

Palaia (a Jewish retelling of OT history books with Christian supplements, preserved in Greek; Jewish material is 1–2 cent. CE)

And Samuel brought the body [namely, of Moses] to the people, he tempted them to make him [namely, Moses] into a god. But Michael, the commander of the heavenly host, came at God's command to get the body and take it away. And Samuel resisted [ἀνθίστατο], and they struggled [διεμάχοντο]. The commander of the host became indignant, and by way of rebuke said "The Lord rebuke you, Devil!" So the Adversary backed off and took to flight. The archangel Michael then took the body of Moses away to the place God had commanded him . . . and no one saw the grave of Moses. (MEB/Berger taken from A. Vassiliev, *Anecdota Graeco-Byzantina* [Moscow, 1893], 188-292, p. 258)

Cf. K. Berger, "Der Streit des Guten und des Bösen Engels um die Seele," *JSJ* 4 (1973), 1-18. This text is the only extant story of the event to which Jude refers. Samuel stands for Sammael, a rabbinic name for the devil. In the context of Jude the issue is how to understand what may be permitted to a pneumatic: even Michael only spoke of the Lord's rebuke and did not rebuke in his own name. Thus a pneumatic must exercise care when he or she begins to speak against angels and spirits. Cf. also no. 639. On Jude 10 (φυσικῶς) cf. no. 482.

920. Jude 14-15

Jubilees 4:16-25 (145–140 BCE)

And in the eleventh Jubilee, Jared took for himself a wife and her name was Baraka, the daughter of Rasuyal, the daughter of his father's brother, as a wife, in the fourth year of the jubilee. And she bore a son for him in the fifth week, in the fourth year of the jubilee. And he called him Enoch.

This one was the first who learned writing and knowledge and wisdom, from [among] the sons of men, from [among] those who were born upon earth. And who wrote in a book the signs of the heaven according to the order of their months, so that the sons of man might know the [appointed] times of the years according to their order, with respect to each of their months. This one was the first [who] wrote a testimony and testified to the children of men throughout the generations of the earth. And their weeks according to jubilees he recounted; and the days of the years he made known. And the months he set in order, and the sabbaths of the years he recounted, just as we made it known to him. And he saw what was and what will be in a vision of his sleep as it will happen among the children of men in their generations until the day of judgment. He saw and knew everything and wrote his testimony and deposited the testimony upon the earth against all the children of men and their generations.

And in the twelfth jubilee in its seventh week, he took for himself a wife and her name was 'Edni, the daughter of Dan'el, his father's brother, as a wife, and in the sixth year of this week she bore a son for him. And he called him Methuselah.

And he was therefore with the angels of God six jubilees of years. And they showed him everything which is on earth and in the heavens, the dominion of the sun. And he wrote everything, and bore witness to the Watchers, the ones who sinned with the daughters of men because they began to mingle themselves with the daughters of men so that they might be polluted. And Enoch bore witness against all of them. And he was taken from among the children of men, and we led him to the garden of Eden for greatness and honor. And behold, he is there writing condemnation and judgment of the world, and all of the evils of the children of men. And because of him none of the water of the Flood came upon the whole land of Eden, for he was put there for a sign and so that he might bear witness against all of the children of men so that he might relate all of the deeds of the generations until the day of judgment. And he offered the incense which is acceptable before the Lord in the evening [at] the holy place on Mount Qater [or "noon"]. (*OTP* 2:62-63)

The quotation from *Jubilees* is only a tiny sample of a vast literature. Enoch is only mentioned briefly in the Old Testament (Gen 5:21-24), and nothing further is made of him in the canonical Hebrew scriptures. Between the Testaments, however, an elaborate Enoch tradition was developed, a whole library of materials attributed to and associated with Enoch. The documents that have come to us as *1, 2,* and *3 Enoch* are themselves composite, representing a much larger number of compositions, and books such as *Jubilees* treat Enoch as source and channel of revealed apocalyptic and wisdom information. He was the ideal figure to whom apocalyptic revelations could be attributed, since he lived before the flood, and since he had been taken to heaven without dying.

Jude 14-15 is the only explicit citation from the Enoch literature in the NT (*1 Enoch* 1:9), but there are numerous allusions, cases of indirect influence, and allusions (Nestle-Aland lists fifty-eight such NT passages, in fourteen NT books).

The Revelation to John

921. Revelation

Inscription from Ephesus (48 BCE)

The cities in Asia along with its [communities] and regions [honor] Gaius Iulius, Son of Gaius, Caesar, High Priest [Pontifex Maximus], Emperor and Consul for the second time, descended from Ares and Aphrodite, the visibly manifest God and universal savior [Σωτήρ] of human life. (MEB/from Leipold and Grundmann)

This is the earliest documentation for the idea of one savior for the whole human race (later examples, e.g. Halicarnassus inscription from Augustus' time). Revelation was written to seven churches in the province of Asia, where for more than a hundred years this kind of enthusiastic affirmation of the divine status of the emperor was promoted. Domitian's encouragement of it was only a link in a long chain.

922. Revelation

Duris the Historian, Athenian Cultic Song for Demetrius Poliorketes (291–290 BCE)

Yes, the greatest and most beloved of the gods
Have appeared to our city:
Here came Demeter and Demetrius
Together the blessing of the hour.
She comes, solemnly to celebrate the sacred mysteries of Kore
He cheerfully tarries, as fitting for a god, beautiful and happy among us.
A splendid scene: the friends all in a circle
He himself in their midst,
The friends like the stars,
But he himself the sun.
You son of Poseidon, the most mighty of gods
And of Aphrodite, receive our greetings.
The other gods must be far distant,
Or have no ears
Or do not even exist, or, if they do, care nothing for us
But you we see as living and present among us
Not of wood and not of stone, but truly present
Thus we pray to you:
Above all, make peace, Most Beloved,
For you are the Lord [Κύριος]. (MEB/*Fragmenta Graecorum Historicorum* 76 F 13)

As the successful Macedonian field marshal Demetrius paraded into Athens for the third time, the enthusiastic Athenians, who needed his help, greeted his arrival as the advent of a god, with singing and dancing in the streets. The historian Duris made a copy of the hymn composed for the occasion. The text from third-century BCE Athens shows both that honoring the ruler as divine was not exclusively a late, eastern development, and was not unusual in Greece after Alexander's time, and that such extravagant language may not have been meant so "literally" as moderns are likely to take it. In the extravagant language of praise, a human being could be acclaimed not only as divine, but as perhaps the only god. This can hardly have been meant as prosaic literalism, since Demeter is celebrated in the same song. The borders between mortals and the gods were more fluid in (non-Jewish) Hellenistic thinking long before NT times.

923. Revelation

Odes of Solomon 8:8-19; 10:1-6; 22:1-12; 28:9-20; 36:1-8; 41:8-10; 42:3-7 (1–2 cent. CE)

[*Ode* 8:8-19 The risen Christ speaks:]
Hear the word of truth,
and receive the knowledge of the Most High.
Your flesh may not understand that which I am about to say to you;
nor your garment that which I am about to declare to you.
Keep my mystery, you who are kept by it;
keep my faith, you who are kept by it.
And understand my knowledge, you who know me in truth;
love me with affection, you who love;
For I turn not my face from my own,
because I know them.
And before they had existed,
I recognized them;
and imprinted a seal on their faces.
I fashioned their members,
and my own breasts I prepared for them,
that they might drink my holy milk and live by it.
I am pleased by them,
and I am not ashamed by them.
For my work are they,
and the power of my thoughts.
Therefore who can stand against my work?
Or who is not subject to them?
I willed and fashioned mind and heart;
and they are my own.
And upon my right hand I have set my elect ones.
And my righteousness goes before them;
and they will not be deprived of my name;
for it is with them.

[*Ode* 10:1-6 The Odist speaks:]
The Lord has directed my mouth by his Word,
and has opened my heart by his Light. . . .
To convert the lives of those who desire to come to him,
and to capture a good captivity for freedom.
[The risen Christ speaks:]
I took courage and became strong and captured the world,
and it became mine for the glory of the Most High, and of God my Father.
And the gentiles who had been scattered were gathered together,
but I was not defiled by my love [for them],
because they had praised me in high places.
And the traces of light were set upon their heart,
and they walked according to my life and were saved,
and they became my people forever and ever.

[*Ode* 22:1-5 The risen Christ speaks:]
He who caused me to descend from on high,
and to ascend from the regions below;
And he who gathers what is in the middle,
and throws them to me;
He who scattered my enemies,
and my adversaries;
He who gave me authority over chains,
so that I might loosen them;
He who overthrew by my hands the dragon with seven heads,
and placed me at his roots that I might destroy his seed;

[*Ode* 28:9-20 The risen Christ speaks:]
Those who saw me were amazed
because I was persecuted.
And they thought that I had been swallowed up,
because I appeared to them as one of the lost.
But my defamation
became my salvation.
And I became their abomination,
because there was no jealousy in me.
Because I continually did good to every man
I was hated.
And they surrounded me like mad dogs,
those who in stupidity attack their masters.
Because their mind is depraved,
and their sense is perverted.
But I was carrying water in my right hand,
and their bitterness I endured by my sweetness.
And I did not perish, because I was not their brother,
nor was my birth like theirs.
And they sought my death but were unsuccessful,

because I was older than their memory;
and in vain did they cast lots against me.
And those who were after me
sought in vain to destroy the memorial of him
who was before them.
Because the mind of the Most High cannot be prepossessed;
and his heart is superior to all wisdom.

[*Ode* 36:1-8 The Odist speaks:]
I rested on the Spirit of the Lord,
and she raised me up to heaven;
And caused me to stand on my feet in the Lord's high place,
before his perfection and his glory,
where I continued praising [him] by the composition of his odes.
[The risen Christ speaks:]
[The Spirit] brought me forth before the Lord's face,
and because I was the Son of Man,
I was named the Light, the Son of God;
Because I was most praised among the praised;
and the greatest among the great ones.
For according to the greatness of the Most High, so she made me;
and according to his newness he renewed me.
And he anointed me with his perfection;
and I became one of those who are near him.
And my mouth was opened like a cloud of dew,
and my heart gushed forth [like] a gusher of righteousness.
And my approach was in peace,
and I was established in the spirit of providence.

[*Ode* 41:8-10 The risen Christ speaks:]
All those who see me will be amazed,
because I am from another race.
For the Father of Truth remembered me;
he who possessed me from the beginning.
For his riches begat me,
and the thought of his heart.

[*Ode* 42:3-12 The risen Christ speaks:]
And I became useless to those who knew me [not],
because I shall hide myself from those who possessed me not.
And I will be with those
who love me.
All my persecutors have died,
and they who trusted in me sought me, because I am living.
Then I arose and am with them,
and will speak by their mouths.
For they have rejected those who persecute them;

and I threw over them the yoke of my love.
Like the arm of the bridegroom over the bride,
so is my yoke over those who know me.
And as the bridal feast is spread out by the bridal pair's home,
so is my love by those who believe in me.
I was not rejected although I was considered to be so,
and I did not perish although they thought it of me.
Sheol saw me and was shattered,
and Death ejected me and many with me.
I have been vinegar and bitterness to it,
and I went down with it as far as its depth. (*OTP* 2:741-71)

As in the canonical psalms of the Hebrew Bible, the Odist introduces first-person oracles from the deity, the risen Christ, without any explicit indication that the speaker is changing from the Odist to Christ (cf. e.g. Ps 89:4, where the speaker shifts from the psalmist to Yahweh with no indication except the content; "You said" is added by the translators).

Additional documentation of the view that the risen Christ spoke by Christian prophets:

The logic of the *Shepherd of Hermas,* who has the revelation conveyed by the ancient Lady, representing the Church, in Vis. 2-4, and by the angel in the Mandates, but all are identified as the Holy Spirit and the Son of God in Sim. 9:1:1. Cf. David Aune, *Prophecy in Early Christianity and the Ancient Mediterranean World* (Grand Rapids: Wm. B. Eerdmans, 1983), 302, 309. The literary/theological manner in which the voice of the exalted Christ is handled is more wooden than in the Apocalypse, however. In the *Shepherd,* the reader can always determine the identity of the speaker, even when the voices are later given new identities. Cf. M. Eugene Boring, "The Voice of Jesus in the Apocalypse of John," NovT 34 (1992), 334-59.

Montanus and the Montanist prophets, as reflected in the patristic quotes from Montanus.

Origen, *Contra Celsum* 7:9. Cf. M. Eugene Boring, *Sayings of the Risen Jesus* (Cambridge: Cambridge University Press, 1982), 128.

The *Book of Elchasai* reports such prophetic speech.

Epistula Apostolorum reports postresurrection conversations.

The *Apocalypse of Peter* may not have had a pre-Easter narrative framework, but reports only the post-Easter revelations of the risen Lord.

924. Revelation

Alexander the Great, in Plutarch, *Parallel Lives,* "Life of Alexander" 27 (680F) (45–125 CE)

Zeus is father of all, but he makes especially his those who are worthy. (LCL)

The worship of the deified emperor played an important role in the context of Revelation. Cf. Plutarch, *Moralia,* "Sayings of Kings and Commanders: Alexander" 180D. The idea of the deity or divine sonship of the ruler has a long and varied history in the Mediterranean world. The term could mean many things, and texts should not be lumped together indiscriminately. A basic difference was between Egypt and the East, where the ruler was always thought to participate in some manner in the divine nature, and the West, where this was not the case. Everett Ferguson's description of a key event symbolizes this difference and the transition of this idea from East to West: "When

Alexander arrived in Egypt, he was welcomed as a deliverer, for the Egyptians had turned against Persian rule in a revival of nationalism and had frequently rebelled against Persia. Thus Alexander was acclaimed as Pharaoh, and he accepted this standing—no doubt gladly, for it meant that he was there not as a robber baron or temple marauder but as the lawful king. As noted above, the Pharaoh was deemed by the Egyptians to have a certain divine character. One of his titles was 'son of Ammon' (a deity accepted by the Greeks as identical with Zeus). A 'desire seized' Alexander to go to the oracle of Ammon at Siwah, deep in the desert of Cyrene. When he arrived, the priest greeted him as 'son of Ammon' and promised him rule over the world. All this was conventional to the priest as the traditional salutation of a Pharaoh. But it was not a common form to Alexander and the Greeks and appears to have made a profound impression on Alexander" (*Backgrounds,* 190). (See also Mark 1:15 above.)

925. Revelation

Wisdom of Solomon 7:1-6 (150 BCE–50 CE)

> I also am mortal, like everyone else,
> a descendant of the first-formed child of earth;
> and in the womb of a mother I was molded into flesh,
> within the period of ten months,
> compacted with blood,
> from the seed of a man and the pleasure of marriage.
> And when I was born, I began to breathe the common air,
> and fell upon the kindred earth;
> my first sound was a cry, as is true of all
> I was nursed with care in swaddling cloths.
> For no king has had a different beginning of existence;
> there is for all one entrance into life, and one way out. (NRSV)

Solomon is pictured as speaking. There is a double contrast. On the one hand, the author wants to make it clear that it was transcendent Wisdom that made Solomon great, not something inherent, and that "Solomon," as a wise seeker after Wisdom, knew and confessed this. But since such a statement stands in contrast with the kingship ideology of the Ancient Near East in general, and especially in contrast to the developing emperor cult, the author also wanted to contrast true kingship and wisdom with the claims of pagan kings and emperors. Revelation stands in this Jewish tradition for which the claims of the emperors were blasphemous.

926. Revelation

Athenaeus, *Deipnosophists* 6.63.253 d-e (307 BCE)

For the highest and dearest of the gods are come to our city. Hither, indeed, the time hath brought together Demeter and Demetrius. She comes to celebrate the solemn mysteries of the Daughter, but he, as is meet for the god, is here in gladness, fair and smiling. Something august he seemeth, all his friends about him, and he himself in their midst, his friends the stars, even as he is the sun. O son of the most mighty god Poseidon and of Aphrodite, hail! For other gods are either far away, or have not ears, or are not, or heed us not at all; but thee we can see in very presence, not in wood and not in stone, but in truth. And so we pray to thee. First bring peace, thou very dear! For thou hast the power. (LCL)

Demetrius attempted to reunite Alexander's empire. When in 307 BCE he recaptured Athens, he was hailed as a savior (σωτήρ), benefactor (ἐυεργέτης), and a god (θεός). In the Greek tradition, the line between gods and human beings was not as sharp and fixed as in the East. Nonetheless, this citation shows that also in the West extravagant titles of divinity could be applied to a human conqueror and ruler shortly after Alexander's time, and with genuine religious feeling.

This tradition was developed among the Greeks especially in Egypt and the East, as is illustrated by the divine titles given to Ptolemy V in the famous Rosetta Stone, dated 196 BCE: "Since King Ptolemy, the ever-living, beloved by Ptah, the God Manifest and Gracious, the Son of King Ptolemy and Queen Arsinoë, the Parent-loving Gods, has done many benefactions to the temples and to those who dwell in them and also to all those subject to his rule, being from the beginning a god born of a god and a goddess like Horus, the son of Isis and Osiris, who came to the help of his Father Osiris [and] being benevolently disposed toward the gods, has consecrated to the temples revenues both of silver and of grain, and has generously undergone many expenses in order to lead Egypt to prosperity and to establish the temples . . . the gods have rewarded him with health, victory, power, and all good things, his sovereignty to continue to him and his children forever."

927. Revelation

Inscription at Eleusis (1 cent. CE)

All the Greeks to the Goddesses and the Emperor. (Ferguson, *Backgrounds*)

This inscription shows how ubiquitous the emperor cult tended to become, how readily it could be combined with the worship of the classical mystery gods, and how blurred the line between mortals and the gods became. Further:

928. Revelation

Inscription of Antiochus I of Commagene (1 cent. BCE)

"The great king Antiochus, the God, the Righteous One, the Manifest Deity," establishes sacrifices "in honor of the gods and in my honor," on an altar set up alongside that of "the great gods." (Nock, *Conversion*)

How common the idea of divine kingship was, but also how pale it had become, is seen from the fact that it could even be included in a child's exercise book: "What is a god? That which is strong. What is a king? He who is equal to the divine" (undated papyrus cited by Nock, *Conversion* 91)

929. Revelation

Suetonius, *Lives of the Caesars*, "Domitian" 13 (early 2 cent. CE)

When he became emperor, he did not hesitate to boast in the Senate that he had conferred their power on both his father and his brother, and that they had but returned him his own; nor on taking back his wife after their divorce, that he had "recalled her to his divine couch." He delighted to hear the people in the amphitheater shout on his feast day: "Good fortune attend our Lord and Mistress." Even more, in the Capitoline competition, when all the people begged him with great unanimity to restore Palfuritus Sura, who had been banished some time before from the Senate, and on that occasion received the prize for oratory, he deigned no reply, but merely had a crier bid them be silent. With no less arrogance he began as follows in issuing a circular letter in the name of his procurators, "Our Master and our God bids that this be done." And so the custom arose of henceforth addressing him in no other way in writing or in conversation. He suffered no statues to be set up in his honor in the Capitol, except of gold and silver and of a fixed weight. (LCL)

Not all the emperors took seriously the view of divine kingship especially popular in the East and often applied to the emperors. (The sober Vespasian at his death commented wryly, "I think I am becoming a god" [Suetonius, *Vespasian* 23].) Domitian was the first emperor since Nero seriously to claim divine titles and status. His intolerance of Christians (not an official persecution) was not only because of their refusal to honor him as a god, however. Domitian attempted to extricate himself from some of his financial troubles by seizing the property of any who belonged to a marginal group that could be suspected of disloyalty (see Suetonius, "Domitian" 12). The Christians naturally became victimized by this state of affairs, and understood it in religious terms. That they were not altogether off target is made clear by the citation below from Dio Cassius.

930. Revelation

Dio Cassius, *Epitome* 67.14.1-3 (40–120 CE)

At this time the road leading from Sinuessa to Puteoli was paved with stone. And the same year Domitian slew, along with many others, Flavius Clemens the consul, although he was a cousin and had a wife Flavia Domitilla, who was also a relative of the emperor's. The charge brought against them both was that of atheism, a charge on which many others who drifted into Jewish ways were condemned. Some of these were put to death, and the rest were at least deprived of their property. Domitilla was merely banished to Pandateria. (LCL)

"Atheism" here means failure to participate in the state religion, a charge to which Jews and Christians were especially subject since they were monotheists who could not incorporate other deities into their religious convictions, and also disdained acknowledging any visible representation of the deity. The execution and banishment of members of the court and imperial family may reflect the influence of Christianity among (a few of) the members of the highest circles, or the confusion that existed for some time among Romans in distinguishing Jews and Christians.

931. Revelation

Claudius' Letter to the Alexandrians (P. London 1912) (41 CE)

Proclamation by Lucius Aemilius Rectus. Seeing that all the populace, owing to its numbers, was unable to be present at the reading of the most sacred and most beneficent letter to the city, I have deemed it necessary to display the letter publicly in order that reading it one by one you may admire the majesty of our god Caesar and feel gratitude for his goodwill toward the city. Year 2 of Tiberius Claudius Caesar Augustus Germanicus Imperator, the 14th of Neus Sebastus.

Tiberius Claudius Caesar Augustus Germanicus Imperator, Pontifex Maximus, holder of the tribunician power, consul designate, to the city of Alexandria greeting. . . . [names given] your ambassadors, having delivered to me the decree, discoursed at length concerning the city, directing my attention to your goodwill toward us, which from long ago, you may be sure, had been stored up to your advantage in my memory; for you are by nature reverent toward the Augusti, as I know from many proofs, and in particular have taken a warm interest in my house, warmly reciprocated, of which fact (to mention the last instance, passing over others) the supreme witness is my brother Germanicus addressing you in words more clearly stamped as his own. Wherefore I gladly accepted the honors given to me by you, though I have no weakness for such things. And first I permit you to keep my birthday as a *dies Augustus* as you have yourselves proposed, and I agree to the erection in their several places of the statues of myself and my family; for I see that you were anxious to establish on every side memorials of your reverence for my house. Of the two golden statues the one made to represent the Pax Augusta Claudiana, as my most honored Barbillus suggested and entreated when I wished to refuse for fear of being thought too offensive, shall be erected in Rome, and the other according to your request shall be carried in procession on name-days in your city; and it shall be accompanied by a throne, adorned with whatever trappings you choose. It would perhaps be foolish, while accepting such great honors, to refuse the institution of a Claudian tribe and the establishment of groves after the manner of Egypt; wherefore I grant you these requests as well, and if you wish you may also erect the equestrian statues given by Itrasius Pollio my procurator. As for the erection of those in four-horse chariots which you wish to set up to me at the entrances into the country, I consent to let one be placed at Taposiris, the Libyan town of that name, another at Pharos in Alexandria, and a third at Pelusium in Egypt. But I deprecate the appointment of a high priest to me and the building of temples, for I do not wish to be offensive to my contemporaries, and my opinion is that temples and such forms of honor have by all ages been granted as a prerogative to the gods alone.

Concerning the requests which you have been anxious to obtain from me, I decide as follows. All those who have become *ephebi* up to the time of my principate I confirm and maintain in possession of the Alexandrian citizenship with all the privileges and indulgences enjoyed by the city, excepting such as by beguiling you have contrived to become *ephebi* though born of servile mothers; and it is equally my will that all the other favors shall be confirmed which were granted to you by former princes and kings and prefects, as the deified Augustus also confirmed them. It is my will that the *neocori* of the temple of the deified Augustus in Alexandria shall be chosen by lot in the same way as those of the said deified Augustus in Canopus are chosen by lot. (LCL)

The letter goes on to respond to the troubles between Jews and the rest of the city that had occasioned an embassy to Rome, providing details of great historical interest. Here, however, the important point is the illuminating ways in which the line between deity and humanity is blurred when referring to the emperor. Claudius modestly and for strategic reasons refuses some divine honors for himself, though these had been proposed by the Alexandrians. He declines to have a temple in Alexandria devoted to him, though incidentally refers to the temple of "the deified Augustus" (Octavian) already there. He is careful to allow specific statues of himself, which would be regarded by many of the people as images of a god, not only after his own death and "deification." The preface to the letter composed by the local Roman official has no hesitation in referring to the living emperor as "our god Caesar."

In addition to the texts cited here (nos. 924-33, see Horace, *Carm.* 1.1.3-6; Statius, *Silvae* 1.6.81-84; Tacitus, *Annals* 2.87; Suetonius, *Lives,* "Augustus" 53.1; Suetonius, *Lives,* "Tiberius" 27.

932. Revelation

Philo, *Embassy to Gaius* 145–154 (15 BCE–50 CE)

The whole habitable world voted him [Augustus] no less than celestial honors. These are so well attested by temples, gateways, vestibules, porticoes. . . . They knew his carefulness and that he showed it in maintaining firmly the native customs of each particular nation no less than of the Romans, and that he received his honors not for destroying the institutions of some nations in vain self-exaltation but in accordance with the magnitude of so mighty a sovereignty whose prestige was bound to be enhanced by such tributes. That he was never elated or puffed up by the vast honors given to him is clearly shown by the fact that he never wished anyone to address him as a god but was annoyed if anyone used the word, and also by his approval of the Jews, who he knew full well regarded all such things with horror. (LCL)

Philo here illustrates the tightrope that Jews (and later, Christians) had to walk in relation to the divine claims made for, and sometimes by, the emperor. Philo joins in the usual extravagant praise of the emperor (esp. in the paragraph preceding the one cited), acknowledges that divine claims were made for the emperor, does not join in them himself, and excuses the emperor, who remained modest and did not insist on being addressed as deity. The author of Revelation engages in no such subtleties, but regards Rome as the agent of Satan and divine honors to the emperor as something not to be minimized. Philo himself condemns the explicit claims to divinity made by Gaius Caligula ("this blasphemous deification of himself to the masses," 77), but attributes it to the personal mental instability of Gaius ("his wild and frenzied insanity," 93), not something inherent in the office of the emperor as such, not a claim made by "good" emperors.

933. Revelation

Pliny the Younger, *Letters* 10:97 (ca. 115 CE)

Pliny, governor of Bithynia, to Trajan the Emperor
I have made it a rule, Lord, to refer everything to you about which I am in doubt. ["Lord" here is Latin *domine,* equivalent of Greek *kurios,* used by Christians only of God and Jesus

as Lord, but claimed as a title by the emperors and esp. important to Domitian in John's time]. For who could better provide direction for my hesitations or instruction for my lack of knowledge?

I have never been present at the interrogation of Christians. Therefore, I do not know how far such investigations should be pushed, and what sort of punishments are appropriate. I have also been uncertain as to whether age makes any difference, or whether the very young are dealt with in the same way as adults, whether repentance [Lat. *paenitentiae*] and renunciation of Christianity is sufficient, or whether the accused are still considered criminals because they were once Christians even if they later renounced it, and whether persons are to be punished simply for the name "Christian" even if no criminal act has been committed, or whether only crimes associated with the name are to be punished.

In the meantime, I have handled those who have been denounced to me as Christians as follows: I asked them whether they were Christians. Those who responded affirmatively I have asked a second and third time, under threat of the death penalty. If they persisted in their confession [Latin *perseverantes,* related to "endurance," Greek *hypomone,* the central virtue for Christians in Revelation], I had them executed. For whatever it is that they are actually advocating, it seems to me that obstinacy and stubbornness must be punished in any case. Others who labor under the same delusion, but who were Roman citizens, I have designated to be sent to Rome.

In the course of the investigations, as it usually happens, charges are brought against wider circles of people, and the following special cases have emerged:

An unsigned placard was posted, accusing a large number of people by name. Those who denied being Christians now or in the past, I thought necessary to release, since they invoked our gods according to the formula I gave them and since they offered sacrifices of wine and incense before your image which I had brought in for this purpose along with the statues of our gods. I also had them curse Christ. It is said that real Christians cannot be forced to do any of these things.

Others charged by this accusation at first admitted that they had once been Christians, but had already renounced it; they had in fact been Christians, but had given it up, some of them three years ago, some even earlier, some as long as twenty-five years ago. All of these worshiped your image and the statues of the gods, and cursed Christ. They verified, however, that their entire guilt or error consisted in the fact that on a specified day before sunrise they were accustomed to gather and sing an antiphonal hymn to Christ as their god and to pledge themselves by an oath not to engage in any crime, but to abstain from all thievery, assault, and adultery, not to break their word once they had given it, and not to refuse to pay their legal debts. They then went their separate ways, and came together later to eat a common meal, but it was ordinary, harmless food. They discontinued even this practice in accordance with my edict by which I had forbidden political associations, in accord with your instructions. I considered it all the more necessary to obtain by torture a confession of the truth from two female slaves, whom they called "deaconnesses." I found nothing more than a vulgar, excessive superstition.

I thus adjourned further hearings, in order to seek counsel from you. The matter seems to me in need of good counsel, especially in view of the large number of accused. For many of every age and class, of both sexes, are in danger of prosecution both now and in the future. The plague of this superstition has spread not only in the cities, but through villages and the countryside. But I believe a stop can be made and a remedy provided. In any case it is now quite clear that the temples, almost deserted previously, are gradually gaining more and more visitors, the long neglected sacred festivals are again regularly observed, and the sacrificial meat, for which buyers have been hard to find, is again being purchased. From this one can easily see what an improvement can be made in the masses, when one gives room for repentance.

The Emperor's response:

My Secundus! You have chosen the right way with regard to the cases of those who have been accused before you as Christians. Nothing exists that can be considered a universal norm for such cases. Christians should not be sought out. But if they are accused and handed over, they are to be punished, but only if they do not deny being Christians and demonstrate it by the appropriate act, i.e. the worship of our gods. Even if one is suspect because of past conduct, he or she is to be acquitted in view of repentance *[paenitentia]*.

Anonymous accusations may not be considered in any trial, for that would be a dangerous precedent, and does not fit our times. (MEB)

This is the earliest document from a Roman hand that lets us see how Christianity looked to those outside the church. Since Pliny refers to those who had withdrawn from Christianity and renounced the Christian faith some twenty-five years previously, the threatening times under Domitian may be meant. The reference to offering incense before the image of Caesar may represent the kind of ritual interpreted as emperor worship and idolatry in Revelation. One gains a sense of the precarious status of Christians in a setting that did not understand them and was too ready to believe the worst, even at the hands of a relatively decent and fair-minded representative of Rome such as Pliny. This letter provides a window into the social and religious setting of Christians not only in Revelation and 1 Peter, but for all of early Christianity at the beginning of the second century.

934. Revelation 1:1

1 Enoch 1:1-2 (1 cent. BCE)

The blessing of Enoch: with which he blessed the elect and the righteous, who would be present on the day of tribulation at [the time of] the removal of all the ungodly ones. And Enoch, the blessed and righteous man of the Lord, took up [his parable] while his eyes were open and he saw, and said, "[This is] a holy vision from the heavens which the angels showed me; and I heard from them everything and I understood. I look not for this generation but for the distant one that is coming." (*OTP* 1:13)

Already in the first lines of *1 Enoch* several common elements shared by Revelation emerge: (1) revelation from heaven; (2) the concept of blessing; (3) the time of tribulation that is to precede the end, in which the recipients of the document are living; (4) the vision of God in the heavens; (5) the interpreting angels; (6) descriptive title in the third person, continuing in first-person address (cf. Tobit 1:1-3).

The contrasts are fundamental: (1) John writes in his own name, and dispenses with the customary literary fiction of a revelation given long ago, sealed up, and preserved until the time of the actual author (cf. 22:10); (2) The christocentric perspective of Revelation. The Enoch literature has a heavenly Messiah/Son of Man only as a marginal figure; for John the revelation is both from and about Jesus Christ (. . . Ἰησοῦ Χριστοῦ of 1:1 is both subjective and objective genitive). On ἐσήμανεν ("show"), cf. no. 449.

935. Revelation 1:4 (sevens)

Apuleius, *Metamorphoses* 11.1 (2 cent. CE)

[In response to the vision of Isis:] Wherefore shaking off my drowsy sleep I arose with a joyful face, and moved by a great affection to purify myself, I plunged my head seven times into the water of the sea; which number of seven is convenable and agreeable to holy and divine things, as the worthy and sage philosopher Pythagoras hath declared. (LCL)

The Apocalypse of John is structured in heptads. Those sevens that are explicitly named: churches (1:4); lampstands (1:12); stars (1:16); spirits (3:1); torches (4:5); seals (5:1); horns of the Lamb (5:6); eyes of the Lamb (5:6); angels (8:2); trumpets (8:2); thunders (10:3); thousands of people (11:13); heads of the beast (12:3); diadems of the beast (12:3; 13:1; 17:3); plagues (15:1); bowls of wrath (16:1); mountains on which the evil city is built (17:9); rulers before the End (17:11). There are also heptads to which the author does not explicitly call attention, such as seven beatitudes (1:3; 14:13; 16:15; 19:9; 20:6; 22:7, 14). Seven was not only a religiously significant number in Jewish tradition (cf. "ἑπτά," TDNT 2:627-35), but had sacred connotations in various streams of Hellenistic tradition. It was related to the number of (then visible and known) heavenly bodies: sun, moon, and five planets.

936. Revelation 1:4

Pausanias, *Description of Greece* 12.10 (2 cent. CE)

Zeus was, Zeus is, Zeus will be, O great Zeus!
[Ζεὺς ἦν, Ζεὺς ἐστίν, Ζεὺς ἔσσεται, ὦ μεγάλε Ζεῦ.]
The earth brings forth fruit, therefore the earth is called Mother! (MEB)

Pausanias is describing the shrine at Delphi. Within the temple of Apollo is the "stone of the Sibyls," which gives Pausanias the occasion to comment on famous Sibyls of the past, and to point out that it was one of the earliest Sibyls that first sang this verse, which became an often-repeated formula. For additional examples, cf. Orpheus, *Fragments* 21a; Theocritus, *Idylls* 17.1-8; Plutarch, *Moralia*, "Isis and Osiris" 354c; Apuleius, *Asclepius* 14.

937. Revelation 1:9-20 (vision of exalted Christ; prophetic commission)

Corpus Hermeticum 1.1-9 (2–4 cents. CE)

[1] Once, when thought came to me of the things that are and my thinking soared high and my bodily senses were restrained, like someone heavy with sleep from too much eating or toil of the body, an enormous being completely unbounded in size seemed to appear

to me and call my name and say to me: "What do you want to hear and see; what do you want to learn and know from your understanding?"

[2] "Who are you?" I asked.

"I am Poimandres," he said, "mind of sovereignty; I know what you want, and I am with you everywhere."

[3] I said, "I wish to learn about the things that are, to understand their nature and to know god. How much I want to hear!" I said.

Then he said to me: "Keep in mind all that you wish to learn, and I will teach you."

[4] Saying this, he changed his appearance, and in an instant everything was immediately opened to me. I saw an endless vision in which everything became light—clear and joyful—and in seeing the vision I came to love it. After a little while, darkness arose separately and descended—fearful and gloomy—coiling sinuously so that it looked to me like a [snake]. Then the darkness changed into something of a watery nature, indescribably agitated and smoking like a fire; it produced an unspeakable wailing roar. Then an inarticulate cry like the voice of fire came forth from it. [5] But from the light . . . a holy word mounted upon the [watery] nature, and untempered fire leapt up from the watery nature to the height above. The fire was nimble and piercing and active as well, and because the air was light it followed after spirit and rose up to the fire away from earth and water so that it seemed suspended from the fire. Earth and water stayed behind, mixed with one another, so that [earth] could not be distinguished from water, but they were stirred to hear by the spiritual word that moved upon them.

[6] Poimandres said to me, "Have you understood what this vision means?"

"I shall come to know," said I.

"I am the light you saw, mind, your god," he said, "who existed before the watery nature that appeared out of darkness. The lightgiving word who comes from mind is the son of god."

"Go on," I said.

"This is what you must know: that in you which sees and hears is the word of the lord, but your mind is god the father; they are not divided from one another for their union is life."

"Thank you," I said.

"Understand the light, then, and recognize it." [7] After he said this, he looked me in the face for such a long time that I trembled at his appearance. But when he raised his head, I saw in my mind the light of powers beyond number and a boundless cosmos that had come to be. The fire, encompassed by great power and subdued, kept its place fixed. In the vision I had because of the discourse of Poimandres, these were my thoughts. [8] Since I was terrified, out of my wits, he spoke to me again. "In your mind you have seen the archetypal form, the preprinciple that exists before a beginning without end." This was what Poimandres said to me.

"The elements of nature—whence have they arisen?" I asked.

And he answered: "From the counsel of god which, having taken in the word and having seen the beautiful cosmos, imitated it, having become a cosmos through its own elements and its progeny of souls. [9] The mind who is god, being androgyne and existing as life and light, by speaking gave birth to a second mind, a craftsman, who, as god of fire and spirit, crafted seven governors; they encompass the sensible world in circles, and their government is called fate." (Copenhaver)

Like John on Patmos, the disciple of Hermes receives a revelation from a gigantic figure and is given an urgent commission to communicate the saving message to others. There is some similarity in the imagery itself, e.g.: the revealer figure is identified as the Word; there are seven subordinate "administrators" in charge of the empirical world; evil is represented by images of darkness, the chaotic sea, and the serpent.

Differences:

1) The precondition of revelation for the Hermetic disciple is the restraint of bodily senses, which are an obstacle to spiritual vision. This mystical dualism plays no role for John, who receives his revelation on the Lord's Day, i.e. in connection with the community's regular worship.

2) The revelation comes in response to his seeking after mystical wisdom, "the things that are." John does not seek the revelation, but is encountered by the divine initiative. The content of the revelation is the mystery of God's historical/eschatological act, not ontological and cosmological mysteries.

3) The revealer in Revelation is identified with a recent historical figure who in his death and resurrection represented the definitive act of God for human salvation. In contrast, in this vision Poimandres remains the exalted figure of the transcendent world. There is some evidence that in some streams and phases of the long and complex Hermetic tradition, Hermes was once an Egyptian sage who had been deified, but this plays no role in his heavenly identity. It appears rather that the name and tradition of an ancient Egyptian sage is given to the heavenly revealer.

4) John is struck down by the impact of the divine holiness (1:17), the typical response of biblical prophets (Isa 6), rather than being fascinated and captivated by the attractiveness of the luminous vision.

Texts of fifty-six vision reports are presented and analyzed in Klaus Berger, "Visionsberichte. Formgeschichtliche Bemerkungen über pagane hellenistische Texte und ihre frühchristlichen Analogien," in Berger et al., eds., *Studien und Texte zur Formgeschichte* (TANZ 7. Tübingen: Francke Verlag, 1992), 177-225. Berger concludes there is no single form "vision report," but points out many similarities and differences between pagan and New Testament texts, with Luke-Acts, esp. Acts, in the closest relation to pagan forms.

938. Revelation 1:9-20

Apuleius, *Metamorphoses* 11.3-4 (2 cent. CE)

I fortuned to fall again asleep upon that same bed; and by and by (for mine eyes were but newly closed) appeared to me from the midst of the sea a divine and venerable face, worshiped even of the gods themselves. Then, by little and little, I seemed to see the whole figure of her body, bright and mounting out of the sea and standing before me: wherefore I propose to describe her divine semblance, if the poverty of my human speech will suffer me, or the divine power give me a power of eloquence rich enough to express it. First she had a great abundance of hair, flowing and curling, dispersed and scattered about her divine neck; on the crown of her head she bare many garlands interlaced with flowers, and in the middle of her forehead was a plain circlet in fashion of a mirror, or rather resembling the moon by the light that it gave forth; and this was borne up on either side by serpents that seemed to rise from the furrows of the earth, and above it were blades of corn set out. Her vestment was of finest linen yielding divers colors, somewhere white and shining, somewhere yellow like the crocus flower, somewhere rosy red, somewhere flaming; and (which troubled my sight and spirit sore) her cloak was utterly dark and obscure covered with shining black, and being wrapped round her from under her left arm to her right shoulder in manner of a shield, part of it fell down, pleated in most subtle fashion, to the skirts of her garment so that the welts appeared comely. Here and there upon the edge thereof and throughout its surface the stars glimpsed, and in the middle of them was placed the moon in mid-month, which shone like a flame of fire; and round about the whole length of the border of that goodly robe was a crown or garland wreathing unbroken, made with all flowers and all fruits. Things quite diverse did she bear: for in her right hand she had a timbrel of brass, a flat piece of metal curved in manner of a girdle, wherein passed not many rods through the periphery of it; and when with her arm she moved these triple cords, they gave forth a shrill and clear sound. In her left hand she bare a cup of gold like unto a boat, upon the handle whereof, in the upper part which is best seen, an asp lifted up his head with a wide-swelling throat. Her odoriferous feet were covered with shoes interlaced and wrought with victorious palm. Thus the divine shape, breathing out the pleasant spice of fertile Arabia, disdained not with her holy voice to utter these words to me. (LCL)

The elements of John's imagery are drawn from the visions of God and angels in the Hebrew Bible, especially Daniel 7 and 10, and Ezekiel 1 and 9. Yet the phenomenon of visions of the deity communicated in literary form was not unknown in the Hellenistic world. There are formal points of similarity, such as descriptions of face, clothing, and feet, reference to the quality of the deity's voice, and the cosmic dimension of the scene indicated by references to stars. Among the striking differences: (1) Apuleius receives his vision in a dream, while John's is a matter of prophetic vision while awake. (2) Apuleius is aware of the inadequacy of human words to describe the deity. John is aware of this, but makes no reference to it here, presenting his description straightforwardly. (3) Isis comes up out of the sea, an impossible image for John with reference to Christ (cf. 11:7; 13:1). (4) In Apuleius the vision is to communicate saving knowledge to Apuleius himself, a matter of his conversion and salvation. After his transformation, Apuleius is invited by the priest to become a member of the order, which he does, but the vision is only for his personal salvation, not a call to an office. For John, the vision is not a call to the prophetic office, which he already has, but it is received as a function of this office, and is not a message of personal salvation, which he already has as a member of the Christian community. On Revelation 1:12 cf. no. 478.

939. Revelation 2–3

Edict of Sextus Sotidius Strabo Libuscidianus (ca. 18 CE)

Sextus Sotidius Strabo Libuscidianus, legate of Ti. Caesar Augustus acting as praetor, declares [λέγει]: It is indeed of all things most inequitable that I should be tightening up by my edict what the two Augustuses, the one the greatest of gods, the other the greatest of leaders [Gk: commanders] most carefully guarded against . . . (Horsley, *New Documents* 1)

This is not a "letter," but the proclamation of a magistrate of the Empire, aware that he stands in a chain of command, intended to regulate the lives of those under his jurisdiction by instruction, promise, and threat. It begins with a descriptive phrase giving the credentials of the one making the promulgation, and reports what he "says" (λέγει, as Rev 2:1, 8, 12, 18; 3:1, 7, 14). It is not a letter but the report of an oral command. Likewise, although Revelation as a whole is a letter using the standard epistolary forms (cf. 1:4-5; 22:21), the messages to the seven churches are in the form of imperial edicts. On the style and function of the imperial edict, cf. M. Benner, *The Emperor Says:*

Studies in the Rhetorical Style in Edicts of the Early Empire (Gothenburg, 1975). (Cf. also no. 943 on Rev 4:11.)

940. Revelation 2:7 (saying about "conquering")

Plutarch, *Moralia*, "Ancient Customs of the Spartans" 40 (45–125 CE)

The boys in Sparta were lashed with whips during the entire day at the altar of Artemis Orthia, frequently to the point of death, and they bravely endured this, cheerful and proud, vying with one another for the supremacy as to which one of them could endure being beaten for the longer time and the greater number of blows. And the one who was victorious was held in especial repute. (LCL)

Analogy: the victor is not the one who subdues others, but the one who endures the most (in Revelation, to death).

Difference: In Revelation, the issue is not competition among the believers as to who can endure the most, but a holding fast against the temptation to apostasy. Similarly in Plutarch's "Vice Cause Unhappiness . . .," §3 (victory in the competition among widows to be burned with their husbands). In Judaism, 4 Maccabees 1:11, 6:33; 4 Ezra 7:127-30; 7:92.

On Revelation 3:7-13, cf. no. 771.

941. Revelation 2:10

3 Maccabees 7:16 (1 cent. CE [?])

But those who had held fast to God even to death and had received the full enjoyment of deliverance began their departure from the city, crowned with all sorts of very fragrant flowers, joyfully and loudly giving thanks to the one God of their ancestors, the eternal Savior of Israel, in words of praise and all kinds of melodious songs. (NRSV)

Third Maccabees is not an apocalyptic work, but the situation it pictures is analogous to that of Revelation. The community of faith is threatened by the evil government. Deliverance is altogether this-worldly. Yet the vocabulary is similar to Revelation's: those who are faithful to death (in 3 Macc those who had not denied the faith even under the threat of imminent death) receive a crown (of flowers). Additional points of contact with Revelation: faith in the one God; those who apostatized are considered "defiled" (7:14); shouts of "Hallelujah" (7:13) and the festive mood of worship.

942. Revelation 4:8-11

Inscription from Stratonikeia (now Eski-Hissar) *CIG* 2, no. 2715 (1 cent. CE)

[Cultic prescription concerning the gods Zeus Panemerius and Hekate:] . . . since to these gods who have thus revealed themselves the whole population brings sacrifices, burns incense in censers, prays to them and offers thanksgiving as they are accustomed to do, and honors them by songs of praise during the procession and the worship services, the Council has decided as follows: henceforth thirty young men shall be chosen from the noble families, who shall be led into the Council Hall every day by the Paidonomos [protector of boys] along with the public guard of boys. They shall be clothed in white, crowned with olive branches, and bear olive branches in their hands. These boys shall be accompanied by a zither player and in the presence of a herald shall sing a hymn of praise determined by the secretary Sosandros, the son of Diomedes. (MEB/Berger)

Revelation 4 thus clearly adopts the contemporary liturgical forms of Asia Minor (cf. Berger, *Formgeschichte,* §83). On the posture assumed in Revelation 4:10 cf. Plutarch, "Fortune Alexander," §3 (to place one's crown at the feet = act of subjugation).

943. Revelation 4:11

Papyrus Copy of an Edict of Titus Haterius Nepos (ca. 120 CE)

Copy of an edict. Titus Haterius Nepos, prefect of Egypt says [λέγει]: our lord and god most manifest Imperator Caesar Trajan Hadrian Augustus having appointed, as you know [NN] as high priest of the gods Augusti and of great Sarapis and in charge of the cults in Alexandria and in Egypt . . . (Horsley, *New Documents* 2) (NN in the trans. is the translator's indication that the appropriate name or act was to be inserted into the formula at this point.)

Horsley points out that the combination "Lord and God" is not common in most of the New Testament, except in the Synoptics and Acts, reflecting the phraseology of Deuteronomy 6. But Revelation has the combination eleven times, which seems to be an intentional reflection (and repudiation) of the usage in the Caesar cult (1:8; 4:8; 4:11; 11:17; 15:3; 16:7; 18:8; 19:6; 21:22; 22:5; 22:6).

944. Revelation 5:1-4

Jubilees 32:20-22 (140 BCE)

And he [Jacob] saw in a vision of the night, and behold an angel was descending from heaven, and there were seven tablets in his hands. And he gave [them] to Jacob, and he read them, and he knew everything that was written in them, which would happen to him and to his sons during all the ages. And he showed him everything that was written on the tablets. (*OTP* 2:118)

As in Revelation, heaven contains a sevenfold document containing the secrets of the future, a document that ordinary mortals may not read. *Jubilees* follows the usual apocalyptic convention: the ancient worthy is given the revelation in a straightforward manner, from which he reads the future destiny unproblematically. Revelation does not indicate the contents of the sealed scroll, but presumably it contains the hidden future. He is not permitted to open or read the scroll. The good news of the revelation is not that the seer is now privy to heavenly information which he may straightforwardly communicate in discursive language, but that the hidden future is in the hands of the exalted Christ. He alone can open it, and the breaking of the seals does not reveal heavenly information which John may communicate, but sets in motion the eschatological events themselves.

945. Revelation 5:1-4

1 Enoch 81:2-3 (1 cent. BCE)

So I looked at the tablet[s] of heaven, read all the writing [on them], and came to understand everything. I read that book and all the deeds of humanity and all the children of the flesh upon the earth for all the generations of the world. At that very moment I blessed the Great Lord, the King of Glory for ever, for he has created all the phenomena in the world. I praised the Lord because of his patience; and I wept on account of the children of the people upon the earth. (*OTP* 1:59)

It was a very ancient Babylonian view that the inscribed heavenly tablets contained the destinies of individuals and nations. Jewish apocalyptic adapted that image in order to offer encouragement to people in stressful situations, often of persecution: the trying times we are forced to endure are not meaningless, but are part of God's plan. When the seer beholds these tablets in the heavenly world and reports them in the world below, the revelation functions as encouragement to the beleaguered community of faith. John's imagery is based on this traditional visionary element, but radically transforms it: he gets to see the scroll, but it is sealed, and only the Messiah can open it. For John as for Enoch, the earthly tribulation of the community of faith is not meaningless but part of the prewritten divine plan. But unlike Enoch, he does not get to view its contents, which are sealed; there is no disclosure of the divine plan until it is put into effect by being opened by the Messiah. The encouraging word is that the book exists, and that it is in the hand of the Messiah; John the seer has no access to it.

946. Revelation 5:1-6

4 Ezra 12:31-33 (late 1 cent. CE)

[The angel speaking to Ezra, interpreting the preceding vision:] And as for the lion whom you saw rousing up out of the forest and roaring and speaking to the eagle and reproving him for his unrighteousness, and as for all his words that you have heard, 32 this is the Messiah whom the Most High has kept until the end of days, who will arise from the offspring of David, and will come and speak with them. He will denounce them for their ungodliness and for their wickedness, and will display before them their contemptuous dealings. 33 For first he will bring them alive before his judgment seat, and when he has reproved them, then he will destroy them. (NRSV)

Written at almost the same time as Revelation, the apocalyptic imagery of 4 Ezra reflects the interpretation of Genesis 49:8-12 that had become traditional: the promised Lion of the tribe of

Judah is the Messiah who will destroy the enemies of the people of God. John's own startling reversal of this imagery is thus not only his independent interpretation of the Genesis passage, but is in direct contrast to contemporary Jewish apocalyptic interpretation.

947. Revelation 6-16

2 Baruch 26-27 (2 cent. CE)

And I answered and said:

That tribulation which will be, will it last a long time; and that distress, will it embrace many years?

And he answered and said to me:

That time will be divided into twelve parts, and each part has been preserved for that for which it was appointed. In the first part: the beginning of commotions. In the second part: the slaughtering of the great. In the third part: the fall of many into death. In the fourth part: the drawing of the sword. In the fifth part: famine and the withholding of rain. In the sixth part: earthquakes and terrors. [the seventh part is absent.] In the eighth part: a multitude of ghosts and the appearances of demons. In the ninth part: the fall of fire. In the tenth part: rape and much violence. In the eleventh part: injustice and unchastity. In the twelfth part: disorder and a mixture of all that has been before. These parts of that time will be preserved and will be mixed, one with another, and they will minister to each other. For some of these parts will withhold a part of themselves and take from others and will accomplish that which belongs to them and to others; hence, those who live on earth in those days will not understand that it is the end of times. (*OTP* 1:630)

As in Revelation, the final period of the earth's history is one of political tumult and natural disasters. These are not haphazard, but precisely arranged, and announced in advance, serving as encouragement to those suffering hard times that they are not living in the midst of blind chaos, but in a history divinely directed and predicted.

948. Revelation 6:9-11

4 Ezra 4:33-37 (late 1 cent. CE)

Then I answered and said, "How long? When will these things be? Why are our years few and evil?" 34 He answered me and said, "Do not be in a greater hurry than the Most High. You, indeed, are in a hurry for yourself, but the Highest is in a hurry on behalf of many. 35 Did not the souls of the righteous in their chambers ask about these matters, saying, 'How long are we to remain here? And when will the harvest of our reward come?' 36 And the archangel Jeremiel answered and said, 'When the number of those like yourselves is completed; for he has weighed the age in the balance, 37 and measured the times by measure, and numbered the times by number; and he will not move or arouse them until that measure is fulfilled.'" (NRSV)

As in Revelation, the pressing question of the author's own situation, "How long?" is placed in the mouths of those already dead and longing for restoration (in Revelation, specifically vindication, which is only implied in 4 Ezra). The same answer is given: the dead must wait until the predetermined number has been completed. In both cases, this functions as assurance: the outrages of the persecuting government are not meaningless chaos, but incorporated in the inscrutable plans of the Almighty. In both cases, the encouraging answer is also that the consummation will occur soon (4 Ezra 4:44-50; Rev 6:11's "a little longer" is of a piece with the near expectation throughout; cf. 1:1, 3; 2:16, 25; 3:11, 20; 10:6-7; 11:2; 12:6, 12; 17:10; 22:6, 7, 10, 12, 20).

In 4 Ezra, the Deity, though "almighty" (13:23) seems subordinate to this predetermined apocalyptic schedule. The author dares to challenge it himself, but cannot bring himself to believe that God also might challenge the apocalyptic timetable (5:34-44, esp. vv. 43-44). In New Testament apocalyptic, there are no "givens" to which God is subject, the system itself is not supreme, and God can rearrange the schedule in order to show mercy (Mark 13:20), i.e. God is truly "almighty" (Rev 1:8; 4:8; 11:17; 15:3; 16:7, 14; 19:6, 15; 21:22).

949. Revelation 6:10

Inscription from Rheneia (Delos) (2–1 cent. BCE)

I invoke and pray to the Most High God, the Lord of Spirits and of all flesh against those who deceitfully poisoned the tragic young woman Heraclea. They unjustly spilled her innocent blood. May the same thing happen to them and to their children! Lord, you who see all, and the angels of God before whom every soul today humbly brings this supplication: avenge this innocent blood, require it, and very quickly! (MEB/from *CIJ* 2, pp. 523-24)

In this Jewish inscription, God is invoked as the avenger of innocent blood, in a noneschatological perspective. In place of the eschatological "How long?" of Revelation 6:10 (which has very close parallels and also an answer in 4 Ezra 4:35-36 and *1 Enoch* 47:1-4), here we find the typical expression of Hellenistic magic, "as soon as possible" (cf. no. 636). Also interesting in this regard is Plutarch, *Moralia*, "Parallel Histories," 9: "When a plague had gained a wide hold among the Romans, Apollo gave an oracle that it would cease if they should appease the wrath of Saturn and the spirits of those who had perished unlawfully" (LCL). Here the divine vengeance is accomplished by human beings.

950. Revelation 8:7-12

b. *Baba Mezia* 59b (2 cent. CE tradition; written much later)

What did R. Aqiba do? He put on black garments and cloaked himself in a black cloak and took his seat before him at a distance of four cubits.

Said to him R. Eliezer, "Aqiba, why is today different from all other days?"

He said to him, "My lord, it appears to me that your colleagues are keeping distance from you."

Then he too tore his garments and removed his shoes, moved his stool and sat down on the ground, with tears streaming from his eyes.

The world was blighted: a third olives, a third wheat, a third barley.

And some say, also the dough in women's hands swelled up. (Neusner, *Talmud*)

The story illustrates not only the great significance attributed to discussions of Torah ("cosmic" significance), but the ease with which sober discussions of points of Halachah could modulate into apocalyptic language, even by the most revered Pharisaic rabbis. Apocalyptic conceptuality should not be thought of as belonging only to the fringes of Jewish life in the period when the New Testament was taking shape.

951. Revelation 8:9-12; 6:6

b. Baba Mezia 59b (2 cent. CE tradition; written much later)

On that day they brought all of the objects that R. Eliezer had declared insusceptible to uncleanness and burned them in fire [as though they were unclean beyond all purification].

They furthermore took a vote against him and cursed him.

They said, "Who will go and inform him?"

Said to them R. Aqiba, "I shall go and tell him, lest someone unworthy go and tell him, and he turn out to destroy the entire world [with his curse]."

What did R. Aqiba do? He put on black garments and cloaked himself in a black cloak and took his seat before him at a distance of four cubits.

Said to him R. Eliezer, "Aqiba, why is today different from all other days?"

He said to him, "My lord, it appears to me that your colleagues are keeping distance from you."

Then he too tore his garments and removed his shoes, moved his stool and sat down on the ground, with tears streaming from his eyes.

The world was blighted: a third olives, a third wheat, a third barley.

And some say, also the dough in women's hands swelled up.

A Tanna taught: There was a great disaster that day, for every place upon which R. Eliezer set his eyes was burned up. (Neusner, *Talmud*)

Rabbi Eliezer is represented in the accompanying circumstances as one who has gone astray and done wrong. The punishment of humanity by the destruction of a part of creation has here, as in the Apocalypse, the function of a warning sign. So too in *Sibylline Oracles* 5.230 an individual figure is addressed (Rome?), and it is said in order to point out her perverse character, ". . . when creation is damaged and [a part] saved again by the Fates" (*OTP* 1:399).

952. Revelation 11:3-12

Ascension of Isaiah 2:8-11 (1 cent. BCE–1 cent. CE)

And also there was great iniquity; and he withdrew from Bethlehem and dwelt on a mountain in a desert place. 9 And Micah the prophet, and the aged Ananias, and Joel and Habakkuk, and Josab his son, and many of the faithful who believed in the ascension into heaven, withdrew and dwelt on the mountain. 10 All of them were clothed in sackcloth, and all of them were prophets; they had nothing with them, but were destitute, and they all lamented bitterly over the going astray of Israel. 11 And they had nothing to eat except wild herbs [which] they gathered from the mountains. . . . (*OTP* 2:158)

For the question of the so far unclarified Jewish background of this passage, one could refer to *Ascension of Isaiah* 1:8-11 (see above, no. 18) and relate to it the hypothesis that here and in Revelation 11:3-12 we have two texts in which material from the same sort of milieu has been worked over (ecstatic prophetic groups with a message of repentance and/or strong criticism of Jerusalem), and which developed similar motifs in two different directions.

Analogies:

1) The clothing and presentation of the preachers of repentance.

2) The martyrological situation: in the place of the godless king Hezekiah in the *Ascension of Isaiah* stands here the eschatological adversary, thought of as a pagan king.

3) The ascension into heaven according to *Ascension of Isaiah* 2:8 (ἀναβῆναι) is realized postmortem in Revelation 11 (v. 12: ἀνάβατε . . . ἀνέβησαν).

4) Description of Jerusalem as Sodom. In *Ascension of Isaiah* 3:10, the false prophet charges: "Know therefore, O king that they (are) false prophets. And he has called Jerusalem Sodom, and the princes of Judah and Jerusalem he has declared (to be) the people of Gomorrah." (*OTP* 2:160). That corresponds to Revelation 11:8.

5) The schema referred to in no. 953 below is realized postmortem in Revelation 11. Obviously the material used in *Ascension of Isaiah* has been elaborated and further developed in Revelation 11 in the direction of an eschatological Adversary and the resurrection.

On Revelation 11:3-12, cf. nos. 131, 219.

953. Revelation 11:8-11

Plutarch, *Moralia*, "On the Delays of the Divine Vengeance" 22 (45–125 CE)

[Thespesius of Soli leads a shameful life and inquires of the oracle of Amphilochos:] He had sent [it appears] to ask the god whether the remainder of his life would be better spent. The god answered that he would do better when he died.

In a sense this actually happened to him not long after. He had fallen from a height and struck his neck, and although there had been no wound, but only a concussion, he died away. On the third day, at the very time of his funeral, he revived. Soon recovering his strength and senses, he instituted a change in his way of life that could hardly be believed . . . (LCL)

In the meantime Thespesius had made a tour of the underworld that corresponds to the type of tours of heaven or hell found in apocalyptic literature, in the course of which he received a new name. Obviously here we have a certain conception of what was supposed to happen in the mystery cult initiations (cf. no. 570 above regarding Apuleius!). Hellenistic Judaism adopts this schema: also Isaiah and Jeremiah lie three days as dead, during this time experience a tour of heaven, and then come back to life (cf. Berger, *Formgeschichte*, 343). In Revelation 11 this schema of representing things that had already received martyrological connotations in Hellenistic Judaism is applied to martyrdom and resurrection.

954. Revelation 11:18

Sirach 11:26-28 (ca. 180 BCE)

For it is easy for the Lord on the day of death
to reward individuals according to their conduct.
An hour's misery makes one forget past delights,
and at the close of one's life one's deeds are revealed.
Call no one happy before his death;
by how he ends, a person becomes known. (NRSV)

Cf. also Sirach 18:24: "Think of his wrath on the day of death, and of the moment of vengeance when he turns away his face" (NRSV). Sirach struggles with the problem of the injustice of the present world, and acknowledges that during the lifetime of good and bad people respectively injustice does not seem to be punished nor righteousness rewarded. Like the classical prophets and the Deuteronomistic theologians, he believed in the justice of God who rewards and punishes according to merit, and like them he did not adopt the notion of a life beyond or an eschatological judgment in which the books are balanced. Unlike the classical prophets, he thinks in terms of the individual rather than the community or nation. He resolves the dilemma by having God reward and punish on the last day of one's earthly life, which supposedly counterbalances the injustice suffered during one's life.

Revelation, like apocalypticism generally, affirmed a future eschatological judgment for the world, and a life beyond this one, in order to affirm the justice of God and the vindication of righteousness.

On Revelation 11:19, cf. no. 495.

955. Revelation 12:1-18

Herodotus, *The Histories*, Book 2.156 (480 BCE)

[Concerning the floating island Chemnis:] Leto received Apollo in charge from Isis and hid him for safety in this island which was before immovable but is now said to float. Apollo and Artemis were (they say) children of Dionysus and Isis, and Leto was made their nurse and preserver; in Egyptian, Apollo is Horus, Demeter Isis, Artemis Bubastis. (LCL)

The text documents an Egyptian myth that is also extant in Greek and Roman versions. In Egypt it is Isis who must hide her child Horus on the floating island from the snake monster Typhon. In Greek this corresponds to the story of Leto, Apollo, Ortygia, and Python. To this belongs also the myth of Apollo's fight against the Python, his flight and being pursued. Cf. also Homer, *Hymns* 3.351ff., and no. 958. Further:

956. Revelation 12:1-18

Euripides, *Iphigeneia in Taurica* 1234-51 (485/84–406 BCE)

A glorious babe in the days of old Leto in Delos bare,
. . . she fled from the . . .

Of the sea encompassed, bringing
From the place where her travail befell
Her babe to the height whence rolled the gushing rills untold,
Where the Wine-god's revels stormy-souled O'er the crests of Parnassus fare; . . .
Was the earth-spawned monster, the dragon, gliding Round the chasm wherein earth's oracle lay. But thou, who wast yet but a babe, yet leaping Babe-like in thy mother's loving embrace, Thou, Phoebus, didst slay him . . . (LCL)

The snatching up of the child to the mountain peak is analogous to the child's being caught up to God's throne in Revelation 11:5. Further:

957. Revelation 12:1-18

Sibylline Oracles 3.132-41 (3–2 cent. BCE)

Whenever Rhea gave birth, the Titans sat by her,
and they tore apart all male children,
but they allowed the females to live and be reared with their mother.
But when Lady Rhea gave birth in the third child-bearing
she brought forth Hera first. When they saw
with their eyes the female species, the Titans, savage men,
went home. Then Rhea bore a male child,
whom she quickly sent away to be reared secretly and in private,
to Phrygia, having taken three Cretan men under oath.
Therefore they named him Zeus, because he was sent away.
Similarly she sent away Poseidon secretly. (*OTP* 1:365)

Here too we have the motif of the threatened child and his secret preservation and rearing, which succeeds. Judaism too has many examples of the motif of salvation and preservation by being caught up to God or to a high mountain, e.g. *1 Enoch* 89:51-52; Pseudo-Philo, *LAB* 48:1 (Elijah/Phinehas lives on the mountain, fed by eagles, until God sends him back now and then to the world below). The version of the myth preserved in the appendix to *2 Enoch* is esp. important: after the boy without a father and—since his mother died before his birth, also without a mother—came to the earth, the archangel Michael, commander of the heavenly host, took him and placed him in paradise for safekeeping, so that he would not perish on the earth. He bears him forth on his wings (cf. nos. 5 and 15). Further:

958. Revelation 12:1-18

Coptic *Apocalypse of Adam* 78-79 (2 cent. CE)

[Declarations of individual kingdoms about the savior(s):] [The fourth] kingdom says [of him] [that] he came [from a virgin. . . . Solomon sought] her, he and Phersalo and Sauel and his armies, which had been sent out. Solomon himself sent his army of demons to seek out the virgin. And they did not find the one whom they sought, but the virgin who was given to them. It was she whom they fetched. Solomon took her. The Virgin became pregnant and gave birth to the child there. She nourished him on a border of the desert. When he had been nourished, he received glory and power from the seed from which he had been begotten. And thus he came to the water. (NHL)

Similarly the reports about the preceding "kingdoms": the virgin-born child is caught up to heaven (or driven out of the city and led to a place in the wilderness), where he is nourished and receives holiness and strength. On the repeated sending of this *Phoster* (prophet of light), cf. as analogy also the text from Pseudo-Philo, *LAB* 48:1 in no. 957 above.

We have here the transfer of the Zeus myth to Solomon and at the same time its transformation. According to the Greek myth (cf. esp. Apollodorus, *Bibliotheca*, ed. I. Bekker, p. 7) Asteria flees from Zeus to avoid having to sleep with him. She transforms herself into a quail and throws herself into the sea. This is the explanation for the old name of Delos (Ortygia = quail). Then Leto unites with Zeus, but flees from Hera, until she comes to Delos, where she bears Artemis and Apollo (cf. above, no. 956). In our text, this is transferred to Solomon: the first virgin is pursued in vain (Asteria; cf. also the crown of stars in Rev 12; "aster" = "star"!). The second virgin becomes pregnant and bears a son "at that place," a reference understandable only on the basis of knowledge of the Greek myth. In the same way, only with this presupposition is the concluding note understandable, "and thus he came to the water," since Delos is an island (that floats on the water). The text exhibits, as does Revelation 12, a deep familiarity with Greek mythical elements, as well as great freedom in their use, as Jewish and Christian authors transformed them (Solomon!). On Solomon and demons, see above, no. 155.

959. Revelation 12:8

Plutarch, *Moralia*, "That We Ought Not to Borrow" 7 (45–125 CE)

And there is no escape to those former pastures and meadows, but they wander like the spirits described by Empedocles, who have been expelled by the gods and thrown out from heaven: Into the waves of the sea they are driv'n by the might of the ether;
Then on the floor of the earth the sea vomits them; earth then ejects them . . . (LCL)

Background: Empedocles, Fragment 115: "There is an oracle of Necessity, an ancient decree of the gods, eternal, sealed fast with broad oaths, that when one of the divine spirits whose portion is long life sinfully stains his own limbs with bloodshed, and following Hate has sworn a false oath—these must wander for thrice ten thousand seasons far from the company of the blessed, being born throughout the period into all kinds of mortal shapes, which exchange one hard way of life for another" (Freeman).

Transgression and fall of heavenly beings to the earth is a mythical motif. In Empedocles it is adopted within the framework of a doctrine of transmigration of souls, while in Revelation it is used as explanation for the tribulation that the community must endure on earth.

Cf. the Coptic "Installation of the Archangel Michael," §3, probably independent of Revelation 12: (Peter to Christ:) "Do all these sins happen because of human beings? Or is it because of Mastemas [the devil]?" (Christ's response:) "It is as you have said: I cast him out of heaven—he fell to the earth. He who sent them [the tribulations] on the earth, until human beings found them" (MEB/Berger).

On Revelation 12:10 (Accuser), cf. nos. 596, 837.

960. Revelation 12:14

2 Baruch 28:1 (1 cent. CE)

But everyone who will understand will be wise at that time. For the measure and the calculation of that time will be two parts: weeks of seven weeks. (*OTP* 1:630)

The three-and-one-half-year period ("a time, two times, and half a time"; 1260 days) important to Revelation's chronology of the End is not arbitrary, but was developed from Daniel's one-half of a week of years (Dan 7:25; 8:14; 9:27; 12:7, 11, 12). The Daniel passage was influential on a broad stream of apocalyptic tradition, as *2 Baruch* illustrates. Under its influence, the three years of drought during Elijah's time became the apocalyptic three and one half years in later references (1 Kgs 17:1; 18:1; Luke 4:25; Jas 5:17).

961. Revelation 13–22

Tacitus, *Histories,* Book 5.13 (55–120 CE)

[On the destruction of Jerusalem:] Prodigies had indeed occurred, . . . contending hosts were seen meeting in the skies, arms flashed, and suddenly the temple was illumined with fire from the clouds. Of a sudden the doors of the shrine opened and a superhuman voice cried: "The gods are departing": at the same moment the mighty stir of their going was heard. Few interpreted these omens as fearful; the majority firmly believed that their ancient priestly writings contained the prophecy that this was the very time when the East should grow strong and that men starting from Judea should possess the world. This mysterious prophecy had in reality pointed to Vespasian and Titus, but the common people, as is the way of human ambition, interpreted these great destinies in their own favor . . . (LCL)

Parallel tradition in Josephus, *Jewish War,* 6.312: "But what more than all else incited them to the war was an ambiguous oracle, likewise found in their sacred scriptures, to the effect that at that time one from their country would become ruler of the world. This they understood to mean someone of their own race, and many of their wise men went astray in their interpretation of it. The oracle, however, in reality signified the sovereignty of Vespasian, who was proclaimed Emperor on Jewish soil" (LCL).

Similarly the Oracle of Hystaspes (2 cent. BCE) in Lactantius, *Divine Institutes* 7.15.19: ". . . the Roman name, by which the world is now ruled, will be taken away from the earth, and the government return to Asia; and the East will again bear rule, and the West be reduced to servitude" (ANF).

As adopted and transmitted in Judaism, *Sib. Or.* 3 350-52: (Asia will recover many times what Rome has taken from them); *Sib. Or.* 3.652-53 (God will send a king from the rising of the sun); cf. also *Sib. Or.* 3 at no. 450.

All these texts are documentation for a widespread expectation: the Roman Empire will pass away and be replaced by a new kingdom from the East. Then the East, now oppressed by Rome, will receive satisfaction. In Revelation this expectation is interpreted in terms of a theology of history and understood eschatologically. A contrary example: The Parthians refer similar prophecies to Mithridates (FGH 87, F 36, p. 246:6, "Oracles from everywhere prophesy power over the civilized world [will return here]"). Further:

962. Revelation 13–22

Potter's Oracle (130 BCE)

Because the Nile will dry up, the unfruitful earth will become parched without having brought forth any fruit. . . . Every year Egypt will suffer terribly by fearful tragedies. The sun will become dark, since it does not want to see the evil of Egypt. Farmers will have to pay taxes for things they have not sown, and there will be civil wars in Egypt, because there will be no food. This race will suffer war and terrible murders, brother against brother and husband against wife. . . . And a king will come from Syria, who will be hated by all people [P: and he will settle down in the city that will later be desolated]. . . . There will be disturbances in the land because of those who have left their own countries. People will move to foreign lands. Friends will murder each other. Each will bemoan his fate, as though it were worse than others'. Then people will unite out of necessity, in order to gain some advantage. Then in the lap of the woman there will be multifarious death . . . and the slaves will be freed, and their masters will beg for their lives, and virgins will be defiled by the men, and the father will displace his son-in-law, and they will marry their own mothers. And they will sacrifice the male children. . . . And the city on the sea will become a dry[ing] place for fishermen['s nets], because the Agathos Daimon [or "good demon"] and Mephis have gone to Memphis, so that those who pass through will say "This was the city that fed the world, in which the whole human race lived." And then Egypt will flourish, when the . . . Dispenser of Good comes forth from the sun, installed in office by the Great Goddess, so that those who are left will pray that those who had already died might be raised to participate in the good life . . . (MEB/from Berger's German; text in L. Koenen, *ZPE* 2 [1968], 178-209, at 201ff., according to P3)

The structure of the text corresponds to the typical apocalyptic catalogs of terrors (cf. Berger, *Formgeschichte,* §77), and the text suggests an Egyptian origin of the genre "historical apocalypse." The "place for spreading [fishermen's] nets" is also found in Ezekiel 26:14. Also the judgment of those who later pass through has biblical analogies (Ezek 27:29-36; Rev 18:15-19).

Particular analogies to Revelation:

1) The turn toward the good times comes about by a change of rulership. As in the texts named above in nos. 957, 961 the new ruler comes from the East ("from the sun").

2) Lament over the desolated city as in Revelation 18.

3) The hostile ruler (here Antiochus III?) is characterized by similar traits as those possessed by the Beast in Revelation, and later the Anti-Christ (cf. nos. 914-15). In addition, the portrayal of economic distress. And note the analogy to the concluding passage of 1 Thessalonians 4:13-18.

On Revelation 14:13, cf. no. 837. On Revelation 18:15-19, cf. no. 962.

963. Revelation 13:1-18

Tacitus, *Histories* 15.44 (55–120 CE)

[Reporting the Great Fire in Rome of 64 and its aftermath:] But all human efforts, all the lavish gifts of the emperor, and the propitiations of the gods did not banish the sinister belief that the conflagration was the result of an order [i.e., of Nero]. Consequently, to get rid of the report, Nero fastened the guilt and inflicted the most exquisite tortures on a class hated for their abominations, called Christians by the populace. Christus, from whom the name had its origin, suffered the extreme penalty during the reign of Tiberius at the hands of one of our procurators [actually, *prefect;* cf. Caesarea inscription], Pontius Pilatus, and a most mischievous superstition thus checked for the moment, again broke out not only in Judea, the first source of the evil, but even in Rome, where all things hideous and shameful from every part of the world find their center and become popular. Accordingly, an arrest was first made of all who pleaded guilty; then, upon their information, an immense multitude was convicted, not so much of the crime of firing the city, as of hatred against mankind. Mockery of every sort was added to their deaths. Covered with the skins of beasts, they were torn by dogs and perished, or were nailed to crosses, or were doomed to the flames and burnt, to serve as nightly illumination when daylight had expired. Nero offered his gardens for the spectacle, and was exhibiting a show in the circus, while he mingled with the people in the dress of a charioteer or stood aloft in a car. Hence, even for criminals who deserve extreme and exemplary punishment, there arose a feeling of compassion; for it was not, as it seemed, for the public good, but to glut one man's cruelty, that they were being destroyed. (LCL)

The image of Nero the emperor who first persecuted Christians burned itself into the consciousness of the Christian community and influenced the picture of the expected eschatological opponent in whom all evil is summed up (though never called "Antichrist" in Revelation), especially in conjunction with the legend that Nero would return. Cf. also *Sibylline Oracles* 4.114-24; 14.137-48; 5.28-34; 5.93-110; 5.137-61; 5.214-27; 5.361-84; Dio Chrysostom, *Discourses* 21.9-10; Suetonius, *Lives of the Caesars,* "Nero" 6.47.

964. Revelation 13:18

Graffito from Pompeii (1 cent. CE)

I love her whose number is 545.

Sibylline Oracles 5:28 (1 cent. CE)

One who has 50 as an initial will be commander. (*OTP* 1.393)

In both Greek and Hebrew, the letters of the alphabet had numerical values. There were no separate signs for numbers, as in the system of Arabic numbers common today. Thus every word was also a numerical sum, a fact which made possible many interpretations of words as numbers and vice versa, serious (as in Revelation) and not serious (as in the graffito above). The numerical value of the name ABRAXAS totaled 365, the number of days in the year, and for this reason played an important role in the magical and astrological symbolism of the Hellenistic world. Thus the numerical value of the name "Jesus" in Greek was 888, a fact apparently generally noticed in the Christian community (cf. the Christian additions to the *Sibylline Oracles* 1.324-30). The "one who has 50 as his initial" refers clearly to Nero, who "declares himself equal to God." While there are several possibilities for understanding the 666 of Revelation 13:18, the most likely is "Nero Caesar" in Hebrew letters: נ = 50; ר = 200; ו = 6; נ = 50; ק = 100; ס = 60; ר = 200, all of which total 666. This interpretation seems to be confirmed by the fact that the alternative spelling of "Nero" without the final ן *totals 616, the figure found in some* MSS of Revelation 13:18.

965. Revelation 14:10-11

4 Ezra 7:61 (late 1 cent. CE)

[God (the revealing angel) speaks:] I will not grieve over the great number of those who perish; for it is they who are now like a mist, and are similar to a flame and smoke—they are set on fire and burn hotly, and are extinguished. (NRSV)

"Ezra" is deeply distressed over the great number that are damned and the few that are saved (cf. no. 597 on Rom 9:1-2). As part of the rationale offered by God for not grieving is the explanation that the damned are not condemned to eternal punishment, but perish quickly. This is in contrast to Revelation, where the punishment is eternal. The contrast, however, is not between the more "merciful" God of 4 Ezra and the "cruel" God of Revelation, but between the rationalistic approach of 4 Ezra, who believes that salvation and damnation can be comprehended within a coherent rational system, and the author of Revelation, who does not attempt this. (Cf. M. Eugene Boring, "Reflection: Universal Salvation and Paradoxical Language" in *Revelation* [Louisville: Westminster/John Knox, 1989], 226-31, and "Revelation 19-21: End Without Closure," *Princeton Seminary Bulletin*, Supplementary Issue, no. 3 [1994], 57-84.

On Revelation 14:13, cf. no. 837.

966. Revelation 14:20

Josephus, *Jewish Wars* 6.406 (37–100 CE)

[Describing the horrors of the destruction of Jerusalem, 70 CE:] . . . they [the Roman soldiers] had no similar feelings for the living, but running everyone through who fell in their way, they choked the alleys with corpses and deluged the whole city with blood, insomuch that many of the fires were extinguished by the gory stream. (LCL)

In both Josephus and Revelation, an unimaginable quantity of blood is associated with the judgment on the city. In Josephus, this is dramatic exaggeration of a historical event, while in Revelation it is part of the surrealistic imagery in the eschatological vision. To make the connection, Revelation introduces "the city," not inherently a part of the vision.

967. Revelation 16:14-16; 19:11-21

Qumran War Scroll (1QM) 1:1-12a (1 cent. CE)

For the M[aster. the Rule of] War on the unleashing of the attack of the sons of light against the company of the sons of darkness, the army of Satan: against the band of Edom,

Moab, and the sons of Ammon, and [against the army of the sons of the East and] the Philistines, and against the bands of the Kittim of Assyria and their allies the ungodly of the Covenant.

The sons of Levi, Judah, and Benjamin, the exiles in the desert, shall battle against them in . . . all their bands when the exiled sons of light return from the Desert of the Peoples to camp in the Desert of Jerusalem; and after the battle they shall go up from there [to Jerusalem?].

[The king] of the Kittim [shall enter] into Egypt, and in his time he shall set out in great wrath to wage war against the kings of the north, that his fury may destroy and cut off the horn of [Israel].

This shall be a time of salvation for the people of God, an age of dominion for all the members of His company, and of everlasting destruction for all the company of Satan. The confusion of the sons of Japheth shall be [great] and Assyria shall fall unsuccored. The dominion of the Kittim shall come to an end and iniquity shall be vanquished, leaving no remnant; [for the sons] of darkness there shall be no escape. [The seasons of right-eous]ness shall shine over all the ends of the earth; they shall go on shining until all the seasons of darkness are consumed and, at the season appointed by God, His exalted greatness shall shine eternally to the peace, blessing, glory, joy, and long life of all the sons of light.

On the day when the Kittim fall, there shall be battle and terrible carnage before the God of Israel, for that shall be the day appointed from ancient times for the battle of destruction of the sons of darkness. At that time, the assembly of gods and the hosts of men shall battle, causing great carnage; on the day of calamity, the sons of light shall battle with the company of darkness amid the shouts of a mighty multitude and the clamor of gods and men to [make manifest] the might of God. And it shall be a time of [great] tribulation for the people which God shall redeem; of all its afflictions none shall be as this, from its sudden beginning until its end in eternal redemption. (Vermes)

The Qumran community resembled early Christianity in being an apocalyptic Jewish sect that saw the promises of Scripture being fulfilled in its own time, and pictured the final resolution of history in terms of a great battle in which God and his people would triumph. Qumran seems to have expected the battle to be a more literal event than did early Christianity. The covenanters of Qumran expected to participate quite literally in the battle themselves. Yet the battle plans have a surrealistic quality about them, and angels and demons participate as well (cf. Eph 6:10-20), and the battle is finally won by God's power, not by human military strategy.

968. Revelation 17:9

4 Ezra 11 (end of 1 cent. CE)

On the second night I had a dream: I saw rising from the sea an eagle that had twelve feathered wings and three heads. I saw it spread its wings over the whole earth, and all the winds of heaven blew upon it, and the clouds were gathered around it. I saw that out of its wings there grew opposing wings; but they became little, puny wings. But its heads were at rest; the middle head was larger than the other heads, but it too was at rest with them. Then I saw that the eagle flew with its wings, and it reigned over the earth and over those who inhabit it. And I saw how all things under heaven were subjected to it, and no one spoke against it—not a single creature that was on the earth. Then I saw the eagle rise upon its talons, and it uttered a cry to its wings, saying, "Do not all watch at the same time; let each sleep in its own place, and watch in its turn; but let the heads be reserved for the last."

I looked again and saw that the voice did not come from its heads, but from the middle of its body. I counted its rival wings, and there were eight of them. As I watched, one wing on the right side rose up, and it reigned over all the earth. And after a time its reign came to an end, and it disappeared, so that even its place was no longer visible. Then the next wing rose up and reigned, and it continued to reign a long time. While it was reigning its end came also, so that it disappeared like the first. And a voice sounded, saying to it, "Listen to me, you who have ruled the earth all this time; I announce this to you before you disappear. After you no one shall rule as long as you have ruled, not even half as long."

Then the third wing raised itself up, and held the rule as the earlier ones had done, and it also disappeared. And so it went with all the wings; they wielded power one after another and then were never seen again. I kept looking, and in due time the wings that followed also rose up on the right side, in order to rule. There were some of them that ruled, yet disappeared suddenly; and others of them rose up, but did not hold the rule.

And after this I looked and saw that the twelve wings and the two little wings had disappeared, and nothing remained on the eagle's body except the three heads that were at rest and six little wings.

As I kept looking I saw that two little wings separated from the six and remained under the head that was on the right side; but four remained in their place. Then I saw that these little wings planned to set themselves up and hold the rule. As I kept looking, one was set up, but suddenly disappeared; a second also, and this disappeared more quickly than the first. While I continued to look the two that remained were planning between themselves to reign together; and while they were planning, one of the heads that were at rest (the one that was in the middle) suddenly awoke; it was greater than the other two heads. And I saw how it allied the two heads with itself, and how the head turned with those that were with it and devoured the two little wings that were planning to reign. Moreover this head gained control of the whole earth, and with much oppression dominated its inhabitants; it had greater power over the world than all the wings that had gone before.

After this I looked again and saw the head in the middle suddenly disappear, just as the wings had done. But the two heads remained, which also in like manner ruled over the earth and its inhabitants. And while I looked, I saw the head on the right side devour the one on the left.

Then I heard a voice saying to me, "Look in front of you and consider what you see." When I looked, I saw what seemed to be a lion roused from the forest, roaring; and I heard how it uttered a human voice to the eagle, and spoke, saying, "Listen and I will speak to you. The Most High says to you, 'Are you not the one that remains of the four beasts that I had made to reign in my world, so that the end of my times might come through them? You, the fourth that has come, have conquered all the beasts that have gone before; and you have held sway over the world with great terror, and over all the earth with grievous oppression; and for so long you have lived on the earth with deceit. You have judged the earth, but not with truth, for you have oppressed the meek and injured the peaceable; you have hated those who tell the truth, and have loved liars; you have destroyed the homes of those who brought forth fruit, and have laid low the walls of those who did you no harm. Your insolence has come up before the Most High, and your pride to the Mighty One. The

Most High has looked at his times; now they have ended, and his ages have reached completion. Therefore you, eagle, will surely disappear, you and your terrifying wings, your most evil little wings, your malicious heads, your most evil talons, and your whole worthless body, so that the whole earth, freed from your violence, may be refreshed and relieved, and may hope for the judgment and mercy of him who made it.'" (NRSV)

This extensive and labored vision report, derived from the imagery of Daniel 7, is like Revelation in that it represents the fourth and final kingdom of Daniel's vision as Rome (in Daniel it stands for the Hellenistic kingdoms of Alexander and his successors), but is unlike Revelation in being detailed and transparent as to its historical meaning. While Revelation's imagery clearly points to Rome, precisely which emperors are intended remains ambiguous.

969. Revelation 19–21

Targum Pseudo-Jonathan on Numbers 11:26 (1–3 cent. CE)

Behold, a king will come forth from the land of Magog at the end of the days. He will assemble kings, who wear crowns, and commanders that bear armor, and all nations will follow him. They will instigate a battle in the land of Israel against the children of the dispersion, but the Lord will be ready to burn the breath of life out of them with the flame of fire that comes forth from beside the throne of his glory. Their dead bodies will fall on the mountains of the land of Israel, and the wild animals of the field and the birds of the sky will come and devour their remains. Afterward all the dead of Israel will be raised and enjoy the good things that have been secretly preserved for them since the beginning, and they will receive the reward for their works. (Bowker)

The phases itemized here correspond in particular to the structure of Revelation 20:8. Differences are that the Targum is concentrated entirely on Israel, and in Revelation the eschatological adversary is divided up into different figures. The animals that devour the corpses have already been met in Revelation at 19:17-21. The Targum lacks a figure corresponding to the Messiah or Logos, simply juxtaposing God and the hostile kings.

On Revelation 19:10; 22:8, cf. no. 805.

970. Revelation 19:13

Palestinian *Targum of Jonathan* Genesis 49:10-11
(7 cent. CE, much earlier materials)

Kings and rulers shall not cease from those of the house of Judah, nor scribes teaching the Law from his descendants, until the time the King Messiah comes, the youngest of his sons, because of whom the people will pine away. How beautiful is the King Messiah who is to arise from among those of the house of Judah. He girds his loins and comes down arranging battlelines against his enemies and slaying kings together with their rulers; and there is no king or ruler who can withstand him. He makes the mountains red with the blood of the slain; his garments are rolled in blood; he is like a presser of grapes. (Maher)

The trajectory of this imagery has three significant moments: (1) Genesis 49:10-12, where the robe of the coming king will be "dipped in the blood of grapes," illustrating the lavish prosperity of the good time coming, when there will be enough wine and milk for all, and vineyards and grapes will be so plentiful and lush that one can tie one's donkey to a grapevine (it will eat it), and do one's laundry in grape juice/wine. (2) This was reinterpreted of the Messianic King, who will dip his garments in real blood—that of his enemies. (3) Revelation's imagery builds on this second hermeneutical phase: the Messianic King will indeed be the victor whose robe is stained with blood, but he will be the Lamb whose own blood takes away sin, and his conquest is his going to the cross.

971. Revelation 20–22

Pseudo-Philo, *Liber Antiquitatum Biblicarum* 3.9-10 (1 cent. CE, probably pre-70)

And God said, "I will never again curse the earth on man's account, for the tendency of man's heart is foolish from his youth; and so I will never destroy all living creatures at one time as I have done. But when those inhabiting the earth sin, I will judge them by famine or by the sword or by fire or by death; and there will be earthquakes, and they will be scattered to uninhabited places. But no more will I destroy the earth by the water of the flood. And in all the days of the earth, seedtime and harvest, cold and heat, spring and fall will not cease day and night until I remember those who inhabit the earth, until the appointed times are fulfilled.

But when the years appointed for the world have been fulfilled, then the light will cease and the darkness will fade away. And I will bring the dead to life and raise up those who are sleeping from the earth. And hell will pay back its debt, and the place of perdition will return its deposit so that I may render to each according to his works and according to the fruits of his own devices, until I judge between soul and flesh. And the world will cease, and death will be abolished, and hell will shut its mouth. And the earth will not be without progeny or sterile for those inhabiting it; and no one who has been pardoned by me will be tainted. And there will be another earth and another heaven, an everlasting dwelling place. (*OTP* 2:306-7)

The Genesis story assumes the permanency of the earth, so that in declaring the faithfulness of God in supplying rain and regular seasons "as long as the earth endures," God has made an "everlasting" covenant with the earth and its inhabitants: there will never again be a judgment like the flood. The author of the targumlike retelling of the Old Testament story understands "as long as the earth endures" to confirm his apocalyptic presuppositions, and uses it as the point of departure to insert a fairly elaborate apocalyptic prediction into the narrative. Such a procedure shows that such ideas were simply in the air in some circles of first-century Judaism, and that the elaborate genre of revealed apocalyptic scenario given to a chosen seer need not be used to communicate it.

In common with Revelation are (1) "dwellers on the earth"; (2) famine, war, fire, death (plague), and earthquakes as the means of God's preliminary judgment prior to the final eschatological judgment; (3) a definite number of years that the earth will endure, i.e. a fixed time for the end of history; (4) judgment according to works; (5) a new heaven and new earth.

972. Revelation 20–22

4 Ezra 7:26-44 (late 1 cent. CE)

For indeed the time will come, when the signs that I have foretold to you will come to pass, that the city that now is not seen shall appear, and the land that now is hidden shall be disclosed. 27 Everyone who has been delivered from the evils that I have foretold shall see my wonders. 28 For my son the Messiah shall be revealed with those who are with him, and those who remain shall rejoice four hundred years. 29 After those years my son the Messiah shall die, and all who draw human breath. 30 Then the world shall be turned back to primeval silence for seven days, as it was at the first beginnings, so that no one shall be left. 31 After seven days the world that is not yet awake shall be roused, and that which is corruptible shall perish. 32 The earth shall give up those who are asleep in it, and the dust those who rest there in silence; and the chambers shall give up the souls that have been committed to them. 33 The Most High shall be revealed on the seat of judgment, and compassion shall pass away, and patience shall be withdrawn. 34 Only judgment shall remain, truth shall stand, and faithfulness shall grow strong. 35 Recompense shall follow, and the reward shall be manifested; righteous deeds shall awake, and unrighteous deeds shall not sleep. 36 The pit of torment shall appear, and opposite it shall be the place of rest; and the furnace of hell shall be disclosed, and opposite it the paradise of delight. 37 Then the Most High will say to the nations that have been raised from the dead, "Look now, and understand whom you have denied, whom you have not served, whose commandments you have despised. 38 Look on this side and on that; here are delight and rest, and there are fire and torments." Thus he will speak to them on the day of judgment— 39 a day that has no sun or moon or stars, 40 or cloud or thunder or lightning, or wind or water or air, or darkness or evening or morning, 41 or summer or spring or heat or winter or frost or cold, or hail or rain or dew, 42 or noon or night, or dawn or shining or brightness or light, but only the splendor of the glory of the Most High, by which all shall see what has been destined. 43 It will last as though for a week of years. 44 This is my judgment and its prescribed order; and to you alone I have shown these things. (NRSV)

Fourth Ezra, written during the same decade as Revelation by a Jewish author to the Jewish community, with no direct literary contacts to Revelation, has numerous points of similarity and contrast, not only in terms of form (revelation by an angel, sevenfold vision, the immediate apocalyptic future revealed in symbolic forms, bizarre animal symbolism), but also in content. The selection printed above manifests the following points of contact with Revelation:

    1)   The approach of the End will be clear to the initiated by signs (v. 26).

    2)   The heavenly city will appear (v. 26). For 4 Ezra, the arrival of the New Jerusalem will also be accompanied by the disclosure of the Promised Land, the true Holy Land created before the world, and only eschatologically revealed.

    3)   The Messiah is identified as the Son of God (though cf. the variations in the ancient versions).

    4)   There will be an intermediate period of eschatological victory, the "days of the Messiah," between the disappearance of the present evil age and the beginning of the age to come. This schema

was brought about by combining the prophetic this-worldly eschatology in which a this-worldly Messianic king would finally rule in the kingdom of God on earth, establishing justice and peace, and the transcendent "other-worldly" eschatology of the apocalyptists, in which salvation comes from the heavenly world in discontinuity with the present age. In 4 Ezra this interregnum lasts 400 years; in Revelation, 1,000 years. In Revelation, the faithful who are alive at the End share the millennial bliss with the faithful martyrs who are raised from the dead. In 4 Ezra, "those who remain" are joined by those who come with the Messiah, but it is not clear whether these are departed saints or heavenly hosts.

5) Both 4 Ezra and Revelation speak of the death of the Messiah. In 4 Ezra, the Messiah dies at the end of this period (v. 29), as a part of the demise of this present age, to which the Messiah belongs. For Revelation, the Messiah who shall appear at the End is the crucified Jesus, who has already lived and died in history. Thus in the theology of Revelation the death of the Messiah is a central event, and redemptive, in a way that is entirely alien to the theology of 4 Ezra, representing the way in which apocalyptic ideas were transformed by being reinterpreted in terms of the actual history of Jesus of Nazareth.

6) The reversion of the world to primeval silence for seven days (v. 30) reflects the creation story of Genesis, in which the precreation silence was broken by the creative word of God, and the universe was created within seven days. Likewise in Revelation, the eschatological realities are portrayed as a new creation.

7) Many of the same features of Revelation's final scenes are found in 4 Ezra: the earth gives up its dead (v. 32); God takes his place on the judgment seat, and good is rewarded and evil punished (vv. 33-35); the contrast between the Pit as the destiny for the unrighteous and the paradisical features of the place prepared for the righteous (vv. 36-38); the new world has no need of sun or moon, for it is illuminated by the glory of God (vv. 39-42).

8) The divine timetable is calculated in reference to the "week of years" (v. 43), an independent development of Daniel that influenced 4 Ezra, Revelation, and other apocalypses.

973. Revelation 20:1-6

Bahman Yascht ("Vohuman Yasn") 3:60-62 West = 9:21-24 Anklesaria (a middle-Persian apocalypse, the older layers of which pre-date the Potter's Oracle [no. 962], therefore prior to 130 BCE; based on the Pahlavi translation of a lost avest. text)

And afterward Sros and Yazat Neryosang go to Kersasp, call her three times, the fourth time (the one from the family of the) Sam stands up victoriously and went straight for Azdahak on the attack. (61) And he paid no attention to his words, and the victorious club struck him on the head, he knocked him down and killed him. Then oppression and hostility depart from the world, and for a thousand years I restore the beginning [of the world]. (62) Then Saosyant will again purify the creation, and the resurrection and the future bodies will come. (MEB/from German trans. of G. Widengren, *Iranische Geisteswelt* [1961], p. 208)

Sros ("the Obedient One") and Yazat Neryosang are heavenly companions and helpers of Ohrmazd, Kersasp from the family of the Sam is a primeval heroic figure, Azdahak is the (demonic) dragon, and Saosyant is the savior of cosmic significance. The expectation of a thousand-year empire is also documented elsewhere in Persian literature, and in fact under the name of Hystaspes (2 cent.

BCE), whose oracle sets forth a seven-thousand-year world-week. The final thousand years brings rest for all things (Aristocritos, *Theosophie*, in Buresch, *Klaros* 1899, p. 95, 11ff., 5 cent. CE) and the reign of justice (Lactantius, *Institutes* 7.14:8; cf. contacts with 2 Pet 3:8, 13). This thousand-year reign corresponds to the Messiah's reign on earth before the coming of the new age as portrayed in the older Jewish texts, yet this time lasts 400 years (4 Ezra 7:28) or 40 years (Hebrew Book of Elijah, in P. Riessler, *Altjüdisches Schrifttum ausserhalb der Bibel* [Heidelberg: F. H. Derle, 1966], p. 237), with the thousand-year period corresponding to the astrologically oriented Iranian witnesses occurring only later in the Coptic Apocalypse of Elijah 3:97-99 (trans.: W. Schrage, *Die Elia–Apocalypse JSHRV* V 3 [Güttersloher: Gerd Muhn, 1980], 273-74 and in Rev 20).

On the derivation of the Iranian conception of the twelve thousand years, the eleventh millennium of which the dragon is bound on the mountain Demawend, later reawakened by Ahriman, and then finally destroyed by Keresasp to prevent a catastrophe, see C. Colpe, "Exkursus III: Zur Eschatologisierung der 'Tausend Jahre,'" in A. Peisl and A. Mohler, eds., *Die Zeit* (Schriften der C.-F.-v. Siemens Stiftung 6), 1983, pp. 225-56. In any case, the picture in Revelation 20 corresponds so precisely to the Iranian, that one must here speak of direct influence. The whole development of the idea of the millennium understood as 1,000 years, not necessarily the interregnum as such, so full of consequences for later generations, had its origin in Iranian eschatology.

974. Revelation 21:1–22:5

4 Ezra 8:51-55 (late 1 cent. CE)

[The angel (God) in response to "Ezra's" lament about the great number of the damned:] But think of your own case, and inquire concerning the glory of those who are like yourself, 52 because it is for you that paradise is opened, the tree of life is planted, the age to come is prepared, plenty is provided, a city is built, rest is appointed, goodness is established and wisdom perfected beforehand. 53 The root of evil is sealed up from you, illness is banished from you, and death is hidden; Hades has fled and corruption has been forgotten; 54 sorrows have passed away, and in the end the treasure of immortality is made manifest. 55 Therefore do not ask any more questions about the great number of those who perish. (NRSV)

This picture of eschatological blessedness has much in common with that of Revelation. There is no literary dependence—both are written about the same time, and draw on the same stock of traditional apocalyptic imagery, which each interprets and uses in his own way. Both have the destruction of death, the restoration of paradise with its tree of life, and the city of God as the final destiny of the redeemed.

The function of the texts in their respective contexts is quite different. In 4 Ezra, the picture of eschatological glory is supposed to provide comfort for "Ezra" who laments the fate of the damned: think about yourself, not about them, and don't ask questions about the fate of others. Because Revelation is not concerned to provide answers within a coherent logical system, it can provide paradoxical pictures of both the terrible fate of the damned (Rev 14:10-11!) and of the glorious destiny of the saved. The despairing mood of introspective soul-searching of 4 Ezra is completely missing, partly because John's theological approach allows him to picture the eschatological future as a glorious destiny for all, including even the persecuting enemy. Cf. no. 597 on Romans 9:1-2 and no. 965 on Revelation 14:10-11, and the literature there given.

975. Revelation 21:1–22:5

Sibylline Oracles 3.767-808 (ca. 140 CE ?)

And then, indeed, he will raise up a kingdom for all ages among men, he who once gave a holy Law to the pious, to all of whom he promised to open the earth and the world and the gates of the blessed and all joys and immortal intellect and eternal cheer.

From every land they will bring incense and gifts to the house of the great God. There will be no other house among men, even for future generations to know, except the one which God gave to faithful men to honor (for mortals will invoke the son of the great God [a later Christian interpolation]). All the paths of the plain and rugged cliffs, lofty mountains, and wild waves of the sea will be easy to climb or sail in those days, for all peace will come upon the land of the good. Prophets of the great God will take away the sword for they themselves are judges of men and righteous kings. There will also be just wealth among men for this is the judgment and dominion of the great God. Rejoice, maiden, and be glad, for to you the one who created heaven and earth has given the joy of the age. He will dwell in you. You will have immortal light. Wolves and lambs will eat grass together in the mountains. Leopards will feed together with kids. Roving bears will spend the night with calves. The flesh-eating lion will eat husks at the manger like an ox, and mere infant children will lead them with ropes. For he will make the beasts on earth harmless. Serpents and asps will sleep with babies and will not harm them, for the hand of God will be upon them. (*OTP* 1:379)

Though incorporated into the official collection of Roman oracles, this is one of several obviously by a Jew (cf. Ancient Author Index), who draws from Isaiah 11 and other Jewish scripture and traditions. The eschatological kingdom will bring the triumph of God over all the world. The temple in the eschatological Jerusalem will be the center not only of Israel's worship, but that of all nations, and not only will national strife cease, but the peace of God will pervade the world of nature. On Revelation 21:11-14, cf. no. 626. On Revelation 22:8, cf. Revelation 19:10 and no. 805.

976. Revelation 22:18-19

Letter of Aristeas 310-11 (140–100 BCE)

[On the translation of the LXX:] As the books were read, the priests stood up, with the elders from among the translators and from the representatives of the "Community," and with the leaders of the people, and said, "Since this version has been made rightly and reverently, and in every respect accurately, it is good that this should remain exactly so, and that there should be no revision." There was general approval of what they said, and they commanded that a curse should be laid, as was their custom, on anyone who should alter the version by any addition or change to any part of the written text, or any deletion either. This was a good step taken, to ensure that the words were preserved completely and permanently in perpetuity. (*OTP* 2:33)

Cf. Philo, *Moses* 2.34 (15 BCE–50 CE; of the LXX translators): Reflecting how great an undertaking it was to make a full version of the laws given by the voice of God, where they could not add or take away or transfer anything, but must keep the original form and shape . . . (LCL). In the Hellenistic world there were no copyright laws. Furthermore, since all manuscripts were copied by hand it was often difficult to determine whether something had been added or modified by a copyist. Thus it was common to attach a threat or curse at the end of a manuscript demanding that it be transmitted as received. The threat in Revelation 22:18-19 corresponds to this general practice. In addition, however, Revelation stands in the Jewish tradition emanating from Deuteronomy 4:2, 12:32, which attributed special sanctity to the wording of the Law which must be transmitted unchanged, as documented in the texts from Aristeas and Philo. Cf. no. 31.

Acknowledgments

The Publisher has made every effort to contact those holding permission to use materials included in this book. On receiving correct information, the Publisher will correct at reprint any instances in which permissions were overlooked, or the Publisher's permission requests received no response before first publication. Grateful acknowledgment is made for permission to use the following:

Excerpts from *Acts of the Pagan Martyrs. Acta Alexandrinorum*, ed. Herbert A. Musurillo; *The Works of Aristotle*, Sir David Ross, ed. and trans.; and *Sidelights on Greek History*, Marcus N. Tod, trans. (Clarendon Press).

Excerpts from *Ancilla*, by K. Freeman, reprinted by permission of the publishers from *Ancilla to the Pre-Socratic Philosophers: A Complete Translation of the Fragments in Diels, Fragmente der Vorsokratiker*, by Kathleen Freeman, Cambridge, Mass.: Harvard University Press, 1948.

Excerpts from *Aramaic Bible*, vol. 1A, "Targum Neofiti 1, Genesis" by Martin McNamara; and from *Targum Pseudo-Jonathan, Genesis* by Michael Maher, *Aramaic Bible* 1B. Copyright © 1992 by The Order of St. Benedict, Inc. Published by The Liturgical Press, Collegeville, Minn. Used with permission.

Three excerpts from B. P. Reardon, *Collected Ancient Greek Novels*. Copyright © 1989 The Regents of the University of California.

Excerpts from the *Babylonian Talmud*, ed. I. Epstein. London, The Soncino Press Ltd., 1935–48.

Excerpts from *Midrash Rabbah*, ed. H. Freedman and Maurice Simon, The Soncino Press.

Excerpts from *Graeco-Roman Literature* by D. Aune; John Dillon and Jackson Hershbell, *On the Pythagorean Way of Life*/Iamblichus; F. Francis and Meeks, eds., *Conflict at Colossae: A Problem in the Interpretation of Early Christianity*; Ronald F. Hock and Edward N. O'Neil, *The Chreia in Ancient Rhetoric*; Luke Timothy Johnson, "The New Testament's Anti-Jewish Slander and the Conventions of Ancient Polemic"; *Paraleipomena Jeremiou*, ed. and trans. Robert A. Kraft and Ann-Elizabeth Purintun; A. J. Malherbe, *Cynic Epistles*, Edward N. O'Neil, *Teles (the cynic teacher)*; Morton Smith, *Tannaitic Parallels to the Gospels*; *Porphyry, the Philosopher, to Marcella*, K. Wicker; "Mithras Liturgy," by Marvin Meyer (Scholars Press/The Society of Biblical Literature).

Excerpt from *The Charismatic Leader and His Followers* by Martin Hengel (Crossroad Publishing Co.).

Excerpts from the *Dead Sea Scrolls in English* by G. Vermes (London: Penguin Books 1962, third ed., 1987), copyright © G. Vermes, 1962, 1965, 1968, 1975, 1987. Reproduced by permission of Penguin Books Ltd.

Excerpts from *Discoveries in the Judean Desert*, vol. 10, ed. Elisha Qimron and John Strugnell; from *Apologia and Florida of Apuleius of Madaura*, by H. E. Butler, *Meditations of Marcus Aurelius*, by A. S. L. Farquharson, *Gnosis: A Selection of Gnostic Texts*, by W. Foerster, ed., *Conversion*, by A. D. Nock,

Hermetica, by W. Scott, and the *Mishnah,* by H. Danby; from the *Panarion of St. Epiphanius, Bishop of Salamis,* by Philip R. Amidon; and from "Apocryphal Jewish Biographies," by E. O. Winstedt *JTS* 9 (1908), by permission of Oxford University Press.

Excerpt from *Documents for the Study of the Gospels* by David R. Cartlidge and David L. Dungan, copyright © 1980 David R. Cartlidge and David L. Dungan. Used by permission of Augsburg Fortress.

Excerpt from *Early Gentile Christianity and Its Hellenistic Background* by Arthur Darby Nock.

Excerpts from E. G. Turner in *JRS* 53 (1963), Society for the Promotion of Roman Studies.

Excerpts from *The Fathers of the Church,* trans. Sister M. Clement Egan; and *Origen, Commentary on the 'Gospel According to John,'* Books 1–10, trans. Ronald Hein (Catholic University of America Press).

Excerpts from the *Greek Magical Papyri in Translation,* H. D. Betz, ed., © the University of Chicago Press.

Excerpt from *The Homeric Hymns* by Andrew Lang (Longman Publishers).

Excerpts from *The Isaiah Targum* by Bruce D. Chilton; and excerpt from *The Aramaic Bible, vol. 13, The Targum of Ezekiel* by Samson H. Levey (Michael Glazier).

Excerpts from Ismar Elbogen's *Jewish Liturgy: A Comprehensive History,* the Jewish Publication Society.

Excerpts from the translations of Jacob Neusner (Atlanta: Scholars Press).

Excerpts from John Bowman, *Samaritan Documents Relating to Their History, Religion, and Life.* Pittsburgh: Pickwick Press, 1977.

Excerpts from the Loeb Classical Library, Harvard University Press.

Excerpt from *Macrobius Saturnalia* trans. Percival Vaughan Davies. Copyright © 1969 by Columbia University Press. Reprinted with permission of the publisher.

Excerpts from *Later Greek Religion* by Edwyn Bevan, J. M. Dent & Sons, publishers.

Four excerpts from *Memar Marqah,* John MacDonald, ed. and trans. (Berlin: Walter de Gruyter).

Excerpt from the *Mishnayoth* ed. Philipp Blackman (London: Judaica Press, 1963).

Excerpts from *Musonius Rufus: "The Roman Socrates,"* by Cora E. Lutz, Yale Classical Studies (1947).

Selected excerpts from the *Nag Hammadi Library in English, Third, Completely Revised Edition* by James M. Robinson, general ed. Copyright © 1988 by E.J. Brill, Leiden, The Netherlands. Reprinted by permission of HarperCollinsPublishers, Inc.

Excerpts from *New Documents Illustrating Early Christianity V. Linguistic Essays* by G. H. R. Horsley; and excerpts from *New Documents Illustrating Early Christianity. A Review of the Greek Inscriptions and Papyri* by G. H. R. Horsley/S. R. Llewelyn (Macquarie University).

ACKNOWLEDGMENTS

Excerpts from *New Testament Apocrypha, I. Gospels and Related Writings* by William Schneelmelcher, ed. (Westminster John Knox Press).

Excerpt from the *New Testament: Proclamation and Parenesis, Myth and History,* Third Edition by Dennis C. Duling and Norman Perrin, copyright © 1994 by Harcourt Brace & Co., reprinted by permission of the publisher.

Excerpts from the *Old Testament Pseudepigrapha* by James H. Charlesworth. Copyright © 1983, 1985 by James H. Charlesworth. Used by permission of Doubleday, a division of Bantam Doubleday Dell Publishing Group, Inc.

Excerpt from *Ovid's Amores,* trans. Guy Lee, John Murray (Publishers) Ltd.

Excerpts from *Pesikta Rabbati,* by W. Braude, and *Fathers According to Rabbi Nathan,* by J. Goldin, copyright 1968, 1955 Yale University Press.

Excerpts from *A Select Library of Nicene and Post-Nicene Fathers of the Christian Church* and *The Ante-Nicene Fathers;* and from *Backgrounds of Early Christianity* by E. Ferguson, Wm. B. Eerdmans Publishing Co.

Excerpts from *Talmudic Anthology* by Lewis I. Newman, with Samuel Spitz (Behrman House).

Excerpts from *The Targums and Rabbinic Literature* by John Westerdale Bowker; *Contra Celsum* by Henry Chadwick; and *Hermetica* by Brian P. Copenhaver (courtesy Cambridge University Press, and Brian P. Copenhaver for excerpts from *Hermetica*).

Excerpt from *Women's Life in Greece and Rome,* by Mary R. Lefkowitz and Maureen B. Fant, eds., copyright 1982. Reprinted by permission of the Johns Hopkins University Press.

Excerpts from the *World of Classical Athens* by Giulio Giannelli. Copyright © 1970 by Giulio Giannelli. Reprinted by permission of the Putnam Publishing Group.

Comparison Chart of Text Numbers

Berger-Colpe Numbers = Present Numbers

Berger-Colpe		Present		Berger-Colpe		Present		Berger-Colpe		Present
1	=	227		49	=	105		98	=	245
2	=	18		50	=	81		98	=	246
3	=	21		51	=	79		99	=	170
4	=	22		52	=	107		100	=	171
5	=	228		53	=	108		101	=	172
6	=	25		54	=	110		102	=	173
7	=	229		55	=	111		103	=	174
8	=	27		56	=	112		104	=	83
9	=	28		57	=	118		105	=	176
10	=	29		58	=	119		106	=	178
11	=	230		59	=	237		107	=	175
12	=	231		60	=	238		108	=	179
13	=	51		61	=	239		109	=	180
14	=	48		62	=	240		110	=	181
15	=	49		63	=	120		111	=	188
16	=	50		64	=	121		112	=	190
17	=	65		65	=	122		113	=	191
18	=	66		66	=	123		114	=	192
19	=	67		67	=	124		115	=	193
20	=	68		68	=	126		116	=	194
21	=	69		69	=	127		117	=	195
22	=	70		70	=	128		118	=	196
23	=	87		71	=	129		119	=	197
24	=	234		72	=	130		120	=	199
25	=	88		73	=	131		121	=	200
26	=	90		74	=	132		122	=	201
27	=	89		75	=	134		123	=	202
28	=	235		76	=	135		124	=	204
29	=	236		77	=	136		125	=	205
30	=	92		78	=	241		126	=	249
31	=	96		79	=	141		127	=	208
32	=	97		80	=	143		128	=	209
33	=	98		81	=	144		129	=	213
34	=	99		82	=	145		130	=	215
35	=	101		83	=	147		131	=	216
36	=	54		84	=	148		132	=	217
37	=	58		85	=	152		132	=	218
38	=	55		86	=	242		133	=	219
39	=	53		87	=	153		134	=	220
40	=	57		88	=	154		135	=	221
41	=	62		89	=	155		136	=	222
42	=	63		90	=	156		137	=	250
43	=	64		91	=	243		138	=	251
44	=	71		92	=	157		139	=	267
44	=	72		93	=	158		140	=	328
45	=	73		94	=	160		141	=	277
46	=	74		95	=	163		142	=	274
47	=	75		96	=	166		143	=	275
48	=	104		97	=	244		144	=	272

COMPARISON CHART OF TEXT NUMBERS

145	=	276	199	=	86	254	=	371
146	=	273	200	=	100	255	=	372
147	=	280	201	=	102	256	=	373
148	=	305	202	=	137	257	=	374
149	=	44	203	=	138	258	=	380
150	=	45	204	=	139	259	=	381
151	=	316	205	=	140	260	=	382
152	=	308	206	=	150	261	=	389
153	=	337	207	=	151	262	=	391
154	=	313	208	=	159	263	=	392
155	=	314	209	=	182	264	=	393
156	=	315	210	=	224	265	=	394
157	=	281	211	=	7	266	=	395
158	=	285	212	=	8	267	=	397
159	=	286	213	=	256	268	=	398
160	=	311	214	=	15	269	=	399
161	=	321	215	=	257	270	=	400
162	=	279	216	=	264	271	=	401
163	=	287	217	=	263	272	=	403
164	=	322	218	=	268	273	=	404
165	=	296	219	=	106	274	=	405
166	=	298	220	=	290	275	=	406
167	=	299	221	=	290	276	=	407
168	=	317	222	=	290	277	=	409
169	=	325	223	=	301	278	=	410
170	=	326	224	=	307	279	=	411
171	=	291	225	=	312	280	=	412
172	=	292	226	=	318	281	=	413
173	=	294	227	=	320	282	=	418
173	=	295	228	=	324	283	=	419
174	=	282	229	=	329	284	=	420
174a	=	310	230	=	330	285	=	421
175	=	319	231	=	331	286	=	422
176	=	344	232	=	332	287	=	423
177	=	343	233	=	333	288	=	424
178	=	5	234	=	334	289	=	425
179	=	10	235	=	335	290	=	427
180	=	11	236	=	336	291	=	429
181	=	12	237	=	338	292	=	431
182	=	13	237a	=	339	293	=	432
183	=	14	238	=	340	294	=	433
184	=	31	239	=	341	295	=	434
185	=	32	240	=	342	296	=	437
186	=	33	241	=	346	297	=	438
187	=	34	242	=	347	298	=	439
188	=	36	243	=	348	299	=	440
189	=	38	244	=	355	300	=	441
190	=	41	245	=	356	301	=	442
191	=	42	246	=	357	302	=	443
192	=	46	247	=	358	303	=	444
193	=	47	248	=	354	304	=	445
194	=	59	249	=	362	305	=	446
195	=	78	250	=	363	306	=	447
196	=	284	251	=	364	307	=	448
197	=	84	252	=	368	308	=	449
198	=	85	253	=	369	309	=	450

310	=	451	361	=	553	414	=	638
311	=	452	362	=	555	415	=	639
312	=	453	363	=	556	416	=	644
313	=	454	364	=	557	417	=	645
313	=	455	365	=	559	418	=	647
314	=	456	366	=	562	419	=	648
315	=	458	367	=	564	420	=	652
316	=	459	368	=	565	421	=	653
317	=	461	369	=	566	422	=	654
318	=	463	370	=	570	423	=	655
319	=	464	371	=	571	424	=	656
319	=	465	372	=	572	425	=	657
319	=	466	373	=	573	426	=	658
319	=	467	374	=	575	427	=	659
320	=	468	375	=	576	428	=	660
321	=	471	376	=	577	429	=	661
322	=	472	377	=	578	430	=	662
323	=	474	378	=	579	431	=	663
324	=	475	379	=	580	432	=	664
325	=	476	380	=	582	433	=	665
326	=	477	381	=	584	434	=	666
327	=	478	382	=	585	435	=	667
328	=	479	383	=	586	436	=	668
329	=	482	384	=	587	437	=	669
330	=	483	385	=	588	438	=	671
331	=	484	386	=	589	439	=	672
332	=	485	387	=	590	440	=	673
333	=	486	388	=	591	441	=	674
334	=	487	389	=	592	442	=	676
335	=	488	390	=	593	443	=	678
336	=	492	391	=	594	444	=	679
337	=	493	392	=	596	445	=	680
338	=	495	393	=	600	446	=	681
339	=	494	394	=	601	447	=	687
340	=	497	395	=	602	448	=	689
341	=	499	396	=	603	448	=	690
342	=	500	397	=	604	449	=	692
343	=	501	398	=	609	450	=	694
344	=	502	399	=	611	451	=	696
345	=	504	400	=	612	452	=	697
345a	=	510	401	=	614	453	=	698
346	=	512	402	=	615	454	=	699
347	=	520	403	=	616	455	=	701
348	=	531	404	=	618	456	=	703
349	=	532	405	=	619	457	=	706
350	=	534	405	=	620	458	=	707
351	=	535	405	=	621	459	=	709
352	=	541	405	=	622	460	=	710
353	=	542	406	=	626	461	=	711
354	=	543	407	=	627	462	=	713
355	=	544	408	=	629	463	=	714
356	=	546	409	=	630	463	=	715
357	=	547	410	=	633	464	=	716
358	=	548	411	=	635	465	=	717
359	=	549	412	=	636	466	=	718
360	=	552	413	=	637	467	=	719

COMPARISON CHART OF TEXT NUMBERS

468	=	720	522	=	784	576	=	868
469	=	721	523	=	800	577	=	869
470	=	722	524	=	802	578	=	870
471	=	723	525	=	803	579	=	871
472	=	724	526	=	786	580	=	872
473	=	725	527	=	804	581	=	873
474	=	726	528	=	805	582	=	874
475	=	727	529	=	807	583	=	875
476	=	728	530	=	787	584	=	876
477	=	729	531	=	789	585	=	877
478	=	730	532	=	810	586	=	878
479	=	731	533	=	790	587	=	880
480	=	732	534	=	811	588	=	881
481	=	733	535	=	791	589	=	882
482	=	734	536	=	792	590	=	883
483	=	735	537	=	793	591	=	884
484	=	736	538	=	794	592	=	885
485	=	740	539	=	795	593	=	887
486	=	741	540	=	798	594	=	889
487	=	739	541	=	812	595	=	891
488	=	737	542	=	813	596	=	896
489	=	742	543	=	814	597	=	897
490	=	743	544	=	815	598	=	899
491	=	744	545	=	817	599	=	901
492	=	746	546	=	819	600	=	903
493	=	747	547	=	820	601	=	905
494	=	748	548	=	821	602	=	906
495	=	749	549	=	822	603	=	907
496	=	752	550	=	824	604	=	908
497	=	754	551	=	827	605	=	909
498	=	755	552	=	828	606	=	910
499	=	756	553	=	829	607	=	911
500	=	757	554	=	830	608	=	912
501	=	758	555	=	831	608	=	913
502	=	759	556	=	834	608	=	914
503	=	760	557	=	835	608	=	915
504	=	763	558	=	836	609	=	916
505	=	763	559	=	837	610	=	917
506	=	764	560	=	838	611	=	919
507	=	765	561	=	839	612	=	940
508	=	766	562	=	840	613	=	942
509	=	767	563	=	843	614	=	949
510	=	768	564	=	850	615	=	951
511	=	769	565	=	851	616	=	952
512	=	770	566	=	853	617	=	953
513	=	771	567	=	854	618	=	955
514	=	772	568	=	855	619	=	956
515	=	773	569	=	856	620	=	957
516	=	774	570	=	858	621	=	958
517	=	775	571	=	859	622	=	959
518	=	776	572	=	861	623	=	961
519	=	777	573	=	865	624	=	962
520	=	778	574	=	866	625	=	969
521	=	780	575	=	867	626	=	973

Bibliography

Primary Sources

(Texts followed by an asterisk are quoted in this volume.)

Amidon, Philip K., trans. *The Panarion of St. Epiphanius, Bishop of Salamis.* New York and Oxford: Oxford University Press, 1990.*

Barrett, C. K. *The New Testament Background: Selected Documents.* Revised and expanded ed. San Francisco: Harper & Row, Publishers, 1989.*

Behr, Charles. *Aelius Aristides: The Complete Works,* vol. 18, *Regarding Sarapis.* Leiden: E.J. Brill, 1981.*

Betz, H. D., ed. *The Greek Magical Papyri in Translation.* Chicago: University of Chicago Press, 1986.*

Blackman, P. *Mishnayoth.* New York: Judaica Press, 1963.*

Bowker, John Westerdale. *The Targums and Rabbinic Literature; an Introduction to Jewish Interpretations of Scripture.* Cambridge: Cambridge University Press, 1969.*

Bowman, John. *Samaritan Documents Relating to Their History, Religion, and Life.* Pittsburgh: Pickwick Press, 1977.*

Braude, W. *Pesiqta Rabbati.* New Haven and London: Yale University Press, 1968.*

Butler, H. E. *The Apologia and Florida of Apuleius of Madaura.* Trans. H. E. Butler. Oxford: Clarendon Press, 1909.*

Cartledge, David R., and David L. Dungan. *Documents for the Study of the Gospels.* Philadelphia: Fortress Press, 1980.*

Chadwick, Henry. *Contra Celsum.* Cambridge: Cambridge University Press, 1953.*

Charlesworth, James H., ed. *Damascus Document, War Scroll, and Related Documents.* Vol. 2, The Princeton Theological Seminary Dead Sea Scrolls Project. Louisville: Westminster/John Knox, and Tübingen: J.C.B. Mohr, 1995.

———, ed. *The Old Testament Pseudepigrapha,* 2 vols. Garden City, N.Y.: Doubleday & Co., 1983, 1985.*

———, ed. *The Rules of the Community and Related Documents.* Vol. 1, The Princeton Theological Seminary Dead Sea Scrolls Project. Louisville: Westminster/John Knox, and Tübingen: J.C.B. Mohr, 1994.

Chilton, Bruce D. *The Isaiah Targum.* Wilmington, Del.: M. Glazier, 1987.*

Copenhaver, Brian P. *Hermetica.* Cambridge: Cambridge University Press, 1992.*

Danby, Herbert. *The Mishnah.* Trans. from the Hebrew with Introductory and Brief Explanatory Notes. London: Oxford University Press, 1933.*

Drower, E. S. *The Canonical Prayerbook of the Mandaeans.* Leiden: E.J. Brill, 1959.*

Eagan, M. Clement. *Persistephanon.* Vol. 43, *The Fathers of the Church,* a new trans. Washington: Catholic University of America Press, 1962.*

———. *Prudentius.* Vol. 52, *The Fathers of the Church,* a new trans. Washington: Catholic University of America Press, 1965.*

Epstein, I., ed. *The Babylonian Talmud.* London: Soncino Press, 1935–48.*

BIBLIOGRAPHY

Farquharson, A. S. L., trans. *Marcus Aurelius, Emperor of Rome, 121–180: Meditations.* No. 9, Everyman's Library. Introduction by D. A. Rees. London: Dent; New York: Dutton, 1961.*

Flemming, J., and H. Duensing. "The Ascension of Isaiah," in Wilhelm Schneelmelcher, ed. *The New Testament Apocrypha.* English trans. by Robert McL. Wilson. 2 vols. Philadelphia: Westminster Press, 1964.*

Foerster, W., ed. *Gnosis: A Selection of Gnostic Texts.* 2 vols. Oxford: Oxford University Press, 1972, 1974.*

Forbes, Clarence A. *Firmicus Maternus: The Error of the Pagan Religions.* New York: Newman Press, 1970.*

Freedman, H., and Maurice Simon, eds. *Midrash Rabbah.* London: Soncino Press, 1939 –.*

Friedlander, Gerald. *Pirké de Rabbi Eliezer.* New York: Hermon Press, 1916; repr., 1963.*

Gifford, Edwin H., trans. *Eusebius, Preparation for the Gospel.* Grand Rapids: Baker Book House, 1981.*

Goldin, Judah, trans. *The Fathers According to Rabbi Nathan.* Yale Judaica Series, vol. 10. New Haven: Yale University Press, 1955.*

Handford, S. A. *Fables of Aesop.* New York: Penguin Books, 1954.*

Heine, Ronald, trans. *Origen, Commentary on the Gospel According to John,* Books 1-10. Washington: Catholic University of America Press, 1989.*

Hennecke, Edgar, and Wilhelm Schneemelcher, eds. *New Testament Apocrypha.* 2 vols. English trans. by Robert McL. Wilson. Philadelphia: Westminster Press, 1963, 1964; vol. 1 revised 1991.*

Hense, Otto, ed. *Iuannis Stabaei Anthologii.* Vol. 4. Berlin: Weidmannos, 1975.*

Horsley, G. H. R. *New Documents Illustrating Early Christianity.* North Ryde, Australia: Macquarie University, 1982.*

Horsley, G. H. R., and S. R. Llewelyn. *New Documents Illustrating Early Christianity.* A Review of the Greek Inscriptions and Papyri published in 1976–1981, I-IV. VI, North Ryde, N. S. W., Australia, 1981–1992.

Hunt, Arthur S. *Select Papyri,* in five vols., with an English trans. by A. S. Hunt and C. C. Edgar. The Loeb Classical Library, vols. 266, 282, 360. Cambridge, Mass.: Harvard University Press; London, Heinemann, 1932.*

Jones, V. S. Vernon. *Aesop's Fables.* New York: Franklin Watts, 1912; repr., 1969.*

Jowett, Benjamin. Translator of Plato, *The Republic,* with the Jowett notes and marginalia. Cleveland and New York: World Publishing Co., 1946.*

Kee, Howard Clark. *The Origins of Christianity.* Englewood, N.J.: Prentice-Hall, 1973.*

Kraft, Robert A., and Ann-Elizabeth Purintun, trans. and eds. *Paraleipomena Jeremiou.* Missoula, Mont.: Society of Biblical Literature, 1972.*

Lang, Andrew. *The Homeric Hymns.* New York: Longmans, Green, and Co., 1899.*

Lathan, R. E. Translator of Lucretius, *On the Nature of the Universe.* New York: Penguin, 1951.*

Layton, B. *The Gnostic Scriptures: A New Translation with Annotations and Introductions.* Garden City, N.Y.: Doubleday & Co., 1987.

LCL = The Loeb Classical Library. Cambridge, Mass.: Harvard University Press; London: Heinemann.*

Leipoldt, Johannes, and Walter Grundmann. *Umwelt des Urchristentums, II, Texte zum neutestamentlichen Zeitalter.* Berlin: Evangelische Verlagsanstalt, 6th ed., 1982.*

———, eds. *Umwelt des Urchristentums,* vol. 2, *Texte zum neutestamentlichen Zeitalter.* 3rd ed. Berlin: Evangelische Verlagsanstalt, 1972.

Levey, Samson H. *The Targum of Ezekiel.* Vol. 13, *The Aramaic Bible.* Wilmington, Del.: M. Glazier, 1987.*

Lewis, Naphtali, and Reinhold Meyer. *Roman Civilization: Sourcebook II, the Empire.* New York: Columbia University Press, 1951–1955.

Llewelyn, S. R. *New Documents Illustrating Early Christianity.* North Ryde, N.S.W.: Ancient History Documentary Research Centre, Macquarie University, 1981.*

Lutz, Cora E. *Musonius Rufus: "The Roman Socrates."* Yale Classical Studies 10. New Haven: Yale University Press, 1947.*

MacDermot, V. *Pistis Sophia*. NHS 9. Leiden: E.J. Brill, 1978.*

MacDonald, John, ed. and trans. *Memar Marqah*. Berlin: Alfred Töpelmann, 1963.*

McNamara, Martin, trans. *Targum Neofiti 1, Genesis*. Collegeville, Minn.: Liturgical Press, 1992.*

Maher, Michael, trans. *Targum Pseudo-Jonathan, Genesis*. Collegeville, Minn.: Liturgical Press, 1992.*

Malherbe, Abraham J. *Moral Exhortation, A Greco-Roman Sourcebook*. Philadelphia: Westminster Press, 1986.

———. *The Cynic Epistles*. SBL Sources for Biblical Study 12. Missoula, Mont.: Scholars Press, 1977.*

Martin, Francis. *Narrative Parallels to the New Testament*. SBL Resources for Biblical Study 22. Atlanta: Scholars Press, 1988.*

Martínez, Florentino García. *The Dead Sea Scrolls Translated: The Qumran Texts in English*. Trans. Wilfred G. E. Watson. Leiden and New York: E.J. Brill, 1994.

Mauer, Ch. "Apocalypse of Peter," in Wilhelm Schneelmelcher, ed. *The New Testament Apocrypha*. Trans. of the Ethiopic text after H. Duensing. English translation by Robert McL. Wilson. 2 vols. Philadelphia: Westminster Press, 1964.*

Meyer, Marvin W., ed. *The Ancient Mysteries: A Sourcebook*. San Francisco: HarperCollins, 1987.*

Meyer, Marvin W., ed. and trans. *The "Mithras Liturgy."* Missoula, Mont.: Scholars Press, 1976.*

Montefiore, C. G., and H. Loewe. *A Rabbinic Anthology: Selected and Arranged with Comments and Introductions*. Philadelphia: Jewish Publication Society of America, 1960; repr. Cleveland: World Publishing Co., 1963.*

Mullachius, G. A. *Fragmenta Philosophorum Graecorum*. Paris: Ambrosio Firmin-Didot, 1865.*

Musurillo, Herbert A., ed. *The Acts of the Pagan Martyrs*. *Acta Alexandrinorum*. Oxford: Clarendon Press, 1954.*

Nahm, Milton C. *Selections from Early Greek Philosophy*. New York: F. S. Crofts & Co., 1934.*

Neusner, Jacob, trans. and ed. *Pesiqta de Rab Kahana: An Analytical Translation*. Brown Judaic Studies; nos. 122-23. Atlanta: Scholars Press, 1987.*

———. *Mekhilta According to Rabbi Ishmael: An Analytical Translation*. Brown Judaic Studies, nos. 148, 154. Atlanta: Scholars Press, 1988.*

———. *Genesis Rabbah: The Judaic Commentary to the Book of Genesis: A New American Translation*. Brown Judaic Studies, nos. 104-6. Atlanta: Scholars Press, 1985.*

———. *Lamentations Rabbah: An Analytical Translation*. Atlanta: Scholars Press, 1989.*

———. *Sifre to Deuteronomy: An Analytical Translation*. Brown Judaic Studies, no. 98. Atlanta: Scholars Press, 1987.*

———. *Sifra to Numbers: An American Translation and Explanation*. Brown Judaic Studies, no. 118. Atlanta: Scholars Press, 1986.*

———. *Song of Songs Rabbah: An Analytical Translation*. Brown Judaic Studies, nos. 197-98. Atlanta: Scholars Press, 1989.*

———. *The Talmud of Babylonia*. Atlanta: Scholars Press.*

———. *Talmud Yerushalmi*. Chicago Studies in the History of Judaism: The Talmud of the Land of Israel. Chicago: University of Chicago Press, 1982–1994.*

———. *The Fathers According to Rabbi Nathan: an Analytical Translation and Explanation*. Atlanta: Scholars Press, 1986.*

———. *The Tosefta*. South Florida Studies in the History of Judaism, no. 10. Atlanta: Scholars Press, 1990.*

Newman, Lewis I., with Samuel Spitz. *Talmudic Anthology*. New York: Behrman House, 1945.*

Newsom, Carol. *Songs of the Sabbath Sacrifice: A Critical Edition*. Harvard Semitic Studies 27. Atlanta: Scholars Press, 1985.*

Nock, Arthur Darby. *Early Gentile Christianity and Its Hellenistic Background*. New York, Evanston, London: Harper & Row, 1964.*

O'Neil, Edward N. *Teles (The Cynic Teacher)*. Missoula, Mont.: Scholars Press for the Society of Biblical Literature, 1977.*

Reardon, B. P. *Collected Ancient Greek Novels*. Berkeley: U. of California Press, 1989.*

Reddish, Mitchell G., ed. *Apocalyptic Literature: A Reader*. Nashville: Abingdon Press, 1990.

Rice, David G., and John E. Stambaugh. *Sources for the Study of Greek Religion*. Missoula, Mont.: Scholars Press for the Society of Biblical Literature, 1979.

Roberts, Alexander, and James Donaldson, eds. *The Ante-Nicene Fathers*. Grand Rapids: Wm. B. Eerdmans. (ANF).*

Robinson, James M., general ed. *The Nag Hammadi Library in English*. 3rd rev. ed. San Francisco: Harper & Row, 1988.*

Ross, Sir David, ed. and trans., *The Works of Aristotle*. Oxford: Clarendon Press, 1952.*

Schaff, Philip, ed. *The Nicene and Post-Nicene Fathers of the Christian Church*. Grand Rapids: Wm. B. Eerdmans. (NF).*

Scheidweiler, Felix. "Gospel of Nicodemus/Acts of Pilate," in William Schneelmelcher, ed., *New Testament Apocrypha, I. Gospels and Related Writings*. Rev. ed. Philadelphia: Westminster Press, 1991.*

Scott, W. *Hermetica: The Ancient Greek and Latin Writings Which Contain Religious or Philosophic Teachings Ascribed to Hermes Trismegistos*. New York and London: Oxford University Press, 1924–1936, repr. 1985.*

Singer, S., trans. *The Authorized Daily Prayer Book of the United Hebrew Congregations of the British Empire/Seder Tefilot Kol Ha-Shanah*. 9th American ed. New York: Hebrew Publishing Co., 193?.*

Smith, Morton. *Tannaitic Parallels to the Gospels*. JBL Monograph Series 6. Philadelphia: Society of Biblical Literature, 1968.*

Stern, Menahem. *Greek and Latin Authors on Jews and Judaism*. Jerusalem: Israel Academy of Sciences and Humanities, 1974–1980.

Taylor, Thomas, trans. *Iamblichus on the Mysteries of the Egyptians, Chaldeans, and Assyrians*. London: Bertram Dobell, 2nd ed. 1895.*

Tod, Marcus N., trans. in *Sidelights on Greek History*. Oxford: Clarendon Press, 1932.*

Turner, E. G. "A Curse Tablet from Nottinghamshire," *Journal of Roman Studies* 53 (1963).*

Vermes, Geza. *The Dead Sea Scrolls in English*. Sheffield: JSOT, 1987.*

Wicker, Kathleen O'Brien, trans. *Porphyry, the Letter to Marcella*. Atlanta: Scholars Press, 1987.*

Secondary Sources

(Texts followed by an asterisk are quoted in this volume.)

Almquist, H. *Plutarch und das Neue Testament. Ein Beitrag zum Corpus Hellenisticum Novi Testamenti*. ASNU XV. Uppsala, 1946.

Aune, David E., ed. *Greco-Roman Literature and the New Testament*. SBL Sources for Biblical Study 21. Atlanta: Scholars Press, 1988.*

Baron, Salo W., and Joseph L. Blau, eds. *Judaism. Postbiblical and Talmudic Period*. Library of Liberal Arts. Indianapolis and New York: Bobbs-Merrill Co., 1954.

Barrett, C. K., and C. J. Thornton, eds. *Texte zur Umwelt des Neuen Testaments*. UTB. 2nd ed. Tübingen, 1991.

Benz, E. *Ideen zu einer Theologie der Religionsgeschichte*. Wiesbaden, 1960.

Berger, Klaus, and Carsten Colpe. *Religionsgeschichtliches Textbuch zum Neuen Testament*. Göttingen: Vandenhoeck & Ruprecht, 1987.

Betz, H. D. *Art. Hellenismus, TRE* 15 (1986): 19-35 (includes good bibliography).

———. *Der Apostel Paulus und die sokratische Tradition. Eine exegetische Untersuchung zu seiner "Apologie" 2 Korinther 10-13*. BHTh 45. Tübingen, 1972.

———. *Lukian von Samosata und das Neue Testament. Religionsgeschichtliche und paränetische Parallelen. Ein Beitrag zum Corpus Hellenisticum Novi Testamenti*. TU 76. Berlin, 1961.

———. "The Mithras Inscriptions of Santa Prisca and the New Testament," *NovT* 10 (1986): 62-80.

———, ed., *Plutarch's Ethical Writings and Early Christian Literature*. SCHNT IV. Leiden, 1978.

———, ed., *Plutarch's Theological Writings and Early Christian Literature*. SCHNT III. Leiden, 1975.

Bevan, Edwyn. *Later Greek Religion*. New York: J. M. Dent & Sons, 1927.*

Bin Gorion, M. J. *Der Born Judas II: Vom rechten Weg, Elias-Geschichten, 1. Reihe: "Der Blindgeborene,"* 208-10.*

Bonhoeffer, A. *Epiktet und das Neue Testament. Religionsgeschichtliche Versuche und Vorarbeiten X.* Giessen, 1911.

Bousset, W. *Kyrios Christos: A History of the Belief in Christ from the Beginnings of Christianity to Irenaeus.* Trans. John E. Steely. Nashville/New York: Abingdon Press, 1970.

Bousset, W. (author)/H. Gressmann (ed.), *Die Religion des Judentums im späthellenistischen Zeitalter,* HNT 21, Tübingen (4)1966 ([3]1926).

Bowker, John Westerdale. *The Targums and Rabbinic Literature; an Introduction to Jewish Interpretations of Scripture.* Cambridge: Cambridge University Press, 1969.

Braun, H. *Gesammelte Studien zum Neuen Testament und seiner Umwelt,* 3rd ed. Tübingen, 1971.

———. *Qumran und das Neue Testament* (Tübingen: J.C.B. Mohr [Paul Siebeck], 1966), 2 vols.

Bultmann, R. *Primitive Christianity in Its Contemporary Setting.* Trans. R. H. Fuller. New York: Meridian Books, 1956.

Burkert, W. *Ancient Mystery Cults.* Trans. John Raffan. Cambridge, Mass., 1987.

———. *Greek Religion.* Trans. John Raffan. Cambridge, Mass., 1985.

Butler, E. M. *Ritual Magic* (cited in Howard Clark Kee. *The Origins of Christianity.* Englewood, N.J.: Prentice-Hall, 1973).*

Clemen, C. *Primitive Christianity and Its Non-Jewish Sources.* Trans. Robert G. Nisbet. New York, 1912.

———. *Religionsgeschichtliche Erklèrung des Neuen Testaments. Die Abhängigkeit des ältesten Christentums von nichtjüdischen Religionen und philosophischen Systemen.* 2nd ed. Giessen, 1924. Repr., Berlin and New York, 1973.

Colpe, C. "Die Funktion religionsgeschichtlicher Studien in der evangelischen Theologie," in C. Colpe, ed., *Theologie, Ideologie, Religionswissenschaft* (ThB 68. Munich, 1980), 40-52.

———. "Nicht 'Theologie der Religionsgeschichte,' sondern 'Formalisierung religionsgeschichtlicher Kategorien zur Verwendung für theologische Aussagen,'" in C. Colpe, ed., *Theologie, Ideologie, Religionswissenschaft* (ThB 68. Munich, 1980), 278-88.

Conzelmann, H. *Gentiles, Jews, Christians: Polemics and Apologetics in the Greco-Roman Era.* Trans. M. Eugene Boring, Minneapolis, 1992; trans. of Hans Conzelmann. *Heiden-Juden-Christen. Auseinandersetzungen in der Literatur der hellenistisch-römischen Zeit. Beiträge zur historischen Theologie,* 62. Tübingen, J.C.B. Mohr (Paul Siebeck), 1981.

Cumont, F. *The Oriental Religions in Roman Paganism,* with an Introductory Essay by Grant Showerman. Chicago and London, 1911.

Deissmann, Adolf. *Light from the Ancient East: The New Testament Illustrated by Recently Discovered Texts of the Graeco-Roman World.* New York: George H. Doran Co., 1927.*

de Zulueta, F. "Violation of Sepulture in Palestine at the Beginning of the Christian Era," *Journal of Roman Studies* 22 (1932).*

Dihle, A. *Greek and Latin Literature of the Roman Empire: from Augustus to Justinian.* Trans. Manfred Malzahn. New York, 1994; trans. of *Griechische und lateinische Literatur der Kaiserzeit.*

Dihle, A. *Griechische Literaturgeschichte.* München, (2)1991.

Dillon, John, and Jackson Hershbell. *On the Pythagorean Way of Life/Iamblichus.* Atlanta: Scholars Press, 1991.*

Doty, William G. *Letters in Primitive Christianity.* Philadelphia: Fortress Press, 1973.

Duling, Dennis C., and Norman Perrin. *The New Testament: Proclamation and Parenesis, Myth and History.* 3rd ed. Fort Worth: Harcourt Brace, 1994.*

Elbogen, Ismar. *Jewish Liturgy: A Comprehensive History.* Trans. Raymond P. Scheindlin, and the 1972 Hebrew ed. edited by Joseph Heinemann, et al. Philadelphia and Jerusalem: Jewish Publication Society and the Jewish Theological Seminary of America, 5753, 1993.*

Ferguson, Everett. *Backgrounds of Early Christianity.* Rev. ed. Grand Rapids, Mich.: Wm. B. Eerdmans Publishing Co., 1993.*

Fiebig, P. *Die Umwelt des Neuen Testamentes. Religionsgeschichtliche und geschichtliche Texte, in deutscher übersetzung und mit Anmerkungen versehen, zum Verständnis des Neuen Testamentes.* Göttingen, 1926.

BIBLIOGRAPHY

Francis, Fred O. "The Background of Embateuein (Col. 2:18) in Legal Papyri and Oracle Inscriptions," in Francis and Meeks, eds., *Conflict at Colossae: A Problem in the Interpretation of Early Christianity* Illustrated by Selected Modern Studies. Sources for Biblical Study 4. Missoula, Mont.: Society of Biblical Literature, 1973.*

Freeman, Kathleen. *Ancilla to the Pre-Socratic Philosophers.* Cambridge, Mass.: Harvard University Press, 1948.*

Geldner, K. F., in A. Bertholet, ed., *Religionsgeschichtliches Lesebuch* 2. Auflage, 1926.*

Giannelli, Giulio. *The World of Classical Athens* [Putnam, 1970].*

Grant, F. C. *Hellenistic Religions.* Liberal Arts Press, 1949.*

Greeven, H. *Das Hauptproblem der Sozialethik in der neueren Stoa und im Urchristentum.* NTF III 4. Gütersloh, 1935.

Grese, W. C. *Corpus Hermeticum XIII and Early Christian Literature,* SCHNT V. Leiden, 1979.

Heinrici, C. F. G. (author), and E. von Dobschütz (editor), *Die Hermes-Mystik und das Neue Testament. Arbeiten zur Religionsgeschichte des Urchristentums* I 1. Leipzig, 1918.

Hengel, M. *Jews, Greeks, and Barbarians: Aspects of the Hellenization of Judaism in the pre-Christian period.* Trans. John Bowden. Philadelphia, 1980.

————. *Judaism and Hellenism: Studies in Their Encounter in Palestine During the Early Hellenistic Period.* Trans. John Bowden. London, 1974.

Hengel, Martin. *The Charismatic Leader and His Followers.* New York: Crossroad, 1981.*

Hock, Ronald F., and Edward N. O'Neil. *The Chreia in Ancient Rhetoric.* Atlanta: Scholars Press, 1986.*

Jackson, F. J. Foakes, and Kirsopp Lake, eds. *The Beginnings of Christianity.* Grand Rapids: Baker Book House, repr. 1979.*

Johnson, Luke Timothy. "The New Testament's Anti-Jewish Slander and the Conventions of Ancient Polemic," *JBL* 108 (1989): 419-41.*

Keyser, P. G. *Sapientia Salomonis und Paulus.* Diss. theol. Halle/Wittenberg, 1971.

Kippenberg, H. G., and G. A. Wewers (Hg.), *Textbuch zur neutestamentlichen Zeitgeschichte,* GNT VIII. Göttingen, 1979.

Klauser, Th. ed., *Reallexikon für Antike und Christentum. Sachwörterbuch zur Auseinandersetzung des Chrisentums mit der antiken Welt (RAC).* Stuttgart seit, 1950.

Koester, H. *History, Culture, and Religion of the Hellenistic Age.* Philadelphiam, 1982; trans. chaps. 1–6 of *Einführung in das Neue Testament.*

Lachs, Samuel Tobias. *A Rabbinic Commentary on the New Testament: The Gospels of Matthew, Mark, and Luke* (Hoboken, N.J.: KTAV Publishing House, 1987).

Lefkowitz, Mary R., and Maureen B. Fant, eds. *Women's Life in Greece and Rome.* Baltimore: Johns Hopkins University Press, 1982.*

Leipoldt, J., and W. Grundmann, eds. *Umwelt des Urchristentums,* vol. 1, *Darstellung des neutestamentlichen Zeitalters.* 4th ed. Berlin: Evangelische Verlagsanstalt, 1975.

————. *Umwelt des Urchristentums,* vol. 3, *Bilder zum neutestamentlichen Zeitalter.* 3rd ed. Berlin: Evangelische Verlagsanstalt, 1973.

Lesky, A. *Geschichte der griechischen Literatur.* Bern/München, (2)1963.

Leuze, R. "Möglichkeiten und Grenzen einer Theologie der Religionsgeschichte," *Kerygma und Dogma* 24 (1978): 230-43.

Lohse, Eduard. *The New Testament Environment.* Trans. John E. Steely. Nashville: Abingdon, 1976.*

Malina, Bruce J. *The New Testament World: Insights from Cultural Anthropology.* Rev. ed. Louisville, Ky.: Westminster/John Knox, 1993.

————. *Windows on the World of Jesus: Time Travel to Ancient Judea.* Louisville, Ky.: Westminster/John Knox, 1993.

Martyn, Lou. *History and Theology in the Fourth Gospel.* Rev. ed. Nashville: Abingdon, 1979.*

Müller, K. "Die Religionsgeschichte Methode. Erwägungen zu ihrem Verständnis und zur Praxis ihrer Vollzüge an neutestamentlichen Texten," *Biblische Zeitschrift* 29 (1985): 161-92.

Murphy, Frederick J. *The Religious World of Jesus: An Introduction to Second Temple Palestinian Judaism.* Nashville: Abingdon Press, 1991.

Murray, Gilbert. *Five Stages of Greek Religion.* Garden City, N.Y.: Doubleday & Co., Anchor Books, 1955.*

Mussies, G. *Dio Chrysostom and the New Testament.* SCHNT II. Leiden, 1972.

———. "Joseph's Dream (Matt 1, 18-23) and Comparable Stories," in *Text and Testimony. Essays on New Testament and Apocryphal Literature in Honour of A. F. J. Klijn.* Ed. T. Baarda et al., 177-86. Kampen, 1988.

Newsome, James D. *Greeks, Romans, Jews: Currents of Culture and Belief in the New Testament World.* Philadelphia: Trinity Press International, 1992.

Nickelsburg, George W. E. *Jewish Literature Between the Bible and the Mishnah.* Philadelphia: Fortress Press, 1981.

Nilsson, M. *A History of Greek Religion.* Trans. from the Swedish by F. J. Fielden, with a preface by Sir James G. Frazer. Oxford, 1925.

Nock, A. D. *Conversion.* London: Oxford University Press, 1961.*

Norden, E. *Agnostos Theos. Untersuchungen zur Formengeschichte religiöser Rede.* Leipzig and Berlin, 1913.

Oates, Whitney J. *The Stoic and Epicurean Philosophers; the Complete Extant Writings of Epicurus, Epictetus, Lucretius, [and] Marcus Aurelius.* New York: Random House, 1940.

Pannenberg, W. "Erwägungen zu einer Theologie der Religionsgeschichte," in W. Pannenberg, *Grundfragen systematischer Theologie* (Göttingen, 1967), 252-95.

Pauly, A. (author), and G. Wissowa, et al., eds. *Paulys Real-Encyclopédie der classischen Altertumswissenschaft.* Stuttgart/München, 1894–1980.

Petzke, G. *Die Traditionen über Apollonius von Tyana und das Neue Testament.* SCHNT I. Leiden, 1970.

———. "Historizität und Bedeutsamkeit von Wunderberichten. Möglichkeiten und Grenzen des religionsgeschichtlichen Vergleichs," in *Neues Testament und christliche Existenz,* fs. für H. Braun. Ed. H. D. Betz and L. Schottroff, 367-85. Tübingen, 1973.

Pfeiffer, R. H. *History of New Testament Times with an Introduction to the Apocrypha.* New York: Harper & Brothers, 1949.

Pohlenz, M. *Die Stoa. Geschichte einer geistigen Bewegung.* 2 vols. 6th ed. Göttingen, 1984.

———. *Vom Zorne Gottes, Eine Studie über den Einfluss der griechischen Philosophie auf das alte Christentum.* FRLANT 12. Göttingen, 1909.

Reitzenstein, R. *Hellenistic Mystery-Religions: Their Basic Ideas and Significance.* Trans. John E. Steely. Pittsburgh, 1978.

Robbins, Vernon K., ed. *Semeia 64: The Rhetoric of Pronouncement.* Atlanta: Scholars Press, 1994. Fourteen articles and responses on the theme "Mediterranean Literature and the New Testament."

Rüd, W. *Die Philosophie der Antike.* Vol. 1. *Von Thales bis Demokrit, Geschichte der Philosophie,* ed. W. Rüd. 2nd ed. München, 1988.

Rose, H. J. *A Handbook of Greek Literature from Homer to the Age of Lucian.* 4th ed., rev. London: Methuen, 1951.

Rostovzeff, M. *The Social and Economic History of the Hellenistic World.* Oxford, 1953.

Sanders, E. P., et al., eds. *Jewish and Christian Self-Definition I-III.* London, 1980–1982.

Schmalzriedt, E., ed. *Hauptwerke der antiken Literaturen. Einzeldarstellungen und Interpretationen zur griechischen, lateinischen und biblisch-patristischen Literatur.* München, 1976.

Schürer, E. *The History of the Jewish People in the Age of Jesus Christ (175 B.C.–A.D. 135).* Trans. T. A. Burkill, et al., rev. and ed. Geza Vermes and Vergus Millar. Edinburgh, 1986 (1973); revised trans. of *Geschichte des jüdischen Volkes im Zeitalter Jesu Christi.*

Sevenster, J. N. *Paul and Seneca. NovT.* S 4. Leiden, 1961.

Siegert, Folker. *Drei hellenistisch-jüdische Predigten.* Tübingen: J.C.B. Mohr (Paul Siebeck), 1980.*

Smith, Morton. *Jesus the Magician.* San Francisco: Harper & Row, 1978.*

BIBLIOGRAPHY

Spiess, E. *Logos spermaticovs. Parallelstellen zum Neuen Testament aus den Schriften der alten Griechen. Ein Beitrang zur christlichen Apologetik und zur vergleichenden Religionserforschung.* Leipzig, 1871 (repr. Hildesheim and New York, 1976).

Stambaugh, John E., and David L. Balch. *The New Testament in Its Social Environment.* Philadelphia: Westminster Press, 1986.

Stowers, Stanley K. *Letter Writing in Greco-Roman Antiquity.* Philadelphia: Westminster Press, 1986.

Strack, H. L., and P. Billerbeck. *Kommentar zum Neuen Testament aus Talmud und Midrasch.* 6 vols. 6th ed. München, 1978.

Strecker, G. *Literaturgeschichte des Neuen Testaments.* Göttingen, 1992.

Tarn, W. *Hellenistic Civilisation.* London, (3)1952.

Tcherikover, V. (author), S. Applebaum (trans.). *Hellenistic Civilization and the Jews.* Philadelphia, 1959.

Temporini, H., and W. Hase, eds. *Aufstieg und Niedergang der römischen Welt. Geschichte und Kultur Roms im Spiegel der neueren Forschung.* Berlin and New York, 1972– (*ANRW*).

Tripp, E. *Crowell's Handbook of Classical Mythology.* New York, 1970.

van der Horst, P. W. *Aelius Aristides and the New Testament.* SCHNT VI. Leiden, 1980.

———. "Chariton and the New Testament. A Contribution to the Corpus Hellenisticum," *NovT* 25 (1983): 348-55.

———. "Cornutus and the New Testament. A Contribution to the Corpus Hellenisticum," *NovT* 23 (1981): 165-72.

———. "Corpus Hellenisticum Novi Testamenti," in *The Anchor Bible Dictionary* (New York: Doubleday & Co., 1992), 1:1157-61, with additional bibliography.

———. "Das Neue Testament und die jüdischen Grabinschriften aus hellenistisch-römischer Zeit." BZ NF 36, 2 (1992): 161-78.

———. "Essays on the Jewish World of Early Christianity." NTOA 14. Freiburg, Schweiz, Göttingen, 1990.

———. "Hellenistic Parrallels to Acts (Chapters 3 and 4)," *JSNT* 35 (1989): 37-46.

———. "Hierocles the Stoic and the New Testament. A Contribution to the Corpus Hellenisticum," *NovT* 17 (1975): 156-60.

———. "Macrobius and the New Testament. A Contribution to the Corpus Hellenisticum," *NovT* 15 (1973): 220-32.

———. "Musonius Rufus and the New Testament, A Contribution to the Corpus Hellenisticum," *NovT* 16 (1974): 306-15.

———. "Pseudo-Phocylides and the New Testament," *ZNW* 69 (1978): 187-202.

———. "The Altar of the 'Unknown God' in Athens (Acts 17:23) and the Cult of 'Unknown Gods' in the Hellenistic and Roman Periods." *ANRW* II 18.2 (1989): 1426-56.

———. *The Sentences of Pseudo-Phocylides.* SVTP IV. Leiden, 1978.

Vielhauer, P. *Geschichte der urchistlichen Literatur. Einleitung in das Neue Testament, die Apogryphen und die Apostolischen Väter.* Berlin and New York, 1975.

Wendland, P. *Die hellenistisch-römische Kultur in ihren Beziehungen zu Judentum und Christentum,* HNT I 2. Tübingen, (4)1972.

Wettstein, J., ed. *Novum Testamentum Graecum.* 2 vols. Amsterdam 1751/1752; repr. Graz, 1962.

White, John L. *Light from Ancient Letters.* Philadelphia: Fortress Press, 1986.

Winstedt, E. O. "Apocryphal Jewish Biographies," *Journal of Theological Studies* 9 (1908).*

Ziegler, K., and W. Sontheimer, eds. *Der Kleine Pauly. Lexikon der Antike. Auf der Grundlage von Paulys Realencyclopädie der classischen Altertumswissenschaft I-V.* Stuttgart and München, 1964–1975 (Kl. Pauly).

Ancient Author Index

(Numbers refer to sections, not pages.)

Greco-Roman Authors and Literature

Achilles Tatius, *Clitophon and Leucippe*, §59
Act Apollonii, §205
Acta Acacii, §494
"Acts of the Alexandrian Martyrs," §§199, 201
Acts of the Pagan Martyrs, "Acta Appiani," §199
Adonis in Origen's *Commentary on Ezekiel*, §447
Aelian, *Variae historiae*, §34
Aelius Aristides
    Discourses, §§169, 405, 468, 483, 814, 831
    "Plato," §818
Aelius Spartianus, *Caracalla*, §634
Aeschines, "Timarch" 185, §537
Aeschylus
    Prometheus, §792
    Seven Against Thebes, §703
Aesop, *Fables*, §§93, 94, 291
Aesop, Life of, 25, §421
Alcidamas, Fragment, §769
Alciphron
    Letters of Courtesans, "Euthydemus," §235
    Letters of Farmers, "Philiscus," §235
Alexander, Life of, 27.9, 680 F, §120
Anaxagoras of Clazomenae fragment, §355
Anthologia Graeca, §245
Apion (soldier), letter to his father, §716
Apollodorus, *Library*, §111
Apollodorus in Pseudo-Demosthenes, §809
Apuleius
    Apologia, §840
    Asclepius, §936
    Florida, §§76, 290
    Metamorphoses, §§194, 387, 519, 563, 570, 935, 938
Aratus of Soli in Cilicia, §520
Archytas, "Law and Righteousness," §547

Aristobulus, Fragment 5, §406
Aristocritos, *Theosophie*, §973
Aristophanes
    Acharnians, §299
    Birds, §336
    Plutus, §405
    Wasps, §405
Aristotle
    Eudemian Ethics, §§136, 241
    Goods and Evils, §34
    Metaphysics, §368
    Nicomachean Ethics, §§153, 241, 492, 540, 541, 564, 627
    On Philosophy, §27
    Politics, §§541, 769, 809, 890
    Rhetoric, §§440, 540, 541
Arius Didymus in Stobaeus, *Anthologium*, §890
Arrian
    Anabasis of Alexander, §74
Asclepius, §§176, 736
Athenaeus, *Learned Banquet*, §§371, 767, 926

Bahman Yascht, §973
Berosos, in Seneca, *Natural Questions*, §901
Bion, from Stobaeus, *Anthologium*, §838
Bundahisn, §710

Callicratidas, *Happiness of a Household*, §894
Callimachus, *Aitia*, §63
Celsus
    Medicine, §76
    True Doctrine, §623
Chariton, *Chaereas and Callirhoe* 3, 3.1-7, §220
Chronicle of Zuqnin, §11
Chrysippus, §694
Chrysippus, Fragment, §§489, 490, 902

ANCIENT AUTHOR INDEX

Cicero
    Cluentius Habitus, §634
    De senectute, §362
    Defense of Rabirius, §208
    Defense of Sextus Roscius, §413
    Divination, §12
    Goods and Evils, §429
    Nature of the Gods, §515
    Republic, §§42, 222, 389
    Soothsayers, §517
Claudian, *Depracatio ad Hadrianum,* §291
Claudius
    Decree, §521
    Letter to the Alexandrians, §931
Cleanthes
    Fragment 527, §799
    Hymn to Zeus, §§43, 356, 518
Cornutus, *Mythology* 27, §364
Cotta, §515
Crates
    Letter to Metrocles 34, §660
    Letter to the Wealthy, §744
    Letters to Hipparchia 28-29, §776

Deed of Divorce, §142
"Delphic Precepts," §884
Demetrios Lacon, *Life of Philonides,* §153
Democritus, Fragments, §§362, 516, 703, 786
Demosthenes, *Exordia,* §279
Demotic narrative, §338
Dio Cassius, §§14, 237, 435, 445, 485, 930
Dio Chrysostom, *Discourse,* §§32, 106, 112,
    263, 313, 407, 540, 576, 584, 611, 685,
    723, 731, 754, 963
Dio Cocceianus, *Oration,* §169
Diodorus Siculus, *History,* §§3, 190, 215, 263,
    335, 365, 371, 496, 760, 765, 815, 839,
    863
Diogenes, an Epicurean, §516
Diogenes, *Epistles,* §§80, 144, 494, 652, 817
Diogenes Laertius
    Lives, §§29, 34, 80, 137, 263, 290, 356
    Lives, "Antisthenes," §§70, 268
    Lives, "Aristippos," §70
    Lives, "Aristotle," §308
    Lives, "Carneades," §213
    Lives, "Cleanthes," §86
    Lives, "Diogenes," §868
    Lives, "Epicurus," §§153, 195, 263, 265, 830
    Lives, "Epitaphs," §1
    Lives, "Plato," §§1, 45
    Lives, "Polemo," §29
    Lives, "Pythagoras," §884
    Lives, "Socrates," §37
    Lives, "Thales," §773
    Lives, "Xenophon," §28

    Lives, "Zeno," §783
Dionysius of Halicarnassus, *Roman Antiquities,*
    §§213, 219, 486, 508
Divorce Certificate from Masada, §35
Duris the historian, §922

Empedocles, Fragments, §§77, 229, 591, 625,
    880, 959
Epictetus
    Discourses, §§38, 44, 78, 84, 148, 197, 275,
        284, 296, 314, 317, 362, 402, 430, 445,
        453, 455, 461, 476, 518, 587, 592, 631,
        637, 645, 650, 660, 661, 662, 664, 665,
        666, 667, 674, 686, 691, 721, 729, 732,
        752, 753, 756, 853, 874
    "Encheiridion," §884
    Fragments, §34
Epicurus, Epistle to Menoeceus, §516
Epigram of the Prefect Julianos of Egypt,
    §245
Eunapius, *Life of Iamblicus,* §376
Euripides
    Bacchanals, §§191, 371
    Fragment, §§191, 244, 580, 711
    Hercules, §703
    Iphigeneia, §956
    Phoenician Maidens, §703
    Daughters of Troy, §703

Florus, *Wars,* §863

Galen
    De Propiorum Animi, §537
    Differences in Impulses, §328
    Dogmas of Hippocrates and Plato, §§628, 673
Greek aphorism, §586
Greek prayer, §64

Heraclitus
    Fragments, §§449, 867, 901
    Letters, §§541, 798
Hermogenes, Ideas, §540
Herodas, *Mime,* §258
Herodotus, *Histories,* §§49, 219, 279, 294, 831,
    955
Hesiod
    Theogony, §611
    Works, §§456, 534
Hierocles, §696
    Commentary, §§607, 727, 740, 742
    "How to Conduct Oneself Toward Gods,"
        §692
    "How to Conduct Oneself Toward One's
        Fatherland," §612
    "On Marriage," §790
    in *Stobaios Anthologii,* §45

Hierocles in Stobaeus 4.22, §654
Hippias of Elis, in Plato, *Protagoras*, §764
Hippocrates
    Letters, §§504, 793
    "On Human Nature," §540
Homer
    Hymns, §§125, 479, 955
    Iliad, §§58, 198, 611, 818
    Odyssey, §§279, 448, 818
Horace
    Carmen Saeculare, §§524, 931
    Odes, §371
    Satires, §674

Iamblichus
    "Life of Pythagoras," §§2, 55, 98, 112, 166, 240, 259, 458, 579, 884
    Mysteries, §357
    Pythagorean Way of Life, §78
    Secret Doctrine, §368
Isis, Hymn to, §417
Isocrates
    Chreia, §§327, 607
    Panegyricus, §112
    "To Demonicus," §§279, 834

Julius Firmicus Maternus, "Pagan Religion," §§447, 571
Justinus, *Historiae Phillippicae*, §863
Juvenal, *Satire*, §640

Krantor in Plutarch, *A Letter to Apollonius*, §565

Lactantius, *Divine Institutions*, §§450, 602, 629, 813, 961, 973
Libanius of Antioch, *Epistles*, §815
Livy, *History*, §§191, 194, 217, 352, 694, 809
Lucian
    Demonax, §66
    "Dialogues on Death," §742
    Hermotimus, or Concerning the Sects, §§242, 720
    "Icaromenippus/Sky Man," §227
    Lover of Lies, §§65, 112, 132, 227, 230
    "Philosophies for Sale," §275
    Saturnalia, §§292, 688
    "The Ship," or "The Wishes," §§54, 55
    True Story, §§374, 477
Lucian of Samosata
    Alexander the False Prophet, §487
    Death of Perigrinus, §§230, 485, 493
Lucretius, *Nature of the Universe*, §§226, 681
Macrobius, *Saturnalia*, §§397, 681, 863
Magical Curse, 309

Marcus Aurelius, *Meditations*, §§41, 276, 381, 604, 695, 876
Martial, *Epigrams*, §640
Maximus of Tyre
    Discourses, §§406, 698, 829
    Lectures 3, "Socrates," §474
Menander, §§285, 828
Musonius Rufus
    Chief End of Marriage?, §§654, 811
    Clothing and Shelter, §§81, 697
    Cutting the Hair, §685
    Daughters Receive Educations?, §895
    Kings Study Philosophy, §89
    Marriage a Handicap?, §143
    One Obey One's Parents?, §§264, 325
    Philosopher Prosecute Anyone?, §638
    Sexual Indulgence, §647
    Women Study Philosophy, §§651, 661

Numenius of Apamea, §840

Oenomaus, §601
Oppianus Cynegetica, §672
Oracle of Hystaspes, §§450, 602, 629, 813, 961
Oracula Leonis MPG 107.1148, §422
Orpheus, Fragments, §936
Orphic gold tablet from the necropolis of Thurioi, §917
Orphic hymn, §802
Ovid
    Amores, §580
    De viris illustr, §215
    Fasti, §§215, 217, 681
    Metamorphoses, §§215, 217, 242, 351, 372, 510, 537

Palaia, §919
Pausanias, *Description of Greece*, §§371, 405, 863, 936
Pausanias, the Son of Pleistonax, §234
Periander, in *Gnomologium Vaticanum*, §717
Petronius, §286
    Satyricon, §307
Philostratus the Elder
    Imagines, §373
    Life of Apollonius, §§7, 55, 61, 88, 119, 132, 153, 198, 227, 228, 230, 290, 373, 474, 815
    Life of Apollonius, Letters, §§106, 240, 326, 772
Photius
    Bibliotheca 242, §571
    Vita Isidori, §571
Pindar, Fragment 121, §705
Plato
    Apology, §§82, 494, 618, 792

Gorgias, §638
Ion, §754
Laws, §§538, 584, 857
Phaedo, §§43, 733, 852
Phaedrus, §§442, 538, 742
Philebus, §882
Protagoras, §§720, 764
Republic, §§205, 428, 437, 492, 589, 696, 852
Sophists, §720
Statesman, §852
Symposium, §§136, 536, 698, 768
Theaetetus, §482
Timaeus, §§364, 702
Plautus, *Curc.,* §§405, 681
Pliny the Elder, *Natural History,* §§12, 76, 372, 840
Pliny the Younger, *Letters,* §§771, 933
Plutarch
  "Aemilius Paulus," §786
  "Agis," §§212, 694
  "Alexander," §§6, 7, 523, 924
  "Antony," §598
  "Being a Busybody," §34
  "Bravery of Women," §775
  "Bride and Groom," §§658, 703
  "Brotherly Love," §138
  "Brutus," §509
  "Caesar," §§203, 212
  "Caius Marius," §425
  "Camillus," §863
  "Cato the Elder," §617
  "Cato the Younger," §156
  "Cleomenes," §107
  "Compliancy," §609
  "Condolence to Apollonius" 18, §§31, 565, 573, 774
  "Customs of the Spartans," §940
  "Deified Julius," §212
  "Delays of Divine Vengeance," §§9, 249, 319, 409, 465, 585, 620, 903, 953
  "Dialogue on Love," §§464, 800
  "Education of Children," §§9, 643, 699
  "Epicurus Makes a Pleasant Life Impossible," §910
  "Exile," §§106, 889
  "Fabius Maximus," §7
  "Fortune of Alexander," §§7, 79, 122, 263, 389, 441, 531, 787
  "Fortune of Romans," §§7, 105, 126, 263, 552
  "Greek Customs," §224
  "Having Many Friends," §241
  "How to Tell a Flatterer," §138
  "Inoffensive Self-Praise," §§120, 622

  "Isis and Osiris," §§137, 418, 486, 557, 619, 671, 706, 748, 786, 805, 936
  "Keeping Well," §578
  "Kings and Commanders," §§1, 120, 341, 891, 924
  "Listening to Lectures," §§96, 318, 615
  "Love of Wealth," §78
  "Marius," §773
  "Men in Power," §591
  Moralia, §§9, 54, 537, 643, 681, 924
  "Numa" 4.2-4, §§7, 215, 219, 478
  "Obsolescence of Oracles," §§54, 132, 364, 534, 671, 672, 684
  "Old Man in Public Affairs," §134
  "Oracle of Delphi," §449
  "Ought Not to Borrow," §959
  "Parallel Stories," §872
  "Pelopidas," §§47, 213
  "Placita philosophorum" 1.3, §355
  "Praising Inoffensively," §85
  "Precepts of Statecraft," §§58, 182, 612, 615, 622, 638, 694, 802
  "Profit by One's Enemies," §§340, 544
  "Progress in Virtue," §§633, 812, 873
  "Pyrrhus," §239
  "Pythian Dialogues," §674
  "Pythian Oracles," §701
  "Reply to Colotes," §780
  "Roman Customs," §65
  "Roman Questions," §§308, 340, 557, 681, 807
  "Romulus," §§104, 141, 218
  "Seven Sages," §§534, 775
  "Sign of Socrates," §478
  "Spartans," §§31, 32, 240, 274, 347, 493, 644, 689
  "Study Poetry," §§621, 627
  "Sufferings," §638
  "Sulla," §74
  "Superstition," §§517, 577, 674, 867
  "Table Talk," §§7, 75, 241, 263, 324, 643, 674, 678, 681, 688, 698
  "Teachings of the Philosophers" 5.19, §711
  "Themistocles," §562
  "Theseus," §§224, 891
  "Tiberius Gracchus," §297
  "Tranquillity of Mind," §499
  "Uneducated Ruler," §§33, 282, 614
  "Vice Cause Unhappiness?," §§204, 674, 784, 940
  "Virtues and Vices," §§633, 799
Polyaenus, *Strategica,* §609
Polybius, *Histories,* §§101, 517, 743, 765
Porphyry
  Antr. Nymph, §843
  cited in Eusebius, §607

(Porphyry, *cont.*)
  "Letter to Marcella" 34, §136
  Life of Pythagoras 29, §484
  On Abstinence, §§432, 749
Posidippus, §668
Posidonius, cited by Galen, §628
Potter's Oracle, §962
Prudentius, *Persistephanon,* §572
Pseudo-Aristotle, *On the Cosmos,* §§535, 858
Pseudo-Asclepius, *Logos Teleios,* §905
Pseudo-Callisthenes, *Life of Alexander,* §§121, 392
Pseudo-Demosthenes, §809
Pseudo-Herodotus, *Life of Homer,* §10
Pseudo-Lucian, *Affairs of the Heart,* §537
Pseudo-Phocylides, §§669, 685, 883
Pseudo-Plato
  Axiochus, §737
  Letter, §877
  Minos, §867
Pythagoras, *Life of Pythagoras,* §55
Pythagorean Letter of Melissa, §892
Pythagorean Letters, §29
Pythagorean Sentences 110, §337

Quintilian, *Declamatio,* §331

Salomo of Bosra's "Bee Book," §450
SEG 4, §§194, 770
Seneca
  Epistles, §§101, 153, 362, 542, 564, 576, 588, 617, 641, 734
  Hercules Oetaeus, §242
  Natural Questions, §901
  On Anger, §§39, 272, 545, 551
  "On Benefits," §276
  "On Despising Death," §734
  "On Leisure," §272
  "On Philosophy and Friendship," §542
  On the Happy Life, §285
  "On the Steadfastness of the Wise," §275
  "On the Usefulness of Basic Principles," §§52, 696
  "On Tranquillity of Mind," §735
  "On Wrath," §542
Sentence of Antiphanes, §828
Sentence of Epictetus, §746
Sentences of Sextus, §757
Sextus Empiricus, *Outlines of Pyrrhonism,* §643
Sextus Sotidius Strabo Libuscidianus, §939
Simplicius, Commentary on Aristotle, §880
Socrates, Letter, §494
Sophocles
  Ajax, §703
  Antigone, §792
  Fragment 194, §316

Fragment 837, §705
Fragment 940, §574
Oedipus Tyrannus, §634
Sotades of Maronea, fragment, §363
Statius, *Silvae,* §931
Stobaeus
  Anthologium, §§42, 45, 363, 420, 547, 654, 660, 668, 696, 698, 726, 828, 838, 858, 890
  Hypothetica, §429
Stoic "Mirror of Duties," §612
Strabo, *Geography,* §§37, 346, 405, 500, 513, 646, 701
Suetonius
  "Augustus," §§7, 14, 524, 931
  "Caligula," §407
  "Claudius," §521
  "Domitian," §929
  "Julius," §§203, 611
  Life of the Caesars, §11
  "Nero," §§19, 179, 610, 641, 963
  "Tiberius," §§521, 524, 931
  "Vespasian," §§188, 237, 435, 929
SVF III, 578-80, §275

Tacitus
  Annals, §§524, 931
  Histories, §§74, 88, 237, 436, 815, 961, 963
"Teaching of vezier of Ptahhotep," §335
Teles
  "On Banishment," §298
  "On Contentment," §331
Teles the Cynic, §662
Themestios, *Speeches,* §437
Theocritus, *Idyls,* §§447, 936
Theon, §327
Theopompus in Plutarch, *Moralia,* "Isis and Osiris," §706
Thucydides, *Peloponnesian War,* §§722, 863
Titus Haterius Nepos, §943
Tyrtaeus, Fragment, §123

Valerius Alexandria, *On the Powers of Nature,* §484
Vettius Valens, *Anthologies,* §799
Virgil
  Aeneid, §§495, 681
  Bucolica, 4 Eclogue, §§256, 835
  Georgica 1.463-68, §213
Vohuman Yasn, §973

Xenophon
  Constitution of the Lacedaemonians, §§643, 766
  Cyropaedia, §263
  Lacedaemonians, §§643, 766

Memorabilia, §§136, 244, 454
Zeno
   in Clement of Alexandria, *Stromata,* §499

Fragment, §902
   in Plutarch, *Moralia,* "Fortune of Alexander," §441

Hellenistic Jewish Literature

Josephus
   Antiquities 2, §§5, 14, 260
   Antiquities 3, §§84, 634, 669
   Antiquities 4, §§84, 494, 764
   Antiquities 5, §§263, 265, 805
   Antiquities 8, §§84, 155
   Antiquities 10, §§69, 202
   Antiquities 11, §§446, 755
   Antiquities 13, §§17, 446, 796
   Antiquities 14, §72
   Antiquities 18, §§16, 17, 107, 191, 839, 898
   Antiquities 19, §407
   Antiquities 20, §§396, 659
   Antiquities 89, §345
   Apion 1, §350
   Apion 2, §§87, 243, 653, 815
   Apion 37, §350
   Apion 170, §605
   Life 7-9, §262
   Life 9-12, §17
   Life 269, §396
   War 1, §§252, 446, 611
   War 2, §§17, 19, 79, 160, 207, 289, 394, 396, 491, 527, 611, 796, 826
   War 5, §526
   War 6, §§170, 266, 293, 961, 966

Letter of Aristeas 306, §§16, 406, 657, 841, 976

Nicolaus of Damascus, §863

Paraleipomena Jeremiou, §290
Philo
   Abraham, §536
   Allegorical Interpretation, §§100, 368, 408, 415, 600, 679, 715, 828
   Animals, §703
   Cain, §484

Cherubim, §§8, 266, 469, 693, 868, 886
Concerning God, §393
Confusion Tongues, §§356, 850
Contemplative Life, §§191, 346, 350, 536
Creation, §§480, 714
Decalogue, §488
Dreams, §§241, 368, 375, 452, 639, 718, 784, 802, 850, 860
Embassy, §§270, 367, 826, 932
Eternity, §101
Every Good Man, §§30, 491
Flaccus, §§200, 473
Flight, §443
Giants, §733
Husbandry, §§520, 726
Jonah, §56
Joseph, §787
Life of Moses, §§87, 146, 240, 260, 349, 383, 409, 446, 463, 649, 653, 702, 712, 725, 728, 752, 797, 833, 841, 976
Migration, §§469, 750
Noah's Work, §§162, 802, 871
Providence, §§100, 617
Questions on Exodus, §§382, 548, 715, 802
Questions on Genesis, §§803, 859
Rewards, §§802, 803
Sobriety, §§429, 469, 764
Special Laws, §§165, 232, 280, 446, 536, 553, 575, 582, 607, 634, 672, 677, 769
Virtues, §§128, 330, 683, 738
Who Is the Heir, §§359, 553, 575, 594
Worse Attack the Better, §575
Pseudo-Philo
   "On Jonah," §56
   LAB, §§131, 155, 200, 501, 626, 711, 724, 791, 827, 957, 958, 971
   "On Samson" 25, §559

Hermetica

Corpus Hermeticum 1, §§419, 567, 593, 607, 741, 794, 854, 937
Corpus Hermeticum 4, §§382, 482
Corpus Hermeticum 5, §§401, 535
Corpus Hermeticum 6, §911
Corpus Hermeticum 7, §730

Corpus Hermeticum 9, §781
Corpus Hermeticum 10, §739
Corpus Hermeticum 11, §§401, 680
Corpus Hermeticum 12, §876
Corpus Hermeticum 13, §§129, 130, 382, 384, 555, 559, 590, 707, 808, 906

Corpus Hermeticum fragment from Stobaeus, §§420, 858
Corpus Hermeticum "Kore Kosmou," §592
Corpus Hermeticum "Letter of Hermes," §778

Hermetica, Fragment 27, §356
Hermetic Sentences, §726
Hermetic tractate *Asclepius*, §368

Inscriptions

Antiochus, §836
Aphrodisia, §§507, 709
Attica, §§670, 832

Bentresch Stele, Egypt, §231

CIG 2, no. 2715, §942
CIG 12 3.330, §190
CIG 1973, §819
CIG 2052.4, 6, §191
CIG 2114 bb, §760
CIJ 683, §760
CIL 6.377, §908
CIL 6.10230, §893
CIL VI.510, §572
CIL VI.3, p. 2244, Nr. 21 521, §221
CIL 6.510, §386
Claros, §806

Delphi, §760
Delphi of Gallio, §522

Egypt, §481
Eleusis, §927
Ephesus, §921
Epidaurus, §§52, 238, 271, 339, 506
Epitaph for a slave, §574
Eski-Hissar, §942

Giaur-Köi in Asia Minor, §804
Graffito from Pompeii, §964

Halicarnassus, §921
Inscr. Lat. Sel. 7212, Statutes of the Association, §687
Inscription 107 BCE, §377
Inscription CII 710, §760
Inscription *IG* 12.3, 178 from Astypalaia, §512
Inscription near Nazareth, §223

Jerusalem LSAM 48.2-3, §§191, 498
Jerusalem Temple, OGIS 598, §526

King Antiochus I of Commagene, §928

Lat. sel. 7215, §687
Lydia, §502

Maroneia, Aretalogy of Isis, §360
Mithras-Inscription, §843

Necropolis of Nikaia, §844
Nottinghamshire, §862

Onassanius, memorial inscription, §221

Pergamon, §653
Philadelphia, §771
Priene, §§225, 226

Regina Inscription, §443
Rheneia (Delos), *CIJ* 2, §949
Rosetta Stone, §926

Santa Prisca Mithraeum in Rome, §§558, 843
Schedia (Egypt), §514
SEG 4 §§194, 770
SIG 3.982 §653
SIG 3.1267 §143
Stratonikeia, §942

Temple of Athena in Pergamum, §303
Tomb Antibes, §108
Tomb inscription, §704
Tomb Thessalonica CIG 1973, §819

Zeus Panamaros, §770

Letters

Alciphron
    Letters of Courtesans, "Euthydemus," §235
    Letters of Farmers, "Philiscus," §235
Claudius, Letter to the Alexandrians, §931

Corpus Hermeticum "Letter of Hermes" 29, §778
Crates
    Letter to Metrocles, §660

Letter to the Wealthy, §744
Letters to Hipparchia, §776

Diogenes
Epistle 7, §80
Epistle 24, §144
Epistle 34, §494
Epistle 38, §814
Epistle 45, §817
Epistle 47, §652

Epicurus, Epistle to Menoeceus 132, §516

Heraclitus
Letter 5, §798
Letter 7, §541
Hippocrates, Letter, §§504, 793

Jerome, Letter 58 to Paulinus, §13

Krantor in Plutarch, *A Letter to Apollonius* 6, §565

Letter of Aristeas 210, §406
Letter of Aristeas 236-38, §657
Letter of Aristeas 301-2, §841
Letter of Aristeas 306, §16
Letter of Aristeas 310-11, §976
Letter of Irene to a grieving family, §820
Letter of the soldier Apion to his father, §716

Libanius of Antioch, *Epistles,* §815
Lucian, *Saturnalia Letters* 3, 32, §688

Mara bar Serapion, Letter to his son, §158

Philostratus
Epistles of Apollonius 43, §326
Epistles of Apollonius 44, §§106, 240
Epistles of Apollonius 67, §772
Pliny the Younger, *Letters* 10.96, §§771, 933
Plutarch, *A Letter to Apollonius* 6, §§565, 573, 774
Porphyry, "Letter to Marcella" 34, §136
Pseudo-Plato, Letter 8 C, §877
Pythagorean Letter of Melissa to Clearete, §892
Pythagorean Letters 2.3, §29

Seneca
Epistle 52, §588
Epistle 94, §576
Epistles 95, §641
Epistles 108, §617
Epistles, "Epistle to Lucilius," §§101, 153, 362, 542, 588
"On Despising Death," Epistle 24, §734
"On Philosophy and Friendship," Epistle 9, §564
Socrates, Letter 1, §494

Mandean and Persian Writings

Cologne Mani-Codex, §760

Left Ginza 3.19, §185

Menog i Xrad, §791

Prayer Book 45, §424

Right Ginza 2.3, §185

True Ginza, §§395, 411
True Ginza 2.3, §427
True Ginza 11, §459
True Ginza 24.10-12, §487

New Testament Apocrypha and Other Early Christian Literature

Acts of Thomas 58, §837
Apocalypse of Adam 78-79, §958
Apocalypse of Elijah 4.7-15, §131
Apocalypse of Paul, §280
Apocalypse of Peter, §§915, 923
Apocryphon of James, §762
Authoritative Teaching, §438

Book of Elchasai, §923

Epistula Apostolorum, §§139, 885, 923

Gospel of Nicodemus/Acts of Pilate, §92
Gospel of Peter, §218
Gospel of Thomas, §§202, 325, 589

Infancy Gospel of Thomas, §260

Kerygma Petrou, §805

Martyrdom of Paul 5, §487
Melchizedek, Tractate from Nag Hammadi 14-20, §866
Pistis Sophia, §§104, 866, 885
Protevangelium of James 18-21, §11
Pseudo-Clementine
    Homilies, §§368, 749

Recognitions, §§399, 679

Second Apocalypse of James, §§174, 762

Testament of Truth, §174
Tripartite Tractate 132.16-29, §777

Papyri

British Museum Papyrus 46, §418

Greek Magical Papyri 1, §§50, 418
Greek Magical Papyri 3, §525
Greek Magical Papyri 4, §§20, 60, 636
Greek Magical Papyri 7, §§132, 471
Greek Magical Papyri 12, §472
Greek Magical Papyri 13, §132

Oracula Leonis MPG 107.1148, §422

P. Köln 57, §191
P. Lond. 46.145-55, §417

P. Oxy. 3.523, §676
P. Oxy. 110, §§191, 676
P. Oxy. 115, §820
P. Oxy. 744, §810
P. Oxy. 1381, §§253, 532, 736
Papyrus BGU 27, §530
Papyrus BGU 37, §530
Papyrus Colon. 7921, §845
Papyrus Copy of an Edict of Titus Haterius Nepos, §943
Papyrus of unknown date, §26
Paris Papyrus 574, §386

Patristica

2 Clement 13, §546
2 Clement 17, §885
2 Clement 19, §885

Acts of SS. Justin, §201

Augustine
    City of God 7, §786
    Confessions 1, §577

Barnabas 6, §843
Barnabas 15, §856

Clement of Alex.
    Exhortation 2, §192
    Exhortation 15, §192
    Protrepikos 119, §191
    Stromata 5, §§402, 499
    Stromata 6, §§450, 805
    Stromata 7, §205
    Stromata 14, §205
    Stromata 43, §450
    Theodotus, §§385, 870
Cyril Alex., *Commentary on Isaiah*, §447
Didache 16, §914
Diognetus 7, §393

Diognetus 10, §393
Epiphanius, *Heresies* 51, §11
Eusebius
    Ecclesiastical History 1, §346
    Preparation for Gospel, §520
    Preparation for Gospel 3, §802
    Preparation for Gospel 6, §601
    Preparation for Gospel 8, §617
    Preparation for Gospel 13, §406

Hippolytus
    Commentary on Daniel 3, §128
    Commentary on Daniel 4, §824
    Refutation 5, §§380, 777

Ignatius
    Ephesians 10, §546
    Polycarp 5, §653

Jerome
    Exposition of Ezekiel 3, §447
    Illustrious Men 2 [Frag. 7], §72
    Letter 58 to Paulinus §3, §13
Justin
    Apology 12, §398
    Apology 21, §219
    Apology 66, §192

Dialogue (Pseudo-Jeremiah Agraphon) 72, §896
Dialogue 8, §422
Dialogue 32, §450
Dialogue 49, §422
Dialogue 78, §11
Dialogue 110, §422

Lactantius
  Div. Inst., §§450, 602, 629, 813, 961, 973

Origen
  Against Celsus 1, §1

Against Celsus 4, §901
Against Celsus 7, §923
Interpretation of John 2, §354

Shepherd of Hermas, §§504, 923
Shepherd of Hermas, Mandates 3, §546
Shepherd of Hermas, Mandates 5, §234
Shepherd of Hermas, Similitudes 9, §923
Shepherd of Hermas, Visions 2, §466

Tertullian, *Apology* 39.15, §§191, 458

Pseudepigrapha and Other Early Jewish Literature

2 Baruch, §§124, 416
2 Baruch 7, §171
2 Baruch 13, §§171, 179
2 Baruch 14, §234
2 Baruch 20, §178
2 Baruch 21, §181
2 Baruch 26-27, §947
2 Baruch 28, §960
2 Baruch 29, §§109, 375, 416, 422
2 Baruch 36, §912
2 Baruch 48, §§171, 172, 543, 566
2 Baruch 51, §§124, 163
2 Baruch 54, §307
2 Baruch 73, §228

3 Baruch 8, §869
3 Baruch 9, §178

1 Enoch, §§137, 805, 920
1 Enoch 1, §§920, 934
1 Enoch 10, §375
1 Enoch 13-16, §639
1 Enoch 15, §897
1 Enoch 21, §897
1 Enoch 25, §718
1 Enoch 37-71, §183
1 Enoch 39, §460
1 Enoch 41, §460
1 Enoch 47, §949
1 Enoch 48, §362
1 Enoch 62, §180
1 Enoch 71, §183
1 Enoch 80, §178
1 Enoch 81, §945
1 Enoch 89, §§443, 957
1 Enoch 91, §743
1 Enoch 95, §609
1 Enoch 97, §312
1 Enoch 106, §126

1 Enoch 108, §362

2 Enoch, §§344, 460, 609, 920, 957
2 Enoch 7, §5
2 Enoch 22, §163
2 Enoch 44, §881
2 Enoch 49, §36
2 Enoch 50, §§145, 273, 344
2 Enoch 53, §369
2 Enoch 61, §460
2 Enoch 64, §369
2 Enoch 65, §743

3 Enoch, §920
3 Enoch 4, §596
3 Enoch 10, §378
3 Enoch 11, 12, 16, §848
3 Enoch 21, §311
3 Enoch 43, §804
3 Enoch 45, §870

Ahiqar, §§277, 320
Apocalypse of Elijah, §625
Apocalypse of Moses 9, §584
Apocalypse of Moses 15, §584
Apocalypse of Moses 20, §§697, 713
Apocalypse of Moses 21, §556
Apocalypse of Moses 23, §584
Apocalypse of Moses 30, §584
Apocalypse of Moses 39, §584
Apocalypse of Sedrach 6.4-6, §332
Apocalypse of Zephaniah 9.1-5, §127
Apocryphal Jewish Biographies, §661
Ascension of Isaiah 2, §§18, 795, 952
Ascension of Isaiah 3, §§202, 952
Ascension of Isaiah 4, §825
Ascension of Isaiah 5, §§152, 202, 209

Book of Elijah (Hebrew), §322

Enosh Apocalypse 55.5-6, §477
Hekhaloth-Text, §851

Joseph and Aseneth 7, §755
Joseph and Aseneth 8, §410
Joseph and Aseneth 15, §§410, 805
Joseph and Aseneth 16, §§193, 419
Joseph and Aseneth 21, §29
Joseph and Aseneth 28, §609
Joseph and Aseneth 29, §609
Jubilees, §805
Jubilees 1, §§547, 743
Jubilees 3, §§143, 697
Jubilees 4, §920
Jubilees 19, §743
Jubilees 22, §§62, 755
Jubilees 31, §560
Jubilees 32, §§467, 944
Jubilees 36, §196
Jubilees 45, §196
Jubilees 50, §87

Life of Adam and Eve, §§431, 444, 749
Lives of the Prophets 21 "Elijah," §127

Mara bar Serapion, §158

Odes of Solomon 8, §923
Odes of Solomon 9, §439
Odes of Solomon 10, §923
Odes of Solomon 18, §909
Odes of Solomon 22, §923
Odes of Solomon 28, §923
Odes of Solomon 30, §423
Odes of Solomon 36, §923
Odes of Solomon 41, §923
Odes of Solomon 42, §923
Oratio Joseph, §354

Psalms of Solomon 17, §167
Psalms of Solomon 18, §822

Sibylline Oracles 1, §§897, 964
Sibylline Oracles 2, §179
Sibylline Oracles 3, §§118, 175, 236, 442, 450,
    813, 957, 961, 975
Sibylline Oracles 4, §963
Sibylline Oracles 5, §963
Sibylline Oracles 5.214-27, §§951, 963, 964
Sibylline Oracles 14.37-148, §963
Sibylline Oracles 767-69, §§450, 822, 961

Targum Pseudo-Jonathan on Genesis 3.9, §379
Te'ezaza Sanbat, §475
Testament of Abraham 8, §311
Testament of Abraham 13.2-7, §§412, 630
Testament of Abraham 16, §§418, 718
Testament of Job, §§216, 487, 873
Testament of Job 4, §147
Testament of Job 10, §497
Testament of Job 18, §102
Testament of Job 38, §390
Testament of Job 39, §216
Testament of Job 48-50, §701
Testament of Joseph 18.2, §609
Testament of Judah 21.1, §864
Testament of Levi 2, §411
Testament of Levi 3, §607
Testament of Levi 5, §805
Testament of Levi 8, §250
Testament of Levi 18, §§21, 864
Testament of Levi 90-93, §899
Testament of Moses 10, §24
Testament of Naphtali 3, §655
Testament of Naphtali 8, §§228, 546, 655
Testament of Reuben 1, §616
Testament of Simeon 2, §§88, 457
Testament of Solomon 6.1-11, §91
Testament of Solomon 15.14, §155
Testament of Solomon 20.1-2, §155

Wisdom Myth, §353

Qumran Documents

1Q27.1, §827
1Q34 2.6, §690
1QH, §§257, 533, 549, 550, 554, 713, 856,
    887
1QM, §§747, 816, 967
1QpHab, §§34, 690, 759, 913
1QS, §§40, 139, 274, 400, 451, 496, 533, 554,
    608, 632, 635, 713, 782, 816, 823, 861,
    864, 918
1QSa, §§248, 864
4Q 169, §761

4Q 175, §864
4Q 185 II.15, §395
4Q 246, §531
4Q 403, §682
4Q Mess ar, §348
4Q psDan Aa, §531
4QMMT, §745
4QpPs37 4.6-8, §745
4QPrNab, §48
11QMelch, §§865, 866
11QPsa 26, §887

CD 1-8, §690
CD 2, §§785, 865
CD 3, §§713, 888
CD 4, §141
CD 5, §840
CD 6, §888

CD 9, §139
CD 10-11, §323
CD 19, §636
1QapGen 20.28-29, §731
1QTemple 64.6-13, §763

Rabbinica

Abot. R. Nat., §§114, 278, 287, 291, 856
b. Arakin, §285
b. Baba Batra, §861
b. Baba Mezia, §§23, 57, 117, 950, 951
b. Berakot, §§44, 45, 47, 135, 211, 251, 288, 404, 529, 648
b. Hagigah, §751
b. Nedarim, §§51, 69
b. Qiddushin, §315
b. Rosh Hashanah, §140
b. Sabbat, §§159, 168, 278, 323, 343
b. Sanhedrin, §§46, 168, 228, 295, 390, 426, 511
b. Sotah 9.15, §§83, 446
b. Suk., §679
b. Ta'anith, §§72, 109, 214, 291, 719
b. Yebamot, §§168, 269, 388
b. Yoma, §§90, 170
Derek Erez 4, §291
Eliyahu Zuta 2, §116
Eighteen Benedictions, §§304, 470
Exodus Rabbah, §484
Genesis Rabbah, §§168, 847
Hagigah 2.1, §624
j. Baba Batra, §350
j. Berakot, §§15, 53
j. Terumot, §62
Kaddish prayer, §305
Lamentations Rabbah, §15
Leviticus Rabbah, §246
m. Abot, §§12, 15, 115, 796, 875
m. Hagigah, §751
m. Ketubot, §656
m. Megilla, §161
m. Pesahim, §189
m. Sota, §900
m. Yadayim, §113
m. Yoma, §254
Megilla, §§161, 841
Mekilta, §§302, 414
Mekilta Beshallah, §§333, 758

Mekilta Deuteronomy, §187
Mekilta Exodus, §§233, 321, 391, 416, 606, 693
Mekilta R. Ishmael, §528
Mekilta R. Simon, §§103, 300
Midrash Deuteronomy, §§162, 334
Midrash Ecclesiastes, §159
Midrash Exodus, §609
Midrash Genesis, §609
Midrash Leviticus Rab., §128
Midrash Numbers, §§112, 115, 162, 779
Midrash Psalms, §§151, 609
Midrash Song of Songs, §§267, 329
Naroaoth 'anse ma'ase, §433
p. Berakot, §§149, 151
p. Sanhedrin, §338
p. Targum of Pseudo-Jonathan, §186
Pesiqta, §§4, 116, 307, 907, 916
Pirke Aboth, §265
Pirke R. Eliezer, §§15, 856
R. Judah, Gerim, §388
Sifra, §§164, 283
Sifre to Deuteronomy, §§157, 583
Sifre to Numbers, §595
Song of Songs Rabbah, §329
t. Berakot, §§251, 648
t. Hagigah, §751
t. Sota, §446
t. Sukka, §679
Tanchuma Ki teze, §150
Tanhumot, Shemot, §260
Targum 1 Chron, §743
Targum Ezekiel, §25
Targum Genesis, §§22, 167, 186, 281, 358, 505, 560, 582, 970
Targum Habakkuk, §71
Targum Isaiah, §§68, 452
Targum Leviticus, §279
Targum Numbers, §§679, 969
Te'ezaza Sanbat, §135
Yalqut, §343

Samaritan Literature

Memar Marqah 2, §400
Memar Marqah 3, §400
Memar Marqah 4, §§403, 855

Memar Marqah 6, §398
Samaritan Decalogue, §399
Samaritan Pentateuch, §399

Subject Index
(Selective)

(Numbers refer to sections, not pages.)

Abortion, §§771, 810

Adam, §§4, 21, 143, 228, 379, 380, 412, 431, 444, 556, 560, 564, 566, 567, 568, 582, 680, 697, 710, 713, 714, 749, 864, 958

Adonis, §§13, 221, 263, 447, 571

Agamemnon, §§58, 537

Akedah, §§22, 505, 560

Alexander the Great, §§6, 12, 14, 74, 79, 80, 120, 121, 122, 144, 263, 341, 441, 486, 523, 767

Allegory, §§8, 78, 95, 98, 157, 170, 415, 428, 463, 600

Amidah, §§116, 304, 470

Andromeda, §3

Angels, §§21, 22, 37, 67, 91, 95, 102, 126, 127, 128, 131, 137, 147, 163, 171, 176, 183, 185, 211, 221, 228, 247, 250, 280, 311, 342, 354, 418, 444, 451, 478, 546, 597, 630, 681, 682, 683, 701, 749, 804, 805, 807, 835, 848, 851, 852, 866, 869, 887, 897, 919, 938, 946

Anger, §§33, 39, 61, 66, 84, 139, 168, 235, 253, 272, 278, 333, 474, 542, 545, 551, 562, 590, 602, 638, 674, 729

Anthropology, §§3, 126, 232, 438, 585, 589, 593, 628, 631, 737, 738, 739, 876, 886, 889, 910

Antichrist, §§179, 219, 912, 915, 962, 963

Antigonus of Soko, §115

Apocalypse, apocalyptic, §§24, 37, 83, 124, 170, 171, 176, 177, 178, 247, 363, 416, 422, 460, 486, 597, 706, 824, 920, 950

Apollo, §§1, 2, 6, 7, 14, 52, 58, 82, 112, 140, 221, 256, 258, 373, 453, 487, 522, 524, 537, 601, 688, 760, 804, 806, 936, 949, 955, 958.

Apollonius, §§7, 31, 55, 61, 88, 119, 132, 198, 228, 229, 230, 290

Apostle, apostolic, §§60, 84, 128, 300, 398, 411, 453, 577, 694, 719, 721, 729, 731, 744, 753, 780, 825, 835, 855

Aretalogy, §§143, 360, 417, 477, 532

Aristeas, §§219, 406, 657, 841, 976

Ascension, §§6, 18, 215, 216, 218, 219, 221, 242, 352, 485, 952

Asceticism, §§17, 79, 616, 649

Asclepius, §§14, 52, 253, 405, 504, 911

Astrology, §§12, 179, 260, 520, 521, 524, 778, 901, 964, 973

Atonement, §§153, 154, 369, 426, 438, 557, 558, 708, 865

Baptism, §§16, 17, 20, 21, 22, 23, 107, 242, 269, 382, 570, 572, 573, 578

Bath Qol, §§23, 109, 117, 211

Beelzebul, §§91, 236

Beliar, §§21, 175, 747, 825, 864

Benefactor, §§89, 120, 122, 225, 270, 407, 461, 926

Bethlehem, §§13, 15, 18

Biography, §§10, 240, 260, 420, 421

Birkat Ha-Minim, §470

Birth, §§1-10, 126, 260, 422, 523, 958

Blasphemy, §§92, 207, 266, 277, 426, 511, 546, 639, 762, 782, 925, 932

Blind, §§52, 88, 237, 238, 321, 330, 433, 434, 435, 436, 457, 764, 782

Blood, §§24, 52, 64, 90, 105, 154, 167, 172, 177, 206, 276, 281, 310, 386, 434, 528, 539, 558, 572, 594, 694, 710, 712, 867, 888, 906, 913, 925, 949, 966, 970

Body, §§38, 694, 695, 696, 802

Book of Life, §301

Born again. See Rebirth

Calendar, §§524, 743, 745, 805, 856

Canon, §§32, 113, 176, 350, 751, 842, 920, 922

Catalog of virtues and vices, §§782, 783, 900

Cave, §§11, 13

Charismatic, §§18, 21

Children, §§19, 417

Children of light, §823

Chreia, §§119, 166, 234, 240, 268, 327, 341, 421, 891

Christian community, §§30, 150, 266, 605, 626, 632, 646, 694, 938, 963, 964

Christology, §§53, 88, 135, 183, 184, 210, 247, 248, 256, 365, 378, 391, 401, 422, 428, 446, 452, 794, 860. *See also* Messiah, messianic

Church, §§58, 134, 148, 258, 345, 438, 444, 470, 516, 522, 577, 631, 632, 639, 670, 687, 695, 733, 771, 802, 809, 822, 824, 908, 921, 923, 935, 939

Circumcision, §§90, 139, 269, 500, 548, 560, 599, 659, 674, 777, 778, 779, 815

Clean/Unclean, §113. *See also* Purity

Cleanthes, §43

Clubs and associations, §687

Comet, §§11, 212, 531

Congregation, §§134, 139, 183, 248, 496, 635, 637, 638, 716, 771, 824, 834, 864, 913

Conversion, §§48, 61, 168, 387, 388, 410, 519, 563, 570, 577, 590, 771, 847, 873

Cosmos, cosmic, §§356, 357, 363, 364, 384, 417, 420, 451, 459, 463, 518, 535, 558, 567, 593, 617, 680, 706, 726, 741, 778, 781, 783, 794, 799, 800, 802, 880, 902, 911, 937, 938, 950, 973

Creation, §§24, 30, 95, 141, 183, 184, 186, 232, 234, 253, 280, 353, 356, 357, 359, 368, 369, 375, 379, 382, 412, 451, 470, 480, 535, 561, 567, 594, 600, 624, 648, 700, 701, 710, 711, 714, 715, 743, 748, 751, 769, 777, 789, 801, 841, 843, 847, 851, 880, 881, 887, 902, 904, 910, 914, 951, 972, 973

Creator, §§8, 24, 95, 196, 201, 216, 304, 358, 359, 366, 378, 385, 417, 420, 475, 534, 553, 561, 596, 600, 648, 726, 848, 880, 887, 904, 918

Crucifixion, §§208, 249, 392, 426, 761, 784

Curse, §§309, 383, 635, 636

Cyclic view of history, §§489, 880

Cynic, §§80, 148, 197, 275, 296, 298, 313, 393, 453, 476, 601, 637, 638, 643, 650, 652, 662, 667, 729, 731, 744, 753, 776, 783, 814, 873

Death, §§5, 6, 19, 72, 76, 77, 82, 108, 122, 123, 131, 132, 153, 154, 155, 176, 188, 189, 198, 199, 203, 204, 206, 207, 208, 210, 211, 212, 213, 214, 215, 220, 221, 224, 242, 289, 290, 330, 331, 340, 360, 363, 369, 376, 386, 387, 410, 418, 424, 431, 433, 438, 442, 443, 447, 459, 476, 493, 516, 527, 534, 536, 555, 557, 563, 564, 565, 566, 568, 570, 571, 572, 573, 574, 575, 578, 585, 597, 638, 651, 704, 706, 707, 709, 711, 718, 719, 721, 730, 733, 734, 737, 738, 740, 741, 742, 751, 792, 795, 799, 817, 819, 820, 866, 883, 892, 896, 917, 923, 929, 931, 937, 941, 947, 954, 962, 971, 972

Decalogue, §§345, 399, 488, 581, 582, 606

Delphi, §§6, 82, 373, 449, 522, 618, 760, 862, 936

Demons, demonic, §§62, 64, 77, 137, 174, 231, 236, 432, 478, 684. *See also* Exorcism

Devil §§24, 61, 228, 546, 919. *See also* Satan, Beliar

Dionysus, §§6, 191, 192, 220, 221, 371, 373, 374, 405, 523, 670, 688, 771, 839, 872, 955

Discipleship, §§28, 29, 61, 86, 98, 124, 152, 153, 229, 326, 327

Divination, §§9, 12, 121, 202, 490, 525, 682, 688, 702, 741

Divine man, §198. *See also* Divine/Human

Divine/Human, §§105, 106, 198, 212, 219, 221, 226, 240, 242, 260, 359, 365, 378, 393, 424, 435, 436, 510, 793, 794, 835, 850, 854, 865, 872, 911, 916, 919, 922, 925, 926, 927, 928, 931, 932, 933

Divinity, §§129, 407

Divorce, §§35, 141, 142, 929

Dream, §§6, 9, 14, 52, 67, 184, 246, 339, 387, 400, 504, 506, 509, 513, 938, 968

Dualism, §§2, 232, 321, 340, 383, 427, 438, 451, 459, 575, 628, 630, 706, 738, 747, 782, 823, 886, 911, 918, 937

Dying and rising gods, §§447, 571

Eating, §§191, 192, 196, 248, 687, 688

Education, §265

Eighteen Benedictions, §470

Elijah, §§72, 83, 127, 131, 179, 214, 216, 219, 322, 326, 422, 485, 625, 663, 701, 835, 879, 900, 915, 957, 960, 973

Emperor cult. *See* Ruler cult

Encomium, §§1, 252, 360, 461, 483, 698, 793, 835

Epicurean, §§153, 458, 516, 711, 779, 910

Epidaurus, §§52, 238, 271, 290, 339, 506

Epilepsy, §63

Epiphany, §839

Equality, §§30, 331, 553, 651, 688, 689, 768, 770, 771, 773, 777, 790, 810, 811, 890, 892, 895

Eschatological judgment, §§37, 185, 395, 412, 639, 692, 742, 821, 824, 954, 971

Eschatology, §§15, 16, 17, 21, 23, 39, 94, 99, 100, 109, 131, 145, 171, 179, 185, 225, 243, 247, 255, 266, 273, 281, 306, 322, 374, 375, 395, 400, 416, 422, 486, 503, 533, 598, 602, 603, 626, 639, 650, 663,

(Eschatology *cont.*)
700, 710, 817, 861, 902, 903, 904

Essene, §§17, 19, 30, 79, 191, 207, 289, 345, 346, 394, 491, 660, 661, 809, 846

Ethics, §§19, 30, 33, 34, 42, 61, 164, 564, 578, 587, 605, 631, 645, 646, 695, 783, 812

Etiological legend, §5

Eucharist, §§191, 192, 194, 345, 424, 687. *See also* Meals, Eating

Eve, §§143, 444, 556, 584, 710, 749

Exorcism, §§21, 48, 60, 61, 65, 73, 91, 132, 155, 230, 636

Faith, §§13, 114, 184, 200, 207, 239, 290, 306, 345, 374, 394, 398, 424, 435, 443, 523, 524, 525, 555, 559, 615, 631, 756, 758, 759, 785, 822, 836, 866, 878, 879, 914, 923, 945

Family, §§35, 148, 325, 327, 331, 332, 417, 580, 612, 634, 652, 654, 656, 658, 663, 666, 668, 790, 809, 810, 811, 890, 894

Fate, §§15, 19, 84, 95, 221, 351, 385, 386, 417, 527, 541, 563, 567, 571, 593, 601, 765, 790, 794, 795, 796, 799, 819, 820, 859, 937, 951, 962

Fertility god, §13

Fire, §§6, 20, 51, 54, 55

Foreknowledge, §490

Forgiveness, §§67, 68, 69, 140, 257, 273, 411, 907

Form criticism, §§88, 98

Free, §§19, 30, 35, 80, 155, 167, 173, 185, 208, 256, 260, 296, 346, 375, 384, 386, 401, 417, 426, 429, 430, 445, 455, 474, 494, 527, 547, 553, 574, 576, 577, 578, 592, 595, 601, 602, 607, 645, 647, 650, 651, 660, 661, 666, 667, 674, 685, 708, 726, 733, 739, 752, 760, 769, 771, 772, 773, 774, 777, 784, 796, 799, 804, 874, 875, 880

Freedom, §§80, 81, 87, 189, 198, 242, 282, 298, 301, 313, 314, 315, 317, 386, 387, 429, 430, 455, 474, 476, 516, 573, 574, 576, 577, 578, 588, 593, 621, 645, 660, 661, 664, 666, 667, 717, 726, 744, 746, 757, 760, 784, 796, 799, 809, 814, 865, 874, 875, 923, 958

Friendship, §§153, 197, 241, 274, 335, 458, 469, 492, 564, 591

Fullness, §368

Gallio Inscription, §522

Gamaliel, §§57, 140, 189, 289, 404, 470

Gematria, §91

Genealogy, §§1, 2, 263

Glossalalia, §§486, 487, 701, 702

Gnosticism, §§174, 186, 357, 384, 385, 427, 438, 459, 567, 624, 886

God, §§10, 111, 120, 125, 126, 401, 402, 500, 518, 519, 520, 607, 631, 671, 693, 794, 830, 858, 876, 948

Godfearer, §507

Gospel, Gospel genre, §§225, 226, 227, 263, 483

Government, §§107, 214, 417, 470, 486, 535, 552, 610, 613, 894, 937, 941, 948, 961

Grace, §§21, 52, 81, 149, 151, 201, 257, 274, 349, 386, 387, 418, 530, 533, 534, 545, 550, 552, 553, 554, 555, 559, 562, 563, 569, 577, 600, 619, 621, 748, 771, 785, 796, 864, 865, 903

Hanina ben Dosa, §§109, 251, 404

Haustafel/Household codes, §§809-11, 890-95

Healing, §§48, 51, 66, 69, 74, 88, 118, 229, 239, 253, 288, 404, 405, 435, 436, 506

Hercules, §§3, 6, 7, 122, 215, 219, 242, 275, 290, 340, 365, 374, 397, 405, 406, 485, 508, 735, 793, 853, 891

Hillel, §§72, 114, 115, 168, 278, 656

History, §§252, 256

History of religions, §§191, 192, 252, 570

Holiness, §§21, 30, 71, 113, 165, 228, 232, 243, 254, 337, 551, 607, 632, 638, 639, 682, 712, 771, 779, 864, 900, 937, 958

Holy Scriptures, §113

Holy Spirit. *See* Spirit

Homosexuality, §§536, 537, 538, 539, 640, 641, 642, 643, 647

Honi the Circle Drawer, §72

Hospitality, §771

Human nature. *See* Anthropology

Humanity (of the Messiah), §§422, 424. *See also* Divine/Human

"I Am" sayings, §§229, 387, 417, 418, 427, 468, 472, 606

Image of God, §§289, 356, 431, 631, 680, 714, 715, 800, 881

Immortality, immortals, §§3, 20, 41, 120, 207, 419, 431, 462, 476, 593, 830

Incest, §633

Initiation, §§192, 193, 194, 387, 410, 419, 482, 536, 539, 555, 563, 570, 571, 624, 705, 771, 804, 835, 843, 873, 953

Inspiration, §§9, 82, 98, 128, 218, 252, 253, 266, 453, 480, 607, 684, 715, 750, 754, 842

Interpretation, §§90, 161, 162, 233, 415

Isis, §§137, 143, 191, 360, 387, 405, 417, 418, 471, 486, 519, 557, 563, 570, 604, 619, 671, 706, 748, 786, 804, 805, 926, 935, 936, 938, 955

Jews, §§30, 118, 133, 158, 168, 169, 174, 175, 214, 233, 252, 266, 356, 375, 388, 396, 397, 407, 473, 498, 507, 508, 514, 521, 524, 526, 553, 603, 604, 644, 674, 693, 708, 745, 756, 760, 761, 797, 805, 815,

816, 826, 831, 833, 840, 859, 899, 930, 931, 932

Johanan B. Zakkai, §§113, 159, 170

John the Baptist, §§16, 107, 616, 871

Justice, §§16, 19, 30, 100, 107, 140, 151, 165, 206, 232, 256, 260, 277, 289, 301, 338, 347, 360, 363, 409, 411, 417, 433, 441, 483, 492, 494, 511, 528, 534, 540, 551, 555, 567, 589, 597, 601, 605, 611, 614, 615, 629, 632, 647, 651, 678, 684, 742, 757, 780, 783, 865, 903, 947, 954, 972, 973

Justification, §§533, 554, 555, 560, 561, 756, 879

Kingdom, §§102, 219

Kingdom of God, kingdom of Heaven, §§24, 25, 26, 77, 93, 94, 102, 103, 131, 167, 219, 286, 305, 450, 475

Language, §§299, 417, 486, 488, 508, 701

Last Judgment. See Eschatological judgment

Law, §§23, 31, 86, 92, 97, 115, 164, 186, 278, 289, 417, 540, 543, 547, 614, 759, 764, 780, 888. See also Torah

Leprosy, §§49, 452

Letter, §§29, 80, 132, 290, 292, 350, 530, 565, 594, 670, 716, 745, 750, 771, 820, 824, 892, 910, 929, 933, 939

Leviathan, §416

Light, §§11, 40, 60, 72, 78, 80, 100, 125, 126, 127, 163, 176, 183, 185, 189, 221, 230, 274, 297, 308, 311, 330, 351, 358, 360, 361, 379, 384, 395, 410, 417, 424, 427, 428, 438, 443, 450, 451, 461, 483, 504, 554, 563, 567, 607, 620, 626, 712, 718, 724, 730, 742, 746, 747, 749, 762, 782, 794, 801, 802, 822, 823, 827, 840, 849, 864, 865, 866, 873, 885, 887,

906, 909, 916, 918, 923, 937, 938, 958, 971, 972, 975

Logos, §§353, 354, 355, 356, 357, 359, 360, 364, 366, 375, 390, 452, 462, 671, 679, 800, 801, 802, 850, 865, 905, 969

Lord and God, §943

Lord's Supper. See Eucharist

Love, §§3, 37, 165, 272, 337, 439, 458, 462, 608, 698, 700, 748, 771, 780, 800

Lust, §33

LXX (Septuagint), §§16, 110, 111, 125, 216, 370, 481, 830, 841, 976

Magi, §§11, 12

Magic, magician, §§20, 50, 60, 64, 71, 72, 75, 309, 434, 435, 471, 472, 487, 523, 525, 563

Mandean, §§395, 411, 418, 424, 427, 459, 461, 791

Manna, §§375, 415, 416, 427, 606, 679

Marriage, §§19, 35, 142, 143, 163, 417, 640, 642, 650, 651, 652, 654, 656, 658, 662, 667, 668, 790, 809, 811, 819, 890

Martyr, §§19, 107, 152, 154, 199, 200, 201, 204, 206, 306, 347, 476, 735, 952

Meals, §§194, 195, 346, 688, 689. See also Eating, Eucharist

Melchizedek, §§5, 600, 865, 866

Memory, §§96, 222, 252, 253, 260, 262, 309, 442, 464, 466, 467, 525, 585, 635, 736, 842, 862, 931. See also Remember

Messiah, messianic, §§4, 15, 24, 68, 83, 167, 248, 348, 389, 403, 422, 450, 531, 864. See also Christology

Messianic banquet, §§109, 248, 416

Messianic secret, §§50, 130, 422. See also Secret

Metatron, §§311, 378, 596, 848, 851

Miracle, §§14, 23, 48, 50, 51, 52, 53, 54, 55, 56, 57, 66, 69,

72, 74, 75, 76, 77, 88, 105, 109, 110, 111, 112, 117, 118, 126, 130, 237, 239, 251, 253, 288, 290, 349, 372, 373, 374, 375, 376, 377, 400, 404, 405, 432, 434, 435, 436, 484, 488, 506

Mithras, §§13, 192, 386, 405, 558, 843, 908

Mixing with the nations, §508

Monotheism, §§118, 475, 693, 930

Mystery cults, §§6, 8, 11, 50, 192, 193, 345, 380, 386, 410, 417, 419, 570, 626, 806, 832, 917

Mystical, §§751, 870, 937

Myth, §§186, 263, 567, 748, 768, 958, 959

Nazarite, §616

Nazoreans, §395

Nero, §§12, 179, 610, 641, 825, 929, 963

Neuer Wettstein, §§510, 541, 863

New birth. See Rebirth

Oath, §§19, 36, 394, 417, 771, 884

Oral tradition, §§23, 114, 115, 116, 117, 168

Orphic, §§6, 802, 917

Parable, §§93, 94, 95, 98, 100, 101, 103, 140, 149, 150, 151, 157, 159, 287, 320, 329, 331, 333

Paradox, §§123, 331, 490, 568, 601, 796, 836, 974

Parents, §§118, 417, 612

Parousia, §§284, 319, 412, 450, 815, 821, 822

Parthians, §§179, 961

Passover, §§189, 190

Patriotism, §612

Pharisees, §§17, 19, 113, 114, 116, 304, 342, 527, 655, 745, 796

Philip of Macedon, §§1, 6

Philosophy, philosophers, §§17, 19, 27, 42, 89, 101, 106, 165, 166, 182, 206, 226, 227, 229, 235, 260, 264, 275, 296, 298, 325,

(Philosophy, *cont.*)
429, 442, 458, 513, 564, 576, 651, 673, 720, 731, 757, 799, 880, 882

Pleroma, §368

Polemic, §169

Poor, §§53, 80, 88, 132, 185, 187, 210, 239, 244, 245, 258, 269, 290, 331, 338, 341, 436, 497, 563, 577, 631, 688, 889

Poverty, §§19, 44, 258, 296, 313, 331, 429, 491, 510, 748, 784

Prayer, §§43, 45, 48, 53, 55, 56, 57, 64, 67, 71, 72, 73, 88, 94, 137, 197, 251, 304, 305, 306, 404, 410, 424, 448, 470, 478, 487, 495, 514, 518, 655, 691, 772, 799, 831, 859

Predestination, §§19, 490, 785, 791, 796, 823

Preexistence, §795

Priest, §§4, 5, 21, 52, 90, 91, 112, 113, 121, 128, 140, 162, 168, 173, 191, 246, 248, 250, 252, 253, 254, 262, 266, 303, 371, 386, 387, 446, 463, 485, 498, 500, 508, 512, 513, 524, 557, 563, 570, 571, 572, 575, 599, 600, 635, 669, 670, 745, 760, 797, 804, 832, 841, 850, 857, 864, 865, 866, 870, 879, 888, 908, 921, 924, 931, 938, 943, 961, 976

Prophecy, prophets, §§4, 6, 9, 12, 18, 23, 82, 98, 115, 121, 127, 152, 172, 179, 202, 205, 209, 236, 247, 253, 266, 310, 311, 326, 399, 400, 404, 437, 446, 487, 524, 649, 653, 702, 824, 923

Proselyte, §§4, 140, 168, 269, 278, 330, 507, 659, 847, 873

Providence, §§100, 154, 206, 225, 253, 280, 313, 314, 356, 386, 392, 534, 570, 617, 639, 671, 817, 923

Pseudepigrapha, §§247, 892, 934

Pseudonymity, §§80, 247, 824

Purity, §§17, 48, 62, 78, 303, 343, 634, 653, 745

Q. (The following sections are usually considered Q-passages:) §§266, 267, 269, 272, 273, 274, 275, 276, 277, 278, 279, 280, 281, 282, 283, 284, 285, 286, 287, 288, 289, 291, 292, 293, 294, 295, 296, 297, 298, 299, 300, 302, 304, 305, 306, 308, 309, 310, 311, 313, 314, 315, 316, 317, 319, 321, 322, 323, 325, 326, 327, 328, 337, 343, 344. (In addition, Q is referred to in the following sections:) 267, 287, 292, 293, 310, 314, 316, 317, 319, 321, 343

Rabbi, §§23, 25, 56, 72, 83, 84, 86, 93, 103, 109, 115, 116

Rabbinic, §§151, 161, 251, 329, 334, 338, 343, 388, 416, 595, 751

Rebirth, §§20, 129, 130, 380, 381, 382, 383, 384, 385, 386, 387, 388, 410, 477, 555, 572, 590, 707, 839, 843

Religion, Greco-Roman, §§377, 417, 443, 472, 515, 517, 518, 520, 524, 646, 695, 799, 868, 930

Remember, §§62, 236, 442, 465, 467, 508, 755, 879, 889

Resurrection, §§6, 13, 75, 76, 83, 163, 218, 222, 290, 387, 442, 443, 462, 708, 710, 821

Resuscitations, §290

Revelation, §§9, 23, 72, 82, 117, 121, 129, 130, 311, 420, 423, 428, 442, 472, 607, 619, 730, 905, 906, 934, 937

Rich, §§19, 30, 43, 144, 146, 244, 245, 292, 312, 313, 314, 337, 338, 393, 429, 447, 491, 627, 646, 662, 688, 744

Romulus, §§14, 104, 105, 141, 215, 217, 218, 219, 351, 352, 485, 515

Ruler cult, §§26, 88, 188, 219, 225, 237, 389, 407, 435,

436, 826, 858, 921, 922, 924, 925, 926, 927, 928, 929, 930, 931, 932, 933

Sabbath, §§87, 90, 109, 133, 135, 232, 233, 269, 323, 406, 674, 682, 856

Sacramental, §424

Sacrifices, §§30, 141, 195, 246

Sadducees, §§17, 19, 113, 116, 527

Sages, §§23, 83, 227, 300. *See also* Wisdom

Salt, §§192, 241

Salvation, §§419, 420, 428, 519, 532, 563, 570

Samaritan, §§162, 236, 396, 397, 398, 399, 400, 403, 855

Satan, §§18, 175, 216, 451, 457, 635, 749

Savior, §§14, 183, 185, 190, 201, 225, 253, 270, 395, 407, 439, 461, 563, 577, 771, 921, 926, 941, 958, 973

Secret, §§250, 801

Septuagint, *See* LXX

Serpent, §§3, 6, 14, 212, 251, 432, 487, 529, 937, 938, 955

Sex ethics, §§303, 644, 646, 647, 653, 656, 771

Shammai, §§114, 115

Simeon the Just, §115

Sin, §§5, 16, 21, 25, 33, 34, 48, 49, 66, 67, 68, 69, 70, 92, 97, 100, 107, 140, 242, 285, 332, 338, 387, 433, 529, 550, 565, 581, 587, 647

Slave, §§7, 30, 61, 87, 100, 108, 115, 120, 126, 173, 201, 208, 272, 289, 296, 313, 331, 346, 421, 429, 430, 457, 469, 491, 498, 502, 521, 545, 567, 573, 574, 576, 577, 578, 593, 595, 600, 623, 646, 647, 651, 660, 661, 726, 746, 760, 764, 769, 770, 771, 772, 773, 776, 777, 781, 794, 799, 809, 826, 844, 845, 846, 890, 892, 933, 962

Socrates, §§27, 28, 37, 43, 82, 112, 158, 201, 244, 282, 474, 478, 482, 489, 494, 618, 651, 666, 731, 748, 754, 773, 780, 792, 852, 874

Solomon, §§60, 91, 150, 155, 167, 174, 210, 261, 329, 358, 361, 390, 423, 431, 439, 442, 462, 480, 503, 539, 561, 652, 801, 822, 849, 909, 923, 925, 958

Son of David, §167

Son of God, §§3, 6, 14, 72, 105, 106, 120, 122, 126, 128, 184, 197, 209, 210, 212, 259, 280, 352, 406, 463, 479, 531, 622, 850, 853, 865, 972

Son of Man, §§92, 152, 180, 183, 184, 389, 412, 450, 533, 603, 923, 934

Sons of light, §§40, 451, 747, 823, 918, 967

Sophists, §§29, 169, 720, 731, 882

Soul, §§2, 9, 11, 20

Spirit, §§7, 20, 21, 29, 60, 71, 82, 83, 92, 128, 266, 395, 402, 488, 547, 548, 559, 639, 781

Spiritual sacrifice, §§30, 246, 501, 607

Star, §§11, 14, 864

State, §§14, 20, 58, 82, 134, 158, 243, 301, 351, 407, 492, 515, 517, 547, 577, 611, 613, 634, 637, 642, 688, 696, 802, 809, 890, 894, 930

Stoic, §§17, 27, 45, 206, 272, 275, 325, 356, 402, 441, 455, 489, 490, 499, 518, 541, 604, 612, 628, 631, 651, 654, 665, 671, 672, 692, 696, 732, 756, 783, 787, 790, 799, 809, 880, 890, 895, 902

Superstition, §§6, 88, 212, 237, 386, 436, 452, 500, 517, 521, 523, 524, 577, 658, 673, 674, 867, 933, 963

Synagogue, §§83, 115, 161, 233, 304, 470, 498, 514, 760

Taheb, §403

Tammuz, §§13, 447

Taurobolium, §§558, 572

Teacher of righteousness, §§745, 759

Teachers, §§86, 115, 226, 327

Teaching, §§101, 419

Temple, §§15, 83, 90, 170, 173, 243, 499, 501, 526, 632, 772

Tithe, §§269, 309, 862, 863

Torah, §§23, 25, 45, 87, 90, 114, 116, 117, 133, 168, 211, 278, 287, 329, 606

Tradition, §§23, 87, 114, 133, 288

Twelfth Benediction, §470

Two powers in heaven, §693

Unclean/Clean, §113

Unwritten law, §723

Virgin, §§1, 11

Vision, §§22, 52, 253, 465, 478, 504, 505, 506, 509, 513, 934, 937

Visionary, §18

Visions, §§11, 938

Washing of hands, §118

Wealth, §§19, 30, 43, 44, 102, 137, 292, 297, 312, 313, 325, 332, 344, 491, 493, 516, 553, 564, 578, 615, 646, 658, 689, 699, 741, 744, 771, 784, 809, 844, 892, 975

Wine, §§190, 196, 228, 248, 346, 372, 373, 375, 416, 424, 617, 670, 970

Wisdom, §§135, 158, 210, 255, 261, 353, 366, 390, 419, 423, 462, 469, 618, 619, 620, 621, 624, 652, 784, 789, 800, 801, 802, 849, 899, 920, 925

Women, §§3, 4, 6, 34, 107, 126, 132, 134, 148, 177, 212, 346, 360, 397, 417, 447, 467, 487, 513, 523, 538, 580, 615, 623, 631, 640, 641, 642, 646, 647, 649, 651, 653, 658, 661, 665, 669, 681, 685, 686, 703, 771, 773, 774, 775, 776, 809, 811, 815, 832, 833, 839, 867, 892, 893, 894, 895, 897, 908, 950, 951

Worship, §§78, 88, 91, 98, 168, 183, 200, 209, 212, 216, 233, 253, 348, 365, 384, 386, 387, 436, 475, 493, 515, 519, 539, 554, 560, 563, 571, 609, 658, 659, 681, 683, 684, 687, 691, 760, 771, 772, 799, 804, 805, 806, 807, 848, 866, 878, 924, 927, 933, 937, 938, 941, 942, 975

Zealot, §§160, 172

Zeus, §§2, 3, 6, 43, 44, 54, 55, 80, 120, 122, 148, 190, 194, 197, 215, 220, 264, 275, 324, 336, 356, 360, 409, 448, 453, 455, 479, 494, 510, 518, 520, 601, 611, 612, 615, 619, 621, 637, 660, 672, 678, 698, 721, 753, 770, 771, 778, 783, 790, 793, 802, 818, 839, 880, 924, 936, 942, 957, 958

Scripture Index

(Numbers refer to sections, not pages.)

GENESIS

1–3	§567
1	§§356, 714
1:1	§356
1:16–2:3	§358
1:27	§141
2	§714
2:2	§232
2:15	§582
2:24	§141
3:9	§379
3:13	§584
3:24	§186
5:21-24	§§216, 920
6:1-6	§897
9:1-17	§511
14	§865
14:17-20	§863
15:6	§§559, 560, 879
18	§510
18:1-16	§872
21:33	§305
22:1-19	§§22, 505, 560
28:18-22	§309
35	§467
37	§457
38:25-26	§281
39–50	§255
49:10-11	§§167, 374, 375, 946, 970

EXODUS

3:6	§161
3:13-15	§472
3:14	§417
4	§409
4:22	§595
7:11	§840
7:22	§840
14	§146
15:1-21	§833
15:22-26	§349
17:1-7	§349
17:8	§609
19:9	§352
19:15	§653
20:11	§232
20:18	§488
20:21b	§399
21:15	§273
22:1	§90
26	§366
34:29-35	§§125, 725

LEVITICUS

10:9	§446
12:2-8	§258
15:18	§653
18:5	§168
18:6-18	§§511, 634
18:22	§536
18:26	§511
19:16	§763
19:18	§§164, 279
20:13	§536
21:1-3	§303
25:10	§270

NUMBERS

6:26	§140
11:26	§969
12:7	§855
20:1-13	§349
21:16-18	§679
22:22-35	§§383, 505

24:17	§11

DEUTERONOMY

4:2	§976
5:15	§232
6:5	§164
8:15-16	§679
10:16	§599
10:17	§140
11:18	§583
12:32	§976
13:1-5	§9
17:17	§141
18:14-22	§§399, 403
19:15-21	§763
21:22-23	§§761, 763
23	§761
23:1	§503
23:3-7	§40
23:18	§536
30:7	§40
32:8-9	§613
32:28	§840
34:7-8	§84

JOSHUA

7:1-26	§496
22	§501

JUDGES

2:1	§128
6:34	§791
13:17	§805

1 SAMUEL

2:1-10	§255
4:17	§225

SCRIPTURE INDEX

2 SAMUEL

6:1-15	§254
24:1	§457

1 KINGS

17:1	§960
17:17-24	§290
18:1	§960
19:19-21	§28

2 KINGS

2:10	§§218, 485, 701
2:16-17	§216
4:18-37	§290
22:44	§802

1 CHRONICLES

4:23	§743
21:1	§457

EZRA

6:9-10	§831
7:13	§311

JOB

9:8	§§110, 111
26:9	§870

PSALMS

2:8-9	§167
5:5	§40
8	§609
8:3-4	§184
14:13-14	§211
26:5	§40
31:5	§211
31:6	§40
34:9	§861
40:8	§197
89:4	§923
90:4	§903
103:3	§69
110:4	§865
116:15	§751
139:21-22	§40

PROVERBS

8:21	§789
8:22-30	§§358, 789
8:22	§800
17:13	§609
20:22	§609

25:16	§751
25:21-22	§608
31	§893

ECCLESIASTES

5:5	§751

ISAIAH

1:8-11	§952
2:3	§447
2:8	§952
6	§937
6:1	§452
6:5	§452
6:9	§433
9:6	§256
11	§975
11:5	§§167, 791
22:13	§709
28:11	§840
33:16-17	§13
52:5	§546
52:7	§865
52:15	§424
53	§154
53:11	§68
56:1	§533
56:3-5	§503
59:17	§791
61:1-4	§§225, 270, 424, 865

JEREMIAH

4:4	§599
9:26	§599
18:20	§609
23:27-28	§9
26:11	§202
26:20-24	§202
31:12	§375
31:31	§690

EZEKIEL

1	§938
2:1	§184
7:7	§§10, 25
9	§938
17:22-24	§101
26:14	§962
27:29-36	§962
31:5-6	§101
36:26-27	§547
44:7	§599

DANIEL

1–6	§255
3:7	§128
3:31–4:34	§48
4	§§19, 824
4:7-10	§101
4:17-19	§101
4:33a	§616
7	§§184, 938, 968
7:13	§352
7:25	§960
8:14	§960
9:27	§960
10	§938
12:4	§345
12:7	§960
12:11	§960
12:12	§960

HOSEA

11:1	§595
12:8-10	§312
14:7	§375

AMOS

7:9	§161
9:13-14	§375

JONAH

1:1-16	§§53, 55, 56

MICAH

5:1	§15
7:6	§83
7:18	§609

HABAKKUK

2:4	§759
3	§179
3:1	§71

ZECHARIAH

14:20-21	§243

TOBIT

1:1-3	§934
4:8	§145
4:9	§145

JUDITH

8:14	§390

8:22 (Vg)   §878

WISDOM OF SOLOMON

1:7   §801
1:13   §431
2:10-20   §§200, 210
2:23-24   §431
3:13-14   §§503, 652
5:4   §442
5:17-22   §791
6:18-19   §462
7:1-6   §925
7:20   §155
7:21-27   §§801, 849
7:22   §801
7:27   §469
8:10   §261
8:21   §657
9:4   §801
9:16-17   §390
11:17   §561
14:21-27   §539
15:11   §480
18:3-4   §361

SIRACH

Prologue   §§350, 370
5:4-6   §569
7:34   §295
10:4   §613
10:14   §255
11:18-19   §312
11:26-28   §954
17:17   §613
18:24   §954
24   §§354, 358
24:8-12   §§354, 366
24:19-22   §419
28:1-6   §609
46:16-17   §448
47:19   §654
48:8   §326
48:11   §822

BARUCH

3:37–4:1   §354

1 MACCABEES

1:53   §599
2:51-60   §§559, 879
7:5   §599
7:9   §599
9:22   §484

2 MACCABEES

5:19   §234
6:14-15   §692
6:18–7:42   §§206, 207
7:23   §561
7:28   §561
7:31   §797
7:38   §§154, 557
8:4   §206
11:13   §797
12:38-45   §708
15:37   §797

3 MACCABEES

1:16   §859
5:7-9   §859
5:25   §859
7:16   §941

4 MACCABEES

1:1   §§306, 581
1:11   §940
2:1-6   §581
4:11   §797
5:2   §797
6:1–18:24   §206
6:1-27   §204
6:12-19   §675
6:27-29   §154
6:33   §940
8:2   §797
8:12-15   §206
9:6   §797
9:7-8   §306
9:10-25   §§206, 797
12:7   §797
16:15   §797
17:9   §797
17:21-22   §§154, 557
18:23   §221

4 EZRA

3:6-8   §§186, 566
3:20   §96
4:11   §390
4:26   §178
4:35-37   §§948, 949
4:38-39   §827
4:44-50   §948
5:4-10   §177
5:18   §437
5:41-42   §821
5:43-45   §904

6:17-24   §177
7:25   §99
7:26-44   §§972, 973
7:33-35   §§700, 972
7:36-42   §972
7:46-50   §568
7:47-61   §§568, 597, 965
7:74   §904
7:92   §940
7:116-20   §568
7:127-30   §940
8:41-45   §96
8:47b-50   §342
8:51-55   §974
9:17   §§96, 97
9:30-37   §§96, 97
10:21-24   §173
11   §968
12:31-33   §946
13   §603
13:1-56   §184
13:3-8   §603
13:16-24   §§822, 948
13:29   §603
13:35-37   §603
14:23-26   §842

5 EZRA

1:28-30, 32 §310

6 EZRA

16:40-46   §663
16:64-66   §837

1 ESDRAS

4:13-41   §698
8:70-71   §508
8:87   §508

MATTHEW

1   §5
1–7   §321
1:1-25   §§1, 2, 3
1:2-17   §§4, 755
1:18–2:23   §9
1:18-25   §§5, 6, 7, 8
1:19   §§5, 10
1:20   §5
2:1-23   §14
2:1-16   §13
2:1-12   §§11, 12
2:5-6   §15
3:1-12   §§16, 266
3:4   §§17, 18

3:7-10	§267	8:5-13	§§287, 288, 289	13:17	§§283, 302
3:7	§§19, 345, 490	8:11	§322	13:24-30	§100
3:10-12	§§20, 267, 269	8:14-17	§52	13:31-32	§101
3:13-17	§§20, 21, 22, 23	8:14-15	§51	13:44-46	§§102, 103, 133
4:1-11	§209	8:20	§§296, 297	13:53-58	§§104, 105
4:2	§728	8:22	§298	13:57	§106
4:3	§209	8:23-27	§§53, 54, 55, 56,	14:1-12	§107
4:6	§209		57, 58	14:6	§108
4:12-17	§§24, 25, 26	8:25	§§58, 59	14:13-21	§109
4:18-22	§§27, 28	8:28-34	§§60, 61, 62	14:22-33	§§58, 110, 111,
4:19	§29	8:31-32	§§63, 64		112
5–7	§§30, 289, 660,	9:1-8	§§65, 66	15:1-20	§§113, 114, 115,
	661	9:2	§§67, 68		116, 117
5:13	§328	9:5-6	§69	15:1-9	§23
5:16	§546	9:12	§70	15:2	§118
5:17-19	§§31, 32	9:18-26	§§71, 72, 73	15:14	§282
5:21-28	§§33, 34, 544	9:20-21	§§74, 75	15:21-28	§119
5:28-29	§§75, 136	9:24	§76	16:1	§119
5:29-30	§34	10:1	§77	16:13-20	§120
5:31-32	§35	10:5-12	§78	16:19	§411
5:33-37	§§36, 394	10:5	§78	16:21-23	§§121, 122
5:37	§36	10:7-14	§79	16:25	§123
5:38-48	§§37, 38, 273	10:8	§78	16:26	§124
5:39	§39	10:9-10	§§80, 81	17:1-9	§§125, 126, 127,
5:40-48	§38	10:13	§299		128, 728
5:40	§277	10:17-25	§637	17:9	§130
5:43-47	§§274, 275, 276,	10:19	§82	17:9-13	§129
	637	10:21	§§78, 83	17:12-13	§131
5:43	§§37, 40, 272,	10:21-22	§176	17:14-21	§132
	274	10:24-25	§§187, 283, 284,	17:22-23	§§121, 122
5:44	§44		300, 302, 414	17:24-27	§133
5:45-48	§41	10:28	§317	18:1-5	§134
5:48	§§277, 280	10:37-39	§§325, 326, 327	18:5	§135
6:1-4	§42	10:40	§§84, 135, 283,	18:6-9	§136
6:7	§43		299, 300	18:10	§137
6:9-15	§§304, 305	11:7-9	§291	18:15-18	§§138, 139, 670
6:10b	§44	11:7	§291	18:20	§§135, 771
6:12b	§471	11:8	§292	18:23-35	§140
6:13	§§45, 306	11:16	§293	19:3-9	§§35, 141, 142
6:19-21	§316	11:17	§§294, 295	19:6	§143
6:22-23	§308	11:28-29	§85	19:9	§142
6:24	§337	11:30	§86	19:12	§140
6:25-34	§§81, 313, 314,	12:1-8	§87	19:16-22	§144
	315	12:9-14	§§88, 89	19:21	§§144, 145
6:30	§677	12:11	§323	19:26	§146
6:33	§313	12:12	§90	19:28	§916
6:34	§§46, 47	12:22-37	§91	19:29	§§147, 148
7:1-5	§47	12:31-32	§92	20:1-16	§§149, 150, 151
7:2	§§281, 609	12:32	§92	20:17-19	§§121, 122
7:3-5	§§285, 286	12:39	§293	20:22	§152
7:7-11	§311	12:44-45	§§86, 155, 293	20:28	§§153, 154
7:12	§§278, 279	12:45	§293	20:30-31	§155
7:13-14	§321	13:1-23	§§95, 96, 97	21:8-9	§156
7:24-27	§287	13:1-52	§§93, 94	21:33-46	§§157, 158
8:1-4	§§48, 49	13:10-17	§98	22	§159
8:4	§§50, 345	13:12	§99	22:1-14	§§282, 325

22:11-14	§159	27:43	§210
22:15-22	§160	27:45-54	§§211, 212, 213
22:23-33	§§161, 162, 710	27:48	§214
22:30	§163	27:51-54	§211
22:32	§417	28:1-20	§§217, 218, 219,
22:34-40	§§164, 165, 166,		220, 221, 222
	278	28:1-8	§§215, 216
22:41-46	§167	28:3	§§221, 222
23:1-36	§169	28:4-5	§222
23:9	§148	28:4	§221
23:15	§§4, 168	28:10	§§221, 222
23:23	§635	28:13	§223
23:25-26	§756	28:16-20	§224
23:34-37	§310	28:20	§§218, 693
23:36	§293		
24:1-15	§§171, 172, 173,	MARK	
	174		
24:1-2	§170	1	§§21, 48
24:4-5	§§175, 417	1:1	§§225, 226, 227
24:7-9	§176	1:4-8	§16
24:15-22	§177	1:4	§107
24:22	§178	1:5	§21
24:30-31	§180	1:6	§§17, 18, 616
24:30	§179	1:7	§21
24:36	§181	1:9-11	§§20, 21
24:48	§319	1:10	§22
25:1-13	§182	1:11	§§22, 23
25:14-30	§§343, 344	1:13	§§228, 728
25:18	§344	1:14-45	§229
25:25-27	§344	1:14-15	§§24, 25
25:25	§343	1:15	§§26, 924
25:31-46	§§183, 184, 185,	1:16-20	§§27, 28
	344, 695	1:17	§29
25:34	§§41, 186	1:21-28	§§61, 230, 231
25:35-40	§§187, 283	1:25	§61
26–27	§637	1:29-34	§52
26:6-13	§188	1:29-31	§51
26:17-29	§189	1:40-45	§§48, 49
26:26-29	§§190, 191, 192,	1:44	§50
	193, 194, 195,	2:1-12	§§65, 66
	196	2:5	§§67, 68
26:28	§§558, 690	2:7	§§66, 67
26:36-46	§859	2:9-10	§69
26:39	§§197, 637	2:12	§88
26:47–		2:17	§70
27:50	§198	2:23-28	§87
26:57–		2:27-28	§§232, 233, 234
27:14	§§199, 200, 201	3:1-6	§§88, 89, 237
26:61	§202	3:4	§§89, 90
27:3-10	§203	3:11	§§72, 89
27:26	§§204, 205	3:20-30	§266
27:28-31	§§205, 473	3:21-22	§§235, 236
27:33-54	§§206, 207	3:22-30	§91
27:35	§208	3:28-29	§92
27:38-43	§209	3:31-35	§§92, 235
27:40	§209	3:34	§148
		3:35	§148
		4:1-34	§§93, 94
		4:1-20	§§95, 96, 97
		4:3-9	§101
		4:11-12	§98
		4:25	§99
		4:30-32	§101
		4:35-41	§§53, 54, 55, 56,
			57, 58
		5:1-20	§§60, 61, 132,
			230, 525
		5:2-3	§62
		5:7	§72
		5:8	§61
		5:8-12	§63
		5:12-13	§§63, 64, 231
		5:21-43	§§71, 72, 73, 88,
			290
		5:22	§498
		5:27-28	§§74, 75
		5:37	§72
		5:39	§76
		5:41	§72
		6:1-6	§§104, 105
		6:2	§104
		6:4	§106, 240
		6:7	§77
		6:8-11	§§78, 79, 80, 81
		6:14-29	§107
		6:14-16	§240
		6:16	§107
		6:22	§108
		6:30-44	§§109, 375
		6:42-52	§§55, 58, 110,
			111, 112
		7:1-23	§113
		7:1-8	§§23, 114, 115,
			116, 117
		7:3	§118
		7:21-22	§783
		7:24-30	§§118, 119
		7:27	§119
		7:28	§119
		7:33	§§118, 434
		8:11	§§119, 213
		8:22-26	§§88, 118, 237,
			238, 239
		8:23	§§239, 434
		8:27-30	§§120, 240
		8:28-29	§240
		8:31-33	§§121, 122, 184
		8:35	§123
		8:36-37	§124
		9	§§728, 835

9:2-13 §795
9:2-10 §§125, 126, 127, 128, 728
9:9 §130
9:9-13 §§129, 384
9:13 §131
9:14-29 §132
9:17-26 §61
9:18 §132
9:25 §132
9:28-29 §132
9:30-32 §§121, 122
9:31 §184
9:33-37 §134
9:36-37 §135
9:37 §135
9:42-50 §136
9:49-50 §241
9:50b §241
10:2-12 §141
10:2-9 §142
10:2-4 §35
10:6 §141
10:9 §143
10:10-12 §142
10:17-22 §144
10:21 §145
10:27 §146
10:29-30 §§147, 148, 817
10:32-34 §§121, 122, 184
10:35-45 §152
10:38 §152
10:38b-39 §242
10:45 §§153, 154
10:47-48 §155
11:8-10 §156
11:16 §243
12:1-12 §§157, 158
12:13-17 §160
12:18-27 §§527, 710
12:25-26 §§161, 162, 163
12:26-27 §§161, 162
12:28 §166
12:28-34 §§164, 165, 166, 211
12:28-31 §278
12:35-37a §167
12:37b-40 §169
12:41-44 §§244, 245, 246
12:43b §246
13 §826
13:1-14 §§171, 172, 173, 174
13:1-2 §170
13:5-6 §§170, 175
13:8 §176

13:9-13 §637
13:11 §82
13:12-13 §§83, 176, 900
13:14-20 §§177, 661
13:20 §§178, 247, 904
13:21-23 §§170, 175
13:22 §914
13:26-27 §§179, 180
13:30 §247
13:32 §181
14 §§188, 201
14–15 §637
14:3-9 §188
14:12-25 §189
14:17-25 §248
14:22-25 §§190, 191, 192, 193, 194, 195, 196
14:24 §690
14:28 §196
14:32-42 §§197, 859
14:35-36 §637
14:36 §§44, 197
14:43– 15:37 §198
14:55– 15:5 §§199, 200, 201
14:56-59 §201
14:58 §§15, 170, 202
15:13-15 §202
15:15 §§204, 205
15:17-20 §§205, 473
15:21-39 §§206, 207
15:21 §249
15:24 §208
15:27-32 §209
15:33-39 §§211, 212, 213
15:36 §214
16:1-20 §§217, 218, 219, 220, 221, 222
16:1-8 §§215, 216
16:8b §250
16:12 §§221, 250
16:16-17 §218
16:18a §251

LUKE

1:1-4 §§252, 253
1:15 §616
1:21 §254
1:26-38 §§1, 2, 3, 6, 7, 8
1:28 §307
1:32 §§8, 531
1:35 §§8, 531
1:42 §307

1:48 §307
1:52 §255
1:67-79 §§256, 758
1:70 §256
1:76 §256
2:1-7 §§1, 2, 3
2:4-20 §15
2:4 §13
2:14 §257
2:24 §258
2:41-52 §§14, 259, 260, 261, 262, 263
2:48-49 §264
2:52 §265
3:1-18 §16
3:1-2 §1
3:3-17 §266
3:3b §107
3:7-9 §§17, 267
3:8 §107
3:9-17 §20
3:10-14 §268
3:16-17 §269
3:21-22 §§20, 21
3:22 §§22, 23
3:23-38 §§1, 4
4:1-13 §209
4:2 §728
4:14-15 §§24, 25
4:16-30 §§104, 105
4:17-21 §270
4:18 §185
4:23-24 §106
4:24 §§106, 240
4:25 §960
4:33-37 §§230, 231
4:38-41 §52
4:38-39 §51
4:41 §89
5:1-11 §§27, 28, 271
5:10 §29
5:12-16 §§48, 49
5:14 §50
5:17-26 §§65, 66
5:20 §§67, 68
5:23-24 §69
5:31 §70
6:1-5 §87
6:6-11 §§88, 89
6:9 §90
6:20-49 §30
6:27-35 §§274, 275, 276
6:27-33 §273
6:27-28 §637
6:27 §272
6:29b §277

6:31	§§278, 279	10:25-28	§§164, 165, 166, 278	16:10-12	§344
6:32	§272			16:13	§337
6:35	§272	10:31	§303	16:19-31	§338
6:36	§280	11:1-4	§§304, 305	16:19*b*	§336
6:37-38	§281	11:4	§306	16:27-31	§338
6:39-40	§282	11:9-13	§311	17	§339
6:40	§§187, 283, 284, 300, 302, 414	11:14-23	§91	17:1-2	§136
		11:16	§119	17:11-19	§339
6:41-42	§§285, 286	11:20	§§73, 301	17:14	§136
6:47-49	§287	11:27	§307	17:23	§175
7:1-10	§§30, 287, 288, 289	11:29	§293	17:33	§123
		11:30-32	§293	17:34-35	§§136, 340
7:5	§289	11:34-36	§308	17:37	§340
7:11-17	§§76, 290, 339	11:34	§310	18	§342
7:24-26	§291	11:42	§§309, 635	18:1-8	§341
7:25	§292	11:49-51	§310	18:7-8	§341
7:31	§293	11:50-51	§293	18:10-14	§342
7:32	§§294, 295	12:4-5	§317	18:18-23	§144
8:1-18	§§93, 94	12:10	§§91, 92	18:22	§145
8:1-15	§95	12:11-12	§§82, 637	18:27	§146
8:4-15	§§96, 97	12:16-21	§312	18:29	§147
8:9-10	§98	12:19*c*	§§312, 709	18:31-34	§§121, 122
8:18	§99	12:22-31	§§313, 314, 315	18:36-40	§155
8:22-25	§§53, 54, 55, 56, 57, 58	12:33-34	§316	19:11-27	§343
		12:42	§318	19:12-27	§344
8:26-39	§§60, 61	12:45	§319	19:21	§343
8:27	§62	12:49-53	§§242, 318	19:35-38	§156
8:32-33	§§63, 64	13:6-7	§320	20:9-19	§§157, 158
8:40-56	§§71, 72, 73	13:18-19	§101	20:20-26	§160
8:44	§§74, 75	13:23-24	§321	20:27-40	§§161, 162, 710
8:52	§76	13:28	§322	20:35-36	§163
9:1-2	§77	14	§324	20:41-44	§167
9:2-5	§78	14:5	§§233, 323	20:45-47	§169
9:3	§81	14:7	§324	21:1-4	§§244, 245, 246
9:3-5	§§79, 80	14:7-11	§324	21:5-20	§§171, 172, 173, 174
9:10-17	§109	14:15-24	§§282, 325		
9:18-21	§120	14:26-27	§§326, 327	21:5-6	§170
9:22	§§121, 122	14:26	§§325, 326	21:8	§175
9:24	§123	14:34-35	§328	21:10-17	§176
9:25	§124	15	§§13, 72	21:14-15	§82
9:28-36	§§125, 126, 127, 128, 728	15:3-10	§329	21:20-24	§177
		15:5	§329	21:27	§§179, 180
9:32	§125	15:6	§329	22–23	§637
9:37-43	§132	15:7	§329	22:7-20	§189
9:43-45	§§121, 122	15:9	§§329, 330	22:15-20	§§190, 191, 192, 193, 194, 195, 196
9:46-48	§134	15:10	§329		
9:48	§135	15:11-32	§§330, 331, 332, 333, 334		
9:58	§§296, 297			22:17-20	§345
9:60	§298	15:19	§334		
10:1-16	§79	15:24	§330	22:19*b*-20	§345
10:4	§81	15:32	§§329, 330	22:19	§195
10:6	§299	16:1-9	§335	22:20	§690
10:16	§§135, 283, 299, 300	16:1	§318	22:25-30	§346
		16:3	§336	22:39-46	§859
10:20	§301	16:8	§823	22:41-42	§§197, 637
10:24	§§283, 302	16:9	§§81, 221, 344	22:47–	

23:46	§198	3:2	§56	7:27	§422
22:55–		3:3-13	§389	7:30	§376
23:5	§§199, 200, 201	3:3-5	§§380, 381, 382,	7:37-38	§§398, 423, 424
23:11	§§205, 473		383, 384, 385,	7:43-46	§425
23:25-38	§209		386, 387, 388,	7:53–	
23:28	§347		410, 480, 558	8:11	§426
23:31	§347	3:8	§375	8:12	§§360, 417, 427,
23:33-48	§§206, 207	3:12	§390		428
23:33	§208	3:13	§§218, 381, 382,	8:20	§376
23:35	§348		391	8:31-36	§430
23:36	§214	3:14	§392	8:31-34	§429
23:44-48	§§212, 213	3:16	§§364, 911	8:44	§§431, 432
23:44-46	§211	3:17	§393	8:48	§§236, 442
23:45	§349	3:18	§§364, 394, 395	9:1-7	§433
23:46	§211	3:19-21	§451	9:6	§§434, 435, 436
24:1-53	§§217, 218, 219,	3:31	§384	9:7	§370
	220, 221, 222	3:34b	§395	9:22	§470
24:1-12	§§215, 216	4	§403	9:33	§433
24:36	§221	4:2	§396	9:34	§§304, 470
24:37-38	§222	4:4-15	§397	10:1-15	§§437, 438
24:44	§350	4:9	§397	10:7	§417
24:48	§222	4:14	§398	10:9	§417
24:50-52	§219	4:19	§§398, 399, 400	10:11	§417
24:51-52	§§218, 240, 348,	4:22-24	§401	10:14	§§417, 439, 440
	351, 352	4:24	§402	10:16	§441
		4:25	§§399, 400, 403	10:20	§442
		4:39	§397	10:27	§440
JOHN		4:42	§§403, 407	11:1-44	§443
1	§§355, 356, 358,	4:44	§§106, 240	11:25	§§417, 427, 443
	364	4:46-54	§§118, 288, 404	11:39	§444
1:1-18	§§353, 390, 801	4:52-53	§288	11:50	§445
1:1-14	§354	5:1-15	§405	11:51	§§266, 446
1:1-3	§§358, 359	5:17	§406	12:1-8	§188
1:1-2	§357	5:18	§§407, 408	12:20	§§447, 448
1:1	§§355, 356, 357,	5:19	§409	12:23	§376
	452	5:21	§410	12:24	§447
1:3	§358	5:22	§411	12:27	§376
1:4	§§360, 361	5:24	§410	12:29	§448
1:10	§362, 363	5:25	§443	12:33	§449
1:12-13	§384	5:27	§412	12:34	§450
1:14	§§354, 359, 364,	5:31-32	§413	12:35-36	§823
	365, 366, 367	5:45	§837	12:36	§451
1:16	§368	5:46	§§283, 414	12:41	§452
1:18	§§354, 364	6:1-13	§§109, 375	12:42	§470
1:29-33	§422	6:11-12	§375	12:44-45	§§84, 452
1:29	§369	6:15-21	§§55, 110, 111,	12:50	§453
1:38	§370		112	13:1-17	§346
1:41	§370	6:26-65	§415	13:1	§376
1:42	§370	6:31	§416	13:15	§§454, 455
2:1-11	§§109, 371, 372,	6:35	§§417, 419	13:16	§§283, 284
	373, 374, 375	6:41	§417	13:17	§456
2:4	§376	6:48	§§417, 418	13:20	§§84, 452
2:11	§377	6:51	§§417, 418	13:27	§457
2:19-21	§15	6:53	§419	13:35	§458
2:24-25	§379	7:4	§420	14:1-6	§459
2:25	§378	7:15	§421	14:2-3	§301
3	§§380, 395				

14:2 §460
14:5-6 §461
14:6 §§417, 427
14:15-16 §462
14:16-17 §463
14:19 §426
14:26 §§464, 465, 466, 467
15:1 §417
15:5 §§427, 468
15:13-15 §458
15:15 §469
15:18-19 §451
16:2 §§304, 470
17:1 §§376, 471
17:4-5 §471
17:4 §471
17:5 §§186, 471
17:6 §472
17:24 §186
18:2– 19:30 §198
18:36-37 §476
19:2-3 §§205, 473
19:9 §474
19:10-11 §476
19:11 §475
19:17-30 §§206, 207
19:17 §249
19:18 §208
19:20 §498
19:25-27 §211
19:35 §477
20:1-23 §§217, 218, 219, 220, 221, 222
20:7 §221
20:13 §221
20:14-18 §219
20:16 §478
20:17 §218
20:19 §479
20:22 §480
20:27 §479
20:28 §481
20:29 §482
20:30 §§377, 483
21:1-14 §271
21:25 §§483, 484

ACTS

1 §701
1–2 §218
1:1-11 §§351, 352
1:3 §§8, 222, 485
1:9-11 §§219, 485

2:6 §486
2:9-11 §486
2:11-13 §§487, 488
2:17-21 §24
2:23 §§489, 490, 796
2:44 §§491, 492, 493
2:45 §493
4:19 §494
4:31 §495
5:1-11 §496
5:29 §494
5:37 §§160, 494
6:1 §§497, 797
6:9 §498
6:15 §128
7 §401
7:6 §886
7:29 §886
7:41 §501
7:48-50 §§500, 501
7:48-49 §499
7:49 §500
7:51-52 §501
7:53 §501
7:54-60 §426
8:9-10 §502
8:26-40 §503
9:1-9 §504
9:5 §504
9:7 §§253, 505
9:12 §506
10:2 §507
10:9-35 §509
10:9-22 §506
10:25-26 §120
10:28 §§486, 508
10:36 §865
11:5-14 §506
13:16 §507
13:26 §507
14:11-15 §120
14:11-13 §510
15:19-21 §511
15:23 §530
15:28 §§252, 512
16:9 §§504, 513
16:13 §514
16:16 §514
16:21 §515
17:6-8 §§200, 512
17:18 §516
17:22-31 §§43, 360, 518, 519
17:22 §517
17:26 §520
17:28 §§518, 520, 604

17:29 §520
18:2 §521
18:12-17 §522
19:13-20 §523
19:19 §§524, 525
20:17-36 §338
20:28 §558
21:27-36 §526
22:6-21 §253
22:9 §§253, 505
23:6-10 §527
23:23-24 §616
23:26 §§530, 616
25:19 §517
26:24 §235
27 §55
27:21-37 §527
28:1-6 §§528, 529
28:3-6 §251

ROMANS

1:1-7 §530
1:3 §531
1:4 §21
1:12-16 §551
1:16 §532
1:17 §533, 534
1:19-21 §535
1:20 §535
1:26-27 §§536, 537, 538, 640, 643
1:28-32 §§539, 783
2:1-11 §551
2:12-15 §540
2:14-15 §§541, 542, 547
2:17-24 §544
2:17-22 §545
2:17 §543
2:19-23 §§282, 546
2:23-24 §§544, 546
2:27-29 §659
2:28 §§547, 548
3:4 §549
3:5 §549
3:6 §549
3:9-25 §550
3:20 §551
3:21– 4:25 §554
3:21– 4:9 §§552, 553
3:21-24a §555
3:21 §534
3:23 §556
3:24-25 §557

3:25	§§557, 558	9:7-13	§600	3:16-17	§§631, 632
3:27	§558	9:14-23	§600	3:22-23	§744
3:28-29	§599	9:19	§601	4:9-10	§694
3:30	§693	10:15	§865	5–10	§633
4:3	§§559, 560, 879	11:15a	§601	5:1-13	§§525, 635, 636
4:13	§§559, 560	11:26	§§602, 603	5:1	§634
4:17	§561	11:33-36	§568	5:3-5	§670
5:1-11	§563	11:36	§§520, 604	5:6-11	§§636, 771
5:1-10	§562	12:1-2	§§518, 607	5:10-11	§783
5:7-8	§564	12:1	§§30, 605, 606	5:11	§§636, 755
5:7	§564	12:4-8	§559	6:1-11	§§637, 638
5:9-10	§813	12:4-5	§607	6:1-8	§§37, 670
5:9	§§558, 564	12:15	§295	6:2-3	§916
5:10	§564	12:17	§609	6:2	§639
5:12-21	§§564, 567, 568	12:17-20	§608	6:3	§639
5:12	§§556, 565, 566	12:19-21	§609	6:6	§§7, 637
6	§387	12:19-20	§277	6:7	§638
6:1-11	§§387, 447	12:20-21	§609	6:9-10	§783
6:1-10	§§570, 571, 572, 573	13:1-7	§§610, 611, 612, 613	6:9	§§640, 641, 642, 643
6:1	§569	13:3	§614	6:12-20	§§646, 647
6:7	§574	13:8	§611	6:12	§§644, 645, 654
6:10	§575	13:9	§278	6:19-20	§631
6:12-23	§§576, 577, 578	13:9-10	§278	6:20	§648
6:13	§578	13:12b-14	§615	7:1-40	§§649, 650, 651, 895
6:15-23	§§430, 595	13:12	§782		
6:17	§579, 780	14:1–		7:1	§§652, 653
7	§593	15:13	§615	7:4	§654
7:2	§809	14:1–		7:5	§§655, 656
7:7-23	§580	15:6	§674	7:7	§657
7:7-13	§583	14:2	§616	7:12-16	§658
7:7-11	§§556, 576, 581	14:6	§§616, 617	7:17-27	§664
7:7	§582	14:14	§§616, 617	7:19	§659
7:11	§584	14:21	§§616, 617	7:20-24	§30
7:12	§547			7:21-23	§§660, 661
7:14	§§547, 585	**1 CORINTHIANS**		7:25-31	§§177, 661
7:15	§§587, 588			7:27	§662
7:17-18	§586	1	§622	7:29-31	§§663, 664, 665, 666
7:19-21	§§587, 588	1:1-3	§530		
7:20	§586	1:18-25	§618	7:32-35	§667
7:22	§§589, 590, 591	1:19–		7:32	§668
7:24	§592	2:7	§§619, 620, 621, 622	7:35	§667
8:1-12	§559			7:36	§668
8:1	§§395, 592	1:26-31	§623	7:37	§669
8:2	§547	2:1-6	§624	7:40	§750
8:4	§659	2:2	§690	8–14	§§670, 688, 832
8:10	§593	2:5-6	§624	8:1-3	§669
8:12	§594	2:6	§624	8:1-2	§673
8:14-17	§595	2:8-9	§626	8:4	§671
8:33	§596	2:9	§§424, 625, 626	8:5-6	§676
8:38	§596	2:10-14	§627	8:5	§670
9	§553	2:10	§626	8:6	§§441, 502, 672
9:1-2	§§597, 700, 965, 974	2:11-18	§635	8:7-13	§§673, 674, 675
		2:14	§628	8:10	§676
9:3	§598	3:1-4	§388	8:11	§690
9:6	§599	3:13-15	§§629, 630	9:9-10	§677

9:19-23	§678	15:33	§709	11:25	§426
10:4	§679	15:35-57	§712	11:32	§522
10:16-17	§196	15:35-54	§711	12:1-10	§§750, 751
10:19-20	§671	15:35-44	§710	12:10	§752
10:20	§62	15:44	§628	12:20	§783
10:23-33	§§673, 674, 675	15:45-49	§§713, 714, 715	13:13	§693
10:23	§§644, 645	15:45-47	§713		
11	§§687, 807	15:46	§§628, 714	GALATIANS	
11:3	§680	15:47-49	§594		
11:4-16	§681	15:51	§715	1–4	§605
11:10	§§682, 683, 684	15:53	§712	1:1-5	§530
11:14	§§685, 686	16:1-4	§670	1:1	§§650, 753, 754
11:17-34	§§196, 670, 687,			2:12	§§754, 755
	688, 689	2 CORINTHIANS		2:13	§§269, 756
11:17-22	§670			2:19	§757
11:23	§721	1:1-2	§530	3:6-14	§758
11:25	§§195, 690	1:3-11	§716	3:6	§§560, 758, 879
11:27-29	§691	1:8-10	§716	3:9	§758
11:30-32	§692	1:9-10	§732	3:11	§§533, 759
11:30-31	§684	1:12	§717	3:13–4:26	§782
12	§559	2:14-16	§§427, 718	3:13	§§760, 761, 762,
12:1–		2:15	§719		763
14:40	§832	2:17	§720	3:14	§758
12:3-6	§693	2:17–		3:19–4:5	§764
12:4-6	§693	3:9	§§698, 721	3:19	§§137, 764
12:8-10	§693	3:3	§§614, 722	3:22	§765
12:12-31	§559	3:6	§§614, 690, 723	3:24	§766
12:12-27	§§694, 695, 696	3:7b	§§724, 725	3:27	§767
12:15-16	§694	3:12	§726	3:28	§§163, 768, 769,
12:21	§694	3:17	§726		770, 771, 772,
12:23	§697	3:18	§§727, 728, 738		773, 774, 775,
12:26	§696				776, 777
12:27-30	§702	4:2	§729	4:3	§799
12:28-31	§694	4:4	§§6, 730	4:9	§778
13	§721	4:5	§731	5–6	§605
13:1-13	§698	4:8	§732	5:1	§430
13:4-7	§783	4:10-12	§733	5:2-12	§778
13:8-13	§699	4:16	§§593, 734	5:2-3	§779
13:12	§700	4:17	§§735, 736	5:13–	
14	§487	5:1-8	§737	6:10	§§771, 778
14:1-40	§§524, 649	5:1-5	§738	5:14	§659
14:1	§701	5:1-4	§730	5:15	§780
14:23-24	§670	5:2-4	§739	5:17	§780
14:26-40	§832	5:2-3	§737	5:19-23	§§781, 782, 783
14:26-28	§702	5:3	§§573, 710, 740,	5:24	§784
14:26	§670		741		
14:34	§703	5:10	§742	EPHESIANS	
14:37-38	§750	5:17	§743		
14:40	§670	5:18-21	§743	1:4-5	§§356, 672
15	§§564, 704, 705,	6:10	§744	1:4	§§186, 785
	707	6:14–		1:7	§558
15:6	§88	7:1	§745	1:22	§802
15:23-24	§710	6:15	§§746, 747	1:23	§803
15:24-26	§§706, 707	8:8	§748	2	§§486, 768
15:28	§707	8:9	§748	2:2	§§91, 137, 786
15:29	§708	11:14	§749	2:12-22	§441
				2:13	§558

2:14-17 §787
2:14 §788
3:9-10 §789
3:19 §§707, 789
4:10 §§707, 789
4:31 §783
5:3-5 §783
5:8 §823
5:19 §§758, 808
5:21–
6:9 §890
5:22–
6:9 §892
5:22-33 §811
5:22-23 §790
5:28-29 §811
5:33 §811
6:5-8 §30
6:10-20 §967
6:11-13 §791
6:14-17 §§490, 791

PHILIPPIANS

1:1-2 §530
1:21 §792
1:27 §798
2:5-11 §742
2:6-11 §§793, 794, 795
2:9-10 §848
2:11 §851
2:12-13 §§490, 796
3 §797
3:5 §797
3:20 §798
4:8-9 §783
4:11-13 §§799, 805
4:11 §799

COLOSSIANS

1:15-20 §361
1:15-17 §§390, 801
1:15 §800
1:18 §§802, 803
1:19 §803
1:20 §558
2 §768
2:6-19 §§804, 805
2:8 §§799, 805
2:12 §805
2:16 §805
2:18 §§682, 804, 806,
807, 848
2:20 §778
3:5 §783
3:8 §783

3:11 §807
3:16 §§758, 808
3:18–
4:1 §§809, 810, 890,
892
3:18 §811
3:22-25 §30

1 THESSALONIANS

1:1 §530
1:6 §812
1:9 §693
1:10 §§603, 813
2:5-6 §814
2:15 §815
2:15-16 §816
2:19 §815
4:5-7 §815
4:6 §817
4:9-12 §516
4:9 §818
4:13 §819
4:13-18 §§820, 821, 962
4:13-17 §822
4:14-17 §896
4:16 §896
5:4-9 §§782, 823
5:8 §791

2 THESSALONIANS

2 §175
2:2 §824
2:3-4 §825
2:4 §826
2:6-7 §827
2:8-12 §§531, 827

1 TIMOTHY

1:9-10 §783
1:9 §§645, 828
1:10 §829
1:17 §830
2–3 §892
2:1-2 §831
2:8-11 §832
2:8 §§118, 832
2:12 §833
3:4-5 §834
3:16 §835
4:7-8 §829
4:12 §836
5:24 §837
6:3 §829
6:4-5 §783

6:10 §838
6:14 §839

2 TIMOTHY

1:10 §839
3:1-9 §83
3:3-4 §783
3:6 §658
3:8 §840
3:16 §§841, 842
4:1-3 §83
4:3 §829

TITUS

1:6 §§141, 842
1:9 §829
2:1-10 §892
2:1-8 §829
2:5 §546
2:13 §839
3:3 §783
3:5 §843

PHILEMON §§30, 844, 845,
846
1-3 §530
10 §847

HEBREWS

1:1-4 §§361, 849
1:1 §§693, 848
1:2 §850
1:3 §849
1:4-14 §§682, 849, 851
1:6 §852
1:8 §849
1:9 §853
2:5-18 §849
2:10 §§850, 853, 854
3:1-6 §§398, 855
3:1 §855
3:12 §510
4:4 §856
4:14–10:18 §857
4:16 §§562, 858
5:7 §859
5:8 §860
5:10 §859
6:4 §861
7:1-28 §§859, 864, 865,
866
7:1-9 §862
7:2 §863
7:3 §§5, 865

7:25	§§369, 866	2:14	§891	10	§§482, 919
8–9	§855	2:18-19	§30	14-15	§920
9:7	§867	2:21-25	§891	19-20	§639
9:12-22	§558	2:22-24	§154	19	§628
9:13	§868	2:23	§204		
9:23	§§868, 869	3:1-7	§§891, 894	**REVELATION**	
10:4	§868	3:1-6	§§892, 893		
10:19	§558	3:7	§895	1:1	§§449, 934, 948
10:20	§870	3:9	§609	1:3	§§935, 948
10:22	§871	3:13	§637	1:4-5	§693
11:9	§886	3:18-20	§897	1:4	§§935, 936
11:13	§886	3:18	§896	1:5	§558
11:17	§364	3:19	§896	1:8	§§417, 943, 948
11:23	§104	3:21	§898	1:9-20	§§253, 509, 937, 938
12:29	§871	4:3	§783		
13:2	§872	4:4	§899	1:12	§§478, 488, 935
13:3-9	§854	4:6	§896	1:16	§935
13:12	§§510, 558	4:12-19	§637	1:17	§§417, 937
13:15	§607	4:17	§899	1:23	§417
				2–3	§939
JAMES		**2 PETER**		2:1	§939
				2:7	§940
1:1	§530	1:4	§§387, 715	2:10	§941
1:2-4	§873	1:5	§900	2:12	§939
1:12-14	§873	1:20	§841	2:16	§948
1:25	§§874, 875	2:10-12	§900	2:18	§939
1:27	§876	2:13-17	§890	2:25	§948
2:8	§877	3	§§743, 901	3:1	§§935, 939
2:12	§877	3:5-7	§§901, 902	3:7-13	§§771, 940
2:20-23	§878	3:5	§901	3:7	§939
2:23	§879	3:8	§§903, 973	3:11	§948
3:6	§880	3:9	§904	3:14	§939
3:9	§881	3:13	§973	3:20	§948
3:15	§§628, 882	3:14-16	§841	3:21	§916
4:14	§883	3:15	§904	4	§942
4:15	§197			4:5	§935
5:12	§§36, 884	**1 JOHN**		4:8-11	§942
5:17	§960			4:8	§§943, 948
5:20	§885	1:5	§§905, 906	4:10	§942
		1:7	§§558, 906	4:11	§943
1 PETER		1:9	§907	5:1-6	§946
		2:1	§369	5:1-4	§§944, 945
1:1	§886	2:9	§908	5:1	§935
1:2	§693	2:11	§909	5:6	§935
1:3	§886	2:15-17	§911	5:13	§742
1:12	§887	2:16	§910	6–16	§947
1:19	§558	2:18	§§912, 913, 914, 915	6:1-6	§83
1:20	§186			6:6	§§83, 951
2:2	§§30, 607	2:21	§913	6:9-11	§§597, 904, 948
2:4-5	§632	3:1	§§916, 917	6:10	§949
2:5	§§30, 607, 888	3:10-12	§431	6:11	§948
2:9	§888	4:6	§918	6:12-17	§24
2:10	§546			7:1-17	§171
2:11	§887	**JUDE**		7:3	§935
2:12	§889			7:13	§941
2:13–3:7	§§809, 890, 894	6	§§137, 918	7:14	§941
2:13-17	§637	8-9	§§639, 918, 919		

8:2	§935	12:8	§959	19:11-12	§179
8:3-5	§137	12:10	§§837, 959	19:13	§970
8:7-12	§950	12:12	§948	19:15	§§167, 948
8:8	§943	12:14	§960	19:17-21	§969
8:9	§951	13	§915	20	§973
8:12	§951	13–22	§§961, 962	20–22	§§971, 972
9:13-14	§171	13:1-18	§§179, 610, 963	20:1-6	§973
9:21	§783	13:1	§938	20:6	§935
10:1-11	§253	13:8	§186	20:7-10	§602
10:3	§935	13:12	§963	20:11	§743
10:6-7	§948	13:18	§§91, 964	21:1–22:5	§§167, 597, 974, 975
11	§952	14:10-11	§§597, 965, 974		
11:2	§948	14:13	§§837, 935, 965	21	§626
11:3-12	§952	14:20	§966	21:1	§743
11:5	§956	15:1	§935	21:8	§783
11:7	§938	15:3	§§943, 948	21:11-14	§975
11:8-11	§953	16:1	§935	21:22	§§943, 948
11:8	§952	16:7	§§943, 948	22:5	§943
11:12	§§219, 952	16:14-16	§967	22:6	§§943, 948
11:13	§935	16:14	§948	22:7	§§935, 948
11:17	§§943, 948	16:15	§935	22:8	§§805, 969, 975
11:18	§954	17:9-11	§§179, 935, 948, 968	22:8-9	§137
11:19	§954			22:10	§§345, 948
12	§§958, 959	18:15-19	§962	22:12	§948
12:1-18	§§955, 956, 957, 958	19–21	§§965, 969	22:15	§783
		19:6	§§943, 948	22:16	§417
12:3	§935	19:9	§935	22:18	§31
12:5	§§15, 167, 179	19:10	§§805, 969, 975	22:18-19	§§32, 253, 976
12:6	§948	19:11-21	§§167, 967	22:20	§948